Second Edition

Introductory Business & Economic Forecasting

Paul Newbold
University of Illinois, Champaign

Theodore Bos
University of Alabama, Birmingham

COLLEGE DIVISION South-Western Publishing Co.

Cincinnati Ohio

Sponsoring Editor: James M. Keefe
Developmental Editor: Alice C. Denny
Production Editor: Sharon L. Smith
Production House: Matrix Productions
Cover Designer: Lotus Wittkopf
Interior Designer: Barbara Libby

HG60BA

Library of Congress Cataloging-in-Publication Data

Newbold, Paul.
    Introductory business and economic forecasting / Paul Newbold,
Theodore Bos. — 2nd ed.
        p.   cm.
    Rev. ed. of: Introductory business forecasting. 1990.
    Includes bibliographical references and index.
    ISBN 0-538-82874-9
    1. Business forecasting—Statistical methods.   I. Bos, Theodore.
II. Newbold, Paul. Introductory business forecasting.   III. Title.
HD30.27.N49   1993
338.5′442—dc20   93-4273
                                                         CIP

1   2   3   4   5   6   7   D1   9   8   7   6   5   4   3
Printed in the United States of America

I(T)P
International Thomson Publishing

South-Western Publishing Co. is an ITP Company. The ITP trademark is used under license.

*P*reface

Forecasting is not simply an important aspect of business management—it is an unavoidable task. No rational decision can be made without, at least implicitly, taking some view of the future. Often in the past, the forecasting activity in many organizations was quite informal. However, over the last several years it has become increasingly well recognized that more formal methods could contribute to increased forecast accuracy, and hence to enhanced quality in decision making. Some knowledge and understanding of these methods is therefore a considerable asset for the well-trained manager.

Our aim in writing this book has been to provide a widely accessible introduction to business forecasting methods. Some of the methods in current use are technically quite complex. However, we have written this text with the intention that it be readily comprehensible to readers who have followed the typical introductory (non-calculus) business statistics course. The level of mathematical and technical sophistication demanded will be no higher than that for such a course. However, subject to this constraint, we attempt to explain not only how the various techniques work, but as far as possible *why* they work. We have tried to write a textbook, not a cookbook. This book should be suitable as a text for both undergraduate and M.B.A. students who have taken an introductory business statistics course. (Chapter 2 of the book provides a brief review of some of the relevant material from such a course.)

We have concentrated heavily on *quantitative* approaches to forecasting. In particular, we have emphasized three approaches: regression analysis, exponential smoothing, and ARIMA (autoregressive integrated moving average) models. All are widely used in business, and we feel that all should be understood by the modern business forecaster. Regression methods are introduced in Chapters 3 and 4 of the book. Following an introduction to time series in Chapter 5, Chapters 6 and 7 cover, respectively, exponential smoothing and ARIMA models. In Chapter 8 we return to regression methods, discussing there the simultaneous equations models often employed in econometric forecasting. Chapter 9 attempts to bring together the regression, exponential smoothing, and

ARIMA approaches to forecasting, discussing relationships among them and possibilities for amalgamation. These seven chapters constitute the central core of the text.

Because of their widespread use, we believe it appropriate that an introduction to quantitative business forecasting methods concentrate most heavily on regression, exponential smoothing, and ARIMA models. However, a good many forecasting methods that do not fit into any of these categories have also been proposed and implemented. In Chapter 10 we introduce some of these, though not at the detailed level of coverage provided by the earlier chapters. Our major goal in this book is to introduce formal quantitative approaches to business forecasting, but we would not wish to give the impression that we do not value sound human judgment in the area. Indeed, we believe that in practice best results will most often be achieved through an alliance between formal methodology and judgment, the latter being most useful for incorporating into the forecast those factors which cannot be accommodated easily within a formal framework. On occasions, purely judgmental approaches to forecasting are employed, and some of these are briefly discussed in Chapter 11.

Chapters 12 and 13 cover two topics that we regard as extremely important. Often forecasts of the same quantity are available, or can be generated, from different sources. It is possible to combine these competing forecasts to achieve an overall composite prediction. The methods most often used in combination of forecasts are remarkably simple; in practice, they have proved to be remarkably successful. Forecasts, once made, are often forgotten. Sometimes, when the eventual outcome has been realized, the forecaster may look back rather casually with pain or pleasure, depending on the relative accuracy of his or her prediction. We feel strongly that this is inadequate. Rather, it is important that forecasts that have been made be systematically evaluated. Only in this way is the analyst likely to learn from experience, and perhaps be in a position to improve future forecast quality. The topic of evaluation is sufficiently important that we are somewhat embarrassed that it appears so late in the text. It does so for technical reasons. One important approach to evaluation requires the combination of forecasts, a topic that is most sensibly covered only after the introduction of individual forecasting methods.

The first and last chapters of the book provide an introduction to, and summary of, business forecasting methods. Both are somewhat opinionated. Not all of our colleagues in the field will share all of our opinions. It is hoped that some of them at least will prove stimulating.

Although various theoretical aspects of forecasting methodology need to be understood, forecasting is essentially a practical activity. We have therefore provided throughout the book many illustrative examples involving the analysis of real data sets. It is hoped that these will facilitate understanding of the techniques, and also illustrate the circumstances in which various methods are useful. Of course, in forecasting, as in many other fields, data analysis is becoming progressively less painful as a result of the proliferation of computer program packages. Our text is liberally sprinkled with sample output from such packages. It is not, however, our aim here to teach the use of any particular packages. In fact, a large number of different programs are available for the analysis of data through some or all of the methods discussed in this book. There are some differences in output style among the programs, but they are sufficiently similar that familiarity with one should be sufficient for an understanding of the output of another.

In preparing this second edition, we have been helped by the comments of many colleagues and students. In particular, we would like to thank the following people for their observations and suggestions:

Joan B. Anderson
University of San Diego

James McCabe
University of Louisville

Ray Y. Chou
Georgia Institute of Technology

Hal McClure
Villanova University

Mark Ferris
St. Louis University

Randolph L. McGee
University of Kentucky

Ed Gamber
Lafayette College

Robert Nau
Duke University

Larry W. Jacobs
Northern Illinois University

James T. Smith
University of North Carolina-
    Chapel Hill

Heejoon Kang
Indiana University

Hikoki Tsurumi
Rutgers University

Shady Kholdy
California State Polytechnic
    University-Pomona

Keith K. Turner
University of Nebraska-Omaha.

The remaining imperfections are, of course, our responsibility.

Paul Newbold
Theodore Bos

Contents

7 ARIMA Models: The Box-Jenkins Approach to Forecasting   258

8 Econometric Forecasting Models, Leading Indicators, and Expectations   387

9 Regression Models, Exponential Smoothing Algorithms, and ARIMA Models: Relationships and Extensions   422

10   Some Other Quantitative Forecasting Methods   449

11   Judgmental Methods and Technological Forecasting   474

12   The Combination of Forecasts   494

13   The Evaluation of Forecasts   522

14   An Overview of Business Forecasting Methods   550

Appendix: Statistical Tables   567

Name Index   574

Subject Index   576

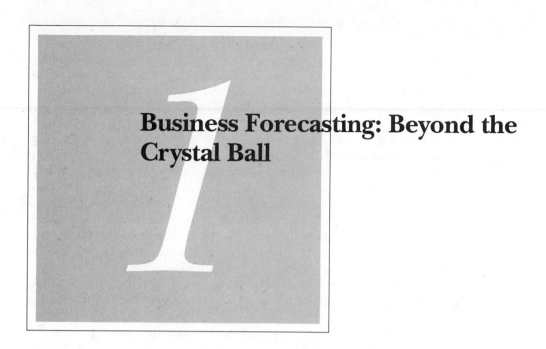

Business Forecasting: Beyond the Crystal Ball

1.1 THE IMPORTANCE OF FORECASTING

What will be the state of your career and your personal life in five years? Faced with such questions, most of us have two reactions. We cannot possibly know with certainty what the future will bring, and we would wish that the future were a little less obscure. All of us have learned to live with the reality of uncertainty, but most of us would feel more comfortable if that uncertainty were diminished somewhat. To a certain extent this reflects natural human curiosity. Throughout the ages such curiosity has provided a market for the services of those who claimed to see the future. Ancient history is replete with stories of consultations of oracles and soothsayers. Fortune tellers, equipped with such aids as tarot cards, crystal balls, and tea leaves, were an integral part of traveling fairs through much of the twentieth century. Today, more people than care to admit it subscribe to astrology to the point of regular reading of horoscopes. There *is* a human instinct to know more of the future. Of course, this is all a matter of degree. Our lives would be very much poorer if we knew with complete certainty everything that the future would bring. For

1

example, the interest in watching a football game would be far lower if we were certain about the eventual outcome. Fortunately, there is no danger that we will ever be able to see the future with such certainty. However, to say that certain knowledge of the future is impossible is not to say that the future must remain totally obscure. The forecaster's aim is to shed a little light, while acknowledging that some element of uncertainty will inevitably remain. It is the demand for more enlightenment about the future that accounts for forecasting being one of the oldest professions.

We have stressed the element of human curiosity in the market for forecasts. However, this is not the only, and certainly not the most important, factor motivating the demand for predictions, even in our day-to-day lives. Indeed, forecasting is inevitable. Whether we want to or not, we all make forecasts quite regularly. This is so because we are all *decision makers*, being required to choose among alternative actions in an uncertain world, where the consequences of these actions cannot be perfectly anticipated. Should we start off on a long journey by car, when there is some prospect of snow? Should we take an apparently attractive job, when we cannot know for sure what will be the status of the prospective employer, or what would be our status with that employer, in a few years' time? Should we invest much of our savings in a speculative project or stock, when the possible gains may be substantial, but the chance of serious loss nonnegligible? We are all faced with the need to make such decisions, and hence at least implicitly with the need to forecast. Presumably, before making decisions whose consequences will have some impact on our lives, we give these matters some thought, gathering whatever relevant information is available, seeking informal advice, and processing that information and advice to the best or our abilities. Of course, the amount of effort spent on these activities will depend on the importance of the decision that is to be made. In making our decisions, we will necessarily attempt to form some picture of the future: the clearer that picture, the greater the faith in the correctness of the decisions made. This discussion of forecasting in everyday life has brought out two important points:

1. Forecasting is an unavoidable activity.
2. Forecasting is an essential input to decision making. The better our forecasts, the better, all else equal, will be the decisions we make.

These same points remain pertinent when we turn our attention to the activities of organizations, whether government or business. Indeed, here the position is even more clear. Businesses cannot avoid planning for the future, in either the short or long term. Manufacturers must necessarily hold inventories of finished products to meet anticipated demand. Failure to meet demand leads to foregone profits, as well as goodwill losses. On the other hand, excessive inventory holdings will result in unnecessary holding costs. Thus, in planning production and inventory holding, manufacturers require regular short-term forecasts of product demand, typically on a month-to-month basis. In planning further ahead, new product developments must be considered, new markets may be investigated, and possibilities for expansion—either at home or abroad—will be studied. Decisions on these questions will have to be taken in the face of an uncertain longer-term future, about which it is obviously desirable to learn as much as possible. Forecasting is an equally important element in the activities of financial institutions. Business now is essentially an international activity, and currency transactions are routinely required. The exchange markets have become so volatile in recent years that the gains from their correct anticipation, and the losses from poor forecasts, can be very substantial. Again, if a bank is to be heavily committed in loans to a particular business sector, such as agriculture or oil, or to particular countries, some view must be taken about relevant future trends in those sectors in assessing capacity to repay. The theme that runs through all of these examples is not simply that forecasts are a vital input to business decision making, but also that the stakes can be very high indeed. High-quality forecasting then should be seen as having a very direct, and possibly quite large, impact on the "bottom line." A little improvement in forecast accuracy can easily translate into substantial gains in profits. Thus, while in our everyday lives we typically make forecasts quite casually and informally, in the business world forecasting is an activity on which it is worth spending a good deal of effort. Klein (1984) provides an excellent discussion and illustration of the value and importance of forecasts to government and business organizations.

Forecasting has been viewed for many years as an important activity in any number of enterprises. However, in the last few years there has been increasing momentum, so that this activity is becoming more widely recognized as having crucial value. In part, the increased attention that has been paid to forecasting may stem from the relatively recent development of new methodological approaches, some of which will be discussed in subsequent chapters of this book. Certainly the rapid development of computing power in the last two decades has also greatly expanded the scope of what can be done at a reasonable cost. However, it appears that the demand for reliable forecasts has increased in part because the need for them is more acute. This is a result of the rapidly changing environment in which we now live. Business must now operate in a world of rapidly evolving technology, of changing national and international market structures, and of critical political developments. In short, stability seems to be a thing of the past, and the future appears more uncertain than ever. Naturally, the anticipation of change has become increasingly important.

We have stressed the point that business forecasting should not be an isolated activity, but rather an integral part of the decision-making process. Indeed, it is difficult to see how rational plans can be developed without forecasts. We have heard it said that a particular corporation does not produce, even internally, forecasts of the sales of its products in various markets. Rather, it operates with a "marketing plan." This seems to misrepresent the nature of the forecast. We would not think of forecasting and planning as separate activities, but rather as two sides of the same coin. After all, what in isolation is a plan? Either it is realistic, in which case it embodies an element of prediction, or it is unrealistic, in which case it is of doubtful value, and indeed could be counterproductive.

1.2   FORECASTING AS ART AND SCIENCE

It is interesting to ask whether there exists, as a coherent intellectual discipline, a subject called "forecasting." On the one hand, the 1980s saw the birth of two journals, aimed at scholars and practitioners, in this area. The *Journal of Forecasting* and the *International Journal of Forecasting* each run to about 500 pages of articles per year. On the other hand, it is easy to have doubts on this question. After all, one presumably consults a meteorologist for weather forecasts, a demographer for population predictions, and an expert on the politics of the Middle East for an assessment of prospective developments in that area. An optimist might even consult an economist if forecasts of macroeconomic trends are wanted! Even if, as is our intention in this book, we restrict attention to the areas of business and economics, it is not difficult to visualize the value of a diversity of expert opinions in these fields. Readers will have encountered, for example, introductions to corporate earnings per share, daily currency exchange rates, national unemployment, and the marketing of new products in different courses, taught by instructors possessing different specialist knowledge. Can it then be useful to lump together the prediction of these quantities in a single course or text? Obviously, if we didn't believe that there is some value in this, we would not have written this book. The point is that certain methodological developments are valuable for considering a range of forecasting problems in business and economics, and indeed in a great many other fields. We have, for example, used essentially the same methodological approach for the prediction of unemployment in the United States and the volume of river flow in Iceland. The appropriate parallel is with a business statistics course, in which are studied techniques that have applications in accounting, finance, economics, marketing, and organizational behavior. These same techniques are also widely applied in many other fields. Since prediction of the future necessarily entails uncertainty, the reader will not be surprised to learn that many of the approaches to forecasting that we will be discussing are grounded in statistical methodology. We hasten to add that it is not our intent to minimize the value of specialist subject matter expertise. Indeed, this necessarily is equally valuable in looking into the future and understanding the past and present. The latter activity is a very desirable prerequisite for the former. We do, however, claim that a valuable set of methodological tools is available to the putative forecaster, and the main objective of this book is to introduce the reader to these tools, rather than concentrating on specific forecasting problems. In practice, for any particular job, it will be necessary to select the appropriate tools, and to use them in an appropriate way. We will try to clarify, at least in broad outline, what types of problems might sensibly be attacked through the various procedures that are introduced in subsequent chapters.

We have asserted that there exists a methodological apparatus for approaching a diversity of forecasting problems. However, that diversity is such that it is unreasonable to expect that there would be a single method that is best, or even suitable, for attacking all prediction questions. Although the methodology of business forecasting does have some coherence, the range of important problems met in practice calls for a range of solution approaches. A corporation may produce a large number of mature products for which sales forecasts up to a year ahead are routinely required on a monthly basis for production and inventory planning purposes. This same corporation may be contemplating a substantial new development in the Middle East, and would like an assessment of political and economic prospects in that region over the next decade or two. One would not reasonably expect to approach these two forecasting problems through the same methods. It is easy to imagine, for example, that the latter would call for considerably more specialist subject matter expertise than would the former. We will have far less to say about those problems for which such specialist knowledge forms the major part of the solution than about those that allow the application of more formal and generally applicable methods.

That there is no single right way to approach all forecasting problems is pretty clear. Indeed, we would be reluctant to claim that there is a single right way to approach any forecasting problem. For one thing, every problem met in practice will have its unique features, and the careful analyst will want to study these before proceeding. Further, even after such careful study, it will often be the case that two or three more or less equally attractive avenues are open. This is not a retreat from our earlier claim to a degree of coherence in the subject matter of forecasting methodology. A number of approaches to forecasting problems have been developed that are soundly and sensibly based, and that have been found to enjoy practical success over a broad range of applications. It is this methodology on which we concentrate in the bulk of this book. Many of these methods are based on the familiar scientific principle of **model building.** A model to represent what is known of past behavior is constructed. That model is then projected to predict the future. The art in forecasting arises through the need to tailor this scientific method to the specific characteristics of individual forecasting problems.

As we will see in later chapters, a number of interesting technical methods for attacking forecasting problems have been developed. It is easy to become so impressed by this technical sophistication that the analyst develops an attachment to a particular methodology and an urge to implement it without giving due consideration to the individual characteristics of the forecasting problem at hand. However, all problems have their unique features, and it is important to pay attention to the problem context before embarking on a complex technical analysis. The questions set out in Figure 1.1 will often provide a useful basis for thinking about the individual ingredients of a forecasting exercise.

In one sense, it seems obvious that such questions should be asked. Their goal, however, is the important one of establishing a working relationship between the forecaster and the client organization. A two-way communication must be established in the interests of both. A manager should not simply commission forecasts of a particular quantity without considerable further elaboration. It is important that the forecaster fully understands the underlying objectives of the exercise. Predictions are generally required to do more than satisfy idle curiosity. As we have stressed, forecasts are an important ingredient of the management decision-making process. The forecaster, who should acquire a good under-

FIGURE 1.1   Questions in a forecasting exercise.

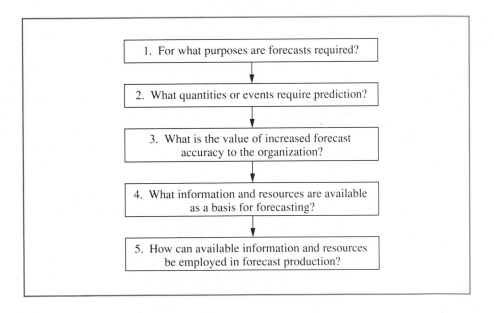

standing of the reliability and limitations of the predictions that will be employed, ought to be thoroughly integrated into decision making. Once the purpose of forecasting has become established, it should become clear precisely what must be predicted. Naturally it is important that this be specified as clearly as possible. Certainly, a broad question on potential developments in the automobile industry is worth asking, and may lead to some interesting conjectures that could influence manufacturers' decision making. However, for many more pressing decisions, there will be far more specific requirements. Not only is it important to know what must be predicted, but it is also necessary to be clear about the relevant forecasting horizon. Again, this depends on the decision maker's objectives. In some applications—for example, the management of corporate cash flow—daily forecasts are needed. On the other hand, even if resources were available to provide them, forecasts of tomorrow's unemployment rate would be of no value to the macroeconomic policy maker. In some applications, where for example a corporation is considering a large investment with a long life, the relevant horizon for forecasts can extend over several years.

Having established what must be predicted and why, the analyst now has some basis for assessing what might be a reasonable methodological approach. Two factors are important in making this choice. First, some thought needs to be given to the amount of effort it is worthwhile to make. In establishing the purpose of the forecasts, it should be possible to assess the potential payoffs from increased forecast accuracy. In some circumstances these payoffs will be very substantial indeed; in some others they will not. There is little point in expending vast resources of time, effort, and money in the production of superior forecasts when a rather crude, simple approach can yield predictions of adequate quality for the purposes at hand. Second, what can be attempted depends on the resources available to the analyst. The forecaster does not simply sit in a comfortable chair and engage in abstract contemplation of an uncertain future. Instead, a study of the past is likely to prove far more rewarding. It is therefore important to have available or to collect information on the past behavior of the variable to be predicted, and on those factors that have influenced the behavior of that variable. Much relevant information will be quantitative, and the amount and reliability of the available data will determine to some extent which analytical techniques can be employed. There is no point in attempting to apply a highly sophisticated statistical methodology to sparse data of poor quality. To the forecaster, the ideal client will have kept meticulous records. Unfortunately, in the real world, departures from this ideal are not uncommon. Good data are valuable, but not the only potentially valuable resource. Subject matter expertise should also be tapped. The judgments of relevant managers can be exploited not only in interpreting the characteristics of the data, but also in understanding the data-generating process. Such judgmental information typically will be subjective and qualitative, and the forecaster needs to assess its worth and determine how best to incorporate it into the forecast-generating mechanism. For example, frequently forecasts generated from some formal quantitative model are subsequently judgmentally modified. In addition to data and expertise, a further resource available to the modern forecaster is a suite of computer programs. Many prewritten packages for use with personal computers are now widely available, and widely used. In our opinion, this is something of a mixed blessing. The attractions are, of course, obvious. Formidable calculations can be accomplished in a fraction of a second, impressive graphical displays can be produced, and large quantities of information can be stored and manipulated. Unfortunately, these developments have, in a sense, made forecast generation too easy. A number of different packages purport to allow the automatic derivation of forecasts of the future of a process, given information on its past. There is an unfortunate tendency toward unwarranted faith in such forecasts, because they are "computer-generated." But there is no universal panacea to be applied to all forecasting problems. No doubt the world would be a more comfortable place if the non-expert, unwilling to make the intellectual effort to understand the structure and limitations of the underlying methodology, could simply push a button to generate invariably reliable predictions. Unfortunately, this option is not truly available. Of course, computer programs are valuable, but the program must be made, or chosen, to fit the problem, not the problem to fit the program.

Having learned as much as possible about the problem at hand, and the resources available, the forecaster must decide on an appropriate approach. Even with adequate prior study of the sort we have just outlined, there will not necessarily be a single "right" approach, though some possibilities should emerge as more attractive and appropriate than others. Many of these approaches are purely quantitative, while others are based entirely on subjective judgment. Often the best approach in practice will involve a marriage of the two types. The more formal methods that we will discuss vary considerably in complexity. Certainly it is easy to be impressed by highly complex methodology, and on many occasions such methods can prove useful. However, in building quantitative models, overelaboration is not a virtue. Rather, the aim should be to describe an admittedly complex real world phenomenon with as simple a model as is reasonable. Experience suggests that relatively simple approaches to forecasting often prove more successful than apparently more sophisticated alternatives. Chatfield (1986) argues a rather extreme variant of this assertion. Our own view is that the forecaster needs to become acquainted with as wide an array as possible of methodological approaches, and to develop insights into their strengths and limitations through practical experience. In this way it should be possible to make an intelligent and informed choice when faced with a new forecasting problem.

1.3 THE LIMITATIONS OF FORECASTING

In our experience, very many managers have an unrealistic attitude toward forecasting. Some are too pessimistic about what can be accomplished, while others are unduly optimistic. Perhaps, as statisticians, we should take comfort in the fact that the average attitude is about right! There are dangers in having either more or less faith in forecasts than is justified. Implicit belief in the reliability of a prediction can persuade the decision maker to underestimate the important element of uncertainty about the future, while extreme skepticism about forecasts can deprive the manager of a valuable aid to decision making.

The future is neither completely knowable nor totally obscure. We can hope to learn something about it, but not everything. The past will generally yield some useful information about the future, but some uncertainty will inevitably remain, for the quantities in which we are interested do not evolve through time according to simple deterministic functions. Inevitably, forecasts will be in error, sometimes spectacularly so. Forecasters in general, and economic forecasters in particular, have over the years endured bad press. In part, this is selective reporting. Accurate forecasts do not make news; dramatically inaccurate ones make for entertaining reading. However, the reputation of unreliability in business and economic forecasts is not completely undeserved. On occasion, the forecasters might have done better. However, it must be accepted that, even with the best available methods, sensibly used, serious errors will sometimes be made. This is inherent in the profession, and the forecaster with a thin skin is well advised to find another occupation. Some quantities are notoriously difficult to predict with consistent, reasonable accuracy, and these are likely to remain so. One can think of the future quantity of interest as being made up of a systematic component, whose value can be anticipated from past behavior, and a random component, whose value is unpredictable. We are saying that for many business and economic variables, the size of this random component is far from negligible.

It is important for users of forecasts to understand that residual uncertainty about the future must inevitably remain, and it is useful to have available some estimate of the magnitude of this uncertainty. However, extreme skepticism about business and economic forecasts, perhaps induced by casual evidence of spectacular failures, is largely unwarranted.

Modern forecasting professionals are not capable of eliminating uncertainty about the future, but they do a pretty good job of anticipating potential trends and characterizing residual uncertainty. This is all that reasonably can be expected, and soundly based forecasts should certainly yield improved decision making, on the average, compared to the alternative of using crude guesses about the future. The degree of success that can be anticipated in any particular forecasting exercise is difficult to predict in advance. Some processes are inherently more difficult to predict than others. It is extremely difficult to forecast yearly changes in stock market prices. Yearly changes in population are easier to anticipate—birth and death rates are fairly stable. Usually we can do better than a crude guess: often we can do much better.

Other than a craving for the mystical, it is more difficult, in light of the well-publicized failures, to see why some managers have more faith in forecasts than is warranted. Two candidates for blame are forecasting courses (and textbooks) and computers. A little exposure to forecasting methodology can quickly convince the manager that a good deal of heavy technical artillery can be turned on forecasting problems. This helps in understanding that part of a process that can be predicted from the past but is no help in forecasting the chance component. No amount of sophisticated mathematics will allow us to predict the outcome of a coin flip! Also, as we noted in the previous section, managers have been tempted to believe that forecasts are endowed with some special quality because they were derived as output from a computer program. Perhaps, as we develop more familiarity with computers, we will learn to question the rationality of placing more faith in programs than we would be prepared to concede to the people who write them!

In this book we will introduce a number of forecasting methods, some of which are quite heavily technical. We will also illustrate the use of some computer programs, delegating to them their proper function—as very rapid calculators—rather than pretending that they are capable of providing a worthwhile substitute for human thought and understanding. We hope to be able to persuade the reader that the modern forecaster can accomplish something of value, but would encourage him or her to keep in mind the inevitable limitations of forecasting.

1.4   FORECASTING AND ORGANIZATIONS

As is clear from survey results reported by Mentzer and Cox (1984), Sparkes and McHugh (1984), and Dalrymple (1987), forecasting methods are widely used in business organizations, and a broad array of forecasting procedures is employed in practice. In this section we briefly discuss the relationship between the forecaster and the organization. Considerably more detailed discussion and illustration is provided by Jenkins (1982), Dino, Riley, and Yatrakis (1982), Miller (1985), and Capon and Hulbert (1985).

A bad model of the forecaster in a business organization would view forecasting as a technical specialty, divorced from central management, except when the forecasting group is needed by senior management decision makers to provide predictions of quantities of interest. Communication between senior management and the forecasters will be limited. Forecasters would have no more than a very general understanding of why predictions are required before the event, or of the use, if any, to which they have been put after the event. Managers would neither know nor care how the forecasts were developed. In those instances where forecasts of a quantity are routinely required over time, a computerized system of transmission will be developed, perhaps without subsequent monitoring, so that senior management is able to key into the management information system and easily extract the "information" about the future that is required. In this model, the forecaster would be relegated to an office at the back of the building, as befits his or her lowly status in the corporate hierarchy. Of course, this office would be equipped with an impressive array of computer hardware and software, and no doubt its shelves would contain books and journals whose contents are viewed as sophisticated games by the "generalists" in the organization who have the responsibility for making the really important decisions. The forecaster would be viewed as a technocrat, with impressive but narrowly focused expertise, to be called on when needed. Not surprisingly, the major goal of ambitious young managers in the forecasting office would be to move out of it.

The model we have just described is (we hope!) at worst a parody of what actually goes on in any real world organization. Its purpose is to emphasize the absurdity of any substantial degree of distance between the forecaster and the decision maker. On the contrary, as we have been at pain to emphasize, the two roles are, or should be, intimately connected. One sensible model, discussed by Jenkins (1982), for establishing such a connection requires the establishment of a forecast formulation committee, involving both forecasters and policy makers. Regardless of the managerial structure established, it is clear that continuous communication between the two groups is essential. As we discussed in Section 1.2, it is important that the forecaster understand the purpose for which forecasts are required. This will influence both the predictions and the development of the forecasts. In practice, many forecasts are of the *conditional*, or "what if" type, to be based on certain assumptions about the future of the organization or the environment in which it operates. It is naturally important that forecasters and policy makers have the same understanding about the assumptions on which predictions are based. The modern forecaster will, of course, possess specialist technical expertise, and neither forecasters nor policy makers will have the time or patience for the full education of the latter in the intricate details of that expertise. Nevertheless, it is useful for forecasters to attempt to explain to policy makers what has been done, and why. Forecasts are likely to be treated more seriously if the policy maker is convinced that they are sensibly founded. Therefore, it is important that the policy maker understands the assumptions underlying the forecasts, and the factors that have been taken into account. Senior managers may have legitimate reservations about some of the assumptions, and may be inclined to judgmentally modify the forecasts in light of factors, about which they have some knowledge, that were not incorporated in the formal forecasting exercise.

In the previous section we discussed the prevalence of inappropriate management attitudes to forecast quality. Some policy makers may need to be persuaded to take the forecasts at all seriously, while others will need to realize the extent of residual uncertainty about the future. One way to achieve this is for the forecaster to hold out some of the most recent data in constructing a forecasting model. The model can then be used to predict these recent outcomes, from a number of starting points, allowing the policy maker to get a reasonable feel for the quality of forecasts likely to be achieved in the future. This provides an excellent means of validating what has been done. In addition, if forecasts are to be continually derived in this way for some time into the future, it is important to continue to monitor forecast performance. This may provide some reassurance to skeptical policy makers. More important, although it is reasonable to expect a well-conceived forecasting model to perform satisfactorily for some time, it is unreasonable to expect it to continue to do so indefinitely. We live in a rapidly evolving world, and assumptions that seem reasonable at one point in time may be much less reasonable at some time in the future. By monitoring prediction quality, the forecaster will continue to learn about the relevant environment of the organization, and be in a position to adapt the forecasting model to that environment.

The details of how the forecaster is integrated into an organization are not terribly important for the purposes of this text. What is most appropriate will differ from one organization to another. What is important is that the forecaster be, as much as possible, a part of the organization, not apart from it.

1.5 FORECASTING METHODS

The bulk of this book is devoted to an exposition of the methodology of business and economic forecasting. These methods are certainly not infallible, nor are the people who use them. Nevertheless, there is enough accumulated experience in their use to claim that the art and science of business forecasting has advanced in respectability well beyond the crystal ball. Our modern computer programs, always allied with intelligent human interpretation, are considerably more useful than a late twentieth-century variant of the fairground fortune teller's paraphernalia. Rather, they aid in a sensible contemplation of the past, which should in turn provide us with useful information about the future. We have also moved well beyond the time in which it justifiably could be argued that, in forecasting, the best work possible involved no more than a few rapid "back-of-the-envelope" calculations. There now exists a body of tried and tested forecasting methods, and the organization that ignores these does so at the cost of unnecessarily poor input to the decision-making process.

As we noted in Section 1.2, there is not one single forecasting method, but many. The procedures in common use range from the very informal to the formal, from the use of unaided human judgment to the exclusive reliance on quantitative models, from the very simple to the highly complex. These different procedures should not be regarded as competitors. They are all available to the forecaster and should be viewed as potential aids to the solution of problems that may arise. It is the broad range of such problems that gives rise to the wide array of potentially useful approaches.

Forecasting problems in practice differ in a number of dimensions. Some are considerably more important than others, and therefore rightly command more time and effort. Some involve short-run prediction, while others require looking much further into the future. The quantity and quality of available relevant information will differ considerably from one problem to another, as will the difficulty in obtaining forecasts of reasonable quality. For relatively stable processes, it can be quite easy to see the picture some distance ahead. For more unstable processes the task is far more difficult. The art in forecasting involves, to some extent, the ability to see in any particular situation what might be accomplished, and to select from the forecaster's bag of tools one or more that might be appropriate for the job at hand.

Often, formal approaches will prove most useful, but there are certainly occasions on which a purely informal approach is best. It may be that the most important factors that will influence the quantity in which we are interested are incapable of formal treatment. Quantitative methods and models are widely used, and becoming more widely so. In our view these developments are entirely positive, but this should not be taken as questioning the value of human judgment. The sensible forecaster will attempt to deploy all of the useful resources at his or her command, and often these will include the very valuable insights of subject matter experts. Many of the most successful forecasting exercises involve a marriage of formal quantitative methods and less formal expert judgment—a marriage that is the more valuable when it is possible to validate the quality of that expertise. Finally, methods that appear simple should not be treated lightly. They may achieve adequate success with a minimum of effort and on occasion may achieve about all that can be achieved. It should be kept in mind that apparent complexity alone is far from guaranteeing success in forecasting.

1.6   A PREVIEW

Our major goal in this book is to introduce some important quantitative approaches to forecasting. We repeat that these approaches are most useful in conjunction with human judgment. Nevertheless, the quantitative methods provide important topics for study in their own right, and it is essential that these be mastered in order to understand modern business and economic forecasting.

In fact, a very large number of forecasting methods, based on a quantitative approach, have been proposed and implemented. We do not attempt an encyclopedic coverage, but instead concentrate on three approaches that seem to be most important and in most general use. These are:

1.   Regression methods
2.   Exponential smoothing algorithms
3.   ARIMA (Box-Jenkins) methods

Both exponential smoothing algorithms and ARIMA (autoregressive integrated moving average) methods, in their basic variants, involve the prediction of future values of a process exclusively on the basis of its own past history. On the other hand, regression analysis is designed to model and understand relationships among processes. Such relationships might then be exploited for forecasting purposes. Both regression and ARIMA analysis rely on the construction of formal statistical models to describe the behavior of observed data. These models might then be projected into the future to develop predictions. By contrast, exponential smoothing does not explicitly require formal model building. Rather, it involves a set of intuitively plausible algorithms which have often proved successful in producing short-term forecasts of reasonable quality, with a minimum of human effort. Each of these three approaches has proved valuable for attacking particular types of forecasting problems.

Since the methods we describe are quantitative in nature, they necessarily are based on statistical principles. It will be assumed that the reader has some knowledge of statistical methods, at the level of an introductory course; Chapter 2 provides a brief review of some of the relevant concepts. Regression methods are introduced, and discussed in some detail in Chapters 3 and 4, while Chapter 8 deals with more complex simultaneous equations regression models frequently employed in modern econometric work.

The important problem of how to predict future values of a process given information on its past takes us into the world of time series analysis. A **time series** is a set of numerical measurements, indexed by time, on some variable of interest, and Chapter 5 introduces one way of viewing such series. Chapters 6 and 7 discuss approaches to forecasting through exponential smoothing algorithms and ARIMA models, respectively. Although regression methods, exponential smoothing algorithms, and ARIMA models constitute distinct topics that are worthy of study in their own right, there are in fact important relationships among them, and Chapter 9 explores the possibilities for their integration.

Our discussion of formal quantitative approaches to forecasting is concluded in Chapter 10 with a very brief review of some procedures not covered in previous chapters. Chapter 11 briefly reviews some purely judgmental methods. In particular, a discussion is provided of technological forecasting, where the judgmental approach seems most obviously suitable.

Chapters 12 and 13 cover two important but often neglected topics—the combination and evaluation of forecasts. On reaching this point the reader will have been exposed to a wide variety of forecasting methods, and might reasonably feel challenged to choose. In fact, often it may not be necessary or desirable to choose a single method or forecast. Instead, forecasts could be combined to produce a composite forecast, whose virtue is roughly the same as investing in a portfolio of stocks, rather than in a single stock. Of course, however plausible or sophisticated the methodology that has been used in producing forecasts, the bottom line test is prediction accuracy, so that the evaluation of forecasts deserves considerable attention.

Finally, in Chapter 14 we provide an overview of the subject, attempting to pull together the various strands developed in previous chapters.

SELECTED BIBLIOGRAPHY

Capon, N. & J. M. Hulbert (1985). The integration of forecasting and strategic planning. *International Journal of Forecasting*, *1*, 123–133.

Chatfield, C. (1986). Simple is best? *International Journal of Forecasting*, *2*, 401–402.

Dalrymple, D. J. (1987). Sales forecasting practices: Results from a United States survey. *International Journal of Forecasting*, *3*, 379–391.

Dino, R. N., D. E. Riley & P. G. Yatrakis (1982). The role of forecasting in corporate strategy: The Xerox experience. *Journal of Forecasting, 1*, 335–348.

Jenkins, G. M. (1982). Some practical aspects of forecasting in organizations. *Journal of Forecasting, 1*, 3–21.

Klein, L. R. (1984). The importance of the forecast. *Journal of Forecasting, 3*, 1–9.

Makridakis, S. (1991). Forecasting in the 21st century. *International Journal of Forecasting, 7*, 123–126.

Mentzer, J. T. & J. E. Cox (1984). Familiarity, application and performance of sales forecasting techniques. *Journal of Forecasting, 3*, 27–36.

Miller, D. M. (1985). The anatomy of a successful forecasting implementation. *International Journal of Forecasting, 1*, 69–78.

Schultz, R. L. (1992). Fundamental aspects of forecasting in organizations. *International Journal of Forecasting, 7*, 409–411.

Sparkes, J. R. & A. K. McHugh (1984). Awareness and use of forecasting techniques in British industry. *Journal of Forecasting, 3*, 37–42.

A Review of Some Basic Concepts in Statistics

2.1 INTRODUCTION

Our discussion in Chapter 1 raised two issues that motivate a review of statistical concepts. First, forecasts of the future very often are based, at least to some extent, on numerical information from the past. Second, since complete precision in forecasting is unattainable, the forecaster must necessarily face uncertainty. The analysis of numerical information and the characterization of uncertainty are the provinces of the statistician, so it is important that the forecaster have a good grasp of statistical concepts.

A study of statistical methods is an essential prerequisite to an understanding of modern forecasting techniques. We have assumed that readers have already taken an introductory statistics course, so we will not provide a detailed introduction to all of the concepts met in such a course. However, it is useful to briefly review some of the statistical ideas that will be met in subsequent chapters of this book.

2.2 RANDOM VARIABLES

The study of uncertainty begins with the concept of **probability,** a concept that allows precise description of the chance of occurrence of some event. Probability of occurrence lies between zero and one and is often thought of as the proportion of times the event would occur in a very large (essentially infinite) number of repeated trials. For example, when a coin is thrown, the probability is one-half that a head will result, meaning that if the coin were thrown many times, the proportion of heads resulting would be very nearly one-half: as the number of throws increases, the proportion of heads approaches one-half. At one extreme, a probability of zero implies that an event will certainly not occur, while a probability of one implies the event's certain occurrence. Between these two extremes, the higher the probability, the more likely is the occurrence of the event.

Suppose that some entity is to be observed and that prior to this observation there is uncertainty as to what will be found. The concept of probability can be used to fully characterize the potential outcomes in such circumstances. A particular case of considerable interest arises when the observed outcome is necessarily numerical. Outcome probabilities in this case can often be very elegantly summarized. A variable that takes on numerical values determined from the observation of an uncertain phenomenon is known as a **random variable.** Here we will concentrate on *continuous* random variables, which can take any numerical value in some range. For example, a corporation manufactures chemicals that are shipped in bags of 20 pounds. Inevitably these will contain some impurities, the amounts differing from one bag to another. The contents of any bag can be analyzed, and the amount of impurity it contains can be determined. If a single bag is selected by some random, or chance, mechanism, there will be some uncertainty before the event about the amount of impurity it contains. It is this uncertain amount, measured in convenient units, such as ounces, that is viewed as a random variable.

To completely characterize the possible outcomes, it is necessary in some way to provide information about the probability that a random variable will take a value in any range. For example, if we let the random variable X denote the amount of impurity, in ounces, in a bag of chemical, we might want to know the probability that between 10 and 15 ounces will be found, which can be written $P(10 < X < 15)$. Two constructs are typically employed for carrying such information.

1. The **cumulative distribution function** $F_X(x)$ of the random variable X determines the probability that the random variable X will be less than the specific value x, for all possible outcomes x; that is

$$F_X(x) = P(X < x) \text{ for all } x$$

Once this is known, probabilities for any interval follow immediately. For example, if X denotes the amount of impurity, in ounces, in a bag of chemical, the probability of finding between 10 and 15 ounces is

$$P(10 < X < 15) = P(X < 15) - P(X < 10)$$
$$= F_X(15) - F_X(10)$$

2. The **probability density function** $f_X(x)$ of the random variable X provides a very useful visual representation of probabilities. This function is constructed so that $f_X(x)$ is non-negative for all x, with the area under the curve $f_X(x)$ between any two possible values equal to the probability that the random variable lies between those values. For example, Figure 2.1 shows the probability density function of the amount, in ounces, of impurity in a bag of chemical. The shaded area is the probability that between 10 and 15 ounces will be found. Notice that the total area under a probability density function is one, since an outcome between $-\infty$ and $+\infty$ is certain.

Expected Values, Mean, and Variance

The probability density function contains all possible information about a random variable. However, it is also very useful to have available numerical summary measures of that information. For example, it would be useful to know the average amount of impurity in all bags of the chemical. The

FIGURE 2.1   Probability density function for amount X, in ounces, of impurity in a bag of a chemical. The shaded area is the probability of between 10 and 15 ounces, $P(10 < X < 15)$.

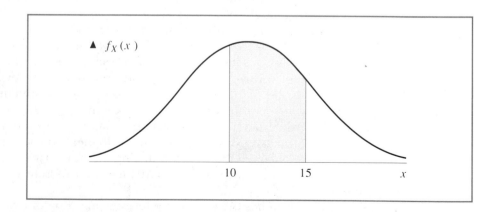

notion of expected values is important in this respect. The **expected value** of a random variable X, denoted $E(X)$, is the average value that would be taken over a very large (essentially infinite) number of trials. The expected value of a random variable is called its **mean,** denoted μ_X, so that

$$\mu_X = E(X)$$

The mean of a random variable obviously carries useful information, because, for example it is valuable to know, on the average, how much impurity is contained in the bags of chemical. Most often, however, the mean alone will not constitute an adequate summary measure. For example, it is certainly useful for a quality control manager to know if impurity levels are low enough that, on the average, a product of adequate quality is being produced. However, concern should remain if this average is attained in circumstances where many bags with quite high impurity contents are balanced by others with very low impurity levels. In this case, the probability of finding a bag of poor quality may be unacceptably high. It is desirable to check for this possibility through a measure of variability, or **dispersion,** about the mean. Such a measure is provided by the **variance,** σ_X^2, of a random variable, defined as the expectation of its squared difference from the mean, so that

$$\sigma_X^2 = E[(X - \mu_X)^2]$$

It is often convenient to describe variability in terms of the original units of measurement, so that the **standard deviation** of a random variable is defined as the (positive) square root of its variance. Consider, for example, an investment in some risky security, such as shares of common stock in a corporation. At the time such an investment is made, the investor will be uncertain about the rate of return that will be obtained, so that this rate can be thought of as a random variable. Obviously, all other things being equal, a high expected rate of return will be preferred. However, also of concern is the degree of risk involved in an investment, so that a high probability of substantial loss is unattractive. High risk, or uncertainty about rate of return, is reflected in a large standard deviation for this random variable. Thus, in assessing a speculative investment, the prudent investor will take into account not only the mean rate of return but also the standard deviation. Given investors' general aversion to risk, efficiency in the securities markets suggests that a higher expected rate of return can only be obtained at the cost of taking on more risk—that is, investing in a security for which the standard deviation of rate of return is also higher.

It is sometimes the case that interest is in a random variable Y that is a linear function of some other random variable X; that is,

$$Y = A + BX$$

where A and B are fixed numbers. Suppose that the random variable X has mean μ_X and standard deviation σ_X. Then it can be shown that the random variable Y has mean and standard deviation

$$\mu_Y = A + B\mu_X \qquad \sigma_Y = |B|\,\sigma_X$$

Related Random Variables

A number of approaches to forecasting exploit relationships among quantities, and in the next two chapters we will introduce methods for building models of such relationships. Any number of variables met in business and economics might reasonably be postulated to exhibit some form of interrelationship. For example, prices of common stock often move in the opposite direction to interest rates. Of course, for some variables we would not reasonably expect to find a relationship of any kind. A pair of random variables is said to be **independent** if the probability that one of them falls in any particular range is the same whatever the value taken by the other. For example, the amount of rainfall in one month in New York City will not provide any useful information about the monthly change in stock market prices. Our judgment about probable values of the latter will be the same whatever we know or believe of the former.

The more interesting case is where some relationship between random variables might reasonably be expected to exist, and here a difficulty arises because, in principle, variables can be related in infinitely many possible ways. Often some progress can be made by considering, at least as a reasonable approximation, the possibility of a **linear association** between a pair of random variables. That is, if data were available, the data points would be distributed around a straight line. This association could be *positive*, so that high values of one variable tend to be associated with high values of the other, and low values of one with low values of the other. For example, we might expect to find such an association between product sales and advertising expenditures. An alternative possibility is of *negative* linear association, where high values of one random variable tend to be associated with low values of the other. We would expect such a relationship, for example, between unemployment and output in an industry, or in the economy at large.

Let X and Y be a pair of random variables, with means μ_X and μ_Y. Consider the product of deviations from the means $(X - \mu_X)(Y - \mu_Y)$. In the case of positive association, when X is relatively large (compared with its mean), Y will tend to be relatively large. Similarly, relatively small values of X will tend to occur in conjunction with relatively small values of Y. Thus we would expect the product $(X - \mu_X)(Y - \mu_Y)$ to be positive. On the other hand, in the case of negative association, relatively high values of one of these random variables will tend to be associated with relatively low values of the other, so that $(X - \mu_X)(Y - \mu_Y)$ can be expected to be negative. The intermediate case, where the expectation of this product is zero, is that of no linear association between the random variables. The expected value of the product $(X - \mu_X)(Y - \mu_Y)$ is called the **covariance** between X and Y; it is denoted C_{XY}, so that

$$C_{XY} = E[(X - \mu_X)(Y - \mu_Y)]$$

If a pair of random variables is independent, the covariance between them is zero. However, zero covariance does not necessarily imply independence: there may be some relationship other than a linear one between the random variables.

The sign of the covariance between a pair of random variables indicates the direction of any linear association between them. However, the magnitude of the covariance does not provide a direct measure of the strength of that association; the size of the covariance depends on the units in which the random variables are measured. For example, suppose that X denotes product price measured in dollars. If instead price were to be measured in cents, so that each observation was simply 100 times its former value, the covariance between price and any other variable would also be 100 times its former value. For many purposes a scale-free measure of the strength of linear association between a pair of random variables is needed. This is provided by their *correlation,* to be discussed in the next chapter.

Often, we are interested in a random variable that is the sum of two (or more) other random variables. Let X and Y be random variables with means μ_X and μ_Y and variances σ_X^2 and σ_Y^2, and let Z be their sum, so that

$$Z = X + Y$$

Then it can be shown that the mean of the sum is the sum of the means, so that

$$\mu_Z = \mu_X + \mu_Y$$

Also, the variance of the sum is

$$\sigma_Z^2 = \sigma_X^2 + \sigma_Y^2 + 2C_{XY}$$

so that, in the special case where the covariance between X and Y is zero, the variance of the sum is the sum of the variances.

The Normal Distribution

In principle, the possible probability structures for the distribution of random variables are endless. It is a remarkable fact that a single family of distributions plays a central role in the theory and practice of statistics. The random variable X is said to follow a **normal distribution** if its probability density function is

$$f_X(x) = \frac{1}{\sqrt{2\pi\sigma^2}} e^{-(x-\mu)^2/2\sigma^2}$$

where $-\infty < x < \infty$, $-\infty < \mu < \infty$, and $0 < \sigma^2 < \infty$. Here, π and e are physical constants, with $\pi = 3.14159\ldots$, and $e = 2.71828\ldots$. The two parameters μ and σ^2 determine a specific normal distribution from this general class: the former is the mean of the distribution, and the latter is its variance. When graphed, the normal probability density function has the appearance of a bell-shaped curve, symmetric around the mean μ, as shown in Figure 2.2. The mean μ determines the center of the distribution, and the variance σ^2 determines the amount of dispersion around the

FIGURE 2.2   Probability density function of a normally distributed random variable.

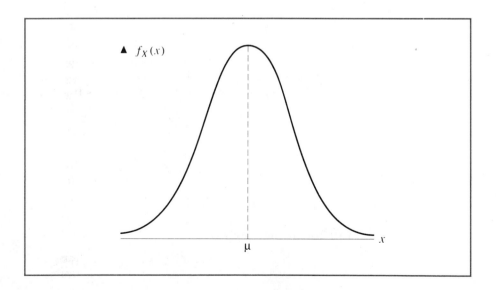

mean; the smaller the variance the more tightly will the probability density function be concentrated around the mean.

It is useful to find probabilities that normally distributed random variables lie in particular ranges. A difficulty in this task arises because we can encounter infinitely many normal distributions, determined by specific values of the mean and variance. This difficulty can be surmounted by employing the fact that any linear function of a normal random variable also has a normal distribution. Let X be a normally distributed random variable with mean μ and variance σ^2. Then, subtracting the mean leaves us with a random variable ϵ, defined from

$$X = \mu + \epsilon \qquad (2.2.1)$$

that has a normal distribution with mean zero and variance σ^2. Then, dividing this random variable by the standard deviation σ yields a random variable

$$Z = \epsilon/\sigma \qquad (2.2.2)$$

having a normal distribution with mean zero and variance one. This is called the **standard normal distribution.**

Once probabilities for the standard normal distribution are known, probabilities for any normal distribution can be found. Table A.1 in the Appendix gives, for selected probabilities α, the numbers z_α such that the probability is α that a standard normal random variable will exceed z_α, that is

$$P(Z > z_\alpha) = \alpha$$

This notation is illustrated in Figure 2.3. Notice that the probability density function of the standard normal random variable is symmetric about its mean of zero, from which it follows that the probability is also α that a standard normal random variable will be less than $-z_\alpha$, so that

$$P(Z < -z_\alpha) = \alpha$$

For example, directly from Table A.1, we see that the probability is 0.025 that a standard normal random variable exceeds 1.960, so that

$$P(Z > 1.960) = 0.025$$

It follows immediately that

$$P(Z < -1.960) = 0.025$$

FIGURE 2.3   Probability density function of the standard normal random variable.

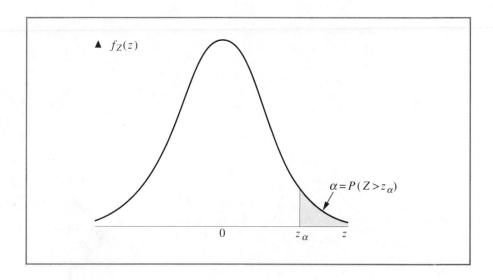

and hence that the probability is 0.95 that a standard normal random variable takes a value between -1.960 and 1.960; that is,

$$P(-1.960 < Z < 1.960) = 0.95$$

This result is illustrated in Figure 2.4.

To see how probabilities for any normal distribution can be found, let X be a normal random variable with mean μ and variance σ^2. It then follows from equations 2.2.1 and 2.2.2 that the random variable

$$Z = \frac{X - \mu}{\sigma}$$

has a standard normal distribution. Thus we have

$$\alpha = P(Z > z_\alpha)$$

$$= P\left[\frac{X - \mu}{\sigma} > z_\alpha\right]$$

$$= P(X > \mu + \sigma z_\alpha)$$

For example, suppose that the amount of impurity in bags of a chemical follows a normal distribution with mean $\mu = 12$ ounces, and standard

FIGURE 2.4   Some probabilities for the standard normal distribution.

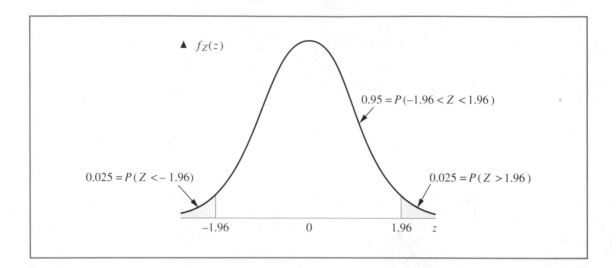

deviation $\sigma = 2$ ounces. We have, denoting weight of impurity by X,

$$0.95 = P(-1.960 < Z < 1.960)$$

$$= P\left[-1.960 < \frac{X - 12}{2} < 1.960\right]$$

$$= P[12 - (1.960)(2) < X < 12 + (1.960)(2)]$$

$$= P(8.08 < X < 15.92)$$

We therefore conclude that 95% of all bags contain between 8.08 and 15.92 ounces of impurity.

In introducing the normal distribution we asserted its central role in statistics. Certainly the formula for the probability density function does not convey any very compelling intuitive appeal of this distribution for the representation of real world phenomena. The graph of this density function is more encouraging. It suggests that the probability of observing values in the central ranges will be quite high, while probabilities for extremely low or extremely high values, in the tails of the distribution, will be much smaller. This agrees with our experience in the observation of many physical quantities—heights and weights of individuals, for example. However, the position occupied by the normal distribution in statistics follows chiefly from a single remarkable result—the *central limit theorem*. Many random variables in which we are most interested are sums or averages of moderately large numbers of other random variables. Given a set of independent random variables, with identical distributions having finite variances, the **central limit theorem** asserts that, as the number of random variables in the set increases, the distribution of their average approaches the normal. This occurs regardless of the distribution of the individual random variables. The normal and related distributions play an important part in statistics because we often deal with sums or averages, or similar functions of random variables, when trying to make inferences about a population on the basis of sample information. In the remainder of the chapter we will explore this inference problem.

2.3   SAMPLING AND SAMPLING DISTRIBUTIONS

A frequently occurring problem arises when we want to learn something about a very large set, or **population,** of numerical values. To collect information on the whole population would be prohibitively expensive and time consuming. Instead, just a subset, or **sample,** of population members is studied. For example, although our interest is in the population of impurity levels in all bags of a chemical shipped by a corporation, only a small subset of bags can be tested. An investigator's focus of interest will be in the whole population: the sample is studied as a way of learning something, or *making inference,* about the population. Since the entire population is not examined, it will be impossible to learn with complete certainty much about it. Even after a careful analysis of the sample data, uncertainty about the population characteristics will necessarily remain. It is this inevitable uncertainty that places the problem of making inference about a population on the basis of sample information firmly in the province of the statistician. Provided that the sample has been chosen by some random mechanism, it should be possible following its analysis to make probability statements that capture elements of our remaining uncertainty about the population. The most straightforward sampling scheme is to select a **simple random sample** of population members. Here, if a sample of n observations is required, it is arranged so that each possible sample of n values is equally likely to be chosen.

The whole structure of a population is summarized in its probability density function or, equivalently, in its cumulative distribution function. However, on the basis of information from a modest-sized sample, it will generally be too ambitious to attempt to learn about these entire functions. For most purposes it should be adequate to make inference about one or two characteristics, or **parameters,** of the population distribution. For example, it may be sufficient to consider the mean and variance of the amounts of impurity in bags of chemicals. This inference must be based on *statistics* computed from the available sample data. For example, suppose that a sample of ten bags is taken: it is natural to base inference about the unknown population mean on the average impurity level in the ten sampled bags—that is, on the **sample mean.**

Now, in the example just discussed we would not expect the sample mean to be precisely equal to the population mean. What we would like is some estimate of how far apart the two are likely to be. This question is attacked through the concept of sampling distributions. The particular sample that is actually taken is just one of a very large number that could have been observed. Different samples of ten bags of chemicals would yield different sample mean impurity contents. The distribution of all possible values of a sample statistic is known as the **sampling distribution** of that statistic.

Suppose that we want to make inference about a population whose values are distributed with unknown mean μ and unknown variance σ^2. A sample of n observations is drawn. We will denote the sample members by $X_1, X_2, \ldots, X_n$. These are viewed as random variables, since prior to taking the observations there will be uncertainty about what values will be found. The distributions of the individual sample members X_i, then, are identical to the population distribution; in particular, each X_i has mean μ and variance σ^2. Further, if simple random sampling is used and the population is very large, these random variables will be independent of one another: the value taken by one will not be affected by the value taken by any other.

For now, suppose that our interest is in making inference about the population mean μ. This will be based on the sample mean

$$\overline{X} = \sum_{i=1}^{n} X_i/n$$

We now need to find the sampling distribution of $\overline{X}$. The mean of this distribution is easily found, since

$$E(\overline{X}) = E\left(\sum_{i=1}^{n} X_i/n\right) = \frac{1}{n} E\left(\sum_{i=1}^{n} X_i\right)$$

Now, using the fact that the mean of a sum is the sum of the means, it follows, since each X_i has mean μ, that

$$E(\overline{X}) = \frac{1}{n} n\mu = \mu$$

Thus the mean of the sampling distribution of the sample mean is the population mean.

The variance of this sampling distribution is

$$\sigma_{\overline{X}}^2 = \text{Var} \left(\sum_{i=1}^{n} X_i/n \right) = \frac{1}{n^2} \text{Var} \left(\sum_{i=1}^{n} X_i \right)$$

Then, since the variance of the sum of independent random variables is the sum of the variances, it follows, since each X_i has variance σ^2, that

$$\sigma_{\overline{X}}^2 = \frac{1}{n^2} n\sigma^2 = \sigma^2/n$$

The standard deviation of the sampling distribution of the sample mean is therefore

$$\sigma_{\overline{X}} = \sigma/\sqrt{n}$$

This quantity is sometimes called the **standard error** of the sampling distribution. Notice that, in sampling from any population, as the number n of sample observations increases, the standard error of the sampling distribution of the sample mean decreases, so that the distribution of the sample mean becomes more tightly concentrated about the true mean. The implication is that, as the sample size increases, the probability that the sample mean differs from the population mean by any fixed amount decreases. This is to be expected, and simply reflects the fact that the more information we collect, the more precise will be our knowledge about the population.

If the distribution of the population members is normal, then it can be shown that the distribution of the sample mean is also normal. Moreover, as a result of the central limit theorem, even if the population distribution is not normal, the distribution of the sample mean will typically be quite close to normal, provided the sample is of at least moderate size. Thus, in most applications, it suffices to take the sampling distribution of the sample mean to be normal, with mean μ and standard deviation $\sigma/\sqrt{n}$. It then follows that the random variable

$$Z = \frac{\overline{X} - \mu}{\sigma_{\overline{X}}} = \frac{\overline{X} - \mu}{\sigma/\sqrt{n}} \qquad (2.3.1)$$

has a distribution that is approximately standard normal. To illustrate this result, suppose that for the population of all bags of chemicals the mean impurity weight is 12 ounces and the standard deviation is 2 ounces. A sample of ten bags is taken, and the sample mean denoted by $\overline{X}$. We have already seen that the probability is 0.95 that a standard normal random variable lies between -1.960 and 1.960. We therefore find

$$0.95 = P(-1.960 < Z < 1.960)$$

$$= P\left[-1.960 < \frac{\overline{X} - 12}{2/\sqrt{10}} < 1.960\right]$$

$$= P\left[-1.960 < \frac{\overline{X} - 12}{0.63246} < 1.960\right]$$

$$= P[12 - (1.960)(0.63246) < \overline{X} < 12 + (1.960)(0.63246)]$$

$$= P(10.76 < \overline{X} < 13.24)$$

We find then that the probability is 0.95 that the sample mean will be between 10.76 and 13.24 ounces—that is, within 1.24 ounces of the population mean.

The calculations of the previous paragraph were made possible through an assumption that the population variance was known. In most practical applications such an assumption will be unrealistic. Typically, when we draw a sample from a population, both the true population mean and variance will be unknown. As a practical matter, even if our only interest is in the population mean, it will be necessary for purposes of inference to use the sample data to learn something about the population variance. This parameter can be estimated by the **sample variance,** defined as

$$s^2 = \sum_{i=1}^{n} (X_i - \overline{X})^2/(n - 1) \qquad (2.3.2)$$

The positive square root of this quantity, the **sample standard deviation,** then provides a natural estimate of the population standard deviation.

When the population standard deviation is unknown, the result in equation 2.3.1 cannot be used directly. It seems natural to replace the unknown σ in equation 2.3.1 by its sample estimate, the sample standard deviation s. However, the resulting distribution is no longer standard normal. In fact, the result is known as the **Student's t** distribution with $(n - 1)$ degrees of freedom, denoted t_{n-1}, so that we can write

$$t_{n-1} = \frac{\overline{X} - \mu}{s/\sqrt{n}} \qquad (2.3.3)$$

The expression "degrees of freedom" requires a little explanation. Essentially, it arises because the sample variance is used to estimate the population variance. For this estimation problem, we have available n observations $X_1, X_2, \ldots, X_n$. However, in effect one of these observations is "lost" because the unknown population mean μ must be estimated by the sample mean $\overline{X}$, leaving the equivalent of $(n - 1)$ observations—or $(n - 1)$ degrees of freedom. Estimation of the population variance is based on the discrepancies from the sample mean

$$X_1 - \overline{X}, X_2 - \overline{X}, \ldots, X_n - \overline{X}$$

However, these do not constitute n independent pieces of information, for if we know any $(n - 1)$ of them, we necessarily know the other, since

$$\sum_{i=1}^{n} (X_i - \overline{X}) = 0$$

The n discrepancies from the sample mean effectively provide $(n - 1)$ independent pieces of information—or **degrees of freedom**—for the estimation of the population variance.

Like the standard normal distribution, the Student's t distribution is symmetric about a mean of zero. The two probability density functions are quite similar in shape, except that the latter has rather heavier tails. For a Student's t distribution with v degrees of freedom, denoted t_v, Table A.2 in the Appendix gives for various values v, and selected probabilities α, numbers $t_{v,\alpha}$, such that the probability is α that $t_{v,\alpha}$ is exceeded by this random variable; that is

$$\alpha = P(t_v > t_{v,\alpha})$$

Since the distribution is symmetric about zero, it follows immediately that

$$P(t_v < -t_{v,\alpha}) = \alpha$$

For example, consider the Student's t distribution with nine degrees of freedom. Directly from the table we see that

$$P(t_9 > 2.262) = 0.025$$

It then follows that

$$P(t_9 < -2.262) = 0.025$$

and hence that

$$P(-2.262 < t_9 < 2.262) = 0.95$$

FIGURE 2.5   Some probabilities for the Student's t distribution with nine degrees of freedom.

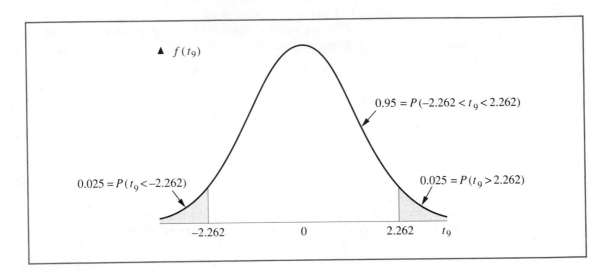

These probabilities are illustrated in Figure 2.5, which is the analogue of Figure 2.4.

It follows from equation 2.3.3 that, for a sample of ten observations,

$$P\left[-2.262 < \frac{\overline{X} - \mu}{s/\sqrt{10}} < 2.262\right] = 0.95$$

Results of this sort, based on the Student's t distribution, are exactly valid if the population distribution is normal. They remain approximately valid, even in moderate-sized samples, for a wide range of non-normal population distributions.

Sampling Distribution of the Sample Variance

In many applications it is important to make inference not only about the population mean, but also about the population variance σ^2. For example, it would be useful to learn about the variability in the levels of impurity in bags of chemicals. Inference about the population variance is based on the sample variance, defined in equation 2.3.2. The sampling distribution of this statistic depends quite critically on the shape of the underlying population distribution. However, it can be shown that, whatever the population distribution, the mean of the sampling distribution of the sample variance is equal to the population variance, that is,

$$E(s^2) = \sigma^2$$

It is precisely to achieve this result that the sample variance is defined as in equation 2.3.2, with division of the sum of squared discrepancies about the sample mean by $(n - 1)$, rather than by n, as would at first sight seem more natural.

If the underlying population distribution is normal, it is known that the random variable

$$\chi^2_{n-1} = (n - 1)s^2/\sigma^2 \qquad\qquad (2.3.4)$$

has a distribution called the *chi-square distribution with $(n - 1)$ degrees of freedom*. Since variances cannot be negative, this random variable can take only non-negative values. Also, its probability density function is not symmetric. Denote by χ^2_ν a chi-square random variable with ν degrees of freedom. For such a random variable, Table A.3 in the Appendix at the back of this book gives numbers $\chi^2_{\nu,\alpha}$ for various values ν and selected probabilities α, such that the probability is α that $\chi^2_{\nu,\alpha}$ is exceeded by this random variable, that is

$$\alpha = P(\chi^2_\nu > \chi^2_{\nu,\alpha})$$

For example, consider the chi-square distribution with nine degrees of freedom. Directly from the table we find that

$$P(\chi^2_9 > 19.02) = 0.025$$

Also from the table we find

$$P(\chi^2_9 > 2.70) = 0.975$$

so that

$$P(\chi^2_9 < 2.70) = 0.025$$

It then follows that

$$P(2.70 < \chi^2_9 < 19.02) = 0.95$$

These probabilities are illustrated in Figure 2.6. Now suppose that, for all bags of chemicals, the standard deviation of impurity weight is $\sigma = 2$

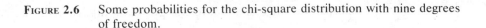

FIGURE 2.6   Some probabilities for the chi-square distribution with nine degrees of freedom.

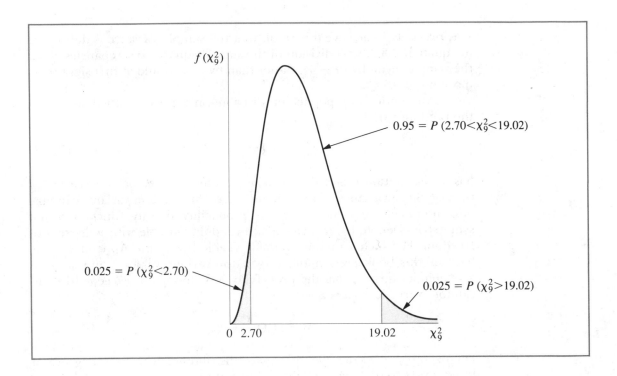

ounces. A sample of ten bags is taken, and the sample variance denoted by s^2. Then, using equation 2.3.4,

$$0.95 = P(2.70 < \chi_9^2 < 19.02)$$
$$= P(2.70 < 9s^2/4 < 19.02)$$
$$= P[(4)(2.70)/9 < s^2 < (4)(19.02)/9]$$
$$= P(1.20 < s^2 < 8.45)$$

Then, taking square roots inside the bracket yields

$$0.95 = P(1.10 < s < 2.91)$$

We have therefore found that, for a sample of ten observations from a population with standard deviation 2, the probability is 0.95 that the sample standard deviation is between 1.10 and 2.91.

It should be repeated that the validity of these calculations is quite heavily dependent on the assumption that the population distribution is normal; they can be quite misleading when sampling from non-normal populations. Inference about a population mean, based on the Student's t distribution, is generally pretty reliable for sampling from a wide range of population distributions. Such inference is said to be *robust* to departures from normality in the population distribution. On the other hand, inference about a population variance, based on the chi-square distribution, is not robust. Fortunately, in the following chapters, where we seek to make inference about future values of some process of interest, the statistics used are essentially analogues of the sample mean, so that an assumption of normality will not be too critical.

2.4 POINT AND INTERVAL ESTIMATION

In forecasting, we attempt in essence to estimate the values that will be taken by some process in the future. The reader will already have met the problem of estimation in the context of sampling from a population, where estimates of parameters such as the mean and variance are required.

Perhaps the type of estimate that most readily springs to mind is a **point estimate**—a single number, computed from the sample data, that constitutes a best guess, or at any rate a good guess about the population parameter of interest. For example, the sample mean, variance, and standard deviation provide quite natural estimators of the population mean, variance, and standard deviation. Table 2.1 shows the results from a random sample of ten observations on impurity levels, in ounces, in bags of chemicals. From these data we find a sample mean of

$$\overline{X} = \sum_{i=1}^{10} X_i/10 = 11.82$$

and a sample variance of

$$s^2 = \sum_{i=1}^{10} (X_i - \overline{X})^2/9 = 5.2262$$

TABLE 2.1   A sample of ten observations on impurity levels (in ounces) in bags of a chemical.

10.7	11.6	8.0	9.0	13.9	15.1	11.2	11.5	14.4	12.8

so that the sample standard deviation is

$$s = 2.286$$

Thus our point estimates of the population mean and standard deviation impurity levels are, respectively, 11.82 and 2.286 ounces.

For these simple point estimation problems, the choice of point estimators seems fairly obvious. However, as we will see in the next two chapters, for less straightforward problems this is not the case. In general, many alternative point estimators of a population parameter may be available, and it will be necessary to make some choice from among them. This can be aided by focusing on desirable properties of estimators, through an examination where possible of the characteristics of their sampling distributions.

In general, let θ denote a population parameter to be estimated, and $\hat{\theta}$ a possible point estimator. The estimator is said to be **unbiased** if the mean of its sampling distribution is equal to the population parameter, that is

$$E(\hat{\theta}) = \theta$$

We have already seen, then, that the sample mean and variance are unbiased estimators of the population mean and variance, that is

$$E(\overline{X}) = \mu \qquad E(s^2) = \sigma^2$$

It is to achieve this latter result that the sum of squared discrepancies from the sample mean is divided by $(n - 1)$ rather than by n in the definition in equation 2.3.2 of the sample variance. The sample standard deviation is not, however, an unbiased estimator of the population standard deviation. All other things equal, unbiasedness is a desirable property in an estimator. The implication is that, if the population were to be sampled a very large number of times, the value of the estimator would, on the average, be equal to that of the parameter being estimated.

Although unbiasedness is an attractive quality in an estimator, it is not by itself a sufficiently strong recommendation. It is little consolation that, on the average, an estimator will be accurate if, in any particular application, the probability is high that it will differ substantially from the true parameter value. This suggests that we should also be concerned about the amount of dispersion about its mean in the sampling distribution of an estimator. The variance of this sampling distribution provides one measure of dispersion, and it is generally desirable that this variance be as small as possible. One unbiased estimator is said to be more **efficient** than another if its sampling distribution has the smaller variance. On some occasions it is possible to demonstrate that a particular point estimator is the most efficient of all possible point estimators. This is the case, for example, for the sample mean and variance when sampling from a normal distribution. More often, an attempt is made to find the most efficient estimator from a broad class of point estimators. As we will see in the next two chapters, the least squares estimators of the parameters of a regression model satisfy such a requirement.

One difficulty in seeking efficient, unbiased point estimators is that for many problems it is simply not possible to find the sampling distributions of candidate estimators: it may also not be possible to find *any* estimators that can be shown to be unbiased. Perhaps surprisingly, it is often easier to learn the statistical properties of estimators in the limiting case where the number of sample observations becomes infinitely large. Let θ be a parameter to be estimated, and $\hat{\theta}_n$ a point estimator based on a sample of n observations. Of course, we would like the probability that $\hat{\theta}_n$ differs from θ by any amount to be as small as possible. Moreover, as the sample size n increases, we would expect this probability to fall. The estimator $\hat{\theta}_n$ is said to be **consistent** for θ if the probability that $\hat{\theta}_n$ differs from θ by any amount, however small, approaches zero as the number n of sample observations approaches infinity. Presumably we would prefer that an estimator have this property, which might be paraphrased as "getting it right" when vast amounts of sample information are available. Admittedly, consistency may be of little comfort to an analyst having just a small sample. Still, if an estimator is inconsistent, it is hard to see how satisfactory performance can be expected in small samples either. The study of the behavior of point estimators as the sample size becomes infinitely large can be taken further. For many consistent estimators $\hat{\theta}_n$, it is possible to show that the sampling distribution of $\sqrt{n}\,\hat{\theta}_n$ approaches the normal as the sample size n approaches infinity. Estimators for which the variance of this normal distribution is as small as possible are said to be **best asymptotic normal.** This concept in infinitely large samples is analogous to the idea of most efficient unbiased estimator in finite samples. An estimation procedure, called the method of *maximum likelihood*, which yields best asymptotic normal estimators for a broad range of problems, is widely used in statistics. We will not discuss its details. This approach has been used for the estimation of the parameters of the time series models to be discussed in Chapter 7.

Confidence Intervals

For many estimation problems, a point estimator alone, however satisfactory its properties, is insufficient. It will typically be valuable also to have some measure of the amount of uncertainty associated with such an estimator. One possibility is to seek an **interval estimate**—a range in which one can have some confidence that the unknown population parameter lies.

Let θ be a parameter that must be estimated on the basis of sample data. Suppose further that two statistics A and B, which are functions of the available sample observations, can be found so that the probability is some specified amount, say $(1 - \alpha)$, that at the same time A is less than θ, and B is bigger than θ; that is,

$$P(A < \theta < B) = 1 - \alpha$$

Then the interval from A and B is called a **confidence interval** with probability content $(1 - \alpha)$, or a $100(1 - \alpha)\%$ confidence interval for the parameter θ.

To illustrate the construction of such intervals, consider the sample of ten observations, given in Table 2.1, on amounts of impurity in bags of chemicals. Both the population mean and population variance are unknown, and the sample data are to be used to make inference about these parameters. We begin by finding confidence intervals for the population mean impurity level. These are based on the Student's t random variable, defined in equation 2.3.3. As we have already seen, for the Student's t random variable with nine degrees of freedom,

$$0.95 = P(-2.262 < t_9 < 2.262)$$

It then follows that

$$0.95 = P\left[-2.262 < \frac{\overline{X} - \mu}{s/\sqrt{10}} < 2.262\right]$$

$$= P(\overline{X} - 2.262\ s/\sqrt{10} < \mu < \overline{X} + 2.262\ s/\sqrt{10})$$

This then defines a 95% confidence interval for the population mean. Substituting the values found for the sample mean and standard deviation, we find the interval

$$11.82 - (2.262)(2.286)/\sqrt{10} < \mu < 11.82 + (2.262)(2.286)/\sqrt{10}$$

or

$$10.18 < \mu < 13.46$$

Thus, a 95% confidence interval for the mean weight of impurity in all bags of this chemical runs from 10.18 to 13.46 ounces. Such confidence intervals can be interpreted as follows: If this population were to be independently and repeatedly sampled, with samples of ten observations drawn, then 95% of all confidence intervals calculated in this way would, over the long run, contain the true population mean. We might therefore say, before drawing the sample, that the probability is 0.95 that the interval we obtain will include μ.

Confidence intervals with other probability contents can be found in the same way. For example, to obtain a 90% confidence interval in this example, we need only note from Table A.2 that the probability is 0.90 that a Student's t random variable with nine degrees of freedom lies between -1.833 and 1.833; that is

$$0.90 = P(-1.833 < t_9 < 1.833)$$

It then follows, using the same argument as before, that a 90% confidence interval for the population mean impurity content is

$$11.82 - (1.833)(2.286)/\sqrt{10} < \mu < 11.82 + (1.833)(2.286)/\sqrt{10}$$

or

$$10.49 < \mu < 13.15$$

Notice that the 95% confidence interval is wider than the 90% confidence interval. This result is quite general. Based on the same information, the greater the probability content the wider will be the confidence interval for any population parameter. This is to be expected; the surer we want to be that a computed interval will contain the parameter, the wider the interval that will be required.

Since the random variable defined in equation 2.3.4 has a chi-square distribution with $(n - 1)$ degrees of freedom, confidence intervals for population variances can also be found, assuming that the population distribution is normal. Our example involves a sample of ten observations, and we have already seen that

$$0.95 = P(2.70 < \chi_9^2 < 19.02)$$

It then follows that

$$0.95 = P(2.70 < 9s^2/\sigma^2 < 19.02)$$
$$= P(9s^2/19.02 < \sigma^2 < 9s^2/2.70)$$

Thus, substituting the observed value of the sample variance, it follows that a 95% confidence interval for the population variance is given by

$$(9)(5.2262)/19.02 < \sigma^2 < (9)(5.2262)/2.70$$

or

$$2.4730 < \sigma^2 < 17.4207$$

Taking square roots, it follows that a 95% confidence interval for the population standard deviation is

$$1.57 < \sigma < 4.17$$

We see then that a 95% confidence interval for the standard deviation of impurity levels in all bags of chemicals runs from 1.57 to 4.17 ounces.

Models and Forecasts

In much statistical work, an important goal is to build a *model* aimed at providing a description of the real world phenomenon under study. Model building involves a good deal of art, as well as a familiarity with statistical science. The real world is a very complex place, and it is impossible to construct a model describing all of the elements that generate actual variables. Indeed, an excess of complexity in model building may be counterproductive. The aim should be to try to represent the major determinants of the variable under study with as simple a structure as is tenable, while taking care to check the adequacy of that structure. Once built, an adequate model can help the analyst in trying to understand the real world phenomenon under study. Fitted models can also be profitably extrapolated forward to produce forecasts. In the next two chapters we will see how regression models can be used to represent relationships among business and economic variables. Here, by way of introducing these ideas, we will discuss the analysis of a random sample from a population with unknown mean and variance from a model-building perspective. Admittedly that particular problem is sufficiently straightforward that the provision of this amount of formality is not really necessary for the analysis. It does, however, provide a useful introduction to some of the concepts of regression analysis through a familiar example.

The objective of model building is to write down an algebraic formulation of the process that might have generated the available data. The resulting model will typically involve a systematic, or deterministic, component. It will inevitably involve a random, or chance, component, since in reality no simple algebraic equation, or system of equations, will be capable of fully explaining the precise values of observed phenomena.

In the case where a random sample of n observations from a population with unknown mean μ and unknown variance σ^2 is taken, the resulting sample observations are denoted $X_1, X_2, \ldots, X_n$. These represent independent random variables, each with mean μ and variance σ^2. We can therefore write

$$X_i = \mu + \epsilon_i \qquad i = 1, 2, \ldots, n \qquad (2.4.1)$$

Subtraction of their mean, μ, from the random variables X_i leaves random variables ϵ_i having mean zero and variance σ^2. Moreover, since the random variables X_i are independent on one another, so are the random variables ϵ_i.

Equation 2.4.1 states that an observation X_i is the sum of a systematic component μ and a random component ϵ_i. This equation, together with specifications or assumptions about the random variables ϵ_i, constitutes the data-generating model for this simple example. These assumptions are:

1. The ϵ_i all have mean zero.
2. The ϵ_i have a common variance, σ^2.
3. The ϵ_i are independent of one another.

As we have seen, the sample mean $\overline{X}$ is typically employed as an estimator of μ. This estimator has the following two interesting properties:

1. Let $\hat{\mu}$ be any point estimator of μ, and consider the sum of squared discrepancies between the observations X_i and $\hat{\mu}$,

$$S = \sum_{i=1}^{n} (X_i - \hat{\mu})^2$$

This sum of squared discrepancies is smallest for the estimator

$$\hat{\mu} = \overline{X}$$

For this reason $\overline{X}$ is called the **least squares** estimator of μ.
2. Consider the class of all estimators of μ that are linear functions of the X_i; that is

$$\hat{\mu} = c_1 X_1 + c_2 X_2 + \cdots + c_n X_n$$

where the c_i are fixed numbers, not depending on the X_i. Then, of all such estimators that are unbiased for μ, the sample mean $\overline{X}$ has the smallest variance. In the terminology introduced earlier in this section, the sample mean is the most efficient estimator of the population mean in this class. It is sometimes called a **best linear unbiased estimator.**

We will leave the proof of these two results as an exercise for the reader. Note that the second does not require an assumption that the ϵ_i have normal distributions: it holds for any distribution with finite variance. If the normality assumption is added to the others that were made, sampling distributions of the estimators of μ and σ^2 can be derived, as discussed in Section 2.3. These allow the derivation of confidence intervals for those two parameters, as we saw earlier in this section. This general approach through model building extends directly to the analysis of regression models, as we will see in Chapters 3 and 4.

Suppose now that another observation is to be drawn from our population. Denote by X_{n+1} the new observation, and consider the problem of forecasting its value. Admittedly this is the least interesting of forecasting problems, but its study yields some useful insights. The new observation can be written

$$X_{n+1} = \mu + \epsilon_{n+1} \qquad (2.4.2)$$

where the random variable ϵ_{n+1} has mean zero, variance σ^2, and is independent of ϵ_i $(i = 1, \ldots, n)$. Looking at equation 2.4.2, it is pretty clear how we would predict X_{n+1}. The right-hand side of this equation is the sum of two parts. The first of these is the unknown population mean μ, which can be estimated by the sample mean $\overline{X}$ of the n available observations. The second term is a random variable ϵ_{n+1} which has a mean of zero, and is independent of any available information. The best we can do then is to predict it by its mean value of zero. Thus our forecast of the next observations X_{n+1} is

$$\hat{X}_{n+1} = \overline{X}$$

The sample mean of the available observations, then, serves as a **point forecast** of the next observation.

It is also useful to have a measure of the uncertainty associated with this forecast. This can be achieved through study of the **forecast error,** the difference between the actual value and its point forecast; that is,

$$X_{n+1} - \hat{X}_{n+1} = -(\overline{X} - \mu) + \epsilon_{n+1} \qquad (2.4.3)$$

Each term on the right-hand side of this expression has mean zero. Hence, the forecast error has mean zero, and the forecast is said to be unbiased. The two terms on the right-hand side of equation 2.4.3 are independent of one another. Thus, the variance of their sum is the sum of their variances, so that the variance of the forecast error is

$$\text{Var}(X_{n+1} - \hat{X}_{n+1}) = \sigma^2/n + \sigma^2 = \sigma^2[(n + 1)/n]$$

If now it is assumed that the population distribution is normal, it follows that the random variable

$$Z = \frac{X_{n+1} - \hat{X}_{n+1}}{\sigma[(n + 1)/n]^{1/2}}$$

has a standard normal distribution. The population standard deviation σ will be unknown, but can be estimated from the n sample observations by the sample standard deviation s. Inference about the future observation X_{n+1} can then be based on the fact that the random variable

$$t_{n-1} = \frac{X_{n+1} - \hat{X}_{n+1}}{s[(n + 1)/n]^{1/2}} \qquad (2.4.4)$$

has a Student's t distribution with $(n - 1)$ degrees of freedom. Confidence intervals for the new observation can be based on this result.

To illustrate, consider the sample of ten observations, given in Table 2.1, on impurity levels in bags of chemicals. An eleventh observation is to be taken, and the forecasting problem is to predict its value. The point forecast is simply the sample mean

$$\hat{X}_{n+1} = \hat{X}_{11} = \overline{X} = 11.82$$

Confidence intervals for future observations are called **interval forecasts.** To obtain interval forecasts, it is only necessary to use the result from equation 2.4.4. We have already seen that, for a Student's t random variable with nine degrees of freedom

$$0.95 = P(-2.262 < t_9 < 2.262)$$

It then follows that

$$0.95 = P\left[-2.262 < \frac{X_{11} - \hat{X}_{11}}{s(11/10)^{1/2}} < 2.262\right]$$

$$= P[\hat{X}_{11} - 2.262s(11/10)^{1/2} < X_{11} < \hat{X}_{11} + 2.262s(11/10)^{1/2}]$$

Thus, substituting the observed value for the sample standard deviation, a 95% confidence interval for the next observation is given by

$$11.82 - (2.262)(2.286)(1.1)^{1/2} < X_{11} < 11.82 + (2.262)(2.286)(1.1)^{1/2}$$

or

$$6.40 < X_{11} < 17.24$$

Hence, a 95% confidence interval for the weight of impurity in the next bag that will be analyzed runs from 6.40 to 17.24 ounces.

The confidence interval found in this example is quite wide, reflecting a good deal of uncertainty about what will be observed next. Inspection of equation 2.4.2 suggests two sources for this uncertainty. First, the true population mean is unknown, and must be estimated from sample data. Second, the distribution of the random variable ϵ_{n+1} has standard deviation σ, reflecting variability among the population members. The first of these two sources of uncertainty can be reduced by basing the forecasts on a larger sample, and hence on a more precise estimate of the population mean; the second, however, is irreducible. This example provides a convenient introduction to some of the features of forecasting problems, particularly those for which regression analysis is appropriate. It is, however, far more straightforward than, and not at all typical of, forecasting problems commonly met in practice. In many real world problems, the appropriate generating model is both more complicated and more interesting than equation 2.4.1.

2.5 HYPOTHESIS TESTING

Hypothesis testing provides another approach to making inference about a population on the basis of sample information. Sample data are employed to check the validity of conjectures, or **hypotheses,** about population parameters. Such hypotheses might specify that a population parameter takes a single specific value, or that the parameter falls in some range. The former type of hypothesis is called **simple,** and the latter **composite.** At the outset, a maintained hypothesis, or **null hypothesis,** about a population parameter is formulated. This hypothesis will be held to be true unless the available sample data contain sufficient contrary evidence. Hypothesis testing, then, can be viewed as the analysis of sample information to assess the strength of evidence against a null hypothesis about a population parameter. The null hypothesis is tested against an **alternative hypothesis**—a conjecture that is assumed to be true if the null hypothesis is false. For example, management of our chemical corporation is concerned that the mean weight of impurity in bags of a chemical does not exceed ten ounces. Strong evidence of a higher average weight will lead to a modification of the production process to improve quality. The null hypothesis, denoted H_0, is that the true mean weight μ is at most ten ounces, that is

$$H_0: \mu \leq 10$$

This is tested against the alternative hypothesis, H_1, that the true mean is bigger than ten ounces,

$$H_1: \mu > 10$$

Having specified null and alterative hypotheses and analyzed the sample data, some decision must be made. In classical statistical hypothesis testing, there are two possible decisions—either to **accept** the null hypothesis or to **reject** it in favor of the alternative. Naturally, it is hoped that the correct decision will be made. This could happen in two ways. Either the null hypothesis could be accepted when it is in fact true, or it could be rejected when it is in fact false. However, since the decision is to be based on sample data, uncertainty about the population will necessarily remain, so it is possible that any decision will be in error. Two types of error are possible:

1. A *Type I* error occurs when a true null hypothesis is rejected.
2. A *Type II* error occurs when a false null hypothesis is accepted.

A decision about a null hypothesis will be based on a **decision rule,** formulated before the data are analyzed. This rule will determine whether the null hypothesis is accepted or rejected, given the sample information. For any decision rule to be applied to sample information there will be nonzero probabilities that both types of error will be made. Adjusting the decision rule to reduce one of these probabilities will necessarily raise the other. In general, practical hypothesis testing proceeds by first fixing at some suitably low level the probability of a Type I error, which is known as the **significance level** of the test. This determines the form of the decision rule that must be used, and in turn the probability of a Type II error. The probability of rejecting a false null hypothesis is known as the **power** of the test. Obviously, for a given significance level, the higher the power of the test the better, and tests are sought having the highest possible power for a fixed significance level and number of sample observations. One way to increase the power of a test, while keeping the significance level unchanged, is to base the test on a larger sample.

We will illustrate the principles of hypothesis testing through the problem of sampling from a normal population with unknown mean μ

and unknown variance σ^2. A sample of n observations is taken, and interest is in the parameter μ. Suppose that we want to test the null hypothesis that the population mean is either equal to some specific value μ_0, or is no bigger than μ_0; that is,

$$H_0: \mu = \mu_0 \quad \text{or} \quad H_0: \mu \leq \mu_0$$

The alternative hypothesis is that the population mean is bigger than μ_0,

$$H_1: \mu > \mu_0$$

Now, if the true mean actually is μ_0, then, as we saw in Section 2.3, the random variable

$$t_{n-1} = \frac{\overline{X} - \mu_0}{s/\sqrt{n}} \qquad (2.5.1)$$

has a Student's t distribution with $(n - 1)$ degrees of freedom. The test decision rule is based on this result. When the sample mean and standard deviation are observed, a realization from the distribution in equation 2.5.1 is available if the true mean is μ_0. This realization provides our test statistic. The null hypothesis will be rejected in favor of the alternative if this realization is a large positive number—that is, if the sample mean $\overline{X}$ is much bigger than the hypothesized mean μ_0. To see how large a value should lead to rejection of the null hypothesis, consider Figure 2.7, depicting the probability density function of the Student's t distribution. Also shown is the number $t_{n-1,\alpha}$, exceeded with probability α by a Student's t random variable with $(n - 1)$ degrees of freedom, so that

$$P(t_{n-1} > t_{n-1,\alpha}) = \alpha$$

Thus, if the true population mean is μ_0, the probability is α that the random variable of equation 2.5.1 will exceed $t_{n-1,\alpha}$. This probability is even lower if the population mean is less than μ_0. It therefore follows that a test with significance level α is provided by the decision rule

$$\text{Reject } H_0 \text{ if } \frac{\overline{X} - \mu_0}{s/\sqrt{n}} > t_{n-1,\alpha}$$

To illustrate, suppose that, using the data of Table 2.1, on amounts of impurity in ten bags of chemicals, we want to test the null hypothesis

$$H_0: \mu \leq 10$$

FIGURE 2.7   The probability is α that a Student's t random variable with $(n - 1)$ degrees of freedom exceeds the number $t_{n-1,\alpha}$.

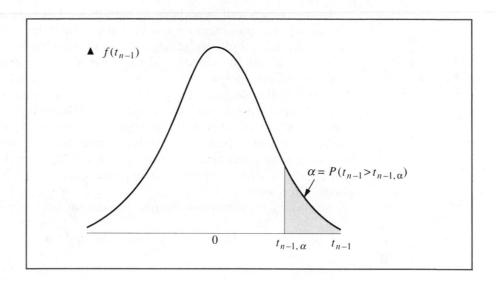

against the alternative

$$H_1: \mu > 10$$

We will use a test with significance level $\alpha = .05$, that is, a 5%-level test. This guarantees that the probability of rejecting the null hypothesis when it is true is at most 0.05. From Table A.2 we find

$$P(t_9 > 1.833) = 0.05$$

Thus, with a 5%-level test, the null hypothesis that the population mean is at most ten ounces is rejected if

$$\frac{\overline{X} - 10}{s/\sqrt{10}} > 1.833$$

Substituting the observed values of the sample mean and standard deviation, we find

$$\frac{\overline{X} - 10}{s/\sqrt{10}} = \frac{11.82 - 10}{2.286/\sqrt{10}} = 2.518$$

Thus the null hypothesis is rejected at the 5%-level, providing strong evidence against the claim that the true mean weight of impurity is no more than ten ounces.

In rejecting a null hypothesis at the 5%-level, we are in effect saying that one of two possibilities must be true. Either the null hypothesis is false, or, in the sample, we have observed an extremely rare event—one that will occur with probability 0.05 when the null hypothesis is true. Now, a null hypothesis can be tested at any significance level an investigator chooses. A null hypothesis that is rejected at one significance level may be accepted at some lower level. Conversely, a null hypothesis that is accepted at one significance level may be rejected at some higher level. Many statistical computer programs produce **probability-values,** or **p-values,** associated with particular test statistics. These are the lowest levels of significance at which certain null hypotheses can be rejected against a specific alternative.

Suppose we want to test the null hypothesis

$$H_0: \mu = \mu_0 \quad \text{or} \quad H_0: \mu \geq \mu_0$$

against the alternative

$$H_1: \mu < \mu_0$$

We would now suspect that the null hypothesis was false if the sample mean was much lower than μ_0. Since the Student's t distribution is symmetric about its mean of zero, it follows that the decision rule for a test of significance level α is

$$\text{Reject } H_0 \text{ if } \frac{\overline{X} - \mu_0}{s/\sqrt{n}} < -t_{n-1,\alpha}$$

A third possibility is that we might want to test the null hypothesis that the population mean is equal to some specific value μ_0,

$$H_0: \mu = \mu_0$$

against the alternative that the true mean is different from μ_0,

$$H_1: \mu \neq \mu_0$$

This is called a **two-sided alternative,** as it permits values of the population mean on both sides of the hypothesized value μ_0.

Again the test is based on the sample realization of the statistic in equation 2.5.1, but now the null hypothesis will be rejected for either very high or very low values of this statistic—that is, if the sample mean is either much bigger than or much smaller than μ_0. To see how the decision rule is formulated, consider Figure 2.8. If we let $t_{n-1,\alpha/2}$ denote the number exceeded with probability $\alpha/2$ by a Student's t random variable with $(n-1)$ degrees of freedom, then

$$P(t_{n-1} > t_{n-1,\alpha/2}) = \alpha/2$$

Also, by the symmetry of the Student's t distribution

$$P(t_{n-1} < -t_{n-1,\alpha/2}) = \alpha/2$$

so that

$$P(t_{n-1} > t_{n-1,\alpha/2} \quad \text{or} \quad t_{n-1} < -t_{n-1,\alpha/2}) = \alpha$$

It therefore follows that a test of significance level α is based on the decision rule

$$\text{Reject } H_0 \text{ if } \frac{\overline{X} - \mu_0}{s/\sqrt{n}} < -t_{n-1,\alpha/2} \quad \text{or} \quad \frac{\overline{X} - \mu_0}{s/\sqrt{n}} > t_{n-1,\alpha/2}$$

For example, for a sample of ten observations, a 5%-level test has decision rule

$$\text{Reject } H_0 \text{ if } \frac{\overline{X} - \mu_0}{s/\sqrt{10}} < -2.262 \quad \text{or} \quad \frac{\overline{X} - \mu_0}{s/\sqrt{10}} > 2.262$$

FIGURE 2.8   The probability is α that a Student's t random variable with $(n-1)$ degrees of freedom is either less than $-t_{n-1,\alpha/2}$ or bigger than $t_{n-1,\alpha/2}$.

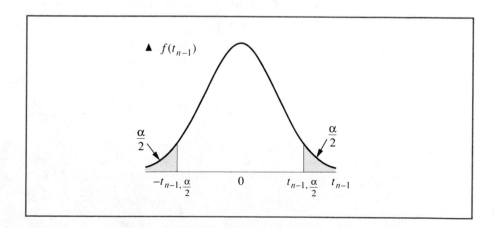

One difficulty with testing a simple null hypothesis against a two-sided alternative is that usually we will know that the null hypothesis is not precisely true. The mean weight of impurity in all bags of chemical, for example, will not be *exactly* ten ounces. Therefore, the null hypothesis will be rejected against the two-sided alternative at any significance level, however trivial the difference between the true and the hypothesized mean, provided that a sufficiently large sample is taken.

Hypothesis Test for Population Variance

It is also possible to test hypotheses about a population variance, σ^2, based on an assumption that the population distribution is normal. Typically, concern is that the variance not be greater than some amount σ_0^2, so that the null hypothesis

$$H_0: \sigma^2 = \sigma_0^2 \quad \text{or} \quad H_0: \sigma^2 \leq \sigma_0^2$$

is tested against the alternative hypothesis

$$H_1: \sigma^2 > \sigma_0^2$$

Given a random sample of n observations, with sample variance s^2, the test is based on the fact that, if the true population variance is σ_0^2, the random variable

$$\chi_{n-1}^2 = (n - 1)s^2/\sigma_0^2 \tag{2.5.2}$$

has a chi-square distribution with $(n - 1)$ degrees of freedom. Now, our null hypothesis will be rejected if the sample variance is much higher than the hypothesized population variance σ_0^2—that is, for high realizations of the statistic in equation 2.5.2. Let $\chi_{n-1,\alpha}^2$ be the number exceeded with probability α by a chi-square random variable with $(n - 1)$ degrees of freedom, so that

$$P(\chi_{n-1}^2 > \chi_{n-1,\alpha}^2) = \alpha$$

Then a test of significance level α follows from the decision rule

$$\text{Reject } H_0 \text{ if } (n - 1)s^2/\sigma_0^2 > \chi_{n-1,\alpha}^2$$

To illustrate, our chemical corporation is concerned that the standard deviation of the weights of impurity in bags of chemicals not exceed 1.5 ounces, that is, that the variance not exceed 2.25. Thus the null hypothesis

$$H_0: \sigma^2 \leq 2.25$$

is to be tested against the alternative

$$H_1: \sigma^2 > 2.25$$

We test this hypothesis using the data of Table 2.1, for which the sample variance is

$$s^2 = 5.2262$$

From Table A.3, we find that for a chi-square distribution with nine degrees of freedom

$$P(\chi_9^2 > 16.92) = 0.05$$

Hence, the decision rule for a 5%-level test is

$$\text{Reject } H_0 \text{ if } 9s^2/2.25 > 16.92$$

Here,

$$9s^2/2.25 = (9)(5.2262)/2.25 = 20.90$$

Thus, the null hypothesis that the population variance is at most 2.25 is rejected at the 5% significance level. The sample data, then, contain strong evidence against that hypothesis.

EXERCISES

2.1 The random variable X has a normal distribution with mean 60 and standard deviation 12.
   (a) The probability is 0.10 that this random variable takes a value less than what number?
   (b) Find the number K such that the probability is 0.90 that the random variable X takes a value between $60 - K$ and $60 + K$.
   (c) The random variable Y is defined by

$$Y = 200 - 2X$$

   Find the mean and standard deviation of Y.

2.2 A particular brand of tire has a lifetime whose distribution is normal with mean 40,000 miles and standard deviation 10,000 miles.
   (a) The probability is 0.95 that one of these tires has a lifetime of more than how many miles?

(b)   Four of these tires are chosen at random. The probability is 0.95 that their average lifetime is more than how many miles?

2.3   A mutual fund has a very large portfolio of stocks. A random sample of nine of these showed the following percentage returns over a year.

8.2	15.7	3.1	4.7	12.8
9.6	18.3	11.4	10.2	

Assume that the population distribution is normal.
(a)   Find the sample mean.
(b)   Find the sample variance.
(c)   Find the sample standard deviation.
(d)   Find a 99% confidence interval for the population mean.
(e)   Find a 95% confidence interval for the population variance.
(f)   Find a 90% confidence interval for the population standard deviation.

2.4   Carefully explain why a 95% confidence interval for a population parameter will be wider than a 90% confidence interval for that parameter based on the same information.

2.5   A random sample of 10 corporations showed the following percentage increases in earnings per share over the last year.

4.3	9.1	7.2	1.3	15.7
12.1	9.4	10.7	2.3	7.4

Assume the population distribution is normal.
(a)   Find the sample mean.
(b)   Find the sample variance.
(c)   Find the sample standard deviation.
(d)   Find a 90% confidence interval for the population mean.
(e)   Find a 90% confidence interval for the population standard deviation.

2.6   A random sample of n observations, $X_1, X_2, \ldots, X_n$, is taken from a population with mean μ. Let $\overline{X}$ denote the sample mean.
(a)   Show that

$$\sum_{i=1}^{n} (X_i - \overline{X}) = 0$$

(b) Using the result in (a), show that, if $\hat{\mu}$ is any number

$$\sum_{i=1}^{n} (X_i - \hat{\mu})^2 = \sum_{i=1}^{n} [(X_i - \overline{X}) + (\overline{X} - \hat{\mu})]^2$$

$$= \sum_{i=1}^{n} (X_i - \overline{X})^2 + n(\overline{X} - \hat{\mu})^2$$

(c) Using the result in (b), show that the sum of squared discrepancies

$$S = \sum_{i=1}^{n} (X_i - \hat{\mu})^2$$

is smallest when

$$\hat{\mu} = \overline{X}$$

2.7 A random sample of n observations, $X_1, X_2, \ldots, X_n$, is taken from a population with mean μ and variance σ^2. Let

$$\hat{\mu} = c_1 X_1 + c_2 X_2 + \cdots + c_n X_n,$$

where the c_i are fixed numbers, be an estimator of μ.
(a) Show that $\hat{\mu}$ is an unbiased estimator of μ if and only if

$$c_1 + c_2 + \cdots + c_n = 1$$

(b) Show that the variance of $\hat{\mu}$ is

$$(c_1^2 + c_2^2 + \cdots + c_n^2)\sigma^2$$

(c) Show that

$$\sum_{i=1}^{n} c_i^2 = \sum_{i=1}^{n} [(c_i - n^{-1}) + n^{-1}]^2$$

$$= \sum_{i=1}^{n} (c_i - n^{-1})^2 + 2n^{-1} \sum_{i=1}^{n} (c_i - n^{-1}) + n^{-1}$$

$$= \sum_{i=1}^{n} (c_i - n^{-1})^2 + n^{-1}$$

if $\hat{\mu}$ is an unbiased estimator of μ.

(d)   Using the results in (b) and (c), show that if $\hat{\mu}$ is an unbiased estimator of μ, its variance is smallest if

$$c_i = n^{-1} \qquad i = 1, 2, \ldots, n$$

that is, $\hat{\mu}$ is the sample mean $\overline{X}$.

2.8   Refer to Exercise 2.3. A tenth observation is to be drawn from this population.
(a)   Find a point forecast for the new observation.
(b)   Find a 95% confidence interval forecast for the new observation.

2.9   Refer to Exercise 2.5. An eleventh observation is to be drawn from this population.
(a)   Find a point forecast for the new observation.
(b)   Find an 80% confidence interval for the new observation.

2.10 A new toy has been introduced into the retail outlets of a large chain of toy stores. A random sample of twelve outlets showed the following results for numbers sold in the first week.

113	102	87	69	111	93
84	98	108	89	96	85

(a)   Find the sample mean.
(b)   Find the sample variance.
(c)   Find the sample standard deviation.
(d)   Test at the 5% level the null hypothesis that the population mean is at least 100.
(e)   Test at the 5% level the null hypothesis that the population standard deviation is at most 10.

2.11 Carefully explain why, if a null hypothesis is rejected against some alternative at the 5% significance level, this same null hypothesis using the same data will be rejected against the same alternative at the 10% significance level.

2.12 Forecasts of earnings per share for major corporations are made by large numbers of financial analysts. For a random sample of eight analysts, the following forecasts, in dollars, for earnings per share of a particular corporation were found.

10.4	14.8	13.7	9.6
12.7	15.8	11.6	12.0

Assume the population distribution is normal.
(a)   Find the sample mean.

(b) Find the sample variance.

(c) Find the sample standard deviation.

(d) Test at the 5% level against a two-sided alternative the null hypothesis that the population mean is $12 per share.

(e) Test at the 5% level the null hypothesis that the population standard deviation is at most $2.

2.13 A null hypothesis has been rejected against an alternative at the 5% significance level. Does this mean that the probability is at least 0.95 that the null hypothesis is false?

2.14 Refer to Exercise 2.12. A forecast from a ninth financial analyst is obtained. Find a 90% confidence interval for this new observation.

2.15 "The normal distribution is often used to describe populations such as heights, weights, and so on, whose values must be positive. But, any normal random variable can take negative values. Therefore, the normal distribution is not appropriate for such populations." Comment on this statement.

SELECTED BIBLIOGRAPHY

Cryer, J. D. & R. B. Miller (1991). *Statistics for Business: Data Analysis and Modeling.* Boston: PWS-Kent.

Mansfield, E. (1991). *Statistics for Business and Economics: Methods and Applications* (4th ed.). New York: W.W. Norton and Company.

McClave, J. T. & P. G. Benson (1991). *Statistics for Business and Economics* (5th ed.). San Francisco: Dellen Publishing Company.

Newbold, P. (1991). *Statistics for Business and Economics* (3rd ed.). Englewood Cliffs, N.J.: Prentice Hall.

Roberts, H. (1991). *Data Analysis for Managers* (2nd ed.). Redwood City, Calif.: Scientific Press.

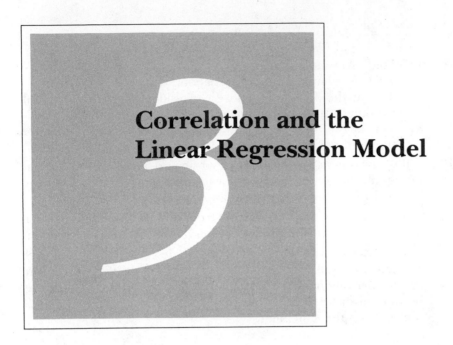

3 Correlation and the Linear Regression Model

3.1 CORRELATION

Often in forecasting one can successfully take advantage of relationships among variables. If relationships that have held in the past continue to do so in the future, successful prediction can be based on the discovery of such regularities in historical data. In this chapter we will discuss the simplest possible case—a linear relation between a pair of random variables.

In Section 2.2 we introduced the covariance as a measure of the linear association between a pair of random variables, noting that this provides an unsatisfactory measure of the strength of association, as its magnitude depends on the units in which the variables are measured. Let X and Y be a pair of random variables, with means μ_X and μ_Y and standard deviations σ_X and σ_Y. The covariance between these random variables is defined as the expected value of the products of discrepancies from their means;

$$C_{XY} = E[(X - \mu_X)(Y - \mu_Y)]$$

The sign of the covariance indicates the direction of any linear association between the random variables. A positive covariance suggests that high values of X tend to be associated with high Y, and low X with low Y. A negative covariance indicates that high values of one of the random variables tend to be associated with low values of the other. If there is no linear association between the random variables, their covariance is zero.

The dependence of the covariance on the units of measurement is easily removed. Division of this quantity by the product of the standard deviations of the random variables yields the **correlation**—a pure scale-free measure of strength of linear association. The correlation then is

$$\rho = C_{XY}/\sigma_X \sigma_Y \qquad (3.1.1)$$

It is possible to demonstrate that the correlation necessarily lies between plus and minus one,

$$-1 \leq \rho \leq 1$$

As we have seen, if there is no linear association between a pair of random variables, their correlation is zero. A correlation of one implies a perfect positive association between the random variables, so that if joint observations were taken on these quantities, the observation points would all lie precisely on an upward-sloping straight line. At the other extreme, a correlation of -1 corresponds to a perfect negative association between the random variables, so that any observation points would fall exactly on a downward-sloping straight line. Between these two extremes, the bigger in absolute value is the correlation between a pair of random variables, the stronger is their linear association. Obviously the stronger is any relationship that can be found, the more valuable is that relationship likely to be, both in understanding the behavior of the system under study and as an aid to forecasting.

To see how the correlation coefficient might be viewed as a measure of the strength of *linear* association between a pair of random variables, suppose that in fact the random variables X and Y are linearly related. Specifically, assume that, given a specific value x for the random variable X, the expected value of Y, $E(Y \mid X = x)$ is a linear function of x. Then it can be shown that this *conditional expectation* of the random variable Y must be

$$E(Y \mid X = x) = \mu_Y + \rho \frac{\sigma_Y}{\sigma_X} (x - \mu_X)$$

The slope of this linear relationship is just the product of the correlation coefficient and the ratio of the two standard deviations. Notice that, when ρ is zero, the expected value of Y is the same whatever value is observed for the random variable X. Otherwise, the larger in absolute value is the correlation coefficient, the greater, all else equal, is the impact of the value taken by X on the expectation of Y—that is, the greater the strength of the linear association between these random variables. In subsequent sections of this chapter we will employ regression models to formulate linear dependence of just this sort.

The correlation coefficient ρ, defined in equation 3.1.1, is a population parameter: in practice, its value will not be precisely known. It can, however, be estimated from sample data. Suppose that we have available a random sample of n pairs of observations $(X_1, Y_1), (X_2, Y_2) \ldots (X_n, Y_n)$ on the random variables X and Y. The correlation between these random variables is estimated by substituting estimates for each of the population parameters on the right-hand side of equation 3.1.1. As in Chapter 2, the population standard deviations are estimated by the corresponding sample standard deviations

$$s_X = \left[\sum_{i=1}^{n} (X_i - \overline{X})^2/(n-1) \right]^{1/2} \qquad s_Y = \left[\sum_{i=1}^{n} (Y_i - \overline{Y})^2/(n-1) \right]^{1/2}$$

where $\overline{X}$ and $\overline{Y}$ are the two sample means. The population covariance is estimated by the sample covariance

$$c_{XY} = \sum_{i=1}^{n} (X_i - \overline{X})(Y_i - \overline{Y})/(n-1)$$

Substitution of these sample statistics for the corresponding population parameters in equation 3.1.1 yields the **sample correlation coefficient**

$$r = \frac{c_{XY}}{s_X s_Y} = \frac{\sum_{i=1}^{n} (X_i - \overline{X})(Y_i - \overline{Y})}{\left[\sum_{i=1}^{n} (X_i - \overline{X})^2 \sum_{i=1}^{n} (Y_i - \overline{Y})^2 \right]^{1/2}} \qquad (3.1.2)$$

Given sample data, the statistic 3.1.2 is readily calculated, and all standard statistical computer program packages provide this facility.

It is sometimes of interest to test, based on the evidence of sample data, the null hypothesis of no linear association between a pair of random variables; that is, that the correlation between them is zero

$$H_0: \rho = 0 \qquad (3.1.3)$$

Naturally, inference about the population correlation is based on the sample correlation 3.1.2, so that, for a given number of sample observations, the more that r differs from zero, the stronger the grounds for doubting the truth of the null hypothesis 3.1.3. In fact, the test is based on the statistic

$$t = r/\sqrt{(1 - r^2)/(n - 2)} \qquad (3.1.4)$$

It can be shown that, when the null hypothesis of zero population correlation is true, the random variable corresponding to the statistic 3.1.4 has a Student's t distribution with $(n - 2)$ degrees of freedom. The precise form of the test then depends on the alternative hypothesis:

1. If the alternative is that the population correlation is positive

$$H_1: \rho > 0$$

the decision rule is, for a test of significance level α,

$$\text{Reject } H_0 \text{ if } \quad r/\sqrt{(1 - r^2)/(n - 2)} > t_{n-2,\alpha}$$

where, in the notation of Section 2.5, $t_{n-2,\alpha}$ is the number exceeded with probability α by a Student's t random variable with $(n - 2)$ degrees of freedom.

2. If the alternative is that the population correlation is negative

$$H_1: \rho < 0$$

the decision rule is, for a test of significance level α,

$$\text{Reject } H_0 \text{ if } \quad r/\sqrt{(1 - r^2)/(n - 2)} < -t_{n-2,\alpha}$$

3. If the alternative hypothesis is the two-sided one that the population correlation is not zero

$$H_1: \rho \neq 0$$

the decision rule is, for a test of significance level α,

$$\text{Reject } H_0 \text{ if } r/\sqrt{(1 - r^2)/(n - 2)} < -t_{n-2,\alpha/2} \quad \text{or} \quad > t_{n-2,\alpha/2}$$

We will not illustrate these correlation calculations here. Our chief interest in correlation is in its connection with regression models, and in its role in the time series model building methods to be discussed in

Chapter 7. In fact, as we will see in Section 3.4, a test for zero correlation can be carried out in the context of linear regression model analysis.

3.2 THE LINEAR REGRESSION MODEL

The concept of correlation postulates a linear association between a pair of random variables. There is, however, no implication about the *direction* of that association. The two variables are treated perfectly symmetrically, so that we might equally well discuss "the correlation between X and Y" or "the correlation between Y and X." **Regression analysis** views the association between variables rather differently. Here we consider that the value taken by one random variable might influence the value taken by another. For example, we might want to assess the effect of advertising expenditure on sales, or the impact of a price increase on the demand for electricity. The two variables are no longer treated symmetrically. Rather, we ask how the value taken by an **independent variable,** X, influences the value of a **dependent variable,** Y. We then speak of *the regression of Y on X.*

Since our concern is with forecasting, we will usually be interested in **time series data**—that is, observations taken over time, generally at equally spaced intervals, on quantities of interest. Accordingly, although regression analysis is equally applicable to other types of data sets, we will employ the subscript t, signifying time, to denote observations. In the case of a pair of random variables (X, Y), a set of n observations over time will be denoted

$$(X_t, Y_t) \qquad t = 1, 2, \ldots, n$$

These observations might be taken at daily, weekly, monthly, quarterly, or annual intervals.

Given just a pair of random variables, X and Y, the goal of regression analysis is to build a model representing the dependence of Y on X. In this chapter we will discuss the simplest model of this sort—the **linear regression model.** The following two considerations underlie the specification of this model:

1. In practice the dependence of one variable on another might conceivably take any number of forms, but, unless a substantial amount of data is available, an exhaustive search among many alternative functional forms is likely to be unrewarding. However, experience suggests that, at least in the range of observations likely to be encountered, an assumption of *linear dependence* will often provide an adequate approximation to the true relationship. In the simplest case, the *expected value* of the dependent variable at time t will be taken to be a linear

function of the realization of the independent variable at time t. Then, denoting by $E(Y_t | X_t)$ the expected value of the dependent variable when the independent variable takes the value X_t, we have the general relation

$$E(Y_t | X_t) = \alpha + \beta X_t \qquad (3.2.1)$$

This relation defines a general straight line, with **intercept** α and **slope** β. In practice, the two parameters α and β will be unknown, and must be estimated from data.

2. In the real world, we do not expect any simple relationship between variables to hold precisely. Thus, while on average it might be reasonable to think of the value of a dependent variable as a simple linear function of an independent variable, the *actual value* observed for the dependent variable will inevitably differ somewhat from its expectation. Writing this discrepancy as ϵ_t, so that

$$\epsilon_t = Y_t - E(Y_t | X_t)$$

we have from equation 3.2.1 the linear regression model

$$Y_t = \alpha + \beta X_t + \epsilon_t \qquad (3.2.2)$$

The term ϵ_t can be viewed as the amalgamation of all those factors, other than the value of the independent variable, that influence the value of the dependent variable. Since we will be uncertain about the value to be taken by ϵ_t at any point in time, this quantity is regarded as a random variable, with mean zero.

Before discussing the fitting of the linear regression model to data, we need to consider the interpretation of the parameters α and β, and also some possible assumptions that might reasonably be made about the random variable ϵ_t. The slope parameter β has an important interpretation. Suppose that the value of the independent variable increases by one unit, from X_t to $X_t + 1$. Then, as in equation 3.2.1, we can write

$$E(Y_t | X_t + 1) = \alpha + \beta(X_t + 1)$$

Subtracting 3.2.1 then gives

$$E(Y_t | X_t + 1) - E(Y_t | X_t) = \alpha + \beta(X_t + 1) - (\alpha + \beta X_t) = \beta$$

We see then that β is *the expected increase in the value of the dependent variable resulting from a one unit increase in the value of the independent variable.*

Substituting $X_t = 0$ in equation 3.2.1 suggests that α is *the expected value of the dependent variable when the independent variable takes the value zero.* Often, however, this interpretation is irrelevant, and may indeed be misleading. For example, the expected demand for electricity when the price is zero is a concept of no practical value. Moreover, even if a linear relationship between expected demand and price of electricity may appear reasonable in the range of electricity prices actually observed, it would be foolish to put much faith in the continuation of this relationship at prices, such as zero, that are well outside that range.

Before any progress can be made in actually fitting the linear regression model to data, it is necessary to make some further assumptions. As a starting point to regression analysis, the following *standard assumptions* are typically made:

1. The quantities X_t are either fixed numbers, chosen for example by a laboratory analyst running an experiment, or they are realizations of random variables that are uncorrelated with the *error terms* ϵ_t.
2. The error terms ϵ_t all have mean zero.
3. The error terms ϵ_t have a common variance, say σ^2.
4. The error terms ϵ_t are not correlated with one another.
5. The values X_t of the independent variable are not all the same.

The first of these assumptions can be viewed in a number of ways. The following is a simple illustration of how it might break down. Suppose that, in addition to X, Y depends on some other variable Z. Then, in effect, Z is incorporated in the error term ϵ. If Z is in fact strongly correlated with X, analysis of the simple linear regression model can yield quite misleading conclusions about the dependence of Y on X. In these circumstances, simple linear regression analysis is inadequate, and it is necessary to consider the more general multiple regression models of Chapter 4, where the value of a dependent variable is permitted to depend on the values taken by several independent variables.

Assumptions 2–4, taken together, suggest that the error terms ϵ_t behave as a random sample of n observations from a population with mean zero. Certainly this will not inevitably be the case in situations where data are passively observed over time, rather than arising through a random sampling scheme. However, an analysis based on these assumptions, which can subsequently be checked, constitutes a reasonable starting point. In this chapter we will take the standard assumptions to hold, discussing the possibility of certain breakdowns in Chapter 4. Of particular concern with time series data is the fourth assumption. Many business and economic processes evolve quite smoothly over time, so that if the dependent variable is above its expected value, for example, in the current period, we might suspect that more likely than not it will also be above its expected value in the next period. Correlation between adjacent error terms in time series data is referred to as the problem of **autocorrelated errors.** We will have much more to say about this problem in Chapter 4.

In practice, the values of the independent variable will almost certainly not all be the same. Assumption 5 is required since, if we do not observe changes in the independent variable it will obviously be impossible to estimate the impact of such changes on the dependent variable.

3.3 FITTING THE LINEAR REGRESSION MODEL

Given a set of n pairs of observations on a dependent and independent variable, we will want to fit the linear regression model 3.2.2—that is, to estimate the intercept and slope parameters, α and β. We will illustrate the calculations with the data of Table 3.1, which shows sixteen quarterly observations on the percentage unemployment rates in the state of Alabama (Y) and the United States as a whole (X). In the regression model the behavior of unemployment in the national economy is used to explain the behavior of unemployment in the state economy. These data are plotted in Figure 3.1, from which it appears that an assumption of linear dependence is quite reasonable. The fitting of a linear regression model to data can be viewed as finding the straight line that in some sense best fits the data points in plots such as Figure 3.1. Looking at that figure, we might feel that we could do a pretty good job of fitting, quite informally by eye, a line through these points. However, the more formal methods that we will employ allow for soundly based inferential statements about the population parameters, and can be extended to more complex problems where simple visual approaches are infeasible.

At least under the standard assumptions about the regression model, made in Section 3.2, the **method of least squares** provides an attractive approach to the estimation of the parameters of a regression model. Let

TABLE 3.1 Quarterly observations on percentage unemployment rate in Alabama (Y) and in the United States (X).

t	Y_t	X_t	t	Y_t	X_t	t	Y_t	X_t
1	7.73	6.30	7	10.33	7.40	12	15.60	10.67
2	8.40	7.33	8	11.13	8.23	13	16.27	10.37
3	9.80	7.67	9	13.33	8.83	14	14.00	10.13
4	9.33	7.40	10	13.63	9.43	15	12.93	9.33
5	10.70	7.43	11	15.00	9.90	16	11.53	8.53
6	10.50	7.40						

FIGURE 3.1   Sixteen quarterly observations on percentage unemployment rate in
Alabama (Y) and the United States (X).

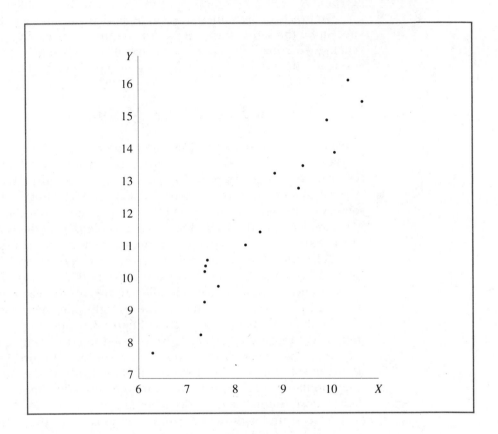

a and b be possible estimates of the regression parameters α and β, leading
to the fitted regression, of the relation between expected, or predicted,
value of the dependent variable, and the independent variable

$$\hat{Y} = a + bX$$

Figure 3.2 shows a possible fitted regression line, together with a single
data point (X_t, Y_t). When the independent variable takes the value X_t, the
value predicted for the dependent variable by this regression line is

$$\hat{Y}_t = a + bX_t$$

The value actually observed for the dependent variable is Y_t. The differ-

FIGURE 3.2 A candidate sample regression line, and the distance from a point to that line.

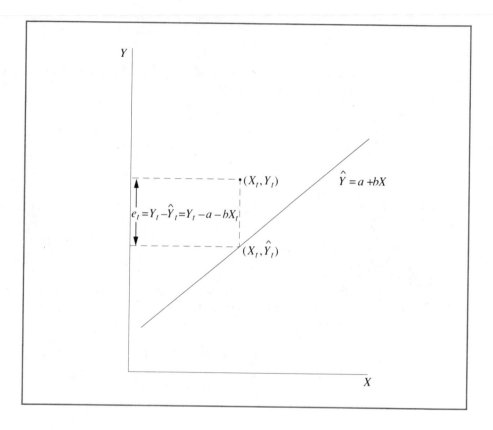

ence between the observed and predicted values of the dependent variable

$$e_t = Y_t - \hat{Y}_t = Y_t - a - bX_t \qquad (3.3.1)$$

is taken as the distance from the data point to the candidate regression line. Notice that distance of a point from a line is not taken as the shortest (perpendicular) distance. Rather, distance is measured along the Y-axis, because the purpose of regression analysis is to use the independent variable to explain the behavior of the dependent variable. The difference between observed and predicted values of the dependent variable then provides a natural measure of the quality of that explanation.

The method of least squares selects that line for which the sum of squared distances from all observation points to the line is as small as possible. Thus, the values a and b are chosen as those numbers for which the sum of squares

$$S = \sum_{t=1}^{n} e_t^2 = \sum_{t=1}^{n} (Y_t - a - bX_t)^2$$

is a minimum. It can be shown that this sum of squares is minimized by the **least-squares estimates**

$$b = \frac{\displaystyle\sum_{t=1}^{n} (X_t - \overline{X})(Y_t - \overline{Y})}{\displaystyle\sum_{t=1}^{n} (X_t - \overline{X})^2}$$

and

$$a = \overline{Y} - b\overline{X}$$

where $\overline{X}$ and $\overline{Y}$ are the sample means of the observations.

For the unemployment data of Table 3.1, the least-squares parameter estimates are

$$a = -4.194 \qquad b = 1.8872$$

Thus the **sample regression line** is

$$\hat{Y} = -4.194 + 1.8872X$$

This line, together with the data points, is shown in Figure 3.3. Visual inspection confirms this as a plausible fit to the given data. The slope of the sample regression line can be interpreted as an estimate that each one percentage point increase (decrease) in the U.S. unemployment rate leads to an expected 1.8872 percentage points increase (decrease) in the Alabama unemployment rate.

We have introduced the method of least squares as an intuitively plausible algorithm for the fitting of a straight line to a set of data points. It is, however, a good deal more than that. After all, the reader could easily think of a number of alternative plausible procedures for fitting lines to data. The widespread practical use of least squares stems from an optimality property provided by the **Gauss-Markov theorem.** Consider the problem of estimating the parameters α and β of the linear regression model 3.2.2, and suppose that the standard assumptions of Section 3.2 do

FIGURE 3.3   Quarterly observations on percentage unemployment rate in
Alabama (Y) and in the United States (X), with the sample
regression line.

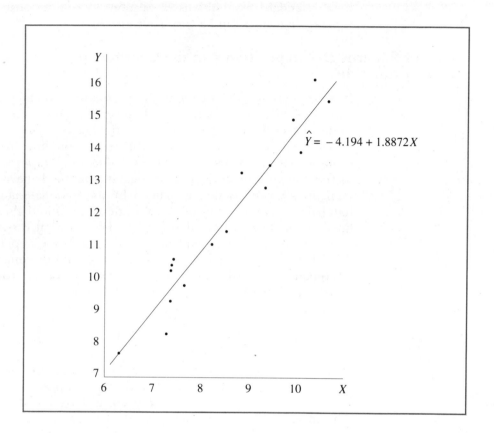

in fact hold. Now, consider the set of all parameter estimators that are
linear functions of observed sample values of the dependent variable; that
is, estimators of the form

$$c_1 Y_1 + c_2 Y_2 + \cdots + c_n Y_n$$

where $c_1, c_2, \ldots, c_n$ are fixed numbers not depending on the Y_t. Then,
according to the Gauss-Markov theorem, of all estimators of the regression
parameters in this class that are unbiased, the least squares estimators
have smallest variance. For this reason, they are often said to be **best
linear unbiased estimators** (BLUE). In the terminology of Section 2.4,
the method of least squares provides the most efficient unbiased point
estimators from a broad class of possible estimators. The Gauss-Markov

theorem provides a powerful motivation for the use of the least squares method in the estimation of the parameters of the linear regression model. However, this approach will not invariably be appropriate. For example, if the standard assumptions of Section 3.2 are seriously violated, least squares estimators can be very poor indeed.

Sums of Squares Decomposition and the Coefficient of Determination

It is certainly useful to compute least squares estimates of the intercept and slope of a regression line. However, to gain some insight into the value of the fitted regression, some further analysis is necessary. It is important to assess how closely the regression line fits the data. For example, looking at Figure 3.3, we get the visual impression of a close fit to our unemployment data. This suggests that the behavior of unemployment in Alabama is well explained by the national rate. On the other hand, if the data points were widely scattered around the sample regression line, we would conclude that we had been less successful in using the independent variable to explain the behavior of the dependent variable.

These considerations suggest that we should be concerned about the discrepancies, or **residuals,** between the values observed for the dependent variable and those predicted by the sample regression line. The larger are these residuals

$$e_t = Y_t - \hat{Y}_t = Y_t - a - bX_t$$

in magnitude, the poorer our achieved explanation of the behavior of the dependent variable. Under the standard assumptions, the error terms ϵ_t in the regression model 3.2.2 are taken to have a common variance σ^2. An unbiased estimator of this error variance is provided by

$$s^2 = \sum_{t=1}^{n} e_t^2/(n - 2) = \sum_{t=1}^{n} (Y_t - a - bX_t)^2/(n - 2) \quad (3.3.2)$$

Notice here that division is by the degrees of freedom number $(n - 2)$. Intuitively this arises because the equivalent of two observations is lost in the estimation of the parameters α and β. For our unemployment data, we found

$$s^2 = 0.482$$

In the next two sections we will see how this statistic is useful in assessing uncertainty about both the least squares parameter estimates and forecasts derived from the sample regression line.

The observed value of the dependent variable can be written as the sum of its predicted value from the sample regression and the residual, that is,

$$Y_t = \hat{Y}_t + e_t$$

Subtracting the sample mean of the dependent variable from each side of this equation then gives

$$Y_t - \overline{Y} = (\hat{Y}_t - \overline{Y}) + e_t \qquad (3.3.3)$$

This expresses the observed discrepancy of the dependent variable from its sample mean as predicted discrepancy plus residual. Squaring each side of equation 3.3.3 and summing over all n observation points, it is possible to show after a little algebra that

$$\sum_{t=1}^{n} (Y_t - \overline{Y})^2 = \sum_{t=1}^{n} (\hat{Y}_t - \overline{Y})^2 + \sum_{t=1}^{n} e_t^2 \qquad (3.3.4)$$

This **sums of squares decomposition** has an interesting interpretation. The quantity on the left-hand side of equation 3.3.4 is called the **total sum of squares** (SST), and can be thought of as the total variability in the sample of the dependent variable about its mean. Regression analysis can be viewed as an attempt to use the behavior of the independent variable to explain this variability in the dependent variable. Since the residuals represent the part of the behavior of the dependent variable that cannot be explained by its linear dependence on the independent variable, the second term on the right-hand side of equation 3.3.4 can be viewed as the part of the total sum of squares unexplained by the regression. This is called the **error** (or **residual**) **sum of squares** (SSE). Hence, the first term on the right-hand side of equation 3.3.4—the **regression sum of squares** (SSR)—is the part of the variability in the dependent variable that *is* explained by the sample regression. For the unemployment data, we found

$$SST = \sum_{t=1}^{n} (Y_t - \overline{Y})^2 = 100.152$$

$$SSR = \sum_{t=1}^{n} (\hat{Y}_t - \overline{Y})^2 = 93.399$$

$$SSE = \sum_{t=1}^{n} e_t^2 = 6.753$$

The proportion of the sample variability in the dependent variable explained by the fitted regression is known as the **coefficient of determination,** R^2, so that

$$R^2 = \frac{\text{SSR}}{\text{SST}} = 1 - \frac{\text{SSE}}{\text{SST}} \qquad (3.3.5)$$

For our unemployment example, then,

$$R^2 = 93.399/100.152 = 0.933$$

Thus, in this sample, 93.3% of the variability in the Alabama unemployment rate is explained by its linear dependence on the United States unemployment rate. This high value for R^2 reflects the tight clustering of the data points around the sample regression line in Figure 3.3. The coefficient of determination is used chiefly as a descriptive statistic to provide a measure of the strength of the relationship in the sample. In fact, the coefficient of determination of the fitted linear regression is simply the square of the sample correlation r, defined in equation 3.1.2. Hence, the sample correlation between the Alabama and U.S. unemployment rates is

$$r = \sqrt{0.933} = 0.97$$

(We can infer that the sign is positive because the slope, b, of the sample regression line is positive.)

On some occasions an **adjusted** (or **corrected**) **coefficient of determination,** $\overline{R}^2$, is calculated by dividing the error sum of squares and total sum of squares in equation 3.3.5 by their associated degrees of freedom. For the linear regression model, the adjusted coefficient of determination is

$$\overline{R}^2 = 1 - \frac{\text{SSE}/(n - 2)}{\text{SST}/(n - 1)}$$

For the unemployment data, we find

$$\overline{R}^2 = 1 - \frac{6.753/14}{100.152/15} = 0.928$$

Unless the number of sample observations is very small, the difference between R^2 and $\overline{R}^2$ will be negligible for the simple linear regression model. However, in the case of multiple regression with several independent variables, to be discussed in Chapter 4, the two statistics can be quite far apart.

3.4 INFERENCE ABOUT THE LINEAR REGRESSION MODEL

It is often required to develop confidence intervals for, or test hypotheses about, the parameters of the linear regression model. The least squares estimators of these parameters are unbiased, and it can be shown that the variances of these estimators are

$$\sigma_a^2 = \sigma^2 \left[\frac{1}{n} + \frac{\overline{X}^2}{\Sigma(X_t - \overline{X})^2} \right]$$

and

$$\sigma_b^2 = \frac{\sigma^2}{\Sigma(X_t - \overline{X})^2}$$

where σ^2 is the variance of the error term ϵ_t in the linear regression model 3.2.2. Unbiased estimators of these quantities, s_a^2 and s_b^2, are obtained by substituting the unbiased estimator s^2, given in equation 3.3.2, for the unknown σ^2. The standard errors of the least squares estimators are then estimated by s_a and s_b. For our unemployment data, these standard errors were found to be

$$s_a = 1.169 \qquad s_t = 0.1356$$

It is common practice, in reporting a sample regression, to incorporate these standard errors, as well as the coefficient of determination (or perhaps the adjusted coefficient). Thus the least squares fit of our unemployment example might be reported as

$$\hat{Y} = -4.194 + 1.8872X \qquad R^2 = 0.933$$
$$(1.169) \quad (0.1356) \tag{3.4.1}$$

Sometimes s_a is omitted, as generally the intercept is of far less interest than the slope.

To make further progress, the most common approach is to add to the other standard assumptions the further assumption that the error terms ϵ_t of the linear regression model have a normal distribution. In that case, it can be shown that the random variable

$$t = (b - \beta)/s_b$$

has a Student's t distribution with $(n - 2)$ degrees of freedom. Similarly, the random variable

$$t = (a - \alpha)/s_a$$

also has a Student's t distribution with $(n - 2)$ degrees of freedom. Confidence intervals and hypothesis tests follow directly from these results.

In the notation of Chapter 2, a $100(1 - \alpha)\%$ confidence interval for the slope of the regression line is therefore given by

$$b - t_{n-2,\alpha/2}s_b < \beta < b + t_{n-2,\alpha/2}s_b$$

In our unemployment example, where there are 16 observations, for a 95% confidence interval, so that $(1 - \alpha) = .95$, and $\alpha/2 = .025$, we find from Table A.2 of the Appendix

$$t_{14,.025} = 2.145$$

that is

$$P(-2.145 < t_{14} < 2.145) = 0.95$$

Thus, a 95% confidence interval for the expected number of percentage points increase in the Alabama unemployment rate following from a one percentage point increase in the United States unemployment rate is

$$1.8872 - (2.145)(0.1356) < \beta < 1.8872 + (2.145)(0.1356)$$

or

$$1.5963 < \beta < 2.1781$$

Now, suppose that β_0 is a hypothesized value of the slope of the true regression line. In precisely the same way as discussed in Section 2.5, there are three possible test procedures.

1. To test either null hypothesis

$$H_0: \beta = \beta_0 \quad \text{or} \quad H_0: \beta \leq \beta_0$$

against the alternative hypothesis

$$H_1: \beta > \beta_0$$

the decision rule is, for a test of significance level α,

$$\text{Reject } H_0 \text{ if } (b - \beta_0)/s_b > t_{n-2,\alpha}$$

2. To test either null hypothesis

$$H_0: \beta = \beta_0 \text{ or } H_0: \beta \geq \beta_0$$

against the alternative hypothesis

$$H_1: \beta < \beta_0$$

the decision rule is, for a test of significance level α,

$$\text{Reject } H_0 \text{ if } (b - \beta_0)/s_b < -t_{n-2,\alpha}$$

3. To test the null hypothesis

$$H_0: \beta = \beta_0$$

against the alternative hypothesis

$$H_1: \beta \neq \beta_0$$

the decision rule is, for a test of significance level α,

$$\text{Reject } H_0 \text{ if } \frac{(b - \beta_0)}{s_b} < -t_{n-2,\alpha/2} \quad \text{or} \quad > t_{n-2,\alpha/2}$$

To illustrate these procedures, we will test the null hypothesis that each one percentage point increase in the United States unemployment rate leads to an expected one percentage point increase in the Alabama unemployment rate, against the alternative that the expected increase in the Alabama rate is higher; that is, we test

$$H_0: \beta = \beta_0 = 1$$

against

$$H_1: \beta > 1$$

For a 1% level test, the decision rule is

$$\text{Reject } H_0 \text{ if } (b - 1)/s_b > t_{14,.01} = 2.624$$

Here we have

$$(b - 1)/s_b = (1.8872 - 1)/0.1356 = 6.543$$

so that the null hypothesis is very clearly rejected. The data contain strong evidence suggesting that a one percentage point increase in the United States unemployment rate leads to an expected increase in the Alabama unemployment rate of greater than one percentage point.

Often it is required to test the null hypothesis that the slope, β, of the regression line is zero. This hypothesis claims that the expected value of the dependent variable is the same, within the linear regression framework, regardless of the value of the independent variable—that is, the dependent variable is not influenced linearly by the independent variable. The test statistic is

$$t = b/s_b$$

This test of the null hypothesis that the regression slope is zero is numerically equivalent to the test that the population correlation is zero, based on the statistic 3.1.4. This should not be surprising, as in each case the test is of no linear relationship between a pair of variables.

The regression methods discussed in this and the following chapter are in such widespread use that prewritten computer program packages for carrying out regression calculations have long been widely available. In fact, for the simple linear regression model of this chapter, the arithmetic burden is not too heavy unless the sample size is large. However, this burden increases substantially for the multiple regression models of Chapter 4. Exhibit 3.1 shows part of the MINITAB program output from the analysis of our unemployment data. There are some differences in output details from one program to another, but the packages yield broadly similar statistics. In our analysis we have labeled the Alabama and United States unemployment rates AL and US. The MINITAB program prints the least squares fitted regression equation. Next, the coefficient estimates are repeated ("Constant" is the intercept term and "US" the slope). Associated with these coefficient estimates are the standard errors (standard deviations). Finally, the "t-ratios" are obtained by dividing the coefficient estimates by their associated standard errors. These are the statistics required for testing the null hypotheses that the corresponding parameters of the regression model are zero. The quantity s is the estimate of the standard deviation of the error term ϵ_t of the regression model—that is, the square root of the statistic s^2 of equation 3.3.2. The MINITAB program gives both the coefficient of determination, R^2, and the adjusted coefficient, $\overline{R}^2$—both expressed as percentages.

In the next part of the output of Exhibit 3.1, the regression, error, and total sum of squares are displayed. The corresponding *mean squares* (MS) are obtained by dividing the sums of squares by their associated degrees of freedom. We will postpone further discussion of these "analysis

Exhibit 3.1 Part of MINITAB program output for regression of Alabama unemployment rate on United States unemployment rate.

```
ROW       US       AL
  1      6.30     7.73
  2      7.33     8.40
  3      7.67     9.80
  4      7.40     9.33
  5      7.43    10.70
  6      7.40    10.50
  7      7.40    10.33
  8      8.23    11.13
  9      8.83    13.33
 10      9.43    13.63
 11      9.90    15.00
 12     10.67    15.60
 13     10.37    16.27
 14     10.13    14.00
 15      9.33    12.93
 16      8.53    11.53

MTB > regr "AL' 1 "US';
SUBC> pred 8.

The regression equation is
AL = - 4.19 + 1.89 US

Predictor       Coef        Stdev      t-ratio
Constant       -4.194       1.169       -3.59
US              1.8872      0.1356      13.92


s = 0.6945      R-sq = 93.3%      R-sq(adj) = 92.8%

Analysis of Variance

SOURCE        DF         SS           MS
Regression     1       93.399       93.399
Error         14        6.753        0.482
Total         15      100.152


    Fit   Stdev.Fit        95% C.I.           95% P.I.
 10.903     0.188     ( 10.501, 11.305)   ( 9.360, 12.447)
```

of variance" calculations until Chapter 4, as they have further use only in the context of the multiple regression model.

The final part of the output reproduced in Exhibit 3.1 provides analysis of a forecasting problem. We will discuss this in the next section.

Before proceeding further we must caution the reader that, although programs such as MINITAB allow the very rapid fitting of regression models, care must be taken that they are appropriately used. For example, if any of the standard assumptions of Section 3.2 are violated, inference based on least squares estimation can be seriously misleading. In particular, in the analysis of time series data the possibility that the error terms are correlated with one another should be checked. We will discuss one procedure for doing so in Chapter 4, merely noting that for this particular example no strong evidence of correlation in the errors was found.

3.5 FORECASTING FROM THE FITTED LINEAR REGRESSION MODEL

Suppose now that interest is in forecasting some future value—say, the next observation Y_{n+1}—of the dependent variable in a regression model. It will be assumed that the linear regression model continues to hold at time $(n + 1)$, so that we can write the quantity to be predicted as

$$Y_{n+1} = \alpha + \beta X_{n+1} + \epsilon_{n+1} \qquad (3.5.1)$$

where X_{n+1} is the value that will be taken by the independent variable at time $(n + 1)$, and ϵ_{n+1} is the error term of that time period. We will further assume that the standard assumptions continue to hold over this extended period, so that ϵ_{n+1} has mean zero, has the same variance as the previous error terms, and is uncorrelated with those error terms. In short, the assumption is that the complete model structure of the observation period will remain in place in the future. Such stability provides some hope of developing reasonably reliable forecasts.

Fitted regression models can be used directly to derive **conditional forecasts** of a dependent variable. In other words, we can ask what value the dependent variable might take in some future time period, given some knowledge of or assumption about the value that will be taken by the independent variable in that time period. For example, the fitted model 3.4.1 could be employed to predict Alabama unemployment rate next quarter, given an assumption that the United States rate that quarter will be 8.0%. Regression models such as this can only be used to obtain **unconditional forecasts** of dependent variables—that is, forecasts of what will actually occur—if forecasts of future values of independent variables are first made available. The regression model is of no value in developing these independent variable forecasts; they must be obtained from some other source.

It is quite easy to see from equation 3.5.1 how we would predict the next value of the dependent variable, given that the next value of the independent variable is X_{n+1}. The right-hand side of that equation is the sum of a deterministic component $(\alpha + \beta X_{n+1})$, and a random component ϵ_{n+1}. The first of these can be estimated by replacing the unknown parameters α and β by their least squares estimates a and b, computed from the available sample data. In addition, since the error term ϵ_{n+1} is uncorrelated with any information known at the time the forecast is made, our best estimate of its realization is the mean zero of this random variable. Thus, the conditional *point forecast* of the next value of the dependent variable is

$$\hat{Y}_{n+1} = a + bX_{n+1} \qquad (3.5.2)$$

To illustrate, suppose that we want to predict the Alabama unemployment rate next quarter, assuming that the United States rate will be 8%. From the fitted model 3.4.1 we have directly

$$\hat{Y}_{n+1} = -4.194 + (1.8872)(8) = 10.9$$

The forecast, then, is for an unemployment rate of 10.9% in Alabama. This is a conditional, or "what if" forecast. We have estimated what the unemployment rate in Alabama will be if the national rate is 8%. Alternatively, we could view our prediction as an unconditional forecast of the Alabama rate if 8% was a forecast of the future United States unemployment rate, obtained, for example, from one of the several agencies that produce U.S. macroeconomic forecasts.

Point forecasts are certainly valuable, and appear to be the exclusive concern of the vast majority of public discussion of business and economic predictions. However, for many purposes it is very important to have available some measure of the uncertainty associated with such forecasts. One way to achieve this is through the calculation of *interval forecasts*. All forecasts will be in error, and a prudent look at the future should incorporate a measure of the magnitude of likely prediction errors. Comparing equations 3.5.1 and 3.5.2 we see that the difference between the predicted and actual values of the dependent variable is

$$\hat{Y}_{n+1} - Y_{n+1} = [(a - \alpha) + (b - \beta)X_{n+1}] - \epsilon_{n+1} \qquad (3.5.3)$$

The forecast error is the sum of two components. The first of these reflects the error made in using the least squares estimates a and b of the parameters α and β. The second arises because in the real world observations do not fall precisely on any regression line, so that Y_{n+1} will certainly not be exactly equal to $(\alpha + \beta X_{n+1})$.

Interval forecasts for the dependent variable are based on the estimated standard deviation of the forecast error 3.5.3. In fact, for the linear regression model, under the standard assumptions, it can be shown that a $100(1 - \alpha)\%$ forecast interval for Y_{n+1} is given by

$$\hat{Y}_{n+1} \pm t_{n-2,\alpha/2} \left[\left(1 + \frac{1}{n} + \frac{(X_{n+1} - \overline{X})^2}{\sum\limits_{t=1}^{n} (X_t - \overline{X})^2} \right) s^2 \right]^{1/2}$$

where $\overline{X}$ is the mean of the n sample observations on the independent variable, and s^2 is the estimated variance 3.3.2 of the regression error terms.

On the right-hand side of the last row of Exhibit 3.1 is shown a 95% interval forecast (or 95% prediction interval) for the Alabama unemployment rate, given that the United States rate will be 8%. This interval runs from 9.4% to 12.4%. Such interval forecasts are routinely available in most regression program packages, such as MINITAB. The reader should be cautioned, however, that these intervals are appropriate only for conditional forecasting. In unconditional forecasting, external predictions of future values of independent variables are required, and the inevitable uncertainty in these predictions should properly be incorporated into wider forecast intervals for future values of the dependent variable.

The last row of Exhibit 3.1 shows also a second interval (labeled 95% C.I.). This interval is not for the actual future value of the dependent variable, but for its expectation $(\alpha + \beta X_{n+1})$. It is therefore not very relevant for the types of forecasting problems with which we are concerned in this book.

We close our discussion of forecasting from linear regression models by noting once again that the analysis of this chapter is based on the standard assumptions of Section 3.2. The approach discussed here can produce quite reliable forecasts in a range of applications when these assumptions hold. However, if the regression errors are strongly autocorrelated, this procedure may generate seriously suboptimal forecasts.

EXERCISES

3.1   The sample correlation is

$$r = c_{XY}/s_X s_Y$$

Show that the statistic 3.1.4 for testing the null hypothesis that the population correlation is zero can be written

$$t = \frac{r}{\sqrt{(1 - r^2)/(n - 2)}} = \sqrt{(n - 2)} \, \frac{c_{XY}}{\sqrt{s_x^2 s_Y^2 - c_{XY}^2}}$$

3.2 Let a and b denote the least squares estimates of the intercept and slope parameters of the linear regression line
   (a) Show that the fitted line

$$\hat{Y} = a + bX$$

   passes through the point of the sample means $(\bar{X}, \bar{Y})$
   (b) Denoting by

$$e_t = Y_t - \hat{Y}_t$$

   the residuals from the fitted line, show that

$$\sum_{t=1}^{n} e_t = 0$$

3.3 Let a and b denote the least squares estimates of the intercept and slope parameters of the linear regression line, and let

$$Y_t = \hat{Y}_t + e_t = (a + bX_t) + e_t$$

(a) Show that

$$\hat{Y}_t - \bar{Y} = b(X_t - \bar{X})$$

and hence that

$$\sum_{t=1}^{n} (\hat{Y}_t - \bar{Y})^2 = b^2 \sum_{t=1}^{n} (X_t - \bar{X})^2$$

(b) Show that

$$\sum_{t=1}^{n} e_t^2 = \sum_{t=1}^{n} [(Y_t - \bar{Y}) - b(X_t - \bar{X})]^2$$

$$= \sum_{t=1}^{n} (Y_t - \bar{Y})^2 - b^2 \sum_{t=1}^{n} (X_t - \bar{X})^2$$

(c) Using the results (a) and (b), deduce the sums of squares decomposition

$$SST = SSR + SSE$$

(d)   Using (a), show that the coefficient of determination is

$$R^2 = \frac{\text{SSR}}{\text{SST}} = \frac{\left[\displaystyle\sum_{t=1}^{n}(X_t - \overline{X})(Y_t - \overline{Y})\right]^2}{\displaystyle\sum_{t=1}^{n}(X_t - \overline{X})^2 \displaystyle\sum_{t=1}^{n}(Y_t - \overline{Y})^2}$$

and hence that the coefficient of determination is the square of the sample correlation coefficient.

3.4   For a sample of 66 monthly returns of 5-year bonds in Japan and the United States, a correlation of 0.293 was found.[1] Suppose that a linear regression of the Japanese returns on the United States returns was estimated. What is the coefficient of determination of this regression? Interpret your result.

3.5   The following linear regression model was estimated through least squares from a sample of 18 annual observations:

$$\hat{Y} = \underset{(0.681)}{1.284} + \underset{(0.102)}{0.237X}$$

where figures in parentheses below parameter estimates are the corresponding estimated standard errors, and

$Y =$ Annual percentage change in value of a firm's sales

$X =$ Annual percentage change in the firm's advertising expenditures

(a)   Interpret the estimated slope of the regression line.
(b)   Find a 95% confidence interval for the slope of the population regression line.

3.6   The following linear regression model was estimated through least squares for a sample of 79 quarterly observations[2];

$$\hat{Y} = \underset{}{0.00027} + \underset{(0.276)}{0.792\ X}$$

    1.   S. Hauser and A. Levy, "Optimal forward coverage of international fixed income portfolios," *Journal of Portfolio Management 17*, no. 4 (1991), 54–59.

    2.   S. B. Park, "Spot and forward rates in the Canadian treasury bill market," *Journal of Financial Economics 10* (1982), 107–114.

where the figure in parentheses below the parameter estimate is the corresponding estimated standard error, and

Y = actual change in Canadian treasury bill spot rate

X = Change in spot rate predicted by the forward rate

(a) Interpret the estimated slope of the regression line.
(b) Test at the 5% level the null hypothesis that the slope of the population regression line is zero against the alternative that the true slope is positive.
(c) Test at the 5% level against a two-sided alternative the null hypothesis that the slope of the population regression line is one
(d) Find and interpret the coefficient of determination of this regression.

3.7 The accompanying table shows, for a period of 23 months, the rate of return (Y) on the stock of Illinois Power Company and a stock market index rate of return (X).

t	X_t	Y_t	t	X_t	Y_t
1	−0.0763	−0.0800	13	0.0493	0.0368
2	0.0595	0.0751	14	0.0149	−0.0740
3	−0.0026	0.0588	15	0.0440	0.1118
4	−0.0997	−0.1042	16	0.0340	−0.1207
5	−0.0615	−0.0194	17	−0.0364	−0.0458
6	−0.0503	−0.0593	18	0.0042	0.0103
7	0.0746	0.1513	19	−0.0406	−0.0678
8	0.0498	0.0365	20	0.0419	0.0146
9	0.0428	0.0211	21	−0.0057	0.0466
10	−0.0157	−0.0276	22	−0.0396	−0.0685
11	0.0522	0.1099	23	0.0002	−0.0147
12	0.0615	0.0415			

(a) Find by least squares the sample regression of Y on X, and interpret the slope of the fitted regression line.
(b) Find and interpret the coefficient of determination for the fitted regression.
(c) Find the sample correlation between the rate of return on the stock of Illinois Power and the rate of return on the market index.
(d) Find a 95% confidence interval for the slope of the population regression line.
(e) Test at the 1% level against at two-sided alternative the null hypothesis that the slope of the population regression line is one.

(f) Test at the 1% level against a two-sided alternative the null hypothesis that the intercept of the population regression line is zero, and interpret your finding.

(g) Find a point forecast of the rate of return on the stock of Illinois Power next month, if the rate of return on the market index is expected to be 0.04.

(h) Find and discuss the implications of a 95% prediction interval for the rate of return on the stock of Illinois Power next month if the rate of return on the market index is expected to be 0.04.

3.8 Let s_X and s_Y denote the sample standard deviations, and c_{XY} the sample covariance.

(a) Show that the unbiased estimator 3.3.2 of the variance of the error term in the linear regression model can be written

$$s^2 = \frac{\sum\limits_{t=1}^{n} e_t^2}{(n-2)} = \frac{s_Y^2 - b^2 s_X^2}{(n-2)}(n-1)$$

$$= \frac{s_X^2 s_Y^2 - c_{XY}^2}{(n-2)s_X^2}(n-1)$$

(b) Using the result in (a), show that the statistic for testing that the slope of the population regression line is zero can be written

$$t = \frac{b}{s_b} = \frac{b(n-1)^{1/2} s_X}{s}$$

$$= \sqrt{(n-2)}\ \frac{c_{XY}}{\sqrt{s_X^2 s_Y^2 - c_{XY}^2}}$$

(c) Comparing the results in Exercises 3.1 and part (b) of this exercise deduce that the tests for no linear association based on the sample correlation coefficient and the slope of the sample regression line are equivalent.

3.9. The accompanying table[3] shows 22 annual observations on retail sales per household (Y) and disposable income per household (X), both in constant dollars, in the United States.

3. Data taken from N. K. Dhalla, "Short-term forecasts of advertising expenditures," *Journal of Advertising Research 19*, no. 1 (1979), 7–14.

t	X_t	Y_t	t	X_t	Y_t
1	9,098	5,492	12	11,307	5,907
2	9,138	5,540	13	11,432	6,124
3	9,094	5,305	14	11,449	6,186
4	9,282	5,507	15	11,697	6,224
5	9,229	5,418	16	11,871	6,496
6	9,347	5,320	17	12,018	6,718
7	9,525	5,538	18	12,523	6,921
8	9,756	5,692	19	12,053	6,471
9	10,282	5,871	20	12,088	6,394
10	10,662	6,157	21	12,215	6,555
11	11,019	6,342	22	12,494	6,755

(a) Find by least squares the sample regression of retail sales on disposable income, and interpret the slope of the fitted regression line.

(b) Find and interpret the coefficient of determination for the fitted regression.

(c) Find a 95% confidence interval for the slope of the population regression line.

(d) Test at the 1% level the null hypothesis that the slope of the population regression line is zero against the alternative that it is positive.

(e) Find a point forecast for retail sales per household next year if it is expected that disposable income per household next year will be $12,600.

(f) Find and discuss the implications of a 95% prediction interval for retail sales per household next year if it is expected that disposable income per household next year will be $12,600.

3.10 The accompanying table shows, for a period of 23 months, the rate of return (Y) on the stock of Vulcan Materials Corporation and a stock market index rate of return (X).

t	X_t	Y_t	t	X_t	Y_t
1	−0.0763	0.0368	13	0.0493	0.0952
2	0.0595	0.0142	14	0.0149	−0.0761
3	−0.0026	0.1748	15	0.0440	0.0471
4	−0.0997	−0.1429	16	0.0340	0.1236
5	−0.0615	−0.0764	17	−0.0364	0.0050
6	−0.0503	0.0376	18	0.0042	−0.0547
7	0.0746	0.1015	19	−0.0406	−0.0158
8	0.0498	0.0855	20	0.0419	−0.0588
9	0.0428	0.0182	21	−0.0057	0.0682
10	−0.0157	−0.0833	22	−0.0396	0.0000
11	0.0522	0.0390	23	0.0002	−0.0106
12	0.0615	0.0500			

(a)   Estimate by least squares the regression of Y on X, and interpret the slope of the sample regression line.

(b)   Find and interpret the coefficient of determination for the fitted regression line.

(c)   Find the sample correlation between the rate of return on the stock of Vulcan Materials and the rate of return on the market index.

(d)   Find a 90% confidence interval for the slope of the population regression line.

(e)   Test at the 1% level against a two-sided alternative the null hypothesis that the slope of the population regression line is one.

(f)   Test at the 1% level against a two-sided alternative the null hypothesis that the intercept of the population regression line is zero, and interpret your finding.

(g)   Find a point forecast for the rate of return on the stock of Vulcan Materials next month, if the rate of return on the market index is expected to be 0.04.

(h)   Find and discuss the implications of a 95% prediction interval for the rate of return on the stock of Vulcan Materials next month if the rate of return on the market index is expected to be 0.04.

SELECTED BIBLIOGRAPHY

Bowerman, B. L. & R. T. O'Connell (1990). *Linear Statistical Models: An Applied Approach.* Boston: PWS-Kent.

Chatterjee, S. & B. Price (1991). *Regression Analysis by Example* (2nd ed.). New York: Wiley.

Draper, N. R. & H. Smith (1981). *Applied Regression Analysis* (2nd ed.). New York: Wiley.

Neter, J., W. Wasserman & M. H. Kutner (1990). *Applied Linear Statistical Models* (3rd ed.). Homewood, Ill.: Richard D. Irwin.

Newbold, P. (1991). *Statistics for Business and Economics* (3rd ed.). Englewood Cliffs, N.J.: Prentice-Hall.

Weisberg, S. (1985). *Applied Linear Regression* (2nd ed.). New York: Wiley.

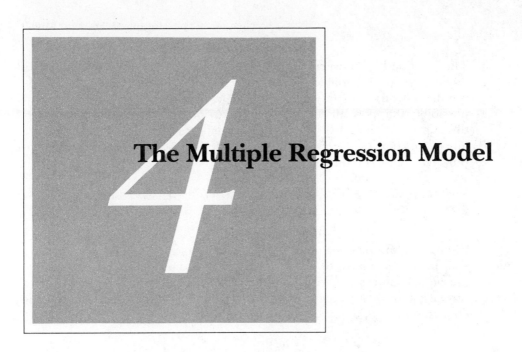

The Multiple Regression Model

4.1 MULTIPLE REGRESSION MODEL: LINEAR AND LOG LINEAR FORMS

The simple linear regression model of Chapter 3 can be useful when the value taken by a dependent variable of interest is influenced by just a single independent variable. However, quite often there are several important influences on the behavior of a dependent variable. For example, the demand for a product may depend not only on the price of that product, but also on the prices of other products and on consumers' incomes. The **multiple regression model** provides a framework for the analysis of such situations.

In general, suppose that the value of a dependent variable, Y, is influenced by K independent variables, $X_1, X_2, \ldots, X_K$. If n sets of observations are taken over time on these variables, the observations will be denoted

$$(X_{1t}, X_{2t}, \ldots, X_{Kt}, Y_t) \qquad t = 1, 2, \ldots, n$$

The relationship between the dependent variable on the one hand and the independent variables on the other might be postulated in a large number of different ways. We will begin with the most straightforward possibility. Suppose that, given the values of the independent variables, the expected value of the dependent variable at time t is assumed to be a linear function of the values taken by the independent variables at that time. We can write this relationship as

$$E(Y_t \mid X_{1t}, X_{2t}, \ldots, X_{Kt}) = \alpha + \beta_1 X_{1t} + \beta_2 X_{2t} + \cdots + \beta_K X_{Kt}$$

$$(4.1.1)$$

where the parameters α, β_1, β_2, $\ldots$, β_K are fixed numbers, whose values will, in practice, have to be estimated from the available data. Naturally, the actual value attained by the dependent variable at time t will differ somewhat from its expectation. We will denote this discrepancy by the *error term* ϵ_t, so that

$$\epsilon_t = Y_t - E(Y_t \mid X_{1t}, X_{2t}, \ldots, X_{Kt})$$

Combining this with equation 4.1.1 yields the **multiple regression model**

$$Y_t = \alpha + \beta_1 X_{1t} + \beta_2 X_{2t} + \cdots + \beta_K X_{Kt} + \epsilon_t \qquad (4.1.2)$$

In the time series context, equation 4.1.2 is said to be a model of **contemporaneous dependence,** since the inherent assumption is that the current value of the dependent variable is influenced only by the current values of the independent variables, and not by earlier values of those variables. In Section 4.4 we will see how this assumption can be relaxed.

To see how the parameters of equation 4.1.2 can be interpreted, consider the situation where one of the independent variables, say X_1, is increased by one unit, while the values of the other independent variables are held constant. Suppose that the value of the first independent variable increases by one unit, from X_{1t} to $X_{1t} + 1$, with the other independent variables remaining unchanged. Then, by analogy with equation 4.1.1, the expected value of the dependent variable will be

$$E(Y_t \mid X_{1t} + 1, X_{2t}, \ldots, X_{Kt})$$

$$= \alpha + \beta_1(X_{1t} + 1) + \beta_2 X_{2t} + \cdots + \beta_K X_{Kt}$$

Subtracting 4.1.1 then yields

$$E(Y_t \mid X_{1t} + 1, X_{2t}, \ldots, X_{Kt}) - E(Y_t \mid X_{1t}, X_{2t}, \ldots, X_{Kt})$$

$$= \alpha + \beta_1(X_{1t} + 1) + \beta_2 X_{2t} + \cdots$$
$$+ \beta_K X_{Kt} - (\alpha + \beta_1 X_{1t} + \beta_2 X_{2t} + \cdots + \beta_K X_{Kt})$$
$$= \beta_1$$

Thus, β_1 is the expected increase in the dependent variable resulting from a one unit increase in the first independent variable when the values of the other independent variables remain fixed. Of course, the parameters $\beta_2, \ldots, \beta_K$ are similarly interpreted. The parameters β_i ($i = 1, \ldots, K$) are sometimes called **partial regression coefficients.** As can be seen, they measure the *separate* influences of the independent variables on the dependent variable.

Setting to zero all of the values of the independent variables in equation 4.1.1 suggests, *in theory*, that the intercept α is the expected value of the dependent variable when all independent variables are zero. In practice, this interpretation is only meaningful and relevant in those rare cases where a value of zero for all the independent variables has worthwhile meaning, and where values of zero are not well outside the range of the available observations.

As in the case of the simple linear regression model of Chapter 3, it is necessary to specify further properties of the multiple regression model before asking how such a model can be fitted to data. As a starting point, it is often useful to consider a set of *standard assumptions*, similar to those of Section 3.2. These assumptions are:

1. The quantities X_{it} ($i = 1, \ldots, K$) are either fixed numbers or they are realizations of random variables that are uncorrelated with the error terms ϵ_t.
2. The error terms ϵ_t all have mean zero.
3. The error terms ϵ_t have a common variance, say σ^2.
4. The error terms ϵ_t are not correlated with one another.
5. There does not exist a set of fixed numbers, $c_0, c_1, c_2, \ldots, c_K$ such that $c_0 + c_1 X_{1t} + c_2 X_{2t} + \cdots + c_K X_{Kt} = 0 \qquad t = 1, 2, \ldots, n$.

The first four of these assumptions are the same as those of Section 3.2. The fifth assumption requires that there does not exist a perfect linear relation among the values of the independent variables in the sample. This assumption is required because the object of multiple regression analysis is to assess the separate linear influences of the independent variables on the dependent variable—that is, to estimate the partial regression coefficients β_i. However, if there is a perfect linear association among the independent variables in the sample, then the sample will simply not contain sufficient information to allow the estimation of these separate effects. This is often referred to as the case of **perfect multicollinearity.** For problems in which we are interested, where data are typically observed passively, there is virtually no chance of finding perfect multicollinearity, so that in practice we need not be concerned about the violation of Assumption 5. However, for such happenstance data, it can often occur that the values of the independent variables are closely, though not perfectly, related. This is known as the problem of **multicollinearity.** In that event, although it will be possible to estimate the parameters of the regression model, the resulting estimators might be quite unreliable due to very large standard errors. Usually, not much can be done about this. It simply reflects the fact that a given data set may not contain very much information about the separate influences of the independent variables on the dependent variable. Although estimators of the partial regression coefficients can be quite imprecise in the presence of serious multicollinearity, good forecasts may still result from the fitted model, provided historical correlation patterns among the independent variables continue to hold in the future.

It is useful to stress the importance of moving from the simple linear regression framework of Chapter 3 to the multiple regression model when there are multiple influences on a dependent variable. Although there might be a huge number of factors having *some* influence on a dependent variable, all *important* influential variables should be included in the list of independent variables $X_1, X_2, \ldots, X_K$. In effect, the influences of the many less important factors will then be subsumed in the regression error term ϵ_t. However, if an important independent variable is omitted from the regression model, its influence will also, in effect, be incorporated into ϵ_t. Then, if the omitted variable is correlated with independent variables included in the model, as is typically the case, Assumption 1 will be violated. This results in the problem of **specification bias.** The usual estimators of the regression parameters will be biased, inference based on these estimates can be seriously misleading, and very poor forecasts could result from the fitted regression model. It is therefore of considerable importance to give a good deal of thought to the question of what might be an appropriate specification for a regression model, appealing where possible to subject matter theory for guidance.

Log Linear Models

The multiple regression model 4.1.2 and the associated standard assumptions can often provide a very useful starting point when thinking about the modeling of relationships among variables. However, it frequently happens that particular modifications or elaborations of the model and assumptions are desirable. For example, although the assumption of a linear relationship will often be adequate, at least within the ranges of values of the variables in which we are interested, this will not always be the case. In some circumstances, subject matter theory, the data, or both may suggest some nonlinear specification.

In business and economic applications, the most commonly used nonlinear formulation is the **log linear model,** which postulates a linear relationship among the *logarithms* of the original variables; that is,

$$\log Y_t = \alpha + \beta_1 \log X_{1t} + \beta_2 \log X_{2t} + \cdots + \beta_K \log X_{Kt} + \epsilon_t$$

$$(4.1.3)$$

The interpretation of the partial regression coefficients of the log linear model is slightly different from those of 4.1.2. In equation 4.1.3, β_i is the expected *percentage* increase in Y resulting from a one *percent* increase in X_i, when the values of all other independent variables remain constant. In Section 4.2 we will illustrate the fitting to data of the model 4.1.3.

One appealing feature of this particular non-linear specification is that there is no great difficulty in its fitting to data. All that is required is that the analyst first take logarithms of all the observations, and then proceed precisely as for the usual linear specification. A number of factors might suggest the desirability of the log linear specification.

1. Subject matter theory or the analyst's intuition often make the log linear form a natural choice. For example, it will often seem more plausible to view relationships in terms of proportional rather than absolute changes. It is natural, for instance, to ask about the expected change in personal consumption, in percentage terms, resulting from a one percent increase in income.

2. A plot of available data might suggest this particular nonlinear form of dependence. Figure 4.1 shows the shapes of relationships between Y and X for which the relationship between $\log Y$ and $\log X$ is linear.

3. If often happens that analysis in logarithms of the original data yields a model whose error terms have more nearly equal variances. Standard Assumption 3 requires that the regression error terms have equal variances. (Violation of this assumption results in a problem known as *heteroscedasticity*.) Taking logarithms dampens the magnitudes of the largest observations, and in this way might mitigate any heteroscedasticity problem.

4. It can also happen that analysis in logarithms of the original data yields a model whose error terms have a more nearly normal distribution. In Section 4.3 we will see that the usual inference about a regression model is based on the assumption that the error terms have a normal distribution. The closer this assumption is to the truth, the more valid will be that inference.

FIGURE 4.1   Examples of log linear dependence.

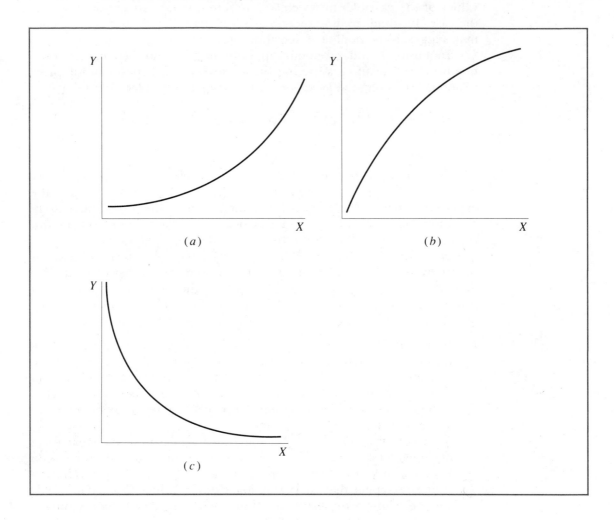

It is quite unrealistic to hope that any simple model and associated assumptions can provide a perfectly accurate description of the complex world in which we live. In adopting the log linear form, the analyst's hope is that, through this simple data transformation, one can achieve a specification that is more nearly linear (in the transformed variables), with error terms that have more nearly equal variances and a more nearly normal distribution. In that case, inference based on the log linear model would be more reliable than inference based on the linear model. We do not wish to claim that the logarithmic transformation is invariably appropriate for time series data: often it will not be. Nevertheless, the log linear specification has often been found useful in modeling the relationships among business and economic time series. When there is doubt as to which of the specifications 4.1.2 and 4.1.3 is more appropriate, a very simple means of discrimination, for which there is some theoretical justification, is to fit both models and select the one for which the coefficient of determination, R^2, is higher.

Dummy Variables

There are occasions on which it might be believed that the process under study has suffered an abrupt *structural change* at some point in time. Such change might be induced, for example, by government policy. One way to model this effect is through the introduction in the regression of an additional independent variable, known as a **dummy variable.**

There are many ways in which an established relationship can be altered by abrupt external forces. Perhaps the most commonly considered possibility is that the external event impacts on the intercept, but not on the partial regression coefficients of the model. The assumption here is that, all other things equal, the external event has increased or decreased the expected value of the dependent variable by some fixed amount. In that case, the regression model (4.1.2) is augmented through the addition of an independent variable—the dummy variable. This variable is defined to take the value 0 at all time periods up to the occurrence of the external event, and 1 thereafter. The coefficient associated with that dummy variable then measures the change in the expected value of the dependent variable, all else equal, from the earlier period to the later period.

One sometimes sees dummy variables employed in time series regressions when data are **seasonal**—that is, the values observed depend on the time of year. For example, regressions might involve data measured quarterly (four times a year) or monthly. The effect of seasonality can be accounted for by incorporating into the regression several dummy variables. The number of dummies required is one less than the number of seasons in the year. For example, for quarterly data, three seasonal dummies would be incorporated into the regression. These can be specified as

$$(1, 0, 0, 0, 1, 0, 0, 0, 1, 0, 0, 0, \ldots)$$
$$(0, 1, 0, 0, 0, 1, 0, 0, 0, 1, 0, 0, \ldots)$$
$$(0, 0, 1, 0, 0, 0, 1, 0, 0, 0, 1, 0, \ldots)$$

In fact, rather than use seasonal dummies, most practitioners typically fit regression models to *seasonally adjusted* data. We will discuss this topic in Chapter 5.

4.2   FITTING THE MULTIPLE REGRESSION MODEL

Given a series of n observations on the dependent and independent variables, we want to estimate the unknown parameters $\alpha, \beta_1, \beta_2, \ldots, \beta_K$ of the multiple regression model 4.1.2. As in Section 3.3, provided that the standard assumptions hold, the method of least squares leads to an estimation algorithm that yields estimators with attractive statistical properties.

Let $a, b_1, b_2, \ldots, b_K$ be possible estimates of $\alpha, \beta_1, \beta_2, \ldots, \beta_K$, leading to the **sample multiple regression**

$$\hat{Y} = a + b_1 X_1 + b_2 X_2 + \cdots + b_K X_K$$

Then, at time t, the value predicted for the independent variable by the sample multiple regression is

$$\hat{Y}_t = a + b_1 X_{1t} + b_2 X_{2t} + \cdots + b_K X_{Kt}$$

The differences between the observed values of the dependent variable and the values predicted by the same multiple regression are the **residuals**

$$e_t = Y_t - \hat{Y}_t = Y_t - a - b_1 X_{1t} - b_2 X_{2t}$$
$$- \cdots - b_K X_{Kt} \qquad t = 1, 2, \ldots, n$$

Obviously, it is sensible to choose the parameter estimates so that the magnitudes of the discrepancies between observed and predicted values of the dependent variable are, on the average, as small as possible. The method of least squares selects those parameter estimates for which the sum of squared residuals is as small as possible: that is, $a, b_1, b_2, \ldots, b_K$ are chosen to minimize the sum of squares

$$S = \sum_{t=1}^{n} e_t^2 = \sum_{t=1}^{n} (Y_t - a - b_1 X_{1t} - b_2 X_{2t} - \cdots - b_K X_{Kt})^2$$

$$(4.2.1)$$

It is possible, using matrix algebra, to derive closed form expressions for the least squares estimates. We will not, however, pursue these details here. Given the very wide availability of computer algorithms for performing the least squares calculations, these expressions are of little practical importance for our purposes. What is important is an understanding that the calculations carry out the intuitively plausible task of minimizing the sum of squared residuals 4.2.1, together with an acknowledgement that

TABLE 4.1   Annual observations on days of incapacity due to sickness per person (Y), male unemployment rate (X_1), ratio of sickness benefits to earnings (X_2), and the real wage rate (X_3) in Great Britain.

t	Y_t	X_{1t}	X_{2t}	X_{3t}
1	12.2	1.5	0.367	1.190
2	12.2	1.2	0.394	1.216
3	11.7	1.3	0.371	1.250
4	11.9	1.7	0.355	1.267
5	12.1	2.4	0.440	1.273
6	12.3	2.5	0.419	1.299
7	11.9	1.9	0.395	1.318
8	12.1	1.9	0.443	1.329
9	12.8	2.5	0.430	1.321
10	12.9	3.1	0.474	1.342
11	13.5	2.0	0.446	1.362
12	13.9	1.8	0.493	1.355
13	14.1	2.0	0.686	1.364
14	15.1	3.2	0.732	1.383
15	15.4	3.4	0.728	1.407
16	15.8	3.3	0.710	1.406
17	15.4	3.6	0.727	1.454
18	15.0	4.7	0.779	1.501
19	15.7	5.1	0.737	1.593
20	16.2	3.6	0.706	1.660

this approach may not be appropriate if any of the standard assumptions is seriously violated.

We will illustrate through an example using data from Great Britain, where days of incapacity due to sickness per person (Y) is related to male unemployment rate (X_1), ratio of sickness benefits to earnings (X_2), and the real wage rate (X_3). Table 4.1 shows twenty annual observations[1] on these variables. We fitted to these data the log linear model

$$\log Y_t = \alpha + \beta_1 \log X_{1t} + \beta_2 \log X_{2t} + \beta_3 \log X_{3t} + \epsilon_t$$

Using the SPSS program, the least squares estimates of the four parameters of this model were found to be

$$a = 2.714 \qquad b_1 = -0.030 \qquad b_2 = 0.316 \qquad b_3 = 0.401$$

1. Data taken from Thomas, R. B., "Wages, sickness benefits, and absenteeism," *Journal of Economic Studies*, 7, no. 1 (1980), 51–61.

Hence the sample multiple regression is

$$\log \hat{Y} = 2.714 - 0.030 \log X_1 + 0.316 \log X_2 + 0.401 \log X_3$$

Keeping in mind that the specification is log linear, the estimated partial regression coefficients are interpreted as follows:

1. It is estimated that, all else remaining the same, a 1% increase in unemployment rate leads to an expected 0.030% decrease in days of incapacity due to sickness per person.
2. It is estimated that, all else remaining the same, a 1% increase in the ratio of sickness benefits to earnings leads to an expected 0.316% increase in days of incapacity due to sickness per person.
3. It is estimated that, all else remaining the same, a 1% increase in the real wage rate leads to an expected 0.401% increase in days of incapacity due to sickness per person.

In Section 3.3 we saw that the **Gauss-Markov theorem** provides a justification for the use of least squares estimators for the simple linear regression model. This theorem extends to the more general multiple regression model. Suppose that the five standard assumptions of Section 4.1 hold. Then, of all unbiased estimators of the regression parameters that are linear functions of the observed values of the dependent variable, the least squares estimators have the smallest variance. They are thus said to be **best linear unbiased estimators** (BLUE). Further, let $d_0, d_1, d_2, \ldots,$ d_K be any fixed numbers, and consider the linear function of the regression parameters

$$d_0\alpha + d_1\beta_1 + d_2\beta_2 + \cdots + d_K\beta_K$$

Then the estimator

$$d_0 a + d_1 b_1 + d_2 b_2 + \cdots + d_K b_K$$

is BLUE for this function. This result is particularly relevant for forecasting. Suppose that we want to predict the next value of the dependent variable, Y_{n+1}, given the next values $X_{1,n+1}, X_{2,n+1}, \ldots, X_{K,n+1}$ of the independent variables. Under the standard assumptions, this amounts to a requirement to estimate

$$\alpha + \beta_1 X_{1,n+1} + \beta_2 X_{2,n+1} + \cdots + \beta_K X_{K,n+1}$$

According to the Gauss-Markov theorem, substituting the least squares estimates for the unknown regression parameters, giving

$$\hat{Y}_{n+1} = a + b_1 X_{1,n+1} + b_2 X_{2,n+1} + \cdots + b_K X_{K,n+1}$$

yields an estimator that is best linear unbiased.

Sums of Squares Decomposition and the Coefficient of Determination

In Section 3.3 we saw how a decomposition of the sum of squared discrepancies of the dependent variable about its sample mean allows a measure of the success of the fitted regression model in explaining the behavior of the dependent variable. Precisely the same decomposition holds for the sample multiple regression. Let $\hat{Y}_t$ denote the fitted or predicted value of the dependent variable at time t from the sample multiple regression, so that

$$\hat{Y}_t = a + b_1 X_{1t} + b_2 X_{2t} + \cdots + b_K X_{Kt}$$

The residuals

$$e_t = Y_t - \hat{Y}_t = Y_t - a - b_1 X_{1t} - b_2 X_{2t} - \cdots - b_K X_{Kt}$$

are the discrepancies between the observed and predicted values of the dependent variable. Then

$$Y_t = \hat{Y}_t + e_t$$

and

$$Y_t - \bar{Y} = (\hat{Y}_t - \bar{Y}) + e_t$$

where $\bar{Y}$ is the sample mean of the dependent variable. It can be shown that squaring both sides of this equation and summing over all observation values yields

$$\sum_{t=1}^{n} (Y_t - \bar{Y})^2 = \sum_{t=1}^{n} (\hat{Y}_t - \bar{Y})^2 + \sum_{t=1}^{n} e_t^2 \qquad (4.2.2)$$

Exactly as in Section 3.3, this expression is interpreted as

Total Sum of Squares = Regression Sum of Squares
+ Error Sum of Squares

or

$$SST = SSR + SSE$$

Thus, the total variability, SST, in the sample of the dependent variable about its mean is expressed as the sum of a component, SSR, reflecting the dependence of Y on the independent variables, and a component, SSE, that can be thought of as unexplained variability in the dependent variable.

Under the standard assumptions, the regression error terms ϵ_t are taken to have a common variance, σ^2. The error sum of squares provides the basis for the estimation of this unknown error variance. Specifically, an unbiased estimator of σ^2 is given by

$$s^2 = \text{SSE}/(n - K - 1) = \frac{\sum\limits_{t=1}^{n} e_t^2}{(n - K - 1)} \qquad (4.2.3)$$

The degrees of freedom, $(n - K - 1)$, are simply the number of observations, n, less the total number of estimated regression parameters, $(K + 1)$.

Exactly as in the simple linear regression case, the **coefficient of determination,** R^2, is defined as the proportion of the sample variability in the dependent variable explained by the fitted regression, so that

$$R^2 = \frac{\text{SSR}}{\text{SST}} = 1 - \frac{\text{SSE}}{\text{SST}} \qquad (4.2.4)$$

For the log linear regression using the data of Table 4.1 we found

$$\text{SSR} = 0.23187 \qquad \text{SSE} = 0.02027 \qquad \text{SST} = 0.25214$$

and

$$R^2 = 0.920$$

We can therefore say that, in this sample, 92.0% of the variability in the logarithms of days of incapacity due to sickness per person is explained by their linear dependence on the logarithms of male unemployment rate, ratio of sickness benefits to earnings, and the real wage rate.

There is a drawback to the use of R^2 that persuades many analysts to prefer the **adjusted** (or **corrected**) **coefficient of determination** as a descriptive measure of the strength of association between the dependent variable on the one hand and the set of independent variables on the other. If *any* independent variable, however irrelevant, is added to a regression model, the sum of squared errors cannot possibly rise, and will almost inevitably fall, at least marginally. Consequently, the addition of an irrelevant independent variable to a regression model will produce at least a modest increase in R^2. It is undesirable to have what is in effect often taken as a measure of the success of a regression exercise be influenced in this way. The corrected coefficient of determination, $\overline{R}^2$, is defined through division of the sums of squares SSE and SST in equation 4.2.4 by their associated degrees of freedom, giving

$$\overline{R}^2 = 1 - \frac{\text{SSE}/(n - K - 1)}{\text{SST}/(n - 1)}$$

For our days of incapacity due to sickness example, the corrected coefficient of determination was found to be

$$\overline{R}^2 = 0.905$$

The addition of a variable to a regression model does not necessarily lead to an increase in the adjusted coefficient of determination. Indeed, in cases where the relationships are very weak, $\overline{R}^2$ can be negative.

Although the coefficient of determination, or the corrected coefficient, is almost invariably reported with practical regression studies, we have serious doubts about the value of either in the context of the analysis of business and economic time series data. The levels of business and economic time series do not behave as a random sample. On the contrary, such processes tend to evolve rather smoothly through time, so that much of their variability is not at all difficult to explain. Accordingly, we really ought to expect to find in practice, exactly as in our example, quite high values for the coefficient of determination. Such high values may reflect the smooth character of the evolution over time of the dependent variable rather than a very strong relationship with the independent variables. In the next section we will see how the sums of squares decomposition and the coefficient of determination provide the basis for a hypothesis test on the set of partial regression coefficients.

4.3 INFERENCE ABOUT THE MULTIPLE REGRESSION MODEL

It is possible, using matrix algebra, to derive closed form expressions for the estimated standard error s_a of the estimated intercept, and the estimated standard errors s_{b_i} $(i = 1, \ldots, K)$ of the partial regression coefficient estimates for the multiple regression model. We will not discuss these details. Regression programs routinely compute these statistics. For the log linear regression fitted to the data of Table 4.1 we found

$$s_a = 0.085 \qquad s_{b_1} = 0.041 \qquad s_{b_2} = 0.055 \qquad s_{b_3} = 0.198$$

The fitted regression equation might then be written out as

$$\log \hat{Y} = \underset{(0.085)}{2.714} - \underset{(0.041)}{0.030} \log X_1 + \underset{(0.055)}{0.316} \log X_2 + \underset{(0.198)}{0.401} \log X_3$$

$$(4.3.1)$$

$$R^2 = 0.920$$

Exhibit 4.1 shows part of the output obtained from the SPSS/PC program when the log linear model was fitted to the data of Table 4.1.

EXHIBIT 4.1   Part of SPSS program output for the fitting of a log linear regression model to the data of Table 4.1.

```
              * * * *   M U L T I P L E   R E G R E S S I O N   * * * *

        Multiple R            .95897
        R Square             .91961
        Adjusted R Square    .90454
        Standard Error       .03559

        Analysis of Variance
                         DF      Sum of Squares      Mean Square
        Regression        3            .23187           .07729
        Residual         16            .02027           .00127

        F =    61.01380     Signif F =   .0000

        ------------------ Variables in the Equation ------------------

        Variable           B        SE B        Beta         T    Sig T
        LNX3             .40117     .19750      .29137      2.031  .0592
        LNX2             .31604     .05512      .79606      5.734  .0000
        LNX1            -.03012     .04056     -.10684      -.743  .4685
        (Constant)      2.71448     .08493                 31.962  .0000


        Durbin-Watson Test =    1.73412
```

See
Table
4.2

The first part of the output contains the coefficient of determination, R^2, and the adjusted coefficient, $\overline{R}^2$. Two further statistics are displayed in this part of the output. The **coefficient of multiple correlation** is simply the square root of R^2. This is the sample correlation between the observed values of the dependent variable and the values predicted by the least squares regression fit. In our example this correlation is 0.959. The **standard error** is the estimated standard deviation of the error terms ϵ_t of the regression model. This is simply the square root of the statistic s^2 of equation 4.2.3. We could interpret this as a measure of how close, in the long run, observed values of the dependent variable are likely to be to values predicted by the true regression model. If the error terms have a distribution that is close to normal, then, in the long run, we would expect approximately 95% of values of the dependent variable generated by the true regression model to be within two standard errors of the predicted values. For our purposes, this is of limited value in assessing the uncertainty that should be associated with forecasts, as it makes no allowance for sampling errors in the estimated regression parameters.

The portion of the output of Exhibit 4.1 headed "Variables in the Equation" displays the least squares parameter estimates and their associated estimated standard errors. The column headed "Beta" shows what are sometimes called *standardized regression coefficients*. These are occasionally calculated as an aid to interpretation, intended to circumvent the difficulty that the magnitudes of the ordinary regression coefficients depend on the units in which the dependent and independent variables are measured. The standardized regression coefficients are obtained by multiplying the estimated partial regression coefficients by the ratios of the sample standard deviations of the independent variables to the sample standard deviation of the dependent variable. (Thus, in the case of the simple linear regression model of Chapter 3, the standardized regression coefficient is the sample correlation between the dependent and independent variables.) For example, from the results in Exhibit 4.1 we can conclude that, all else equal, it is estimated that an increase of one standard deviation in the logarithm of real wage rate leads to an expected increase of 0.291 standard deviation in the logarithm of days of incapacity due to sickness per person.

Inference about the parameters of a multiple regression model is generally based on the further assumption that the regression error terms ϵ_t follow a normal distribution. If this assumption together with the standard assumptions of Section 4.1 holds, it can be shown that the random variables

$$t = (a - \alpha)/s_a \qquad t_i = (b_i - \beta_i)/s_{b_i} \qquad (i = 1, 2, \ldots, K)$$

all have Student's t distributions with $(n - K - 1)$ degrees of freedom.

Confidence intervals for and hypothesis tests about the regression parameters follow from these results.

To illustrate, we will find a 95% confidence interval for the parameter β_3 in the log linear regression model of the data of Table 4.1. Here we have

$$n = 20 \qquad K = 3$$

so that, from Table A.2 of the Appendix, we require

$$t_{n-K-1,\alpha/2} = t_{16,.025} = 2.120$$

Then, the required 95% confidence interval is

$$0.401 - (2.120)(0.198) < \beta_3 < 0.401 + (2.120)(0.198)$$

or

$$-0.02 < \beta_3 < 0.82$$

Thus, a 95% confidence interval for the effect on days of incapacity due to sickness per person of a 1% increase in real wage rate, all else equal, runs from a decrease of 0.02% to an increase of 0.82%.

Suppose now that our interest is in testing hypotheses about the partial regression coefficients. Let $\beta_{i,0}$ be a hypothesized value of the parameter β_i. There are three possible test procedures:

1. To test either null hypothesis

$$H_0: \beta_i = \beta_{i,0} \quad \text{or} \quad H_0: \beta_i \leq \beta_{i,0}$$

against the alternative hypothesis

$$H_1: \beta_i > \beta_{i,0}$$

the decision rule is, for a test of significance level α,

$$\text{Reject } H_0 \text{ if} \qquad \frac{(b_i - \beta_{i,0})}{s_{b_i}} > t_{n-K-1,\alpha}$$

2. To test either null hypothesis

$$H_0: \beta_i = \beta_{i,0} \quad \text{or} \quad H_0: \beta_i \geq \beta_{i,0}$$

against the alternative hypothesis

$$H_1: \beta_i < \beta_{i,0}$$

the decision rule is, for a test of significance level α,

$$\text{Reject } H_0 \text{ if } \quad \frac{(b_i - \beta_{i,0})}{s_{b_i}} < -t_{n-K-1,\alpha}$$

3. To test the null hypothesis

$$H_0: \beta_i = \beta_{i,0}$$

against the two-sided alternative hypothesis

$$H_1: \beta_i \neq \beta_{i,0}$$

the decision rule is, for a test of significance level α,

$$\text{Reject } H_0 \text{ if } \quad \frac{(b_i - \beta_{i,0})}{s_{b_i}} < -t_{n-K-1,\alpha/2} \quad \text{or} \quad >t_{n-K-1,\alpha/2}$$

Often, the null hypothesis of interest is that the regression parameter is zero. Tests of this hypothesis, then, are based on the statistics

$$t = b_i/s_{b_i}$$

that is, on the ratios of the least squares parameter estimates to the associated standard errors. These statistics are computed in the SPSS program output in Exhibit 4.1 in the column headed "T". The next column, headed "Sig T", shows the p-values for tests against two-sided alternatives. These are the lowest levels of significance at which the null hypothesis that the regression parameters are zero can be rejected against the alternative hypotheses that the true parameters are different from zero. To obtain p-values for tests against one-sided alternatives, the figures in the "Sig T" column should be divided by two. For example, from Exhibit 4.1, we see that the null hypothesis that β_3 is zero can be rejected against the alternative that β_3 is not equal to zero at all significance levels above 5.92%. This null hypothesis can be rejected against the alternative that β_3 is bigger than zero at all significance levels above 2.96%.

The hypothesis that a partial regression coefficient is zero is of interest since this is the hypothesis that, all else equal, the value taken by the dependent variable is not linearly influenced by the value of the corresponding independent variable. Looking at the Sig T column of Exhibit 4.1, and assuming that our regression model specification is adequate, the evidence that the ratio of sickness benefits to earnings influences days of incapacity due to sickness is quite overwhelming. Also, there is fairly strong evidence that the real wage rate is an influential variable. However, the evidence that, all else equal, incapacity due to sickness depends on the unemployment rate is very weak.

The final entry in Exhibit 4.1 shows the Durbin-Watson test statistic. This statistic is used to test the hypothesis that the regression error terms are not correlated with one another against a particular pattern of error correlations whose presence might be suspected in time series data. The inferential procedures discussed in this section depend for their validity on the assumption that the regression error terms are uncorrelated. If this assumption is false, these procedures can be seriously misleading. We will return to this issue in Section 4.5.

A Test on All the Partial Regression Coefficients

We have seen how the hypothesis that a particular partial regression coefficient is zero can be tested. It is of some interest to test the null hypothesis that *all* the partial regression coefficients are zero; that is, the hypothesis

$$H_0: \beta_1 = \beta_2 = \cdots = \beta_K = 0 \qquad (4.3.2)$$

In a sense this is a very pessimistic hypothesis. If it were true, the expected value of the dependent variable would be the same whatever the values of the independent variables, so that, taken as a set, the independent variables would have no linear influence on the dependent variable.

Now, since the coefficient of determination measures the proportion of variability of the dependent variable in the sample explained by the fitted regression, we might expect that a test of the null hypothesis 4.3.2 would be based on R^2, or the sums of squares decomposition. This is in fact the case. All else equal, the larger is R^2, or equivalently the larger is the regression sum of squares compared with the error sum of squares, the more inclined would we be to suspect that the null hypothesis 4.3.2 is false. In fact, the test statistic that is employed is

$$F = \frac{\text{SSR}/K}{\text{SSE}/(n - K - 1)} = \frac{(n - K - 1)}{K} \frac{R^2}{(1 - R^2)} \quad (4.3.3)$$

Under the hypothesis 4.3.2, it can be shown that this statistic has a distribution known as the **F-distribution,** with numerator degrees of freedom K and denominator degrees of freedom $(n - K - 1)$. Notice that this random variable depends on two different degrees of freedom. Let us denote by F_{v_1, v_2} a random variable having an F-distribution with numerator degrees of freedom v_1 and denominator degrees of freedom v_2. For significance levels $\alpha = 0.05, 0.01$, Table 4 in the Appendix at the back of this volume gives the numbers $F_{v_1, v_2, \alpha}$ that are exceeded with probability α by the F_{v_1, v_2} random variable; that is,

$$P(F_{v_1, v_2} > F_{v_1, v_2, \alpha}) = \alpha$$

To test the null hypothesis 4.3.2, the statistic 4.3.3 is calculated. The null hypothesis is rejected at significance level α if this test statistic is bigger than the tabulated value $F_{K, n-K-1, \alpha}$.

These calculations are sometimes set out in a table known as an **analysis of variance** table. The general format is shown in Table 4.2. The three *sources of variation,* each with an associated degrees of freedom, are identified. Next, the sums of squares corresponding to the decomposition of Section 4.2 are entered. Dividing the sums of squares by the corresponding degrees of freedom yields the **mean squares.** (Notice that the mean squared error MSE is the statistic s^2 of 4.2.3, providing an unbiased estimate of the variance of regression error terms.) Finally, the ratio of the regression mean square to the error mean square provides the test statistic 4.3.3. For our log linear regression of the data of Table 4.1, Exhibit 4.1 shows some of these analysis of variance calculations. We see that the test statistic 4.3.3 is

$$F = 61.01$$

This could be compared with the tabulated values of the F-distribution in Table 4 of the Appendix. However, that is not necessary with the SPSS program, which computes the p-value of the test (labeled "Signif F"). It can be seen that the p-value is negligibly small, so that the null hypothesis that the three partial regression coefficients are all zero can be rejected at a very low significance level. The evidence against the hypothesis that,

TABLE **4.2**   General format of the analysis of variance table for multiple regression.

Source of Variation	Degrees of Freedom	Sum of Squares	Mean Square	F-ratio
Regression	K	SSR	MSR = SSR/K	F = MSR/MSE
Error	$n - K - 1$	SSE	MSE = SSE/$(n - K - 1)$	
Total	$n - 1$	SST		

taken together, the logarithms of male unemployment rate, ratio of sickness benefits to earnings, and the real wage rate do not linearly influence the logarithm of days of incapacity due to sickness per person is overwhelming.

Occasionally, in fitting multiple regression models to real data, one encounters a perplexing result. On one hand there may be no strong evidence of significance of any of the individual partial regression coefficients, yet, on the other hand, the null hypothesis that all of these coefficients are zero is clearly rejected. This can arise as a consequence of severe multicollinearity in the data. There may be strong evidence of some dependence, but the data may not be sufficiently informative to allow very precise disentangling of the separate influences of the independent variables on the dependent variable.

A Test on a Subset of the Partial Regression Coefficients

We have seen how to test hypotheses on individual partial regression coefficients, and also on the complete set of coefficients. Occasionally one encounters the intermediate problem, where it is required to test the null hypothesis that some subset of the partial regression coefficients are all zero. Suppose we want to test that M of these coefficients are zero, where M is a number less than K. The independent variables can be relabeled so that $X_1, X_2, \ldots, X_M$ denote those variables whose associated coefficients are to be tested. The null hypothesis, then, is

$$H_0: \beta_1 = \beta_2 = \cdots = \beta_M = 0$$

The test of this hypothesis proceeds as follows:

1. Estimate the full regression of Y on all K independent variables X_1, $X_2, \ldots, X_K$, and record the error sum of squares SSE.
2. Estimate the regression of Y on the $(K - M)$ independent variables $X_{M+1}, \ldots, X_K$, and record the error sum of squares SSE*.
3. For a test of significance level α, the null hypothesis is rejected if

$$\frac{(\text{SSE*} - \text{SSE})/M}{\text{SSE}/(n - K - 1)} > F_{M, n-K-1, \alpha}$$

The logic behind this test follows from the fact that, if the set of independent variables $X_1, \ldots, X_M$ really has no influence on the dependent variable, given that the other $(K - M)$ variables are to be used, the two regressions in 1 and 2 above should fit almost equally well; their error sums of squares should be quite close. If the error sum of squares from the full regression is much smaller, this would suggest that at least one of the variables $X_1, \ldots, X_M$ makes a significant contribution toward explaining the behavior of the dependent variable.

4.4 LAGGED DEPENDENT VARIABLES

A potential weakness of the time series regression models that we have discussed thus far is that they are static in character. The current value of the dependent variable is assumed to be influenced only by the current values of the independent variables. In some applications such a specification would be unnecessarily and implausibly restrictive. For example, the funds committed to investment by a corporation are likely to depend not only on its current earnings, but also on its stream of past earnings.

To see a simple way in which a more dynamic relationship might be postulated, consider the case of a dependent variable Y and a single independent variable X. We now allow the expected value of the dependent variable at the current time period to be influenced by the values taken by the independent variable at the current and all previous time periods. In practice, to make any progress, some structure must be imposed on the dynamics of this relationship. It will often be plausible to assume that the impacts of recent values of the independent variable are stronger than those of more distant values. One model that captures this structure is

$$Y_t = \delta + \beta X_t + \beta\gamma X_{t-1} + \beta\gamma^2 X_{t-2} + \beta\gamma^3 X_{t-3} + \cdots + u_t$$

$$(4.4.1)$$

In this expression, u_t is an error term with mean zero, while δ, β, and γ are fixed parameters. It will be assumed that the parameter γ has a value between zero and one. The implication of equation 4.4.1, then, is that a one-unit increase in the independent variable in the current time period leads to an expected increase of β units in the dependent variable in the current time period, a further expected increase of $\beta\gamma$ units in the next time period, an additional expected increase of $\beta\gamma^2$ units two time periods ahead, and so on. Notice that the implication of this specification, together with the assumption that the value of the parameter γ is between zero and one, is that the impact of a change in the independent variable on current and future values of the dependent variable is strongest initially, and weakens exponentially further into the future, so that the impact on very distant future values of the dependent variable will be negligible. This type of structure has a good deal of intuitive appeal.

For practical analysis, an alternative equivalent specification of the model is preferable. This can be derived by first replacing t by $(t - 1)$ in equation 4.4.1, giving

$$Y_{t-1} = \delta + \beta X_{t-1} + \beta\gamma X_{t-2} + \beta\gamma^2 X_{t-3} + \cdots + u_{t-1}$$

Multiplying through this equation by γ, and subtracting from equation 4.4.1 gives

$$Y_t - \gamma Y_{t-1} = \delta(1 - \gamma) + \beta X_t + u_t - \gamma u_{t-1}$$

This can be written

$$Y_t = \alpha + \beta X_t + \gamma Y_{t-1} + \epsilon_t \qquad (4.4.2)$$

where

$$\alpha = \delta(1 - \gamma) \qquad \epsilon_t = u_t - \gamma u_{t-1}$$

In the formulation 4.4.2, the expected value of the dependent variable in the current time period is expressed as a linear function of the current value of the independent variable and the value of the dependent variable in the previous time period. This last term is known as a **lagged dependent variable.**

In the case where a dependent variable is influenced by K independent variables, $X_1, X_2, \ldots, X_K$, a natural extension of the model 4.4.2 is

$$Y_t = \alpha + \beta_1 X_{1t} + \beta_2 X_{2t} + \cdots + \beta_K X_{Kt} + \gamma Y_{t-1} + \epsilon_t$$

$$(4.4.3)$$

This model is in the familiar form of the usual multiple regression specification, with the addition on the right-hand side of the lagged dependent variable and associated parameter γ. The presence of the lagged dependent variable in equation 4.4.3 alters the usual interpretation of the regression parameters. Following our discussion of equation 4.4.1, it can be seen that, with the values of the other independent variables held fixed, an increase of one unit in the independent variable X_i leads to an expected increase of β_i units in the dependent variable in the current time period, a further expected increase of $\beta_i\gamma$ units in the next time period, an additional expected increase of $\beta_i\gamma^2$ units two time periods ahead, and so on. The total, or *long run*, expected increase in the dependent variable over current and all future time periods is

$$\beta_i + \beta_i\gamma + \beta_i\gamma^2 + \beta_i\gamma^3 + \cdots = \beta_i/(1 - \gamma) \qquad (4.4.4)$$

The model 4.4.3, incorporating a lagged dependent variable with associated coefficient γ between zero and one, has often been found to provide a good representation of business and economic processes. A number of theoretical explanations of why this should be so have been advanced; here we briefly discuss two of them.

Adaptive Expectations

For ease of exposition, we will again restrict attention to the case where a dependent variable Y is influenced by a single independent variable X. To make matters more concrete, suppose that we are interested in the dependence of corporate investment on corporate earnings. Now, earnings in the current time period may be influenced by extraordinary items, and hence not representative of what might be expected in the future. Corporate decision makers may prefer to base current investment strategy, not on current earnings, but on the **expected future earnings stream;** that is, on earnings expected in future time periods. Let Y_t denote investment at time t, and suppose that at time t the corporation expects future earnings of X_t^* per period. Then, the value of investment made at time t might be represented by the model

$$Y_t = \delta + \lambda X_t^* + u_t \qquad (4.4.5)$$

where δ and λ are fixed parameters, and u_t is an error term with mean zero.

As it stands, the formulation 4.4.5 is of no value for practical analysis, as the expected earnings X_t^* will be unobservable. To achieve a model representing the behavior of observable variables, some assumption must be made about the way in which expectations are formed. One intuitively plausible possibility is to assume a process of adaptive expectations formation[2]

$$X_t^* = (1 - \gamma)X_t + \gamma X_{t-1}^* \qquad 0 < \gamma < 1 \qquad (4.4.6)$$

where X_t denotes actual earnings at time t. According to this expression, the expectation at time t is a weighted average of the expectation at the previous time period and the actual value in the current time period.

Equations 4.4.5 and 4.4.6 can be amalgamated to yield a model linking the observable processes Y_t and X_t. To achieve this, we substitute $(t - 1)$

---

2.   In Chapter 6 we will see that expectations formed in this way can be regarded as forecasts derived from the simple exponential smoothing algorithm. They are also optimal forecasts when the series X_t is generated by the ARIMA(0, 1, 1) model of Chapter 7.

for t in 4.4.5, giving

$$Y_{t-1} = \delta + \lambda X^*_{t-1} + u_{t-1}$$

Multiplying through this expression by γ, and subtracting from equation 4.4.5, gives

$$Y_t - \gamma Y_{t-1} = \delta(1 - \gamma) + \lambda(X^*_t - \gamma X^*_{t-1}) + u_t - \gamma u_{t-1}$$
$$= \delta(1 - \gamma) + \lambda(1 - \gamma)X_t + u_t - \gamma u_{t-1}$$

by virtue of equation 4.4.6. It therefore follows that

$$Y_t = \alpha + \beta X_t + \gamma Y_{t-1} + \epsilon_t$$

where

$$\alpha = \delta(1 - \gamma) \qquad \beta = \lambda(1 - \gamma) \qquad \epsilon_t = u_t - \gamma u_{t-1}$$

This is precisely the lagged dependent variable model 4.4.2.

Partial Adjustment

Again, consider the case of a relationship between a dependent variable Y and a single independent variable X. Suppose, for example, that Y_t represents consumers' expenditures in period t, and X_t denotes consumers' disposable income in that time period. The premise of the **partial adjustment hypothesis,** in the context of this example, is that an increase in disposable income from one time period to the next will lead to a new level of desired consumption expenditure, but consumers will only be able to make part of the desired adjustment in expenditure from one time period to the next. This seems reasonable, since it is difficult, for example, to abruptly alter behavior patterns.

If disposable income in period t is X_t, we assume that desired consumption Y^*_t in that time period is simply the linear function

$$Y^*_t = \delta + \lambda X_t \qquad (4.4.7)$$

where δ and λ are fixed parameters. Then, since Y_{t-1} is the actual consumption expenditure in period $(t - 1)$, an adjustment $(Y^*_t - Y_{t-1})$ is required to achieve the desired level in period t. Suppose, however, that the actual adjustment $(Y_t - Y_{t-1})$ that can be made is, on the average, only a proportion $(1 - \gamma)$ of the desired adjustment. We can then write

$$Y_t - Y_{t-1} = (1 - \gamma)(Y^*_t - Y_{t-1}) + \epsilon_t \qquad 0 < \gamma < 1 \quad (4.4.8)$$

where ϵ_t is a random variable with mean zero. To achieve a model linking observable quantities, it is necessary to eliminate the desired value, Y_t^*, of the dependent variable, since this quantity cannot be directly observed. Substituting equation 4.4.7 into equation 4.4.8 gives

$$Y_t - Y_{t-1} = (1 - \gamma)(\delta + \lambda X_t - Y_{t-1}) + \epsilon_t$$

so that

$$Y_t = \delta(1 - \gamma) + \lambda(1 - \gamma)X_t + \gamma Y_{t-1} + \epsilon_t$$

Hence, we can write

$$Y_t = \alpha + \beta X_t + \gamma Y_{t-1} + \epsilon_t$$

where

$$\alpha = \delta(1 - \gamma) \qquad \beta = \lambda(1 - \gamma)$$

Thus we have again arrived at the lagged dependent variable model 4.4.2.

Fitting to Data a Model with a Lagged Dependent Variable

Suppose now that we have available observations on a dependent variable and K independent variables and want to fit the model 4.4.3. We will assume that data are available for time periods $t = 1, 2, \ldots, n$, and that the previous value, Y_0, of the dependent variable has been observed. The model 4.4.3 can then be fitted by least squares in the usual way, treating the lagged dependent variable as if it were another independent variable. The usual least squares-based inferential procedures of Section 4.3 are then typically applied, though strictly speaking they only become valid as the number of sample observations approaches infinity; they are, however, approximately valid in moderate-sized samples. This least squares approach is only appropriate under the standard assumptions, where the error terms ϵ_t have mean zero, constant variance, are uncorrelated with one another, and are not correlated with the independent variables X_1, $X_2, \ldots, X_K$.

To illustrate, consider the data of Table 4.3, which shows 34 consecutive quarterly observations from Japan on quantity of imports (Y), real gross national product (X_1), and the ratio of import prices to domestic prices (X_2). Also shown is the observed quantity of imports from the previous quarter. We analyzed these data in logarithms, fitting the model

$$\log Y_t = \alpha + \beta_1 \log X_{1t} + \beta_2 \log X_{2t} + \gamma \log Y_{t-1} + \epsilon_t$$

TABLE 4.3   Quarterly observations on quantity of imports (Y), real gross
national product (X_1), and ratio of import prices to domestic prices
(X_2) in Japan.

t	Y_t	X_{1t}	X_{2t}	t	Y_t	X_{1t}	X_{2t}
0	78.7			18	108.2	96.6	0.9323
1	80.4	78.2	0.8264	19	98.0	97.9	1.0567
2	84.0	79.7	0.8391	20	104.0	98.3	1.0494
3	80.9	81.2	0.8484	21	96.6	99.5	0.9781
4	86.5	82.4	0.8188	22	100.8	100.0	0.9427
5	89.7	83.1	0.7986	23	97.9	101.5	0.9449
6	91.7	83.8	0.8060	24	97.0	102.1	1.0010
7	89.8	85.3	0.7886	25	93.6	103.0	1.0214
8	89.7	86.9	0.7611	26	101.1	103.0	0.9787
9	88.5	87.0	0.7345	27	103.3	104.1	0.9663
10	91.3	88.4	0.6854	28	96.7	105.6	0.9895
11	90.6	88.4	0.6608	29	92.1	106.5	1.0391
12	94.5	89.4	0.6150	30	95.1	106.9	1.0459
13	95.0	90.4	0.5487	31	94.1	107.1	0.9364
14	102.1	91.6	0.5447	32	95.5	108.3	0.8975
15	104.2	92.9	0.5970	33	94.6	109.9	0.9190
16	106.7	94.5	0.6695	34	108.2	110.8	0.8878
17	105.8	95.5	0.7916				

This model was fitted using the ordinary SPSS multiple regression
program, treating $\log Y_{t-1}$ as if it were just a third independent variable.
Part of the SPSS program output is shown in Exhibit 4.2. We will
concentrate on the segment of output headed "Variables in the Equation."
The right-hand side variables are labeled LNRGNP (logarithm of real
gross national product), LNPRC (logarithm of ratio of import prices to
domestic prices), and LNIMP1 (logarithm of quantity of imports lagged
one time period). From the output of Exhibit 4.2, we then find that the
fitted model is

$$\log \hat{Y}_t = 0.504 + 0.261 \log X_{1t} - 0.108 \log X_{2t} + 0.626 \log Y_{t-1}$$
$$\quad (0.440) \quad (0.111) \qquad\quad (0.045) \qquad\qquad (0.122)$$

$$(4.4.9)$$

where figures in brackets below the coefficient estimates are the corresponding estimated standard errors.

   Keeping in mind that the analysis is of the logarithms of the original
data, the coefficient estimates can be interpreted as follows:

1. For a constant ratio of import prices to domestic prices, each 1%

EXHIBIT 4.2   Part of SPSS program output for the fitting of a log linear regression model with lagged dependent variable to the data of Table 4.3.

```
                 * * * *   M U L T I P L E   R E G R E S S I O N   * * * *


      Multiple R             .86109
      R Square              .74147
      Adjusted R Square     .71562
      Standard Error        .04117

      Analysis of Variance
                           DF      Sum of Squares      Mean Square
      Regression            3             .14585           .04862
      Residual             30             .05085           .00170

      F =      28.67997     Signif F =  .0000



      ----------------- Variables in the Equation -------------------

      Variable             B          SE B         Beta          T    Sig T

      LNRGNP           .26071        .11057       .34554       2.358   .0251
      LNPRC           -.10781        .04546      -.26583      -2.371   .0243
      LNIMP1           .62594        .12203       .65285       5.129   .0000
      (Constant)       .50434        .43963                    1.147   .2604


      Durbin-Watson Test =      2.31581
```

increase in real gross national product leads to an expected 0.261% increase in import quantity in the current quarter, a further $(0.261)(0.626) = 0.163\%$ expected increase in the next quarter, an additional $(0.261)(0.626)^2 = 0.102\%$ expected increase two quarters ahead, and so on. From 4.4.4, we estimate a total long run expected increase in the current and all future time periods of

$$\frac{0.261}{(1 - 0.626)} = 0.698\%$$

2. For constant real gross national product, we estimate that a 1% increase in the ratio of import prices to domestic prices leads to an expected 0.108% decrease in import quantity in the current period, a further $(0.108)(0.626) = 0.068\%$ expected decrease in the next

quarter, an additional $(0.108)(0.626)^2 = 0.042\%$ expected decrease two quarters ahead, and so on. The total long run expected decrease in the current and all future time periods is estimated as

$$\frac{0.108}{(1 - 0.626)} = 0.289\%$$

Confidence intervals for, and hypothesis tests on, the regression parameters can be carried out in the usual way. For illustration, we derive a 95% confidence interval for the parameter β_2. Since there are 34 sets of observations, and the model 4.4.9 involves four fitted parameters, we require from Table A.2 of the Appendix

$$t_{30,.025} = 2.042$$

Hence, the 95% confidence interval for β_2 is

$$-0.108 - (2.042)(0.045) < \beta_2 < -0.108 + (2.042)(0.045)$$

or

$$-0.200 < \beta_2 < -0.016$$

Thus, with real gross national product fixed, a 95% confidence interval for the expected decrease in import quantities in the current quarter, resulting from a 1% increase in the ratio of import prices to domestic prices runs from 0.016% to 0.200%.

It is interesting to note, from the Sig T column of Exhibit 4.2, that the p-value of the test of the null hypothesis that the coefficient on the lagged dependent variable is zero is very small indeed. This strongly suggests the desirability of including the lagged dependent variable in the model, and certainly argues the inadequacy of the ordinary static model for the representation of these data.

The lagged dependent variable model 4.4.3, or its log linear variant, are frequently fitted to business and economic time series data. Empirical evidence often suggests its adequacy, and, as we have seen, a number of theoretical arguments can be advanced in its support. Nevertheless, this is by no means the only dynamic specification that might reasonably be tried. For example, terms in higher lagged dependent variables, Y_{t-2}, Y_{t-3}, etc., could be added, as could terms in lagged values of the independent variables. Experimentation with such alternatives allows consideration of a rich array of possible dynamic specifications. We will discuss in Chapter 9 a general class of dynamic time series models.

4.5 AUTOCORRELATED ERRORS

Since our interest is in forecasting, we have concentrated in this and the previous chapter on fitting regression models to time series data. The method of least squares, and the inferential procedures that flow from it, are generally appropriate when the standard assumptions of Section 4.1 hold, and the overwhelming majority of empirical regression analysis is based on least squares. However, in the context of time series data we might suspect that the assumption that the regression errors are uncorrelated with one another will often fail to hold. These errors are the discrepancies between the observed and expected values of the dependent variable. Now, business and economic time series tend to evolve quite smoothly through time, so we might suspect that if the observed value of a dependent variable is above its expectation in one time period, it is more likely than not to be higher than its expectation in the following period. This suggests the possibility of a positive correlation between regression errors in adjacent time periods, which would constitute a violation of the fourth of the standard assumptions of Section 4.1. A pattern of correlation through time in the errors of a regression model is referred to as the problem of **autocorrelated errors.**

If regression errors are seriously autocorrelated, it is inappropriate to proceed with the usual least squares methods. In particular, the application of these methods to regression models with autocorrelated errors leads to the following consequences:

1. The least squares estimators of the parameters of the model 4.1.2 will still be unbiased, but they will no longer be efficient. It is possible to find estimators with smaller variances. The Gauss-Markov theorem does not hold when the regression errors are autocorrelated.

2. Application of the usual inferential procedures of Section 4.3 can yield seriously misleading conclusions. In the presence of severe autocorrelation in the regression errors, the true probability contents of confidence intervals and the true significance levels of tests can be very different than those reported by least squares algorithms that are based on the assumption of no autocorrelation in the errors.

3. If autocorrelation in the regression errors is ignored, forecasts derived from the fitted model can be seriously inefficient. This is so, not only because the regression parameter estimators will be inefficient, but also because any autocorrelation present in the regression errors can be exploited in the production of superior forecasts.

Checking for autocorrelated errors, and modifying the usual estimation and inference procedures to allow for them, is no mere academic exercise.

It can make a serious impact on our understanding of the system under study, and on the quality of any forecasts that are developed. One illustration of this is provided by Granger and Newbold (1974), elaborating on point 2 above. These authors demonstrated in a simulation study that, if severe autocorrelated errors are ignored, the analyst can be led very often to conclude that there is a very significant relationship between variables, when in fact none exists. The possibility of "discovering" *spurious regressions* in this manner was illustrated by Box and Newbold (1971) in the context of a practical forecasting problem.

In theory, the error terms of a regression model could exhibit any number of possible correlation patterns over time. In this chapter we will concentrate on just a single possible pattern—one that has been employed in practical applications far more than all others. We will outline some further possibilities in Chapters 7 and 9. The most commonly employed model of autocorrelation is predicated on the belief that we would expect to find the strongest correlations between error terms that are closest to one another in time, with correlations weakening for errors further apart in time. A simple and intuitively appealing structure of this sort follows when the correlation is ρ between error terms adjacent in time, ρ^2 between error terms two time periods apart, ρ^3 between error terms three time periods apart, and so on. Letting, as usual, ϵ_t denote the error at time t, the assumption is that

$$\text{Corr. } (\epsilon_t, \epsilon_{t-1}) = \rho \quad \text{Corr. } (\epsilon_t, \epsilon_{t-2}) = \rho^2 \quad \text{Corr. } (\epsilon_t, \epsilon_{t-3}) = \rho^3$$

and, in general,

$$\text{Corr. } (\epsilon_t, \epsilon_{t-j}) = \rho^j \quad j = 1, 2, 3, \ldots \quad (4.5.1)$$

Since ρ is a correlation coefficient, its absolute value cannot exceed one, and will typically be less than one, so that equation 4.5.1 implies a pattern of geometrically declining correlation magnitudes as the separation in time of regression errors increases.

It is possible to show,[3] provided that the regression error terms all have mean zero and the same variance, that the autocorrelation pattern 4.5.1 implies the model of autocorrelated error behavior

$$\epsilon_t = \rho\epsilon_{t-1} + a_t \quad -1 < \rho < 1 \quad (4.5.2)$$

where the random variables a_t have zero means, constant variances, and are not correlated with one another—that is, they satisfy the standard

---

3. This result is demonstrated in Section 7.5, where more general models of autocorrelation behavior are also considered.

assumptions about the statistical behavior of regression errors. The formulation 4.5.2 is called the **first order autoregressive model.** In the remainder of this section we will see how to test for the presence of autocorrelated errors in the context of this formulation, and how to estimate the parameters of a regression model in the presence of this type of autocorrelated errors.

A Test for Autocorrelated Errors

Assume a relationship between a dependent variable, Y, and K independent variables, $X_1, X_2, \ldots, X_K$, represented by the multiple regression model 4.1.2. This model contains no lagged dependent variables. The problem of autocorrelated errors in models with lagged dependent variables requires separate treatment, and will be discussed later in this section. We assume that the regression errors ϵ_t are generated by the first-order autoregressive model 4.5.2, and require to test the null hypothesis of no autocorrelation in these errors. This is the hypothesis

$$H_0: \rho = 0 \qquad (4.5.3)$$

In most applications we would suspect the possibility of positive correlation between adjacent errors, so that the null hypothesis 4.5.3 would be tested against the alternative hypothesis

$$H_1: \rho > 0$$

Several alternative tests of this hypothesis have been proposed and implemented, but by far the most frequently applied in practice is the **Durbin-Watson test.** This test is based on the residuals from the least squares fit of the model 4.1.2. Then, if $a, b_1, b_2, \ldots, b_K$ are the least squares estimates of the regression parameters, the residuals are

$$e_t = Y_t - a - b_1 X_{1t} - b_2 X_{2t} - \cdots - b_K X_{Kt} \qquad t = 1, 2, \ldots, n$$

The Durbin-Watson test statistic is

$$d = \frac{\sum_{t=2}^{n} (e_t - e_{t-1})^2}{\sum_{t=1}^{n} e_t^2} \qquad (4.5.4)$$

To see the rationale behind this statistic, notice that it can be written

$$d = \frac{\sum\limits_{t=2}^{n} e_t^2}{\sum\limits_{t=1}^{n} e_t^2} + \frac{\sum\limits_{t=1}^{n-1} e_t^2}{\sum\limits_{t=1}^{n} e_t^2} - 2 \frac{\sum\limits_{t=2}^{n} e_t e_{t-1}}{\sum\limits_{t=1}^{n} e_t^2}$$

Now, unless the number of observations n is quite small, the first two terms on the right-hand side of the expression will be very close to one, so that we can write to a close approximation

$$d \simeq 2(1 - r) \qquad\qquad (4.5.5)$$

where

$$r = \frac{\sum\limits_{t=2}^{n} e_t e_{t-1}}{\sum\limits_{t=1}^{n} e_t^2}$$

is the sample correlation between adjacent residuals. Since these residuals estimate the regression errors ϵ_t, r provides a natural estimate of the correlation ρ between adjacent errors. It follows that, if the null hypothesis 4.5.3 of no autocorrelation is true, we would expect to find a value close to two for the Durbin-Watson d statistic. In the presence of serious positive autocorrelation in the regression errors, we would expect to find a value well below two for this statistic.

Let d_α be the number such that, when the null hypothesis 4.5.3 is true,

$$P(d < d_\alpha) = \alpha$$

Then, a test of significance level α of the null hypothesis against the alternative of positive autocorrelation would reject the null hypothesis when the statistic 4.5.4 is less than d_α. Unfortunately, however, the distribution of the Durbin-Watson statistic under the null hypothesis depends on the values of the independent variables, and it is obviously infeasible to tabulate percentage points of the distribution for all possible values of these variables. It is known that, whatever the values taken by the independent variables, it is possible to find two statistics whose distributions lie on either side of that of d under the null hypothesis. Consequently, we are able to find a pair of numbers, $d_{L,\alpha}$ and $d_{U,\alpha}$, such

that

$$d_{L,\alpha} \le d_\alpha \le d_{U,\alpha}$$

These limits are tabulated in Table A.5 of the Appendix at the back of this volume for significance levels $\alpha = 0.05, 0.01$ and various values of sample size, n, and number of independent variables, K. Once the statistic d of equation 4.5.4 has been calculated, there are three possible decisions:

1. If $d < d_{L,\alpha}$, H_0 is rejected
2. If $d > d_{U,\alpha}$, H_0 is accepted
3. If $d_{L,\alpha} < d < d_{U,\alpha}$, the test is inconclusive.

The position is illustrated in Figure 4.2. The Durbin-Watson test is somewhat unusual because of the existence of an inconclusive region, bounded by $d_{L,\alpha}$ and $d_{U,\alpha}$. It is sometimes called the *bounds test*.

In Exhibit 4.1, we see that for the log linear regression on the data of Table 4.1, the Durbin-Watson test statistic is

$$d = 1.734$$

Since the regression is based on 20 observations, with three independent variables, we find from Table A.5 of the Appendix that, for a 5% level test, the Durbin-Watson statistic should be compared with

$$d_{L,.05} = 1.00 \qquad d_{U,.05} = 1.68$$

Therefore, the null hypothesis of no autocorrelation in the errors of this regression is accepted against the alternative of positive autocorrelation with a test of significance level 5%. We find no strong evidence of autocorrelated errors in this model.

As is the case in the example just discussed, when the sample size is small, the inconclusive region of the Durbin-Watson test can be quite

FIGURE 4.2   Decision rule for Durbin-Watson test of null hypothesis of no autocorrelation in regression errors against the alternative of positive correlation.

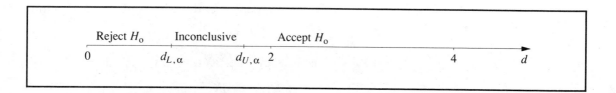

wide. This is frustrating, as in practice some decision on how to proceed must be taken. Some authors appear to take anything other than a clear rejection of the null hypothesis of no autocorrelation as a welcome signal that nothing else need be done. Our own preference is to err on the side of caution, correcting for possible autocorrelated errors when a 5% level test yields a statistic in the inconclusive region.

Occasionally, particularly when the dependent variable represents period to period changes in some quantity of interest, it is desirable to test against the alternative hypothesis of negative autocorrelation in the regression errors. The procedure is precisely the same as that just described, except that at the outset the statistic d is replaced by $4 - d$.

Estimation of Regression Models with Autocorrelated Errors

When there is strong indication of the presence of autocorrelated errors in a regression model, it is, as we have seen, dangerous to proceed with ordinary least squares methods. Fortunately, alternative estimation procedures, with appealing statistical properties, are available. The model to be estimated can be regarded as a pair of equations:

$$Y_t = \alpha + \beta_1 X_{1t} + \beta_2 X_{2t} + \cdots + \beta_K X_{Kt} + \epsilon_t \quad (4.5.6a)$$

$$\epsilon_t = \rho \epsilon_{t-1} + a_t \quad (4.5.6b)$$

In this model, it is the error terms $a_;yt$ that obey the standard assumptions. Our problem is to jointly estimate the $(K + 2)$ unknown parameters α, $\beta_1, \beta_2, \ldots, \beta_K, \rho$. Several alternative procedures have been proposed for this purpose. Here we will discuss just one of them—the **Cochrane-Orcutt method.**

To see the rationale for this estimation procedure, first replace t by $(t - 1)$ in equation 4.5.6a, giving

$$Y_{t-1} = \alpha + \beta_1 X_{1,t-1} + \beta_2 X_{2,t-1} + \cdots + \beta_K X_{K,t-1} + \epsilon_{t-1}$$

Multiplying through this equation by ρ and subtracting from equation 4.5.6a then gives

$$Y_t - \rho Y_{t-1} = \alpha(1 - \rho) + \beta_1(X_{1t} - \rho X_{1,t-1}) + \cdots$$
$$+ \beta_K(X_{Kt} - \rho X_{K,t-1}) + \epsilon_t - \rho \epsilon_{t-1}$$

It then follows from equation 4.5.6b that

$$Y_t - \rho Y_{t-1} = \alpha(1 - \rho) + \beta_1(X_{1t} - \rho X_{1,t-1}) + \cdots$$
$$+ \beta_K(X_{Kt} - \rho X_{K,t-1}) + a_t \qquad (4.5.7)$$

We can view equation 4.5.7 as a regression equation with dependent variable $(Y_t - \rho Y_{t-1})$ and K independent variables $(X_{1t} - \rho X_{1,t-1})$, ..., $(X_{Kt} - \rho X_{K,t-1})$. The error terms a_t have zero means, constant variances, and are not autocorrelated. Therefore, if the autocorrelation parameter were known, since the standard assumptions are satisfied we could obtain best linear unbiased estimators by applying ordinary least squares to the regression of $(Y_t - \rho Y_{t-1})$ on $(X_{1t} - \rho X_{1,t-1})$, ..., $(X_{Kt} - \rho X_{K,t-1})$. This would yield directly estimates of $\alpha(1 - \rho)$, β_1, β_2, ..., β_K. An estimate of α could then be obtained by dividing the estimate of $\alpha(1 - \rho)$ by $(1 - \rho)$. In practice, the parameter ρ will be unknown. However, we may be able to proceed by replacing that parameter in equation 4.5.7 by an estimate.

These considerations underlie the Cochrane-Orcutt approach, which is an *iterative* method, beginning with a set of initial parameter estimates and proceeding through a cycle of iterative improvements of these estimates. This approach has the following steps:

1. First fit the model 4.5.6a by ordinary least squares, yielding the parameter estimates $\hat{\alpha}^{(1)}$, $\hat{\beta}_1^{(1)}$, ..., $\hat{\beta}_K^{(1)}$.

2. An estimate of the error terms ϵ_t of equation 4.5.6a is obtained as

$$\hat{\epsilon}_t^{(1)} = Y_t - \hat{\alpha}^{(1)} - \hat{\beta}_1^{(1)} X_{1t} - \cdots - \hat{\beta}_K^{(1)} X_{Kt}$$

These quantities are used to estimate the autocorrelation parameter ρ by

$$\hat{\rho}^{(1)} = \frac{\sum\limits_{t=2}^{n} \hat{\epsilon}_t^{(1)} \hat{\epsilon}_{t-1}^{(1)}}{\sum\limits_{t=1}^{n} (\hat{\epsilon}_t^{(1)})^2}$$

3. Following from equation 4.5.7 fit by ordinary least squares the regression of $(Y_t - \hat{\rho}^{(1)} Y_{t-1})$ on $(X_{1t} - \hat{\rho}^{(1)} X_{1,t-1})$, ..., $(X_{Kt} - \hat{\rho}^{(1)} X_{K,t-1})$. The estimated partial regression coefficients provide the next step estimates $\hat{\beta}_1^{(2)}$, ..., $\hat{\beta}_K^{(2)}$. Dividing by $(1 - \hat{\rho}^{(1)})$ the estimated intercept of this regression provides the new estimate $\hat{\alpha}^{(2)}$.

4. Steps 2 and 3 are now repeated iteratively. The new regression

parameter estimates are used to obtain a new estimate of the auto-correlation parameter, which in turn is employed to derive new estimates of the regression parameters, and so on. This cycle of iterations is continued until the parameter estimates converge, so that successive iterations achieve negligible revisions.

The Cochrane-Orcutt procedure is arithmetically tedious, though it requires only an ordinary multiple regression program. In fact, programs to perform the calculations involved in this and some alternative proce-dures for fitting regression models with autoregressive errors are quite widely available. To illustrate, we will analyze the data of Table 4.4. The table shows 39 quarterly observations on bank borrowing (Y) in millions of dollars and the difference (X) between the discount rate and the U.S. Treasury bill rate. We will assume a simple linear relationship

$$Y_t = \alpha + \beta X_t + \epsilon_t \qquad (4.5.8)$$

The SPSS program analysis of these data is shown in Exhibit 4.3. The first half of the printout is for the fitting of equation 4.5.8 by ordinary least squares, as would be appropriate if the error terms ϵ_t obeyed the standard assumptions. However, it can be seen that the Durbin-Watson test statistic is

$$d = 1.222$$

For a regression based on 39 observations, with one independent variable,

TABLE 4.4 Quarterly observations on bank borrowing (Y) in millions of dollars and the difference (X) between the discount rate and the U.S. Treasury bill rate.

t	Y_t	X_t	t	Y_t	X_t	t	Y_t	X_t
1	242	0.32	14	146	0.86	27	988	−0.03
2	170	0.30	15	67	0.49	28	710	−0.04
3	338	0.12	16	246	0.36	29	138	0.95
4	657	0.02	17	464	0.22	30	142	0.92
5	307	0.16	18	146	0.34	31	476	−0.44
6	579	0.05	19	849	0.18	32	557	−0.27
7	683	0.04	20	839	−0.04	33	601	0.20
8	1593	−0.34	21	993	0.25	34	921	0.29
9	1202	−0.01	22	769	0.26	35	903	−0.04
10	423	−0.11	23	792	0.16	36	906	−0.49
11	468	0.21	24	688	−0.21	37	635	0.69
12	441	0.40	25	834	−0.08	38	425	1.04
13	189	0.62	26	1005	−0.29	39	225	0.52

EXHIBIT 4.3   Part of the SPSS program output for the fitting of a linear regression model to the data of Table 4.4, including correction for first order autoregressive errors.

```
         * * * *   M U L T I P L E   R E G R E S S I O N   * * * *

Multiple R            .61406
R Square              .37707
Adjusted R Square     .36024
Standard Error     276.12241

Analysis of Variance
                    DF      Sum of Squares        Mean Square
Regression           1       1707623.15950      1707623.15950
Residual            37       2821012.58409        76243.58335

F =     22.39694      Signif F =  .0000


------------------ Variables in the Equation ------------------

Variable           B          SE B         Beta         T     Sig T

DIFF        -568.19119     120.06049      -.61406     -4.733   .0000
(Constant)   693.94588      49.99478                  13.880   .0000


Durbin-Watson Test =  1.22235


FINAL PARAMETERS:

Estimate of Autocorrelation Coefficient

Rho                    .4630304
Standard Error of Rho  .14772373
Mean Squared Error   60109.933

Cochrane-Orcutt Estimates

Multple R            .48784934
R-Squared            .23799697
Adjusted R-Squared   .19445394
Standard Error     253.06069
Durbin-Watson        1.7721175


            Analysis of Variance:

              DF   Sum of Squares      Mean Square
Regression     1        700055.0        700054.98
Residuals     35       2241389.9         64039.71


            Variables in the Equation:

                    B          SEB         BETA            T         SIG T
DIFF        -394.36031     119.27565    -.48784934    -3.3062934   .00219215
CONSTANT     669.24759      79.93128        .          8.3727869   .00000000
```

we find from Table A.5 that, for a 1% level test, the observed value of the test statistic should be compared with

$$d_{L,.01} = 1.24 \qquad d_{U,.01} = 1.34$$

Hence, the null hypothesis of no autocorrelation in the regression errors can be rejected against the alternative of positive autocorrelation even at the 1% significance level. Given such strong evidence of autocorrelated errors, it is prudent to ignore any other statistics from the ordinary least squares fit, however strong is the apparent relationship, as measured for example by t-statistics or by the coefficient of determination, R^2.

The second half of the output in Exhibit 4.3 results from the application of the Cochrane-Orcutt procedure. Parameter estimates and associated estimated standard errors are shown. The full estimated model, in the form 4.5.6 is, then,

$$Y_t = 669 - 394\, X_t + \epsilon_t \qquad (4.5.9a)$$
$$ (80) \quad (119)$$

$$\epsilon_t = 0.463\epsilon_{t-1} + a_t \qquad (4.5.9b)$$
$$ (0.148)$$

where, as usual, figures in brackets are estimated standard errors. In the Cochrane-Orcutt procedure, standard errors follow from the final application of least squares to the regression 4.5.7, with the final estimate of the autocorrelation parameter ρ (in this case, 0.463) substituted. The estimate of the regression slope implies that a one-unit increase in the difference between the discount rate and the U.S. Treasury bill rate leads to an expected decrease of 394 million dollars in bank borrowing. From the Sig T column in the final part of Exhibit 4.3, we see that the null hypothesis that the slope of the population regression line is zero can be rejected against a two-sided alternative at all significance levels above 0.22%, providing very strong evidence of a relationship between the two variables. From equation 4.5.9b we see that the estimated correlation between adjacent regression error terms is 0.463.

The SPSS output for the Cochrane-Orcutt estimation procedure displays the coefficient of determination, R^2. In fact, this relates to the final stage regression 4.5.7, with the final estimate of the parameter ρ substituted for the unknown true value. This is not, then, directly comparable with the usual coefficient of determination, and does not have a very interesting interpretation. This occurs because the dependent variable being explained by this regression is not the level Y_t of the series;

it is the partial difference $(Y_t - 0.463Y_{t-1})$ in our example. However, the appropriate F-test that all partial regression coefficients are zero is the one based on this Cochrane-Orcutt R^2, used as in 4.3.3. This is equivalent to the analysis of variance displayed in the second part of Exhibit 4.3, not that of the first part.

Autocorrelated Errors in Regressions with Lagged Dependent Variables

Autocorrelated errors in regression models, such as those of Section 4.4, with lagged dependent variables, raise particularly serious problems. On one hand, the consequences of ignoring autocorrelated errors in this case are, if anything, even more severe. On the other hand, the Durbin-Watson test and the Cochrane-Orcutt estimation procedure are not appropriate in the presence of lagged dependent variables.

If ordinary least squares is applied to a regression equation with no lagged dependent variable, then in the presence of autocorrelated errors, the least squares parameter estimators are inefficient, although they are unbiased. In regressions with lagged dependent variables and autocorrelated errors, least squares parameter estimators are inconsistent. As the number of sample observations increases, the distributions of these estimators do not converge to the true parameter values. In this sense, autocorrelated errors constitute a more serious problem in regressions with lagged dependent variables.

The Durbin-Watson test is used to detect autocorrelated errors in regression models with no lagged dependent variables. However, when lagged dependent variables are in the model, the Durbin-Watson test statistic is biased towards two—that is, against the detection of autocorrelated errors. Of course, it is still possible to compute the Durbin-Watson test statistic when a regression with lagged dependent variables is estimated by ordinary least squares. However, a modification of the usual test procedure is now required. The most commonly applied approach is through **Durbin's h test,** which is approximately valid in moderately large samples. The regression equation is estimated by ordinary least squares, and the usual Durbin-Watson statistic d of equation 4.5.4 computed. Following equation 4.5.5 this leads to an estimate of the autocorrelation parameter

$$r = 1 - d/2$$

Durbin's h test statistic is then

$$h = r[n/(1 - ns_c^2)]^{1/2} \qquad (4.5.10)$$

where n is the number of observations and s_c is the estimated standard error of the estimator of the parameter multiplying the lagged dependent variable in the regression model. Under the null hypothesis of no auto-correlation, this statistic has approximately a standard normal distribution in moderately large samples. The null hypothesis of no autocorrelation in the regression errors is rejected against the alternative of positive corre-lation between adjacent errors for large positive values of the statistic 4.5.10. For example, from Table A.1 of the Appendix, it follows that, for a 5% level test, the null hypothesis would be rejected if h exceeds 1.645. (Similarly, if the alternative is of negative autocorrelation, the null hy-pothesis would be rejected at the 5% level if $h < -1.645$).

We will apply this test to the example of Section 4.4 on 34 quarterly observations of Japanese imports. From Exhibit 4.2, we find

$$n = 34 \qquad s_c = 0.122 \qquad d = 2.316$$

Then,

$$r = 1 - d/2 = 1 - 2.316/2 = -0.158$$

suggesting, if anything, some possibility of negative autocorrelation. Using equation 4.5.10, the test statistic is

$$h = (-0.158)[34/[1 - (34)(.122)^2]]^{1/2} = -1.311$$

The magnitude of this value of the test statistic is not unduly large compared with the percentage points of the standard normal distribution, given in Table A.1 of the Appendix. For example, since $-1.645 < -1.311 < 1.645$, the null hypothesis of no autocorrelation in the regression errors is not rejected against a two-sided alternative at the 10% significance level.

Suppose now that we want to estimate a regression model with a lagged dependent variable, and errors assumed to follow a first order autoregressive process; that is,

$$Y_t = \alpha + \beta_1 X_{1t} + \beta_2 X_{2t} + \cdots + \beta_K X_{Kt} + \gamma Y_{t-1} + \epsilon_t$$

$$\epsilon_t = \rho \epsilon_{t-1} + a_t$$

where, as previously, the a_t are uncorrelated with one another. Now, through precisely the same argument that led us to equation 4.5.7, we have

$$Y_t - \rho Y_{t-1} = \alpha(1 - \rho) + \beta_1(X_{1t} - \rho X_{1,t-1}) + \cdots$$

$$+ \beta_K(X_{Kt} - \rho X_{K,t-1}) + \gamma(Y_{t-1} - \rho Y_{t-2}) + a_t$$

$$(4.5.11)$$

Unfortunately, however, the Cochrane-Orcutt procedure does not in such cases generally achieve convergence to satisfactory point estimates. One possibility, since the error terms a_t in equation 4.5.11 satisfy the standard assumptions, is the direct approach of applying least squares, selecting the parameter estimates $a, b_1, \ldots, b_K, c, r$ for which the sum of squares

$$S = \sum [Y_t - rY_{t-1} - a(1 - r) - b_1(X_{1t} - rX_{1,t-1}) - \cdots$$
$$- b_K(X_{Kt} - rX_{K,t-1}) - c(Y_{t-1} - rY_{t-2})]^2$$

$$(4.5.12)$$

is a minimum. However, this problem is not in the standard format of the usual multiple regression problem, since the error term a_t in equation 4.5.11 is a *nonlinear* function of the parameters $\alpha, \beta_1, \ldots, \beta_K, \gamma, \rho$. Consequently, standard linear regression programs are inapplicable. Instead, a **nonlinear regression** program is required to solve the problem of minimizing equation 4.5.12. Such programs are widely available. In the absence of access to such a program, one can proceed by first selecting a grid of possible values for the autocorrelation parameter ρ. For each chosen value, the regression 4.5.11 can then be estimated by ordinary least squares, with $(Y_t - \rho Y_{t-1})$ regressed on $(X_{1t} - \rho X_{1,t-1}), \ldots, (X_{Kt} - \rho X_{K,t-1}), (Y_{t-1} - \rho Y_{t-2})$. The fitted regression chosen is that with the smallest sum of squared errors.

In this section we have concentrated on regression equations whose errors obey a first order autoregressive model. In Chapter 9 we will briefly discuss some more general possibilities.

4.6 FORECASTING FROM THE MULTIPLE REGRESSION MODEL

Exactly as in our discussion of Section 3.5, a fitted multiple regression model is directly applicable to the problem of *conditional forecasting*. Forecasts of the values that will be taken in future time periods by the dependent variable can be directly derived, *assuming particular future values for the independent variables*. To obtain *unconditional forecasts* for the dependent variable, it is necessary first to develop predictions of future values of the independent variables. The regression model is of no help in forecasting the independent variables: these forecasts must be obtained from some other source.

The most straightforward case is where forecasts are required from the static multiple regression model 4.1.2, whose error terms ϵ_t obey the standard assumptions. The point forecast problem here is a direct generalization of that for the simple linear regression model, discussed in Section 3.5. Let $a, b_1, b_2, \ldots, b_K$ be the least squares estimates of the parameters α, β_1, β_2, $\ldots$, β_K, and suppose that, standing at time n, we want to predict the value that the dependent variable will take in some future time period, $(n + h)$. Assuming that, at time $(n + h)$, the independent variables take the values $X_{1,n+h}$, $X_{2,n+h}$, $\ldots$, $X_{K,n+h}$, the required point forecast is

$$\hat{Y}_{n+h} = a + b_1 X_{1,n+h} + b_2 X_{2,n+h} + \cdots + b_K X_{K,n+h} \qquad h = 1, 2, \ldots$$

Many multiple regression computer packages allow the computation of interval forecasts (that is, prediction intervals). It should be noted, however, that such intervals are only appropriate for the problem of conditional forecasting. They take no account of uncertainty in the forecasts of future values of the independent variables, required to develop unconditional forecasts of the dependent variable. If a log linear regression model has been fitted, a straightforward approach to forecasting is to first predict future values of the logarithm of the dependent variable, and then to take antilogarithms of these predictions.

Consider next the lagged dependent variable model 4.4.3, with error terms ϵ_t assumed to satisfy the standard assumptions. Suppose that we are standing at time n, and require a forecast of the next value, Y_{n+1}, of the dependent variable. The quantity to be predicted, then, is

$$Y_{n+1} = \alpha + \beta_1 X_{1,n+1} + \beta_2 X_{2,n+1} + \cdots + \beta_K X_{K,n+1} + \gamma Y_n + \epsilon_{n+1}$$

To obtain a point forecast, the unknown parameter values α, β_1, β_2, $\ldots$, β_K, γ in this expression can be replaced by their least squares estimates a, b_1, b_2, $\ldots$, b_K, c. Also, since the random error term ϵ_{n+1} has mean zero and is, by assumption, uncorrelated with anything that is known at the time the forecast is made, the best that can be done is to predict that it will take the value zero. This suggests that, if at time $(n + 1)$ the independent variables take the values $X_{1,n+1}$, $X_{2,n+1}$, $\ldots$, $X_{K,n+1}$, the point forecast for the dependent variable should be

$$\hat{Y}_{n+1} = a + b_1 X_{1,n+1} + b_2 X_{2,n+1} + \cdots + b_K X_{K,n+1} + cY_n \qquad (4.6.1)$$

Notice that this expression involves Y_n, which is simply the most recent observation on the dependent variable.

Suppose now that forecasts of the dependent variable two time periods ahead are required on the basis of a fitted lagged dependent variable model of the form 4.4.3. The value of the dependent variable at time $(n + 2)$ can be written

$$Y_{n+2} = \alpha + \beta_1 X_{1,n+2} + \beta_2 X_{2,n+2} + \cdots$$
$$+ \beta_K X_{K,n+2} + \gamma Y_{n+1} + \epsilon_{n+2}$$

Again, least squares estimates can be substituted for the unknown parameters, and zero for the future error term. In addition, this expression involves the value, Y_{n+1}, of the dependent variable at time $(n + 1)$, which will be unknown when the forecast is to be made. We will, however, have available the point forecast of this quantity, obtained from equation 4.6.1. Replacing Y_{n+1} by its forecast $\hat{Y}_{n+1}$, we then obtain, as a two periods ahead point forecast for the dependent variable, assuming the independent variables take the values $X_{i,n+h}$ $(i = 1, \ldots, K; h = 1, 2)$.

$$\hat{Y}_{n+2} = a + b_1 X_{1,n+2} + b_2 X_{2,n+2} + \cdots$$
$$+ b_K X_{K,n+2} + c\hat{Y}_{n+1}$$

Continuing in this way, it can be seen that, standing at time n, point forecasts for the dependent variable h time periods ahead are obtained from

$$\hat{Y}_{n+h} = a + b_1 X_{1,n+h} + \cdots + b_K X_{K,n+h} + c\hat{Y}_{n+h-1}$$
$$h = 1, 2, 3, \ldots \qquad \hat{Y}_n = Y_n$$

Notice that, if unconditional forecasts of the dependent variable are required, forecasts of the independent variables will be needed for *all* future time periods up to and including time $(n + h)$.

Next we turn to the problem of forecasting from a fitted regression model whose errors follow a first order autoregressive process, as in equation 4.5.6. The form 4.5.6a is *not* the most suitable for forecasting, as the error terms ϵ_t are autocorrelated. For example, the future error ϵ_{n+1} will be correlated with ϵ_n, ϵ_{n-1}, ... Since this future error is correlated with information that is available at the time the forecast is made, its best prediction will *not* be zero.

The most straightforward approach is to transpose the model 4.5.6 to the form 4.5.7, which involves error terms a_t that are not correlated with one another. That is,

$$Y_t = \alpha(1 - \rho) + \beta_1(X_{1t} - \rho X_{1,t-1}) + \cdots \qquad (4.6.2)$$
$$+ \beta_K(X_{Kt} - \rho X_{K,t-1}) + \rho Y_{t-1} + a_t$$

Suppose that, standing at time n, we want to forecast the next value, Y_{n+1}, of the dependent variable. From equation 4.6.2, the quantity to be predicted is

$$Y_{n+1} = \alpha(1 - \rho) + \beta_1(X_{1,n+1} - \rho X_{1n}) + \cdots$$
$$+ \beta_K(X_{K,n+1} - \rho X_{Kn}) + \rho Y_n + a_{n+1}$$

In this expression, we can replace the unknown parameters α, β_1, ..., β_K, ρ by suitable estimates a, b_1, ..., b_K, r, obtained for example from the Cochrane-Orcutt procedure. Also, since the zero mean error process a_t is not autocorrelated, the best prediction of all its future values will be zero. Hence, standing at time n, and given that the independent variables will take the values $X_{1,n+1}$, ..., $X_{K,n+1}$ in the next time period, our point forecast of the dependent variable in that time period is

$$\hat{Y}_{n+1} = a(1 - r) + b_1(X_{1,n+1} - rX_{1n}) + \cdots \qquad (4.6.3)$$
$$+ b_K(X_{K,n+1} - rX_{Kn}) + rY_n$$

Notice that this expression involves the most recent observations Y_n, X_{1n}, ..., X_{Kn} on the dependent and independent variables.

If forecasts two time periods ahead are required, the quantity to be predicted is

$$Y_{n+2} = \alpha(1 - \rho) + \beta_1(X_{1,n+2} - \rho X_{1,n+1}) + \cdots$$
$$+ \beta_K(X_{K,n+2} - \rho X_{K,n+1}) + \rho Y_{n+1} + a_{n+2}$$

Again, estimates can be substituted for the unknown parameters, and zero for the future value of the random error term. Also, the unknown future value of the dependent variable, Y_{n+1}, can be replaced by its forecast, $\hat{Y}_{n+1}$, obtained from equation 4.6.3. This yields the conditional point forecast

$$\hat{Y}_{n+2} = a(1 - r) + b_1(X_{1,n+2} - rX_{1,n+1}) + \cdots$$
$$+ b_K(X_{K,n+2} - rX_{K,n+1}) + r\hat{Y}_{n+1}$$

Continuing in this way if, standing at time n, conditional point forecasts of the dependent variable at time $(n + h)$ are required, we have

$$\hat{Y}_{n+h} = a(1 - r) + b_1(X_{1,n+h} - rX_{1,n+h-1}) + \cdots$$
$$+ b_K(X_{K,n+h} - rX_{K,n+h-1}) + r\hat{Y}_{n+h-1} \qquad (4.6.4)$$
$$h = 1, 2, 3, \ldots \qquad \hat{Y}_n = Y_n$$

Notice again that unconditional prediction requires forecasts of the independent variables at all future time periods up to and including time $(n + h)$.

To illustrate this procedure, we return to the example of Section 4.5 on quarterly bank borrowing. The data are given in Table 4.4, and the fitted model, obtained through the Cochrane-Orcutt procedure, in equations 4.5.9. From these equations we obtain the fitted model in transposed form

$$Y_t = 669(1 - 0.463) - 394(X_t - 0.463X_{t-1}) + 0.463Y_{t-1} + a_t$$

or

$$Y_t = 359 - 394(X_t - 0.463X_{t-1}) + 0.463Y_{t-1} + a_t$$

Suppose now that we want to predict bank borrowing in the next quarter, assuming that the difference between the discount rate and the U.S. Treasury bill rate in that quarter will be

$$X_{n+1} = X_{40} = 0.40$$

Direct application of equation 4.6.4 then yields the point forecast

$$\hat{Y}_{40} = 359 - 394(X_{40} - 0.463X_{39}) + 0.463Y_{39}$$
$$= 359 - 394[0.40 - (0.463)(0.52)] + (0.463)(225)$$
$$= 400 \text{ million dollars}$$

where the values X_{39} and Y_{39} were obtained from Table 4.4.

Suppose also that the difference between the discount rate and the U.S. Treasury bill rate two quarters ahead will be

$$X_{n+2} = X_{41} = 0.30$$

Using equation 4.6.4 again, the point forecast for bank borrowing two quarters ahead is

$$\hat{Y}_{41} = 359 - 394(X_{41} - 0.463X_{40}) + 0.463\hat{Y}_{40}$$
$$= 359 - 394[0.30 - (0.463)(0.40)] + (0.463)(400)$$
$$= 499 \text{ million dollars}$$

Continuing in this way, forecasts of bank borrowing as far ahead as required can be obtained, given further future assumed values for the difference between the discount rate and the U.S. Treasury bill rate. These forecasts can be viewed as unconditional if $X_{n+1} = 0.40$, $X_{n+2} = 0.30$, and so on are regarded as forecasts of future values of the difference between the discount rate and the U.S. Treasury bill rate, obtained from some external source.

Notice that the form of the forecast function 4.6.4 for regression models with first order autoregressive errors is quite different from that for the case where the errors are not autocorrelated. It is for this reason that we asserted in Section 4.5 that ignoring autocorrelated errors when they are present leads to additional inefficiency in the forecasts beyond that induced by the use of inefficient ordinary least squares parameter estimators.

4.7 TREND CURVES

We turn now to a topic that is in one sense related to, but in another sense quite different in spirit from, the regression methods discussed in this and the previous chapter. Again we will assume that interest is in forecasting future values of some variable Y, and that n consecutive observations through time, $Y_1, Y_2, \ldots, Y_n$, are available. In **trend curve** (or **growth curve**) analysis, it is assumed that the value taken by Y at time t is some function of time, and a random error term, ϵ_t, so that we can write

$$Y_t = f(t, \epsilon_t) \qquad (4.7.1)$$

In practice, a number of simple parametric forms for this function might be postulated, and the unknown parameters involved would be estimated from the available data. The fitted functions could then be projected forward to obtain forecasts of future values. The relationship of this approach to forecasting to regression methods lies in the fact that least squares procedures are employed to estimate the unknown parameters of models from the general class of equation 4.7.1. However, regression analysis, as we have described it to this point, rests on the postulation of *behavioral relationships*. Given interest in a dependent variable, an appeal is made to subject matter theory to suggest independent variables whose behavior might influence it, and perhaps also to suggest an appropriate structural form and dynamic specification for the relationship. Trend curve analysis is quite different; an attempt is made to discover some simple function that might describe the evolution through time of a variable. No appeal is made to subject matter theory to suggest possibly relevant *causal* models. Rather, it is hoped that a plot of the observations against time might point, through visual graphical inspection, to a simple approximate deterministic relationship between an observation value and its location in time.

In practice, a number of trend curves of this sort have been fitted to data, and used for forecasting. Here we will briefly introduce five of them, concentrating on the deterministic elements, so that ϵ_t in equation 4.7.1 is temporarily set to zero. These curves are graphed in Figure 4.3, where we have assumed, as is often the case, that the series of interest is growing over time.

1. The simplest possibility is the **linear trend**

$$Y_t = \alpha + \beta t \qquad \beta > 0$$

shown in Figure 4.3(a). Here α and β are fixed parameters, and the series grows by a constant absolute amount β in each time period.

2. For some time series a more plausible pattern of growth is provided by the **exponential function**

$$Y_t = \alpha \exp(\beta t) \qquad \alpha > 0, \quad \beta > 0$$

where α and β are fixed parameters, and we employ the notation $\exp(x) = e^x$, where $e = 2.71828. \ldots$. This function is graphed in Figure 4.3(b), from which it can be seen that growth is at a faster rate than linear. In fact, the exponential function implies a constant percentage growth rate.

3. Both the linear trend and the exponential function imply unbounded growth. In some circumstances it seems plausible to expect that growth of a time series will not continue beyond some level. This concept is particularly popular in the marketing literature, where trend curves with upper limits, or **saturation levels,** are often fitted. This idea could apply to the behavior of sales of mature products, or more usually to the levels of market penetration of such products. For example, if we are interested in the percentage of all homes with a telephone, this percentage can never exceed 100%. One trend curve with an upper limit is the **modified exponential function**

$$Y_t = \alpha - \beta \exp(-\gamma t) \qquad \alpha > 0, \quad \beta > 0, \quad \gamma > 0$$

where α, β, and γ are fixed parameters. This curve is drawn in Figure 4.3(c), and has an upper limit α. Notice that growth of the modified exponential function is everywhere slower than linear.

4. In marketing, it is widely believed that, following initial introduction, products achieve an early rapid growth rate in sales, followed by a more mature period of slower growth, and with some upper limit on what is attainable. In this view, growth curves should have an S-

FIGURE 4.3   Some deterministic trend curves.

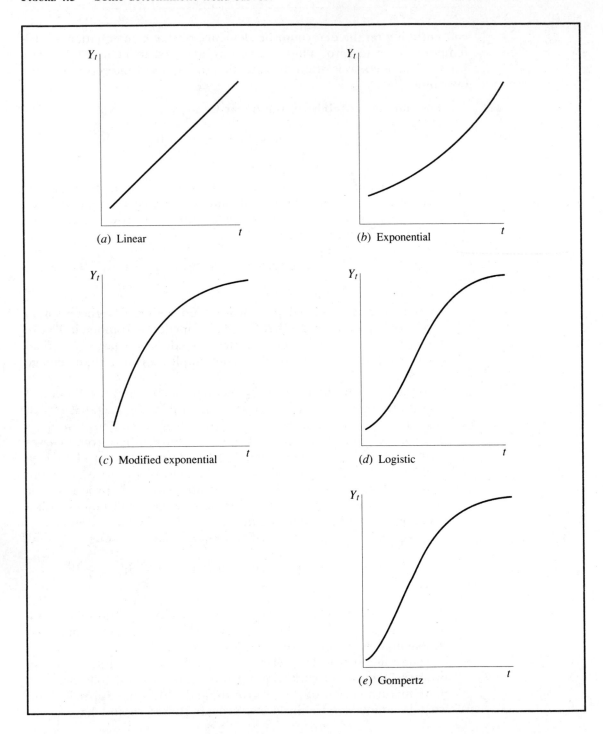

(*a*) Linear

(*b*) Exponential

(*c*) Modified exponential

(*d*) Logistic

(*e*) Gompertz

shaped appearance. One curve with this shape is the **logistic function**

$$Y_t = \frac{\alpha}{1 + \beta \exp(-\gamma t)} \qquad \alpha > 0, \quad \beta > 0, \quad \gamma > 0$$

where α, β, and γ are fixed parameters. Part of such a function is drawn in Figure 4.3(d). Initially growth is faster than linear, but eventually becomes slower than linear, with a saturation level at α.

5. Another function with an *S*-shaped appearance is provided by the **Gompertz curve**

$$Y_t = \alpha \exp[-\beta \exp(-\gamma t)] \qquad \alpha > 0, \quad \beta > 0, \quad \gamma > 0$$

where α, β, and γ are fixed parameters. Part of this function is shown in Figure 4.3(e). It is quite similar to the logistic function. One difference is that, for the logistic function, the curve moves from faster than linear growth to slower than linear growth—known as the point of inflection—when Y_t is at precisely half the saturation level α. The Gompertz curve also has saturation level α, but its point of inflection occurs at $\alpha \exp(-1) = 0.37\alpha$—that is, at 37% of the saturation level.

In practice, no observed time series will precisely follow one of these, or any other, simple functional forms. Indeed, experience suggests that observed data tend to be scattered very widely around any conceivable trend curve. Nevertheless, it is certainly possible to re-introduce the error term in equation 4.7.1 and, given data, to estimate the parameters of a trend curve. For example, for the linear function we can write

$$Y_t = \alpha + \beta t + \epsilon_t$$

Then, if it is assumed that the error terms ϵ_t satisfy the standard assumptions, the parameters α and β can be estimated by ordinary least squares, exactly as in Chapter 3, with the time term t playing the part of the independent variable. This variable simply takes the values 1, 2, . . . , n over the observation period. Once the equation has been estimated, forecasts are obtained in the usual way. In this case, of course, that simply implies projecting the fitted trend line into the future.

For the exponential function, it is most straightforward to take logarithms before adding the error term, giving

$$\log Y_t = \alpha^* + \beta t + \epsilon_t$$

where $\alpha^* = \log \alpha$. If it is assumed that these error terms ϵ_t satisfy the standard assumptions, then the parameters α^* and β can be estimated by least squares, regressing the logarithms of the observed series on time. For the other three trend curves that we have discussed, parameter estimation is rather less straightforward. Least squares can still be employed, but now a nonlinear regression algorithm is required. We will not devote space to these details.

Authors of textbooks inevitably inject their own prejudices, if only through topic coverage and emphasis. We certainly intend to follow this precedent, though we would naturally prefer to replace the word prejudices in the previous sentence with expertise and insight. The present topic is a case in point. The world of applied forecasting is filled by many weird and wonderful techniques. Fortunately, many of the most weird— a number of which are grossly inferior to the crystal ball—are so little used that we can, in good conscience, ignore them altogether. However, some approaches about which we have considerable skepticism remain in disturbingly widespread use. Too often, deterministic trend functions are fitted, often by ordinary least squares methods, by marketing professionals and others charged with business forecasting responsibilities. Our reservations about the wisdom of this approach can be summarized as follows:

1. In our experience, rarely if ever will a careful analysis of a real business or economic time series suggest the suitability of these trend functions *with errors that are not autocorrelated*. Of course, one could proceed by building a model incorporating errors with an autocorrelation structure. However, the problem is often so severe that it will be inadequate to rely exclusively on the first order autoregressive error structure of Section 4.5. The analyst will have to consider the more general class of possibilities discussed in Chapter 7, and, in the context of regression analysis, in Chapter 9.

2. If one is interested in forecasting just a short distance ahead, it is considerably more important to be able to predict deviations from any apparent long-term trend structure than it is to adequately capture that structure in a model. In fact, this is simply another way of emphasizing the importance of an adequate specification of the autocorrelation properties of the error terms.

3. It is in forecasting over the longer term that trend curves apparently come into their own. They can be projected forward over any desired horizon, leading to very easily derived forecasts of future values. Unfortunately, the world is so unkind that what appears to be a well-established trend over an observed stretch of data very frequently becomes illusory in the light of subsequent experience. A particular trend function may appear to provide a good fit of time series data. In fact, a number of different trend curves may appear to fit observed

data almost equally well. However, when these trend curves are projected forward, they tend to diverge quite rapidly, leaving the analyst with a bewildering and wide array of possible forecasts from which to choose. Those eventually selected could perform very poorly. Granger (1967), Newbold (1973), and Freedman, Rothenberg and Sutch (1983) make these points quite well. These last authors fit both linear and exponential trends to U.S. data on income per capita for the period 1959–69. Both appear to fit the data very well. However, when projected forward to the year 2000, the latter gives forecasts 25% above the former. In our view, the long-term future is sufficiently obscure that forecasting from simplistic trend functions is hopelessly naive.

4. The trend curve analysis discussed in this section assumes a *fixed*, or *deterministic* trend, taken to hold over all time. In our experience, business and economic time series simply do not behave in this way. Rather, they appear to exhibit *local* trend that evolves through time in a *stochastic*, or random, manner. In Chapters 6 and 7 we will discuss some methods that have proved useful in forecasting time series that behave in this way.

We have deliberately not included an example in this section, because we know of no business or economic time series that we would choose to predict through this kind of trend curve analysis. The notion in the marketing literature of a saturation level for the sales or market penetration of a product is, of course, not without appeal. (We are reminded, however, that not so many years ago trend extrapolations were used to predict the imminent exhaustion of the world's oil reserves. Shortly after these forecasts were made, thanks to OPEC-induced price rises, the world's known reserves of oil actually *increased* over a period of several years.) The idea of a saturation level permeates a number of diverse areas, such as track and field records. We can safely assume, for example, that the 100 meters will never be run in 5 seconds, or the mile in 2 minutes. There must be *some* bounds. Unfortunately, when models with bounds or saturation levels are fitted to business, economic, or other types of data, these bounds are often estimated very imprecisely, and frequently the estimates turn out to be quite unreliable. For example, in 1954 the mile was run in less than 4 minutes for the first time. The world record had fallen very little over many years. Any model, incorporating a lower bound, fitted at that time would have been hopelessly pessimistic about what could subsequently be achieved.

A more complete discussion of growth curve analysis—and one that is considerably more upbeat than ours—is provided by Meade (1984). Some further applications are discussed by Dino (1985), Kunisawa and Horibe

(1986), and Bewley and Fiebig (1988). For our part, we are content to repeat the oft-quoted words of Cairncross[4]

A trend is a trend is a trend
But the question is, will it bend?
Will it alter its course,
Through some unforeseen force,
And come to a premature end?

EXERCISES

4.1   The accompanying table[5] shows 25 annual observations on percentage profit margin (Y), net revenues per deposit dollar (X_1), and number of offices (X_2) for U.S. savings and loans associations. Assume a model of the form

$$Y_t = \alpha + \beta_1 X_{1t} + \beta_2 X_{2t} + \epsilon_t$$

where ϵ_t is a random error term.

t	Y_t	X_{1t}	X_{2t}	t	Y_t	X_{1t}	X_{2t}
1	0.75	3.92	7,298	14	0.84	3.78	6,672
2	0.71	3.61	6,855	15	0.79	3.82	6,890
3	0.66	3.32	6,636	16	0.70	3.97	7,115
4	0.61	3.07	6,506	17	0.68	4.07	7,327
5	0.70	3.06	6,450	18	0.72	4.25	7,546
6	0.72	3.11	6,402	19	0.55	4.41	7,931
7	0.77	3.21	6,368	20	0.63	4.49	8,097
8	0.74	3.26	6,340	21	0.56	4.70	8,468
9	0.90	3.42	6,349	22	0.41	4.58	8,717
10	0.82	3.42	6,352	23	0.51	4.69	8,991
11	0.75	3.45	6,361	24	0.47	4.71	9,179
12	0.77	3.58	6,369	25	0.32	4.78	9,318
13	0.78	3.66	6,546				

(a)   Fit by least squares the multiple regression model, and interpret the parameter estimates.

(b)   Find and interpret the coefficient of determination.

(c)   Find a 95% confidence interval for the parameter β_1.

4.   Cairncross, A., "Economic forecasting," *Economic Journal, 79* (1969): 797–812.

5.   Data taken from Spellman, L. J., "Entry and profitability in a rate-free savings and loan market." *Quarterly Review of Economics and Business, 18,* no. 2 (1978): 87–95.

(d)   Test at the 5% significance level the null hypothesis

$$H_0: \beta_2 = 0$$

against the alternative hypothesis

$$H_1: \beta_2 < 0$$

(e)   Test at the 1% significance level the null hypothesis

$$H_0: \beta_1 = \beta_2 = 0$$

(f)   Test at the 5% significance level the null hypothesis that the error terms ϵ_t are not correlated with one another, against the alternative they follow a first order autoregressive process with positive parameter.

(g)   It is expected that, in the next two years, the independent variables will take the values

$$X_{1,26} = 4.70 \qquad X_{1,27} = 4.80 \qquad X_{2,26} = 9{,}350$$
$$X_{2,27} = 9{,}400$$

Find point forecasts of percentage profit margins for savings and loan associations in these two years.

4.2 (a)   When an important independent variable is omitted from a regression model, quite misleading results can emerge. This is the problem of specification bias. Using the data of Exercise 4.1, fit by least squares the simple linear regression of Y on X_1, and comment on the results.

(b)   If an important independent variable is omitted from a regression model, this can be reflected in strongly autocorrelated error terms. Comment on the value of the Durbin-Watson test statistic from the fitted regression in part (a), and on the implications of this result.

4.3   Refer to the data of Table 4.1, and to the fitted regression 4.3.1. It is expected that, in the next two years, the independent variables will take the values

$$X_{1,21} = 3.8 \qquad X_{2,21} = 0.700 \qquad X_{3,21} = 1.670$$
$$X_{1,22} = 4.0 \qquad X_{2,22} = 0.690 \qquad X_{3,22} = 1.680$$

Find point forecasts of days of incapacity due to sickness per person for these two years.

4.4 Sometimes, when the estimated value of a regression parameter is small in magnitude, compared with the estimated standard error, an analyst will drop the corresponding variable from the regression, and re-estimate the model. Following inspection of equation 4.3.1, estimate the regression of log Y on log X_2 and log X_3, and discuss the results. Using the same values for future values of the independent variables as in Exercise 4.3, obtain from the new fitted model point forecasts of days of incapacity due to sickness per person for the next two years. Compare these with the forecasts of Exercise 4.3.

4.5 Refer to the data of Table 4.3, and to the model 4.4.9 fitted to these data. It is expected that, in the next two quarters, the independent variables will take the values

$$X_{1,35} = 106.0 \qquad X_{1,36} = 105.0$$
$$X_{2,35} = 0.9000 \qquad X_{2,36} = 0.9400$$

Obtain point forecasts of Japanese quantity of imports in these two quarters.

4.6 (a) In Section 4.4 we considered separately the possibilities of adaptive expectations and partial adjustment models. It is entirely possible that these phenomena could occur jointly. Let Y_t denote the actual value of a dependent variable, and X_t the actual value of an independent variable, at time t. Denote by Y_t^* the desired value for the dependent variable at time t, and by X_t^* the expectation per period of future values of the independent variable, formed at time t. Assume that the desired level of the dependent variable is related to the expected value of the independent variable by

$$Y_t^* = \delta + \lambda X_t^*$$

that expectations of the independent variable are formed through

$$X_t^* = (1 - \gamma)X_t + \gamma X_{t-1}^*$$

and that the partial adjustment mechanism for the dependent variable

$$Y_t - Y_{t-1} = (1 - \omega)(Y_t^* - Y_{t-1}) + u_t$$

holds. In these expressions, δ, λ, γ, and ω are fixed parameters, and u_t is a random error term with mean zero. Show that these three equations imply

$$Y_t = \alpha + \beta X_t + \gamma_1 Y_{t-1} + \gamma_2 Y_{t-2} + \epsilon_t$$

where

$$\alpha = \delta(1 - \omega)(1 - \gamma) \qquad \beta = \lambda(1 - \omega)(1 - \gamma)$$
$$\gamma_1 = (\omega + \gamma) \qquad \gamma_2 = -\omega\gamma$$

and

$$\epsilon_t = u_t - \gamma u_{t-1}$$

(b) Following from this discussion of part (a), fit to the data of Table 4.3 the model

$$\log Y_t = \alpha + \beta_1 \log X_{1t} + \beta_2 \log X_{2t} + \gamma_1 \log Y_{t-1}$$
$$+ \gamma_2 \log Y_{t-2} + \epsilon_t$$

and discuss the results.

4.7 In Section 4.6, we discussed separately the forecasting of future values of a dependent variable from models with a lagged dependent variable, and from models with first-order autoregressive errors. From this discussion, it is possible to see how point forecasts of a dependent variable should be derived from a model with *both* a lagged dependent variable and first order autoregressive errors. Consider the model

$$Y_t = \alpha + \beta_1 X_{1t} + \cdots + \beta_K X_{Kt} + \gamma Y_{t-1} + \epsilon_t$$
$$\epsilon_t = \rho\epsilon_{t-1} + a_t$$

where the errors a_t have mean zero, constant variance, and are uncorrelated with one another. Assuming that suitable estimates of the parameters $\alpha, \beta_1, \ldots, \beta_K, \gamma, \rho$ are available, explain how you would obtain conditional point forecasts of future values of the dependent variable.

4.8 (a) The linear trend model

$$Y_t = \alpha + \beta t + \epsilon_t$$

is to be fitted by least squares to the time series $Y_1, Y_2, \ldots,$ Y_n. Show that the least squares estimates of the parameters β

and α are, respectively,

$$b = \frac{12 \sum_{t=1}^{n} tY_t}{n(n^2 - 1)} - \frac{6\bar{Y}}{(n - 1)}$$

where $\bar{Y}$ is the sample mean of the Y_t, and

$$a = \bar{Y} - b(n + 1)/2$$

(b)   The exponential trend model is to be fitted in the form

$$\log Y_t = \alpha + \beta t + \epsilon_t$$

to the time series $Y_1, Y_2, \ldots, Y_n$. Find expressions for the least squares estimates of β and α.

4.9   The multiple regression model 4.1.2, with K independent variables, is estimated by least squares from a sample of n observations. Let R^2 be the coefficient of determination and $\bar{R}^2$ the corrected coefficient of determination.

(a)   Show that

$$R^2 = 1 - \frac{(n - K - 1)}{(n - 1)} (1 - \bar{R}^2)$$

(b)   Show that

$$\bar{R}^2 = 1 - \frac{(n - 1)}{(n - K - 1)} (1 - R^2)$$

(c)   Show that the statistic 4.3.3 for testing the null hypothesis that all of the partial regression coefficients are zero can be written

$$F = \frac{(n - K - 1)}{K} \frac{\bar{R}^2}{(1 - \bar{R}^2)} + \frac{1}{(1 - \bar{R}^2)}$$

4.10   The following regression was fitted by ordinary least squares to 30 annual observations on time series data

$$\log \hat{Y}_t = 1.31 - 0.27 \log X_{1t} + 0.53 \log X_{2t} - 0.82 \log X_{3t}$$
$$\qquad\qquad (0.17) \qquad\quad (0.21) \qquad\qquad (0.30)$$

$$\bar{R}^2 = 0.615 \qquad d = 0.496$$

where

Y_t = Number of business failures
X_{1t} = Volume of industrial production
X_{2t} = Short term interest rate
X_{3t} = Value of new business orders placed

Figures in brackets below parameter estimates are the corresponding estimated standard errors.

(a) Interpret, in the context of the assumed model, the estimated parameter on $\log X_{3t}$.
(b) Interpret the corrected coefficient of determination, $\overline{R}^2$.
(c) Briefly explain why $\overline{R}^2$ might be preferred to R^2 for purposes of interpretation.
(d) What null hypothesis can be tested through the Durbin-Watson statistic? Carry out this test for the present problem, using a 1% significance level.
(e) Given your findings in (d), what are the consequences of proceeding with the ordinary least squares-estimated model? Explain what you would do next.
(f) Estimate the correlation between adjacent error terms in this model.

4.11 The following regression was fitted by ordinary least squares to 32 annual observations on time series data

$$\log \hat{Y}_t = 2.52 - 0.62 \log X_{1t} + 0.92 \log X_{2t}$$
$$(0.28) \qquad\qquad (0.38)$$

$$+ 0.61 \log X_{3t} + 0.16 \log X_{4t}$$
$$(0.21) \qquad\qquad (0.12)$$
$$R^2 = 0.638 \qquad d = 0.615$$

where figures in brackets below parameter estimates are the corresponding estimated standard errors, and

Y_t = Quantity of U.S. wheat exported
X_{1t} = Price of U.S. wheat on world markets
X_{2t} = Quantity of U.S. wheat harvested
X_{3t} = Measure of income in countries purchasing U.S. wheat
X_{4t} = Price of barley on world markets

(a) Interpret, in the context of the assumed model, the estimated parameter on $\log X_{1t}$.
(b) Interpret the coefficient of determination, R^2.
(c) Find the corrected coefficient of determination, $\overline{R}^2$.

(d) Test the null hypothesis that the regression errors are not correlated with one another against the alternative that they obey a first order autoregressive model with positive parameter.

(e) Given your finding in (d), is it possible with the information provided to validly test the null hypothesis that, all else equal, income in countries purchasing U.S. wheat has no impact on the quantity of U.S. wheat exported?

4.12 An agricultural economist believes that the amount of beef consumed (Y) in tons in a year in the United States depends on the price of beef (X_1) in dollars per pound, the price of pork (X_2) in dollars per pound, the price of chicken (X_3) in dollars per pound, and income per household (X_4) in current dollars. The following sample regression was obtained through ordinary least squares, using time series of 30 annual observations:

$$\log \hat{Y}_t = 0.044 - 0.529 \log X_{1t} + 0.217 \log X_{2t}$$
$$\phantom{\log \hat{Y}_t = 0.044} (0.168) \phantom{\log X_{1t} +} (0.103)$$

$$+ 0.193 \log X_{3t} + 0.416 \log X_{4t}$$
$$(0.106) \phantom{\log X_{3t} +} (0.163)$$

$$R^2 = 0.704 \qquad d = 1.758$$

where figures in brackets below parameter estimates are the corresponding estimated standard errors.

(a) Interpret, in the context of the assumed model, the estimated parameter on $\log X_{2t}$.

(b) Find and interpret a 90% confidence interval for the parameter on $\log X_{1t}$ in the true regression.

(c) Test the null hypothesis that the four variables ($\log X_{1t}$, $\log X_{2t}$, $\log X_{3t}$, $\log X_{4t}$) do not, as a set, have any linear influence on $\log Y_t$.

(d) Carefully explain the value of calculating the Durbin-Watson d statistic in time series regressions. What can be learned from that statistic in the present case?

4.13 A market researcher is interested in the average amount of money per year spent by college students on clothing. From 25 years of annual data the following estimated regression was obtained through ordinary least squares

$$Y_t = 50.72 + 0.124X_{1t} + 0.271X_{2t} + 0.451Y_{t-1} + \epsilon_t$$
$$ (0.047) \phantom{X_{1t} +} (0.213) \phantom{X_{2t} +} (0.136)$$

$$d = 1.821$$

where figures in brackets below coefficient estimates are the corresponding estimated standard errors, and

Y_t = Expenditure per student on clothes, in real dollars
X_{1t} = Disposable income per student (after the payment of tuition, fees, room and board), in real dollars
X_{2t} = Index of advertising, aimed at the student market, on clothes

(a) Test at the 5% level, against the obvious one-sided alternative, the null hypothesis that, all else equal, advertising does not affect expenditures on clothes in this market.

(b) Find a 95% confidence interval for the parameter on X_{1t} in the true regression model.

(c) With advertising level held fixed, what would be the expected impact over time of a $1 increase in real disposable income per student on clothing expenditure?

(d) Test the null hypothesis that the error terms ϵ_t are not autocorrelated against the alternative that they follow a first-order autoregressive model with positive parameter.

4.14 The accompanying table shows 36 annual observations on real imports (Y_t) and real gross national product (X_t) in the United States. Consider the log linear lagged dependent variable model

$$\log Y_t = \alpha + \beta \log X_t + \gamma \log Y_{t-1} + \epsilon_t$$

(a) Fit by least squares the log linear lagged dependent variable model, and write a full report on your findings, including a test for autocorrelated errors.

t	Y_t	X_t	t	Y_t	X_t	t	Y_t	X_t
1	62.9	1380.0	13	90.0	1973.3	25	252.0	2826.7
2	64.8	1435.3	14	98.4	2087.5	26	282.0	2958.6
3	61.7	1416.2	15	111.7	2208.4	27	309.3	3115.1
4	66.6	1494.9	16	117.1	2271.3	28	346.3	3192.3
5	70.8	1525.7	17	130.6	2365.6	29	372.4	3187.2
6	71.9	1551.1	18	137.4	2423.3	30	371.6	3248.7
7	71.0	1539.3	19	143.9	2416.2	31	335.7	3166.0
8	77.2	1629.1	20	148.9	2484.8	32	345.1	3279.1
9	77.5	1665.2	21	168.2	2608.5	33	410.6	3501.4
10	76.4	1708.7	22	196.3	2744.0	34	403.9	3607.4
11	82.0	1799.4	23	250.1	2729.3	35	422.3	3713.3
12	84.8	1873.3	24	219.8	2695.0	36	462.6	3818.0

(b) It is expected that, in the next three years, real gross national product will be

$$X_{37} = 3900 \qquad X_{38} = 4020 \qquad X_{39} = 4100$$

Predict real imports for these years.

4.15   The following regression was fitted by ordinary least squares to 14
       annual observations.[6]

$$\hat{Y}_t = -3.248 + \underset{(0.023)}{0.101}\, X_{1t} - \underset{(0.080)}{0.244}\, X_{2t} + \underset{(0.009)}{0.057}\, X_{3t}$$

$R^2 = 0.93$

where

Y_t = Year-end share of assets in U.S. bank subsidiaries held by
       foreigners, as a percentage of total assets

X_{1t} = Annual change, in billions of dollars, in foreign direct
        investment in the U.S. (excluding finance, insurance, and
        real estate)

X_{2t} = Bank price-earnings ratio

X_{3t} = Index of the exchange value of the dollar

Figures in brackets below parameter estimates are the corresponding
estimated standard errors.

(a)   Interpret the estimated coefficient on X_{3t}.
(b)   Find a 95% confidence interval for the true coefficient on X_{2t}.
(c)   Test against a two-sided alternative the null hypothesis that
      the true coefficient on X_{1t} is zero.

4.16   The accompanying table shows 30 annual observations on personal
       consumption expenditures (Y_t), disposable personal income (X_{1t})
       and interest rates (X_{2t}) in the United States. Consider the model

$$\log Y_t = \alpha + \beta_1 \log X_{1t} + \beta_2 \log X_{2t} + \gamma \log Y_{t-1} + \epsilon_t$$

t	Y_t	X_{1t}	X_{2t}	t	Y_t	X_{1t}	X_{2t}
1	1025	1123	4.5	9	1457	1600	8.0
2	1069	1170	4.5	10	1492	1668	9.9
3	1108	1207	4.6	11	1538	1728	5.7
4	1170	1291	4.6	12	1622	1797	5.3
5	1236	1366	4.5	13	1690	1916	8.0
6	1299	1431	5.6	14	1674	1899	10.8
7	1338	1493	5.6	15	1712	1932	7.9
8	1406	1551	6.3	16	1804	2001	6.8

6.   Hultman, C. W. and L. R. McGee, "Factors affecting the foreign bank
presence in the U.S.," *Journal of Banking and Finance, 12* (1989), 383–396.

t	Y_t	X_{1t}	X_{2t}	t	Y_t	X_{1t}	X_{2t}
17	1884	2067	6.8	24	2249	2470	12.0
18	1961	2167	9.1	25	2355	2543	9.9
19	2004	2213	12.7	26	2446	2635	8.3
20	2000	2214	15.3	27	2516	2671	8.2
21	2024	2249	18.9	28	2607	2801	9.3
22	2051	2262	14.9	29	2657	2869	10.9
23	2146	2332	10.8	30	2682	2893	10.0

(a) Fit the model by least squares and write a full report on your findings.

(b) Indicate how the model can be used for forecasting.

4.17 The accompanying table shows 21 annual observations on energy consumption (Y_t), energy prices (X_{1t}) and gross domestic product (X_{2t}) in Korea. Consider the model

$$\log Y_t = \alpha + \beta_1 \log X_{1t} + \beta_2 \log X_{2t} + \gamma \log Y_{t-1} + \epsilon_t$$

t	Y_t	X_{1t}	X_{2t}	t	Y_t	X_{1t}	X_{2t}
1	120	37	248	12	1246	102	576
2	221	39	271	13	1346	107	618
3	321	40	286	14	1449	103	691
4	425	40	324	15	1553	100	756
5	526	61	351	16	1656	100	808
6	628	64	376	17	1761	92	909
7	730	62	425	18	1868	88	1018
8	834	63	467	19	1975	76	1135
9	938	62	513	20	2082	70	1205
10	1043	71	552	21	2193	66	1313
11	1144	92	540				

(a) Fit the model by least squares and write a full report on your findings.

(b) Indicate how the model can be used for forecasting.

SELECTED BIBLIOGRAPHY

Bewley, R., & D. G. Fiebig (1988). A flexible logistic growth model with applications in telecommunication. *International Journal of Forecasting, 4,* 177–192.

Box, G. E. P., & P. Newbold (1971). Some comments on a paper of Coen, Gomme and Kendall. *Journal of the Royal Statistical Society A, 134,* 229–240.

Dino, R. N. (1985). Forecasting the price evolution of new electronic products. *Journal of Forecasting, 4,* 39–60.

Draper, N. R., & H. Smith (1981). *Applied Regression Analysis* (2nd ed.). New York: Wiley.

Freedman, D., T. Rothenberg, & R. Sutch (1983). On energy policy models. *Journal of Business and Economic Statistics, 1,* 24–32.

Granger, C. W. J. (1967). Simple trend fitting for long range forecasting. *Management Decision,* 29–34.

Granger, C. W. J. & P. Newbold (1974). Spurious regressions in econometrics. *Journal of Econometrics, 2,* 111–120.

Granger, C. W. J. & P. Newbold (1986). *Forecasting Economic Time Series* (2nd ed.). Orlando, Fl.: Academic Press.

Gujarati, D. N. (1988). *Basic Econometrics* (2nd ed.). New York: McGraw-Hill.

Johnson, A. C., M. B. Johnson, & R. C. Buse (1987). *Econometrics: Basic and Applied.* New York: Macmillan.

Kunisawa, K. & Y. Horibe (1986). Forecasting international telecommunications traffic by the data translation method. *International Journal of Forecasting, 2,* 427–434.

Maddala, G. S. (1988). *Introduction to Econometrics.* New York: Macmillan.

Meade, N. (1984). The use of growth curves in forecasting market development—a review and appraisal. *Journal of Forecasting, 3,* 429–451.

Mendenhall, W. & T. Sincich (1986). *A Second Course in Business Statistics: Regression Analysis* (2nd ed.). San Francisco: Dellen.

Myers, R. H. (1986). *Classical and Modern Regression with Applications.* Boston: Duxbury Press.

Neter, J., W. Wasserman, & M. H. Kuntner (1990). *Applied Linear Statistical Models* (3rd ed.). Homewood, Ill.: Richard D. Irwin.

Newbold, P. (1973). *Forecasting Methods.* London: Her Majesty's Stationery Office.

Newbold, P. (1991). *Statistics for Business and Economics* (3rd ed.). Englewood Cliffs, N.J.: Prentice-Hall.

Pindyck, R. S. & D. L. Rubinfeld (1981). *Econometric Models and Economic Forecasts* (2nd ed.). New York: McGraw-Hill.

Weisberg, S. (1985). *Applied Linear Regression* (2nd ed.). Wiley: New York.

Wonnacott, T. H. & R. J. Wonnacott (1981). *Regression: A Second Course in Statistics.* New York: Wiley.

Young, P. & J. K. Ord (1989). Model selection and estimation for technological growth curves. *International Journal of Forecasting, 5,* 501–513.

An Introduction to Time Series and Their Components

5.1   DISTINCTIVE FEATURES OF TIME SERIES DATA

Managers face a very wide range of forecasting problems, each with unique features. Nevertheless, whatever the problem, forecasts will have to be based on currently available information. To some extent the characteristics of the useful information will be problem-specific: it might, for example, be quantitative, qualitative, or both. However, one particular type of information is almost invariably useful when available, and its analysis constitutes an important ingredient in the forecast-generating mechanism. If one is asked to predict future values for such quantities as product sales, corporate earnings, domestic interest rates, or foreign currency exchange rates, an important and obvious question—typically, the first that should be asked—is how these quantities have behaved in the past. When forecasting, we try to study the past in the hope that the knowledge gained will help in forming an educated assessment of the future. If the focus of interest is, for example, the prediction of future sales of a product, it would almost certainly be valuable to have available a record of the evolution of the sales of this product in the past. A record, over time, of the numerical value of a quantity is called a **time series.** Generally, observations on a time series will be available at equally spaced intervals of time, such as daily, monthly, quarterly, or annually, and in our subsequent discussion this will be assumed. Since the study of time series data of this sort is likely to be a valuable part of the attack on a forecasting problem, it is important to understand how business and economic time series data might behave, and in this chapter we will explain the characteristics of time series. For some problems it may be entirely appropriate to base forecasts of future values of a quantity such as product sales *exclusively* on past values of that quantity. However, for many forecasting problems, other information will also be valuable. In either case, study of the time series behavior of the quantity to be predicted should constitute an important element of the forecasting process.

To make our discussion more concrete, suppose that we have available a time series of ten years of quarterly observations on the sales of a product. Now, traditional statistical methodology is aimed at the analysis and interpretation of numerical information, so it seems natural to turn to that methodology for guidance in understanding our data. Unfortunately, procedures such as those reviewed in Chapter 2 will typically not be applicable without modification to this problem. This is so because of a critically important distinction between time series data and the types of data sets that traditional statistical methods were developed to analyze. The traditional methods rely for their validity on the assumption that the data are a *random sample* drawn from some population. Put another way, it is assumed that the sample observations are *independent* of one another, so that a relatively high value for one would tell us nothing at all about whether another is likely to be relatively high or low. Occasionally, observed time series, such as rates of return in speculative markets, appear to exhibit such behavior, but in practice this will be the exception rather than the rule. Consider, for example, what might be expected from forty consecutive quarterly observations on product sales. Sales level will depend to some extent on the state of the national economy; when this is healthy, it would be reasonable to expect relatively high sales for a wide range of products, but when the economy is in recession sales of many products necessarily suffer. Now, the status of the economy does not vary randomly over time between boom and bust, but evolves rather smoothly. This suggests that, if sales of our product were relatively buoyant last quarter, they are more likely than not to remain so in the current quarter. Other factors, such as consumers' tastes and competitors' strategies, which affect the sales of a product, will have similar effects, so that the market environment faced by the product is not likely to change too dramatically from one quarter to the next. Our discussion suggests that we would not expect independence of the time series observations, but *positive correlation* between observations close to one another in time. Many business and economic time series possess a further feature of non-independence. For example, sales of a great many products exhibit **seasonality,** so that they are likely, all else equal, to rise and fall at specific times each year. As a trivial example, a great deal more ice cream is sold in summer than in winter. Seasonal behavior can be observed in the sales of many products and in the earnings of most corporations. In addition, macroeconomic time series such as gross national product and its components, unemployment and inflation rates, are seasonal.

The fact that time series data do not behave as a random sample dictates the development of special statistical methods for their analysis. Indeed, **time series analysis** has evolved as a distinct branch of statistics. The time series analyst's problem can be viewed in two ways:

1. How can valid statistical methods be developed to circumvent the non-independence in time series data?
2. Can the non-independence in time series data *be exploited* to help understand the process being studied, and perhaps predict its future behavior?

Viewed in terms of the first question, the non-independence in time series is a nuisance, causing difficulties that must be overcome. We met this issue in Chapter 4 when discussing regression models with *autocorrelated errors*. When the error terms in a regression equation exhibit patterns of correlation through time, the usual method of analysis based on least squares is suboptimal, and indeed can yield seriously misleading conclusions. As we saw in Chapter 4, this traditional approach must be modified for regression models with autocorrelated errors. In this sense, if the goal is to understand a system of relationships, as through regression analysis, the special features present in time series data can cause difficulties which must be circumvented by modifying the traditional statistical methods.

There is, however, a positive aspect to the structure of time series data, as suggested by the second of our questions. This view is relevant when the goal is to produce forecasts. The non-independence of time series data suggests that what will happen in the future will not be independent of what has happened in the past. When we observe a time series, we observe additional useful information beyond that contained in a random sample: we know the dates at which observations were recorded. It is therefore possible to study historical patterns of dependency in an observed time series, and to use what has been learned about these patterns to estimate what is likely to happen in the future. Viewed in this way, the distinctive features of time series data are not a nuisance to the forecaster; they are a valuable basis for the derivation of predictions.

It is important, then, to try to characterize the special features of time series data, and to understand the kinds of patterns that might be observed.

One approach, on which we will concentrate in this chapter, is to think of an observed time series as a compound of several *components*, each with specific features.

5.2   THE COMPONENTS OF A TIME SERIES

It can be useful to think of the value actually observed for some quantity, such as product sales, as the net result of a number of distinct factors. Then, an observation on a time series can be viewed as resulting from an underlying model involving several components. In the previous section, we briefly introduced such a component. If the progression of a time series is such that a more or less stable pattern within each year is regularly found on a year-to-year basis, the series is said to exhibit seasonality. The process generating the data can then be viewed as having a **seasonal component.** It is well known that a strong seasonal component is present in many business and economic time series, and can arise for a number of reasons. In practice, seasonality is typically due, either directly or indirectly, to the weather or to institutional calendar arrangements such as the timing of public holidays or school vacations.

Seasonality is generally not the only source of regularity in the movement through time of a series. Often some broad upward or downward movement that we will call **trend** is also present. For example, product sales may experience a steady increase, at least for a couple of years. In designating this behavior as resulting from a **trend component,** we do not wish to suggest the expectation of fixed patterns of trend over many years, as would be implied, for example, by a constant 10% growth rate in sales each year. Rather, for business and economic time series, it is more realistic to view the trend as smoothly changing over time. It is this overall smooth pattern that is identified as trend—a much weaker and more useful requirement than that of a constant pattern that could be depicted by some simple function such as a straight line over the whole period for which the time series is observed. We will return to this important point later in this section.

To illustrate time series components, Table 5.1 gives seven years of quarterly sales data, which are graphed in Figure 5.1. The most striking feature, which is clear from both the table and the graph, is the very strong seasonal component in these data; sales are invariably very much higher in the first quarter of each year than in any other. This pronounced seasonal pattern so dominates the time series that it is rather difficult to see clearly its other characteristics. However, a further look at Figure 5.1 suggests a downward trend, that eventually becomes quite pronounced, in the middle of the series, followed by a sharp recovery. The tendency for strong seasonality to blur other characteristics is not uncommon in

TABLE 5.1   Quarterly product sales over seven years.

Year	Quarter			
	1	2	3	4
1	897	476	376	509
2	967	529	407	371
3	884	407	310	338
4	900	448	344	274
5	740	261	289	319
6	1,036	602	536	349
7	1,050	633	435	415

FIGURE 5.1   Quarterly product sales over seven years.

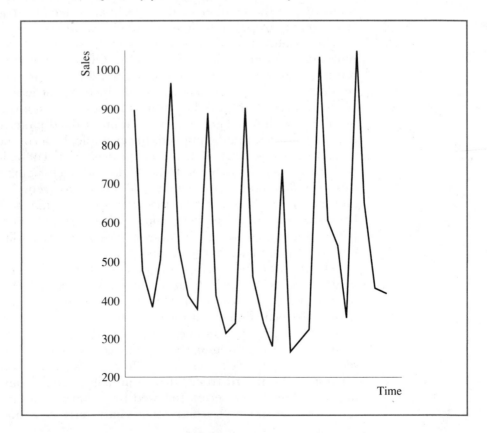

business and economic time series. For that reason it is often useful to try to extract the seasonal component, a procedure known as **seasonal adjustment,** to get a clearer picture of the other features of a time series. We will see how this can be done in sections 4 and 5 of this chapter.

If the only components of a time series were regular seasonal patterns and smooth trend-like behavior, the graph of the series would present a very smooth pattern with regular seasonality superimposed, and a casual look at such a graph would rightly suggest that quite accurate predictions could easily be obtained. Unfortunately, the real world is not so kind. Typically, besides these regular components, observed time series will also have a strong **irregular component,** which induces a jaggedness in the graph of the series, and whose future values are difficult, if not impossible, to predict with much accuracy. The irregular component can be thought of in much the same way as the error term in a regression equation. It arises from a myriad of different causes that individually may not be of any great importance, but whose combined effect can be substantial. Just as simple regression relationships between variables do not hold precisely in the real world, time series are not made up exclusively of nice, easily characterized regular components.

It is sometimes useful to think of a model generating the observed value (X_t) of a time series as a function of trend (T_t), seasonal (S_t), and irregular (I_t) components. The two simplest possibilities of this sort are the **additive components model**

$$X_t = T_t + S_t + I_t$$

and the **multiplicative components model**

$$X_t = T_t \, S_t \, I_t$$

These are not, however, the only possibilities. For example, we might view trend as additive and the seasonal factor as multiplicative, leading to the model

$$X_t = (T_t + I_t)S_t$$

Such models are often called **unobserved components models,** because in practice, although we observe the actual values X_t, the individual components themselves will not be observed. One approach to the analysis of time series involves an attempt, given an observed series, to estimate the values of the individual components. Many approaches to this problem have been proposed and implemented; in subsequent sections of this chapter we introduce a particularly simple possibility based on *moving averages*.

On occasion, a further component, the **cyclical component,** is introduced into unobserved components models. This is intended to capture periodic oscillatory behavior, other than that associated with seasonality, in a time series. It is generally associated with the business cycle in a national economy.

Now, it is instinctive to require that anything characterized as a cycle exhibit some regularity and be of constant duration, like the seasonal component. Certainly this would be a great asset in attempting to estimate such an entity. Unfortunately, to the extent that business cycles can be identified from historical records, it is clear that both their lengths and magnitudes, as measured by differences between peaks and troughs, are far from constant. Hence, given a series of just a few years' data, it will be difficult and perhaps impossible to distinguish between cyclical behavior and smoothly evolving trend. For this reason it is generally preferable to view the component T_t as a combination of trend and cycle, so that it might be designated the **trend-cycle component.** Only on rare occasions will it be useful to attempt to disentangle these two components. To illustrate, Table 5.2 and Figure 5.2 show thirty years of annual sales data. It is clear from the graph that there is some smoothness in the progression through time of these sales; that is, the time series clearly has a regular component. After an initial decline to a trough in year 6, sales climb to a peak in years 13–15, after which the general tendency is downward. It is difficult to say whether this behavior is cyclical or an evolving trend pattern involving decline, recovery, and further decline. The data really contain insufficient evidence on which to base a well-founded attempt to distinguish between the two. It may be worthwhile, however, to extract the irregular component which gives Figure 5.2 its rather jagged appearance. In the next section we describe a procedure for doing so, producing a smoother picture of the trend-cycle.

TABLE 5.2   Annual product sales over thirty years.

Year	Sales	Year	Sales	Year	Sales
1	1,813	11	2,162	21	1,693
2	1,650	12	2,337	22	1,871
3	1,822	13	2,608	23	1,899
4	1,778	14	2,518	24	1,693
5	1,520	15	2,641	25	1,633
6	1,103	16	2,178	26	1,666
7	1,266	17	1,928	27	1,575
8	1,478	18	1,911	28	1,395
9	1,431	19	1,991	29	1,389
10	1,767	20	1,788	30	1,297

FIGURE 5.2   Annual product sales over 30 years.

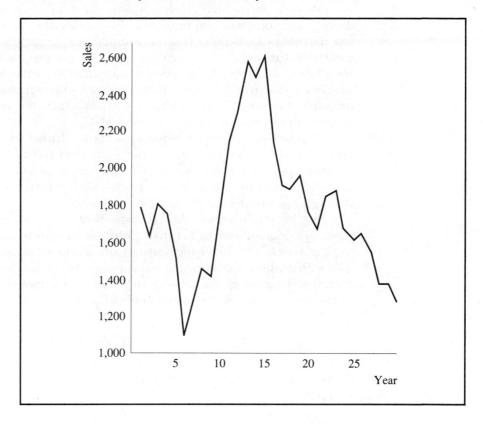

Global and Local Trend and Seasonality

In Chapter 4 we briefly discussed the fitting to time series data of **global trend models,** such as straight lines, using regression methods. The implicit assumption here is that the presumed trend pattern remains fixed over the whole span of time for which the series is observed and, for forecasting purposes, that it will continue to do so into the future. For example, if the linear trend model

$$X_t \doteq \alpha + \beta t + \epsilon_t$$

is fitted, where ϵ_t is an error term, the assumption is of steady upward or downward movement, with constant expected period-to-period change at all points in time. Now, global trend models have been found useful in some forecasting exercises, particularly when there is good reason to expect specific trend functions, as might occur, for example, when market saturation is anticipated. However, for most practical purposes, when dealing with business and economic time series, this view of trend is far too narrow to be useful. The more modern approach is to contemplate **local trend models,** where growth rates are not assumed to be constant for all time, but instead might evolve smoothly over time. We have already suggested that trend be viewed in this way; this approach considerably broadens the set of real-world problems to which the unobserved components model can be sensibly applied.

In practice, seasonality often appears to exhibit more stability over time in business and economic series than does trend. Nevertheless, the modern approach to seasonal adjustment and time series model building is not restricted to global models; it allows for evolving seasonal patterns through models of local seasonality.

In Chapter 6 we will discuss some forecasting algorithms based on the assumption of local rather than global patterns of trend and seasonality in time series. The widespread use of these and other forecasting procedures that shun the stronger assumption of global behavior strongly indicates the value of the broader view that allows time-changing behavior in the trend and seasonal components of a time series.

5.3 SMOOTHING A TIME SERIES USING MOVING AVERAGES

As already indicated, Figure 5.2 shows a series of thirty annual observations on product sales and has a rather jagged appearance, suggesting the presence of an important irregular component. It is often useful, in trying to get a clear picture of the underlying regularities in a time series, to soften the effects of the irregular behavior, producing a *smoother* picture of the evolution of the process. Now, jaggedness in graphs such as Figure 5.2 arises because of abrupt changes in a series, so that an observation differs substantially from its immediate neighbors. This suggests that a smoother picture can be achieved by averaging the value observed at any point in time with the values of closely neighboring observations.

To illustrate, consider again the annual sales data of Table 5.2, which is reproduced as the series X_t in Table 5.3. To get a clearer picture of the trend pattern, we compute in Table 5.3 the new series X_t^* by averaging all sets of five consecutive values of the original series. The resulting series is called a **moving average** of the original. The first value that can be calculated in this way is

TABLE 5.3   Product sales (X_t) and 5-point moving averages (X_t^*).

t	X_t	X_t^*	t	X_t	X_t^*	t	X_t	X_t^*
1	1,813		11	2,162	2,061	21	1,693	1,848
2	1,650		12	2,337	2,278	22	1,871	1,789
3	1,822	1,717	13	2,608	2,453	23	1,899	1,758
4	1,778	1,575	14	2,518	2,456	24	1,693	1,752
5	1,520	1,498	15	2,641	2,375	25	1,633	1,693
6	1,103	1,429	16	2,178	2,235	26	1,666	1,592
7	1,266	1,360	17	1,928	2,130	27	1,575	1,532
8	1,478	1,409	18	1,911	1,959	28	1,395	1,464
9	1,431	1,621	19	1,991	1,862	29	1,389	
10	1,767	1,835	20	1,788	1,851	30	1,297	

$$X_3^* = \frac{X_1 + X_2 + X_3 + X_4 + X_5}{5}$$

$$= \frac{1,813 + 1,650 + 1,822 + 1,778 + 1,520}{5} = 1,717$$

We designate this value X_3^* because year 3 is at the center of the 5 years being averaged. The second value of this series of moving averages is

$$X_4^* = \frac{X_2 + X_3 + X_4 + X_5 + X_6}{5}$$

$$= \frac{1,650 + 1,822 + 1,778 + 1,520 + 1,103}{5} = 1,575$$

and so on. The complete series X_t^* is given in Table 5.3 and graphed in Figure 5.3, from which it is clear that the series of moving averages is very much smoother than the original series of Figure 5.2.

In general, the smoothed series computed in Table 5.3 can be expressed as

$$X_t^* = \frac{X_{t-2} + X_{t-1} + X_t + X_{t+1} + X_{t+2}}{5} \qquad (t = 3, 4, \ldots, 28)$$

Two points should be noted. First, when the series is smoothed in this way, two observations are lost at the beginning and two more at the end of the series. Those at the beginning may not be of much concern, but if we are interested in forecasting, loss of information on the two most recent time periods certainly makes the task more difficult. Second, note that the smoothed series is *centered*, so that X_t is the central value in the calculation of X_t^*. Hence, at any point in time, the smoothed value is the

FIGURE 5.3   Simple 5-point moving averages of annual product sales data.

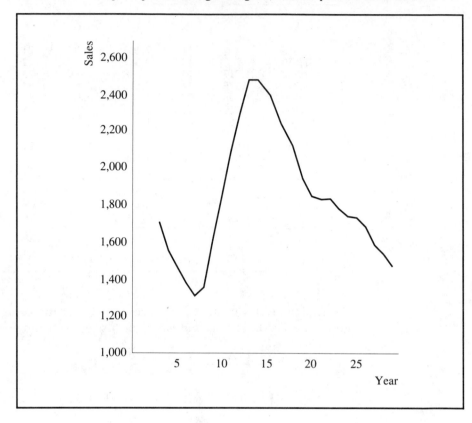

average of the observed value at that time and the two previous and two following observations. Thus, compared with the original series, the smoothed series defined in this way is not shifted in time. For this reason, it is natural to base the moving averages, where possible, on an odd number of observations.

The series X_t^* computed in Table 5.3 is called a *simple centered 5-point moving average*. The word *simple* implies that a simple average is taken. The choice of five points for averaging is somewhat arbitrary; in principle, any odd number could have been used. In general, for any positive integer m, the **simple centered $(2m + 1)$-point moving average** of the time series $X_1, X_2, \ldots, X_n$ is given by

$$X_t^* = \frac{X_{t-m} + \cdots + X_{t-1} + X_t + X_{t+1} + \cdots + X_{t+m}}{2m + 1}$$

$$(t = m + 1, \ldots, n - m)$$

Notice that m observations will be lost at each end of the smoothed series.

The use of *simple* averages, though perhaps obvious, is also rather arbitrary, and indeed may be undesirable. If we are interested in preserving information about what happened in 1992, it is unreasonable to give the same weight to observations from 1990 and 1994 as to the observation from 1992 in calculating the smoothed value of the series for that year. This suggests the possibility of abandoning simple averages in favor of **weighted averages,** where most weight is given to the central observation and least weight to those observations furthest from the center. For example, if five points are to be used, one possible scheme of this sort would be

$$X_t^* = \frac{X_{t-2} + 2X_{t-1} + 4X_t + 2X_{t+1} + X_{t+2}}{10} \qquad (t = 3, \ldots, n - 2)$$

One way to achieve weighted averages of this sort is through the repeated application of simple averaging. For example, suppose we calculate a simple 3-point average of the observed series X_t, giving

$$X_t^* = \frac{X_{t-1} + X_t + X_{t+1}}{3} \qquad (t = 2, \ldots, n - 1) \quad (5.3.1)$$

Then, a simple 3-point average of the series X_t^* gives the new series

$$X_t^{**} = \frac{X_{t-1}^* + X_t^* + X_{t+1}^*}{3} \qquad (t = 3, \ldots, n - 2) \quad (5.3.2)$$

It follows from equations 5.3.1 and 5.3.2 that the smoothed series X_t^{**} can be expressed in terms of the original observations X_t as

$$X_t^{**} = \frac{X_{t-2} + 2X_{t-1} + 3X_t + 2X_{t+1} + X_{t+2}}{9} \qquad (t = 3, \ldots, n - 2)$$

The series X_t^{**} is called a 3×3 moving average of X_t, the notation implying that X_t^{**} is a simple 3-point moving average of a simple 3-point moving average of X_t.

We have introduced the moving averages technique as a mechanism for smoothing a time series so that the impact of the irregular component is dampened, giving a picture of the evolution of a process that is easier to interpret. As a graphical tool of this sort, there is no doubt that this type of analysis can often be useful. However, if we return to our more formal concept of an unobserved components model, what has been achieved? We began with the time series of Figure 5.2, which has both a trend-cycle and an irregular component. In using moving averages to derive the smoother series of Figure 5.3, we might say that the irregularity has been (at least largely) removed. In this sense it could be claimed that, in the series X_t^* of Table 5.3, we have isolated the trend-cycle component, or at least derived an estimate of it. (Correspondingly, the irregular component would be estimated as the difference between X_t and X_t^*.) Indeed, much of the early work on the analysis of business and economic time series proceeded along these lines, using moving averages to obtain component estimates. There is, however, a serious reservation about this approach—it is undesirably and unnecessarily arbitrary. After all, as we have indicated, there are any number of plausible and reasonable alternatives to the simple 5-point moving averages calculated in Table 5.3. More or less than five points could have been employed, and any number of weighted average schemes might have been used in place of simple averages. Thus, any number of alternative estimates of the trend component could plausibly have been computed for the series. However, there is no way to determine which of these alternatives is most appropriate for any given data set purely from visual examination of a time series. The more modern approach to time series analysis involves the formal fitting to data, through efficient statistical techniques, of a *model*: the specific model achieved would then suggest how the components of a series should be estimated. Models might, as we will see in Chapter 7, be designed to represent the observed time series. Alternatively, as will be briefly discussed in Chapter 10, individual models for the constituent components might be postulated. In either case, the properties of the data will suggest an appropriate method for estimating components, rather than relying on the arbitrary choice of some moving average scheme.

5.4   USING MOVING AVERAGES TO EXTRACT THE SEASONAL COMPONENT

We have seen how moving averages can be used to smooth a time series for nonseasonal data, and hence produce an estimate of the trend component. In this section we discuss the use of moving averages in the estimation of unobserved components for seasonal data, illustrating with the quarterly product sales data of Table 5.1, which are reproduced as the series X_t in Table 5.4.

Now, for quarterly data, since each set of four consecutive observations will contain exactly one from each quarter, a series of 4-point moving averages should be largely free from seasonality. The first value that can be calculated for this series is the average of X_1, X_2, X_3, X_4. Notice that the average has center between time period two and time period three,

TABLE 5.4   Quarterly product sales (X_t) and 2×4 moving averages (X_t^{**}).

t	X_t	X_t^*	X_t^{**}	t	X_t	X_t^*	X_t^{**}
1	897			15	344		471.5
						451.5	
2	476			16	274		428.125
		564.5				404.75	
3	376		573.25	17	740		397.875
		582				391	
4	509		588.625	18	261		396.625
		595.25				402.25	
5	967		599.125	19	289		439.25
		603				476.25	
6	529		585.75	20	319		518.875
		568.5				561.5	
7	407		558.125	21	1,036		592.375
		547.75				623.25	
8	371		532.5	22	602		627
		517.25				630.75	
9	884		505.125	23	536		632.5
		493				634.25	
10	407		488.875	24	349		638.125
		484.75				642	
11	310		486.75	25	1,050		629.375
		488.75				616.75	
12	338		493.875	26	633		625
		499				633.25	
13	900		503.25	27	435		
		507.5					
14	448		499.5	28	415		
		491.5					

so that we will denote it $X_{2.5}^*$. This is

$$X_{2.5}^* = \frac{X_1 + X_2 + X_3 + X_4}{4} = \frac{897 + 476 + 376 + 509}{4} = 564.5$$

Similarly, the next value is

$$X_{3.5}^* = \frac{X_2 + X_3 + X_4 + X_5}{4} = \frac{476 + 376 + 509 + 967}{4} = 582$$

Continuing in this way, the remaining values, which are shown in Table 5.4, can be calculated. Given a series $X_1, X_2, \ldots, X_n$, the general formula is

$$X_{t+.5}^* = \frac{X_{t-1} + X_t + X_{t+1} + X_{t+2}}{4} \qquad (t = 2, \ldots, n - 2) \quad (5.4.1)$$

We have succeeded in using moving averages to compute a series X_t^* that is free from strong seasonality, but a difficulty remains. The locations of the values of this series do not correspond to those of the original series. This problem can be rectified by averaging adjacent pairs of values of the series X_t^*. For example, the average of $X_{2.5}^*$ and $X_{3.5}^*$ is

$$X_3^{**} = \frac{X_{2.5}^* + X_{3.5}^*}{2} = \frac{564.5 + 582}{2} = 573.25$$

This gives us a value centered at time period three. The remaining values of the series X_t^{**}, calculated in this way, are shown in Table 5.4 and graphed in Figure 5.4. The general formula is

$$X_t^{**} = \frac{X_{t-.5}^* + X_{t+.5}^*}{2} \qquad (t = 3, \ldots, n - 2) \qquad (5.4.2)$$

so that two observations have been lost at the beginning of this series, and two more at the end. Of course, combining equations 5.4.1 and 5.4.2, the

FIGURE 5.4   2 × 4 moving average of quarterly product sales data.

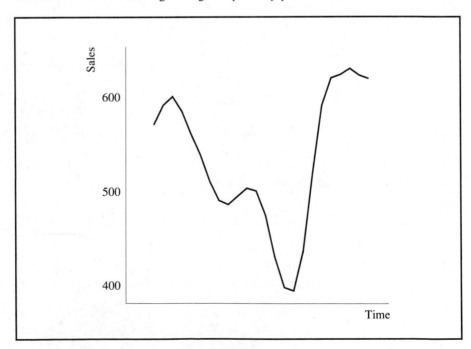

series X_t^{**} can be expressed as a weighted moving average of the original series X_t

$$X_t^{**} = \frac{X_{t-2} + 2X_{t-1} + 2X_t + 2X_{t+1} + X_{t+2}}{8} \qquad (t = 3, \ldots, n-2)$$

In the terminology introduced in Section 5.3, X_t^{**} is 2×4 moving average of X_t—that is, it is a simple 2-point moving average of a simple 4-point moving average. Naturally, given monthly rather than quarterly data, we would compute a 2×12 moving average.

What has been accomplished in deriving the series X_t^{**} of Table 5.4? Of course, as was our purpose, we have removed the seasonality from the original product sales data. However, recalling our discussion of Section 5.3, the application of moving averages also smooths out the irregular component in a time series. Accordingly, we can view the series X_t^{**} as an estimate of the trend-cycle component. This is quite clear from the graph in Figure 5.4. Not only does this appear to be free from noticeable seasonality, it has a rather smooth appearance, suggesting that no strong irregularity remains. Certainly, the historical trend behavior is a good deal easier to see from Figure 5.4 than from the graph of the original data in Figure 5.1. After an initial brief increase, there is a long period of decline, broken only by a modest and brief recovery. This is followed by a sharp sustained recovery to an apparent plateau that is somewhat higher than the previous peak.

For many purposes, an estimate of trend of this sort is precisely what is required. However, it is also thought valuable to produce a series from which the seasonal component only has been extracted, leaving in the irregular component as well as the trend. This is the **seasonal adjustment problem,** on which a good deal of effort has been expended by time series analysts, particularly those employed by government agencies charged with the responsibility of publishing seasonally adjusted values of important economic time series. Several rather complicated approaches to this problem have been proposed and implemented. Some of these will be briefly discussed in the next section. Here we introduce a particularly simple procedure, the seasonal index method, that often performs quite satisfactorily.

The premise of the **seasonal index method** is that the effect of seasonality will be to modify the value observed in any given period of the year by a constant proportionate amount compared with what would have been observed in the absence of seasonality. The proportional adjustment factors, one for each period of the year, are called **seasonal indices.** We illustrate the estimation of these indices for the quarterly product sales data of Table 5.4.

The estimates of the seasonal indices are obtained by comparing each observation X_t with the corresponding trend estimate X_t^{**}. The first value for which this is possible is the third observation; that is, the value for the third quarter of the first year. The actual observation, 376, is to be compared with the trend estimate, 573.25, so that the observation is a proportion

$$\frac{X_3}{X_3^{**}} = \frac{376}{573.25} = 0.6559$$

of the trend estimate. Ratios of observations-to-trend values, calculated in this way, are set out in Table 5.5. We have seen that, in the third quarter of the first year, actual product sales are only 65.59% of the trend value. This discrepancy is caused partly by seasonality, and partly by irregularity in the time series of product sales. Given an observation for just a single year, it would be impossible to disentangle the separate effects of these factors. However, if observation-to-trend ratios are calculated for the third quarter for several years, the effects of irregularities can be averaged out, leaving us with an estimate of the impact of seasonality on third quarter sales.

Table 5.5 shows six years of observation-to-estimated trend ratios for the third quarter. One possibility is to average these ratios to estimate the influence of seasonality in the third quarter. However, given such a small number of observations, the median is preferable to the mean for this purpose, as it attaches less weight to extreme values. For six observations, the median is the average of the third and fourth when the observations are arranged in ascending order. Thus, from Table 5.5 we have

Median Third Quarter $(X/X^{**}) = (0.6579 + 0.7292)/2 = 0.6936$

TABLE 5.5   Calculation of seasonal indices for quarterly product sales data.

Year	1	2	3	4	Totals
1			0.6559	0.8647	
2	1.6140	0.9031	0.7292	0.6967	
3	1.7501	0.8325	0.6369	0.6844	
4	1.7884	0.8969	0.7296	0.6400	
5	1.8599	0.6581	0.6579	0.6148	
6	1.7489	0.9601	0.8474	0.5469	
7	1.6683	1.0128			
Median	1.7495	0.9000	0.6936	0.6622	4.0053
Seasonal Index	1.7472	0.8988	0.6927	0.6613	4

Corresponding values for the other quarters are also reported in Table 5.5. One further, usually modest, adjustment needs to be made. Since the average effect of seasonality over a calendar year should lead neither to an increase nor to a decrease in the seasonality-free process, we would like seasonal indices that average one. This can be achieved by multiplying each median observation-to-estimated-trend ratio by (4/4.0053), since these four ratios sum to 4.0053. Thus, for the third quarter we find

$$\text{Third Quarter Seasonal Index} = (4/4.0053)0.6936 = 0.6927$$

The seasonal indices for the four quarters are given in the last line of Table 5.5. These indices can be interpreted as estimating, for example, that the effect of seasonality is to reduce product sales in the third quarter of the year to 69.27% of the level that otherwise would have resulted.

Given this interpretation, the procedure for finding the seasonally adjusted series is clear; each of the original observations is divided by the seasonal index for the appropriate period of the year. The seasonally adjusted product sales data are shown in Table 5.6, and graphed in Figure 5.5. These are obtained from the original data of Table 5.1 by dividing each first quarter value by 1.7472, each second quarter value by 0.8988, each third quarter value by 0.6927, and each fourth quarter value by 0.6613. For example, for the first quarter of the first year the seasonally adjusted figure is (897/1.7472) = 513.

It is interesting to compare the series graphed in Figures 5.4 and 5.5. In the former, both seasonal and irregular components have been extracted, leaving an estimate of trend-cycle, while in the latter only the seasonal component has been removed. Certainly the graph in Figure 5.5 appears to be free from any obvious seasonality. Also it depicts the same general movements through time as that of Figure 5.4, but has a far more jagged and erratic appearance. This indicates a considerable amount of

TABLE 5.6   Quarterly product sales seasonally adjusted by the seasonal index method.

Year	Quarter			
	1	2	3	4
1	513	530	543	770
2	553	589	588	561
3	506	453	448	511
4	515	498	497	414
5	424	290	417	482
6	593	670	774	528
7	601	704	628	628

Figure 5.5   Seasonally adjusted product sales, calculated by the seasonal index method.

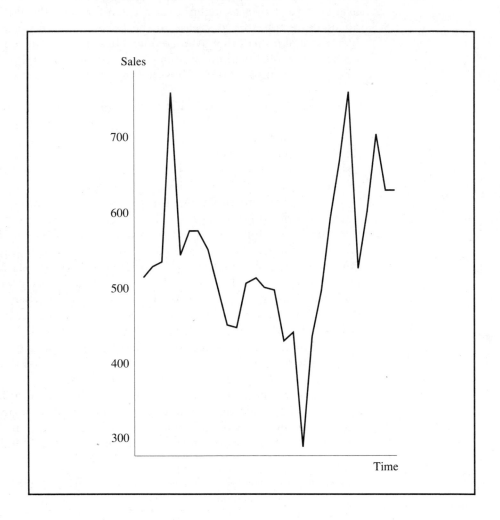

irregularity in these product sales data. Particularly noticeable is the extremely high value for the fourth quarter of the first year, compared to its neighbors. This indicates a very sharp increase, not subsequently sustained, in sales in this quarter, once the effects of seasonality are taken into account.

Since the seasonally adjusted data of Table 5.6 incorporate both trend-cycle and irregular components, and the series X_i^{**} is an estimate of trend-cycle, the irregular component can be estimated by subtracting the X_i^{**}

values from the corresponding values in the seasonally adjusted series. We will illustrate these calculations in Section 5.6.

5.5 THE SEASONAL ADJUSTMENT OF TIME SERIES

As we have seen, many business and economic time series have a strong seasonal component, and much effort is spent on the extraction of this component in the production of seasonally adjusted series. Seasonal adjustment has long been a particular concern of government statisticians, and the weekly, monthly, and quarterly movements of macroeconomic variables invariably are reported on a seasonally adjusted basis when the raw data exhibit seasonality. This service seems to be valued by users, as media discussions of developments in, for example, the money supply, unemployment rates, and gross national product growth are based exclusively on the seasonally adjusted figures. Scholarly and professional analyses of these quantities typically are similarly based. Interestingly, the publication of seasonally adjusted data is far less common in the private sector. For example, although quarterly corporate earnings are generally strongly seasonal, they are reported only on an unadjusted basis. However, when a corporation's most recent earnings figure is reported in the financial press, more often than not it is compared with the corresponding value for the same quarter of the previous year—a process that can be viewed as a crude form of seasonal adjustment. Moreover, when financial analysts study corporate earnings, or business statisticians examine monthly product sales, they often find it convenient to seasonally adjust the raw data as part of a more detailed analysis.

It is clearly the case that the acquisition of seasonally adjusted data is valued by a wide variety of users. In a survey of developments in this area, Bell and Hillmer (1984) identify three motives for seasonal adjustment, listed here from most to least compelling:

1. Seasonal adjustment allows reliable comparison of observations at different points in time.
2. If the aim is to try to understand relationships among economic or business variables through a regression analysis, for instance, this task is generally believed to be easier once the complicating factor of seasonality has been purged from the data.
3. Seasonal adjustment may be a useful element in an approach to the production of short-term forecasts of future values of a time series.

In practice, it is the first of these motives that is the least controversial, and the one which persuades government agencies to expend effort on the production of seasonally adjusted data. Given a plot of a strongly seasonal time series, such as that graphed in Figure 5.1, the seasonal component can dominate the picture, making it very difficult to distinguish other possibly interesting behavior patterns. Once seasonality has been removed, the behavior of the other components becomes more transparent, as for example in Figure 5.5. That this is the major motivation for seasonal adjustment appears also to be the opinion of Bell and Hillmer, who conclude: "Seasonal adjustment is done to simplify data so that they may be more easily interpreted by statistically unsophisticated users without a significant loss of information." In this view, seasonal adjustment forms a valuable part of a preliminary, or exploratory, data analysis, allowing through graphical inspection a useful visual feel for time series data, perhaps as a prelude to performing a more sophisticated analysis.

When economists or business analysts build models linking variables of interest, far more often than not their analysis is based on seasonally adjusted data. They believe that whereas the focus of interest is in, and subject matter theory is developed in terms of, the underlying constructs and their relationships, seasonality merely enters the system through extraneous and not very interesting causes such as the weather and position in the calendar. Moreover, seasonality can be a nuisance to the model builder. Just as seasonality in a time series renders identification of the behavior of the other components more difficult, seasonality in a set of time series can make it harder to detect interrelationships among them. In Chapter 8 we will discuss the quite complex systems of relationships that have been devised to model economic behavior. To the model builder the complexity of these relationships poses sufficient challenges, without having to worry about the extra complication of seasonality. For this reason, model builders have usually found the temptation to work with seasonally adjusted data irresistible. However, this practice is not free from difficulties. It is well known that the process of seasonal adjustment itself can lead to the distortion of underlying relationships. The hope must be that when this distortion arises, it is not too severe. The view in the applied economics profession appears to be that the costs of any distortion thus induced will be outweighed by the benefits from the relative ease in modeling adjusted data. We know of no hard evidence for or against this view. Although this issue is interesting and important, it will not be pursued further here, as that would take us far from our main focus of interest, which is forecasting.

The view that seasonal adjustment might constitute the first step in a forecasting exercise appears also to be based on the thought that seasonality is a nuisance. Consequently, once seasonality has been removed, the analyst can focus on predicting the adjusted series—possibly further broken down into trend and irregular components—multiplying each predicted future value of the adjusted series by the most recently available estimates of the seasonal factors. For example, if this approach is used to forecast the quarterly product sales series of Table 5.1, we would first seasonally adjust. If the seasonal index method is used, this would yield the adjusted series of Table 5.6, for which forecasts must then be found. To forecast future values for the actual sales, each adjusted series forecast would be multiplied by the appropriate seasonal factor, taken from the last row of Table 5.5. For example, each first quarter forecast of the adjusted series would be multiplied by 1.7472, and so on. We will return to the issue of forecasting in the next section.

The seasonal index method, described in Section 5.4, is a straightforward, easy-to-understand approach that can yield adequate seasonal adjustment. However, the major procedures in current use are a good deal more complex. They differ from the seasonal index method in two important respects. First, the modern view is that the assumption of a fixed seasonal pattern over time is inadequate to describe the behavior of many economic time series; the possibility of an evolving seasonal pattern is allowed. Second, there is concern about the impact on adjustment methods of odd outlying extreme observations, and special procedures are incorporated to minimize their impact. Outliers are a particular concern here since, for example, if ten years of monthly data are analyzed, only ten January observations will be available. If one of these happens to be extreme, a false impression of the impact of seasonality in this month will be created unless care is taken.

The historical development of seasonal adjustment has been a long one, and will not be pursued here; the interested reader is referred to Dagum (1978), Nerlove, Grether, and Carvalho (1979), Pierce (1980), and Bell and Hillmer (1984). Given our earlier discussion, it is important to emphasize that workers in this field long ago recognized that models of fixed trend and seasonality were inadequate for business and economic data. In turn, the concentration on local trend and seasonality suggested that seasonal adjustment methods be based on moving averages. The seasonal adjustment procedure that is still most widely used in practice was developed, through a number of versions, by Julius Shiskin and his colleagues at the United States Bureau of the Census. The final version, variant X-11 of the Census Bureau approach, was first described in Shiskin, Young, and Musgrave (1967). More accessible and succinct descriptions of the important aspects of this method are provided by Wallis (1974, 1982). The X-11 method is rather *ad hoc*, having developed through a combination of intuitive plausibility and practical experience as a procedure that should work well for a wide variety of time series, rather than one that is in any sense optimal for specific series. Its details are very complicated, and need not detain us here. However, it is interesting to note from Young (1968) that apart from special treatment of outliers, the X-11 estimates can be written to a good approximation as relatively straightforward moving averages. For example, for monthly data, the Census X-11 procedure can be approximated by the following three steps:

1. Given a monthly seasonal time series X_t, compute the series of 2×12 moving averages

$$X_t^* = \frac{X_{t-6} + 2x_{t-5} + 2X_{t-4} + \cdots + 2X_t + \cdots + 2X_{t+4} + 2X_{t+5} + X_{t+6}}{24}$$

2. Subtract the 2×12 moving averages from the original observations, giving

$$Z_t = X_t - X_t^*$$

Thus, if the series is viewed as being generated by an additive components model, X_t^* estimates trend-cycle, and Z_t is the sum of the seasonal and irregular components.

3. The seasonal component at time t, S_t, is estimated by

$$\hat{S}_t = \frac{Z_{t-36} + 2Z_{t-24} + 3Z_{t-12} + 3Z_t + 3Z_{t+12} + 2Z_{t+24} + Z_{t+36}}{15}$$

Notice that this approximation to the Census X-11 procedure for the seasonal adjustment of monthly time series yields at any time an estimate that is a linear function of the observation of interest and the 42 observations on either side of it. In consequence, exactly as we noted for moving average methods in Sections 5.3 and 5.4, when moving averages are applied, information is lost at each end of a time series. Special modifications are needed to recover this information.

To understand the problem, suppose that we have just observed the value of a time series in September, 1994. Ideally, to obtain the seasonally adjusted figure for the current month, we would want to weigh this observation not only with those from the last three and a half years, but also with those from the next three and a half years. Of course, this is impossible. Faced with a desire to use these future observations were they available, a natural and practical solution is to use instead their forecasts. It seems clear that the better the forecasts used, the better will be the seasonal adjustment. In fact, Census X-11 does not ostensibly employ forecasts in this way to resolve the problem of lost end values, employing instead an approach that is rather arbitrary and unsatisfactory. Wallis (1982) demonstrates that this is tantamount to using suboptimal forecasts, assuming that the components of a time series behave in the way implied by the X-11 adjustment for central values of a series. The notion that the seasonal adjustment of the most recent observations involves the solution of a forecasting problem was exploited directly in the development at Statistics Canada of the X-11 ARIMA method, described by Dagum (1975, 1978). The name is derived from the fact that forecasts are obtained from ARIMA models, which will be discussed in Chapter 7. In fact, X-11 ARIMA involves the application of the standard X-11 algorithm to a time series augmented with forecasts for just the next year.

In order to estimate the seasonal component for the month of September in 1994, it will be necessary to use forecasts either explicitly or implicitly, in place of the unknown future values that ideally would be employed in the moving averages. As time moves on, these future observations become available, and their use would lead to a better estimate of the seasonal component in this month. Thus, for example, standing in September 1996, a better estimate than that originally found of the September 1994 seasonal factor can be achieved. For this reason, initial seasonally adjusted figures undergo periodic revision, and often it is quite substantial. This should not be seen as a weakness in seasonal adjustment techniques, but an inevitable consequence of the fact that acquisition of additional relevant information leads to superior estimates. A number of empirical studies have concluded that, on average, the magnitudes of these revisions are smaller for X-11 ARIMA than for basic X-11. In this sense, the explicit injection of soundly based forecasts into the seasonal adjustment appears to lead to superior initial seasonally adjusted figures.

Although the most widely used, X-11 and X-11 ARIMA are by no means the only seasonal adjustment algorithms that have been developed and implemented. Of particular note is the SABL procedure, developed at Bell Laboratories, and reported in Cleveland, Dunn, and Terpenning (1978). It differs from X-11 in two important respects. First, it makes heavy use of graphical analysis; second, it uses methods, such as moving medians in place of moving averages, that are designed to minimize the impact of extreme outlying observations.

All of the seasonal adjustment procedures described thus far are essentially *ad hoc*, being designed to be applicable, generally without substantial manual intervention, to a broad range of time series. They were developed on the basis of intuitive plausibility and experience, but without specific consideration of the possibility of building models to represent individual time series. In the last few years, there has been some interest in basing the seasonal adjustment of time series on formal models fitted to the available data. These include the seasonal ARIMA models, to be introduced in Chapter 7, and the so-called structural models that will be briefly discussed in Chapter 10.

5.6 Components Estimation and Forecasting

We have seen that the use of moving averages to yield estimates of the components of a time series can provide graphical insight into the behavior over time of that series. Undoubtedly, such an understanding may be very valuable in formulating an attack on the problem of how best to go about forecasting future values of the time series. However, whether such a components decomposition can usefully form the basis for a forecasting exercise is far more problematic.

Attempts to develop forecasts of a time series from components estimates as derived in Section 5.4 have been based on this notion: Once the individual components have been identified, their projection into the future should be relatively straightforward. Forecasts of individual components could then be amalgamated to produce forecasts of the overall time series. This notion has a good deal of intuitive appeal, but turns out to be much less attractive when one begins to explore in detail how such an approach might be put into practice. In part, difficulty arises because of the arbitrary nature of the moving average scheme chosen to estimate the components, and in part because it is often unclear how best to predict the trend-cycle component from these estimates.

To illustrate, consider further the components estimation procedure discussed in detail in Section 5.4, where, for quarterly data, a 2×4 moving average is applied to isolate trend, and the seasonal index method is used to estimate fixed multiplicative seasonal factors. In effect, then, the assumption is a components model of the form

$$X_t = (T_t + I_t)S_t \qquad (5.6.1)$$

We now discuss, in increasing order of difficulty, the prediction of the three constituent components. First, in embracing the seasonal index method, the assumption of a fixed seasonal pattern has already been made, and estimates of the constant seasonal factors derived. It is natural to assume that this same pattern will persist into the future, and to employ the four quarterly seasonal factor estimates as forecasts of future values of the corresponding multiplicative seasonal components.

Having eliminated seasonality, it is usual to think of the irregular component as representing random unpredictable deviations about a smooth underlying trend. In this view, since past experience provides no information about whether future deviations will be above or below the trend curve, the best that can be done is to forecast future values of the irregular component to be zero. The intellectual difficulty in this approach is that the choice of moving average scheme used to segregate the irregular from the other components is, as we have already seen, to some extent arbitrary. But, if the irregular component computed from one such scheme truly is unpredictable from its past, the irregular component computed from some other equally plausible scheme will generally not be. However, leaving this reservation aside, if a moving average components decomposition is employed, it may be reasonable to take zero as a close approximation to the best that can be done in predicting the irregular component. Thus, if we denote by $\hat{X}_n(h)$ the forecast of the future value X_{n+h}, made at time n, we have from equation 5.6.1

$$\hat{X}_n(h) = \hat{T}_n(h)\hat{S}_n(h)$$

where $\hat{T}_n(h)$ and $\hat{S}_n(h)$ are the corresponding forecasts of the trend and seasonal components. For example, suppose that we want to forecast future values of the quarterly product sales data of Section 5.4. Standing at the end of year seven, the first value to be predicted is that for the first quarter of year eight. Given the estimated seasonal indices of Table 5.5, the required forecast is simply 1.7472 times the predicted trend-cycle value for the first quarter of year eight. Similarly, the next forecast of actual sales will be 0.8988 times the predicted trend-cycle value for the second quarter of year eight.

The problem that remains is how to predict future values of the trend-cycle component. It is sometimes proposed that a graph of the sample estimates of this component will suggest some simple function, such as a straight line, or a quadratic or exponential function that can be fitted by regression methods, as seen in Chapter 4. This is rarely the case, and such an approach will frequently be unsatisfactory in practice. Consider, for example, the trend-cycle estimates graphed in Figure 5.4 for our quarterly sales data. There is certainly no obvious choice of function that might be fitted to this graph. One way out of this dilemma is to simply extrapolate the figure into the future graphically by visual inspection. This approach, which has been called **bold freehand extrapolation,** is the crudest form of judgmental forecasting, and one that is hard to recommend. However, it may on occasion produce serviceable rough and ready forecasts when great precision is not needed. Generally, though, a more formal approach is preferred.

The approach to forecasting we have just outlined might best be described as "quick and dirty," and we would generally prefer to employ a procedure based on a somewhat firmer foundation. Apart from the reservations already mentioned, the seasonal index method will rarely be the preferred method of seasonal adjustment. It will typically be preferable to allow the possibility of an evolving seasonal pattern rather than assuming global seasonality. A procedure that has been employed successfully in forecasting seasonal business and economic time series involves three steps. First, X-11 is used to generate a seasonally adjusted series. Next, the seasonally adjusted series is predicted using Holt's exponential smoothing algorithm, which we will discuss in Chapter 6. Finally, the most recent X-11 seasonal components estimates are used to modify the predictions of the seasonally adjusted series to yield forecasts of the original series. In the very large empirical study reported by Makridakis et al. (1982) that compared the quality of forecasts from several methods applied to real data sets, this procedure performed quite well.

If forecasts are to be based on time series components derived through moving averages, the procedure described in the previous paragraph may be the best that can be done. It is quick and inexpensive to apply, given access to the X-11 computer program, and may often yield adequately accurate predictions. However, we retain reservations about this or any approach based on the decomposition methods of this chapter. In part, this is because the inevitable arbitrariness, including that in X-11, in the choice of the weighted average schemes used can lead to components estimates that are themselves difficult to predict. In short, the decomposition of a time series into components in this fashion might well make the forecasting problem harder rather than easier. Furthermore, as we saw in Section 5.5, the estimation of the seasonally adjusted figures, and consequently of all the constituent components of a time series, for the most recent time periods, logically involves the prior solution of the forecasting problem as an input in the solution of the seasonal adjustment problem rather than the converse.

The alternative view, which forms the basis of most modern approaches to the prediction of a time series, is that the components should be analyzed jointly rather than attempting to break them out through moving averages. Three general lines of attack of this sort have been employed.

1. Exponential smoothing algorithms, to be discussed in Chapter 6, provide estimates of current trend and seasonal factors that are simultaneously updated each time a new observation becomes available. This approach is also somewhat *ad hoc*, but has enjoyed considerable success and popularity in routine sales forecasting for inventory control purposes.

2. More formally, given observations on a time series, a model appropriately chosen from a broad class might be fitted. This model can then be projected forward to obtain forecasts of future values. The ARIMA class of models, to be discussed in Chapter 7, has been found to be very useful for this purpose.

3. An alternative formal model building approach, which we briefly discuss in Chapter 10, explicitly recognizes the intuitive appeal of components decomposition, and involves the specification of possible models for each component. The estimation, from available data, of the model parameters then yields directly estimates of components in the sample period, together with forecasts of future values. This

seems preferable to the essentially arbitrary choice of moving average schemes for the same purpose.

Having written a chapter of this length on components estimation through moving averages, we feel obliged to end on a positive note. We have already indicated skepticism about the merits of basing a forecasting exercise on such a decomposition. However, we believe this technique has the more modest value to the forecaster of providing valuable insights into the structure of a time series of interest. These insights can be useful inputs into a subsequent, more formal analysis on which forecasts are to be based. We see the methods of this chapter as tools of preliminary or exploratory data analysis, allowing an investigator the opportunity to form a visual appreciation of some of the characteristics of the data before attempting a more sophisticated analysis of them.

To illustrate, let us see what can be learned about the series of quarterly product sales from the analysis of Section 5.4. Looking at the three components estimates in turn, we find:

1. These sales data have a very strong seasonal component, dominated by the recurrence of very high sales in the first quarter of each year. This is already quite obvious from the graph of the raw data in Figure 5.1 or even from casual inspection of those data in Table 5.1. The point is emphasized by the estimated seasonal indices in the last row of Table 5.5, suggesting that the first quarter seasonal behavior has the effect of raising sales about 75% above trend values.

2. The estimated trend-cycle component is graphed in Figure 5.4, which shows quite abrupt swings in direction from sharp decline to steep and substantial growth. The forecaster will have to recognize that such swings are likely to be difficult to anticipate. Consequently, it must be expected that *any* procedure used to predict this time series from its own past history could yield quite inaccurate forecasts a few quarters into the future.

3. The size of the irregular component can be gauged by comparing the graphs of the estimated trend-cycle component (Figure 5.4) and the seasonally adjusted series (Figure 5.5), an exercise that, as we have already suggested, indicates that the magnitudes of the irregular component can be far from negligible. Irregular component estimates can be found by subtracting the trend-cycle estimates, X_i^{**} of Table 5.4 from the corresponding seasonally adjusted sales figures of Table 5.6. The results are set out in Table 5.7. This reveals values in the fourth quarter of year 1, the second quarter of year 5, and the third and fourth quarters of year 6 that are certainly large when compared with trend sales levels. A very sensible response in such circumstances is to return to the data source and try to discover the causes for these extreme observations. It may be that data have been incorrectly

TABLE 5.7   Irregular component estimates for quarterly product sales data.

| | | Quarter | | |
Year	1	2	3	4
1			−30	181
2	−46	3	29	28
3	1	−36	−39	17
4	12	−1	25	−14
5	26	−106	−22	−37
6	1	43	141	−110
7	−28	79		

recorded, or that unusually high values are due to the filling of the odd, extremely large order, while unusually low values result from shipping difficulties or other extraneous factors not reflecting true product demand. Another possibility is that sales made in one quarter were incorrectly recorded in the next. In circumstances such as these, it would be sensible to make appropriate modifications to the original observations before proceeding to further analysis. Unfortunately, it frequently happens that such explanations of extreme observations are not forthcoming. The question of what, if anything, should then be done is a difficult one. It is known that extreme observations can exert a strong and undesirable influence on least squares estimates, as in the regression estimation discussed in Chapters 3 and 4. One possibility is to use some alternative estimation technique in place of least squares. An alternative is to modify the original observations and proceed with least squares methods on the modified data. There is no consensus as to the desirable degree of this sort of modification. We tend toward the side of caution. After all, the original data represent real observations on the process of interest, and it is hard to be sanguine about the sophisticated analysis of a heavily modified data set having little resemblance to anything that was truly observed or actually happened. We suggest a modest modification that would replace any value of the irregular series outside the range ±2.5 sample standard deviations with a value at the appropriate end-point of that region. Now, the irregular component should have mean zero (though the mean of the sample estimates will differ somewhat from zero). Therefore, we find the sample standard deviation of the irregular component estimates $\hat{I}_t$ ($t = 3, \ldots, 26$) of Table 5.7 to be

$$\left(\sum_{t=3}^{26} \hat{I}_t^2 / 24 \right)^{1/2} = 63.5$$

Hence, we modify values outside the range $\pm(2.5)(63.5) = \pm159$. The only irregular value qualifying for modification by this criterion is that for the fourth quarter of year 1, where we would substitute 159 for 181. In terms of the original series of Table 5.1 then, we would subtract 22 times the fourth quarter seasonal factor (0.6613) from the observed value, substituting 494 for 509. The impact of such a modification will be to allow this observation to exert less influence on the forecasting process. Whatever is done about modifying series with large irregular values, it must be realized that, to the extent that these occur in the future, such occurrences will be largely unpredictable on the basis of previous observations on a time series. Thus, even in the short run, the possibility of quite large forecast errors must be anticipated. Inspection of the fourth quarter figures in Table 5.7 suggests a further possibility. These figures for the irregular component estimates get steadily and markedly lower over the years. It could be that the assumption of a fixed seasonal pattern was inappropriate for this time series.

To summarize, our analysis to date leads us to conclude that sales of this product are highly seasonal, but because of the behavior of its trend and irregular components it is difficult to be optimistic about the likely accuracy of forecasts of future sales based exclusively on past sales data. We prefer to characterize this position as realistic rather than pessimistic. It is important to recognize that, in the real world, some time series are a good deal more difficult to project accurately than others. It can certainly be useful to know that the series at hand falls into the difficult category. If it is particularly important to management to have, if possible, relatively accurate forecasts for such a series, it may be worthwhile to search for other relevant information that can be incorporated into the forecasting process.

We have seen that the simple moving average techniques of this chapter can provide the forecaster with useful information and insights. However, it will generally be preferable to base forecasts of time series on the more formal and less arbitrary methods to be discussed in subsequent chapters rather than employ these components estimates as the sole basis for forecasting.

EXERCISES

5.1   What is meant in saying that a time series can be viewed as being made up of components? Provide examples of business and economic time series in which you would expect to find strong evidence of (i) trend (ii) seasonality (iii) irregularity.

5.2   The table shows hourly earnings in U.S. manufacturing over a period of 24 months.

Month	Earnings	Month	Earnings	Month	Earnings
1	10.58	9	10.84	17	11.05
2	10.67	10	10.87	18	11.02
3	10.48	11	10.81	19	11.06
4	10.59	12	10.93	20	11.11
5	10.67	13	10.94	21	11.15
6	10.74	14	10.96	22	11.19
7	10.74	15	11.05	23	11.22
8	10.80	16	10.83	24	11.17

(a)   Graph this time series and discuss its behavior.

(b)   Compute the series of simple centered 5-point moving averages. Graph the smoothed series and discuss its properties.

5.3   The table shows U.S. state unemployment insurance benefits (seasonally adjusted at annual rates in millions of dollars) over a period of 24 quarters.

Quarter	Benefits	Quarter	Benefits	Quarter	Benefits
1	14832	9	13076	17	15196
2	15088	10	13508	18	16016
3	15864	11	13140	19	16996
4	16440	12	13040	20	17868
5	16244	13	12708	21	20400
6	15012	14	13524	22	23448
7	14460	15	13940	23	26833
8	13948	16	14596	24	26323

(a)   Graph this time series and discuss its behavior.

(b)   Calculate the series of simple centered 5-point moving averages. Graph the smoothed series and discuss its behavior.

5.4   A smoothed series is to be calculated from a series X_t ($t = 1, 2, \ldots, n$) through a 5×3 moving average. Find an expression for the smoothed series in terms of the original observations on X_t.

5.5   The table shows the evolution of the value of the United States dollar in terms of number of dollars per International Monetary Fund special drawing right over a period of 30 months.

(a)   Graph this series and discuss its behavior.

(b)   Calculate the series of simple centered 5-point moving averages. Graph this smoothed series and comment on its behavior.

(c)   Calculate the series of 3×3 moving averages. Graph the smoothed series and discuss its properties.

	Year 1	Year 2	Year 3
January	0.975	1.111	1.268
February	0.959	1.156	1.264
March	0.991	1.138	1.286
April	0.991	1.176	1.306
May	0.993	1.143	1.287
June	0.998	1.178	1.278
July	1.037	1.204	
August	1.035	1.207	
September	1.059	1.213	
October	1.072	1.187	
November	1.093	1.210	
December	1.098	1.223	

5.6   The table shows annual percentage change in the consumer price index in the United States over 21 years.

Year	CPI % change	Year	CPI % change	Year	CPI % change
1	1.6	8	3.3	15	11.3
2	3.1	9	6.2	16	13.5
3	2.8	10	11.0	17	10.4
4	4.2	11	9.1	18	6.2
5	5.4	12	5.8	19	3.2
6	5.9	13	6.5	20	4.3
7	4.3	14	7.6	21	3.6

(a)   Graph this time series and discuss its behavior.

(b)   Calculate the series of simple centered 5-point moving averages. Graph this smoothed series and comment on its behavior.

(c)   Compute the series of 3×3 moving averages. Graph this series and comment on the resulting picture.

5.7   The table shows the rates on 6-month Certificates of Deposit in the United States over a period of 36 months.

Month	Rate	Month	Rate	Month	Rate
1	8.81	13	8.21	25	7.95
2	9.28	14	8.12	26	7.64
3	9.36	15	8.17	27	7.17
4	9.71	16	8.26	28	6.51
5	10.40	17	8.48	29	6.50
6	10.13	18	8.57	30	6.16
7	9.60	19	8.48	31	6.03
8	9.09	20	8.28	32	6.26
9	8.59	21	8.12	33	6.25
10	8.56	22	7.99	34	5.79
11	8.75	23	8.06	35	5.60
12	8.45	24	8.05	36	5.32

(a)   Draw a graph of the time series and discuss its behavior.

(b)   Compute the series of 3 × 3 moving averages. Draw a graph of the smoothed series and comment on its behavior.

5.8   What is meant by the seasonal adjustment of a time series? What is the value of having access to seasonally adjusted data?

5.9   The table shows quarterly earnings per share of a corporation over a period of seven years.

	Quarter			
Year	1	2	3	4
1	34	53	46	102
2	50	68	56	126
3	56	86	68	156
4	60	98	85	171
5	62	104	94	202
6	71	122	108	230
7	83	140	127	271

(a)   Using a 2 × 4 moving average, estimate the trend component, and graph this series.

(b)   Using the seasonal index method, derive and graph the series of seasonally adjusted earnings per share.

(c)   What can be learned from the components estimates for this time series?

5.10   The table shows quarterly plant and equipment expenditures (in billions of dollars) over a period of seven years.

	Quarter			
Year	1	2	3	4
1	19.38	22.01	21.86	25.20
2	21.50	24.73	25.04	28.48
3	24.10	28.16	28.23	31.92
4	25.82	28.43	27.79	30.74
5	25.87	29.70	30.41	34.52
6	29.20	33.73	34.82	38.06
7	32.35	37.89	38.67	44.91

(a)   Draw a graph of this time series and discuss its behavior.

(b)   Estimate the trend component by computing a series of 2 × 4 moving averages. Graph the resulting series and discuss its behavior.

(c)   Use the seasonal index method to obtain a seasonally adjusted series. Graph the resulting series and discuss its behavior.

(d) What can be learned from the components estimates for this time series?

5.11 The table shows the value of quarterly sales of a corporation over six years.

Year	Quarter			
	1	2	3	4
1	600	830	820	1,070
2	730	1,030	900	1,140
3	840	1,190	1,020	1,250
4	970	1,670	1,430	1,680
5	1,160	1,450	1,570	1,820
6	1,220	2,140	1,750	2,040

(a) Graph this series and discuss its properties.
(b) Using a 2×4 moving average, estimate the trend component, and graph this series.
(c) Using the seasonal index method, obtain and graph the series of seasonally adjusted sales values.
(d) What can be learned from the components estimates for this time series?

5.12 The table shows quarterly product sales over a period of seven years.

Year	Quarter			
	1	2	3	4
1	786	668	863	807
2	802	670	885	805
3	579	423	904	851
4	430	409	1,120	958
5	681	468	1,192	833
6	764	449	1,021	639
7	694	609	1,130	688

(a) Graph this series and discuss its properties.
(b) Using a 2×4 moving average, estimate the trend component, and graph this series.
(c) Using the seasonal index method, obtain and graph the series of seasonally adjusted product sales.
(d) What can be learned from the estimated components for this time series?

SELECTED BIBLIOGRAPHY

Bell, W. R., & S. C. Hillmer (1984). Issues involved with the seasonal adjustment of economic time series. *Journal of Business and Economic Statistics, 2,* 291–320.

Cleveland, W. S., D. H. Dunn, & I. J. Terpenning (1978). SABL: A resistant seasonal adjustment procedure with graphical methods for interpretation and diagnosis. In A. Zellner (Ed.), *Seasonal Analysis of Economic Time Series.* Washington, DC: U.S. Department of Commerce, Bureau of the Census.

Croxton, F. E., D. J. Cowden, & B. W. Bolch (1969). *Practical Business Statistics.* Englewood Cliffs, N.J.: Prentice-Hall.

Dagum, E. B. (1975). Seasonal factor forecasts from ARIMA models. *Bulletin of the International Statistical Institute, 46,* 203–216.

Dagum, E. B. (1978). *A comparison and assessment of seasonal adjustment methods for employment and unemployment statistics* (National Commission on Employment and Unemployment Statistics, Background Paper No. 5). Washington, DC: Government Printing Office.

Frecka, T. J., P. Newbold, & P. A. Silhan (1991). Seasonal adjustment at the corporate level using X-11 procedures. *Advances in Quantitative Analysis of Finance and Accounting, 1B,* 39–53.

Makridakis, S., A. Anderson, R. Carbone, R. Fildes, M. Hibon, R. Lewandowski, J. Newton, E. Parzen, & R. Winkler (1982). The accuracy of extrapolation (time series) methods. *Journal of Forecasting, 1,* 111–153.

Nerlove, M., D. M. Grether, & J. L. Carvalho (1979). *Analysis of Economic Time Series: A Synthesis.* Orlando. Fl.: Academic Press.

Pierce, D. A. (1980). A survey of recent developments in seasonal adjustment. *The American Statistician, 34,* 125–134.

Shiskin, J., A. H. Young, & J. C. Musgrave (1967). *The X-11 variant of the Census Method II seasonal adjustment program.* (Technical Paper No. 15). U.S. Department of Commerce, Bureau of Economic Analysis.

Wallis, K. F. (1974). Seasonal adjustment and relations between variables. *Journal of the American Statistical Association, 69,* 18–31.

Wallis, K. F. (1982). Seasonal adjustment and revision of current data: Linear filters for the X-11 method. *Journal of the Royal Statistical Society A, 145,* 76–85.

Young, A. H. (1968). Linear approximation to the Census and BLS seasonal adjustment methods. *Journal of the American Statistical Association, 63,* 445–457.

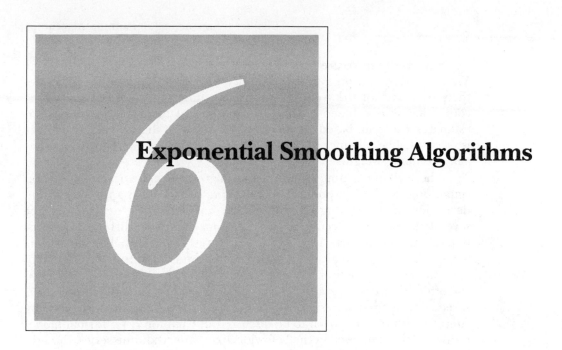

6 Exponential Smoothing Algorithms

6.1 INTRODUCTION TO EXPONENTIAL SMOOTHING

In Chapter 5 we saw that it can be useful to view a time series as made up of trend, seasonal, and irregular components. For some purposes, particularly seasonal adjustment, it is valuable to have estimates of these components over the whole period of observation of a series. The procedures discussed in Chapter 5 were based on *centered moving averages*, where the observation at the time period of interest is averaged, not necessarily using equal weights, with observations on either side of it. Of course, toward the ends of a series, some modifications of this approach will be needed since it is impossible to include in the averages observations that have not yet occurred. Now, if the focus of interest is forecasting the future rather than reviewing the historical record, the relevant quantities to be estimated are the most recent trend and seasonal terms. These can then be projected forward to derive predictions of future values of the time series. This estimation problem and its solution is the basis of *exponential smoothing*, an approach to short-term forecasting that is widely used in industry (see the discussion in Gardner, 1985).

Suppose that we are standing at time t, having available observations $X_t, X_{t-1}, X_{t-2}, \ldots$ on a time series. If we want to estimate, for example, the parameters of the trend component at time t, these estimates will of course have to be based on the data that are at hand. As in Chapter 5, estimates are again based on weighted averages, so that the original series is *smoothed*. The schemes used in these calculations employ sets of *exponentially* declining weights.

There is not a unique forecasting algorithm known as exponential smoothing. Rather, **exponential smoothing** is a general approach to the derivation of forecasting algorithms that has led to the development of several alternative procedures, based to some extent on different assumptions about the characteristics of the time series of interest. The algorithms in popular use are typically justified on grounds of intuitive plausibility and successful practical experience in their application. Exponential smoothing is therefore a somewhat ad hoc approach to the problem of forecasting a time series on the basis of its own past. In particular, by contrast with the approach to be discussed in Chapter 7, no formal model is directly fitted to explain the behavior of an observed time series, though, beginning with Muth (1960), a number of authors have shown that particular exponential smoothing algorithms do yield optimal forecasts for time series generated by specific models. The decision to base forecasts on some exponential smoothing algorithm is rather arbitrary. The hope, founded on accumulated experience, is that such an approach is *robust*, in the sense that good quality forecasts will be obtained for a broad range of time series.

In subsequent sections of this chapter we will outline the structures of a number of exponential smoothing algorithms. In general, these algorithms have quite simple and intuitively appealing forms, the necessary calculations are easily programmed, information storage requirements are minimal, and application is largely routine so that relatively little skilled labor needs to be tied up. These features render exponential smoothing algorithms particularly attractive when forecasts of a very large number of time series are needed on a regular basis. Specifically, these procedures were developed for, and are currently widely used in, routine sales forecasting for inventory control purposes. Typically, short-term forecasts are required, on a monthly basis, for demand for a great many mature product lines. In these circumstances it may not be feasible or, given the costs involved, desirable to devote a great deal of time and effort to the tailoring of specific forecasting procedures to the observed properties of each individual sales series. The extra forecast precision and consequent inventory cost savings may fail to compensate for the additional costs incurred. What may be required instead is an inexpensive algorithm whose application yields adequate short-term forecasts for at least the great majority of series that need to be predicted. In such circumstances, both ease of application and a successful track record render exponential smoothing algorithms particularly attractive.

6.2 SIMPLE EXPONENTIAL SMOOTHING

We begin our discussion with the simple exponential smoothing algorithm, which is appropriate for forecasting certain types of time series, and which forms the basis for a wide range of algorithms that have been successfully employed in practice to predict many other types of series. The simple exponential smoothing algorithm is appropriate for nonseasonal time series with no predictable upward or downward trend. The aim for such series is to estimate the current level. This level estimate is then used as the forecast of all future values of the series.

Our time series, then, is viewed as having a mean, but no upward or downward trend. However, as in our discussion in Chapter 5, this mean is not globally fixed over all time, but rather changes, or evolves, through time. Thus, expected sales of a product can be quite different today than they were a few years ago. Although mean sales evolve over time, the basis of simple exponential smoothing is the assumption that future changes in the mean are unpredictable. Our most recent estimate of the mean, denoted as the current *level* of the time series, is therefore the appropriate forecast of all future values. Of course, as new data become available, previous estimates of the level should be modified, and hence new forecasts obtained.

Suppose that we are standing at time t and have available current and past observations $X_t, X_{t-1}, X_{t-2}, \ldots$ on a time series. How might the level of this series at time t be estimated? Two extreme possibilities are available:

1. The level could be estimated as the simple average of all the available observations. The use of this simple average to forecast the future would imply that, in computing predictions, the same weight is given to observations in the distant past as to the most recent data. In a great many applications this will be unappealing, as it is surely reasonable to believe that the most recent observations will contain more relevant information about what is likely to happen in the future than will the experience of many years ago. This argument suggests that, if the estimate of current level is to be based on an average of the available data, it should be a *weighted average*, in which most weight is given to the most recent observations, and relatively little weight to those from the distant past.
2. The current observation itself could be used to estimate current level. This implies that the latest available observation on a time series would be used as the forecast of all future values. By contrast with the simple

average, where all observations are weighted equally, here all of the weight is assigned to the most recent observation. Although it is well known that for certain time series, particularly prices in speculative markets, this is just about the best that can be done. We would often be unhappy with having to depend on just a single observation which could incorporate a large irregular element. Rather, some smoothing will frequently be desirable, in the spirit of the procedures of Chapter 5.

Simple exponential smoothing allows a compromise between these two extremes. The current level of a series at time t is estimated as a weighted average of the observations $X_t, X_{t-1}, X_{t-2}, \ldots$. Most weight is given to the most recent observation, with weights decreasing for more distant observations through a system of exponentially decreasing weights. Specifically, weight α is assigned to X_t, weight $\alpha(1 - \alpha)$ to X_{t-1}, weight $\alpha(1 - \alpha)^2$ to X_{t-2}, and so on, where α is a number between zero and one. The estimated level of the time series made at time t is, then,

$$L_t = \alpha X_t + \alpha(1 - \alpha)X_{t-1} + \alpha(1 - \alpha)^2 X_{t-2} \qquad (6.2.1)$$
$$+ \alpha(1 - \alpha)^3 X_{t-3} + \cdots$$

Notice that this is a true weighted average since the weights sum to one, that is

$$\alpha + \alpha(1 - \alpha) + \alpha(1 - \alpha)^2 + \alpha(1 - \alpha)^3 + \cdots = 1$$

For example, if we set $\alpha = 0.4$, formula 6.2.1 gives the level estimate

$$L_t = 0.4X_t + 0.24X_{t-1} + 0.144X_{t-2} + 0.0864X_{t-3} + \cdots$$

Now, although formula 6.2.1 provides a definition of the level estimate, it is not in convenient form for easy computation. The exponential smoothing algorithm is obtained by writing, in the same form as equation 6.2.1, the estimated level at time $(t - 1)$ as

$$L_{t-1} = \alpha X_{t-1} + \alpha(1 - \alpha)X_{t-2} + \alpha(1 - \alpha)^2 X_{t-3} + \cdots$$
$$(6.2.2)$$

Multiplying through equation 6.2.2 by $(1 - \alpha)$ yields

$$(1 - \alpha)L_{t-1} = \alpha(1 - \alpha)X_{t-1} + \alpha(1 - \alpha)^2 X_{t-2} \qquad (6.2.3)$$
$$+ \alpha(1 - \alpha)^3 X_{t-3} + \cdots$$

Finally, subtracting the left- and right-hand sides of equation 6.2.3 from those of 6.2.1 yields

$$L_t - (1 - \alpha)L_{t-1} = \alpha X_t$$

or

$$L_t = \alpha X_t + (1 - \alpha)L_{t-1} \qquad 0 < \alpha < 1 \qquad (6.2.4)$$

Formula 6.2.4, which is sometimes called the **recurrence form** of the simple exponential smoothing algorithm, is particularly convenient for computation, involving simple repetitive calculations and minimal information storage requirements. At the current time period t, the new estimate of level is a weighted average of the previous level estimate, L_{t-1}, and the new observation, X_t. The weight given to each is determined by the value the analyst chooses to use for the parameter α, which is called the **smoothing constant.** Notice that, once a value for the smoothing constant has been chosen, it is not necessary to store the whole past history of the time series. Only the most recent observation and the last estimate of level are needed. As we already indicated, the current level estimate is used to predict all future observations. Thus, if $\hat{X}_t(h)$ denotes the forecast of X_{t+h}, made at time t,

$$\hat{X}_t(h) = L_t \qquad h = 1, 2, 3, \ldots \qquad (6.2.5)$$

To illustrate the calculations involved, Table 6.1 shows 30 years of annual product sales, labeled $X_1, X_2, \ldots, X_{30}$. To start off the algorithm 6.2.4, it is necessary to set an *initial value* for the smoothed series. In exponential smoothing this is typically done rather arbitrarily. An obvious

TABLE 6.1 Application of simple exponential smoothing ($\alpha = 0.3$) to annual sales data.

t	X_t	L_t	t	X_t	L_t	t	X_t	L_t
1	103	103	11	82	94.00	21	102	103.31
2	86	97.90	12	123	102.70	22	101	102.61
3	84	93.73	13	106	103.69	23	112	105.43
4	84	90.81	14	103	103.48	24	104	105.00
5	92	91.17	15	99	102.14	25	105	105.00
6	92	91.42	16	106	103.30	26	116	108.30
7	94	92.19	17	107	104.41	27	100	105.81
8	102	95.13	18	115	107.59	28	128	112.47
9	103	97.49	19	95	103.81	29	109	111.43
10	103	99.15	20	104	103.87	30	122	114.60

choice is to set the first level estimate equal to the first observation; that is,

$$L_1 = X_1$$

This choice should have minimal effect on the final result, unless the time series is very short. Then, given

$$L_1 = X_1 = 103$$

formula 6.2.4 can be applied recursively for $t = 2, 3, \ldots$. Using smoothing constant $\alpha = 0.3$, we find

$$L_2 = 0.3X_2 + 0.7L_1 = (0.3)(86) + (0.7)(103) = 97.9$$

Next, we can calculate

$$L_3 = 0.3X_3 + 0.7L_2 = (0.3)(84) + (0.7)(97.9) = 93.73$$

Continuing in this way, the level estimates $L_4, L_5, \ldots, L_{30}$ can be found. These are entered in Table 6.1. Given these data, sales forecasts for all future years are, according to equation 6.2.5, simply the most recent level estimate, L_{30}. Thus, rounding to the nearest integer, we have

$$\hat{X}_{30}(h) = L_{30} = 115 \qquad h = 1, 2, 3, \ldots$$

This time series and the forecasts for the next five years are graphed in Figure 6.1. At first sight it might seem surprising that, although the observed series exhibits considerable variability, the forecasts for all future years are the same. It must be made clear that we are not making the prediction that product sales level will be identical in each of the next five years. Rather, given the observed data, each of these individual forecasts is the best that can be achieved. We are saying that as a result of irregularities in the structure of the series, sales in year 32 will almost certainly differ from sales in year 31. However, the observed data provide no useful information about what this difference will be, so the best prediction is that it will be zero. It is a feature of all time series forecasting methods that the forecast function is a good deal smoother than the observed series. This is simply a reflection of the unpredictability of irregular behavior.

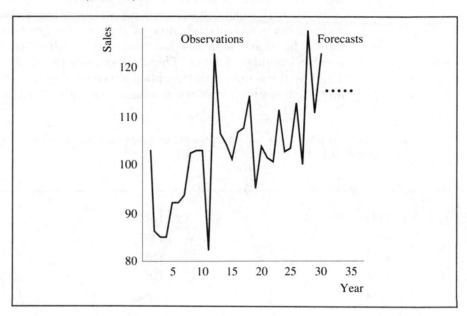

FIGURE 6.1   Annual sales and forecasts from simple exponential smoothing ($\alpha = 0.3$).

Choice of Smoothing Constant

To this point we have said nothing about the value to be used for the smoothing constant, except that it is generally restricted to lie between zero and one. Even this restriction is not universally accepted; some authors note that a value between one and two also yields stable estimates of current level. However, such values render more tenuous the usual justifications for exponential smoothing discussed earlier in this section. For most purposes, a restriction to the narrower range is satisfactory, and certainly intuitively more plausible.

The value of a smoothing constant for an exponential smoothing algorithm can be chosen either subjectively or objectively. If the analyst has experience in the application of this approach, then, for a given series, it might be satisfactory to select a value that has yielded reliable forecasts for similar time series. This possibility can be quite attractive when the analyst is required to produce sales forecasts for many closely related product lines.

A second possibility for the judgmental choice of the smoothing constant is through visual inspection of the observed data. From formula 6.2.4 it is obvious that the simple exponential smoothing predictor is a weighted average, in which weight α is attached to the most recent observation and weight $(1 - \alpha)$ to the previous estimate of level. A graph of the time series can be useful in assessing appropriate weights. If the time series appears to evolve quite smoothly, it is reasonable to give relatively high weight to the most recent observation. On the other hand, if the progression through time of the series is quite erratic, less weight should be attached to the last observation, which could incorporate a sizeable irregular element. These considerations are illustrated in Figure 6.2. The three time series graphed there were generated from processes for which simple exponential smoothing with smoothing constants 0.1,

FIGURE 6.2   Generated time series for which simple exponential smoothing yields optimal forecasts. (a) $\alpha = 0.1$ (b) $\alpha = 0.5$ (c) $\alpha = 0.9$.

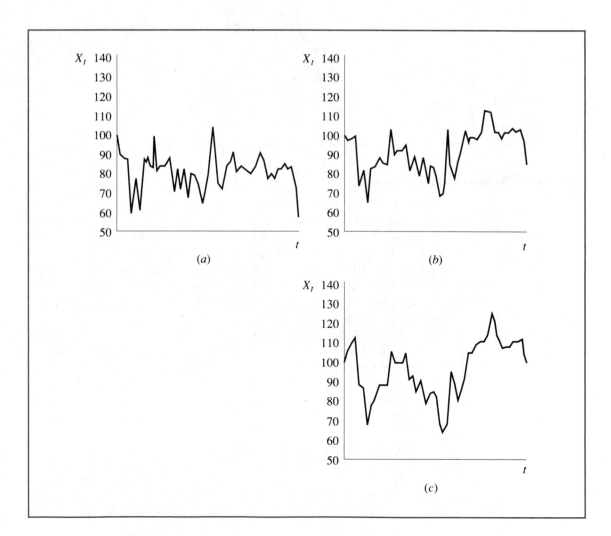

0.5, and 0.9 yields optimal forecasts. They also clarify how the choice of smoothing constant depends on the characteristics of a time series. The graph in part (a) of Figure 6.2 has a very jagged appearance. A large change in one direction is very likely to be followed by a large change in the opposite direction. In such circumstances it would be very poor strategy to give much weight to the last available observation in forecasting future values. In fact, the best choice of smoothing constant here is 0.1. As we move through the intermediate case in part (b) of the figure to the series graphed in part (c), increasing smoothness can be noted. Thus, the series in part (c) exhibits a wandering behavior so that distant experience can be very far removed from the current value, which appears to evolve from the previous one in generally modest steps. For such series it is best, in forming forecasts, to give high weight to the most recent observation, and consequently very little weight to all previous data. The best choice of smoothing constant for the series of Figure 6.2(c) is $\alpha = 0.9$. If the progression in Figure 6.2 is continued to the extreme case where $\alpha = 1$, a slightly smoother series yet will result. An example of a time series of this sort, where the current observation is the best forecast of the future, is provided by the prices of common stocks.

We do not claim that the visual judgmental choice of smoothing constant is either easy or reliable without a good deal of experience. The task is considerably more difficult for more elaborate exponential smoothing algorithms that may involve two or three different smoothing constants (to be discussed in subsequent sections of this chapter). For this reason, a more objective means of selecting smoothing constant values is desirable. One possibility is to try several different values, using each to calculate forecasts of the observed data series, and then select that value which has proved most successful. Typically, this choice is based on the quality of one-step-ahead forecasts. Suppose the analyst has available a time series of n observations, denoted $X_1, X_2, \ldots, X_n$. Then, after initialization, the algorithm 6.2.4 can be employed, for any value α, to compute the level estimates $L_2, L_3, \ldots, L_n$. As we have seen, the forecast of X_t, made at time $t - 1$ is L_{t-1}, so that

$$\hat{X}_{t-1}(1) = L_{t-1} \qquad t = 3, \ldots, n$$

Denoting by e_t the error in this forecast, we have

$$e_t = X_t - L_{t-1} \qquad t = 3, \ldots, n \qquad (6.2.6)$$

For any choice of smoothing constant, the set of in-sample, one-step forecast errors in equation 6.2.6 can be calculated. It seems reasonable to prefer the value of α that yields forecast errors that are smallest in magnitude. It is useful to choose a grid of values for the smoothing constant, say $\alpha = 0.1, 0.2, \ldots, 0.9$, calculate the corresponding error series with equation 6.2.6, and then choose for subsequent use that value of α for which the sum of squared one-step forecast errors

$$S = \sum_{t=3}^{n} e_t^2$$

is smallest. This and similar objective approaches to the choice of smoothing constants certainly adds to the computational cost of employing an exponential smoothing algorithm. However, given modern computing power, it is likely that these additional costs will be more than balanced by the benefits from better quality forecasts. Notice also that, once a value has been chosen for the smoothing constant, it will still be unnecessary to store the whole past history of a time series.

Error-Correction Form of the Algorithm

The recurrence form, 6.2.4, of the simple exponential smoothing algorithm is quite satisfactory for purposes of computation. However, an alternative form yields useful insight into the structure of the predictor. As before, denote the forecast of X_t made at time $(t - 1)$ and the corresponding forecast error by

$$\hat{X}_{t-1}(1) = L_{t-1} \qquad e_t = X_t - L_{t-1}$$

Substitution for X_t in equation 6.2.4 then gives

$$L_t = \alpha(L_{t-1} + e_t) + (1 - \alpha)L_{t-1}$$

or

$$L_t = L_{t-1} + \alpha e_t \qquad 0 < \alpha < 1 \qquad (6.2.7)$$

This is known as the **error-correction form** of the simple exponential smoothing algorithm.

According to equation 6.2.7 the estimate of level at time t is the sum of the previous estimate of level and a multiple of the error that was made in the prediction of X_t at time $(t - 1)$. We might therefore think of the forecasting system as learning from past prediction errors. If L_{t-1} turns out to be a perfect forecast of X_t, so that the error e_t is zero, there is no good reason to modify this level estimate. However, suppose that this forecast is less than the actual outcome, so that the forecast error is positive. It seems natural to react to this error by increasing the estimate of the level of the series; the larger the error, the greater the adjustment that is made. This is precisely what is implied in formula 6.2.7. Conversely, if the forecast of X_t exceeds the actual outcome, the level estimate will be proportionately reduced.

The error-correction form 6.2.7 also sheds some light on the part played by the smoothing constant. It can be seen that, the larger is α, the larger the adjustment that is made to the level estimate when a given forecast error is observed. For series, such as that of Figure 6.2(a), with a very jagged, erratic appearance, only a small adjustment would be desirable, since it appears that any substantial increase or decrease in the value of the series is likely to be reversed, the process quite possibly returning to something close to its previous level. On the other hand, for smoother series, such as that of Figure 6.2(c), it is important that the forecasting algorithm tracks any changes, requiring a high value for the smoothing constant.

6.3 HOLT'S LINEAR TREND ALGORITHM

The simple exponential smoothing algorithm yields constant forecasts for all future values of a time series. In some situations, the observed data will contain information that allows the anticipation of future upward or downward movements. In that case, rather than a constant forecast function, some trending function would be preferable. The simplest possibility of this sort is a *linear trend forecast function*. It is not necessary that the time series exhibit a fixed linear trend; this will rarely, if ever, be the case for business and economic series. Instead, we consider the possibility of evolving local linear trend over time. Holt (1957) developed an exponential smoothing algorithm that allows for local linear trend in a time series. In this section, we continue to concentrate on the nonseasonal case, postponing to Section 6.4 a discussion of forecasting algorithms for series with a seasonal component.

Just as in simple exponential smoothing, an estimate of the *current level* of the time series is required. Also, since upward or downward movement is to be anticipated, we also need an estimate of the *current slope*, or change in level, of the series. **Holt's linear trend algorithm** provides estimates of level and slope that adapt over time as new observations become available. The recurrence form of this algorithm is

$$L_t = \alpha X_t + (1 - \alpha)(L_{t-1} + T_{t-1}) \qquad 0 < \alpha < 1 \quad (6.3.1a)$$

$$T_t = \beta(L_t - L_{t-1}) + (1 - \beta)T_{t-1} \qquad 0 < \beta < 1 \quad (6.3.1b)$$

where L_t and T_t are estimates of level and slope at time t, and α and β are smoothing constants, whose values are generally between zero and one. Equations 6.3.1 are in similar form to the simple exponential smoothing algorithm 6.2.4, and have similar justifications. Standing at time $(t - 1)$, the latest estimates of level and slope are L_{t-1} and T_{t-1}, which suggest a new level $(L_{t-1} + T_{t-1})$ for time t, since the level is expected to increase by the amount of the slope. At time t, we obtain the new observation X_t, providing further information about the level of the series at that time. In equation 6.3.1a the level at time t is estimated as a weighted average of X_t and $(L_{t-1} + T_{t-1})$. The new observation also provides additional information about the slope of the series. Slope at time t is estimated in equation 6.3.1b as a weighted average of the most recent change in estimated levels, $(L_t - L_{t-1})$, and the previous slope estimate, T_{t-1}.

Equations 6.3.1 are in very convenient form for the computation through recursive calculations of level and slope estimates. Again, minimal storage is required, since only the most recent slope and level estimates need to be retained, together with the last observation on the time series. Standing at time t, we will have available the estimates L_t and T_t. Forecasts of future observations then follow from an assumption of a continued period-by-period increase in the amount of the latest slope estimate from a base provided by the latest level estimate. Thus, the forecast of X_{t+h} made at time t is

$$\hat{X}_t(h) = L_t + hT_t \qquad h = 1, 2, 3, \ldots \qquad (6.3.2)$$

Figure 6.3 shows data generated from a process for which it is known that Holt's linear trend algorithm (in this particular case, with both smoothing constants equal to 0.5) yields optimal forecasts. Comparison of this picture with the graphs of Figure 6.2 indicates the circumstances in which Holt's algorithm rather than simple exponential smoothing is appropriate. Notice that the series of Figure 6.3 exhibits periods of pronounced general upward and downward trend, together of course with inevitable irregularities. This trend pattern is far from constant over the entire observation period, but instead evolves gradually through time.

To illustrate the calculations required for the Holt algorithm, we consider again the series of 30 annual product sales figures that were discussed in Chapter 5 and are set out in Table 5.2. For convenience, the data are reproduced in the X_t column of Table 6.2. We will use smoothing constants $\alpha = 0.5$ and $\beta = 0.3$, so that the algorithm is

$$L_t = 0.5X_t + 0.5(L_{t-1} + T_{t-1})$$
$$T_t = 0.3(L_t - L_{t-1}) + 0.7T_{t-1}$$

As with all exponential smoothing algorithms, initial values are required

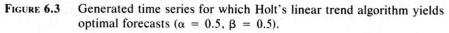

FIGURE 6.3   Generated time series for which Holt's linear trend algorithm yields optimal forecasts ($\alpha = 0.5$, $\beta = 0.5$).

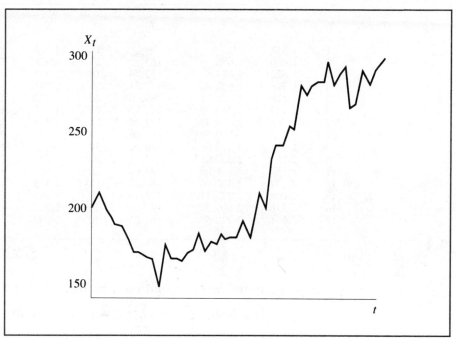

to start up the calculations. A number of possibilities are available. One simple solution is to set

$$L_2 = X_2 \qquad T_2 = X_2 - X_1$$

and begin the calculations with $t = 3$. For the data of Table 6.2, we then have

$$L_2 = 1{,}650 \qquad T_2 = 1{,}650 - 1{,}813 = -163$$

Then, for year three,

$$L_3 = 0.5X_3 + 0.5(L_2 + T_2) = (0.5)(1{,}822)$$
$$+ 0.5(1{,}650 - 163) = 1{,}654.5$$

and

$$T_3 = 0.3(L_3 - L_2) + 0.7T_2 = 0.3(1{,}654.5 - 1{,}650)$$
$$+ (0.7)(-163) = -112.75$$

TABLE 6.2   Application of Holt's linear trend algorithm ($\alpha = 0.5$, $\beta = 0.3$) to annual sales data.

t	X_t	L_t	T_t	t	X_t	L_t	T_t
1	1,813			16	2,178	2,533.68	62.15
2	1,650	1,650	−163	17	1,928	2,261.91	−38.03
3	1,822	1,654.5	−112.75	18	1,911	2,067.44	−84.96
4	1,778	1,659.88	−77.31	19	1,991	1,986.74	−83.68
5	1,520	1,551.28	−86.70	20	1,788	1,845.53	−100.94
6	1,103	1,283.79	−140.93	21	1,693	1,718.79	−108.68
7	1,266	1,204.43	−122.46	22	1,871	1,740.56	−69.55
8	1,478	1,279.98	−63.06	23	1,899	1.785.01	−35.35
9	1,431	1,323.96	−30.95	24	1,693	1,721.33	−43.85
10	1,767	1,530.01	40.15	25	1,633	1,655.24	−50.52
11	2,162	1,866.08	128.93	26	1,666	1,635.36	−41.33
12	2,337	2,166.00	180.23	27	1,575	1,584.52	−44.18
13	2,608	2,477.11	219.49	28	1,395	1,467.67	−65.98
14	2,518	2,607.30	192.70	29	1,389	1,395.34	−67.89
15	2,641	2,720.50	168.85	30	1,297	1,312.23	−72.45

Continuing in this way, we find for year four,

$$L_4 = 0.5X_4 + 0.5(L_3 + T_3) = (0.5)(1,778)$$
$$+ 0.5(1,654.5 - 112.75) = 1,659.875$$
$$T_4 = 0.3(L_4 - L_3) + 0.7T_3 = 0.3(1,659.875 - 1,654.5)$$
$$+ (0.7)(-112.75) = -77.3125$$

The remaining estimates, found in the same way and rounded to two decimal places, are given in Table 6.2. Notice in particular how the slope estimates track the evolving trend pattern in this time series.

Having reached this point, forecasts of future values are easily found using equation 6.3.2. Standing at time 30, the forecasts are

$$\hat{X}_{30}(h) = L_{30} + hT_{30} = 1,312 - 72h \qquad h = 1, 2, 3, \ldots$$

where the level and slope estimates have been rounded to the nearest integer. Sales forecasts for the next five years are therefore 1,240, 1,168, 1,096, 1,024, 952. The time series and these forecasts are graphed in Figure 6.4. As we have already noted, it is a property of this algorithm that the forecast function is a straight line.

Choice of Smoothing Constants

Holt's linear trend algorithm depends on two smoothing constants, α and β defined in equation 6.3.1, both of which must be fixed before forecasts

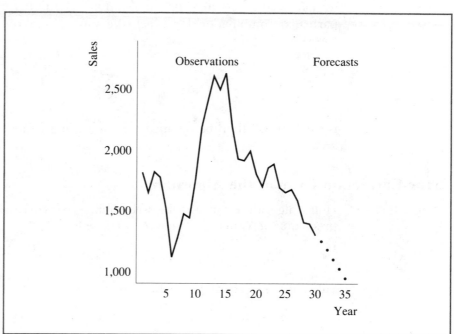

FIGURE 6.4   Annual sales and forecasts from Holt's linear trend algorithm (α = 0.5, β = 0.3).

can be obtained. As was the case for simple exponential smoothing, these values can be chosen subjectively or objectively. It is certainly possible that successful past experience with similar series can be called upon, but basing the choice on a visual examination of a plot of the data is more tricky here. As before, as the evolution of the level of the time series appears smoother, the appropriate value for α becomes higher. Similarly, if the slope appears to change quite smoothly over time, this suggests a relatively high value for the smoothing constant β. In practice, however, it can be quite difficult to make these two judgments simultaneously.

The smoothing constants can also be chosen as those values minimizing the sum of squared one-step forecast errors over the observation period. Given a time series $X_1, X_2, \ldots, X_n$, suppose as in our example that, after setting initial values, the algorithm 6.3.1 is applied for $t = 3, 4, \ldots, n$. Then, the forecast of X_t, made at time $(t - 1)$ is

$$\hat{X}_{t-1}(1) = L_{t-1} + T_{t-1} \qquad t = 4, \ldots, n$$

so that the forecast error will be

$$e_t = X_t - \hat{X}_{t-1}(1) = X_t - L_{t-1} - T_{t-1} \qquad t = 4, \ldots, n$$

In practice a grid of possible pairs of values (α, β) of the smoothing constants can be tried; for example, we might examine the 25 combinations with $\alpha = 0.1, 0.3, 0.5, 0.7, 0.9$ and $\beta = 0.1, 0.3, 0.5, 0.7, 0.9$. The particular combination for which the sum of squared one-step forecast errors

$$S = \sum_{t=4}^{n} e_t^2$$

is smallest will then be retained for forecasting future values of the time series.

Error-Correction Form of the Algorithm

Holt's algorithm can also be written in error-correction form. For the prediction of X_t made at time $(t - 1)$, we have

$$\hat{X}_{t-1}(1) = L_{t-1} + T_{t-1} \qquad e_t = X_t - L_{t-1} - T_{t-1}$$

Substitution in equation 6.3.1a yields

$$L_t = \alpha(L_{t-1} + T_{t-1} + e_t) + (1 - \alpha)(L_{t-1} + T_{t-1})$$
$$= L_{t-1} + T_{t-1} + \alpha e_t$$

Substituting this result in equation 6.3.1b we then obtain

$$T_t = \beta(T_{t-1} + \alpha e_t) + (1 - \beta)T_{t-1}$$
$$= T_{t-1} + \alpha\beta e_t$$

The error-correction form of Holt's linear trend algorithm is therefore

$$L_t = L_{t-1} + T_{t-1} + \alpha e_t \qquad 0 < \alpha < 1 \qquad (6.3.3a)$$
$$T_t = T_{t-1} + \alpha\beta e_t \qquad 0 < \beta < 1 \qquad (6.3.3b)$$

These equations indicate how forecast errors lead to modifications of previously made level and slope estimates. Suppose that, at time $(t - 1)$, we were fortunate enough to have made a perfect forecast of X_t, so that the error e_t is zero. This happy outcome will cause no revision in our estimate of the slope, while the previous level estimate L_{t-1} is simply updated at time t by adding on the slope estimate T_{t-1}. However, if the forecast is below the actual outcome, so that the error e_t is positive, we might suspect the cause to be a greater than anticipated level, or an increased slope. In fact, the algorithm reacts by raising both the level and slope estimates at time t above those that would have been made in the case of a perfect forecast. These adjustments are proportional to the size of the forecast error. Similarly, downward adjustments to the level and slope estimates will be made if the forecast of X_t is higher than the actual outcome. The magnitudes of the modifications made when forecast errors of any given size are observed depend on the values of the smoothing constants. A small value of α, which is appropriate for a series with erratic level, implies a relatively modest modification of the previously implied level estimate. Similarly, a small value of β, as would be used for series with erratic slope, leads to only a minor adjustment to the previous slope estimate. Notice that the size of the slope estimate adjustment depends also on the smoothing constant α. This is reasonable, for, if the behavior of the level of a series is erratic, we would not want this behavior to be interpreted as a change in slope. A low value of α in equation 6.3.3b guards against this possibility.

6.4   THE HOLT-WINTERS ALGORITHM FOR SEASONAL TIME SERIES

The major advantage of exponential smoothing algorithms lies in their ability to produce quite reliable short-term forecasts relatively quickly for a large collection of time series. This is particularly valuable as an input to inventory management, for which monthly, or perhaps quarterly, sales forecasts are needed. However, for a great many products, sales have a strong seasonal component, so that it is obviously desirable to extend exponential smoothing algorithms to allow for seasonality. Holt's algorithm was extended in this way by Winters (1960). In fact, there are two possible lines of development, depending on whether seasonality is taken to be additive or multiplicative. In the additive seasonality framework, we view the removal of seasonality from a series as requiring the subtraction of a seasonal factor, whereas if multiplicative seasonality is assumed then seasonality would be purged through division by a seasonal factor. We will introduce both the additive and multiplicative variants of the **Holt-Winters algorithm.**

Additive Seasonality

Retaining the notation of the previous section, given observations X_t on a time series, estimates L_t and T_t of current level and slope are again required. In addition, for each time period it is necessary to estimate an additive seasonal factor F_t. Denote by s the number of periods per year, so that $s = 4$ for quarterly data and $s = 12$ for monthly data. Then, if we are standing at time t, the last available seasonal factor estimate for this period of the year will be F_{t-s}, obtained from the corresponding period of last year. In common with the exponential smoothing algorithms discussed in previous sections, the Holt-Winters algorithm employs a new observation to update previous estimates, with a recurrence form using weighted averages. These updating equations are

$$L_t = \alpha(X_t - F_{t-s}) + (1 - \alpha)(L_{t-1} + T_{t-1}) \qquad 0 < \alpha < 1$$

$$(6.4.1a)$$

$$T_t = \beta(L_t - L_{t-1}) + (1 - \beta)T_{t-1} \qquad 0 < \beta < 1 \quad (6.4.1b)$$

$$F_t = \gamma(X_t - L_t) + (1 - \gamma)F_{t-s} \qquad 0 < \gamma < 1 \qquad (6.4.1c)$$

where α, β, and γ are smoothing constants. Equation 6.4.1a, which yields the current level estimate, is very similar to the corresponding equation 6.3.1a of Holt's linear trend algorithm. Again, before X_t is observed, the projected level at time $(t - 1)$ is $(L_{t-1} + T_{t-1})$. The new observation X_t involves a seasonal component, so that, in assessing the level of the series, we subtract F_{t-s}, the last available estimate of the seasonal factor for this period of the year. Then, in equation 6.4.1a, current level is estimated as a weighted average of $(X_t - F_{t-s})$ and $(L_{t-1} + T_{t-1})$. Equation 6.4.1b, through which the estimate of current slope is obtained, is identical to equation 6.3.1b of Holt's linear trend algorithm. Finally, in equation 6.4.1c, the estimate of the current seasonal factor for the period of the new observation is derived. The latest available seasonal factor estimate for this period is F_{t-s}, and additional information about this factor is obtained by subtracting from the new observation estimated current level. The new seasonal factor estimate is then obtained as a weighted average. Notice that, once this estimate of the seasonal factor for a period has been calculated, it will not be updated until another year has elapsed.

The repetitive nature of the calculations in equations 6.4.1 make them ideally suited for programming on an electronic computer. Storage requirements are simply the most recent observation, the latest level and slope estimates, and the last s seasonal factor estimates—one for each period of the year.

Standing at time t, the forecast of X_{t+h} is obtained by projecting forward h periods the latest slope estimate, with the latest level estimate as base, and then adding on the last available seasonal factor estimate for the period of the year in which time $t + h$ occurs. Thus, the forecast is

$$\hat{X}_t(h) = L_t + hT_t + F_{t+h-s} \qquad h = 1, 2, \ldots, s$$

$$= L_t + hT_t + F_{t+h-2s} \qquad h = s + 1, s + 2, \ldots, 2s$$

$$(6.4.2)$$

and so on. The forecast function is a straight line, with superimposed additive seasonal factors.

To illustrate this algorithm, we consider again the series of quarterly sales figures discussed in Chapter 5, and tabulated in Table 5.1: The data are shown in the X_t column of Table 6.3. We will compute forecasts using the smoothing constants $\alpha = 0.3$, $\beta = 0.4$, and $\gamma = 0.5$, so that from equation 6.4.1 the recurrence equations are

$$L_t = 0.3(X_t - F_{t-4}) + 0.7(L_{t-1} + T_{t-1}) \qquad (6.4.3a)$$

$$T_t = 0.4(L_t - L_{t-1}) + 0.6T_{t-1} \qquad (6.4.3b)$$

$$F_t = 0.5(X_t - L_t) + 0.5F_{t-4} \qquad (6.4.3c)$$

Initial values are required to start up the calculations, and any number of alternatives have been proposed and employed. A particularly simple procedure that has been found to work well in practice (Chatfield 1978)

TABLE 6.3   Application of Holt-Winters additive seasonal algorithm ($\alpha = 0.3$, $\beta = 0.4$, $\gamma = 0.5$) to quarterly sales data.

t	X_t	L_t	T_t	F_t
1	897			332.50
2	476			−88.50
3	376			−188.50
4	509	564.50	0	−55.50
5	967	585.50	8.40	357.00
6	529	600.98	11.23	−80.24
7	407	607.20	9.23	−194.35
8	371	559.45	−13.56	−121.97
9	884	540.22	−15.83	350.39
10	407	513.24	−20.29	−93.24
11	310	496.37	−18.92	−190.36
12	338	472.21	−21.02	−128.09
13	900	480.72	−9.21	384.84
14	448	492.43	−0.84	−68.83
15	344	504.42	4.29	−175.39
16	274	476.73	−8.50	−165.41
17	740	434.31	−22.07	345.27
18	261	387.52	−31.96	−97.68
19	289	388.21	−18.90	−137.30
20	319	403.84	−5.09	−125.12
21	1,036	486.35	29.95	447.46
22	602	571.31	51.96	−33.49
23	536	638.28	57.96	−119.79
24	349	629.60	31.31	−202.86
25	1,050	643.40	24.30	427.03
26	633	667.34	24.16	−33.92
27	435	650.48	7.75	−167.64
28	415	646.13	2.91	−216.99

starts the calculations at the first period of the second year, with slope for the last period of the first year set at zero, so that in our example we would have

$$T_4 = 0$$

The initial level estimate, required for the final period of the first year, is taken to be the average of the observations in that year. Thus we set

$$L_4 = \frac{(X_1 + X_2 + X_3 + X_4)}{4}$$

$$= \frac{(897 + 476 + 376 + 509)}{4} = 564.5$$

This initial level estimate is then subtracted from the observations to obtain the first year seasonal factors, so that

$$F_1 = 897 - 564.5 = 332.5 \qquad F_2 = 476 - 564.5 = -88.5$$

$$F_3 = 376 - 564.5 = -188.5 \qquad F_4 = 509 - 564.5 = -55.5$$

Equations 6.4.3 can then be applied in turn for $t = 5, 6, \ldots$. For quarter five, we obtain

$$L_5 = 0.3(X_5 - F_1) + 0.7(L_4 + T_4)$$

$$= 0.3(967 - 332.5) + 0.7(564.5 + 0) = 585.5$$

$$T_5 = 0.4(L_5 - L_4) + 0.6T_4 = 0.4(585.5 - 564.5)$$

$$+ (0.6)(0) = 8.4$$

$$F_5 = 0.5(X_5 - L_5) + 0.5F_1 = 0.5(967 - 585.5)$$

$$+ (0.5)(332.5) = 357$$

Similarly, for quarter six,

$$L_6 = 0.3(X_6 - F_2) + 0.7(L_5 + T_5)$$

$$= 0.3(529 + 88.5) + 0.7(585.5 + 8.4) = 600.98$$

$$T_6 = 0.4(L_6 - L_5) + 0.6T_5 = 0.4(600.98 - 585.5)$$

$$+ (0.6)(8.4) = 11.232$$

$$F_6 = 0.5(X_6 - L_6) + 0.5F_2 = 0.5(529 - 600.98)$$

$$+ (0.5)(-88.5) = -80.24$$

The calculations continue this way through the final observation period, yielding the results given, to two decimal places, in Table 6.3.

To compute forecasts of future sales, we require the latest slope and level estimates, and the last year's seasonal factors; these are

$$L_{28} = 646.13, \quad T_{28} = 2.91, \quad F_{25} = 427.03, \quad F_{26} = -33.92,$$
$$F_{27} = -167.64, \quad F_{28} = -216.99$$

Then, using equation 6.4.2, the forecasts for next year are

$$\hat{X}_{28}(1) = L_{28} + T_{28} + F_{25} = 646.13 + 2.91 + 427.03 = 1{,}076$$
$$\hat{X}_{28}(2) = L_{28} + 2T_{28} + F_{26} = 646.13 + (2)(2.91) - 33.92 = 618$$
$$\hat{X}_{28}(3) = L_{28} + 3T_{28} + F_{27} = 646.13 + (3)(2.91) - 167.64 = 487$$
$$\hat{X}_{28}(4) = L_{28} + 4T_{28} + F_{28} = 646.13 + (4)(2.91) - 216.99 = 441$$

Similarly, for the following year,

$$\hat{X}_{28}(5) = L_{28} + 5T_{28} + F_{25} = 646.13 + (5)(2.91) + 427.03 = 1{,}088$$
$$\hat{X}_{28}(6) = L_{28} + 6T_{28} + F_{26} = 646.13 + (6)(2.91) - 33.92 = 630$$
$$\hat{X}_{28}(7) = L_{28} + 7T_{28} + F_{27} = 646.13 + (7)(2.91) - 167.64 = 499$$
$$\hat{X}_{28}(8) = L_{28} + 8T_{28} + F_{28} = 646.13 + (8)(2.91) - 216.\,99 = 452$$

Continuing in this way, forecasts as far ahead as required can be derived. Figure 6.5 shows the series and the forecasts up to eight quarters ahead.

As with other exponential smoothing algorithms, the smoothing constants for the Holt-Winters algorithm can be chosen either subjectively or objectively, as those values for which the sum of squared in-sample one-step forecast errors is smallest. However, it is particularly difficult to reliably select the values of three different smoothing constants from visual inspection of a plotted time series.

The algorithm 6.4.1 can also be written in error-correction form. From equation 6.4.2, the one-step ahead forecast at time $(t - 1)$, and associated forecast error are

$$\hat{X}_{t-1}(1) = L_{t-1} + T_{t-1} + F_{t-s} \qquad e_t = X_t - L_{t-1} - T_{t-1} - F_{t-s}$$

$$(6.4.4)$$

Substitution in equation 6.4.1a gives

$$L_t = \alpha(L_{t-1} + T_{t-1} + e_t) + (1 - \alpha)(L_{t-1} + T_{t-1}) \qquad (6.4.5)$$
$$= L_{t-1} + T_{t-1} + \alpha e_t$$

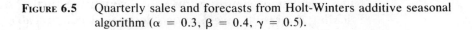

FIGURE 6.5   Quarterly sales and forecasts from Holt-Winters additive seasonal
algorithm ($\alpha = 0.3$, $\beta = 0.4$, $\gamma = 0.5$).

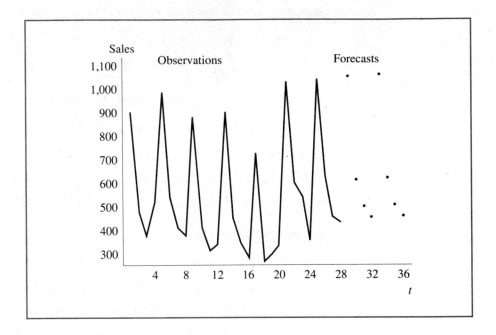

Substituting this result in equation 6.4.1b yields

$$T_t = \beta(T_{t-1} + \alpha e_t) + (1 - \beta)T_{t-1}$$

$$= T_{t-1} + \alpha\beta e_t$$

Finally, from equations 6.4.1c, 6.4.4 and 6.4.5, we find

$$F_t = \gamma[(L_{t-1} + T_{t-1} + F_{t-s} + e_t) - (L_{t-1} + T_{t-1} + \alpha e_t)]$$

$$+ (1 - \gamma)F_{t-s}$$

$$= F_{t-s} + \gamma(1 - \alpha)e_t$$

The error-correction form of the Holt-Winters additive seasonal algorithm
is therefore

$$L_t = L_{t-1} + T_{t-1} + \alpha e_t \qquad 0 < \alpha < 1 \qquad (6.4.6a)$$

$$T_t = T_{t-1} + \alpha\beta e_t \qquad 0 < \beta < 1 \qquad (6.4.6b)$$

$$F_t = F_{t-s} + \gamma(1 - \alpha)e_t \qquad 0 < \gamma < 1 \qquad (6.4.6c)$$

Notice that the first two of these equations are precisely the same as the error-correction equations 6.3.3 in Holt's linear trend algorithm. According to equation 6.4.6c, at time t the seasonal factor is obtained by adding to the seasonal factor for the same period of the previous year a multiple of the one-step forecast error made in predicting X_t. Thus, for example, if X_t is underpredicted, the seasonal factor for this period is increased. The larger the smoothing constant γ, the larger the adjustment made for any given forecast error. Thus, in line with our previous discussion, a high value of γ is desirable for a series with a smoothly changing seasonal pattern, while a lower value would be preferable if the seasonal pattern is more erratic.

Multiplicative Seasonality

The Holt-Winters algorithm is employed more often in a variant that assumes a multiplicative seasonal factor. Retaining our previous notation, but now with F_t denoting a multiplicative rather than an additive seasonal factor, the recurrence form of the algorithm is

$$L_t = \alpha X_t / F_{t-s} + (1 - \alpha)(L_{t-1} + T_{t-1}) \qquad 0 < \alpha < 1$$

$$\text{(6.4.7a)}$$

$$T_t = \beta(L_t - L_{t-1}) + (1 - \beta)T_{t-1} \qquad 0 < \beta < 1 \quad \text{(6.4.7b)}$$

$$F_t = \gamma X_t / L_t + (1 - \gamma)F_{t-s} \qquad 0 < \gamma < 1 \qquad \text{(6.4.7c)}$$

The second of these equations is identical to equation 6.4.1b. The only differences in the first and third equations in 6.4.7 from the corresponding equations of 6.4.1 arise because now we view an observation as the *product* of level and a seasonal factor. For this reason, the forecast of X_{t+h}, made at time t, is now obtained from

$$\begin{aligned} \hat{X}_t(h) &= (L_t + hT_t)F_{t+h-s} \qquad h = 1, 2, \ldots, s \\ &= (L_t + hT_t)F_{t+h-2s} \qquad h = s + 1, \; s + 2, \ldots, 2s \end{aligned} \qquad \text{(6.4.8)}$$

and so on.

To illustrate, we again derive forecasts of our quarterly sales series, with smoothing constants $\alpha = 0.3$, $\beta = 0.4$, and $\gamma = 0.5$. The recurrence equations 6.4.7 are then

$$L_t = \frac{0.3X_t}{F_{t-4}} + 0.7(L_{t-1} + T_{t-1}) \qquad \text{(6.4.9a)}$$

$$T_t = 0.4(L_t - L_{t-1}) + 0.6T_{t-1} \qquad \text{(6.4.9b)}$$

$$F_t = \frac{0.5X_t}{L_t} + 0.5F_{t-4} \qquad \text{(6.4.9c)}$$

The initial values for slope and level, as before, are set at

$$T_4 = 0 \quad L_4 = 564.5$$

However, since now the seasonal factors are multiplicative, these factors for the first year are set at

$$F_1 = 897/564.5 = 1.589017 \quad F_2 = 476/564.5 = 0.843224$$
$$F_3 = 376/564.5 = 0.666076 \quad F_4 = 509/564.5 = 0.901683$$

Equations 6.4.9 are then applied in turn for $t = 5, 6, \ldots$. For quarter five, this yields

$$L_5 = \frac{0.3X_5}{F_1} + 0.7(L_4 + T_4)$$

$$= 0.3\left(\frac{967}{1.589017}\right) + 0.7(564.5 + 0) = 577.71569$$

$$T_5 = 0.4(L_5 - L_4) + 0.6T_4$$

$$= 0.4(577.71569 - 564.5) + (0.6)(0) = 5.286276$$

$$F_5 = \frac{0.5X_5}{L_5} + 0.5F_1 = 0.5\left(\frac{967}{577.71569}\right)$$

$$+ (0.5)(1.589017) = 1.631425$$

Then, for quarter six we find

$$L_6 = 0.3\frac{X_6}{F_2} + 0.7(L_5 + T_5) = 0.3\left(\frac{529}{0.843224}\right)$$

$$+ 0.7(577.71569 + 5.286276) = 596.30758$$

$$T_6 = 0.4(L_6 - L_5) + 0.6T_5 = 0.4(596.30758 - 577.71569)$$

$$+ (0.6)(5.286276) = 10.608521$$

$$F_6 = 0.5\frac{X_6}{L_6} + 0.5F_2 = 0.5\left(\frac{529}{596.30758}\right)$$

$$+ (0.5)(0.84324) = 0.865175$$

The calculations are continued in this way through the last observation period, giving the results shown in Table 6.4.

TABLE 6.4   Application of Holt-Winters multiplicative seasonal algorithm
($\alpha = 0.3$, $\beta = 0.4$, $\gamma = 0.5$) to quarterly sales data.

t	X_t	L_t	T_t	F_t
1	897			1.589
2	476			0.843
3	376			0.666
4	509	564.50	0	0.902
5	967	577.72	5.29	1.631
6	529	596.31	10.61	0.865
7	407	608.15	11.10	0.668
8	371	556.92	−13.83	0.784
9	884	542.72	−13.98	1.630
10	407	511.24	−20.98	0.831
11	310	482.48	−24.09	0.655
12	338	450.22	−27.36	0.767
13	900	461.63	−11.85	1.790
14	448	476.65	−1.10	0.885
15	344	490.42	4.85	0.678
16	274	453.81	−11.74	0.686
17	740	433.48	−15.17	1.748
18	261	381.27	−29.99	0.785
19	289	373.72	−21.01	0.726
20	319	386.49	−7.50	0.755
21	1,036	443.05	18.12	2.043
22	602	552.91	54.82	0.937
23	536	646.96	70.51	0.777
24	349	640.82	39.85	0.650
25	1,050	630.62	19.83	1.854
26	633	658.02	22.86	0.949
27	435	644.54	8.32	0.726
28	415	648.53	6.59	0.645

The quantities needed to derive forecasts of future sales are, from Table 6.4,

$$L_{28} = 648.53, \quad T_{28} = 6.59, \quad F_{25} = 1.854, \quad F_{26} = 0.949,$$
$$F_{27} = 0.726, \quad F_{28} = 0.645$$

Forecasts are then found from equation 6.4.8. For the next year, we find

$$\hat{X}_{28}(1) = (L_{28} + T_{28})F_{25} = (648.53 + 6.59)1.854 = 1,215$$
$$\hat{X}_{28}(2) = (L_{28} + 2T_{28})F_{26} = (648.53 + 13.18)0.949 = 628$$
$$\hat{X}_{28}(3) = (L_{28} + 3T_{28})F_{27} = (648.53 + 19.77)0.726 = 485$$
$$\hat{X}_{28}(4) = (L_{28} + 4T_{28})F_{28} = (648.53 + 26.36)0.645 = 435$$

In the same way, the forecasts for the following year are

$$\hat{X}_{28}(5) = (L_{28} + 5T_{28})F_{25} = (648.53 + 32.95)1.854 = 1{,}263$$

$$\hat{X}_{28}(6) = (L_{28} + 6T_{28})F_{26} = (648.53 + 39.54)0.949 = 653$$

$$\hat{X}_{28}(7) = (L_{28} + 7T_{28})F_{27} = (648.53 + 46.13)0.726 = 504$$

$$\hat{X}_{28}(8) = (L_{28} + 8T_{28})F_{28} = (648.53 + 52.72)0.645 = 452$$

These forecasts are very similar to those from the additive seasonal algorithm, except in the first quarter of each year where the multiplicative seasonal algorithm yields appreciably higher forecasts. The observations in the first quarter of the year differ substantially from the seasonality-free level for this time series, and it is precisely in such circumstances that the choice of multiplicative or additive assumed seasonality can be expected to make a significant difference.

The algorithm 6.4.7 can also be written in error-correction form, though because of the multiplicativity this is not quite so elegant as for other algorithms. It follows from equation 6.4.8 that the one-step forecast made at time $(t - 1)$ and associated error are

$$\hat{X}_{t-1}(1) = (L_{t-1} + T_{t-1})F_{t-s} \qquad e_t = X_t - (L_{t-1} + T_{t-1})F_{t-s}$$

$$(6.4.10)$$

Substitution of equation 6.4.10 into equation 6.4.7a gives

$$L_t = \alpha \left[(L_{t-1} + T_{t-1}) + \frac{e_t}{F_{t-s}} \right] + (1 - \alpha)(L_{t-1} + T_{t-1})$$

$$= L_{t-1} + T_{t-1} + \frac{\alpha e_t}{F_{t-s}}$$

$$(6.4.11)$$

Next, substitution of equation 6.4.11 into equation 6.4.7b yields

$$T_t = \beta \left(T_{t-1} + \frac{\alpha e_t}{F_{t-s}} \right) + (1 - \beta)T_{t-1}$$

$$= T_{t-1} + \frac{\alpha \beta e_t}{F_{t-s}}$$

Finally, from equations 6.4.7c, 6.4.10 and 6.4.11 we find for the seasonal factor

$$F_t = \frac{\gamma[(L_{t-1} + T_{t-1})F_{t-s} + e_t]}{L_t} + (1 - \gamma)F_{t-s}$$

$$= \frac{\gamma(L_t F_{t-s} - \alpha e_t + e_t)}{L_t} + (1 - \gamma)F_{t-s}$$

$$= F_{t-s} + \gamma(1 - \alpha)\frac{e_t}{L_t}$$

The error-correction form of the Holt-Winters multiplicative seasonal algorithm is then

$$L_t = L_{t-1} + T_{t-1} + \frac{\alpha e_t}{F_{t-s}} \qquad 0 < \alpha < 1$$

$$T_t = T_{t-1} + \frac{\alpha\beta e_t}{F_{t-s}} \qquad 0 < \beta < 1$$

$$F_t = F_{t-s} + \frac{\gamma(1 - \alpha)e_t}{L_t} \qquad 0 < \gamma < 1$$

In practice, the algorithmic calculations can be carried out either with these equations or with the recurrence equations 6.4.7.

As we have seen, the Holt-Winters additive and multiplicative algorithms can yield quite different forecasts of future values of a time series, so that the choice between them may not be a matter of indifference. For any particular data set this selection might involve much the same considerations as the choice of values for smoothing constants. Experience with similar data sets may suggest a preference for one algorithm or the other. A graph of the observed time series might also offer useful guidance. If the amplitudes of the seasonal oscillations are roughly constant, additive seasonality is suggested. On the other hand, a multiplicative seasonal would be indicated if these amplitudes seemed to be proportional to the level of the time series. However, as we have indicated earlier, we are skeptical of the reliability of graphical inspection of this sort. A more objective approach is to try both algorithms, proceeding with the one for which the sum of squared one-step forecast errors in-sample is smaller. What we are proposing, then, is that both algorithms 6.4.1 and 6.4.7 be applied to the given data. In each case, smoothing constants should be chosen objectively, based on the quality of in-sample forecasts. (The same values of the smoothing constants will not necessarily be optimal for both algorithms.) Finally, the quality of in-sample forecasts for the two algorithms, each with its optimal smoothing constants, can be compared. Certainly this involves considerably more computational effort than running just one of the algorithms with a single set of smoothing constants, chosen subjectively. However, unless the analyst has good reason to believe that a particular choice is likely to lead to satisfactory forecasts, the objective approach is the safer course. Some further detailed discussion on the practical implementation of the Holt-Winters algorithm is provided by Chatfield and Yar (1988).

6.5 Some Other Exponential Smoothing Algorithms

The exponential smoothing algorithms discussed in the previous sections of this chapter are very straightforward to implement and have been successfully used in many practical forecasting exercises. However, they represent only a small subset of the algorithms of this type in current use. There are many variants, which can be viewed as modifications of, or closely related to, these procedures. Gardner (1985) provides a comprehensive discussion of exponential smoothing algorithms. Here we will briefly discuss a few of them.

Exponential Trend Algorithms

The algorithms of Sections 6.3 and 6.4 project linear trend forecast functions, the latter with superimposed seasonal factors. In many applications this will be quite appropriate. However, on occasion it may be preferable to employ predictors projecting a rate of growth (or decline) that is either faster than or slower than linear. In either case this can be achieved with relatively minor modifications of the algorithms discussed in the previous two sections. The possibilities are illustrated in Figure 6.6 which shows linear trend, exponential trend, and damped trend forecast functions. The exponential trend function allows the projection of a *constant growth rate*, while the damped trend function will be appropriate if the analyst is uncomfortable in projecting far into the future continuing growth at a rate as steep as linear.

Allowance for exponential trend is easily made. We retain our previous notation, but now with T_t denoting growth rate rather than linear slope. The three algorithms of Sections 6.3 and 6.4 are then modified as follows:

1. *The non-seasonal case*
   Since T_t now denotes growth rate, in the absence of any evolution in trend the level at time t would simply be the product of the previous

FIGURE 6.6 Three possible trend forecast functions.

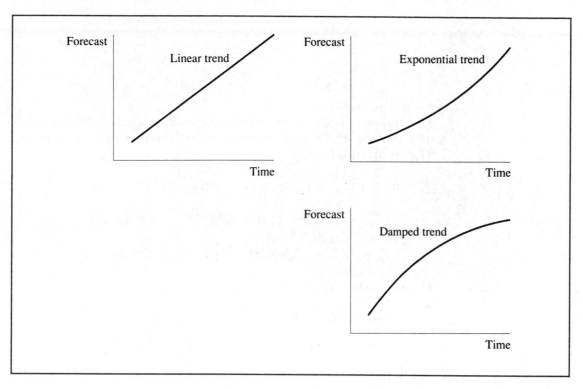

level and growth rate. Thus, the algorithm (6.3.1) is modified to the recurrence form

$$L_t = \alpha X_t + (1 - \alpha)L_{t-1}T_{t-1} \qquad 0 < \alpha < 1$$

$$T_t = \frac{\beta L_t}{L_{t-1}} + (1 - \beta)T_{t-1} \qquad 0 < \beta < 1$$

At time t, forecasts are obtained by projecting the most recent growth rate T_t from the most recent level L_t, so that the forecast of X_{t+h} is

$$\hat{X}_t(h) = L_t T_t^h \qquad h = 1, 2, \ldots$$

Since the one-step forecast error is

$$e_t = X_t - \hat{X}_{t-1}(1) = X_t - L_{t-1}T_{t-1}$$

it follows after a little algebra that the error-correction form of this algorithm is

$$L_t = L_{t-1}T_{t-1} + \alpha e_t \qquad 0 < \alpha < 1$$

$$T_t = T_{t-1} + \frac{\alpha\beta e_t}{L_{t-1}} \qquad 0 < \beta < 1$$

2. *Additive seasonality*

The Holt-Winters additive seasonal algorithm equation 6.4.1 is modified in a similar way to allow for exponential rather than linear trend. The recurrence form is

$$L_t = \alpha(X_t - F_{t-s}) + (1 - \alpha)L_{t-1}T_{t-1} \qquad 0 < \alpha < 1$$

$$T_t = \frac{\beta L_t}{L_{t-1}} + (1 - \beta)T_{t-1} \qquad 0 < \beta < 1$$

$$F_t = \gamma(X_t - L_t) + (1 - \gamma)F_{t-s} \qquad 0 < \gamma < 1$$

The forecast of X_{t+h} made at time t is

$$\hat{X}_t(h) = L_t T_t^h + F_{t+h-s} \qquad h = 1, 2, \ldots, s$$

$$= L_t T_t^h + F_{t+h-2s} \qquad h = s + 1, \ s + 2, \ldots, 2s$$

and so on.

In addition, since the one-step forecast errors are

$$e_t = X_t - \hat{X}_{t-1}(1) = X_t - L_{t-1}T_{t-1} - F_{t-s}$$

the error-correction form of the algorithm can be derived as

$$L_t = L_{t-1}T_{t-1} + \alpha e_t \qquad 0 < \alpha < 1$$

$$T_t = T_{t-1} + \frac{\alpha\beta e_t}{L_{t-1}} \qquad 0 < \beta < 1$$

$$F_t = F_{t-s} + \gamma(1 - \alpha)e_t \qquad 0 < \gamma < 1$$

3. *Multiplicative seasonality*

The multiplicative seasonal algorithm 6.4.7 is modified in analogous fashion in the presence of exponential trend. The recurrence form is

$$L_t = \frac{\alpha X_t}{F_{t-s}} + (1 - \alpha)L_{t-1}T_{t-1} \qquad 0 < \alpha < 1$$

$$T_t = \frac{\beta L_t}{L_{t-1}} + (1 - \beta)T_{t-1} \qquad 0 < \beta < 1$$

$$F_t = \frac{\gamma X_t}{L_t} + (1 - \gamma)F_{t-s} \qquad 0 < \gamma < 1$$

The forecast of X_{t+h} made at time t is

$$\hat{X}_t(h) = L_t T_t^h F_{t+h-s} \qquad h = 1, 2, \ldots, s$$
$$= L_t T_t^h F_{t+h-2s} \qquad h = s + 1, \quad s + 2, \ldots, 2s$$

and so on.

Further, since the one-step forecast errors are

$$e_t = X_t - \hat{X}_{t-1}(1) = X_t - L_{t-1}T_{t-1}F_{t-s}$$

it follows after some algebra that the error-correction form of the algorithm is

$$L_t = L_{t-1}T_{t-1} + \frac{\alpha e_t}{F_{t-s}} \qquad 0 < \alpha < 1$$

$$T_t = T_{t-1} + \frac{\alpha\beta e_t}{(L_{t-1}F_{t-s})} \qquad 0 < \beta < 1$$

$$F_t = F_{t-s} + \frac{\gamma(1 - \alpha)e_t}{L_t} \qquad 0 < \gamma < 1$$

When it is felt that both exponential trend and multiplicative seasonality are appropriate, an alternative approach is available. The Holt-Winters additive seasonal algorithm equation 6.4.1 can be applied to the logarithms of the observed series, rather than to the raw data. This approach will yield directly forecasts of future values of the logarithms of the time series, so that taking antilogarithms of these forecasts produces predictions for the original series.

Damped Trend Algorithms

Sometimes an investigator is uncomfortable with projecting an estimated local slope far into the future, suspecting rather that the series is likely to level out. In that case, the damped trend forecast function of Figure 6.6 might be attractive. This can be achieved by arguing that an observed slope T_t at time t suggests slope ϕT_t at time $(t + 1)$, slope $\phi^2 T_t$ at time

$(t + 2)$, slope $\phi^3 T_t$ at time $(t + 3)$, and so on, where ϕ is the **damping factor,** with a value between zero and one. The smaller the value of the parameter ϕ, the greater will be the amount of damping of the trend in the forecast function. Then, if L_t is the level of the series at time t, we would predict, in the absence of seasonality, X_{t+1} by $L_t + \phi T_t$, X_{t+2} by $L_t + (\phi + \phi^2)T_t$, and so on. The algorithms of Sections 6.3 and 6.4 are easily modified to generate predictors with damped trend.

1. *The nonseasonal case*

   With T_{t-1} denoting the slope of the series at time $(t - 1)$, in the absence of evolution in trend we would expect in the next time period a slope of ϕT_{t-1}, with this amount added to the previous level. Hence, the algorithm 6.3.1 is modified to the recurrence form

$$L_t = \alpha X_t + (1 - \alpha)(L_{t-1} + \phi T_{t-1})$$

$$0 < \alpha < 1 \qquad 0 < \phi \le 1 \quad (6.5.1a)$$

$$T_t = \beta(L_t - L_{t-1}) + (1 - \beta)\phi T_{t-1} \qquad 0 < \beta < 1$$

$$(6.5.1b)$$

Standing at time t, forecasts are obtained by projecting from the most recent level a damping of the most recent slope, so that the forecast of X_{t+h} is

$$\hat{X}_t(h) = L_t + \sum_{i=1}^{h} \phi^i T_t \qquad h = 1, 2, \ldots$$

In order to apply this algorithm to generate forecasts from a given data set, the values of three parameters, α, β, and ϕ, must be chosen. The most reliable approach is the objective one, where that set of values for which the sum of squared one-step in-sample forecast errors is minimum is selected; that is, we choose those values for which

$$S = \sum_{t=4}^{n} [X_t - (L_{t-1} + \phi T_{t-1})]^2$$

is smallest. Notice that Holt's linear trend algorithm, 6.3.1, is simply the special case of equation 6.5.1 with the damping factor ϕ equal to one. Therefore, if this value of the damping factor is included in the objective search for the values of the parameters of equation 6.5.1, the data could indicate a preference for the simpler Holt algorithm rather than the more elaborate algorithm with ϕ strictly less than one.

Since the one-step forecast error for this algorithm is

$$e_t = X_t - \hat{X}_{t-1}(1) = X_t - L_{t-1} - \phi T_{t-1}$$

it is straightforward to show that the error-correction form is

$$L_t = L_{t-1} + \phi T_{t-1} + \alpha e_t \qquad 0 < \alpha < 1 \qquad 0 < \phi \leq 1$$
$$T_t = \phi T_{t-1} + \alpha\beta e_t \qquad 0 < \beta < 1$$

2. *Additive seasonality*

Modification of the Holt-Winters additive seasonal algorithm 6.4.1 to generate predictions in which the trend is damped proceeds along similar lines. The recurrence form is

$$L_t = \alpha(X_t - F_{t-s}) + (1 - \alpha)(L_{t-1} + \phi T_{t-1})$$
$$0 < \alpha < 1 \qquad 0 < \phi \leq 1$$
$$T_t = \beta(L_t - L_{t-1}) + (1 - \beta)\phi T_{t-1} \qquad 0 < \beta < 1$$
$$F_t = \gamma(X_t - L_t) + (1 - \gamma)F_{t-s} \qquad 0 < \gamma < 1$$

The forecast of X_{t+h} made at time t is

$$\hat{X}_t(h) = L_t + \sum_{i=1}^{h} \phi^i T_t + F_{t+h-s} \qquad h = 1, 2, \ldots, s$$

$$= L_t + \sum_{i=1}^{h} \phi^i T_t + F_{t+h-2s} \qquad h = s+1, s+2, \ldots, 2s$$

and so on.

Further, since the one-step forecast errors are

$$e_t = X_t - \hat{X}_{t-1}(1) = X_t - L_{t-1} - \phi T_{t-1} - F_{t-s}$$

it follows, after a little algebra, that the error-correction form of the algorithm is

$$L_t = L_{t-1} + \phi T_{t-1} + \alpha e_t \qquad 0 < \alpha < 1 \qquad 0 < \phi \leq 1$$
$$T_t = \phi T_{t-1} + \alpha\beta e_t \qquad 0 < \beta < 1$$
$$F_t = F_{t-s} + \gamma(1 - \alpha)e_t \qquad 0 < \gamma < 1$$

3. *Multiplicative seasonality*
    A similar modification of the Holt-Winters multiplicative seasonal algorithm, equation 6.4.7, yields the recurrence form

$$L_t = \frac{\alpha X_t}{F_{t-s}} + (1-\alpha)(L_{t-1} + \phi T_{t-1}) \qquad 0 < \alpha < 1 \qquad 0 < \phi \le 1$$

$$T_t = \beta(L_t - L_{t-1}) + (1-\beta)\phi T_{t-1} \qquad 0 < \beta < 1$$

$$F_t = \frac{\gamma X_t}{L_t} + (1-\gamma)F_{t-s} \qquad 0 < \gamma < 1$$

The forecast of X_{t+h} made at time t is

$$\hat{X}_t(h) = \left(L_t + \sum_{i=1}^{h} \phi^i T_t\right) F_{t+h-s} \qquad h = 1, 2, \ldots, s$$

$$= \left(L_t + \sum_{i=1}^{h} \phi^i T_t\right) F_{t+h-2s} \qquad h = s+1, \; s+2, \ldots, 2s$$

and so on.

In addition, since the one-step forecast errors are

$$e_t = X_t - \hat{X}_{t-1}(1) = X_t - (L_{t-1} + \phi T_{t-1})F_{t-s}$$

it follows, after some algebra, that the error-correction form of the algorithm is

$$L_t = L_{t-1} + \phi T_{t-1} + \frac{\alpha e_t}{F_{t-s}} \qquad 0 < \alpha < 1 \qquad 0 < \phi \le 1$$

$$T_t = \phi T_{t-1} + \frac{\alpha \beta e_t}{F_{t-s}} \qquad 0 < \beta < 1$$

$$F_t = F_{t-s} + \frac{\gamma(1-\alpha)e_t}{L_t} \qquad 0 < \gamma < 1$$

A difficulty with these two seasonal damped trend algorithms is that they involve four parameters whose values need to be determined—the three smoothing constants, α, β, and γ, and the damping factor, ϕ. Indeed, in a survey of exponential smoothing procedures, Gardner (1985) excludes these algorithms from consideration explicitly for this reason. It is not at all clear to us why an algorithm with three parameters should be perfectly acceptable while one with four parameters is unworthy of any consideration. However, an increase in the number of parameters does raise two problems when their values must be chosen from sample data. First, the more free parameters for which a search for optimal values must be carried out, the greater the computational cost, though given modern computing power a search over four parameters is no longer an overwhelming burden. More seriously, a heavily parameterized algorithm violates the *principle of parsimony*, which dictates the choice of the simplest forecast function that seems to capture the major features of the data. It is well known that, while overly elaborate functions can appear to provide a very good fit of sample data, their projection forward for forecasting can yield disappointingly poor results. Whether these considerations automatically disqualify any algorithm with four parameters is problematic. Since extreme parsimony is most critical when data are very scarce, perhaps the best advice is to restrict the use of these algorithms to situations where moderately long series of observations are available.

Brown's Double Smoothing Algorithm

In Section 6.3 we saw how Holt's linear trend algorithm could be used to predict non-seasonal time series for which a linear trend forecast function is appropriate. An alternative approach was developed by Brown (1959) and discussed further by Brown and Meyer (1961). This procedure can be set out in a number of different equivalent ways. One involves using the simple exponential smoothing algorithm of Section 6.2 twice, leading to the name *double smoothing*. The observed series X_t is smoothed according to equation 6.2.4, yielding the series $L_t^{(1)}$. This series is then smoothed again, using the same smoothing constant, to produce the doubly smoothed series $L_t^{(2)}$. The algorithmic calculations then can be written as

$$L_t^{(1)} = \alpha X_t + (1 - \alpha)L_{t-1}^{(1)} \qquad (6.5.2a)$$

$$L_t^{(2)} = \alpha L_t^{(1)} + (1 - \alpha)L_{t-1}^{(2)} \qquad (6.5.2b)$$

Notice, by contrast with the Holt linear trend algorithm, that the Brown double smoothing algorithm rests on just a single smoothing constant, α. It can be shown that, if the time series exhibits local linear trend, the appropriate forecast of X_{t+h}, made at time t, is

$$\hat{X}_t(h) = 2L_t^{(1)} - L_t^{(2)} + h\left(\frac{\alpha}{1 - \alpha}\right)(L_t^{(1)} - L_t^{(2)}) \qquad h = 1, 2, \ldots$$

$$(6.5.3)$$

On the surface, this predictor appears to be an alternative to that of Section 6.3. However, the Brown predictor is merely a special case of the Holt predictor. To understand this, note that the forecast function, equation 6.5.3, can be expressed as

$$\hat{X}_t(h) = L_t + hT_t \qquad h = 1, 2, \ldots$$

where

$$L_t = 2L_t^{(1)} - L_t^{(2)} \qquad T_t = \left(\frac{\alpha}{1 - \alpha}\right)(L_t^{(1)} - L_t^{(2)}) \quad (6.5.4)$$

Then, using equations 6.5.2 and 6.5.4, it follows after some tedious but straightforward algebra, whose details we omit, that

$$L_t = \alpha^* X_t + (1 - \alpha^*)(L_{t-1} + T_{t-1}) \qquad (6.5.5a)$$

$$T_t = \beta^*(L_t - L_{t-1}) + (1 - \beta^*)T_{t-1} \qquad (6.5.5b)$$

where

$$\alpha^* = \alpha(2 - \alpha) \qquad \beta^* = \alpha/(2 - \alpha) \qquad (6.5.6)$$

It can be seen that equation 6.5.5 is in precisely the form of the recurrence equations 6.3.1 of Holt's linear trend algorithm. That the Brown algorithm is simply a special case of the Holt algorithm follows by noting from equation 6.5.6 that the smoothing constants α^* and β^* satisfy

$$\alpha^* = \frac{4\beta^*}{(1 + \beta^*)^2}$$

If Holt's linear trend algorithm is applied, with the two smoothing constants chosen through the minimization of the sum of squared, in-sample, one-step forecast errors, values that satisfy or are close to satisfying this restriction could be obtained. In this sense, the observed data can determine whether its restricted variant, the Brown algorithm, is appropriate in any particular application.

Since the double smoothing algorithm is, in effect, a special case of Holt's linear trend algorithm, it follows, using equation 6.5.6 to specialize equation 6.3.3, that one way to write the Brown algorithm in error-correction form is

$$L_t = L_{t-1} + T_{t-1} + \alpha(2 - \alpha)e_t \qquad 0 < \alpha < 1$$
$$T_t = T_{t-1} + \alpha^2 e_t$$

where, as usual, e_t denotes the one-step forecast error.

Since Brown's double smoothing algorithm is, in fact, no more than a special case of the procedure of Section 6.3, our main interest in double smoothing is not as a distinctive forecasting procedure. Rather, it is a member of an interesting general class of exponential smoothing algorithms which provide a valuable insight into the important concepts of *local* trend and seasonality. We now proceed to discuss these algorithms.

General Exponential Smoothing

A general procedure that generates many alternative exponential smoothing algorithms was developed by Brown (1962). Although this approach is usually called **general exponential smoothing,** this name is rather misleading since it does not include as special cases many exponential smoothing algorithms in common use. To illustrate general exponential smoothing, suppose that an analyst wishes to develop, as appropriate for a particular data set, a linear predictor, so that standing at time t the forecast of X_{t+h} will be of the form

$$\hat{X}_t(h) = a_1(t) + ha_2(t) \qquad h = 1, 2, \ldots \qquad (6.5.7)$$

where the quantities $a_1(t)$ and $a_2(t)$ are the intercept and slope of the linear forecast function. Notice that these parameters depend on t. Thus, the linear predictor used need not be the same over all time, but instead can evolve as new data become available. This corresponds to our notion that the trend in the time series is local rather than global. In order to implement a forecasting procedure of this sort, it is necessary to determine appropriate values for $a_1(t)$ and $a_2(t)$. To see how this might be done, suppose we project back the function 6.5.7 over the data observation period, which ends at time t, and begins at time one. This is done by setting $h = 0, -1, -2, \ldots, (1 - t)$ in equation 6.5.7. Thus we have:

Time t; $h = 0$; Observed value X_t;
   Value of equation 6.5.7 $a_1(t)$
Time $(t - 1)$; $h = -1$; Observed value X_{t-1};
   Value of equation 6.5.7 $a_1(t) - a_2(t)$

Time $(t - 2)$; $h = -2$; Observed value X_{t-2};
   Value of equation 6.5.7 $a_1(t) - 2a_2(t)$

$$\vdots$$

Time 1; $h = 1 - t$; Observed value X_1;
   Value of equation 6.5.7 $a_1(t) - (t - 1)a_2(t)$

In general, then, we see that for the sample period, we have

Observed value X_{t-j}; Value of equation 6.5.7 $a_1(t) - ja_2(t)$;
   $j = 0, 1, \ldots, (t - 1)$

A reasonable strategy for choosing the values of $a_1(t)$ and $a_2(t)$, then, might be to pick those numbers for which the values of the forecast function extrapolated back, $a_1(t) - ja_2(t)$, are in some sense closest to the actual observations X_{t-j}. Recalling our discussion of linear regression in Chapter 3, the method of least squares immediately springs to mind as a tool for this task. This suggests selecting those values for which the sum of squares

$$S = \sum_{j=0}^{t-1} [X_{t-j} - (a_1(t) - ja_2(t))]^2 \qquad (6.5.8)$$

is a minimum. This would be appropriate if our time series were generated by the *global* linear trend model

$$X_{t-j} = a_1(t) - ja_2(t) + \epsilon_{t-j} \qquad j = 0, 1, \ldots, (t - 1)$$

where the ϵ_{t-j} are error terms with zero means, fixed variances, and no autocorrelation. However, as we have frequently indicated, such global trend models rarely provide a good description of the behavior of real business and economic time series.

If instead we think in terms of a locally evolving linear trend pattern, with the most recent estimate of trend to be projected forward for forecasting, an interesting modification of equation 6.5.8 is suggested. The difficulty with that expression as it stands is that, in forming the sum of squares, the same weight is given to the current time period t as to less relevant distant time periods. A better alternative, given an assumption of local linear trend, would be to discount information from the past. Thus, if we attach weight one to the squared discrepancy between the observation and the forecast function in the current time period, we might attach weight δ to the previous period, weight δ^2 to the period before that, and so on, where δ is some number between zero and one and is called a **discount factor.** Then, in place of equation 6.5.8, $a_1(t)$ and $a_2(t)$

are chosen to minimize

$$S^* = \sum_{j=0}^{t-1} \delta^j [X_{t-j} - a_1(t) + j a_2(t)]^2 \qquad 0 < \delta < 1 \qquad (6.5.9)$$

This approach is known as the method of **discounted least squares.** In fact, it can be shown that discounted least squares applied to a linear trend function in this way yields Brown's double smoothing predictor, equations 6.5.2, 6.5.3, with smoothing constant $\alpha = (1 - \delta)$. What is interesting about this way of looking at that predictor is the light that is shed on the distinction between viewing trend as a local and as a global phenomenon. In the latter case forecast functions would be derived through ordinary least squares, whereas certain exponential smoothing algorithms, developed to allow for local trend, are equivalent to the estimation of trend functions by discounted least squares.

Now, the linear trend forecast function is just one of any number of forecast functions that might be employed. The class of general exponential smoothing algorithms follows from the application of discounted least squares to a range of possible forecast functions. Brown proposed polynomials, exponentials, sines and cosines, and linear combinations of all of these. In general, consider the forecast of X_{t+h}, made at time t,

$$\hat{X}_t(h) = a_1(t) f_1(h) + a_2(t) f_2(h) + \cdots + a_k(t) f_k(h) \qquad h = 1, 2, \ldots$$

$$(6.5.10)$$

where $f_1(h), f_2(h), \ldots, f_k(h)$ are k functions of time. For example, equation 6.5.7 is the special case of equation 6.5.10 with

$$k = 2 \qquad f_1(h) = 1 \qquad f_2(h) = h$$

Then, generalizing equation 6.5.9 the values $a_1(t), a_2(t), \ldots, a_k(t)$ are obtained by minimizing

$$S^* = \sum_{j=0}^{t-1} \delta^j [X_{t-j} - a_1(t) f_1(-j) - \cdots - a_k(t) f_k(-j)]^2 \qquad 0 < \delta < 1$$

$$(6.5.11)$$

In fact, it is not necessary to compute the minimum of 6.5.11 anew each time period. Rather, it can be shown that the parameters $a_i(t)$ can be updated each time period through an appropriate error-correction algorithm. We will not pursue these details here.

Perhaps the most obvious extension of the linear trend predictor 6.5.7 is to polynomial predictors of higher degree. In fact, the corresponding discounted least squares approach can be shown to be equivalent to an extension of double smoothing to triple smoothing, and more generally multiple smoothing. However, as Gardner (1985) argues, this elaboration is "of little practical interest in business and economic forecasting." Quite simply, real data virtually never support the case for its implementation.

A more interesting possibility arises in the analysis of seasonal data, where sine and cosine functions can be employed to represent smooth seasonal patterns. For example, a possible forecast function with linear trend and this type of seasonal pattern is

$$\hat{X}_t(h) = a_1(t) + a_2(t)h + a_3(t) \cos (2\pi h/s) + a_4(t) \sin (2\pi h/s)$$

where s is the number of seasonal periods. This can be extended by adding further sine and cosine terms to, for example,

$$\hat{X}_t(h) = a_1(t) + a_2(t)h + a_3(t) \cos (2\pi h/s) + a_4(t) \sin (2\pi h/s)$$
$$+ a_5(t) \cos (4\pi h/s) + a_6(t) \sin (4\pi h/s)$$

An alternative approach to seasonality in the discounted least squares framework, explored by Groff (1973), Sweet (1981), and McKenzie (1984), is to use seasonal dummy variables in place of sines and cosines.

An apparent advantage of the general exponential smoothing algorithm is that forecasts depend on the specification of just a single parameter—the discount factor δ. Suppose, for example, that a seasonal time series is to be predicted. In Section 6.4 we saw that the Holt-Winters algorithm for this purpose rests on three smoothing constants, whose values must be set. Thus, if the values of these parameters are to be chosen objectively through the minimization of the sum of one-step in-sample squared forecast errors, this search will be more time consuming for the Holt-Winters predictor than for the general exponential smoothing predictor. In fact, this apparent strength of general exponential smoothing may well be a weakness. Harrison (1965) and Ameen and Harrison (1984) have argued that the notion that forecasts can reliably be based on just a single parameter in the seasonal case is just too good to be true. It is quite likely that trend and seasonal patterns will evolve at different rates, suggesting in effect that different discount factors are needed for each. These authors develop a number of extensions of general exponential smoothing and the simple discounted least squares procedure to allow different evolutionary rates for trend and seasonality.

6.6 EXPONENTIAL SMOOTHING AND MODELS FOR TIME SERIES DATA

Exponential smoothing, as we have seen, provides a large collection of forecasting algorithms that have been developed and implemented over the years. This development has been largely pragmatic rather than systematic. Forecasting procedures have been proposed on the basis of intuitive plausibility, and have survived as a result of successful practical applications. In practice, most implementations of exponential smoothing are somewhat unsystematic, in the sense that a particular algorithm is often chosen on the basis of judgment and experience, or because it is a favorite of the analyst. Indeed, in any specific application it is not at all clear how a systematic search for an appropriate algorithm from what is virtually an endless list of possibilities might be organized. To some extent this is inevitable, reflecting the pragmatic philosophy behind the development of exponential smoothing methods. This philosophy contrasts with the *statistical model-building* approach to data analysis.

Indeed, it is rather remarkable that the development and understanding of exponential smoothing algorithms is quite separate from anything that is studied in the typical Statistics course. At whatever level of rigor such courses are taught, their basis will almost inevitably involve certain fundamental concepts. These include uncertainty (as measured by probability), random variables, inference (estimation, hypothesis testing, confidence intervals), and model building (for example, regression). The reader will have found very little of this of any value in attempting to understand the rationale behind exponential smoothing. This is inevitable, as the development of these algorithms owes very little to the foundations of statistics. A more traditional statistical approach to forecasting would rest on the concept of model building.

Statistical model building is certainly not limited to the analysis of time series data. For example, the regression models of Chapters 3 and 4 have been fitted to many types of data from a broad range of subject areas. The objective is to develop a model of the data-generating process, which provides good forecasts. This generally involves the following elements:

1. The investigator has in mind a *class of models* as possible generators of the given data. These models will not be purely deterministic, since it is inevitable that an investigator will be unable to predict any new observation with complete certainty. Statistical, or *stochastic*, models explicitly incorporate an element of uncertainty in the data-generating mechanism.

2. A specific model from the general class of models is fitted to the observed data. This exercise involves three stages:

    (a) On the basis of subject matter theory, evidence in the data, or some combination of the two, a specific model is tentatively chosen for further analysis from the broad class of models.

    (b) The selected model will typically involve unknown parameters. Using the available data, these parameters are estimated through efficient statistical methods. For example, in Chapters 3 and 4 we saw that, given certain assumptions, the parameters of a regression model can be efficiently estimated through the method of least squares.

    (c) Since the investigator cannot be sure that the initially chosen model will be appropriate, it is important to check that it adequately describes the observed data. Any inadequacies detected may suggest some alternative model specification. The process of model selection, parameter estimation and model checking is then continued iteratively until a suitable model is achieved.

3. Once a satisfactory model has been achieved, it can be employed to learn about the real world system under study, or to derive forecasts of out-of-sample values.

When one compares this statistical model-building approach with our previous discussion of the practical implementation of exponential smoothing algorithms, a number of distinctions are clear. First, properly speaking, these algorithms are not models at all, and were not formulated as such. Rather, they are simply a set of algebraic formulae that might be appropriate in particular instances for the generation of forecasts. This being the case, it should not be surprising that some of the elements of statistical model-building methodology are difficult, if not impossible, to incorporate into practical exponential smoothing applications. In fact, given the choice of a particular algorithm, data can be used in the objective choice of smoothing constants through the minimization of the sum of one-step in-sample squared forecast errors. This is, in effect, parameter estimation under a different name. However, as Gardner (1985) notes, exponential smoothing lacks both a systematic approach to the selection of an appropriate algorithm and a completely convincing methodology for checking the appropriateness of the algorithm chosen. This seems to be an inevitable consequence of the fact that exponential smoothing algorithms were not developed within the framework of statistical models. Given that the algorithms in current use were proposed in a rather haphazard *ad hoc* manner, it is hardly surprising that there exists no systematic framework for choosing an appropriate algorithm from this group for any specific forecasting exercise. In addition, in the statistical model-building framework, the appropriateness of an assumed model is typically checked by testing it against some more elaborate model. This possibility is not available in a framework in which data-generating models are not explicitly specified. In fact, when exponential smoothing predictors are employed, some attempt is often made to verify their adequacy, using procedures that we will discuss in Section 6.8.

In Chapter 7 we will discuss a statistical model-building methodology for time series data. We will see how the model building approach outlined here can be used to fit to given data an appropriate model from a general class—the *autoregressive integrated moving average models*—and how the particular model achieved in this way can be extrapolated forward to generate forecasts. In this approach then, for any specific problem, the form of the forecast function employed is determined by the properties of the observed data.

In fact, it can be shown that particular exponential smoothing algorithms yield optimal forecasts for time series generated by specific stochastic models, and that forecasts generated by some of these algorithms are identical to predictions that would be obtained by projecting forward certain models. This point will be explored considerably more in Chapter 9, where we examine the relationships among some forecasting methods. The distinction between forecasting through exponential smoothing algorithms and through the construction of statistical models is not so much in the forecast functions that are used, but in the determination of the form of the forecasts in any individual application. The model building approach provides the analyst with a framework in which the appropriate forecast function can be determined from a careful analysis of the observed data, so that the method of prediction is tailored to the properties of a given time series. It is far from clear that the exponential smoothing approach is well-suited to this purpose.

In contrasting exponential smoothing and statistical model building as approaches to the problem of predicting future values of a time series given past data, it is not our intention to claim that the former is intrinsically inferior, much less that it is worthless in practice. On the contrary, these approaches have been developed with different types of forecasting problems in mind, and naturally each is better suited for the type of problem for which it was designed. It frequently happens that forecasts of a large collection of time series are required quickly on a regular basis. In these circumstances it will be very expensive, even if it is possible, to devote skilled human resources to the task of building individual models for all of the time series in the collection. At much lower cost, an appropriately chosen exponential smoothing algorithm typically can provide forecasts of adequate quality. On the other hand, if the analyst has just a few series for which it is important to derive forecasts that are as reliable as possible, it would be rash to merely apply some particular exponential smoothing algorithm without any assurance that something much better might not be possible. Certainly, in some situations, individual exponential smoothing algorithms will generate forecasts that are optimal, or close to optimal, but in any particular application there is no guarantee that this will be the case. If the resources are available, it is preferable to give some time and thought to the properties of an observed time series, allowing these properties, through the construction of a statistical model, to determine how forecasts are to be obtained. The value of the exponential smoothing approach is not that it is likely to yield optimal, or nearly optimal, forecasts in specific applications. However, both the logic behind their construction and a wealth of accumulated practical experience suggest that these algorithms will produce quite good forecasts for a wide range of time series of the sort likely to be met in business and economic applications. On the other hand, it is inevitable that from time to time the analyst will meet series for which her or his favorite exponential smoothing algorithm is ill-suited. Situations of this sort are both most easily detected and best catered for in the statistical model-building approach, where individual series characteristics are brought out and incorporated into the choice of appropriate model.

Although forecasting from particular exponential smoothing algorithms is equivalent to prediction from certain statistical models, the lack of explicit model specification in the development of exponential smoothing methods does lead to some problems and difficulties. We have already discussed the selection of, and verification of the adequacy of, the exponential smoothing algorithm to be used in this context. In the next section we consider two other problems that essentially arise for this same reason.

6.7 Two Problems in Exponential Smoothing: Initial Values and Interval Forecasts

In this section we briefly discuss two problems that can arise in the practical implementation of exponential smoothing algorithms. Although these problems appear to have very little in common, in fact they arise from a common source—the absence of a formal statistical model in the usual specification of the algorithms. Specifically, we will consider the following:

1. As we have already seen, in order to get the algorithmic calculations started, it is necessary to set *initial values* for such quantities as level, slope, and seasonal factors. In the early sections of this chapter, we employed very simple, but somewhat arbitrary, solutions to this problem.
2. The forecasts of future values considered so far have been **point**

forecasts—that is, single numbers that in some sense represent a best bet. For many problems, such as routine sales forecasting for inventory control, where the forecasts are inputs to a formal decision-making process, this is all that is required. However, it is often desirable to have some measure of the uncertainty attached to these forecasts. This can be achieved through provision of an **interval forecast**—a range in which the analyst can be pretty sure that the true value lies. This requirement is equivalent to that for the provision of confidence intervals as well as point estimates in classical statistical parameter estimation problems.

Initial Values

The very simple procedures described in previous sections for the setting of initial values should in fact be quite adequate for most purposes. The particular choice made will introduce an effect into the values obtained for early estimates of level, slope, and the seasonal factors. However, as the algorithmic computations proceed through the observation period of the series, the influence of this initial choice becomes less and less significant, so that, unless the time series is very short, the particular initial values selected will have very little impact on the forecasts of future observations. In effect, the initial values introduce into the calculations a transient value whose importance dies out as more data points are incorporated.

In spite of the fact that the simple approach to the initial values problem is generally quite satisfactory, a number of practitioners and scholars have felt it to be intellectually unsatisfying, and have therefore sought more sophisticated solutions. A wide array of possibilities, most of which are summarized by Gardner (1985), have been proposed. One approach is to use regression methods. For example, if the additive seasonal variant of the Holt-Winters algorithm of Section 6.4 is to be used, a regression of the observations on a linear trend plus seasonal dummy variables could be estimated. Since we do not believe that business and economic time series are at all well-described by such global models, it would be best to fit this regression to just a few observations from the beginning of the time series rather than to all of the available data. An alternative possibility for seasonal time series is to apply the decomposition methods of Chapter 5 to obtain initial estimates of the seasonal factors. For example, suppose that multiplicative seasonality is assumed, and the Holt-Winters predictor is to be employed. As a first step, the seasonal index method of Section 5.4 could be applied. The seasonal indices could then be taken as initial values for the seasonal factors. To get initial values for slope and level, each of the first few observations would be divided by the appropriate seasonal factor, and a linear regression of the adjusted observations on time estimated.

Although they involve considerable additional calculations, these approaches to the initial value problem are still *ad hoc*, and unsatisfactorily arbitrary. Ledolter and Abraham (1984) have proposed a more appealing possibility, based on **backcasting,** where the exponential smoothing algorithm is first applied to a time series in reverse order, as if the objective were to forecast observations from the past—that is, to "backcast." To illustrate, consider Holt's linear trend algorithm of Section 6.3, and suppose that the observed time series consists of n observations, labeled $X_1, X_2, \ldots, X_n$. If our aim were to backcast the values at time $t = 0$, $t = -1$, and so on, we could apply the algorithm 6.3.1 to the series in reverse order. Then, if L_t^* and T_t^* denote the level and slope estimates at time t, we would have

$$L_{n-j}^* = \alpha X_{n-j} + (1-\alpha)(L_{n-j+1}^* + T_{n-j+1}^*) \qquad j = 2, \ldots, (n-1)$$

$$T_{n-j}^* = \beta(L_{n-j}^* - L_{n-j+1}^*) + (1-\beta)T_{n-j+1}^*$$

with the calculations initialized through the simple choice

$$L_{n-1}^* = X_{n-1} \qquad T_{n-1}^* = X_{n-1} - X_n$$

Then, L_t^* provides an estimate of the level of the series at time 1, and T_t^* an estimate of the backward-looking slope. The usual Holt algorithm 6.3.1 can now be applied to the series in correct order, beginning with $t = 2$, and using the initial values

$$L_1 = L_1^* \qquad T_1 = -T_1^*$$

The proposal of Ledolter and Abraham to employ backcasting was motivated by the correspondence between particular exponential smoothing algorithms and certain statistical models. This suggests that, where possible, the most satisfactory solution to the initial value problem is to simply transpose the algorithm to the equivalent stochastic model form. (We will see how this can be done in Chapter 9.) In effect, the problems of initial values and parameter estimation (or equivalently, choice of smoothing constants) are then handled simultaneously, without recourse to arbitrary ad hoc procedures. We repeat, however, that in practice there will often be little gain from these more sophisticated approaches to the initial values problem. Typically the very simple methods used in earlier sections will be quite satisfactory.

Makridakis and Hibon (1991) have reviewed a number of procedures in common use for setting initial values. According to these authors, the most prevalent approach in practice is the regression method, applied to *all* the available data. Although this procedure is implemented in many widely available computer programs for exponential smoothing, its intellectual foundation is, as we have indicated, very insecure. Where a choice is available, we continue to prefer the backcasting approach. Makridakis and Hibon evaluated several different choices of initial values in terms of their effect on forecast quality for a large collection of nonseasonal time series, concluding that the impact of initial value choice on forecast quality was minimal. It is easy to see why this should be so. Consider again the simple exponential smoothing algorithm (6.2.4), where the initial level is set at some number L_1. Then, by repeated application of (6.2.4), it follows that

$$L_t = \alpha X_t + \alpha(1 - \alpha)X_{t-1} + \alpha(1 - \alpha)^2 X_{t-2}$$
$$+ \cdots + \alpha(1 - \alpha)^{t-2}X_2 + \alpha(1 - \alpha)^{t-1}L_1$$

Notice that the initial value, L_1, appears only in the final term of this expression, where it is multiplied by $\alpha(1 - \alpha)^{t-1}$. Since $0 < \alpha < 1$, this multiple will be negligible for moderately large t. A similar argument applies to other nonseasonal algorithms. However, for seasonal time series, estimates of seasonal factors are updated only once each year, so that a sound choice for initial values of these factors may be more critical.

Interval Forecasts

In estimating a population parameter, such as the slope of a regression line, from sample data, we do not expect to achieve a perfectly precise estimate. Similarly, in predicting future values of a time series, perfectly accurate forecasts should not be expected. One way to characterize uncetainty in parameter estimation is through the provision of confidence intervals. In the same way, prediction intervals can be found to characterize uncertainty in forecasting. Now, an understanding of this uncertainty springs from recognition of the presence of a chance, or random, element in the mechanism that generates the observed data. Statistical models provide the natural structure for the specification and analysis of this randomness. Indeed, the objective of statistical model building is the description of the random as well as the deterministic element in the data-generating process. It follows that the obvious, and perhaps the only really satisfactory, way to develop interval forecasts is through the analysis of a carefully specified statistical model. In Chapter 7 we will see how interval forecasts as well as point forecasts can be derived from models fitted to time series data. Now, the procedures we have outlined for the calculation of point forecasts from exponential smoothing algorithms involve no explicit random element, so that there is no natural framework in these algorithms for the provision of interval forecasts. However, as we will discuss in detail in Chapter 9, it is possible in some cases to find statistical models for which particular exponential smoothing algorithms yield optimal point forecasts. Corresponding interval forecasts could then be obtained by expressing the exponential smoothing algorithms in the equivalent model form.

Although transposition of the exponential smoothing algorithm to statistical model form seems to be the most satisfactory approach to the derivation of interval forecasts, there are three reservations about the general applicability of this procedure:

1. For some exponential smoothing algorithms, including those with multiplicative seasonality or exponential growth, it is either extremely difficult or impossible to find the equivalent statistical model form.
2. Even when the equivalent statistical model is known, the analyst may not have available appropriate computer programs for the confidence interval calculations.
3. The philosophy behind the majority of exponential smoothing implementations is not that completely optimal point forecasts are being derived, but that this technique should yield forecasts that are pretty good for a wide variety of time series. This being the case, consideration of the model for which the algorithm yields optimal forecasts may not be strictly correct, and possibly not appropriate.

Given these considerations, it may be worthwhile to seek some way of developing at least approximately valid interval forecasts without going through the stochastic model framework.

It seems reasonable to base uncertainty about the forecasts of future values on the observed quality of forecasts that have been made in the past. This suggests that in-sample forecast errors could provide a basis for deriving interval forecasts. Suppose that the time series $X_1, X_2, \ldots,$ X_n is available, and that forecasts of future values of this series are to be obtained from an exponential smoothing algorithm. Then the algorithm can also be used to forecast the given sample values. As before, let $\hat{X}_t(h)$ denote the forecast of X_{t+h} made at time t. We denote by $e_t(h)$ the corresponding forecast error, so that

$$e_t(h) = X_{t+h} - \hat{X}_t(h)$$

The average squared forecast errors in-sample are then

$$S^2(h) = \sum_{t=m+1}^{n-h} e_t^2(h)/(n - h - m) \qquad h = 1, 2, \ldots \quad (6.7.1)$$

In equation 6.7.1 we have assumed that the first forecast used in the calculations is not made at the time of the first observation, but rather after a few time periods have elapsed, say at time $t = m + 1$. This allows the transient introduced by the setting of initial values in the exponential smoothing algorithm to die out somewhat, and should provide more reliable estimates. The quantities defined in equation 6.7.1 can be viewed as estimates of the h-steps forecast error variances. If, in addition, the assumption is made that the forecast errors are normally distributed, the properties of the normal distribution can be used to derive confidence intervals in the usual way. For example, the following would provide interval forecasts for X_{n+h}, made at time n:

$$95\% \text{ interval: } \hat{X}_n(h) \pm 1.96S(h)$$
$$75\% \text{ interval: } \hat{X}_n(h) \pm 1.15S\ (h) \qquad h = 1, 2, \ldots$$
$$50\% \text{ interval: } \hat{X}_n(h) \pm 0.675S\ (h)$$

This simple procedure should be fairly reliable unless the analyst has available only a small amount of data on which to base the estimates from equation 6.7.1.

It is sometimes thought that forecast quality might evolve over time, rather than being fixed, and procedures to allow for this possibility have been proposed. Two of these are discussed by Bretschneider (1986). One modification of equation 6.7.1 estimates forecast error variance as a weighted average rather than a simple average of squared forecast errors, through the simple exponential smoothing algorithm. Thus, if $V_t(h)$ denotes the estimate of h-step forecast error variance, made at time t, we compute

$$V_t(h) = \alpha e_t^2(h) + (1 - \alpha)V_{t-1}(h) \qquad 0 < \alpha < 1 \qquad h = 1, 2, \ldots$$

$$(6.7.2)$$

where α is a smoothing constant. Confidence intervals for future values are then found by substituting $V_{n-h}^{1/2}(h)$ for $S(h)$ in the previous formulae. One difficulty with this approach is that, since the true forecast error variances are never observed, there is no objective way to choose the value of the smoothing constant α to be used in equation 6.7.2. It should be noted also that, although the use of an expression such as 6.7.2 in conjunction with an exponential smoothing algorithm seems natural, this is not necessarily the case. It does not follow that, because level, slope, and seasonal factors evolve over time, forecast error variance must also evolve over time. On the contrary, statistical models implying evolution of trend and seasonality but constant forecast error variances have been found to provide very good representations of many business and economic time series. This fact, combined with the inevitable arbitrariness in the choice of α in equation 6.7.2, suggests a general preference for the simpler equation 6.7.1 unless the analyst has strong reasons for believing that uncertainty about the future is likely to change, in some relatively smooth fashion, over time.

Yar and Chatfield (1990) discuss a computationally straightforward procedure for finding interval forecasts for exponential smoothing algorithms yielding forecasts that are linear functions of the available data. Their approach rests heavily on the assumption that the algorithm used generates optimal forecasts. As we have already noted, such an assumption may be difficult to justify, but if it is made, computational savings follow, as only the one-step mean squared error, $S^2(1)$ of (6.7.1), is required. Estimates of forecast error variance further ahead depend only on $S^2(1)$ and the smoothing constants. Specifically, in place of $S^2(h)$, $h = 2, 3, \ldots$, calculated from (6.7.1), the following can be employed:

1. For simple exponential smoothing, with smoothing constant α

$$S^2(h) = [1 + (h - 1)\alpha^2]S^2(1)$$

2. For Holt's linear trend algorithm, with smoothing constants α and β

$$S^2(h) = \left[1 + (h - 1)\alpha^2\left(1 + h\beta + \frac{1}{6}h(2h - 1)\beta^2\right)\right]S^2(1)$$

$$(6.7.3)$$

We will illustrate the use of this formula in Section 6.9.

3. For the additive seasonality variant of the Holt-Winters algorithm, with smoothing constants α, β, and γ

$$S^2(h) = \left[1 + \sum_{i=1}^{h-1} v_i^2\right]S^2(1)$$

where

$$v_i = \alpha + i\alpha\beta + \gamma(1 - \alpha)g_i$$

where $g_i = 1$ if i is an integer multiple of the seasonal period s, and $g_i = 0$ otherwise.

Calculations based on these expressions are straightforward to implement, but it should be emphasized that their validity depends heavily on the assumption that the algorithms are yielding at least approximately optimal forecasts. Chatfield and Yar (1991) show that this approach can be extended to the multiplicative seasonality variant of the Holt-Winters algorithm. However, in this case the solution is somewhat less straightforward, and a number of possibilities are available, depending on what is assumed about the structure of the time series.

6.8 TRACKING FORECAST PERFORMANCE

The great advantage of exponential smoothing algorithms in many applications where forecasts of a large number of time series are routinely required is that these algorithms are *fully automatic*. Once a particular algorithm has been chosen, and values determined for the smoothing constants, forecasts can be calculated on-line without further manual intervention as new observations are recorded. Naturally, such an approach is very cost-efficient. However, there will inevitably be some unease about the routine production of forecasts in this way over time without some quality assurance. It is important that the analyst be alerted by the system if poor forecasts are being produced; forecast performance should be monitored, or *tracked*. Of particular value are tracking mechanisms that are themselves fully automatic, so that the system is routinely monitored, with warning signals produced when performance deteriorates for the prediction of any particular series. The analyst is then free to take some corrective action, perhaps modifying the forecast algorithm in use or employing a different algorithm for those series causing difficulties while continuing with the routine generation of predictions for the majority of series for which performance has been satisfactory.

A number of fully automatic tracking signals have been implemented in conjunction with exponential smoothing algorithms. These are discussed by Gardner (1983, 1985). McClain (1988) provides an evaluation of the performance of some signals in common use. Here we will discuss the approach of Trigg (1964). The object is to detect *bias* in the forecasts, and to signal if the system is consistently generating predictions either above or below the actual realized values of the series. The procedure is based on the one-step forecast errors

$$e_t = X_t - \hat{X}_{t-1}(1)$$

Now, in the absence of any bias, the values of these errors should be distributed about zero, so that the average error should be relatively small compared with the average absolute error. In fact, rather than using simple averages, Trigg's tracking signal, in the spirit of other exponential smoothing calculations, is based on weighted averages with exponentially declining weights. Specifically, the weighted average error and weighted average absolute error are obtained from the algorithm

$$E_t = \delta e_t + (1 - \delta)E_{t-1} \qquad 0 < \delta < 1 \qquad (6.8.1a)$$

$$D_t = \delta \, | \, e_t \, | + (1 - \delta)D_{t-1} \qquad\qquad (6.8.1b)$$

The tracking signal at time t is then defined as

$$TS_t = E_t/D_t \qquad\qquad (6.8.2)$$

Bias would be indicated by large absolute values of the tracking signal.

At this point a very tricky question must be faced. How large is large? In practice, the computed tracking signal must be compared with appropriately chosen control limits, determined so that, while there is a good chance that serious bias in the forecasts will be signaled, not too many false alarms will be raised. Now, this is precisely the issue faced in classical statistical hypothesis testing, where a test statistic is compared with appropriately chosen bounds. However, these bounds are derived from the statistical model assumed to have generated the data, while, as we saw in Section 6.6, much of the development of exponential smoothing methods has proceeded in the absence of any assumed generating model. In our particular context, the question boils down to what is assumed about the autocorrelations of the one-step forecast errors e_t. Now, if the exponential smoothing algorithm yields forecasts that are optimal or close to optimal for the process that actually generates the time series, the e_t will be uncorrelated with one another, or nearly so. Then it can be shown to a close approximation that, for low values of δ in equation 6.8.1, in the absence of bias, the tracking signal will have a normal distribution with mean zero and standard deviation

$$\sigma_{TS} = \frac{1.2\delta}{\sqrt{(2\delta - \delta^2)}}$$

It then follows that, for a 5% level test—if the signal is to be outside the control limits only 5% of the time in the absence of bias—these bounds should be set at $\pm 1.96 \, \sigma_{TS}$. Similarly, for a 1% level test, bounds of $\pm 2.575 \, \sigma_{TS}$ are used. Trigg recommends setting δ in equation 6.8.1 at 0.1, in which case

$$\sigma_{TS} = 0.275$$

Then we have:

5% level limits: ± 0.54
1% level limits: ± 0.71

The difficulty with this approach is that the appropriate control limits depend quite critically on the assumption that the one-step forecast errors are not too seriously autocorrelated. If an exponential smoothing algorithm is applied routinely to a very large collection of time series, it may well be that for some of these the particular algorithm used will produce forecasts that are far from optimal and highly autocorrelated one-step forecast errors will be produced. For such series, the test for bias just discussed will not be valid. However, we prefer this approach, since any other will have to be based on some assumed generating model, and if this model is truly one in which the analyst has faith, an exponential smoothing algorithm should not be used if it produces severely suboptimal forecasts for data generated by that model. It is very desirable, in addition to checking for bias, to test also for autocorrelation in the one-step forecast errors, as this would suggest the possibility of improving the quality of the forecasts through use of an alternative algorithm. Gardner (1983) introduces a tracking signal for the detection of autocorrelated one-step forecast errors.

Tracking signals can be useful in alerting the analyst to situations where some modification of the forecasting algorithm may be desirable. This may require some intervention from the forecasting manager, but it is tempting to ask if the fully automatic nature of exponential smoothing can be retained by making these modifications automatically, perhaps through adjustments of the smoothing constants. A number of procedures for the **adaptive control of smoothing constants** have been proposed. These allow the smoothing constants to be adjusted each time period, as a new observation becomes available. The simplest of these, due to Trigg and Leach (1967), employs Trigg's tracking signal in conjunction with the simple exponential smoothing algorithm. Suppose that the forecasting algorithm has moved out of control, in the sense that it appears to be producing biased forecasts. The algorithm might be adapted to this circumstance by giving relatively more weight to the most recent observations. Trigg and Leach propose that the usual simple exponential smoothing algorithm be modified by resetting the smoothing constant at each time period to the absolute value of the tracking signal, equation 6.8.2. Writing α_t for the value of the smoothing constant used at time t, the full algorithm is then

$$e_t = X_t - \hat{X}_{t-1}(1) = X_t - L_{t-1}$$

$$E_t = \delta e_t + (1 - \delta)E_{t-1} \qquad 0 < \delta < 1$$

$$D_t = \delta \, | \, e_t \, | + (1 - \delta)D_{t-1}$$

$$\alpha_t = | \, TS_t \, | = \frac{| \, E_t \, |}{D_t}$$

$$L_t = \alpha_t X_t + (1 - \alpha_t)L_{t-1}$$

TABLE 6.5   Application of Trigg-Leach method ($\delta = 0.1$) to annual sales data.

t	X_t	e_t	E_t	D_t	TS_t	α_t	L_t
1	103						103.00
2	86					0.30	97.90
3	84	-13.90				0.30	93.73
4	84	-9.73				0.30	90.81
5	92	1.19				0.30	91.17
6	92	0.83				0.30	91.42
7	94	2.58	-3.81	5.65	-0.67	0.67	93.16
8	102	8.84	-2.54	5.97	-0.43	0.43	96.92
9	103	6.08	-1.68	5.98	-0.28	0.28	98.63
10	103	4.37	-1.07	5.82	-0.18	0.18	99.44
11	82	-17.44	-2.71	6.98	-0.39	0.39	92.67
12	123	30.33	0.59	9.31	0.06	0.06	94.60
13	106	11.40	1.67	9.52	0.18	0.18	96.61
14	103	6.39	2.15	9.21	0.23	0.23	98.10
15	99	0.90	2.02	8.38	0.24	0.24	98.31
16	106	7.69	2.59	8.31	0.31	0.31	100.71
17	107	6.29	2.96	8.11	0.36	0.36	103.00
18	115	12.00	3.86	8.50	0.45	0.45	108.46
19	95	-13.46	2.13	8.99	0.24	0.24	105.27
20	104	-1.27	1.79	8.22	0.22	0.22	104.99
21	102	-2.99	1.31	7.70	0.17	0.17	104.48
22	101	-3.48	0.83	7.28	0.11	0.11	104.08
23	112	7.92	1.54	7.34	0.21	0.21	105.75
24	104	-1.75	1.21	6.78	0.18	0.18	105.43
25	105	-0.43	1.05	6.15	0.17	0.17	105.36
26	116	10.64	2.01	6.60	0.30	0.30	108.60
27	100	-8.60	0.95	6.80	0.14	0.14	107.40
28	128	20.60	2.91	8.18	0.36	0.36	114.74
29	109	-5.74	2.05	7.93	0.26	0.26	113.26
30	122	8.74	2.72	8.01	0.34	0.34	116.22

To illustrate, we apply this procedure to the annual sales data of Table 6.1, which are reproduced in the X_t column of Table 6.5. We will use $\delta = 0.1$, the value typically recommended by practitioners. To start the calculations, we set

$$L_1 = X_1 = 103$$

Also, to allow some information for initial estimates of mean error and mean absolute error, the first five forecasts will be calculated with a fixed smoothing constant, set at 0.3, as when these data were analyzed through simple exponential smoothing in Table 6.1. Thus

$$\alpha_t = 0.3 \qquad L_t = 0.3X_t + 0.7L_{t-1} \qquad t = 2, \ldots, 6$$

Hence we find the five forecast errors

$$e_t = X_t - L_{t-1} \qquad t = 3, \ldots, 7$$

These results are recorded in Table 6.5. Then, for initial estimates of mean error and mean absolute error, we take the simple averages

$$E_7 = \frac{(e_3 + \cdots + e_7)}{5} = \frac{(-13.90 + \cdots + 2.58)}{5} = -3.806$$

$$D_7 = \frac{(|e_3| + \cdots + |e_7|)}{5} = \frac{(13.90 + \cdots + 2.58)}{5} = 5.646$$

The initial value of the tracking signal is therefore set at

$$TS_7 = E_7/D_7 = -3.806/5.646 = -0.6741$$

Hence, the smoothing constant to be used in year seven is

$$\alpha_7 = |TS_7| = 0.6741$$

The algorithm now proceeds with adaptive smoothing constant, so that

$$L_7 = 0.6741X_7 + 0.3259L_6$$

$$= (0.6741)(94) + (0.3259)(91.42) = 93.1592$$

We then have, for year eight,

$$e_8 = X_8 - L_7 = 102 - 93.1592 = 8.8408$$

so that

$$E_8 = 0.1e_8 + 0.9E_7 = (0.1)(8.8408) + (0.9)(-3.806) = -2.54132$$

$$D_8 = 0.1|e_8| + 0.9D_7 = (0.1)(8.8408) + (0.9)(5.646) = 5.96548$$

Then

$$TS_8 = -2.54132/5.96548 = -0.426 \qquad \alpha_8 = 0.426$$

and

$$L_8 = (0.426)(102) + (0.574)(93.1592) = 96.92$$

Proceeding in this way we find the results set out in Table 6.5.

Since forecasts are based on the simple exponential smoothing algorithm, the prediction of all future values is the latest estimate of level, so that

$$\hat{X}_{30}(h) = L_{30} = 116 \qquad h = 1, 2, \ldots$$

This differs only trivially from the forecast of 115, obtained in Section 6.2 through simple exponential smoothing with smoothing constant fixed at 0.3. In fact, it can be seen from Table 6.5 that, in this particular application, the value of α_t is for the most part relatively stable at quite low levels. This reflects a failure of the tracking signal to detect much evidence of any substantial bias in the forecasts. In some applications of the Trigg-Leach approach, the value of the tracking signal can exhibit considerably more volatility, so that the value used for α_t swings quite strongly over time. Whether or not this extreme variability is necessarily helpful in securing superior forecast performance is open to debate.

Gardner (1985) discusses a number of other procedures for adaptive control of the smoothing parameters both in simple exponential smoothing and other algorithms. He notes that the empirical evidence on the efficacy of this approach is rather mixed. Indeed, some of the larger empirical studies suggest a preference for the simpler methods where smoothing constants are held fixed.

6.9   EXPONENTIAL SMOOTHING CALCULATIONS WITH PERSONAL COMPUTERS

In previous sections of this chapter we have emphasized the computational simplicity of exponential smoothing algorithms, and certainly the arithmetic can be carried out using a calculator. However, unless the time series of interest is very short, this exercise is rather tedious. The wide availability of personal computers and suitable programs should allow most of our readers to try out some of the techniques of this chapter with a minimum of pain. In this section we will illustrate the generation of exponential smoothing forecasts using two programs available on personal computers. The first example applies Holt's linear trend algorithm of Section 6.3 using the spreadsheet program of LOTUS 1-2-3. In the second example the SPSS program is used to derive forecasts based on the Holt-Winters multiplicative seasonal algorithm of Section 6.4. These programs are quite suitable for the prediction of individual time series. However, in some applications forecasts of a large number of series will be required as inputs to an inventory control system. In that case, exponential smoothing algorithms will typically form part of a very much larger Materials Resource Planning program.

The LOTUS 1-2-3 spreadsheet program is a popular example of the many good electronic spreadsheet programs that are currently available. The utility of such spreadsheets is that both data and results—inputs and outputs—are readily visible. Spreadsheets can be useful tools for the forecaster, especially for exponential smoothing techniques, since

1. modifications to initial conditions, smoothing constants, and data can be easily made.
2. special features, which may not have been included in prewritten programs such as SPSS, can often be easily incorporated.
3. provided that the user's personal computer has graphics, plots of the raw data and predicted values can readily be viewed—something that is of great value when one is changing a smoothing constant, or initial condition.

If the exponential smoothing algorithm used has at most two smoothing constants, it is quite straightforward to use LOTUS 1-2-3 to calculate the in-sample sum of squared forecast errors over a grid of values for the smoothing constants, and thus for the user to determine the values of the smoothing constants that minimize the in-sample sum of squared forecast errors. However, this task is very cumbersome when there are three or more smoothing constants, unless the user writes a macro (or program) for this purpose.

The SPSS computer program for personal computers contains a module TRENDS which incorporates many algorithms for the analysis of time series, including several exponential smoothing procedures. Grid searches for optimal in-sample values for smoothing constants are available as part of this program. Thus, for example, the Holt-Winters algorithm of Section 6.4 is more easily applied through SPSS TRENDS than through LOTUS 1-2-3 if the user does not wish to prespecify smoothing constant values.

LOTUS 1-2-3 Spreadsheet

Spreadsheet programs such as LOTUS 1-2-3 allow the entry of numbers, words, and calculations into cells. In LOTUS 1-2-3 these cells are labeled with a column letter and row number, so that, for example, the cell B5 is the fifth row of column B. Exhibit 6.1 shows screen views from the application of Holt's linear trend algorithm, as described in Section 6.3, to a series of fifty annual observations on the number of active oil wells in the United States. These data are given in Table 6.6.

In Exhibit 6.1, the row and column labels of the spreadsheet are in the shaded borders. Part (a) of the exhibit shows the first screen, with calculations for a particular pair of smoothing constants ($\alpha = 0.8$, $\beta = 0.6$).

Exhibit 6.1 Screens from LOTUS 1-2-3, using Holt's linear trend algorithm to forecast number of active oil wells in the United States.

```
F7: (F2) [W14] @SUM(F14..F60)/1000000000                          READY
```

	A	B	C	D	E	F	G
1	Holt's Linear Trend Algorithm on LOTUS 1-2-3						
2	DATA: Number of Active Oil Wells in US						
3						Sum of squared	
4						one step ahead	
5						forecasts	
6			Alpha	Beta		(in billions)	
7			0.8	0.6		4.70	
8							
9		t	X(t)	L(t)	T(t)	Forecast	e(t)*e(t)
10							
11		1	333070				
12		2	340990	340990.0	7920.0		
13		3	349450	347758.0	7228.8		
14		4	363030	359975.6	10222.1	354986.8	64693066
15		5	369640	367707.1	8727.7	370197.7	311007
16		6	380390	377853.4	9578.9	376434.9	15643101
17		7	389010	386778.7	9186.7	387432.3	2489125
18		8	399960	397323.7	10001.7	395965.4	15956883
19		9	404840	403336.7	7680.5	407325.5	6177470
20		10	407170	406403.3	4883.4	410945.2	14252433

(a)

```
E63: (F1) +$C$60+(A63-$A$60)*$D$60                                READY
```

	A	B	C	D	E	F	G
1	Holt's Linear Trend Algorithm on LOTUS 1-2-3						
2	DATA: Number of Active Oil Wells in US						
3						Sum of squared	
4						one step ahead	
5						forecasts	
6			Alpha	Beta		(in billions)	
7			0.8	0.6		4.70	
8							
9		t	X(t)	L(t)	T(t)	Forecast	e(t)*e(t)
10							
56		46	526835	519207.9	14709.8	479711.3	2220647656
57		47	537523	533860.0	14675.2	533917.7	12998341
58		48	557009	552379.2	16981.6	548535.1	71806182
59		49	580142	574589.4	20118.8	569360.8	116234403
60		50	603290	597549.9	21823.8	594708.2	73646869
61		51				619373.7	
62		52				641197.5	
63		53				663021.2	
64		54				684845.0	
65							

(b)

Exhibit 6.1   *(Continued)*

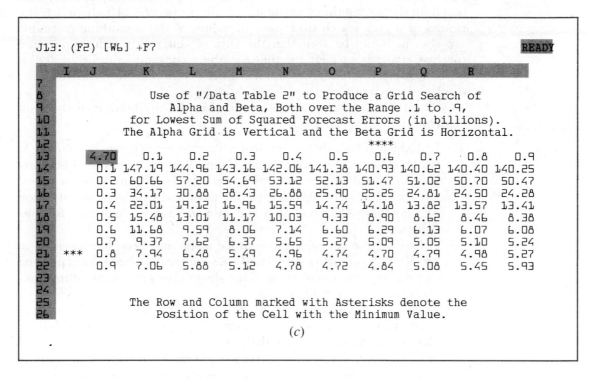

```
J13: (F2) [W6] +F7                                                    READY

     I  J      K      L      M      N      O      P      Q      R
 7
 8            Use of "/Data Table 2" to Produce a Grid Search of
 9              Alpha and Beta, Both over the Range .1 to .9,
10          for Lowest Sum of Squared Forecast Errors (in billions).
11          The Alpha Grid is Vertical and the Beta Grid is Horizontal.
12                                                      ****
13     4.70    0.1    0.2    0.3    0.4    0.5    0.6    0.7    0.8    0.9
14      0.1 147.19 144.96 143.16 142.06 141.38 140.93 140.62 140.40 140.25
15      0.2  60.66  57.20  54.69  53.12  52.13  51.47  51.02  50.70  50.47
16      0.3  34.17  30.88  28.43  26.88  25.90  25.25  24.81  24.50  24.28
17      0.4  22.01  19.12  16.96  15.59  14.74  14.18  13.82  13.57  13.41
18      0.5  15.48  13.01  11.17  10.03   9.33   8.90   8.62   8.46   8.38
19      0.6  11.68   9.59   8.06   7.14   6.60   6.29   6.13   6.07   6.08
20      0.7   9.37   7.62   6.37   5.65   5.27   5.09   5.05   5.10   5.24
21 *** 0.8   7.94   6.48   5.49   4.96   4.74   4.70   4.79   4.98   5.27
22      0.9   7.06   5.88   5.12   4.78   4.72   4.84   5.08   5.45   5.93
23
24
25          The Row and Column marked with Asterisks denote the
26             Position of the Cell with the Minimum Value.

                                  (c)
```

Table 6.6   Number of active oil wells in the United States.

Year	Oil Wells	Year	Oil Wells	Year	Oil Wells	Year	Oil Wells
1	333070	14	426280	27	591158	40	497378
2	340990	15	437880	28	594917	41	497631
3	349450	16	448680	29	596385	42	500333
4	363030	17	465870	30	588675	43	499110
5	369640	18	474990	31	588225	44	508000
6	380390	19	488520	32	589203	45	484311
7	389010	20	498940	33	583302	46	526835
8	399960	21	511200	34	565289	47	537523
9	404840	22	524010	35	553920	48	557009
10	407170	23	551170	36	542227	49	580142
11	412220	24	569273	37	530990	50	603290
12	415750	25	574905	38	517318		
13	421460	26	583141	39	508443		

Part (b) shows the final screen, including forecasts for the next four years based on these smoothing constants. Finally, in part (c) of Exhibit 6.1, the results of a grid search over pairs of values of the smoothing constants are shown. It can be seen that the sum of squared in-sample one-step forecast errors is smallest for the smoothing constant values $\alpha = 0.8$, $\beta = 0.6$, suggesting that we should indeed proceed with the forecasts displayed in part (b).

The following elements are included in this application of the Holt algorithm:

1. In Exhibit 6.1(a), (b) we see that a time index is given in column A, while the data series is set out in column B, successive rows containing information about successive time periods. These entries begin in row 11, earlier rows being reserved for titles and headings, specification of smoothing constants, and the sum of squared, one-step forecast errors.

2. Values for the smoothing constants, alpha and beta, are assigned to specific cells—in this case C7 and C8—rather than being incorporated directly into the calculations. This allows changes in smoothing constant values to be easily made.

3. The Holt algorithm proceeds by calculating, at each time period, current level and trend, here denoted $L(t)$ and $T(t)$. Separate columns, C and D, contain these calculations.

4. Since the intention is to perform a grid search for the best smoothing constant values, two further columns are required at this stage. In column E, elements of this column headed by Forecast contain calculations for the prediction of the current observation $X(t)$, *made at the previous time period*. The values "$e(t)*e(t)$" shown in column F are the squared forecast errors.

5. To start off the algorithm, initial values for level and trend are set as

$$L(2) = X(2) \qquad T(2) = X(2) - X(1)$$

in cells C12 and D12, respectively.

6. From this point we can employ the repetitive nature of the algorithmic calculations

$$L(t) = \alpha X(t) + (1 - \alpha)[L(t-1) + T(t-1)]$$
$$T(t) = \beta[L(t) - L(t-1)] + (1 - \beta)T(t-1) \qquad t = 3, 4, \ldots, 50$$

The necessary instructions need only be inputted for the first set of these calculations—that is, for $t = 3$ (row 13). This can be done by describing the relative positions of the entries for $X(t)$, $L(t)$ and $T(t)$, while using the fixed cell positions for alpha and beta. Thus, after the initial value, the $L(t)$ column entries are: (the number in C7) times (the number to the left) plus (one minus the number in C7) times (the number above). Similarly, after the initial value, the $T(t)$ column entries are: (the number in D7) times (the number to the left minus the number in the previous row to the left) plus (one minus the number in D7) times (the number above). Also, the entries in the Forecast column are the sum of the $T(t)$ and $L(t)$ entries from the previous row. Finally, $e(t)*e(t)$ is the square of the difference between the column B and column E entries for the same row. These instructions can then be copied through to the end of the data set ($t = 50$, row 60, in this particular example). The sum of squared errors is entered in cell F7 in our example.

7. When these calculations are completed, forecasts of future values, based on the particular smoothing constants used, are easily found. The forecast for time $50 + h$ is simply L(50) plus h times T(50). These forecasts are displayed in rows 61–64 of Exhibit 6.1(b).

8. A grid search for the values of alpha and beta that minimize the sum of squared, in-sample, one-step forecast errors can be performed with LOTUS 1-2-3 using the /DT2, or Data Table 2, command. The results are shown in Exhibit 6.1(c). The value in the top left corner of the table, cell J13 (which is in reverse color, denoting that the cursor is resting here), specifies which calculation will be carried out for the given combination of parameters, here alpha and beta. The top left corner of the screen displays format and formula contents of cell J13. As we already noted, in this particular example, the minimum sum of squared forecast errors occurs when alpha is 0.8 and beta is 0.6.

With very little further arithmetic, it is possible to use formula (6.7.3) to calculate interval forecasts. For the optimum values of the smoothing constants, we see from Exhibit 6.1 that the sum of squared one year ahead forecasts errors is 4.70×10^9. Since this sum is based on 47 forecasts, then, as in (6.7.1), the one year ahead forecast error variance is estimated as

$$S^2(1) = 4.70 \times 10^9/47 = 1.00 \times 10^8$$

The forecasts are based on smoothing constants $\alpha = 0.8$, $\beta = 0.6$. Substitution of these values in formula (6.7.3) gives

$$S^2(2) = 2.6384 \; S^2(1) \qquad S^2(3) = 5.7360 \; S^2(1)$$
$$S^2(4) = 10.7536 \; S^2(1)$$

Finally, we can find, for example, 75% prediction intervals from

$$\hat{X}_n(h) \pm 1.15 \; S(h)$$

Reading the point forecasts directly from part (b) of Exhibit 6.1, we find the following 75% prediction intervals for the next four years

$$619{,}374 \pm 11{,}500$$

$$641{,}198 \pm 18{,}680$$

$$663{,}021 \pm 27{,}542$$

$$684{,}845 \pm 37{,}712$$

SPSS/PC TRENDS

The module TRENDS of the SPSS/PC program allows the analysis of time series through a number of different exponential smoothing algorithms. Here we will apply the Holt-Winters algorithm with multiplicative seasonality to a series of 132 monthly observations on shipments of machine tools of cutting and forming types. The data are given in Table 6.7.

Part of the output is shown in Exhibit 6.2. The user can specify initial values for the seasonal factors (expressed as percentages), level, and trend. If, as in our example, this is not done, the program implements an initialization procedure discussed by Gardner (1985). The program performs a grid search over smoothing constant values, which are denoted here alpha, gamma, delta, corresponding respectively to our α, β, γ of Section 6.4. The ten sets of values leading to the smallest sums of squared, one-step, in-sample forecast errors are printed out. From the output, we see that the optimal choice is (0.4, 0.2, 0.4). Accordingly, in the final part of Exhibit 6.2 we computed forecasts based on these smoothing constants. The output segment displayed shows fitted values—one-step forecasts— for the last few observations, and predicted shipments for the next twelve

TABLE 6.7   Shipments of machine tools of metal cutting and forming types (millions of dollars).

Year	Jan	Feb	Mar	Apr	May	Jun	Jul	Aug	Sep	Oct	Nov	Dec
1	156.3	175.1	200.6	173.4	162.2	182.5	148.7	124.3	187.4	163.1	177.0	209.5
2	145.1	168.7	183.2	176.8	185.7	222.3	167.7	145.0	211.5	193.1	220.0	262.9
3	209.3	201.6	272.4	243.0	255.7	293.0	208.5	215.4	263.8	266.9	274.5	280.5
4	244.6	280.4	333.2	305.1	322.7	350.6	267.7	285.4	346.8	380.1	361.3	399.2
5	330.8	355.5	460.0	343.1	374.7	475.7	327.0	311.0	411.3	439.9	400.2	463.3
6	389.0	422.2	477.2	347.4	411.4	508.9	367.2	325.4	441.5	406.9	408.2	490.9
7	383.6	359.7	411.1	303.5	295.9	409.2	250.4	257.2	275.9	200.7	193.5	264.2
8	162.9	158.4	176.3	150.9	135.9	183.1	122.4	113.1	131.7	145.5	147.7	237.9
9	113.0	147.3	189.3	158.8	210.1	203.5	182.0	164.4	210.8	207.8	211.8	275.8
10	137.9	166.3	227.7	169.8	177.3	239.0	194.8	215.9	244.0	199.3	199.2	374.4
11	145.9	202.6	248.8	209.6	229.6	311.9	190.1	151.4	208.0	242.8	166.8	272.0

Exhibit 6.2 Part of SPSS program output for the prediction of shipments of machine tools of cutting and forming types through the Holt-Winters algorithm with multiplicative seasonality.

```
Results of EXSMOOTH procedure for Variable TOOLS
MODEL = LM (Linear trend, multiplicative seasonality)        Period = 12

Seasonal indices:


             Seasonal
  Period       index
     1         84.174
     2         92.278
     3        112.324
     4         92.237
     5         98.441
     6        119.962
     7         86.489
     8         81.993
     9        105.834
    10         99.558
    11        100.495
    12        126.215


  Initial values:       Series           Trend
                     169.51083          .36069

DFE = 119.

The 10 smallest SSE's are:    Alpha    Gamma    Delta          SSE
                              .4000    .2000    .4000    104542.67299
                              .4000    .2000    .5000    104949.29091
                              .3000    .3000    .3000    104989.63305
                              .4000    .2000    .3000    105121.24279
                              .3000    .3000    .2000    105442.96655
                              .3000    .4000    .2000    105826.71795
                              .3000    .3000    .4000    105900.76384
                              .4000    .2000    .6000    106306.21673
                              .3000    .4000    .1000    106385.18622
                              .4000    .2000    .2000    106630.92324


  The SSE is:    Alpha    Gamma    Delta          SSE
                 .4000    .2000    .4000    104542.67299
```

Exhibit 6.2   (*Continued*)

Case#	TOOLS	FIT#1
109	137.9	186.67992
110	166.3	188.89071
111	227.7	215.41477
112	169.8	179.66644
113	177.3	188.80535
114	239.0	211.96053
115	194.8	162.93279
116	215.9	164.13517
117	244.0	235.67028
118	199.3	239.69432
119	199.2	228.42879
120	374.4	285.96174
121	145.9	200.35190
122	202.6	212.18869
123	248.8	264.65817
124	209.6	206.17773
125	229.6	225.22889
126	311.9	277.96563
127	190.1	219.97260
128	151.4	197.07324
129	208.0	204.88314
130	242.8	186.44946
131	166.8	212.97247
132	272.0	276.32501
133	.	142.27791
134	.	176.11120
135	.	218.29341
136	.	174.68541
137	.	186.34280
138	.	228.95338
139	.	157.60670
140	.	142.49386
141	.	174.87413
142	.	167.87866
143	.	148.02102
144	.	221.02739

FIGURE 6.7   Monthly shipments of machine tools, and forecasts for the next twelve months.

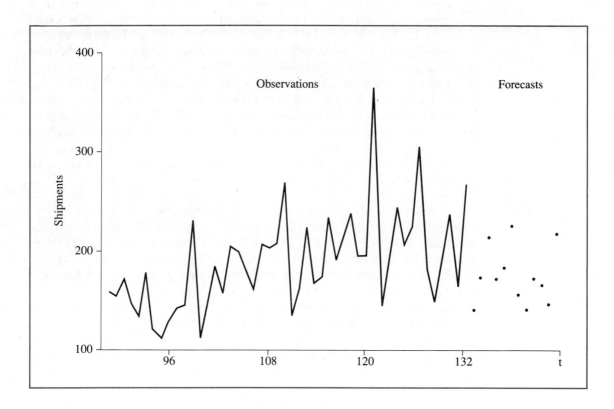

months. The last four years of data, together with forecasts for the next twelve months are graphed in Figure 6.7.

6.10   THE ROLE OF EXPONENTIAL SMOOTHING IN BUSINESS FORECASTING

Because a wide diversity of forecasting problems arise in the business environment, it would be unrealistic to expect that a single methodological approach would be invariably appropriate. Certainly neither we nor its most enthusiastic proponents would make this claim for exponential smoothing. This approach has two serious limitations that restrict its applicability.

1. Often forecasts of future values of a time series can be considerably improved through the incorporation of information on related time series, such as within the framework of regression models, as discussed in Chapters 3 and 4. It is very difficult to satisfactorily extend exponential smoothing algorithms to incorporate information beyond that contained in the history of the series to be predicted.

2. Even when a time series is to be predicted on the basis of its own past alone, it must be expected that difficult or atypical data sets, for which the usual standard methods do not work well, will be met on occasion. In such circumstances, an approach based on careful model building, where the forecast function is tailored to the observed data characteristics, would be desirable. In Chapter 7 we will discuss such an approach.

A summary of these reservations might suggest that, if the development of particularly accurate forecasts is sufficiently important and adequate resources are available, a more elaborate methodology than exponential smoothing might be preferred. However, many industrial forecasting systems require the regular routine production of forecasts for a great many time series. Great accuracy for predictions of individual series will not be of paramount importance, and budget and other resource constraints will prohibit the devotion of much effort to the development of appropriate procedures for every series. In such circumstances, a fully automatic forecasting algorithm is essential, and exponential smoothing methods are almost invariably chosen by practitioners. Certainly we know of no convincing evidence in favor of any alternative. In business applications, exponential smoothing algorithms seem to exhibit the property of *robustness*, which is highly desirable in routine forecasting. The forecasts produced may be capable of improvement, with some effort, but they are generally pretty good for a wide variety of time series met in practice. As to which particular exponential smoothing algorithms are most useful in practical forecasting exercises of this sort, it is impossible to be dogmatic. To some extent, practitioners tend to have their own favorites, and the accumulated empirical evidence that exists, summarized by Gardner (1985), is not completely definitive. Our own preference is for the algorithms of Sections 6.2 through 6.4. They have simple, intuitively appealing forms, and seem to have been successful in many practical implementations.

We do not wish to leave the reader with the impression that exponential smoothing algorithms are necessarily a poor second best to elaborate time series model-building methods, used only when forced on the analyst by various circumstances. In fact, in a number of large-scale empirical studies, such as Reid (1975), Newbold and Granger (1974), Makridakis and Hibon (1979), and Makridakis, et al. (1982), various exponential smoothing algorithms have been found to perform quite well, *in the aggregate*, compared with time series model-building methods.

EXERCISES

6.1 Discuss the limitations of forecasting future values of a time series as the average of all past values. Why might weighted averages be preferred? Explain how simple exponential smoothing involves, in effect, a particular scheme of weighted averages.

6.2 Suppose that the series X_t is to be predicted through simple exponential smoothing. Let L_t denote the estimate of level, and e_t the error made in the prediction of X_t at time $(t - 1)$. If α denotes the smoothing constant, show that

$$L_{t-1} - (1 - \alpha)L_{t-2} = \alpha X_{t-1}$$

$$= X_t - (1 - \alpha)X_{t-1} - [e_t - (1 - \alpha)e_{t-1}]$$

and hence that

$$X_t - X_{t-1} = e_t - (1 - \alpha)e_{t-1}$$

6.3 The accompanying table shows U.S. local government employment in thousands over a period of 25 months.

Month	Employment	Month	Employment	Month	Employment
1	10,849	10	11,098	18	11,098
2	10,980	11	10,202	19	11,298
3	10,973	12	10,040	20	11,363
4	10,609	13	10,817	21	11,353
5	10,829	14	11,184	22	11,441
6	11,022	15	11,334	23	11,304
7	11,100	16	11,283	24	10,352
8	11,099	17	10,934	25	10,177
9	11,195				

(a) Use simple exponential smoothing, with smoothing constant 0.4, to predict future values of this series.
(b) Graph the time series, together with forecasts for the next five months.

6.4   The accompanying table shows average U.S. manufacturing weekly hours worked over a period of 25 months.

Month	Hours	Month	Hours	Month	Hours
1	40.9	10	41.1	18	40.2
2	41.0	11	40.5	19	39.9
3	41.3	12	40.8	20	40.1
4	41.0	13	41.3	21	40.1
5	40.6	14	40.9	22	40.3
6	40.4	15	40.8	23	40.9
7	40.7	16	41.3	24	40.4
8	39.8	17	40.8	25	40.9
9	40.9				

(a)   Use simple exponential smoothing, with smoothing constant 0.3, to predict future values of this series.

(b)   Graph the time series, together with forecasts for the next five months.

(c)   Use the method of Trigg and Leach, with $\delta = 0.1$, to derive forecasts through simple exponential smoothing with an adaptive smoothing constant.

6.5   Exponential smoothing is used to provide forecasting algorithms that are not explicitly based on the specification of a formal statistical model. Discuss the consequences, and some of the difficulties that can arise, in the absence of a formal model specification.

6.6   The accompanying table shows the U.S. 6-months certificate of deposit rate over a period of 30 months.

Month	Rate	Month	Rate	Month	Rate
1	9.60	11	8.48	21	7.17
2	9.09	12	8.57	22	6.51
3	8.59	13	8.48	23	6.50
4	8.56	14	8.28	24	6.16
5	8.75	15	8.12	25	6.03
6	8.45	16	7.99	26	6.26
7	8.21	17	8.06	27	6.25
8	8.12	18	8.05	28	5.79
9	8.17	19	7.95	29	5.60
10	8.26	20	7.64	30	5.32

(a)   Use simple exponential smoothing, with smoothing constants 0.2, 0.4, 0.6, 0.8, to predict future values of the time series.

(b) Which value of the smoothing constant would you choose to use for further forecasting?

6.7 Suppose that the series X_t is to be predicted through Holt's linear trend algorithm, with smoothing constants α and β. Let L_t and T_t denote the estimates of level and slope, and e_t the error made in the prediction of X_t at time $(t - 1)$.

(a) Show that

$$T_{t-1} - 2T_{t-2} + T_{t-3} = \alpha\beta(e_{t-1} - e_{t-2})$$

(b) Show that

$$L_{t-1} - 2L_{t-2} + L_{t-3} = \alpha\beta e_{t-2} + \alpha(e_{t-1} - e_{t-2})$$

(c) Using the results in (a) and (b), show that

$$X_t - 2X_{t-1} + X_{t-2}$$
$$= e_t - (2 - \alpha - \alpha\beta)e_{t-1} + (1 - \alpha)e_{t-2}$$

6.8 Consider again the data of Exercise 6.6 on the 6-months certificate of deposit rate

(a) Use Holt's linear trend algorithm, with smoothing constants $\alpha = 0.5, \beta = 0.2$, to obtain forecasts for the next five months.

(b) Faced with such a time series, discuss how you would decide whether to use simple exponential smoothing or Holt's linear trend algorithm.

6.9 The accompanying table shows U.S. manufacturing hourly earnings over a period of 25 months.

Month	Earnings	Month	Earnings	Month	Earnings
1	10.53	10	10.84	18	11.05
2	10.58	11	10.87	19	11.02
3	10.67	12	10.81	20	11.06
4	10.48	13	10.93	21	11.11
5	10.59	14	10.94	22	11.15
6	10.67	15	10.96	23	11.19
7	10.74	16	11.05	24	11.22
8	10.74	17	10.83	25	11.17
9	10.80				

(a) Use Holt's linear trend algorithm, with smoothing constants $\alpha = 0.4, \beta = 0.6$, to predict the time series.

(b) Graph the series together with forecasts for the next five months.

6.10 The accompanying table shows the number of active oil wells (in thousands) in the United States over a period of 30 years.

Year	Wells	Year	Wells	Year	Wells
1	511	11	588	21	498
2	524	12	589	22	500
3	551	13	583	23	499
4	569	14	565	24	508
5	575	15	554	25	484
6	583	16	542	26	527
7	591	17	531	27	538
8	595	18	517	28	557
9	596	19	508	29	580
10	589	20	497	30	603

(a) Use Holt's linear trend algorithm with all sixteen combinations of values of smoothing constants, $\alpha = 0.2, 0.4, 0.6, 0.8$ and $\beta = 0.2, 0.4, 0.6, 0.8$, to predict this series over the next five years.

(b) Which values of the smoothing constants would you choose to use for further forecasting?

6.11 The accompanying table shows plant and equipment expenditures in billions of dollars in the United States over a period of seven years.

	Quarter			
Year	1	2	3	4
1	19.38	22.01	21.86	25.20
2	21.50	24.73	25.04	28.48
3	24.10	28.16	28.23	31.92
4	25.82	28.43	27.79	30.74
5	25.87	29.70	30.41	34.52
6	29.20	33.73	34.82	38.06
7	32.35	37.89	38.67	44.91

(a) Use the Holt-Winters algorithm with additive seasonality, and with smoothing constants $\alpha = 0.5$, $\beta = 0.2$, $\gamma = 0.3$ to derive forecasts for the next eight quarters.

(b) Repeat part (a), but now assuming multiplicative seasonality.

6.12 Suppose that, in general exponential smoothing, a constant predictor

$$\hat{X}_t(h) = a(t) \qquad h = 1, 2, \ldots$$

is required. The value of $a(t)$ is chosen to minimize

$$S = \sum_{j=0}^{t-1} \delta^j [X_{t-j} - a(t)]^2 \qquad 0 < \delta < 1$$

(a)   Show that the value of $a(t)$ for which S is a minimum is

$$a(t) = (1 - \delta) \sum_{j=0}^{t-1} \frac{\delta^j X_{t-j}}{(1 - \delta^t)}$$

and hence that

$$a(t - 1) = (1 - \delta) \sum_{j=0}^{t-2} \frac{\delta^j X_{t-1-j}}{(1 - \delta^{t-1})}$$

(b)   Show that
$$a(t) - \delta a(t - 1) \simeq (1 - \delta)X_t$$

provided that t is moderately large, so that we can take $\delta^t \simeq \delta^{t-1} \simeq 0$.

(c)   Discuss the result in (b) in terms of the simple exponential smoothing algorithm.

6.13   The accompanying table shows monthly retail sales of apparel, in billions of dollars, over four years.

		Year		
	1	2	3	4
January	3.43	4.34	4.59	5.05
February	3.15	4.17	4.40	4.73
March	4.12	5.06	5.72	6.59
April	4.27	5.55	5.96	6.17
May	4.26	5.53	6.09	6.79
June	4.18	5.49	5.66	6.12
July	4.04	4.90	5.42	5.95
August	4.56	5.68	6.60	7.11
September	4.31	5.47	5.90	6.45
October	4.62	5.59	6.31	6.83
November	5.17	6.47	7.27	7.57
December	7.91	9.55	10.38	11.43

(a)   Use the Holt-Winters algorithm with additive seasonality, and with smoothing constants $\alpha = 0.2$, $\beta = 0.4$, $\gamma = 0.3$, to derive forecasts for the next twelve months.

(b)   Repeat part (a), but now assuming multiplicative seasonality.

6.14   Suppose that the simple constant predictor

$$\hat{X}_t(h) = L_t \qquad h = 1, 2, \ldots$$

is to be used, with L_t taken as the unweighted average of all available observations

$$L_t = \frac{(X_1 + X_2 + \cdots + X_t)}{t}$$

Show that

$$L_t = t^{-1}X_t + (t - 1)t^{-1}L_{t-1}$$

Compare this with simple exponential smoothing.

6.15   The accompanying table shows 48 monthly observations on an index of newspaper advertising.

t	X_t	t	X_t	t	X_t	t	X_t
1	91.9	13	97.9	25	97.5	37	96.6
2	83.3	14	91.3	26	99.6	38	101.0
3	104.2	15	109.9	27	114.8	39	116.4
4	102.9	16	121.7	28	121.4	40	103.6
5	115.5	17	116.6	29	119.6	41	108.3
6	104.3	18	111.1	30	111.1	42	105.4
7	93.8	19	99.8	31	102.9	43	88.8
8	96.6	20	92.7	32	95.8	44	101.6
9	102.2	21	93.8	33	100.1	45	96.9
10	119.3	22	108.0	34	102.0	46	109.1
11	118.2	23	123.3	35	124.2	47	117.3
12	105.8	24	109.1	36	110.0	48	98.8

(a)   Use the Holt-Winters algorithm with additive seasonality, and with smoothing constants $\alpha = 0.4$, $\beta = 0.6$, $\gamma = 0.5$, to derive forecasts for the next twelve months.

(b)   Repeat part (a), but now assuming multiplicative seasonality.

(c)   Faced with such a time series, discuss how you would decide whether to use the additive or multiplicative seasonality variant of the algorithm.

SELECTED BIBLIOGRAPHY

Ameen, J. R. M., & P. J. Harrison (1984). Discounted weighted estimation. *Journal of Forecasting, 3*, 285–296.

Bretschneider, S. (1986). Estimating forecast variance with exponential smoothing: some new results. *International Journal of Forecasting, 2*, 349–355.

Brown, R. G. (1959). *Statistical Forecasting for Inventory Control.* New York: McGraw-Hill.

Brown, R. G. (1962). *Smoothing, Forecasting and Prediction of Discrete Time Series.* Englewood Cliffs, N.J.: Prentice-Hall.

Brown, R. G., & R. F. Meyer (1961). The fundamental theorem of exponential smoothing. *Operations Research, 9*, 673–685.

Chatfield, C. (1977). Some recent developments in time series analysis. *Journal of the Royal Statistical Society A, 140*, 492–510.

Chatfield, C. (1978). The Holt-Winters forecasting procedure. *Applied Statistics, 27*, 264–279.

Chatfield, C., & M. Yar (1988). Holt-Winters forecasting: some practical issues. *The Statistician, 37*, 129–140.

Chatfield, C., & M. Yar (1991). Prediction intervals for multiplicative Holt-Winters. *International Journal of Forecasting, 7*, 31–37.

Chow, W. M. (1965). Adaptive control of the exponential smoothing constant. *Journal of Industrial Engineering, 16*, 314–317.

Cox, D. R. (1961). Prediction by exponential weighted moving averages and related methods. *Journal of the Royal Statistical Society B, 23*, 414–422.

Fildes, R. (1979). Quantitative forecasting—the state of the art: extrapolative methods. *Journal of the Operational Research Society, 30*, 691–710.

Gardner, E. S. (1983). Automatic monitoring of forecast errors. *Journal of Forecasting, 2*, 1–21.

Gardner, E. S. (1984). The strange case of the lagging forecasts. *Interfaces, 14*, 47–50.

Gardner E. S. (1985). Exponential smoothing: the state of the art. *Journal of Forecasting, 4*, 1–28.

Gardner, E. S., & D. G. Dannenbring (1980). Forecasting with exponential smoothing: some guidelines for model selection. *Decision Sciences, 11*, 370–383.

Gilchrist, W. G. (1967). Methods of estimation using discounting. *Journal of the Royal Statistical Society B, 29*, 355–369.

Gilchrist, W. G. (1976). *Statistical Forecasting*. London: Wiley.

Godolphin, E. J., & P. J. Harrison (1975). Equivalence theorems for polynomial-projecting predictors. *Journal of the Royal Statistical Society B, 37*, 205–215.

Golder, E. R., & J. G. Settle (1976). Monitoring schemes in short-term forecasting. *Operational Research Quarterly, 27*, 489–501.

Groff, G. K. (1973). Empirical comparison of models for short-range forecasting. *Management Science, 20*, 22–31.

Harrison, P. J. (1965). Short-term sales forecasting. *Applied Statistics, 14*, 102–139.

Harrison, P. J. (1967). Exponential smoothing and short-term sales forecasting. *Management Science, 13*, 821–842.

Harrison, P. J., & O. L. Davies (1964). The use of cumulative sum (CUSUM) techniques for the control of routine forecasts of product demand. *Operations Research, 12*, 325–333.

Holt, C. C. (1957). Forecasting seasonal and trends by exponentially weighted moving averages. Office of Naval Research. (Memorandum 52).

Ledolter, J., & B. Abraham (1984). Some comments on the initialization of exponential smoothing. *Journal of Forecasting, 3*, 79–84.

Makridakis, S., A. Anderson, R. Carbone, R. Fildes, M. Hibon, R. Lewandowski, J. Newton, E. Parzen, & R. Winkler (1982). The accuracy of extrapolation (time series) methods. *Journal of Forecasting, 1*, 111–153.

Makridakis, S., & M. Hibon (1979). Accuracy of forecasting: an empirical investigation. *Journal of the Royal Statistical Society A, 142*, 97–145.

Makridakis, S., & M. Hibon (1991). Exponential smoothing: the effect of initial values and loss functions on post-sample forecasting accuracy. *International Journal of Forecasting, 7*, 317–330.

McClain, J. O. (1988). Dominant tracking signals. *International Journal of Forecasting, 4*, 563–572.

McKenzie, E. (1978). The monitoring of exponentially weighted forecasts. *Journal of the Operational Research Society, 29*, 449–458.

McKenzie, E. (1984). General exponential smoothing and the equivalent ARMA process. *Journal of Forecasting, 3*, 333–344.

Muth, J. F. (1960). Optimal properties of exponentially weighted forecasts. *Journal of the American Statistical Association, 55*, 299–306.

Nerlove, M., & S. Wage (1964). On the optimality of adaptive forecasting. *Management Science, 10*, 207–224.

Newbold, P., & T. Bos (1989). On exponential smoothing and the assumption of deterministic trend plus white noise data-generating models. *International Journal of Forecasting, 5,* 523–527.

Newbold, P., & C. W. J. Granger (1974). Experience with forecasting univariate time series and the combination of forecasts. *Journal of the Royal Statistical Society A, 137,* 131–165.

Reid, D. J. (1975). A review of short-term projection techniques. In H. A. Gordon (Ed.), *Practical Aspects of Forecasting.* London: Operational Research Society.

Sweet, A. L. (1981). Adaptive smoothing for forecasting seasonal series. *AIIE Transactions, 13,* 243–248.

Theil, H., & S. Wage (1964). Some observations on adaptive forecasting. *Management Science, 10,* 198–206.

Trigg, D. W. (1964). Monitoring a forecasting system. *Operational Research Quarterly, 15,* 271–274.

Trigg, D. W., & A. G. Leach (1967). Exponential smoothing with an adaptive response rate. *Operational Research Quarterly, 18,* 53–59.

Winters, P. R. (1960). Forecasting sales by exponentially weighted moving averages. *Management Science, 6,* 324–342.

Yar, M., & C. Chatfield (1990). Prediction intervals for the Holt-Winters forecasting procedure. *International Journal of Forecasting, 6,* 127–137.

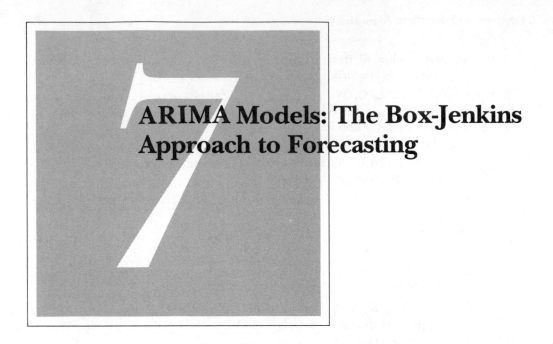

7 ARIMA Models: The Box-Jenkins Approach to Forecasting

7.1 BUILDING MODELS FOR FORECASTING

The practical problem to be discussed in this chapter is, with one possible caveat, the same as that considered in Chapter 6. Based exclusively on information from its own past, forecasts of future values of a time series are required. In the exponential smoothing approach, a particular forecasting algorithm is applied to a time series without first making a careful and thorough study of the properties of that series. We now assume that the investigator has available the resources for such a study, and intends to develop a forecast function that is appropriate for series with the observed properties. The particular algorithm eventually chosen for forecasting, then, will be determined through an examination of the behavior of the observed time series. The first step in such an approach is an attempt to fit a stochastic model to the given set of time series data. The goal is for this fitted model to provide a reasonably close approximation to the process that actually generates the data. If this can be achieved, we can then ask how best to predict future values for a given series.

In this chapter, the model-building approach to forecasting a time series will be discussed. In pursuing this approach, answers must be provided to three questions:

1. What class of models might be considered as possible generators of observed time series?
2. How should the analyst proceed to fit a specific model from the general class to a given data set?
3. How are forecasts of future values developed from the fitted model?

In an extremely influential book, Box and Jenkins (1970) attacked the forecasting problem within this framework. They proposed the use of a class of models called *autoregressive integrated moving average (ARIMA) models*, and developed a methodology for fitting to data an appropriate member of this class. In this chapter we will describe and illustrate the Box-Jenkins approach.

Forecasts of future observations are to depend on the observed time series data; that is, the forecasts will be *functions* of the given data, where the particular function used in any implementation will be determined by the model that has been fitted. Now, in principle, there are infinitely many possible forecast functions from which a choice could be made. However, as a practical matter, some limitations must be imposed before much progress can be made. The ARIMA model-building approach is based on the following two restrictions:

1. The forecasts are linear functions of the sample observations.
2. The aim is to find efficiently parameterized models—that is, models that provide an adequate description of the characteristics of an observed time series with as few parameters as possible.

The restriction to linear forecast functions is not something that is *a priori* desirable. Rather, it is very often a practical necessity. Given a limited amount of data, it is simply impossible in any systematic way to investigate the merits of all possible forecasting functions. The set of linear functions still provides a very rich class of possibilities, and should prove adequate for most purposes. In fact, as we will see, some modest extension of this class is quite feasible through the analysis of simple transformations, such as logarithms, of the data. The importance of efficiently parameterized models should be stressed. Both practical experience and common sense suggest that, given a limited amount of data, it is easy to find a model with a large number of parameters to achieve a good fit to the sample data, but post-sample forecasts developed from such models are likely to be disappointingly poor. For example, given a time series of forty observations, a polynomial of degree thirty nine in time will provide a perfect fit. However, surely one could not be optimistic about the quality of forecasts from the projection forward of this fitted model. An excellent strategy in building models for forecasting is to seek the simplest possible model—that is, the model with the fewest parameters—that appears to provide an adequate description of the major features of the data. In this way the analyst can have some faith that the achieved model depicts genuine regularities in the data-generating process, and hence that it should provide reliable forecasts. This preference for relatively simple models is sometimes known as the **principle of parsimony.**

The ARIMA models, and the associated model-building methodology, are best introduced by restricting attention to nonseasonal time series. Accordingly, we will postpone to Section 7.11 a discussion of model-building and forecasting for seasonal series. Before considering the full ARIMA class, it will be useful to examine an important subclass of these models—*pure autoregressive models*. These models have immediate intuitive appeal, are very easily fitted to data, and in many applications will yield quite adequate forecasts. We have already met autoregressive models in our discussion in Chapter 4 of regression equations with autocorrelated errors. In Section 7.2 we will see how these models can be used in the time series prediction problem. In Sections 7.3–10 we extend this analysis to the broader autoregressive integrated moving average class of models.

7.2 FORECASTING FROM AUTOREGRESSIVE MODELS

In Chapter 4 we saw that, for regressions involving time series data, it is important to check for the possibility of autocorrelated errors, and that the **first-order autoregressive model** can be useful in representing auto-correlation in regression errors. This same model can also be useful in representing the behavior of some observed time series. Let $X_1, X_2, \ldots,$ X_n denote a series of n observations for which forecasts are required. As a possible generating process for these data we could consider the first-order autoregressive model

$$X_t = C + \phi_1 X_{t-1} + a_t \qquad (7.2.1)$$

In equation 7.2.1, ϕ_1 is the autoregressive parameter, and a_t is a random variable, assumed to have zero mean and constant variance at all time periods t. It is further assumed that a_t is not autocorrelated, so that there is no correlation between a_t and the error in any other time period. Thus the a_t are taken to have the properties of the error terms in a regression equation when the standard assumptions for the regression model hold. In addition, the parameter C is included in the model 7.2.1 to allow for the fact that the time series X_t can have non-zero mean.

Given our assumptions about the first-order autoregressive model 7.2.1, the value X_t, observed at time t, can be viewed as the sum of two parts, a quantity $(C + \phi_1 X_{t-1})$ that will be known at time $(t - 1)$, and an unpredictable random term a_t, uncorrelated with anything known previously. Then, standing at time $(t - 1)$, since the random variable a_t has mean zero, the best forecast of X_t will be $(C + \phi_1 X_{t-1})$. Notice that, if the first-order autoregressive model is indeed the true data-generating process, forecasts of future values of the time series depend only on the most recent observation. Certainly there are many real time series for which such a forecast does indeed appear to be optimal. However, it is natural to suspect that it will often be desirable to base forecasts on more than just a single observation. This suggests an extension of the simple model 7.2.1.

Suppose that we want to base forecasts on the *two* most recent observations. This suggests the specification of the model

$$X_t = C + \phi_1 X_{t-1} + \phi_2 X_{t-2} + a_t \qquad (7.2.2)$$

where the past value X_{t-2}, with associated parameter ϕ_2, has been incorporated into the model. The formulation 7.2.2 is called a **second-order autoregressive model.** More generally, for any positive integer p, we could require that forecasts of future values be a linear function of the p most recent observations, suggesting the generating model

$$X_t = C + \phi_1 X_{t-1} + \phi_2 X_{t-2} + \cdots + \phi_p X_{t-p} + a_t \quad (7.2.3)$$

This is the **autoregressive model of order p,** denoted $AR(p)$.

Given sample data, a relatively straightforward approach to time series forecasting is based on the fitting of autoregressive models. Assume for now that the autoregressive order p has been determined. It then remains to estimate the parameters $C, \phi_1, \ldots, \phi_p$ of equation 7.2.3. The fact that the random variable a_t has the properties of the error terms of a regression equation under the standard assumptions suggests the use of least squares. Thus equation 7.2.3 can be treated as a multiple regression model, with dependent variable X_t and p independent variables $X_{t-1}, \ldots, X_{t-p}$. The sum of squares to be minimized is

$$S = \sum_{t=p+1}^{n} (X_t - C - \phi_1 X_{t-1} - \cdots - \phi_p X_{t-p})^2$$

where summation begins at time $(p + 1)$ since X_1 is the first available observation. It follows that an ordinary multiple regression computer program can be used to estimate the parameters of an autoregressive model.

In any practical application of this approach it is necessary to select the autoregressive order, p. One possibility is to fit a sequence of autoregressions for all possible orders up to some maximum contemplated level. We could then compare the estimated autoregressive parameter of highest order in a model with its estimated standard error, and drop that parameter if its estimate is insignificant at some level. In this way, the hypothesis that the model is $AR(p - 1)$ against the alternative that it is $AR(p)$ can be tested with the usual t-statistic, though the choice of significance level for such tests is quite arbitrary. The more modern approach is to employ an **order estimation criterion.** Again, all models up to some maximum order, say p_{max}, are fitted; that is, we estimate 7.2.3 for values $p = 1, 2, \ldots, p_{max}$. The fitted models are then compared using criteria which reflect both their closeness of fit to the data and the number of parameters estimated. Two criteria of this sort are in very common use. These are the Akaike Information Criterion (AIC) and the Schwartz Bayesian Criterion (SBC). The latter is often called the Bayesian Information Criterion (BIC). In the context of our model, these are defined as

$$AIC(p) = n \log \hat{\sigma}_p^2 + 2p \qquad (p = 1, \ldots, p_{max}) \quad (7.2.4)$$

$$SBC(p) = n \log \hat{\sigma}_p^2 + p \log n \qquad (p = 1, \ldots, p_{max}) \quad (7.2.5)$$

where $\hat{\sigma}_p^2$ is the estimated error variance when an $AR(p)$ model is fitted, so that

$$\hat{\sigma}_p^2 = \sum_{t=p+1}^{n} \frac{\hat{a}_t^2}{(n - p)}$$

where the $\hat{a}_t$ are the residuals from the fitted models. The value of p chosen is then the one for which the criterion is smallest. In fact, a number of alternative formulations of these criteria are stated in the literature and calculated in computer packages. However, since these are increasing functions of equations 7.2.4 and 7.2.5, in practice it does not matter which formulation is employed. The decision as to whether to base model choice on AIC or SBC *can* affect the conclusion reached. The two criteria differ in their second terms, which are penalty functions for extra parameters; these terms increase in value as extra parameters are added to the model.

Often AIC and SBC will lead to the same model choice. Moreover, even when different models are selected, the chosen models will frequently yield very similar forecasts. It is not possible to be dogmatic on the question of which criterion is preferable for practical use. To some extent this depends on the way the model selection problem is viewed. If we think of autoregressive order p as a parameter to be estimated, it is known that

SBC yields consistent estimates, while AIC is inconsistent, tending in large samples to produce estimates that are higher than the true value. This suggests a preference for SBC. On the other hand, if we do not think of the autoregressive model specification as correct, but as an approximation to some unknown generating model, it may be sensible to follow AIC in choosing the more elaborate model, in the hope that this may provide a better approximation. To some extent the choice might be dictated by the strength of the analyst's attachment to the principle of parsimony. If a choice has to be made, our own slight preference is for AIC when fitting autoregressive models. However, when comparing the more general ARIMA models to be discussed in later sections of this chapter, we tend toward SBC. Alternatively, if the two approaches lead to quite different forecasts, it might pay to consider the combination of these forecasts, using methods to be discussed in Chapter 12.

To illustrate the approach to fitting autoregressive models to time series data discussed here, we analyze a set of 252 daily observations on volume of shares traded on the New York Stock Exchange. These data are provided in the appendix at the end of this chapter. As we have indicated, autoregressive models can be fitted using standard multiple regression programs. However, there are also several packages that have been written for the fitting of ARIMA time series models. Autoregressive models are members of the general ARIMA class, so that the time series packages can be used for fitting these models. We have used here the SPSS/PC time series package, which produces estimates of the model parameters, and routinely calculates the corresponding AIC and SBC statistics. In Section 7.9 we will discuss in detail the output of this package in the broader context of fitting ARIMA models. Here we show in Table 7.1 the values of AIC and SBC for autoregressive orders up to five.

Both criteria select the AR(1) model. The SPSS program analyzes the model in a slightly different form from 7.2.3. The series mean μ is first subtracted from each observation, and equation 7.2.3 without the intercept C is fitted to the deviations; that is

$$\dot{X}_t = X_t - \mu \qquad (7.2.6a)$$

$$\dot{X}_t = \phi_1 \dot{X}_{t-1} + \phi_2 \dot{X}_{t-2} + \cdots + \phi_p \dot{X}_{t-p} + a_t \qquad (7.2.6b)$$

TABLE 7.1   Values of AIC and SBC criteria for autoregressions fitted to daily stock volume.

p:	1	2	3	4	5
AIC:	2,203.5	2,204.8	2,204.1	2,206.1	2,205.8
SBC:	2,210.6	2,215.4	2,218.2	2,223.7	2,226.9

The two forms are equivalent, since substitution of equation 7.2.6a into 7.2.6b yields

$$(X_t - \mu) = \phi_1(X_{t-1} - \mu) + \phi_2(X_{t-2} - \mu)$$
$$+ \cdots + \phi_p(X_{t-p} - \mu) + a_t$$

so that

$$X_t = (1 - \phi_1 - \phi_2 - \cdots - \phi_p)\mu + \phi_1 X_{t-1}$$
$$+ \phi_2 X_{t-2} + \cdots + \phi_p X_{t-p} + a_t$$

which is precisely equation 7.2.3 with

$$C = (1 - \phi_1 - \phi_2 - \cdots - \phi_p)\mu$$

The fitted first-order autoregressive model, which will be used for forecasting the daily volume series, was

$$\dot{X}_t = X_t - 91.01 \qquad \dot{X}_t = 0.567\dot{X}_{t-1} + a_t$$
$$(2.76) \qquad\qquad (0.052)$$

where figures in parentheses beneath coefficient estimates are the corresponding estimated standard errors. The estimated model can easily be expressed in the form of equation 7.2.1. We have

$$(X_t - 91.01) = 0.567(X_{t-1} - 91.01) + a_t$$

so that

$$X_t = (1 - 0.567)91.01 + 0.567X_{t-1} + a_t$$

or

$$X_t = 39.41 + 0.567X_{t-1} + a_t \qquad (7.2.7)$$

Once an autoregressive model has been fitted to data, it is quite straightforward to project forward the fitted model to calculate forecasts. Suppose we are standing at time n, and let $\hat{X}_n(h)$ denote the forecast of X_{n+h}. The first forecast required is of X_{n+1}. Setting $t = (n + 1)$ in the AR(p) model 7.2.3 gives

$$X_{n+1} = C + \phi_1 X_n + \phi_2 X_{n-1} + \cdots + \phi_p X_{n-p+1} + a_{n+1}$$

Now, the random variable a_{n+1} has mean zero, and is uncorrelated with anything that is known at time n, so that the best prediction of this term is simply zero. This suggests for X_{n+1} the forecast

$$\hat{X}_n(1) = C + \phi_1 X_n + \phi_2 X_{n-1} + \cdots + \phi_p X_{n-p+1}$$

For the prediction of X_{n+2},

$$X_{n+2} = C + \phi_1 X_{n+1} + \phi_2 X_n + \cdots + \phi_p X_{n-p+2} + a_{n+2}$$

This expression involves the unknown X_{n+1}, for which the forecast $\hat{X}_n(1)$ can be substituted. Then, since the best prediction of the random variable a_{n+2} is zero, the forecast of X_{n+2} is

$$\hat{X}_n(2) = C + \phi_1 \hat{X}_n(1) + \phi_2 X_n + \cdots + \phi_p X_{n-p+2}$$

Arguing in exactly the same way, the forecast of X_{n+3} is

$$\hat{X}_n(3) = C + \phi_1 \hat{X}_n(2) + \phi_2 \hat{X}_n(1) + \phi_3 X_n + \cdots + \phi_p X_{n-p+3}$$

In general, then, the forecast of X_{n+h} for a series generated by the AR(p) model 7.2.3 can be written

$$\hat{X}_n(h) = C + \phi_1 \hat{X}_n(h-1) + \phi_2 \hat{X}_n(h-2)$$
$$+ \cdots + \phi_p \hat{X}_n(h-p) \qquad h = 1, 2, 3, \ldots \quad (7.2.8)$$

In this expression, forecasts of known observations are simply the observations themselves; that is,

$$\hat{X}_n(j) = X_{n+j} \qquad j \le 0$$

Specializing equation 7.2.8 to the case of the first-order autoregressive model 7.2.7 fitted to our daily stock volume data, only the most recent observation

$$X_n = X_{252} = 80.26$$

is needed for forecasting. The forecast of the next day's volume is then

$$\hat{X}_{252}(1) = 39.41 + (0.567)(80.26) = 84.9174$$

The forecast for two days ahead is

$$\hat{X}_{252}(2) = 39.41 + (0.567)(84.9174) = 87.5582$$

TABLE 7.2   Forecasts for daily stock volume.

Time	253	254	255	256	257	258
Forecast	84.92	87.56	89.06	89.90	90.39	90.66

Continuing in this way, forecasts as far ahead as required can be calculated. Table 7.2 shows forecasts for the next six trading days. As we will see in Section 7.10, given one of the standard ARIMA model-building programs, interval forecasts can also be found.

In terms of our discussion of time series model-building in Section 7.1, the approach discussed in this section postulates a class of possible generating models—the autoregressive models 7.2.3, of some finite order p. The given data are then used to determine an appropriate model from that class; that is, to suggest an appropriate value for autoregressive order p, as well as to estimate the unknown parameters of the chosen model. In this way, the form of the forecast function eventually used is determined by the observed characteristics of the data. For our example of daily stock volume, it appears that the best approach is to base forecasts of all future values exclusively on the most recent observation. (In fact, when these data are examined in the broader framework to be discussed in subsequent sections of this chapter, no very compelling grounds for preferring any other model over the first-order autoregressive emerge.)

7.3   BEYOND PURE AUTOREGRESSIVE MODELS

This chapter is the longest in the book. It would be the shortest if we believed that autoregressive models of relatively low orders were invariably adequate for representing business and economic time series. After a modest modification of the methods of Section 7.2 to deal with seasonal time series, we would be done. Unfortunately, a number of considerations, the most important of which is accumulated practical experience in the analysis of real data, suggest the desirability of considering a broader class of models. Before proceeding to a detailed discussion of these models, we outline our reservations about the exclusive reliance on low-order pure autoregressive models.

The autoregressive models, and the procedures described in Section 7.2 for fitting them, are quite straightforward and have a good deal of intuitive appeal. Nevertheless, restriction to this approach can result in considerable costs in terms of forecast accuracy. One rather technical objection to the autoregressive models follows from the consideration of two types of **aggregation.** Many business and economic time series met in practice are aggregates of a number of constituent series. For example, the total sales of a product is the sum of sales in different regions, or in different markets. In addition, macroeconomic time series, such as gross national product, consumption, or investment are formed from the aggregation of information from many diverse sources. Unfortunately, even if individual time series are pure autoregressions, their sum typically is not, unless the constituent autoregressive models happen to have identical parameters. Granger and Morris (1976) provide a detailed discussion of this point. Many business and economic time series are necessarily **time aggregates;** that is, the observations are formed by summing or averaging information over time. Obviously, monthly product sales are obtained by summing sales figures for each day of the month. Again, if a time series is generated by a pure autoregressive model, its time aggregate typically is not. In a sense, the points we have made here are somewhat academic. After all, if pure autoregressive models happen to fit well to actual data, there is no practical objection to their use for forecasting. However, it does follow that the intuitive appeal of autoregressive models as a natural representation of time series is rather superficial. They are not quite as plausible as they appear at first sight.

Now, no model is intended to be truth. A model is just a convenient approximation to a complex reality. An autoregressive model of sufficiently high order can generally be found to provide a close approximation to any data-generating process likely to be met in business and economic applications. The difficulty is that the autoregressive order required to achieve an adequate approximation may be quite high. In fitting a high-order autoregressive model to a relatively short data set, the analyst is in danger of violating the principle of parsimony. If a large number of parameters must be estimated, while an apparently good fit of the sample data might be achieved, the forecasts from the fitted model could be quite poor. This suggests the possibility of working with a broader class of models in the hope that a relatively sparsely parameterized member of the class can be found to fit well a broad range of the types of time series likely to be met in practice. Davies and Newbold (1980) illustrate the loss in forecast accuracy that can result when autoregressive models are used to approximate the data-generating process.

To amplify the point made in the previous paragraph, and also to motivate important extensions of the autoregressive class of models, it is useful to consider again the simple exponential smoothing predictor of Section 6.2. Recall that, if this algorithm is adopted, the forecast of X_t, made at time $(t - 1)$, is

$$\hat{X}_{t-1}(1) = \alpha X_{t-1} + \alpha(1 - \alpha)X_{t-2}$$
$$+ \alpha(1 - \alpha)^2 X_{t-3} + \alpha(1 - \alpha)^3 X_{t-4} + \cdots$$

where α is the smoothing constant. Now, if this forecast is optimal, the one-step errors

$$a_t = X_t - \hat{X}_{t-1}(1)$$

should have mean zero, and be uncorrelated with one another. Therefore, we can write

$$X_t = \alpha X_{t-1} + \alpha(1 - \alpha)X_{t-2} + \alpha(1 - \alpha)^2 X_{t-3}$$
$$+ \alpha(1 - \alpha)^3 X_{t-4} + \cdots + a_t \quad (7.3.1)$$

This is in autoregressive form

$$X_t = \phi_1 X_{t-1} + \phi_2 X_{t-2} + \phi_3 X_{t-3} + \phi_4 X_{t-4} + \cdots + a_t$$

with

$$\phi_j = \alpha(1 - \alpha)^{j-1} \quad j = 1, 2, \ldots$$

However, in theory this autoregressive specification has infinitely many parameters ϕ_j, each a function of the single smoothing constant α. In practice, for large values of j the ϕ_j will be negligibly small, so that the infinite sum in equation 7.3.1 could be truncated, and a finite order autoregressive model should provide an adequate approximation. However, for low values of α, the ϕ_j only die out very slowly, so that many autoregressive terms would be needed. The fitting of an autoregressive model with many parameters in a situation where there is just a single unknown parameter, α, clearly violates the principle of parsimony.

To see how this difficulty can be avoided through an alternative model specification, we can write, in line with equation 7.3.1,

$$X_{t-1} = \alpha X_{t-2} + \alpha(1 - \alpha)X_{t-3} + \alpha(1 - \alpha)^2 X_{t-4} + \cdots + a_{t-1}$$

Multiplying through this equation by $(1 - \alpha)$ and subtracting the result from equation 7.3.1 yields

$$X_t - (1 - \alpha)X_{t-1} = \alpha X_{t-1} + a_t - (1 - \alpha)a_{t-1}$$

or

$$X_t - X_{t-1} = a_t - (1 - \alpha)a_{t-1} \quad (7.3.2)$$

The model 7.3.2 has two important features that are incorporated in the general ARIMA class of models, which we will use in subsequent sections to represent time series behavior. First, it includes the term $(1 - \alpha)a_{t-1}$—that is, a multiple of the random error from period $(t - 1)$. This is known as a **moving average term,** and is not present in the pure autoregressive specification. Second, notice that the left-hand side of equation 7.3.2 is the change in the observed time series from one period to the next. This is sometimes called the **first difference** of the series. That first differences can play an important part in the modeling of business and economic time series is quite plausible. For example, in trying to predict what product sales will be next year, this year's sales level seems a reasonable place to start. Then, we would like an explanation in our models, as far as possible, of the change in sales from one year to the next.

The general ARIMA class of models, on which our subsequent analysis will be based, incorporates both of these features. It will often be useful to analyze differences of a time series, and models with moving averages and autoregressive terms will be considered. Many of the other exponential smoothing algorithms discussed in Chapter 6 also lead to models involving both differencing and moving average terms. It is not our intention merely to write down stochastic generating models that yield the same forecasts as particular exponential smoothing algorithms. However, the widespread success enjoyed by these algorithms should not be ignored, and it is desirable where possible to incorporate their equivalent models into any general class of models intended as candidates for representing business and economic time series. As we have noted, exponential smoothing algorithms yield predictions, different from those generated by pure autoregressive models, with intuitively appealing forms. All of this suggests that we need to move beyond pure autoregressive models when analyzing business and economic time series data.

7.4 STATIONARITY AND AUTOCORRELATIONS

In building stochastic models for time series, we are in effect viewing an observed time series as a set of realizations of random variables. A useful way to think of this is to imagine a very large number of ordered lists of values. The particular time series that we actually see can be regarded as one of these lists, chosen at random.

When it is claimed that information on the past behavior of a time series is of some value in predicting the future, the implicit assumption is that there is some *regularity* in the process generating the series. If observations arose in an entirely haphazard way, the position of the forecaster would be hopeless. Accordingly, the models that are postulated as possible generators of a series must exhibit some regularity in their behavior over time to be at all useful. A frequently valuable way to view such regularity is through the concept of *stationarity*. This concept can be expressed in different forms. Here we will concentrate on *weak stationarity*, which is the relevant variant when attention is confined to linear predictors.

The time series X_t is said to be **weakly stationary** if the following three properties are satisfied:

1. The *mean* of the series is the same at all points in time. Then, writing this fixed mean as μ, we have

$$E(X_t) = \mu \qquad \text{for all } t$$

2. The *variance* of the series is the same at all points in time. Thus, if σ_x^2 denotes this fixed variance, we can write

$$\text{Var } (X_t) = E[(X_t - \mu)^2] = \sigma_x^2 \qquad \text{for all } t$$

3. The *covariance* between any two values of the series depends only on their distance apart in time, not on their absolute location in time. Then, we can denote by γ_k the covariance between any two values separated by k time periods, so that

$$\text{Cov } (X_t, X_{t-k}) = E[(X_t - \mu)(X_{t-k} - \mu)] = \gamma_k \qquad \text{for all } t$$

It is possible to relax, or to modify, the assumption of weak stationarity and still make some progress in the analysis of a time series. However, some simplifying assumption of this sort is obviously essential. For example, suppose that we reject property (1) and decline to admit any structure *a priori* for the evolution through time of the mean of the process. Then, given a series of n observations, we would have to estimate n different means—one for each time period. Already we have as many unknown parameters as data points, and this before we have begun to worry about variances and covariances. Obviously in these circumstances nothing constructive can be done. The assumption of weak stationarity is by no means invariably appropriate in practice. Nevertheless, experience suggests that it can very often form a useful basis for the development of statistical models from which reliable forecasts can be made.

Now, the aim of the forecaster is to seek to explain what will happen in the future in terms of what is already known. In this sense, the mean and variance of a time series are of limited value. The most relevant information is likely to come from the covariances γ_k, defined in property 3 above. For example, a positive covariance between X_t and X_{t-1} suggests, for daily data, that a relatively high value today is more likely than not to be followed by a relatively high value tomorrow. The set of covariances γ_k are called the **autocovariances** of a time series. The assumed stability over time of these covariances allows their exploitation in forecasting, and also allows their estimation from sample data. Given an observed time series, $X_1, X_2, \ldots, X_n$, natural estimates for the mean, variance and autocovariances, given an assumption of weak stationarity, are provided by the sample mean

$$\overline{X} = \frac{1}{n} \sum_{t=1}^{n} X_t$$

the sample variance

$$s_x^2 = \frac{1}{n} \sum_{t=1}^{n} (X_t - \overline{X})^2$$

and the **sample autocovariances**

$$c_k = \frac{1}{n} \sum_{t=k+1}^{n} (X_t - \overline{X})(X_{t-k} - \overline{X}) \qquad k = 1, 2, \ldots$$

As we discussed in Chapter 3, covariances are difficult to interpret because their magnitudes depend on the units of measurement of the data. It is invariably preferable to work with correlations, which provide a scale-free measure of the strength of linear association. The correlations between values of a time series separated by k time periods are called the **autocorrelations** of the process, and denoted ρ_k, so that

$$\rho_k = \text{Corr}(X_t, X_{t-k})$$

Then, from the definition of correlation,

$$\rho_k = \frac{\text{Cov}(X_t, X_{t-k})}{\sqrt{\text{Var}(X_t)\,\text{Var}(X_{t-k})}} = \frac{\gamma_k}{\sigma_x^2} \qquad\qquad (7.4.1)$$

since, by property 2 of weak stationarity, X_t and X_{t-k} have common variance σ_x^2.

The autocorrelations of a weakly stationary time series obey the following:

1. Since the correlation between a random variable and itself is necessarily one, it follows that

$$\rho_0 = 1$$

2. Given stationarity, the correlation between X_t and X_{t+k} is the same as that between X_t and X_{t-k}, so that

$$\rho_{-k} = \rho_k$$

The autocorrelations of a time series provide the natural framework for studying and summarizing linear associations between observations separated by various amounts of time. It is often useful to graph the set of autocorrelations ρ_k; $k = 0, 1, 2, \ldots$. This graph is called a **correlogram.** The simplest possible example of this sort is the process

$$X_t = a_t$$

where a_t has mean zero, constant variance, and

$$\text{Corr } (a_t, a_s) = 0 \qquad \text{for all } t \neq s$$

Time series analysts often call such a process **white noise,** and this is of course precisely the structure postulated for the error terms of a regression equation by the standard assumptions. The autocorrelations are then

$$\rho_0 = 1$$
$$\rho_k = 0 \qquad k = 1, 2, \ldots$$

so that the correlogram takes the particularly simple form shown in Figure 7.1. The correlogram of many processes met in practice is far more interesting than this, and the examination of a correlogram helps provide

FIGURE 7.1 The correlogram of white noise.

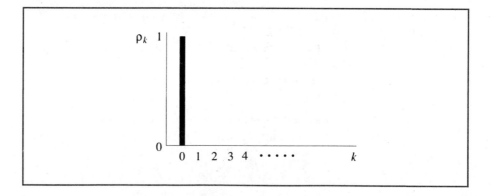

an understanding of the evolution of a time series. Indeed, there is a one-to-one correspondence between the correlogram and the various models to be discussed in Sections 7.5 through 7.7 for stationary time series. That is, knowledge of the correlogram implies knowledge of the generating model, and vice versa. For this reason, the correlogram is an extremely important tool in time series model-building.

Of course, given just a sample of observations, the true autocorrelations will never be precisely known, and similarly it will be impossible to learn with certainty what is the true generating model. However, it follows from the definition of equation 7.4.1 that the autocorrelations of a process can be estimated by the corresponding **sample autocorrelations**

$$r_k = \frac{c_k}{s_x^2} = \frac{\sum\limits_{t=k+1}^{n} (X_t - \overline{X})(X_{t-k} - \overline{X})}{\sum\limits_{t=1}^{n} (X_t - \overline{X})^2} \qquad k = 1, 2, \ldots$$

In subsequent sections of this chapter, it will be seen that the sample autocorrelations of an observed time series can be very useful in suggesting the form of the generating model. It should be repeated that, if the *true* autocorrelations were known, so also would be the generating model. However, since in practice only the sample autocorrelations will be available, the analyst will only be able to make an educated guess about the structure of the generating model. The ability to distinguish among alternative possible generating models depends on the quality of the sample autocorrelations as estimators of the true autocorrelations; that is, on the sampling distributions of the sample autocorrelations. It is known that, for moderately large sample sizes, the sample autocorrelations are approximately normally distributed. The sample autocorrelations r_k of white noise have means zero, and variances that, to a close approximation, are given by

$$\text{Var}\ (r_k) \simeq \frac{(n - k)}{n(n + 2)}$$

A slightly cruder approximation that is sometimes used, and is adequate provided that k is small relative to n, is

$$\text{Var}\ (r_k) \simeq \frac{1}{n}$$

Given an assumed normal distribution, the magnitudes of sample autocorrelations are often assessed through comparison with bounds of ± 2 standard errors, so that we could use $\pm 2[(n - k)/n(n + 2)]^{1/2}$. These would be appropriate for testing at the 5% significance level the null hypothesis that the population autocorrelations are zero.

Figure 7.2 shows the sample correlogram for a series of 100 observations generated by a white noise process, together with ± 2 standard error limits. By contrast with the corresponding true autocorrelations, the sample autocorrelations will, of course, not be precisely zero. However, they can be expected to be relatively small, with, on average, just 5% of them outside the ± 2 standard error limits. An analyst, presented with the sample results graphed in Figure 7.2 would conclude that there is very little evidence in the data to suggest other than that the true autocorrelations of the process are all zero, and hence that the generating model is simply white noise, perhaps with a non-zero mean.

For the analyst to reasonably expect to be able to deduce the generating model from an examination of the sample autocorrelations, it is important that, on the average, these sample quantities be relatively close to the corresponding population values; that is, that the standard errors of the sample autocorrelations be quite low. Now, these standard errors are decreasing functions of the number n of observations available. Consequently, in order to proceed with much confidence, a moderately long series of observations is needed. For example, given a series of $n = 25$

FIGURE 7.2   A sample correlogram for white noise (n = 100).

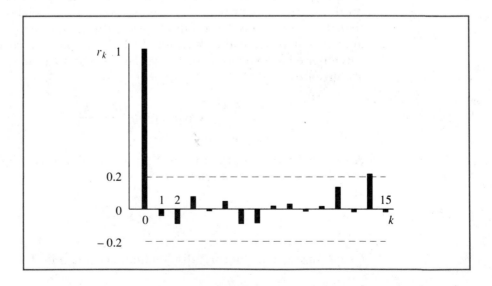

FIGURE 7.3   From sample data to inference about time series generating model.

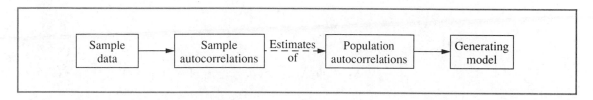

observations, ± 2 standard error limits will be approximately $\pm 2n^{-1/2} = \pm 0.4$. This is an enormously wide range, given that we know that any correlation must be in the range ± 1, and it would be difficult to be optimistic about being able to distinguish between a wide array of possible generating models given sample autocorrelations based on such a short series. Generally, to proceed with the methods to be discussed in later sections of this chapter, at least 40–50 observations are required. This requirement is often given as a criticism of the ARIMA model-building approach to forecasting. Such an attitude is unreasonable. A more logical reaction is that, given relatively little information, one should not expect to be able to learn much with any great certainty. When only short time series are available an approach exclusively through pure autoregressive models, as discussed in Section 7.2, will often be about the best that can be done.

We now assume that sufficient data are available to allow the analyst to consider the possibility of a wider class of generating models. The general procedure that will be followed is outlined in Figure 7.3. We have seen that, given a sample of time series observations, sample autocorrelations can be routinely calculated. These are estimates of the corresponding true, or population, quantities, the quality of the estimates depending on the amount of sample data available. Finally, as we have already indicated, particular generating models are associated with specific correlograms. Thus, in the next four sections of this chapter, where various time series models are to be introduced, it will be necessary to derive the autocorrelation patterns corresponding to these models.

7.5 PROPERTIES OF AUTOREGRESSIVE MODELS

In Section 7.2, we discussed and illustrated the fitting to time series data of autoregressive models. These models constitute an important sub-class of the general class of models we will be considering, and in this section we will derive some of their properties. To begin, suppose that a time series X_t is generated by the simple first-order autoregressive model. Then, if the series has mean μ, we can write

$$\dot{X}_t = X_t - \mu$$

and

$$\dot{X}_t = \phi_1 \dot{X}_{t-1} + a_t \qquad -1 < \phi_1 < 1 \qquad (7.5.1)$$

where a_t is white noise. The requirement that the absolute value of the autoregressive parameter ϕ_1 be less than one is known as the **stationarity condition,** since it ensures that a series generated in this way will be weakly stationary.

We will now derive the autocorrelations of a process generated by a first-order autoregressive model. To begin, note from equation 7.5.1 that we can write

$$\dot{X}_t = \phi_1 \dot{X}_{t-1} + a_t$$
$$= \phi_1(\phi_1 \dot{X}_{t-2} + a_{t-1}) + a_t = \phi_1^2 \dot{X}_{t-2} + a_t + \phi_1 a_{t-1}$$

Then, substituting for X_{t-2} gives

$$\dot{X}_t = \phi_1^3 \dot{X}_{t-3} + a_t + \phi_1 a_{t-1} + \phi_1^2 a_{t-2}$$

Continuing in this way, it follows that for any positive integer T

$$\dot{X}_t = \phi_1^T \dot{X}_{t-T} + a_t + \phi_1 a_{t-1} + \phi_1^2 a_{t-2} + \cdots + \phi_1^{T-1} a_{t-T+1}$$

Now, as T becomes large, given the stationarity condition, ϕ_1^T becomes negligibly small, so that $\dot{X}_t$ can be written in terms of the whole past history of the white noise process as

$$\dot{X}_t = a_t + \phi_1 a_{t-1} + \phi_1^2 a_{t-2} + \phi_1^3 a_{t-3} + \cdots \qquad (7.5.2)$$

Then, since each a_{t-j}, $j = 0, 1, 2, \ldots$ has mean zero, it follows that $\dot{X}_t$ has mean zero, and hence as postulated that X_t has mean μ.

We now seek expressions for the autocovariances

$$\gamma_k = E[(X_t - \mu)(X_{t-k} - \mu)] = E(\dot{X}_t \dot{X}_{t-k})$$

First, multiplying equation 7.5.2 by a_{t+j} and taking expectations gives

$$E(a_{t+j} \dot{X}_t) = E(a_{t+j} a_t) + \phi_1 E(a_{t+j} a_{t-1}) + \phi_1^2 E(a_{t+j} a_{t-2}) + \cdots$$

Then, for any $j > 0$, since a_t is white noise, each expectation on the right-hand side of this expression is zero, so that

$$E(\dot{X}_t a_{t+j}) = 0 \qquad j = 1, 2, 3, \ldots \qquad (7.5.3)$$

Next, multiply equation 7.5.1 by $\dot{X}_{t-k}$ and take expectations, giving

$$E(\dot{X}_t \dot{X}_{t-k}) = \phi_1 E(\dot{X}_{t-1} \dot{X}_{t-k}) + E(a_t \dot{X}_{t-k})$$

Now, by definition, the left-hand side of this expression is the autocovariance γ_k and the first expectation on the right-hand side is the autocovariance γ_{k-1}. The final term on the right-hand side is zero, by equation 7.5.3, for $k > 0$, so that

$$\gamma_k = \phi_1 \gamma_{k-1} \qquad k = 1, 2, 3, \ldots$$

Finally, since the autocorrelations are obtained by division of the autocovariances by the variance, it follows on dividing through this equation by the variance of the series that

$$\rho_k = \phi_1 \rho_{k-1} \qquad k = 1, 2, 3, \ldots \qquad (7.5.4)$$

(That the series does indeed have finite variance follows by squaring both sides of equation 7.5.2 and taking expectations.)

The result in equation 7.5.4 and its generalization to other models with autoregressive terms is extremely important. The autocorrelations of the first-order autoregressive process now follow immediately for, since $\rho_0 = 1$, we have from equation 7.5.4

$$\rho_1 = \phi_1 \rho_0 = \phi_1 \qquad \rho_2 = \phi_1 \rho_1 = \phi_1^2 \qquad \rho_3 = \phi_1 \rho_2 = \phi_1^3$$

and so on. Thus, it follows that the autocorrelations are

$$\rho_k = \phi_1^k \qquad k = 0, 1, 2, \ldots$$

We see then that the autoregressive parameter ϕ_1 is the correlation ρ_1 between observations adjacent to one another in time. Further, given the stationarity condition, it follows that, as the lag k between observations increases, the magnitude of the autocorrelation dies out toward zero, according to an exponential decay. Figure 7.4 shows the correlograms of first-order autoregressive processes with parameters -0.5, 0.5, and 0.9. For negative ϕ_1, the autocorrelations alternate in sign, whereas for positive ϕ_1, they are all positive. Provided the autoregressive parameter is not zero, all autocorrelations are non-zero. They do, however, decay toward zero as the lag k increases; the smaller $|\phi_1|$ is, the more rapid this decay.

FIGURE 7.4   Correlograms for first-order autoregressive models. (a) $\phi_1 = -0.5$,
(b) $\phi_1 = 0.5$, (c) $\phi_1 = 0.9$.

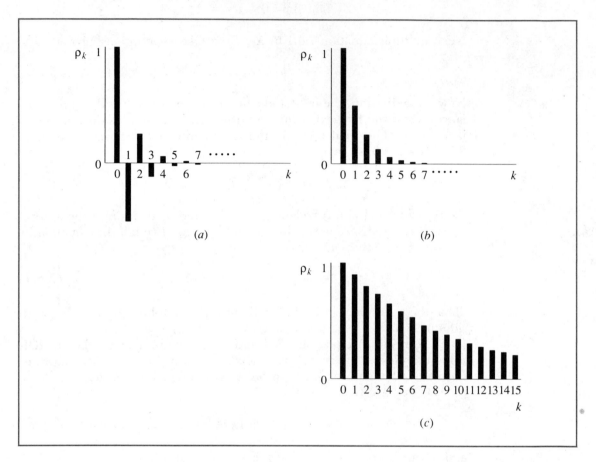

More generally, the time series X_t is said to be generated by an *autoregressive model of order p* that is often denoted AR(p), if

$$\dot{X}_t = X_t - \mu$$

and

$$\dot{X}_t = \phi_1\dot{X}_{t-1} + \phi_2\dot{X}_{t-2} + \cdots + \phi_p\dot{X}_{t-p} + a_t \qquad (7.5.5)$$

where a_t is white noise. We will assume that the series is stationary, a requirement which imposes certain restrictions on the values that can be jointly taken by the autoregressive parameters ϕ_1, ϕ_2, ..., ϕ_p. In that case, it can be shown that X_t has mean μ, and that the autocorrelations obey

$$\rho_k = \phi_1\rho_{k-1} + \phi_2\rho_{k-2} + \cdots + \phi_p\rho_{k-p} \qquad k = 1, 2, 3, \ldots$$

$$(7.5.6)$$

Equations 7.5.6, of which equation 7.5.4 is a special case, are called the **Yule-Walker equations.** They can be solved either for the autocorrelations in terms of the autoregressive parameters, or for the autoregressive parameters in terms of the autocorrelations. As we will see, the Yule-Walker equations form the basis for a very useful approach to the detection of pure autoregressive behavior in a time series. The formula 7.5.6 is derived in the appendix to this chapter.

For stationary autoregressive processes, the autocorrelations again decay toward zero as the lag k increases. The shape of this decay, which can be exponential, sinusoidal, or a mixture of the two, is dictated by equations 7.5.6. To illustrate, consider the AR(2) process

$$\dot{X}_t = \phi_1\dot{X}_{t-1} + \phi_2\dot{X}_{t-2} + a_t$$

Then, specializing the Yule-Walker equations 7.5.6 to the case $p = 2$, and setting in turn $k = 1, 2$, it follows, since $\rho_0 = 1$ and $\rho_{-1} = \rho_1$, that

$$\rho_1 = \phi_1 + \phi_2\rho_1 \qquad \rho_2 = \phi_1\rho_1 + \phi_2$$

Hence, we find

$$\rho_1 = \frac{\phi_1}{1 - \phi_2} \qquad \rho_2 = \frac{\phi_1^2}{1 - \phi_2} + \phi_2$$

Further autocorrelations then follow from

$$\rho_k = \phi_1\rho_{k-1} + \phi_2\rho_{k-2} \qquad k = 3, 4, \ldots$$

Figure 7.5 shows correlograms for AR(2) processes with $(\phi_1, \phi_2) = (1.6, -0.64)$, $(0.4, 0.45)$, and $(1.3, -0.6)$. Notice in every case that the autocorrelations decay towards zero, though the three patterns of decay are quite different.

FIGURE 7.5   Correlograms for second-order autoregressive models. (a) $\phi_1 = 1.6$, $\phi_2 = -0.64$, (b) $\phi_1 = 0.4$, $\phi_2 = 0.45$, (c) $\phi_1 = 1.3$, $\phi_2 = -0.6$.

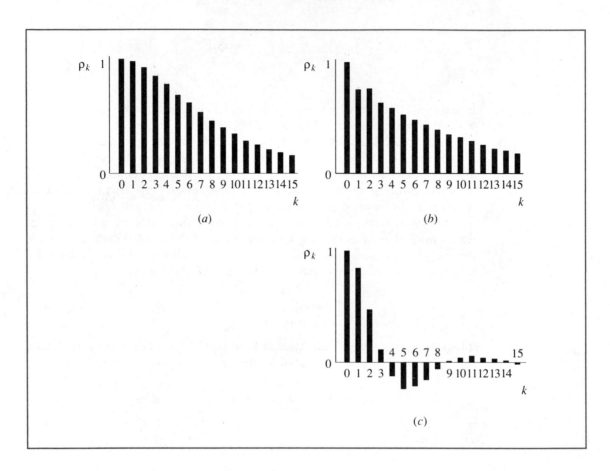

The Back-Shift Operator Notation

At this point it is convenient to introduce a notation that is often used in conjunction with autoregressive and other time series models. We define the operator B on the index of any time series X_t such that B shifts the series back one period in time; thus,

$$BX_t \equiv X_{t-1}$$

The operator can be repeated, so that in general for any integer j,

$$B^j X_t \equiv X_{t-j}$$

Using this notation, the autoregressive model 7.5.5 can be written

$$\dot{X}_t = \phi_1 B \dot{X}_t + \phi_2 B^2 \dot{X}_t + \cdots + \phi_p B^p \dot{X}_t + a_t$$

or

$$(1 - \phi_1 B - \phi_2 B^2 - \cdots - \phi_p B^p)\dot{X}_t = a_t$$

Hence, the autoregressive model can be expressed as

$$\phi(B)\dot{X}_t = a_t$$

or, equivalently

$$\phi(B)(X_t - \mu) = a_t$$

where $\phi(B)$ is the function of the back-shift operator B given by

$$\phi(B) = 1 - \phi_1 B - \phi_2 B^2 - \cdots - \phi_p B^p$$

The introduction of the back-shift operator provides a convenient short-hand notation for writing out autoregressive models, as well as other time series models to be discussed in subsequent sections of this chapter.

Partial Autocorrelations

We have seen how, using the Yule-Walker equations, the correlogram for any autoregressive model can be found. However, it is not at all easy to determine from visual examination of plots such as those in Figures 7.4 and 7.5 what is the order p of the autoregression, or indeed whether the generating model is truly purely autoregressive. The problem becomes even more difficult when one takes into account that the true autocorrelations will be unknown in practice, and that any inference will have to be based on their sample estimates. It is important to be able to recognize pure autoregressive behavior. A widely used procedure for doing so follows from using the Yule-Walker equation 7.5.6.

Suppose that the generating model of a time series is AR(k), and let $\phi_{k1}, \phi_{k2}, \ldots, \phi_{kk}$ denote the autoregressive parameters. Then it follows from equation 7.5.6 that

$$\rho_j = \phi_{k1}\rho_{j-1} + \phi_{k2}\rho_{j-2} + \cdots + \phi_{kk}\rho_{j-k} \qquad j = 1, 2, \ldots, k$$

$$(7.5.7)$$

Now, for given values of the autocorrelations, equations 7.5.7 constitute a set of k simultaneous linear equations in the k autoregressive parameters. These equations can therefore be solved for these parameters. For any process, the solution of equation 7.5.7 for the last parameter ϕ_{kk} yields the **partial autocorrelation of order k** of the process. Assume now that the true generating model is AR(p), where $p \leq k$. Clearly, if $p = k$, ϕ_{kk} will be the last autoregressive parameter, and will differ from zero. On the other hand, if $p < k$, we can think of the AR(p) model as an AR(k) model in which the last $k - p$ parameters are zero. In particular, then, the partial autocorrelation ϕ_{kk} will be zero. This establishes the important conclusion that, for an AR(p) model, the partial autocorrelation of order p is non-zero, but all partial autocorrelations of orders higher than p will be zero, that is

$$\phi_{kk} = 0 \qquad k = p + 1, p + 2, \ldots$$

Therefore knowledge of the partial autocorrelations of a process would provide a very easy way to recognize pure autoregressive behavior of any order. A plot of ϕ_{kk} against the lag k has a very distinctive shape, involving an abrupt cutoff, with all values equal to zero at lags higher than the true autoregressive order p.

In practice, the partial autocorrelations will not be known with certainty as they depend on the unknown population autocorrelations. They can be estimated through replacement of the true autocorrelations in equations 7.5.7 by their sample estimates. Thus, the **sample partial autocorrelation of order k** is $\hat{\phi}_{kk}$ obtained by solving the set of equations

$$r_j = \hat{\phi}_{k1} r_{j-1} + \hat{\phi}_{k2} r_{j-2} + \cdots + \hat{\phi}_{kk} r_{j-k} \qquad j = 1, 2, \ldots, k$$

$$(7.5.8)$$

Setting $r_0 = 1$ and $r_{-j} = r_j$, it follows from equations 7.5.8 that

$$\hat{\phi}_{11} = r_1$$

and $\hat{\phi}_{22}$ is obtained by solving the pair of equations

$$r_1 = \hat{\phi}_{21} + \hat{\phi}_{22} r_1 \qquad r_2 = \hat{\phi}_{21} r_1 + \hat{\phi}_{22}$$

giving

$$\hat{\phi}_{22} = \frac{(r_2 - r_1^2)}{(1 - r_1^2)}$$

Continuing in this way, sample partial autocorrelations of higher order can be found. In fact, efficient computational algorithms are available for finding sample partial autocorrelations and these are programmed in standard time series computer packages.

It is known that, for moderately large sample size n, the sample partial autocorrelations of order greater than p for an AR(p) process have a distribution that is approximately normal, with mean zero and standard error $n^{-1/2}$. To assess their significance, the sample partial autocorrelations are typically compared with limits $\pm 2n^{-1/2}$. This gives the analyst a good opportunity to detect pure autoregressive behavior in an observed time series. To illustrate, Figure 7.6 shows the first twenty sample partial autocorrelations for the series of 252 daily observations on volume of shares traded, discussed in Section 7.2. Also shown are the two standard error limits, $\pm 2(252)^{-1/2} = \pm 0.126$. Judged by this criterion, the first sample partial autocorrelation is very large, while the remainder are relatively small. Only the one at lag six is a little outside the two standard error bounds, an occurrence that can reasonably be put down to chance. This suggests that the first-order autoregressive model, fitted to these data in Section 7.2, is indeed appropriate. In Section 7.2, we concluded that, from the class of pure autoregressive models, the first-order model was the best choice. The sample partial autocorrelations of Figure 7.6 indicate that there is little to be gained in looking beyond this simple model for other possible data-generating processes for these data.

FIGURE 7.6   Sample partial autocorrelations for daily stock volume.

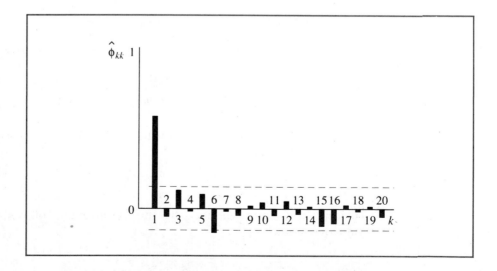

7.6　Moving Average Models

In Section 7.3 we suggested that the class of pure autoregressive models will not invariably be adequate for the representation of non-seasonal business and economic time series. In this section we introduce some different possible generating models, in which the value of a time series is expressed as a linear function of current and past values of a white noise process. The simplest model of this sort is the **first-order moving average model,** often denoted MA(1). The time series X_t is said to be generated by a first-order moving average model if

$$X_t - \mu = \dot{X}_t = a_t - \theta_1 a_{t-1} \tag{7.6.1}$$

where θ_1 is a fixed parameter and a_t is white noise.

Since the white noise process has mean zero, it follows immediately from equation 7.6.1 that $\dot{X}_t$ has mean zero, and hence that X_t has mean μ. The variance of the process X_t is

$$
\begin{aligned}
\mathrm{Var}(X_t) = E(\dot{X}_t^2) &= E[(a_t - \theta_1 a_{t-1})^2] \\
&= E(a_t^2) + \theta_1^2 E(a_{t-1}^2) - 2\theta_1 E(a_t a_{t-1})
\end{aligned}
$$

Since a_t is white noise, the last expectation on the right-hand side of this expression is zero, so that, if σ_a^2 denotes the variance of the white noise process,

$$\mathrm{Var}(X_t) = (1 + \theta_1^2)\sigma_a^2$$

The first autocovariance of this process is

$$
\begin{aligned}
\gamma_1 = E(\dot{X}_t \dot{X}_{t-1}) &= E[(a_t - \theta_1 a_{t-1})(a_{t-1} - \theta_1 a_{t-2})] \\
&= E(a_t a_{t-1}) - \theta_1 E(a_t a_{t-2}) \\
&\quad - \theta_1 E(a_{t-1}^2) + \theta_1^2 E(a_{t-1} a_{t-2})
\end{aligned}
$$

Since a_t is white noise, only one of the expectations on the right-hand side is non-zero, so that

$$\gamma_1 = -\theta_1 \sigma_a^2$$

Dividing this autocovariance by the variance, it follows that the first autocorrelation is

$$\rho_1 = \frac{-\theta_1}{(1 + \theta_1^2)}$$

The other autocovariances follow in the same way, so that

$$\gamma_k = E(\dot{X}_t \dot{X}_{t-k}) = E[(a_t - \theta_1 a_{t-1})(a_{t-k} - \theta_1 a_{t-k-1})]$$

$$= E(a_t a_{t-k}) - \theta_1 E(a_{t-1} a_{t-k}) - \theta_1 E(a_t a_{t-k-1})$$

$$+ \theta_1^2 E(a_{t-1} a_{t-k-1})$$

Now, for any $k > 1$, it follows since a_t is white noise that each of the expectations on the right-hand side of this expression is zero, and hence that the autocovariance and the corresponding autocorrelation are zero. We have therefore established that, for an MA(1) process, the autocorrelation of order one is non-zero, but all autocorrelations of order greater than one will be zero, that is

$$\rho_k = 0 \qquad k = 2, 3, \ldots$$

The correlogram for the first-order moving average process is quite distinctive, with only zero values beyond lag one. Figure 7.7 shows correlograms for two first-order moving average models. The only non-

FIGURE 7.7   Correlograms for first-order moving average models. (a) $\theta = -0.8$, (b) $\theta = 0.8$.

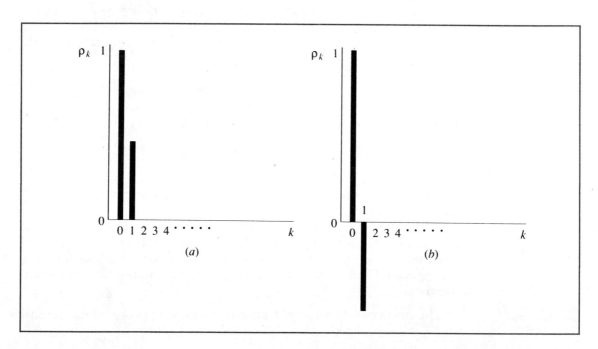

zero value is at lag one, the sign of this correlation being the opposite of that of the moving average parameter θ_1.

The first-order moving average model can be generalized by allowing further lagged white noise terms. The time series X_t is said to be generated by a **moving average model of order q,** denoted MA(q), if

$$X_t - \mu = \dot{X}_t = a_t - \theta_1 a_{t-1} - \theta_2 a_{t-2} - \cdots - \theta_q a_{t-q} \quad (7.6.2)$$

where θ_1, θ_2, . . . , θ_q are moving average parameters and a_t is, as usual, white noise. Clearly this process has mean μ. Also, arguing in exactly the same way as for the MA(1) process, it is quite straightforward to show that, for an MA(q) process, the autocorrelation of order q is non-zero, but all autocorrelations of orders higher than q will be zero, that is

$$\rho_k = 0 \quad k = q + 1, q + 2, \ldots$$

The correlogram for a moving average process then is quite distinctive, exhibiting an abrupt cut-off after lag q. This fact should help the analyst recognize pure moving average behavior, and determine the order of a moving average generating model. Of course, in practice, sample auto-correlations must be used to estimate the corresponding population quantities. These sample estimates can then be compared with the two standard error limits discussed in Section 7.4 to assess the evidence against the hypothesis that population autocorrelations are zero. We will illustrate this approach to the recognition of moving average behavior in Section 7.9.

The moving average model 7.6.2 can be efficiently written in back-shift operator notation as

$$X_t - \mu = \theta(B)a_t$$

where

$$\theta(B) = 1 - \theta_1 B - \theta_2 B^2 - \cdots - \theta_q B^q$$

This, of course, corresponds to the formulation introduced in Section 7.5 for the pure autoregressive model.

For moving average processes, the partial autocorrelations do not cut off, but rather decay toward zero with increasing lag length. The contrasts in the behavior of autocorrelations and partial autocorrelations for pure autoregressions and pure moving averages are very important, and worth repeating.

1. The autocorrelations, ρ_k, of a pure autoregressive process decay toward

zero with increasing lag length k. By contrast, for a pure moving average process of order q, the autocorrelations cut off abruptly—they are all zero for k bigger than q.

2. The partial autocorrelations, ϕ_{kk}, of a pure moving average process decay toward zero with increasing lag length k. By contrast, for a pure autoregressive process of order p, the partial autocorrelations cut off abruptly—they are all zero for k bigger than p.

Because of these properties, sample autocorrelations and sample partial autocorrelations are computed by time series analysts to help determine whether the fitting to data of pure autoregressive or pure moving average models of particular orders might be appropriate. However, in practice, since sample estimates must be used, this decision is a good deal more tricky than it would be if the true autocorrelations and partial autocorrelations were known.

7.7 AUTOREGRESSIVE MOVING AVERAGE MODELS

The models of Section 7.5 contain no moving average terms, while those of Section 7.6 contain no autoregressive terms. It is clearly possible to write down generating model equations that involve both autoregressive and moving average terms. In fact, practical experience suggests that it is worthwhile to do so, as **mixed autoregressive moving average models** can provide excellent representations of actual stationary time series using relatively few unknown parameters. Sometimes adequate representation of a series with pure autoregressions or pure moving averages can only be achieved with quite high-order models, while a model involving both autoregressive and moving average terms requires a relatively small total number of parameters. The principle of parsimony then suggests that the mixed autoregressive moving average formulation is an attractive alternative.

The stationary time series X_t, with mean μ, is said to be generated by an *autoregressive moving average model of order* (p, q), denoted ARMA(p, q), if

$$\dot{X}_t - \phi_1 \dot{X}_{t-1} - \cdots - \phi_p \dot{X}_{t-p} = a_t - \theta_1 a_{t-1} - \cdots - \theta_q a_{t-q}$$

$$(7.7.1)$$

where a_t is white noise and

$$\dot{X}_t = X_t - \mu$$

Equivalently, in back-shift operator notation, the ARMA(p, q) model can be written

$$\phi(B)(X_t - \mu) = \theta(B)a_t$$

where

$$\phi(B) = 1 - \phi_1 B - \cdots - \phi_p B^p \qquad \theta(B) = 1 - \theta_1 B - \cdots - \theta_q B^q$$

The requirement that the process is stationary imposes certain restrictions on the values that can be taken jointly by the autoregressive parameters $\phi_1, \phi_2, \ldots, \phi_p$.

Pure autoregressive and pure moving average models can be viewed as special subclasses of the general class of autoregressive moving average models. Setting $q = 0$ in equation 7.7.1 yields a pure autoregressive model, so that the AR(p) process could be designated ARMA(p, 0). Similarly, setting $p = 0$ in equation 7.7.1 produces a pure moving average model, so the MA(q) process could be denoted ARMA(0, q).

It can be shown that the autocorrelations, ρ_k, of an ARMA(p, q) process satisfy the relationships

$$\rho_k = \phi_1 \rho_{k-1} + \phi_2 \rho_{k-2} + \cdots + \phi_p \rho_{k-p} \qquad (7.7.2)$$
$$k = q + 1, q + 2, q + 3, \ldots$$

This result is established in the appendix to this chapter. Equations 7.7.2 are in precisely the same form as the Yule-Walker equations 7.5.6 for stationary pure autoregressive processes. Thus, we can think of the autoregressive parameters as determining the eventual shape of the autocorrelation pattern as the lag increases, while the moving average parameters play a part in determining the initial q autocorrelations. In practice an attempt to recognize particular autoregressive moving average models given a time series of observations can be based on noting patterns similar to equation 7.7.2 in the sample autocorrelations. Unless the autoregressive and moving average orders, p and q, are very small this can be quite difficult. However, experience suggests that models with a small total number of parameters will often provide adequate representations of actual data sets. Certainly, the principle of parsimony argues that we should begin by looking for such models.

The simplest mixed autoregressive moving average process arises when a time series is generated by the ARMA(1, 1) model

$$\dot{X}_t - \phi_1 \dot{X}_{t-1} = a_t - \theta_1 a_{t-1}$$

It can be shown that the first autocorrelation for this process is

$$\rho_1 = \frac{(1 - \phi_1\theta_1)(\phi_1 - \theta_1)}{1 - 2\phi_1\theta_1 + \theta_1^2}$$

Then, specializing equation 7.7.2, the remaining autocorrelations decay toward zero according to

$$\rho_k = \phi_1\rho_{k-1} \qquad k = 2, 3, \ldots$$

The distinction between the ARMA(1, 1) process and the AR(1) process is that, for the former

$$\rho_1 \neq \phi_1\rho_0$$

that is

$$\rho_1 \neq \phi_1.$$

Figure 7.8 shows the correlogram of the ARMA(1, 1) process with $\phi_1 = 0.9$, $\theta_1 = 0.5$. Notice that a steady exponential decay of the autocorrelations sets in after a delay of one lag.

As we have seen, for ARMA(p, q) processes with $p \neq 0$, the autocorrelations do not cut off, but rather decay toward zero. Similarly, it can be

FIGURE 7.8   Correlogram for ARMA(1, 1) model; $\phi_1 = 0.9$, $\theta_1 = 0.5$.

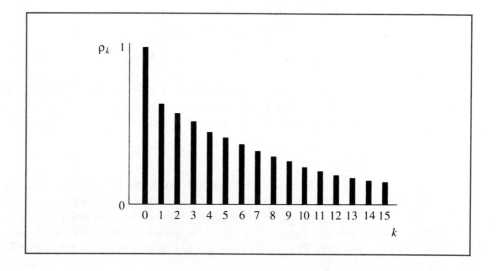

shown that, if $q \neq 0$, the partial autocorrelations decay toward zero rather than cutting off. This behavior of mixed autoregressive moving average models is in contrast to the properties we have already noted of pure autoregressive and pure moving average models. This lack of abrupt cut-offs in either the autocorrelations or the partial autocorrelations makes it more difficult in practice to distinguish among alternative mixed autoregressive moving average specifications than it is to identify either pure autoregressive or pure moving average behavior.

7.8 AUTOREGRESSIVE INTEGRATED MOVING AVERAGE MODELS

Autoregressive moving average models have been successfully used to represent the behavior of stationary time series over a very wide field of practical applications. However, for the levels of many business and economic time series, the assumption of stationarity is neither realistic nor supported by empirical observation. Stationarity requires, among other things, that the series has a fixed mean over time, but often such a concept lacks credibility. Does it make sense, for example, to think of some fixed mean level throughout time for an interest rate series, such as the 30-day Treasury bill rate, or for the exchange rate between the currencies of two countries? It really does not. In the same way, the concept of a true mean over time for the level of product sales is difficult to take seriously. Fortunately, it turns out that the stationary models of Sections 7.5–7.7 very often are appropriate for the representation of a simple transformation of business and economic time series. Although the levels of a time series may not be stationary, frequently period-to-period changes, or **first differences**, of the series will be stationary. Thus, if the observed series is X_t, the series of changes

$$W_t = X_t - X_{t-1} = (1 - B)X_t$$

will be stationary. It may therefore be reasonable to fit a stationary model to the first differences of an observed time series. The simplest case of this sort is where the first differences of a series are white noise, so that

$$X_t - X_{t-1} = a_t$$

This is known as the **random walk model,** and has been found to provide a good description of the behavior of prices in speculative markets, providing empirical support for the efficient markets hypothesis of finance theory. Figure 7.9 shows a plot of data generated by a random walk model. The general shape is not dissimilar to what has been observed in

FIGURE 7.9   A random walk.

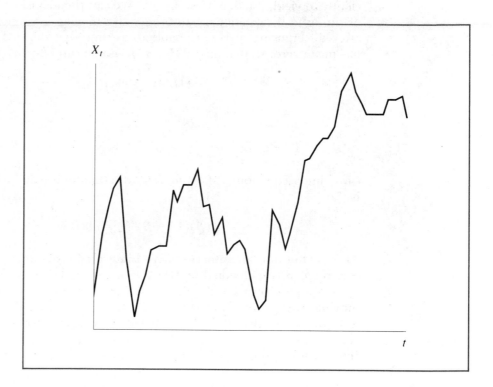

the behavior of stock market prices and currency exchange rates. Notice that this time series does not appear to oscillate about some fixed mean, to whose neighborhood it tends to return. Rather it exhibits wandering behavior that is typical of series that require differencing to induce stationarity.

It sometimes happens that a single differencing does not yield a stationary series, but that second differencing—differencing the series of first differences—will do so. Just occasionally, even further differencing is required. In general, a series may require differencing some number d times to induce stationarity, so that

$$W_t = (1 - B)^d X_t \qquad (7.8.1)$$

is a stationary series. Almost invariably for business or economic time series the appropriate value for d is either 0, 1, or 2. A process for which some differencing is required to achieve stationarity is called an **integrated process.**

Suppose that an observed time series X_t has been differenced sufficiently to yield a stationary series W_t. We can then consider the possibility of fitting to W_t a stationary autoregressive moving average model. Often, after differencing, it is reasonable to assume that the differenced series has mean zero, so that an ARMA(p, q) model can be written

$$\phi(B)W_t = \theta(B)a_t \qquad (7.8.2)$$

where

$$\phi(B) = 1 - \phi_1 B - \cdots - \phi_p B^p \qquad \theta(B) = 1 - \theta_1 B - \cdots - \theta_q B^q$$

Combining equations 7.8.1 and 7.8.2, the model for the original series X_t is

$$\phi(B)(1 - B)^d X_t = \theta(B)a_t \qquad (7.8.3)$$

This is known as an **autoregressive integrated moving average model of order (p, d, q),** denoted ARIMA(p, d, q). Here, p is the number of autoregressive terms, d the degree of differencing, and q the number of moving average terms in the model. In this notation then, the random walk model is ARIMA(0, 1, 0). If the differenced series has some non-zero mean μ, as might be appropriate for a series of steadily growing sales figures, for example, the model 7.8.3 is extended to

$$\phi(B)[(1 - B)^d X_t - \mu] = \theta(B)a_t$$

The autoregressive integrated moving average class of models is the most general we will consider for fitting to nonseasonal time series. These models have proved to be very successful in business and economic applications. For example, in Section 7.3 we saw that the simple exponential smoothing predictor, with smoothing constant α, yields optimal forecasts for series generated by the model

$$X_t - X_{t-1} = a_t - (1 - \alpha)a_{t-1}$$

This is an ARIMA(0, 1, 1) model; that is, first differences obey a first-order moving average process. The success that has been enjoyed by the simple exponential smoothing predictor suggests the desirability of considering time series models involving both differencing and moving average terms. The series graphed in Figure 6.2 of Section 6.2 are examples of data generated by ARIMA(0, 1, 1) models. It can also be shown that Holt's linear trend algorithm of Section 6.3 yields optimal forecasts for series generated by particular ARIMA(0, 2, 2) models. An example of a time series generated by such a model was shown in Figure

6.3. In Chapter 9 we will discuss in considerably more detail the relationships between exponential smoothing algorithms and ARIMA models. The practical success of various exponential smoothing predictors and the fact that many of these predictors are equivalent to forecasting from specific members of the ARIMA class of models certainly suggests that these models should prove to be valuable forecasting tools. However, the justification for the ARIMA model-building approach to forecasting certainly does not rest exclusively on this relationship. The ARIMA class is much wider than the array of alternatives typically considered in implementations of exponential smoothing, and it often happens that data suggest a particular model for which there is no exponential smoothing equivalent. Moreover, an approach through model building allows the development of a well-structured procedure for determining an appropriate model, and hence an appropriate forecast function, tailored to the observed historical behavior of a given time series. In Section 7.9 we will describe and illustrate such a procedure.

Recognition that the data-generating process is integrated—that is, that differencing is required to produce stationarity—can be achieved through examination of the sample autocorrelations of a time series. It is known that, for integrated processes, the sample autocorrelations r_k exhibit very smooth behavior, rather than decaying quickly toward zero, for moderately high lags k. Some examples of this type of behavior will be provided in Section 7.9, where integrated processes are fitted to real time series. A further possibility is to regard the need for differencing as a null hypothesis to be tested. (See, for example, Dickey, Bell, and Miller, 1986.)

Why be concerned at all about differencing? After all, the differencing element in equation 7.8.3 could simply be incorporated into the autoregressive component. One reason is that, if the generating model is indeed integrated, it is very difficult to learn anything more from the sample autocorrelations and partial autocorrelations of the undifferenced series. This feature appears to dominate everything else, so that it can be almost impossible to determine, for example, how many autoregressive and moving average terms are involved in the generating model. In practice, time series analysts generally proceed by first determining what level of differencing is needed. Next, the sample autocorrelations and partial autocorrelations of the differenced series are employed to suggest autoregressive and moving average orders. This is the approach to time series model selection that will be applied in Section 7.9.

7.9 FITTING ARIMA MODELS TO DATA

The class of ARIMA models has been found to give an adequate parsimonious representation of a wide variety of actual time series. Box and

Jenkins (1970) developed a methodology for fitting models from this class to data. In this section we will outline and illustrate that methodology. The approach involves the iterative three-stage cycle set out in Figure 7.10. The first, and in practice the trickiest, step requires the *selection* of a specific model from the general class; that is, the analyst must determine the appropriate degree, d, of differencing, and also the autoregressive and moving average orders, p and q, of the ARMA model to be fitted to the differenced series. These decisions are based on the evidence in sample statistics that can readily be computed from the given time series data. Specifically, as suggested in previous sections, the behavior of the sample autocorrelations and sample partial autocorrelations of the time series and its first one or two differences is examined. This involves at least as much art as science: The judgment of the analyst, based on experience, is important. The choice of model will not necessarily be obvious or clear-cut. On occasion it may be desirable to carry forward not just one, but two or more models for subsequent analysis, postponing the final choice until the contending models have been more thoroughly investigated. Also, any decision made at the initial model selection stage is not irrevocable. If, on fuller analysis, the chosen model turns out to be unsatisfactory, it can be abandoned in favor of some alternative.

Unless the sample autocorrelations suggest that the appropriately differenced series is simply white noise, the chosen model will involve unknown autoregressive or moving average parameters, or both. At the second stage, these parameters are estimated using efficient statistical methods. Finally, the adequacy with which the fitted model describes the data is checked. Any lack of adequate fit that is revealed may suggest some alternative specification, so that the cycle of model selection, param-

FIGURE 7.10   An approach to ARIMA model-building.

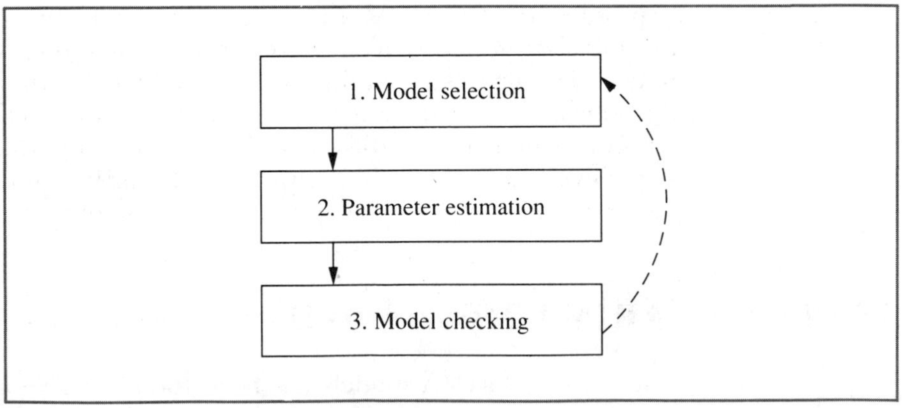

eter estimation, and model checking is repeated until a satisfactory fitted model is finally achieved.

Model Selection

In Sections 7.5 through 7.8 we have already, in effect, set out and justified the ingredients of an approach to ARIMA model selection, based on the sample autocorrelations and sample partial autocorrelations of a time series and its first one or two differences. We now pull together these ingredients.

1. The first decision to be made is the amount of differencing necessary to produce a stationary time series. This decision can be based on visual examination of a plot of the sample autocorrelations. The need for further differencing is indicated when this plot exhibits a very smooth pattern at high lags, rather than a quicker decay to values scattered close to zero.

2. Once an appropriate degree of differencing has been determined, autoregressive and moving average orders are selected by examining the sample autocorrelations and sample partial autocorrelations *of the differenced series*. The characteristics of pure autoregressive and pure moving average behavior are most easily spotted, so that it is natural to look first for these. However, it should be kept in mind that, on occasion, a superior and less heavily parameterized representation may be available through a mixed autoregressive moving average model, and this possibility should be checked:

   (a) For a pure autoregressive model of order p, all partial autocorrelations of order higher than p are zero. Evidence for such behavior is provided by comparing the corresponding sample partial autocorrelations with two standard error limits, that is with $\pm 2n^{-1/2}$. On the other hand, the autocorrelations of a pure autoregressive model do not abruptly cut off, but rather decay toward zero.

   (b) For a pure moving average model of order q, all autocorrelations of order higher than q are zero. To detect such behavior the corresponding sample autocorrelations are compared with two standard error limits; that is, with $\pm 2[(n - k)/n(n + 2)]^{1/2}$, or more simply and slightly more crudely, with $\pm 2n^{-1/2}$. The partial autocorrelations of a pure moving average process do not abruptly cut off, but decay toward zero.

   (c) Finally, for an ARMA(p, q) model, with both p and q bigger than zero, neither the autocorrelations nor the partial autocorrelations exhibit abrupt cut-off. It is known that, for this process, the autocorrelations ρ_k decay toward zero according to

$$\rho_k = \phi_1 \rho_{k-1} + \phi_2 \rho_{k-2} + \cdots + \phi_p \rho_{k-p}$$
$$k = q + 1, q + 2, \ldots$$

The identification of mixed autoregressive moving average models depends on the ability of the analyst to recognize similar patterns in the sample autocorrelations. In principle, this would seem to be a horribly difficult task, and in practice it can indeed be quite tricky. However, the field of search is not too large; experience suggests that very often a good representation can be achieved with very small values for p or q or both.

The intricacies of model selection are best absorbed through examples, and through the acquisition of practical experience. In this section we will discuss three cases of ARIMA model fitting. In the exercises at the end of the chapter there are further series for practice. Before proceeding, however, it is important to stress here the principle of parsimony. The search is not for a very elaborate model, but for the simplest model that appears to adequately represent the data. Thus, in making an initial choice, the analyst should attempt to proceed, if this seems tenable, with a model containing just a very small number of parameters. If something more elaborate is required, this should be indicated at the model checking stage.

Parameter Estimation

Assume now that a particular model from the general ARIMA class has been selected for fuller analysis—that is, specific values have been chosen for p, d, and q. The next step is to estimate the unknown parameters of that model. (In practice, as we have already noted, it will sometimes be useful to carry more than one model forward from the model selection stage. In that case it will be necessary to estimate the unknown parameters of all these competing models, selecting among them according to closeness of fit to the data.)

The object, then, is to estimate the parameters of a stationary autoregressive moving average process that may follow from the differencing of an observed time series. Suppose that we have available n observations, denoted $X_1, X_2, \ldots, X_n$, on the levels of a time series. If it is necessary to difference this series d times before obtaining a stationary series, which we will denote W_t, then d observations will be lost, leaving

$(n - d)$ values for the differenced series

$$W_t = (1 - B)^d X_t \qquad t = d + 1, d + 2, \dots, n$$

If the stationary process W_t has mean μ, and is generated by an ARMA(p, q) model, we can write

$$(W_t - \mu) - \phi_1(W_{t-1} - \mu) - \cdots - \phi_p(W_{t-p} - \mu)$$
$$= a_t - \theta_1 a_{t-1} - \cdots - \theta_q a_{t-q} \qquad (7.9.1)$$

This model involves $(p + q + 1)$ unknown parameters $\mu, \phi_1, \dots, \phi_p, \theta_1, \dots, \theta_q$ which must be estimated. Frequently, after differencing, it is reasonable to assume that the differenced series has mean zero, in which case the parameter μ can be dropped. More generally, when this assumption is untenable, the series mean is simply viewed as an additional parameter to be estimated together with the $(p + q)$ autoregressive and moving average coefficients.

A number of alternative procedures have been proposed and implemented for the estimation of the parameters of the model 7.9.1. These various procedures will typically yield quite similar estimates when the sample size is large. However, for shorter series, there can be larger differences, particularly if the model involves substantial moving average terms. Here we will briefly discuss the approach that is most simply described. It is based on least squares, involving the minimization of the sum of squares of the white noise error terms, and is sometimes called **conditional least squares.** To implement this approach, it is necessary to express the white noise errors as functions of the observed data and the unknown parameters. Specifically, it follows from equation 7.9.1 that

$$a_t = (W_t - \mu) - \phi_1(W_{t-1} - \mu) - \cdots - \phi_p(W_{t-p} - \mu)$$
$$+ \theta_1 a_{t-1} + \cdots + \theta_q a_{t-q} \qquad t = (p + d + 1), \dots, n \qquad (7.9.2)$$

This sequence is started at time $(p + d + 1)$, since the first observation on the differenced series is W_{d+1}; thus, from $t = (p + d + 1)$ on, the values for the differenced series required on the right-hand side of equation 7.9.2 will all be available. However, to get the calculations started, it is still necessary to specify the first few values of the white noise series. This can be done by setting them to their means of zero; that is, we set

$$a_t = 0 \qquad t = (p + d - q + 1), \dots, (p + d) \qquad (7.9.3)$$

Given these initial values, equation 7.9.2 can then be used to compute the a_t for any specific set of parameters μ, ϕ_1, ϕ_2, $\ldots$, ϕ_p, θ_1, $\ldots$, θ_q. The sum of squares of the white noise errors is then

$$S = \sum_{t=p+d+1}^{n} a_t^2 \qquad\qquad (7.9.4)$$

The least squares parameter estimates are then those values of the parameters for which this sum of squares is a minimum.

The sum of squared errors in equation 7.9.4 is a very complicated function of the unknown parameters. Computational algorithms for the numerical minimization of this and related functions are widely available. These algorithms, based on *nonlinear regression procedures*, have been incorporated in special computer packages for the analysis of ARIMA models. In addition to point estimates, they allow the computation of associated standard errors, so that confidence intervals for the parameters can be found, and the statistical significance of the estimates tested. These inferential procedures are based on the fact that, given a moderately large sample size, the parameter estimators have distributions that are close to normal.

As we have already indicated, a number of alternative parameter estimation procedures are in common use. This can be somewhat frustrating to the practitioner, who needs to be aware that the standard ARIMA computer packages will yield somewhat different parameter estimates using identical data sets. Very often these differences will be of no great practical significance, in the sense that quite similar forecasts will result. The simple conditional least squares procedure, for instance, might be viewed as somewhat unsatisfactory because of the rather arbitrary way in which the first few values of the white noise series are set to zero in equation 7.9.3. The alternative estimation procedures, which we will not discuss in detail here, can be viewed as attempts to treat this initial values problem more carefully. When different estimation procedures do yield significantly different results, our preference, based to some extent on evidence discussed by Ansley and Newbold (1980), is for an approach through *full maximum likelihood*. This approach is implemented in a few computer program packages, including SPSS and SAS.

Model Checking

In any statistical model-building exercise, it is important to check that the achieved model adequately represents the given data. This is particularly important in the context of ARIMA model building, given the admittedly and necessarily imprecise nature of our approach to model selection.

Initially, a specific model is tentatively chosen, but the analyst must be prepared to abandon or modify this model if checks suggest its inadequacy.

Two major approaches to model checking have traditionally been used. First, a more elaborate model—that is, one containing *additional parameters*—can be estimated, and the statistical significance of the extra parameter estimates checked. Thus, if an ARMA(p, q) model has been fitted, an alternative model with either one or two extra autoregressive terms or one or two extra moving average terms can be tried. It is not, however, a good strategy to add *both* extra autoregressive and extra moving average terms, because if the model is adequately specified, the additional parameters will in effect cancel out. Consequently, the augmented model will be difficult and costly to estimate and the resulting parameter estimators will have very large variances. For example, suppose that the time series W_t is white noise, so that

$$W_t = a_t$$

If we were to fit the ARMA(1, 1) model

$$(1 - \phi_1 B)W_t = (1 - \theta_1 B)a_t$$

any pair of parameter values with $\phi_1 = \theta_1$ would yield the correct model.

A second approach to model checking is based on the fact that, if the model is correctly specified, the error terms a_t will be white noise; that is, all autocorrelations of these errors will be zero. In practice, the true errors a_t will be unknown, but they are estimated by the residuals from the fitted model. If $\hat{\mu}, \hat{\phi}_1, \ldots, \hat{\phi}_p, \hat{\theta}_1, \ldots, \hat{\theta}_q$ are the parameter estimates, the residuals satisfy

$$\hat{a}_t = (W_t - \hat{\mu}) - \hat{\phi}_1(W_{t-1} - \hat{\mu})$$
$$- \hat{\phi}_p(W_{t-p} - \hat{\mu}) + \hat{\theta}_1 \hat{a}_{t-1} + \cdots + \hat{\theta}_q \hat{a}_{t-q}$$

The autocorrelations of the errors are then estimated by the **residual autocorrelations**

$$\hat{r}_k = \frac{\sum\limits_{t=k+1}^{n} \hat{a}_t \hat{a}_{t-k}}{\sum\limits_{t=1}^{n} \hat{a}_t^2} \qquad k = 1, 2, \ldots$$

If the assumed model is adequate, these residual autocorrelations, which are routinely calculated by time series computer packages, should be close to zero. They are typically compared with limits $\pm 2[(n - k)/n(n + 2)]^{1/2}$ or $\pm 2n^{-1/2}$ to assess their significance. However, this can be somewhat misleading as, for low k, the true standard error of $\hat{r}_k$ can be a good deal smaller than $n^{-1/2}$, depending on the actual model specification. Besides looking at individual residual autocorrelations, it is common to ask whether, taken as a group, the first few of them are bigger than would be expected if the error terms were indeed white noise. The resulting test is sometimes called a **portmanteau test** since, by contrast with the approach in which a slightly more elaborate model is fitted, no simple specific alternative to the assumed model is postulated. Rather, the test is designed to detect any of a wide variety of alternative specifications.

The portmanteau test statistic that is usually calculated in practice is due to Ljung and Box (1978), and is based on the squares of the first M residual autocorrelations, where M is a moderately large number—typically at least ten. The Box-Ljung statistic, which is a modification of an earlier proposal of Box and Pierce (1970), is

$$Q = n(n + 2) \sum_{k=1}^{M} (n - k)^{-1} \hat{r}_k^2 \qquad (7.9.5)$$

It is known that, provided M is moderately large, if an assumed ARMA(p, q) specification is correct, the statistic 7.9.5 has a distribution close to the chi-square with $(M - p - q)$ degrees of freedom. Model inadequacy would be indicated by large absolute values for the residual autocorrelations, and consequently large values for the statistic 7.9.5. Accordingly, the hypothesis that the assumed specification is correct would be rejected for a value of Q exceeding tabulated upper tail points of the chi-square distribution.

In the remainder of this section we will illustrate the Box-Jenkins model-building methodology with three examples. The three data sets are given in the appendix to this chapter. The reader is cautioned that different computer packages will produce somewhat different output, both in terms of form and specific numerical values. This is particularly so for parameter estimation.

Example 7.1.   Exhibit 7.1 shows part of the output from the MINITAB program for the analysis of a series of $n = 149$ daily observations on the percent advances of number of issues traded on the New York Stock Exchange. The first part of the output shows the sample autocorrelations and sample partial autocorrelations for this time series. For high lags, the sample autocorrelations are all very small, and do not follow a very smooth pattern, so that there is no evidence to suggest this series needs differencing to induce stationarity. Accordingly, the aim is to fit an autoregressive

EXHIBIT 7.1 Part of MINITAB program output for analysis of percent advances of number of issues traded.

```
ACF of ADVANCES

          -1.0 -0.8 -0.6 -0.4 -0.2  0.0  0.2  0.4  0.6  0.8  1.0
          +----+----+----+----+----+----+----+----+----+----+
  1   0.211                             XXXXXX
  2   0.004                             X
  3   0.005                             X
  4   0.080                             XXX
  5   0.003                             X
  6   0.011                             X
  7   0.037                             XX
  8  -0.111                          XXXX
  9  -0.061                           XXX
 10  -0.014                             X
 11  -0.016                             X
 12  -0.021                            XX
 13   0.007                             X
 14  -0.076                           XXX
 15   0.004                             X
 16   0.035                             XX
 17   0.015                             X
 18  -0.069                           XXX
 19  -0.009                             X
 20  -0.053                            XX


PACF of ADVANCES

          -1.0 -0.8 -0.6 -0.4 -0.2  0.0  0.2  0.4  0.6  0.8  1.0
          +----+----+----+----+----+----+----+----+----+----+
  1   0.211                             XXXXXX
  2  -0.042                            XX
  3   0.014                             X
  4   0.080                             XXX
  5  -0.033                            XX
  6   0.022                             XX
  7   0.032                             XX
  8  -0.141                          XXXXX
  9  -0.002                             X
 10  -0.006                             X
 11  -0.025                            XX
 12   0.011                             X
 13   0.011                             X
 14  -0.089                           XXX
 15   0.061                             XXX
 16   0.010                             X
 17  -0.010                             X
 18  -0.056                            XX
 19   0.010                             X
 20  -0.071                           XXX
```

301

EXHIBIT 7.1   *(Continued)*

```
Final Estimates of Parameters
Type       Estimate    St. Dev.   t-ratio
MA   1      -0.2182     0.0805     -2.71
Constant    38.586      1.107      34.85
Mean        38.586      1.107

No. of obs.:  149
Residuals:    SS = 18070.9  (back forecasts excluded)
              MS =   122.9  DF = 147

Modified Box-Pierce chi-square statistic
Lag               12           24           36           48
Chi-square   4.3(DF=11)   12.6(DF=23)  26.6(DF=35)  38.6(DF=47)


ACF of Error

           -1.0 -0.8 -0.6 -0.4 -0.2  0.0  0.2  0.4  0.6  0.8  1.0
            +----+----+----+----+----+----+----+----+----+----+
  1   0.001                           X
  2   0.006                           X
  3  -0.014                           X
  4   0.086                          XXX
  5  -0.016                           X
  6   0.001                           X
  7   0.062                          XXX
  8  -0.117                         XXXX
  9  -0.035                          XX
 10  -0.005                           X
 11  -0.009                           X
 12  -0.025                          XX
 13   0.030                          XX
 14  -0.087                         XXX
 15   0.016                           X
 16   0.027                          XX
 17   0.026                          XX
 18  -0.078                         XXX
 19   0.014                           X
 20  -0.031                          XX
```

moving average model to the undifferenced series. The sample autocorrelations and sample partial autocorrelations of this series must now be examined to suggest appropriate autoregressive and moving average orders. To assess their significance, these quantities can be compared with limits $\pm 2n^{-1/2} = \pm 2(149)^{-1/2} = \pm 0.164$. Judged by this criterion, the first sample autocorrelation is quite large, whereas the others are small, suggesting the possibility of a first-order moving average model. Also, whereas the first sample partial autocorrelation is large, the remainder are small, so that a first-order autoregressive model is also a possibility. The fact that the second sample autocorrelation is somewhat smaller than the second sample autocorrelation suggests a slight preference for the moving average model, so we proceed with the ARIMA(0, 0, 1) specification. In fact, in a case like this, where the parameters are relatively small, fitted MA(1) and AR(1) models will yield very similar forecasts.

The next part of the output in Exhibit 7.1 shows the results of fitting a first-order moving average model to the percent advances series. In general, an ARMA(p, q) model can be written either as

$$(X_t - \mu) - \phi_1(X_{t-1} - \mu) - \cdots - \phi_p(X_{t-p} - \mu)$$
$$= a_t - \theta_1 a_{t-1} - \cdots - \theta_q a_{t-q}$$

or, equivalently,

$$X_t - \phi_1 X_{t-1} - \cdots - \phi_p X_{t-p} = C + a_t - \theta_1 a_{t-1} - \cdots - \theta_q a_{t-q}$$

where

$$C = (1 - \phi_1 - \cdots - \phi_p)\mu$$

In the MINITAB output, C is the "constant" and μ is the "mean." Of course, for pure moving average models these are the same.

The model fitted to the percent advances data is

$$X_t = C + a_t - \theta_1 a_{t-1}$$

and we see from the program output that the point estimates of the two parameters are

$$\hat{C} = 38.586 \qquad \hat{\theta}_1 = -0.218$$

The fitted model then is

$$X_t = 38.586 + a_t + 0.218 a_{t-1} \qquad (7.9.6)$$
$$(1.107) \qquad\qquad (0.081)$$

where the figures in parentheses below the parameter estimates are the corresponding estimated standard errors, or standard deviations. Notice that the estimated moving average parameter is quite large compared with its standard error; the t-ratio is -2.71. Since the parameter estimates are approximately normally distributed, this t-ratio can be compared with significance points of the standard normal distribution, and strongly suggests the desirability of including the moving average term in the model.

The output also shows the sum of squares of the residuals, $\hat{a}_t$, from the fitted model. Division of this sum of squares by its associated degrees of freedom (the number of observations less the number of parameters estimated) yields the residual mean square 122.9. This provides an estimate of the variance of the white noise error term, a_t, that, as we will see in Section 7.10, is used to estimate forecast error variances. In particular, 122.9 is the estimated error variance for forecasting percent advances one day ahead with this model. Since there seemed to be some possibility that a first-order autoregressive model might be appropriate for these data, we also fitted that model, though the details have been omitted from Exhibit 7.1. The resulting residual mean square was 123.1. Since the two models have the same number of parameters, this suggests a preference for the moving average model.

The remaining output in Exhibit 7.1 is useful in checking the adequacy of the fitted first-order moving average model. The modified Box-Pierce chi-square statistics are the quantities of equation 7.9.5 for different values of M. As indicated in the output, these statistics should be compared with critical points of the chi-square distribution with $(M - 1)$ degrees of freedom, since here the total number of estimated autoregressive and moving average parameters is one. These comparisons provide no substantial grounds for doubting the adequacy of the fitted model. Also shown are the first 20 autocorrelations of the residuals from the fitted model. These are all small compared with limits $\pm 2n^{-1/2} = \pm 0.164$, so that again there is little reason to question the adequacy of our first-order moving average model. We also fitted MA(2) and MA(3) models to these data. The results, which are not shown, provided estimates that were insignificantly different from zero for the additional parameters. It therefore seems reasonable to proceed with the fitted model equation 7.9.6 for forecasting future values of this time series.

Example 7.2.   Exhibit 7.2 shows part of the output from the SPSS program for the analysis of a series of $n = 56$ annual observations on the number of private housing units started per 1000 of population in the United States. In the first part of this exhibit the sample autocorrelations and partial autocorrelations of the series are shown. Notice that, for high lags, the sample autocorrelations remain moderately large and follow a smooth pattern. This indicates a need for differencing to achieve a stationary time series. In the SPSS output the sample autocorrelations are accompanied by values of the Box-Ljung statistic, equation 7.9.5, computed from the time series observations. This is useful in checking whether an observed time series might be white noise, though this is clearly not the

EXHIBIT 7.2 Part of SPSS program output for analysis of private housing units started per thousand of population.

```
Autocorrelations:    HOUSTART

     Auto- Stand.
Lag  Corr.  Err. -1 -.75 -.5 -.25  0  .25  .5  .75  1  Box-Ljung  Prob
                 +----+----+----+----+----+----+----+----+
  1  .874   .130                .  :****.************    45.113   .000
  2  .682   .129                .  :****.*********       73.124   .000
  3  .534   .128                .  :****.******          90.631   .000
  4  .461   .127                .  :****.****           103.897   .000
  5  .400   .125                .  :****.***            114.078   .000
  6  .338   .124                .  :****.**             121.505   .000
  7  .277   .123                .  :****.*              126.603   .000
  8  .236   .122                .  :*****               130.364   .000
  9  .197   .120                .  :****.               133.044   .000
 10  .121   .119                .  :** .                134.081   .000
 11  .067   .118                .  :*  .                134.403   .000
 12  .040   .116                .  :*  .                134.519   .000
 13  .011   .115                .  *   .                134.527   .000
 14 -.056   .114                . *:   .                134.768   .000
 15 -.142   .112              .***:   .                136.357   .000
 16 -.217   .111             ****:   .                 140.171   .000
 17 -.244   .110            *.***:   .                 145.126   .000
 18 -.239   .108            *.***:   .                 150.012   0.0
 19 -.237   .107            *.***:   .                 154.933   0.0
 20 -.221   .105             ****:   .                 159.333   0.0

Plot Symbols:      Autocorrelations *      Two Standard Error Limits.

Total cases:  56    Computable first lags:   55

Partial Autocorrelations:   HOUSTART

     Pr-Aut- Stand.
Lag  Corr.  Err. -1 -.75 -.5 -.25  0  .25  .5  .75  1
                 +----+----+----+----+----+----+----+----+
  1  .874   .134                .  :****.************
  2 -.345   .134              **.****:   .
  3  .163   .134                .  :*** .
  4  .130   .134                .  :*** .
  5 -.121   .134                . **:   .
  6  .044   .134                .  :*  .
  7 -.010   .134                .  *   .
  8  .028   .134                .  :*  .
  9 -.050   .134                . *:   .
 10 -.192   .134              .****:   .
 11  .196   .134                .  :****.
 12 -.077   .134                . **:   .
 13 -.131   .134                .***:   .
 14 -.080   .134                . **:   .
 15 -.102   .134                . **:   .
 16 -.035   .134                . *:   .
 17  .043   .134                .  :*  .
 18 -.008   .134                .  *   .
 19 -.006   .134                .  *   .
 20  .071   .134                .  :*  .

Plot Symbols:      Autocorrelations *      Two Standard Error Limits .

Total cases:  56    Computable first lags:  55
```

Exhibit 7.2   (*Continued*)

```
Autocorrelations:     HOUSTART
Transformations:  difference (1)
      Auto- Stand.
 Lag  Corr.  Err.  -1 -.75 -.5 -.25   0  .25  .5  .75   1   Box-Ljung  Prob.
                   +----+----+----+----+----+----+----+----+
   1   .271  .131                       . :*****             4.273    .039
   2  -.156  .130                     . ***:    .            5.705    .058
   3  -.266  .129                     *****:    .            9.963    .019
   4  -.027  .128                       . *:    .           10.008    .040
   5   .008  .126                       . *     .           10.013    .075
   6  -.028  .125                       . *:    .           10.064    .122
   7  -.102  .124                       . **:   .           10.748    .150
   8   .000  .122                       . *     .           10.748    .216
   9   .198  .121                       . :****.            13.431    .144
  10  -.063  .120                       . *:    .           13.707    .187
  11  -.130  .118                     . ***:    .           14.920    .186
  12  -.035  .117                       . *:    .           15.011    .241
  13   .153  .116                       . :***  .           16.751    .211
  14   .081  .114                       . :**   .           17.251    .243
  15  -.046  .113                       . *:    .           17.416    .295
  16  -.197  .112                     ****:     .           20.546    .197
  17  -.104  .110                       . **:   .           21.435    .207
  18   .012  .109                       . *     .           21.447    .257
  19  -.068  .107                       . *:    .           21.845    .292
  20  -.237  .106                     *.***:    .           26.863    .139
Plot Symbols:      Autocorrelations *    Two Standard Error Limits .
Total cases:  56     Computable first lags after differencing:  54

Partial Autocorrelations:   HOUSTART
Transformations:  difference (1)
     Pr-Aut- Stand.
 Lag  Corr.  Err.  -1 -.75 -.5 -.25   0  .25  .5  .75   1
                   +----+----+----+----+----+----+----+----+
   1   .271   .135                      . :*****
   2  -.247   .135                    *****:    .
   3  -.168   .135                    . ***:    .
   4   .080   .135                      . :**   .
   5  -.097   .135                      . **:   .
   6  -.058   .135                      . *:    .
   7  -.082   .135                      . **:   .
   8   .028   .135                      . :*    .
   9   .171   .135                      . :***  .
  10  -.258   .135                    *****:    .
  11   .028   .135                      . :*    .
  12   .064   .135                      . :*    .
  13   .042   .135                      . :*    .
  14  -.002   .135                      . *     .
  15  -.048   .135                      . *:    .
  16  -.103   .135                      . **:   .
  17  -.042   .135                      . *:    .
  18  -.077   .135                      . **:   .
  19  -.104   .135                      . **:   .
  20  -.259   .135                    *****:    .
Plot Symbols:      Autocorrelations *     Two Standard Error Limits .
Total cases:  56     Computable first lags after differencing:  54
```

Exhibit 7.2 (*Continued*)

```
FINAL PARAMETERS:

Number of residuals   55
Standard error         1.3863685
Log likelihood        -94.725826
AIC                   195.45165
SBC                   201.47365


               Analysis of Variance:

              DF    Adj. Sum of Squares    Residual Variance
Residuals     52             100.77670           1.92201776


               Variables in the Model:

               B           SEB         T-RATIO    APPROX. PROB.
MA1     -.29712449    .13229081    -2.2459948      .02897923
MA2      .17797542    .13777047     1.2918256      .20212956
MA3      .33166858    .13421127     2.4712424      .01677738


Covariance Matrix:

                 MA1          MA2          MA3
MA1         .01750086    .00498925   -.00118424
MA2         .00498925    .01898070    .00521324
MA3        -.00118424    .00521324    .01801267


Correlation Matrix:

                 MA1          MA2          MA3
MA1        1.0000000     .2737472    -.0666993
MA2         .2737472    1.0000000     .2819438
MA3        -.0666993     .2819438    1.0000000
```

case with these data. The probabilities attached to these statistics are the lowest significance levels at which the null hypothesis of white noise can be rejected.

Having decided that differencing is necessary, the next step is to examine the sample autocorrelations and sample partial autocorrelations of the first differenced series. These are shown, together with two standard error limits in the next part of Exhibit 7.2. The pattern of these sample autocorrelations at high lags is not at all smooth, so that further differencing is unnecessary. Compared with their standard errors, the first three sample autocorrelations are at least moderately large, while the next

EXHIBIT 7.2   (*Continued*)

```
     Autocorrelations:    ERR#1       Error for HOUSTART from ARIMA

          Auto- Stand.
     Lag  Corr.  Err. -1  -.75  -.5 -.25   0   .25  .5   .75   1  Box-Ljung  Prob.
                        +----+----+----+----+----+----+----+----+
       1   .016  .131                    .     *   .                  .014    .905
       2   .053  .130                    .    :*   .                  .181    .914
       3  -.002  .129                    .     *   .                  .181    .981
       4  -.031  .128                    .    *:   .                  .241    .993
       5  -.025  .126                    .     *   .                  .280    .998
       6   .038  .125                    .    :*   .                  .373    .999
       7  -.086  .124                    .   **:   .                  .857    .997
       8  -.072  .122                    .    *:   .                 1.204    .997
       9   .209  .121                    .    :****.                 4.170    .900
      10  -.142  .120                    .  ***:   .                 5.575    .850
      11  -.056  .118                    .    *:   .                 5.796    .887
      12  -.012  .117                    .     *   .                 5.807    .925
      13   .069  .116                    .    :*   .                 6.159    .940
      14  -.014  .114                    .     *   .                 6.173    .962
      15  -.028  .113                    .    *:   .                 6.237    .975
      16  -.148  .112                    .***:   .                   7.998    .949
      17  -.142  .110                    .***:   .                   9.661    .917
      18  -.034  .109                    .    *:   .                 9.758    .940
      19  -.035  .107                    .    *:   .                 9.862    .956
      20  -.231  .106                  *.***:   .                   14.650    .796

     Plot symbols:     Autocorrelations *     Two Standard Error Limits .
```

several values are quite small, suggesting the possibility of an MA(3) model for the series of first differences. However, much the same pattern is also present in the sample partial autocorrelations, so that an AR(3) model might be appropriate. Given these two potential specifications, it seems reasonable also to consider the two mixed models with three parameters—the ARMA(2, 1) and ARMA(1, 2) models. Given this degree of uncertainty about what might be the best choice, we decided at this stage to carry forward four models for further analysis.

In general, we compare fitted ARIMA models through the SBC criterion, introduced in Section 7.2. This is particularly valuable when the competing models involve different numbers of parameters. When, as here, the models have the same number of parameters, the residual mean square could also be used for comparison. The SBC statistics for the four models under consideration are shown in Table 7.3. These results indicate preference for the ARIMA(0, 1, 3) model. Only analysis related to this model is shown in Exhibit 7.2.

TABLE 7.3   Values of SBC criterion for ARIMA models fitted to private housing units started per 1,000 of population.

Model	(3, 1, 0)	(2, 1, 1)	(1, 1, 2)	(0, 1, 3)
SBC	202.46	202.71	203.10	201.47

The SPSS model estimation algorithm computes both AIC and SBC statistics, as well as the variance and standard error of the residuals from the fitted model. The residual variance, or mean square, here indicates an estimated error variance of 1.92 for the one-year-ahead prediction of private housing units started per 1000 of population. The model fitted is of the form

$$(1 - B)X_t = a_t - \theta_1 a_{t-1} - \theta_2 a_{t-2} - \theta_3 a_{t-3}$$

The point estimates of the three moving average parameters are

$$\hat{\theta}_1 = -0.297 \qquad \hat{\theta}_2 = 0.178 \qquad \hat{\theta}_3 = 0.332$$

The fitted model then is

$$(1 - B)X_t = a_t + 0.297 a_{t-1} - 0.178 a_{t-2} - 0.332 a_{t-3} \qquad (7.9.7)$$
$$\quad (0.132) \qquad (0.138) \qquad (0.134)$$

where the figures in parentheses below the parameter estimates are the associated estimated standard errors. The estimation algorithm also computes the estimated covariance and correlation matrices of the parameter estimators. A very large positive or negative correlation between two estimators can indicate that two parameters are doing more or less the same job, and consequently that one or the other, but possibly not both, are needed in the model. The analyst might then try the simpler models implied by dropping each of these parameters. However, in the present example, such a course of action is not indicated.

In the final part of Exhibit 7.2 the residual autocorrelations from the fitted model are shown, together with their associated standard errors. Most of the first 20 residual autocorrelations are very small. Only those at lags 9 and 20 are even moderately large, and it seems reasonable to attribute to chance values of this size at such long lags. Certainly these would not lead us to seriously question the adequacy of our fitted model. Neither would the reported values for the Box-Ljung statistic 7.9.5. For example, we see that, for a test based on the first $M = 10$ residual autocorrelations, the null hypothesis that the model is correctly specified can only be rejected at significance levels of 85.0% or more. Similarly, 79.6% is the lowest significance level for rejecting the model specification when the test is based on the first 20 residual autocorrelations. In addition, we fitted ARIMA(1, 1, 3) and ARIMA(2, 1, 3) models. The estimates of the additional parameters were statistically insignificant. We conclude then that the fitted model, equation 7.9.7, can be carried forward with some confidence for forecasting future private housing starts.

Example 7.3.   Our third example is a series of 50 annual observations on the number of active oil wells in the United States. Part of the SPSS program output from our analysis of these data is shown in Exhibit 7.3. The sample autocorrelations of the undifferenced series exhibit very smooth behavior at high lags, so that it seems quite clear that the series of levels is not stationary. Turning now to the sample autocorrelations of the first differenced series, these quantities also are not terribly small for high lags, and seem to follow quite a smooth pattern. This suggests the desirability of further differencing. Next, the sample autocorrelations of the second differenced series provide no grounds for further differencing, so that an ARIMA(p, 2, q) model is indicated. The sample autocorrelations and sample partial autocorrelations of the second differenced series are examined to suggest autoregressive and moving average orders. Compared with their standard errors, the first two sample autocorrelations are large, whereas the remainder are quite small, suggesting an MA(2) model for the series of second differences. Similarly, the first two sample partial autocorrelations are moderately large, while most of the remainder are small, so that an AR(2) model is possible. Given that these two-parameter models are under consideration, it might also be useful to include the ARMA(1, 1) specification for the second differenced series. A fourth possibility arises from noting that, although the second sample partial autocorrelation is moderately large, it is still within the two standard error bounds. It might therefore be useful to consider the simpler ARIMA(1, 2, 0) model.

Table 7.4 shows the values of the SBC criterion when these four models were fitted. The smallest value is for the ARIMA(0, 2, 2) model,

TABLE 7.4   Values of SBC criterion for ARIMA models fitted to number of active oil wells.

Model	(1, 2, 0)	(2, 2, 0)	(1, 2, 1)	(0, 2, 2)
SBC	1,023.4	1,024.4	1,024.5	1,023.3

Exhibit 7.3   Part of SPSS program output for analysis of number of active oil wells.

```
Autocorrelations:    OILWELLS

      Auto- Stand.
Lag   Corr.  Err. -1  -.75  -.5 -.25   0   .25  .5   .75  1   Box-Ljung   Prob.
                    +----+----+----+----+----+----+----+----+
  1   .925   .137                    . :****.**************      45.421     .000
  2   .849   .136                    . :****.************        84.483     .000
  3   .769   .134                    . :****.**********         117.232     .000
  4   .691   .133                    . :****.*********          144.252     .000
  5   .609   .132                    . :****.*******            165.695     0.0
  6   .540   .130                    . :****.******             182.955     0.0
  7   .462   .129                    . :****.****               195.855     0.0
  8   .388   .127                    . :****.***                205.191     0.0
  9   .315   .126                    . :****.*                  211.484     0.0
 10   .243   .124                    . :*****                   215.331     0.0
 11   .176   .122                    . :****.                   217.402     0.0
 12   .110   .121                    . :**  .                   218.228     0.0
 13   .048   .119                    . :*   .                   218.390     0.0
 14  -.012   .118                    .  *   .                   218.400     0.0
 15  -.066   .116                    . *:   .                   218.725     0.0
 16  -.116   .114                    . **:  .                   219.760     0.0
 17  -.158   .113                    . ***: .                   221.730     0.0
 18  -.200   .111                    ****:  .                   224.982     0.0
 19  -.236   .109                   *.***:  .                   229.664     0.0
 20  -.267   .107                   *.***:  .                   235.824     0.0

Plot Symbols:      Autocorrelations *    Two Standard Error Limits .

Total cases:  50    Computable first lags:  49

Partial Autocorrelations:   OILWELLS

       Pr-Aut- Stand.
Lag   Corr.   Err. -1  -.75  -.5 -.25   0   .25  .5   .75  1
                    +----+----+----+----+----+----+----+----+
  1   .925    .141                   . :*****.**************
  2  -.047    .141                   .  *:   .
  3  -.067    .141                   .  *:   .
  4  -.032    .141                   .  *:   .
  5  -.075    .141                   .  *:   .
  6   .043    .141                   .   :*  .
  7  -.114    .141                   . **:   .
  8  -.021    .141                   .   *   .
  9  -.047    .141                   .  *:   .
 10  -.053    .141                   .  *:   .
 11  -.011    .141                   .   *   .
 12  -.069    .141                   .  *:   .
 13  -.018    .141                   .   *   .
 14  -.052    .141                   .  *:   .
 15  -.023    .141                   .   *   .
 16  -.028    .141                   .  *:   .
 17  -.011    .141                   .   *   .
 18  -.052    .141                   .  *:   .
 19  -.027    .141                   .  *:   .
 20  -.011    .141                   .   *   .

Plot Symbols:      Autocorrelations *    Two Standard Error Limits .

Total cases:  50    Computable first lags:  49
```

Exhibit 7.3 *(Continued)*

```
Autocorrelations:   OILWELLS

Transformations:  difference (1)

       Auto- Stand.
  Lag  Corr.  Err.  -1  -.75  -.5  -.25   0   .25   .5   .75   1   Box-Ljung  Prob.
                    +----+----+----+----+----+----+----+----+
    1  .404   .139              .       :*****.**              8.514    .004
    2  .551   .137              .       :****.******          24.636    .000
    3  .387   .136              .       :****.***             32.787    .000
    4  .362   .134              .       :****.**              40.074    .000
    5  .215   .133              .       :****.               42.692    .000
    6  .140   .131              .       :***  .               43.832    .000
    7  .060   .130              .       :*    .               44.047    .000
    8 -.027   .128              .      *:     .               44.090    .000
    9 -.083   .127              .     **:     .               44.522    .000
   10 -.203   .125              .   ****:     .               47.155    .000
   11 -.236   .123              .  *****:     .               50.813    .000
   12 -.341   .122           **.*****:     .               58.656    .000
   13 -.323   .120            *.*****:     .               65.897    .000
   14 -.310   .118            *.*****:     .               72.754    .000
   15 -.256   .117              *****:     .               77.574    .000
   16 -.304   .115            *.*****:     .               84.560    .000
   17 -.228   .113              *****:     .               88.603    .000
   18 -.191   .111               ****:     .               91.549    .000
   19 -.159   .110               .***:     .               93.662    .000
   20 -.109   .108               . **:     .               94.695    .000

Plot Symbols:     Autocorrelations *    Two Standard Error Limits .

Total cases:  50    Computable first lags after differencing:  48

Partial Autocorrelations:   OILWELLS

Transformations:  difference (1)

       Pr-Aut- Stand.
  Lag  Corr.   Err.  -1  -.75  -.5  -.25   0   .25   .5   .75   1
                     +----+----+----+----+----+----+----+----+
    1  .404   .143              .       :*****.**
    2  .463   .143              .       :*****.***
    3  .123   .143              .       :**   .
    4  .016   .143              .       *     .
    5 -.126   .143              .    ***:     .
    6 -.144   .143              .    ***:     .
    7 -.084   .143              .     **:     .
    8 -.083   .143              .     **:     .
    9 -.054   .143              .      *:     .
   10 -.143   .143              .    ***:     .
   11 -.112   .143              .     **:     .
   12 -.151   .143              .    ***:     .
   13 -.048   .143              .      *:     .
   14  .080   .143              .       :**   .
   15  .132   .143              .       :***  .
   16 -.050   .143              .      *:     .
   17 -.056   .143              .      *:     .
   18 -.011   .143              .       *     .
   19 -.022   .143              .       *     .
   20  .008   .143              .       *     .

Plot Symbols:     Autocorrelations *    Two Standard Error Limits .

Total cases:  50    Computable first lags after differencing:  48
```

EXHIBIT 7.3 (*Continued*)

```
    Autocorrelations:   OILWELLS

    Transformations:  difference (2)

        Auto- Stand.
    Lag Corr.  Err.  -1  -.75  -.5 -.25   0   .25  .5   .75   1   Box-Ljung  Prob.
                    +----+----+----+----+----+----+----+----+
     1  -.648  .140        *******.*****:       .           21.472    .000
     2   .276  .138                .   :******              25.461    .000
     3  -.099  .137                . **:      .             25.988    .000
     4   .034  .135                .  :*      .             26.052    .000
     5   .084  .134                .  :**     .             26.443    .000
     6  -.068  .132                . *:       .             26.705    .000
     7   .030  .131                .  :*      .             26.758    .000
     8  -.035  .129                . *:       .             26.831    .001
     9   .060  .127                .  :*      .             27.051    .001
    10  -.050  .126                . *:       .             27.207    .002
    11   .058  .124                .  :*      .             27.423    .004
    12  -.096  .122                . **:      .             28.034    .005
    13  -.003  .121                .  *       .             28.034    .009
    14  -.034  .119                . *:       .             28.114    .014
    15   .087  .117                .  :**     .             28.663    .018
    16  -.090  .115                . **:      .             29.273    .022
    17   .007  .114                .  *       .             29.277    .032
    18  -.010  .112              .    *    .                29.285    .045
    19  -.013  .110              .    *    .                29.299    .061
    20   .077  .108              .    :**  .                29.802    .073

    Plot Symbols:     Autocorrelations *    Two Standard Error Limits .

    Total cases:  50    Computable first lags after differencing:  47

    Partial Autocorrelations:   OILWELLS

    Transformations:  difference (2)

        Pr-Aut- Stand.
    Lag Corr.  Err.  -1  -.75  -.5 -.25   0   .25  .5   .75   1
                    +----+----+----+----+----+----+----+----+
     1  -.648  .144        *******.*****:          .
     2  -.248  .144                .*****:         .
     3  -.068  .144                . *:       .
     4  -.014  .144                .  *       .
     5   .174  .144                .  :***    .
     6   .164  .144                .  :***    .
     7   .075  .144                .  :*      .
     8  -.032  .144                . *:       .
     9  -.001  .144                .  *       .
    10  -.037  .144                . *:       .
    11   .024  .144                .  *       .
    12  -.069  .144                . *:       .
    13  -.207  .144              . ****:      .
    14  -.302  .144              *******:     .
    15  -.109  .144                .  **:     .
    16  -.021  .144                .  *       .
    17   .001  .144                .  *       .
    18   .036  .144                .  :*      .
    19   .014  .144                .  *       .
    20   .120  .144                .  :**     .

    Plot Symbols:     Autocorrelations *    Two Standard Error Limits .

    Total cases:  50    Computabable first lags after differencing: 47
```

EXHIBIT 7.3   (*Continued*)

```
FINAL PARAMETERS:

Number of residuals  48
Standard error       9632.1059
Log likelihood       -507.78834
AIC                  1019.5767
SBC                  1023.3191


            Analysis of Variance:
            DF     Adj. Sum of Squares  Residual Variance
Residuals   46        4338673739.5          92777464.7


            Variables in the Model:

            B           SEB        T-RATIO    APPROX. PROB.
MA1    .85587819    .13776893    6.2124182    .00000013
MA2   -.37224308    .13960143   -2.6664705    .01054288


Covariance Matrix:

            MA1          MA2
MA1    .01898028    -.01199400
MA2   -.01199400     .01948856


Correlation Matrix:

            MA1          MA2
MA1    1.0000000    -.6236243
MA2   -.6236243     1.0000000


Autocorrelations:   ERR#1      Error for OILWELLS from ARIMA

    Auto- Stand.
Lag Corr.  Err. -1  -.75  -.5  -.25  0  .25  .5  .75  1  Box-Ljung  Prob.
                  +----+----+----+----+----+----+----+----+
  1   .000  .140                  .    *    .              .000    .997
  2   .026  .138                  .   :*    .              .035    .983
  3  -.059  .137                  .  *:     .              .220    .974
  4   .093  .135                  .   :**   .              .691    .952
  5   .168  .134                  .   :***  .             2.268    .811
  6   .011  .132                  .    *    .             2.275    .893
  7  -.002  .131                  .    *    .             2.275    .943
  8   .017  .129                  .    *    .             2.293    .971
  9   .092  .127                  .   :**   .             2.816    .971
 10   .007  .126                  .    *    .             2.819    .985
 11  -.079  .124                  .  **:    .             3.223    .987
 12  -.257  .122              *****:        .             7.611    .815
 13  -.190  .121               .****:       .            10.093    .686
 14  -.053  .119                  . *:      .            10.291    .741
 15   .047  .117                  .   :*    .            10.452    .790
 16  -.102  .115                  .  **:    .            11.234    .795
 17  -.093  .114                  .  **:    .            11.898    .806
 18  -.033  .112                  .  *:     .            11.983    .848
 19   .028  .110                  .   :*    .            12.047    .884
 20   .005  .108                  .    *    .            12.049    .914

Plot Symbols:     Autocorrelations *     Two Standard Error Limits .
```

with which we will therefore proceed. The remainder of the output shown in Exhibit 7.3 relates exclusively to that model.

The model to be fitted then is

$$(1 - B)^2 X_t = a_t - \theta_1 a_{t-1} - \theta_2 a_{t-2}$$

The estimated parameters were

$$\hat{\theta}_1 = 0.856 \qquad \hat{\theta}_2 = -0.372$$

From the SPSS output, then, we see that the fitted model can be written

$$(1 - B)^2 X_t = a_t - 0.856 a_{t-1} + 0.372 a_{t-2} \qquad (7.9.8)$$
$$(0.138) \qquad (0.140)$$

where figures in parentheses below parameter estimates are the corresponding estimated standard errors. The fact that the estimate of the second moving average parameter is large compared with its standard error—the t-ratio is -2.67—indicates that the simpler ARIMA(0, 2, 1) model would not be adequate.

The final part of Exhibit 7.3 shows the autocorrelations of the residuals from the fitted model, equation 7.9.8. These are mostly very small. Only one is outside the two standard error limits—a result that can be expected by chance. Moreover, the large residual autocorrelation is at a lag of 12 years, which certainly suggests no plausible alternative specification. The Box-Ljung statistics also are very reassuring. For example, based respectively on the first 10 and on the first 20 residual autocorrelations, the hypothesis that the ARIMA(0, 2, 2) specification is correct can only be rejected at the 98.5% and the 91.4% significance levels. We also tried fitting some more elaborate models to this time series, but the estimates of the extra parameters were statistically insignificant. Accordingly, we can proceed with some confidence to base forecasts on the fitted model 7.9.8.

7.10 FORECASTING FROM FITTED ARIMA MODELS

Once an ARIMA model has been fitted to a time series, the projection of that model forward to derive forecasts of future values is quite straightforward. The general ARIMA(p, d, q) model can be written

$$(1 - \phi_1 B - \cdots - \phi_p B^p)[(1 - B)^d X_t - \mu] = (1 - \theta_1 B - \cdots - \theta_q B^q) a_t$$

However, for forecasting, the autoregressive and differencing terms can be amalgamated, and the model is expressed as

$$(1 - \Phi_1 B - \cdots - \Phi_{p+d} B^{p+d}) X_t = C + (1 - \theta_1 B - \cdots - \theta_q B^q) a_t$$

$$(7.10.1)$$

where

$$1 - \Phi_1 B - \cdots - \Phi_{p+d} B^{p+d} = (1 - \phi_1 B - \cdots - \phi_p B^p)(1 - B)^d$$

and

$$C = (1 - \phi_1 - \cdots - \phi_p)\mu$$

The form 7.10.1 of the model is, then,

$$X_t = C + \Phi_1 X_{t-1} + \cdots + \Phi_{p+d} X_{t-p-d}$$
$$+ a_t - \theta_1 a_{t-1} - \cdots - \theta_q a_{t-q}$$

$$(7.10.2)$$

Suppose now that, standing at time n, we want to predict the future value X_{n+h}. Setting $t = n + h$ in equation 7.10.2, the quantity to be predicted is

$$X_{n+h} = C + \Phi_1 X_{n+h-1} + \cdots + \Phi_{p+d} X_{n+h-p-d}$$
$$+ a_{n+h} - \theta_1 a_{n+h-1} - \cdots - \theta_q a_{n+h-q}$$

$$(7.10.3)$$

This equation forms the basis for forecasting through the substitution on the right-hand side of estimates and forecasts for unknown quantities. This is achieved as follows:

1. The parameters $C, \Phi_1, \ldots, \Phi_{p+d}, \theta_1, \ldots, \theta_q$ are replaced by their estimates, derived from the parameter estimation stage of the model building cycle. We will denote the estimates $\hat{C}, \hat{\Phi}_1, \ldots, \hat{\Phi}_{p+d}, \hat{\theta}_1, \ldots, \hat{\theta}_q$.
2. For $t \leq n$, X_t will be a known observation. For $t > n$, X_t is replaced by its forecast made at time n.
3. For $t \leq n$, the error term a_t is replaced by its estimate, the residual $\hat{a}_t$ from the fitted model. For $t > n$, the unknown a_t is replaced by its best forecast, zero.

It then follows from equation 7.10.3 that the forecast of X_{n+h} is given by

$$\hat{X}_n(h) = \hat{C} + \hat{\Phi}_1 \hat{X}_n(h-1) + \cdots + \hat{\Phi}_{p+d} \hat{X}_n(h-p-d)$$
$$+ \hat{a}_{n+h} - \hat{\theta}_1 \hat{a}_{n+h-1} - \cdots - \hat{\theta}_q \hat{a}_{n+h-q} \qquad h = 1, 2, \ldots$$

$$(7.10.4)$$

where

$$\hat{X}_n(j) = X_{n+j} \qquad j \le 0$$

and

$$\hat{a}_{n+j} = 0 \qquad j > 0$$

Using equation 7.10.4 in turn for $h = 1, 2, \ldots$, forecasts as far ahead as required can easily be computed. These calculations are programmed in standard ARIMA packages, which also allow the computation of interval forecasts. The confidence intervals are based on an assumption that the white noise error terms a_t are normally distributed, and are generally quite reliable. We will not discuss here the algebraic details underlying the derivation of confidence intervals around the forecasts.

To illustrate, consider again the series of observations on the number of active oil wells in the United States, discussed in Example 7.3 of Section 7.9. The fitted model, equation 7.9.8, can be written

$$X_t = 2X_{t-1} - X_{t-2} + a_t - 0.856a_{t-1} + 0.372a_{t-2}$$

Thus, standing at the final observation year, time $n = 50$, the prediction algorithm 7.10.4 is

$$\hat{X}_{50}(h) = 2\hat{X}_{50}(h-1) - \hat{X}_{50}(h-2) + \hat{a}_{50+h}$$
$$- 0.856\hat{a}_{49+h} + 0.372\hat{a}_{48+h} \qquad h = 1, 2, \ldots$$

$$(7.10.5)$$

The last two observations on this series were

$$X_{50} = 603290 \qquad X_{49} = 580142$$

while the last two residuals, obtained from the estimation algorithm, were

$$\hat{a}_{50} = 752 \qquad \hat{a}_{49} = 2900$$

EXHIBIT 7.4   Point and 95% interval forecasts from SPSS program, derived from fitted ARIMA(0,2,2) model, for number of active oil wells.

```
        Case#    OILWELLS       FIT#1          LCL#1          UCL#1

         51          .        626874.1165   607841.2477   646266.9853
         52          .        650738.1048   621269.7826   680206.4269
         53          .        674602.0930   630952.0633   718252.1228
         54          .        698466.0813   637741.5816   759190.5809
         55          .        722330.0695   642234.1674   802425.9717
         56          .        746194.0578   644756.6712   847631.4444
         57          .        770058.0461   645516.5403   894599.5518
         58          .        793922.0343   644660.3997   943183.6689
         59          .        817786.0226   642299.7201   993272.3251
         60          .        841650.0108   638523.5495   1044776.472
```

Setting $h = 1$ in equation 7.10.5, the forecast for the number of active oil wells next year is

$$\hat{X}_{50}(1) = 2\hat{X}_{50}(0) - \hat{X}_{50}(-1) + \hat{a}_{51} - 0.856\hat{a}_{50} + 0.372\hat{a}_{49}$$

$$= 2X_{50} - X_{49} - 0.856\hat{a}_{50} + 0.372\hat{a}_{49}$$

$$= 2(603290) - 580142 - (0.856)(752)$$

$$+ (0.372)(2900) = 626873$$

Similarly, setting $h = 2$ in equation 7.10.5, the forecast for two years ahead is

$$\hat{X}_{50}(2) = 2\hat{X}_{50}(1) - \hat{X}_{50}(0) + \hat{a}_{52} - 0.856\hat{a}_{51} + 0.372\hat{a}_{50}$$

$$= 2\hat{X}_{50}(1) - X_{50} + 0.372\hat{a}_{50}$$

$$= 2(626873) - 603290 + (0.372)(752) = 650736$$

Arguing in the same way, it follows that forecasts further ahead are given by

$$\hat{X}_n(h) = 2\hat{X}_n(h - 1) - \hat{X}_n(h - 2) \qquad h = 3, 4, \ldots$$

Exhibit 7.4 shows point forecasts, together with lower and upper limits of 95% confidence intervals, up to ten years ahead, obtained from the SPSS program. The point forecasts differ very slightly from those calculated above due to rounding errors.

7.11 SEASONAL ARIMA MODELS AND FORECASTING

The ARIMA models that we have discussed and fitted so far lead to forecasts of future observations that are linear functions of the available data, almost inevitably with most weight given to the most recent few observations. However, if the time series of interest is seasonal, a rather different pattern of weights on past observations would be desirable in forecasting the future. For example, suppose that we have a series of monthly sales figures for a product whose demand is seasonal. In October 1994 we would expect sales for November 1994 to be closely related to sales in the previous few months—that is, to sales in October, September, August 1994, and so on. However, exclusive concentration on just the last few months would fail to capture important seasonality in the series. In predicting sales for November 1994, it would be sensible, in the presence of seasonality, to give extra weight to observations from the last few Novembers—to November 1993, November 1992, and so on. In this section we introduce an extension of the ARIMA class of models that generates forecast functions of this type.

Let X_t denote the time series of interest, observed with s periods per year, so that $s = 4$ for quarterly data and $s = 12$ for monthly data. Suppose that it is possible to find a linear transformation of this series yielding a nonseasonal series Z_t. This transformation may be of the general ARIMA form, but with relationships between observations s periods apart—that is, for monthly data, between observations of the same month in different years. For example, in place of regular differencing, this transformation may involve *seasonal differencing*, so that we would compute

$$X_t - X_{t-s} = (1 - B^s)X_t = Z_t$$

Thus, for monthly series, the series of seasonal differences will be made up of the change from one January to the next, the change from one February to the next, and so on. Now, it is possible that this simple seasonal differencing will be sufficient to yield a series Z_t that is free from seasonality. However, generally this will not be the case. It may be that further seasonal differencing, or *seasonal autoregressive* or *seasonal moving average* terms will also be required. In general, we consider the possibility of D seasonal differences, P seasonal autoregressive terms and Q seasonal moving average terms, so that the nonseasonal series Z_t is defined from

$$(1 - \Phi_1 B^s - \cdots - \Phi_p B^{Ps})(1 - B^s)^D X_t$$
$$= (1 - \Theta_1 B^s - \cdots - \Theta_Q B^{Qs})Z_t \qquad (7.11.1)$$

where the Φ_i and Θ_j are fixed seasonal autoregressive and moving average parameters.

If the series Z_t of equation 7.11.1 is nonseasonal, it could be represented by the regular ARIMA(p, d, q) model

$$(1 - \phi_1 B - \cdots - \phi_p B^p)(1 - B)^d Z_t = (1 - \theta_1 B - \cdots - \theta_q B^q)a_t$$

$$(7.11.2)$$

where a_t is white noise. Amalgamating equations 7.11.1 and 7.11.2 then yields the model

$$(1 - \phi_1 B - \cdots - \phi_p B^p)(1 - \Phi_1 B^s - \cdots - \Phi_P B^{Ps})$$

$$\times (1 - B)^d (1 - B^s)^D X_t$$

$$= (1 - \theta_1 B - \cdots - \theta_q B^q)(1 - \Theta_1 B^s - \cdots - \Theta_Q B^{Qs})a_t$$

$$(7.11.3)$$

The class of models from equation 7.11.3 has been widely used to represent seasonal business and economic time series. They are called **multiplicative seasonal ARIMA(p, d, q)(P, D, Q)$_s$ models.** Notice that both regular and seasonal differencing are allowed, and that the model for the differenced series may include both regular and seasonal autoregressive and moving average terms. The general model form, equation 7.11.3, certainly looks rather formidable, and the reader might conjecture that the task of fitting to given data an appropriate member of this class is horribly difficult. In fact, experience suggests otherwise. Very simple members of this class are typically found to adequately represent actual time series. For example, only very rarely is a value higher than two required for any of the orders p, d, q, P, D, or Q. Moreover, very often a total of no more than two or three fitted parameters is needed.

One specific member of the class 7.11.3 merits special comment. The ARIMA(0, 1, 1)(0, 1, 1)$_s$ model is

$$(1 - B)(1 - B^s)X_t = (1 - \theta_1 B)(1 - \Theta_1 B^s)a_t \qquad (7.11.4)$$

This is sometimes called the **airline model,** as it was fitted to the logarithms of monthly numbers of international airline passengers by Box and Jenkins (1970). Notice that this model involves one regular difference and one seasonal difference. It is very common indeed to find that this transformation is needed to yield stationarity for seasonal business and economic time series. Thus, the stationary series to be modeled is

$$W_t = (1 - B)(1 - B^s)X_t = X_t - X_{t-1} - X_{t-s} + X_{t-s+1}$$

Then, if X_t is generated by the airline model 7.11.4, the stationary series

W_t follows the multiplicative first-order moving average process

$$W_t = (1 - \theta_1 B)(1 - \Theta_1 B^s)a_t \qquad (7.11.5)$$
$$= a_t - \theta_1 a_{t-1} - \Theta_1 a_{t-s} + \theta_1 \Theta_1 a_{t-s-1}$$

Given that a_t is white noise, it follows immediately from equation 7.11.5 that W_t has mean zero. The seasonal ARIMA model 7.11.3 can be extended by subtracting any nonzero mean from the differenced series. The autocovariances of the differenced series W_t can be found directly from equation 7.11.5 as

$$\gamma_k = E(W_t W_{t-k}) = E[(a_t - \theta_1 a_{t-1} - \Theta_1 a_{t-s} + \theta_1 \Theta_1 a_{t-s-1})$$
$$\times (a_{t-k} - \theta_1 a_{t-k-1} - \Theta_1 a_{t-k-s} + \theta_1 \Theta_1 a_{t-k-s-1})]$$

Then, since a_t is white noise, it follows after a little algebra that

$$\gamma_0 = (1 + \theta_1^2)(1 + \Theta_1^2)\sigma_a^2$$
$$\gamma_1 = -\theta_1(1 + \Theta_1^2)\sigma_a^2$$
$$\gamma_k = 0 \qquad k = 2, \ldots, s - 2$$
$$\gamma_{s-1} = \theta_1 \Theta_1 \sigma_a^2$$
$$\gamma_s = -\Theta_1(1 + \theta_1^2)\sigma_a^2$$
$$\gamma_{s+1} = \theta_1 \Theta_1 \sigma_a^2$$
$$\gamma_k = 0 \qquad k = s + 2, s + 3, \ldots$$

where σ_a^2 is the variance of the white noise error series a_t. Dividing the autocovariances by the variance γ_0 then yields the autocorrelations

$$\rho_1 = \frac{-\theta_1}{(1 + \theta_1^2)}$$

$$\rho_{s-1} = \rho_{s+1} = \frac{\theta_1 \Theta_1}{(1 + \theta_1^2)(1 + \Theta_1^2)}$$

$$\rho_s = \frac{-\Theta_1}{(1 + \Theta_1^2)}$$

$$\rho_k = 0 \qquad k = 2, \ldots, s - 2, s + 2, s + 3, \ldots$$

Figure 7.11 shows the correlogram for a series W_t generated by the model 7.11.5 with $s = 12$, $\theta_1 = 0.8$, $\Theta_1 = 0.5$. The regular first-order

FIGURE 7.11   Correlogram for series W_t
generated by $W_t = (1 - 0.8B) \times (1 - 0.5B^{12})a_t$.

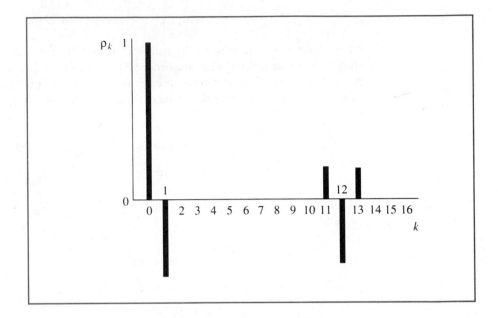

moving average term induces a non-zero autocorrelation at lag one, and the seasonal first-order moving average term induces a non-zero autocorrelation at lag 12. Notice also that echo effects are also observed at lags 11 and 13, so that

$$\rho_{11} = \rho_{13} = \rho_1\rho_{12}$$

The remaining autocorrelations are all zero, so that in practice this model is quite easy to detect from the sample autocorrelations.

We have concentrated on the airline model because experience suggests that it crops up frequently in practice. It has been found for a great many business and economic series that this particular model, or a member of the seasonal ARIMA class that is very close to it, provides an excellent representation. To see one reason why this might be so, we consider the forecast function that results when the airline model is fitted. The calculation of point forecasts for seasonal ARIMA models proceeds in exactly the way described in Section 7.10 for the nonseasonal case. Thus, if the series X_t is generated by an airline model, it follows by specializing equation 7.10.4 that the forecast of X_{n+h} at time n is given by

$$\hat{X}_n(h) = \hat{X}_n(h - 1) + \hat{X}_n(h - s) - \hat{X}_n(h - s - 1)$$

$$h = s + 2, s + 3, \ldots$$

A consequence of this result is that the forecast function for the airline model is a linear trend with superimposed seasonal dummy variables. This is precisely the forecast function implied by the Holt-Winters algorithm with additive seasonality, discussed in Section 6.4, though the two procedures do *not* produce identical forecasts. This particular forecast function has a certain amount of intuitive appeal, so that it should not be surprising that it is common experience to find appropriate a model leading to forecasts of this form.

The airline model is not invariably appropriate, however. The analyst will want to examine the observed properties of a time series carefully, and to fit to the data the model that seems to be the best choice from the general seasonal ARIMA class. We now show how the model-building methodology of Section 7.9 can be extended to the seasonal case. Again, this involves the three stages of model selection, parameter estimation, and model checking.

Model Selection

Selecting an appropriate seasonal ARIMA model can be quite tricky. The best strategy is to begin by looking for the simplest possible model that appears to be compatible with the characteristics of the sample data: more elaborate possibilities can then be entertained at the model checking stage. Also, the analyst should be prepared to try a little experimentation, carrying forward two or three alternative models for subsequent analysis in cases of uncertainty. As in the nonseasonal case, it is necessary to first decide on the amount of differencing required, and then on the autoregressive and moving average orders of a model to be fitted to the differenced series.

1.   To decide on the amount of differencing, the sample autocorrelations of the original series and some differenced versions are examined. It is usual practice to look at the sample autocorrelations of X_t, $(1 - B)X_t$, $(1 - B^s)X_t$, and $(1 - B)(1 - B^s)X_t$, though on occasion further differencing of one type or another might be indicated. The necessity for further regular differencing will be suggested by smooth behavior in the sample autocorrelations at moderately high lags. High sample autocorrelations at multiples of the seasonal period s indicate that further seasonal differencing may be desirable.

2. The next step is to examine the sample autocorrelations and sample partial autocorrelations of the differenced series

$$W_t = (1 - B)^d(1 - B^s)^D X_t$$

As before, these sample quantities are compared with two standard error limits.

(a) Pure moving average behavior is indicated when most of the sample autocorrelations are small. If the generating model is pure moving average, with q regular and Q seasonal moving average terms, the first q autocorrelations will be nonzero, as will autocorrelations at lags js ($j = 1, \ldots, Q$). In addition, the echo effect will lead to nonzero autocorrelations for q lags on either side of those at multiples of the seasonal period.

(b) Pure autoregressive behavior is detected by finding in the sample partial autocorrelations patterns similar to those induced in the sample autocorrelations by pure moving average behavior.

(c) For models with both autoregressive and moving average terms, neither the sample autocorrelations nor the sample partial autocorrelations exhibit abrupt cut-offs, but rather decay toward zero. The eventual pattern of the decay in the autocorrelations is determined by the autoregressive terms. For example, if the autoregressive component is $(1 - \phi_1 B)(1 - \Phi_1 B^s)$, the autocorrelations ρ_k eventually obey

$$\rho_k = \phi_1 \rho_{k-1} + \Phi_1 \rho_{k-s} - \phi_1 \Phi_1 \rho_{k-s-1}$$

This pattern sets in after a delay whose length is determined by the moving average component of the model. We do not want to pretend that recognition of any but the simplest mixed models is at all straightforward from visual examination of the sample autocorrelations. Indeed, these models are most often found through a process of experimentation, when the analyst carries forward several models for comparison. It is perhaps best in the seasonal case to think of model selection as suggesting an area for further search rather than pinpointing a single model for further analysis.

Parameter Estimation

In moving from the nonseasonal to the seasonal case, no new principles in parameter estimation are involved. The least squares procedure discussed in Section 7.9 can be routinely extended to the seasonal case. Once again several alternative estimation algorithms are available, and if the sample size is very large these should yield quite similar estimates. However, for seasonal models, particularly those with important moving average components, differences in estimates based on moderate sample sizes can be non-negligible. Our preference for estimation based on full maximum likelihood, as for example through SPSS or SAS, is particularly pronounced in the seasonal case.

Model Checking

The general approach to the checking of seasonal models is the same as for nonseasonal models. Again, extra parameters can be added to the fitted model, though now both seasonal and regular parameters should be tried. For example, the model 7.11.5 could be elaborated by adding both a regular and a seasonal moving average term, giving

$$W_t = (1 - \theta_1 B - \theta_2 B^2)(1 - \Theta_1 B^s - \Theta_2 B^{2s})a_t$$

The significance of the estimates of the extra parameters is assessed as usual through comparison with the corresponding estimated standard errors.

Residual autocorrelations are also a valuable aid in the assessment of the adequacy of a fitted model. High values in the first few residual autocorrelations would suggest inadequacy in the specification of the regular part of the model. Similarly, high values for residual autocorrelations at lags that are multiples of the seasonal period s suggest that the specification of the seasonal part of the model is inadequate. The significance of the first several residual autocorrelations, taken as a group, can again be assessed through the Box-Ljung portmanteau statistic, equation 7.9.5. This is now compared with tabulated values of the chi-square distribution with $(M - p - q - P - Q)$ degrees of freedom, since the total number of fitted parameters is $(p + q + P + Q)$.

We conclude this section with the discussion of four examples. The data are given in the appendix to this chapter. The practical aspects of ARIMA model building are best understood through numerical examples rather than the study of general principles, and readers are encouraged to attempt the analysis of other data sets, including those given in the chapter exercises.

Example 7.4. Our first example is of a series of 76 quarterly observations on plant and equipment expenditures. In Exhibit 7.5 we illustrate the analysis of this series with some output from the SAS program. We begin by determining the amount of differencing needed through examining the sample autocorrelations. In SAS, the standard errors associated with the sample autocorrelations differ from those reported in SPSS. In short,

Exhibit 7.5   Part of SAS program output for analysis of plant and equipment expenditures.

```
                              ARIMA PROCEDURE

                    NAME OF VARIABLE      =       LOGX
                    MEAN OF WORKING SERIES=     2.8883
                    STANDARD DEVIATION    =    0.455886
                    NUMBER OF OBSERVATIONS=         76
                          AUTOCORRELATIONS


  LAG COVARIANCE CORRELATION -1 9 8 7 6 5 4 3 2 1 0 1 2 3 4 5 6 7 8 9 1        STD
    0   0.207832    1.00000   |                        |*******************|       0
    1   0.188764    0.90825   |                        |******************  |   0.114708
    2   0.185768    0.89384   |                     .  |******************   |   0.186725
    3   0.173107    0.83292   |                    .   |*****************    |   0.236413
    4   0.175831    0.84603   |                    .   |*****************    |   0.272301
    5   0.156969    0.75527   |                  .     |***************      |   0.304932
    6   0.152607    0.73428   |                  .     |***************      |   0.328626
    7   0.139732    0.67233   |                 .      |*************.       |   0.349548
    8   0.141831    0.68243   |                .       |**************.      |   0.366168
    9   0.123725    0.59531   |                .       |************  .      |   0.382537
   10   0.119908    0.57695   |               .        |************  .      |   0.394539
   11   0.108076    0.52002   |               .        |**********   .      |   0.405488
   12   0.110205    0.53026   |              .         |***********  .      |   0.41417
   13  0.0928588    0.44680   |              .         |*********    .      |   0.423009
   14  0.0889479    0.42798   |              .         |*********    .      |   0.429173
   15  0.0772724    0.37180   |              .         |*******      .      |   0.434753
   16  0.0787813    0.37906   |             .          |********     .      |   0.438916
   17  0.0618164    0.29743   |             .          |******       .      |   0.443203
   18  0.0575886    0.27709   |             .          |******       .      |   0.445822
   19   0.045888    0.22079   |             .          |****         .      |   0.448082
   20   0.047468    0.22840   |             .          |*****        .      |   0.449511
   21  0.0320432    0.15418   |             .          |***          .      |   0.451036
   22   0.028932    0.13921   |             .          |***          .      |   0.451729
   23  0.0192217    0.09249   |             .          |**           .      |   0.452293
   24   0.022145    0.10655   |             .          |**           .      |   0.452541
                            '.' MARKS TWO STANDARD ERRORS
```

SPSS reports the standard errors computed on the assumption that a series is white noise, whereas in SAS the standard error associated with the kth sample autocorrelation is that appropriate for checking that the generating model is moving average of order $k - 1$.

We decided to analyze the logarithms of this time series since the series exhibits much more variability at high levels than low. The sample autocorrelations of the undifferenced series behave quite smoothly at high lags, suggesting the necessity for some differencing. The sample auto-correlations of $(1 - B)X_t$ are persistently high at lags that are multiples of four, so that seasonal differencing seems to be required. In addition,

Exhibit 7.5 (*Continued*)

```
                        ARIMA PROCEDURE

                NAME OF VARIABLE      =      LOGX
                PERIOD(S) OF DIFFERENCING=1.
                MEAN OF WORKING SERIES= 0.0229033
                STANDARD DEVIATION    = 0.135502
                NUMBER OF OBSERVATIONS=      75

                        AUTOCORRELATIONS

LAG COVARIANCE CORRELATION -1 9 8 7 6 5 4 3 2 1 0 1 2 3 4 5 6 7 8 9 1      STD
  0  0.0183607   1.00000  |                    |********************|       0
  1 -0.0128861  -0.70183  |      **************|           .        |     0.11547
  2  0.00885299  0.48217  |               .    |*********            |     0.162691
  3 -0.0131068  -0.71385  |      **************|            .        |     0.180743
  4  0.0167157   0.91040  |              .     |******************   |     0.215074
  5 -0.0123295  -0.67151  |       *************|           .         |     0.261456
  6  0.00840072  0.45754  |               .    |********* .          |     0.283521
  7 -0.0123823  -0.67439  |      *************|            .          |     0.2932
  8  0.0157161   0.85596  |             .     |*****************     |     0.3132
  9 -0.0115252  -0.62771  |      .************|               .       |     0.342976
 10  0.00790058  0.43030  |          .        |*********      .       |     0.357966
 11 -0.0118621  -0.64606  |      . *************|              .       |     0.364797
 12  0.0146387   0.79728  |         .         |****************      |     0.379746
 13 -0.0107564  -0.58584  |      .  ***********|               .      |     0.401455
 14  0.00745538  0.40605  |         .         |********       .      |     0.412687
 15 -0.011141   -0.60679  |      .  ***********|                .     |     0.41798
 16  0.0138579   0.75476  |         .         |**************    .    |     0.429564
 17 -.00997625  -0.54335  |         .      ***********|             . |     0.446896
 18  0.00707258  0.38520  |         .         |*********         .    |     0.455619
 19 -0.0104016  -0.56651  |         .   ***********|              .   |     0.459941
 20  0.012834    0.69899  |         .         |*************        . |     0.469153
 21 -.00913944  -0.49777  |         .     **********|             .   |     0.482839
 22  0.00651971  0.35509  |         .         |*******           . |     0.489633
 23 -.00969401  -0.52798  |        .    ***********|              . |     0.493055
 24  0.0118669   0.64632  |        .          |************        . |     0.500536
                  '.' MARKS TWO STANDARD ERRORS
```

the sample autocorrelations of $(1 - B^4)X_t$, which are not shown in Exhibit 7.5, behave quite smoothly at high lags, suggesting that regular differencing is needed. Finally, turning to the sample autocorrelations of $(1 - B)(1 - B^4)X_t$ there are moderately large sample autocorrelations at lags one, four, and five. The sample partial autocorrelation at lag one is large, but the next two are very small. Also, note that whereas the sample autocorrelations at lags 8, 12, 16 are small, the partial autocorrelations at these lags are larger. These considerations suggest that a model with one

EXHIBIT 7.5   *(Continued)*

```
                            ARIMA PROCEDURE

                 NAME OF VARIABLE        =      LOGX
                 PERIOD(S) OF DIFFERENCING=1,4.
                 MEAN OF WORKING SERIES=0.00293797
                 STANDARD DEVIATION      = 0.0300151
                 NUMBER OF OBSERVATIONS=        71

                            AUTOCORRELATIONS

LAG COVARIANCE CORRELATION -1 9 8 7 6 5 4 3 2 1 0 1 2 3 4 5 6 7 8 9 1        STD
  0 .000900908   1.00000  |                    |********************|        0
  1 .000286547   0.31806  |                 .  |******              |     0.118678
  2 .000096483   0.10710  |                 .  |**    .             |     0.130132
  3 -1.887E-05  -0.02095  |                 .  |     .              |     0.131367
  4 -.00031408  -0.34862  |            *******|     .              |     0.131414
  5 -0.0002499  -0.27739  |             ******|     .              |     0.143851
  6 -5.182E-05  -0.05752  |                 . *|     .              |     0.151198
  7 -3.035E-05  -0.03368  |                 .  *|    .              |     0.151505
  8 -6.860E-05  -0.07615  |                 . **|    .              |     0.151611
  9 .000020871   0.02317  |                 .  |     .              |     0.152149
 10 .000057988   0.06437  |                 .  |*    .              |     0.152198
 11 -8.069E-06  -0.00896  |                 .  |     .              |     0.152581
 12 -7.155E-05  -0.07942  |                 . **|    .              |     0.152589
 13 .000045482   0.05048  |                 .  |*    .              |     0.15317
 14 -.00010308  -0.11441  |                 . **|    .              |     0.153404
 15 .000044809   0.04974  |                 .  |*    .              |     0.154601
 16 .000164961   0.18311  |                 .  |****  .             |     0.154826
 17 .000035992   0.03995  |                 .  |*    .              |     0.157847
 18 .000086262   0.09575  |                 .  |**   .              |     0.157989
 19 8.877E-06    0.00985  |                 .  |     .              |     0.158804
 20 -6.774E-05  -0.07520  |                 . **|    .              |     0.158813
 21 -3.398E-05  -0.03771  |                 .  *|    .              |     0.159314
 22 3.653E-06    0.00405  |                 .  |     .              |     0.159439
 23 -.00014864  -0.16499  |                 . ***|    .             |     0.159441
 24 -.00015949  -0.17704  |                 . ****|    .            |     0.161828
                     '.' MARKS TWO STANDARD ERRORS


              PARTIAL AUTOCORRELATIONS

LAG              CORRELATION -1 9 8 7 6 5 4 3 2 1 0 1 2 3 4 5 6 7 8 9 1
  1               0.31806  |                 .  |******              |
  2               0.00660  |                 .  |     .              |
  3              -0.06329  |                 .  *|    .              |
  4              -0.36273  |            *******|     .              |
  5              -0.08294  |                 . **|    .              |
  6               0.12098  |                 .  |**   .              |
  7              -0.01584  |                 .  |     .              |
  8              -0.23757  |             *****|     .              |
  9              -0.04452  |                 .  *|    .              |
 10               0.13816  |                 .  |***  .              |
 11              -0.02185  |                 .  |     .              |
 12              -0.27708  |             ******|     .              |
 13               0.07324  |                 .  |*    .              |
 14              -0.02930  |                 .  *|    .              |
 15               0.16526  |                 .  |***  .              |
 16              -0.00331  |                 .  |     .              |
 17              -0.10468  |                 . **|    .              |
 18               0.09419  |                 .  |**   .              |
 19               0.02309  |                 .  |     .              |
 20              -0.00553  |                 .  |     .              |
 21              -0.00786  |                 .  |     .              |
 22               0.04390  |                 .  |*    .              |
 23              -0.21136  |                 .****|    .             |
 24              -0.15668  |                 . ***|    .             |
```

EXHIBIT 7.5 (*Continued*)

```
              ARIMA: MAXIMUM LIKELIHOOD ESTIMATION

                                APPROX.
          PARAMETER    ESTIMATE     STD ERROR    T RATIO  LAG
          MA1,1        0.664127     0.101486       6.54    4
          AR1,1        0.296324     0.11481        2.58    1

          VARIANCE  ESTIMATE =.000625094
          STD ERROR ESTIMATE = 0.0250019
          AIC              =  -317.94
          SBC              =  -313.42
          NUMBER OF RESIDUALS=      71


                  CORRELATIONS OF THE ESTIMATES

                              MA1,1    AR1,1
                    MA1,1      1.000    0.006
                    AR1,1      0.006    1.000


              AUTOCORRELATION CHECK OF RESIDUALS

        TO    CHI-
       LAG  SQUARE DF  PROB              AUTOCORRELATIONS
        6    8.30   4  0.081 -0.057  0.139  0.043  0.098 -0.234  0.134
       12   10.30  10  0.415  0.004 -0.060 -0.066  0.101 -0.024 -0.068
       18   15.12  16  0.516  0.039 -0.062 -0.048  0.160 -0.024  0.130
       24   23.83  22  0.356 -0.105 -0.004 -0.038  0.091 -0.247 -0.008
              AUTOCORRELATION PLOT OF RESIDUALS
```

```
LAG  COVARIANCE  CORRELATION -1 9 8 7 6 5 4 3 2 1 0 1 2 3 4 5 6 7 8 9 1      STD
 0   .000625094    1.00000   |                    |********************|       0
 1   -3.552E-05   -0.05683   |              .    *|    .               |    0.118678
 2   .000087015    0.13920   |              .     |***  .              |    0.119061
 3   .000026941    0.04310   |              .     |*    .              |    0.121331
 4   .000061552    0.09847   |              .     |**   .              |    0.121547
 5   -.00014622   -0.23392   |          *****|    .                    |    0.122665
 6   .000083456    0.13351   |              .     |***  .              |    0.128795
 7   2.747E-06     0.00439   |              .     |     .              |    0.13073
 8   -3.748E-05   -0.05996   |              .    *|     .              |    0.130732
 9   -4.154E-05   -0.06645   |              .    *|     .              |    0.131119
10   .000063149    0.10102   |              .     |**   .              |    0.131592
11   -1.501E-05   -0.02401   |              .     |     .              |    0.13268
12   -4.254E-05   -0.06806   |              .    *|     .              |    0.132741
13   .000024479    0.03916   |              .     |*    .              |    0.133232
14   -3.877E-05   -0.06203   |              .    *|     .              |    0.133394
15   -2.999E-05   -0.04797   |              .    *|     .              |    0.1338
16   .000100231    0.16035   |              .     |***  .              |    0.134042
17   -1.481E-05   -0.02370   |              .     |     .              |    0.136716
18   .00008114     0.12981   |              .     |***  .              |    0.136774
19   -6.542E-05   -0.10466   |              .   **|     .              |    0.138499
20   -2.700E-06   -0.00432   |              .     |     .              |    0.139608
21   -2.403E-05   -0.03844   |              .     |     .              |    0.13961
22   .000056876    0.09099   |              .     |**   .              |    0.139759
23   -.00015431   -0.24685   |          .*****|    .                   |    0.140591
24   -4.698E-06   -0.00752   |              .     |     .              |    0.146568
                      '.' MARKS TWO STANDARD ERRORS
```

Exhibit 7.5   (*Continued*)

| | SAS | |
OBS	XACT	XFOR
55	25.04	24.5111
56	28.48	28.4125
57	24.10	23.9325
58	28.16	27.8748
59	28.23	28.2429
60	31.92	31.9631
61	25.82	26.8393
62	28.43	29.5687
63	27.79	28.0120
64	30.74	31.2162
65	25.87	25.3477
66	29.70	29.5829
67	30.41	29.5487
68	34.52	34.4537
69	29.20	28.8809
70	33.73	33.4858
71	34.82	33.9454
72	38.06	39.5714
73	32.35	31.6044
74	37.89	37.2420
75	38.67	38.6174
76	44.91	43.2291
77	.	38.2671
78	.	44.3424
79	.	45.0709
80	.	50.9726
81	.	43.0926
82	.	49.8177
83	.	50.6012
84	.	57.2154
85	.	48.3674
86	.	55.9148

regular autoregressive term and one seasonal moving average term might be adequate. Accordingly, we fitted the model

$$(1 - \phi_1 B)(1 - B)(1 - B^4)X_t = (1 - \Theta_1 B^4)a_t$$

From the next part of the SAS program output, we find that the fitted model is

$$(1 - 0.296B)(1 - B)(1 - B^4)X_t = (1 - 0.664B^4)a_t \quad (7.11.6)$$
$$\quad (0.115) \qquad\qquad\qquad\qquad\qquad (0.101)$$

The estimated parameters are both quite large compared with their estimated standard errors.

The great majority of the residual autocorrelations from this fitted model are very small, though there are moderately large values at lags 5 and 23. Though the latter of these can certainly be safely ignored, some analysts may opt for a somewhat more exotic model to take care of the former. However, since it is only of moderate size, our preference for simple models wherever possible inclines us against such a course. The portmanteau test statistics based on the first 12 and 24 residual autocorrelations cause no concern. The null hypothesis that the assumed model is correctly specified can only be rejected at the 41.5% and 35.6% significance levels through these tests. The final part of Exhibit 7.5 shows actual and fitted values from this model for the last few observation periods, together with forecasts for the next ten quarters.

Example 7.5. In Exhibit 7.6 part of the SPSS program output for the analysis of 288 monthly observations on factory sales of U.S. passenger cars is shown. The sample autocorrelations of the undifferenced series are persistently high, and follow quite smooth patterns at high lags. For the first differenced series, we find high sample autocorrelations at lags that are multiples of twelve, indicating the desirability of seasonal differencing. The pattern at high lags of the sample autocorrelations of the seasonally differenced series, $(1 - B^{12})X_t$, is quite smooth, so that regular differencing also seems to be needed. The sample autocorrelations of the series $(1 - B)(1 - B^{12})X_t$ indicate no need for further differencing.

Inspection of the sample autocorrelations of the series $(1 - B)(1 - B^{12})X_t$ suggests that a pure moving average model might be appropriate for this series. The first two sample autocorrelations are moderately large, and the twelfth is very large, compared with the standard errors. Moreover, the moderately large value at lag 11 could be the result of an echo effect in the multiplicative seasonal model. It seems likely then that the ARIMA$(0, 1, 2)(0, 1, 1)_{12}$ model will yield an adequate fit to these data.

The model to be fitted then is of the form

$$(1 - B)(1 - B^{12})X_t = (1 - \theta_1 B - \theta_2 B^2)(1 - \Theta_1 B^{12})a_t$$

From the SPSS output, it can be seen that the fitted model is

$$(1 - B)(1 - B^{12})X_t$$

$$= (1 - 0.321B - 0.299B^2)(1 - 0.734B^{12})a_t \quad (7.11.7)$$
$$\quad (0.057) \quad (0.057) \quad\quad\quad (0.046)$$

All three parameter estimates are very large compared with their estimated standard errors.

Exhibit 7.6   Part of SPSS program output for analysis of factory sales of U.S. passenger cars.

```
Autocorrelations:   PASSCARS
      Auto- Stand.
Lag   Corr.  Err.  -1  -.75  -.5  -.25   0   .25   .5   .75   1    Box-Ljung   Prob.
                   +----+----+----+----+----+----+----+----+
 1    .571   .059                        . :*.*********          94.861      .000
 2    .164   .059                        . :*.*                 102.689      .000
 3    .113   .058                        . :**                  106.444      .000
 4    .164   .058                        . :*.*                 114.315      .000
 5    .210   .058                        . :*.**                127.296      .000
 6    .266   .058                        . :*.***               148.323      .000
 7    .197   .058                        . :*.**                159.852      0.0
 8    .131   .058                        . :*.*                 164.965      0.0
 9    .036   .058                        . :*.                  165.343      0.0
10    .046   .058                        . :*.                  165.966      0.0
11    .367   .058                        . :*.*****             206.619      0.0
12    .604   .057                        . :*.*********         316.982      0.0
13    .269   .057                        . :*.***               338.913      0.0
14   -.045   .057                      .*: .                    339.526      0.0
15   -.081   .057                      **: .                    341.542      0.0
16   -.012   .057                      . * .                    341.584      0.0
17    .062   .057                        . :*.                  342.760      0.0
18    .097   .057                        . :**                  345.682      0.0
19    .019   .057                        . * .                  345.791      0.0
20   -.048   .057                      .*: .                    346.519      0.0
21   -.135   .057                    *.*: .                     352.229      0.0
22   -.126   .056                    *.*: .                     357.176      0.0
23    .174   .056                        . :*.*                 366.764      0.0
24    .397   .056                        . :*.******            416.665      0.0
25    .101   .056                        . :**                  419.903      0.0
26   -.195   .056                    **.*: .                    431.973      0.0
27   -.199   .056                    **.*: .                    444.655      0.0
28   -.094   .056                      **: .                    447.479      0.0
29   -.024   .056                        . * .                  447.664      0.0
30   -.000   .056                        . * .                  447.664      0.0
31   -.065   .055                      .*: .                    449.048      .000
32   -.134   .055                    *.*: .                     454.947      .000
33   -.208   .055                    **.*: .                    469.178      .000
34   -.172   .055                    *.*: .                     478.867      .000
35    .147   .055                        . :*.*                 485.959      .000
36    .341   .055                        . :*.*****             524.506      .000

Plot Symbols:     Autocorrelations  *      Two Standard Error Limits .

Total cases:  288    Computable first lags:    287
```

EXHIBIT 7.6 (*Continued*)

```
Autocorrelations:   PASSCARS

Transformations: difference (1)

      Auto- Stand.
Lag   Corr.  Err. -1  -.75  -.5 -.25   0   .25  .5  .75   1   Box-Ljung   Prob.
                   +----+----+----+----+----+----+----+----+
  1  -.025  .059                     .*: .                      .187      .665
  2  -.415  .059             ******.*: .                      50.203      .000
  3  -.119  .059                   **: .                       54.305      .000
  4   .002  .058                   . * .                       54.306      .000
  5  -.011  .058                   . * .                       54.343      .000
  6   .150  .058                   . :*.*                      61.000      .000
  7  -.003  .058                   . * .                       61.002      .000
  8   .034  .058                   . :*.                       61.344      .000
  9  -.125  .058                   **: .                       65.980      .000
 10  -.363  .058             *****.*: .                       105.486      .000
 11   .100  .058                   . :**                      108.468      .000
 12   .665  .058                   . :*.**********            241.851      0.0
 13  -.023  .057                   . * .                      242.018      0.0
 14  -.322  .057             ****.*: .                        273.603      0.0
 15  -.125  .057                 *.*: .                       278.375      0.0
 16  -.006  .057                   . * .                      278.385      0.0
 17   .044  .057                   . :*.                      278.993      0.0
 18   .135  .057                   . :*.*                     284.609      0.0
 19  -.011  .057                   . * .                      284.649      0.0
 20   .022  .057                   . * .                      284.798      0.0
 21  -.112  .057                  **: .                       288.717      0.0
 22  -.341  .057            *****.*: .                        325.018      0.0
 23   .091  .056                   . :**                      327.596      0.0
 24   .603  .056                   . :*.*********             442.351      0.0
 25   .001  .056                   . * .                      442.352      0.0
 26  -.340  .056            *****.*: .                        479.063      0.0
 27  -.130  .056                 *.*: .                       484.452      0.0
 28   .041  .056                   . :*.                      484.997      0.0
 29   .054  .056                   . :*.                      485.926      0.0
 30   .106  .056                   . :**                      489.527      0.0
 31   .007  .056                   . * .                      489.541      .000
 32   .005  .055                   . * .                      489.549      .000
 33  -.129  .055                 *.*: .                       494.963      .000
 34  -.330  .055            *****.*: .                        530.626      .000
 35   .144  .055                   . :*.*                     537.449      .000
 36   .570  .055                   . :*.********              644.736      .000

Plot Symbols:     Autocorrelations *    Two Standard Error Limits .

Total cases: 288   Computable first lags after differencing:  286
```

Exhibit 7.6 (*Continued*)

```
    Autocorrelations:   PASSCARS

    Transformations:  seasonal difference (1 at 12)

          Auto- Stand.
    Lag   Corr.  Err.  -1  -.75  -.5 -.25   0   .25  .5  .75   1   Box-Ljung  Prob.
                       +----+----+----+----+----+----+----+----+
      1   .664   .060                       . :*.***********     122.860   .000
      2   .459   .060                       . :*.*******         181.798   0.0
      3   .380   .060                       . :*.******          222.372   0.0
      4   .287   .060                       . :*.****            245.552   0.0
      5   .216   .059                       . :*.**              258.786   0.0
      6   .229   .059                       . :*.***             273.634   0.0
      7   .233   .059                       . :*.***             289.103   0.0
      8   .207   .059                       . :*.**              301.353   0.0
      9   .131   .059                       . :*.*               306.318   0.0
     10   .078   .059                       . :**                308.056   0.0
     11  -.014   .059                       . *.                 308.115   0.0
     12  -.232   .059                    ***.*: .                323.783   0.0
     13  -.185   .059                     **.*: .                333.777   0.0
     14  -.120   .058                       **: .                338.013   0.0
     15  -.108   .058                       **: .                341.466   0.0
     16  -.112   .058                       **: .                345.140   0.0
     17  -.079   .058                       **: .                346.968   0.0
     18  -.083   .058                       **: .                349.031   0.0
     19  -.111   .058                       **: .                352.686   0.0
     20  -.127   .058                      *.*: .                357.504   0.0
     21  -.123   .058                       **: .                362.055   0.0
     22  -.166   .058                      *.*: .                370.342   0.0
     23  -.220   .057                     **.*: .                385.022   0.0
     24  -.218   .057                     **.*: .                399.442   0.0
     25  -.160   .057                      *.*: .                407.268   0.0
     26  -.119   .057                       **: .                411.592   0.0
     27  -.139   .057                      *.*: .                417.572   0.0
     28  -.117   .057                       **: .                421.826   0.0
     29  -.105   .057                       **: .                425.245   0.0
     30  -.132   .057                      *.*: .                430.675   0.0
     31  -.113   .057                       **: .                434.666   .000
     32  -.104   .057                       **: .                438.092   .000
     33  -.084   .056                       **: .                440.316   .000
     34  -.085   .056                       **: .                442.619   .000
     35  -.015   .056                       . * .                442.690   .000
     36  -.018   .056                       . * .                442.789   .000

    Plot Symbols:     Autocorrelations *      Two Standard Error Limits .

    Total cases:  288     Computable first lags after differencing: 275
```

EXHIBIT 7.6 (*Continued*)

```
     Autocorrelations:   PASSCARS

     Transformations:  difference (1), seasonal difference (1 at 12)

          Auto- Stand.
     Lag  Corr.  Err.  -1  -.75  -.5 -.25   0   .25  .5   .75   1    Box-Ljung   Prob.
                       +----+----+----+----+----+----+----+----+
       1  -.195  .060                  **.*: .                      10.611      .001
       2  -.188  .060                  **.*: .                      20.427      .000
       3   .021  .060                    . * .                      20.547      .000
       4  -.032  .060                    .*: .                      20.838      .000
       5  -.124  .060                   **: .                       25.182      .000
       6   .014  .059                    . * .                      25.234      .000
       7   .043  .059                    . :*.                      27.768      .001
       8   .073  .059                    . :*.                      27.284      .001
       9  -.025  .059                    . * .                      27.459      .001
      10   .051  .059                    . :*.                      28.220      .002
      11   .185  .059                    . :*.**                    38.048      .000
      12  -.393  .059              *******.*: .                     82.855      .000
      13  -.027  .059                    .*: .                      83.062      .000
      14   .076  .059                    . :**                      84.761      .000
      15   .025  .058                    . * .                      84.937      .000
      16  -.054  .058                    .*: .                      85.789      .000
      17   .055  .058                    . :*.                      86.690      .000
      18   .033  .058                    . :*.                      87.022      .000
      19  -.016  .058                    . * .                      87.096      .000
      20  -.027  .058                    .*: .                      87.307      .000
      21   .061  .058                    . :*.                      88.440      .000
      22   .021  .058                    . * .                      88.567      .000
      23  -.082  .058                   **: .                       90.584      .000
      24  -.082  .057                   **: .                       92.602      .000
      25   .024  .057                    . * .                      92.778      .000
      26   .093  .057                    . :**                      95.404      .000
      27  -.063  .057                    .*: .                      96.614      .000
      28   .014  .057                    . * .                      96.672      .000
      29   .059  .057                    . :*.                      97.744      .000
      30  -.066  .057                    .*: .                      99.082      .000
      31   .014  .057                    . * .                      99.144      .000
      32  -.023  .056                    . * .                      99.312      .000
      33   .035  .056                    . :*.                      99.693      .000
      34  -.106  .056                   **: .                      103.224      .000
      35   .109  .056                    . :**                     107.003      .000
      36   .053  .056                    . :*.                     107.913      .000

     Plot Symbols:     Autocorrelations *     Two Standard Error Limits .

     Total cases:  288     Computable first lags after differencing:  274
```

Exhibit 7.6   (*Continued*)

```
     Partial Autocorrelations:    PASSCARS

     Transformations:  difference (1), seasonal difference (1 at 12)

       Pr-Aut- Stand.
     Lag  Corr.  Err. -1  -.75  -.5  -.25   0   .25   .5   .75   1
                      +----+----+----+----+----+----+----+----+
        1  -.195  .060                      **.*: .
        2  -.235  .060                     ***.*: .
        3  -.077  .060                       **: .
        4  -.099  .060                       **: .
        5  -.185  .060                      **.*: .
        6  -.107  .060                       **: .
        7  -.064  .060                      .*: .
        8   .036  .060                      . :*.
        9  -.019  .060                      . * .
       10   .057  .060                      . :*.
       11   .249  .060                      . :*.***
       12  -.284  .060                   ****.*: .
       13  -.097  .060                       **: .
       14  -.104  .060                       **: .
       15  -.018  .060                      . * .
       16  -.089  .060                       **: .
       17  -.097  .060                       **: .
       18  -.041  .060                      .*: .
       19  -.062  .060                      .*: .
       20   .004  .060                      . * .
       21   .050  .060                      . :*.
       22   .075  .060                      . :**
       23   .119  .060                      . :**
       24  -.213  .060                      **.*: .
       25  -.124  .060                       **: .
       26   .001  .060                      . * .
       27  -.056  .060                      .*: .
       28  -.078  .060                       **: .
       29  -.054  .060                      .*: .
       30  -.088  .060                       **: .
       31  -.014  .060                      . * .
       32  -.081  .060                       **: .
       33   .095  .060                      . :**
       34  -.080  .060                       **: .
       35   .169  .060                      . :*.*
       36  -.066  .060                      .*: .

     Plot Symbols:     Autocorrelations *      Two Standard Error Limits .

     Total cases:  288      Computable first lags after differencing:  274
```

EXHIBIT 7.6 (*Continued*)

```
FINAL PARAMETERS:

Number of residuals   275
Standard error        .09112031
Log likelihood        265.17126
AIC                   -524.34251
SBC                   -513.4922


              Analysis of Variance:

              DF   Adj. Sum of Squares      Residual Variance
Residuals     272        2.3398211                 .00830291


              Variables in the Model:

             B          SEB        T-Ratio    APPROX. PROB.
MA1     .32147272    .05726452    5.613820       .00000005
MA2     .29854464    .05726358    5.213517       .00000038
SMA1    .73396060    .04627721   15.860086      0.0


Covariance Matrix:

            MA1            MA2           SMA1
MA1     .00327923    -.00149099     -.00025187
MA2    -.00149099     .00327912      .00021915
SMA1   -.00025187     .00021915      .00214158


Correlation Matrix:

            MA1            MA2           SMA1
MA1    1.0000000     -.4546844      -.0950450
MA2    -.4546844     1.0000000       .0826989
SMA1   -.0950450      .0826989      1.0000000
```

The residual autocorrelations from the fitted model 7.11.7 are all very small. The Box-Ljung statistics, based on the first 12, 24, and 36 residual autocorrelations indicate that the hypothesis that the model specification is correct can only be rejected at significance levels of 82.8%, 76.4%, and 68.4% respectively. In addition, none of the more elaborate alternative models that we tried produced significantly superior fits. Accordingly, the fitted model 7.11.7 is used to yield forecasts of future factory sales. Predictions for the next ten months, together with 95% confidence limits, are shown in the final part of Exhibit 7.6. Figure 7.12

EXHIBIT 7.6 (*Continued*)

```
Autocorrelations:   ERR#1      Error for PASSCARS from ARIMA

       Auto- Stand.
  Lag  Corr.  Err. -1  -.75  -.5 -.25   0   .25  .5  .75   1   Box-Ljung  Prob.
                    +----+----+----+----+----+----+----+----+
    1  -.003  .060                       . * .                    .003    .955
    2   .018  .060                       . * .                    .095    .953
    3   .004  .060·                      . * .                    .099    .992
    4  -.056  .060                       .*: .                    .987    .912
    5  -.087  .060                      **: .                    3.144    .678
    6   .002  .059                       . * .                   3.145    .790
    7   .004  .059                       . * .                   3.150    .871
    8   .043  .059                       . :*.                   3.683    .885
    9   .030  .059                       . :*.                   3.937    .916
   10  -.031  .059                      .*: .                    4.209    .937
   11   .100  .059                       . :**                   7.103    .791
   12   .033  .059                       . :*.                   7.423    .828
   13  -.099  .059                      **: .                   10.295    .670
   14  -.033  .059                      .*: .                   10.605    .717
   15  -.049  .058                      .*: .                   11.314    .730
   16  -.096  .058                      **: .                   14.021    .597
   17   .026  .058                       . :*.                  14.216    .652
   18  -.011  .058                       . * .                  14.254    .712
   19   .025  .058                       . * .                  14.435    .758
   20  -.012  .058                       . * .                  14.475    .806
   21   .055  .058                       . :*.                  15.368    .804
   22  -.064  .058                      .*: .                   16.600    .785
   23  -.004  .058                       . * .                  16.605    .828
   24  -.085  .057                      **: .                   18.776    .764
   25  -.046  .057                      .*: .                   19.414    .777
   26   .005  .057                       . * .                  19.421    .818
   27  -.074  .057                      .*: .                   21.104    .781
   28  -.037  .057                      .*: .                   21.520    .803
   29   .063  .057                       . :*.                  22.743    .788
   30  -.077  .057                      **: .                   24.565    .746
   31   .045  .057                       . :*.                  25.193    .759
   32  -.039  .056                      .*: .                   25.681    .778
   33   .039  .056                       . :*.                  26.164    .795
   34  -.089  .056                      **: .                   28.675    .726
   35   .092  .056                       . :**                  31.336    .646
   36  -.020  .056                       . * .                  31.459    .684

Plot Symbols:    Autocorrelations *    Two Standard Error Limits .

Case# PASSCARS     FIT#1       LCL#1        UCL#1

   289      .       .65003      .47060       .82946
   290      .       .62168      .40484       .83852
   291      .       .69522      .46792       .92252
   292      .       .68481      .44750       .92211
   293      .       .70060      .45369       .94751
   294      .       .69841      .44226       .95456
   295      .       .52670      .26164       .79177
   296      .       .47254      .19884       .74624
   297      .       .61229      .33023       .89435
   298      .       .69173      .40155       .98192
```

FIGURE 7.12   Factory sales of U.S. passenger cars with point forecasts (dashed)
and 95% confidence limits (dotted).

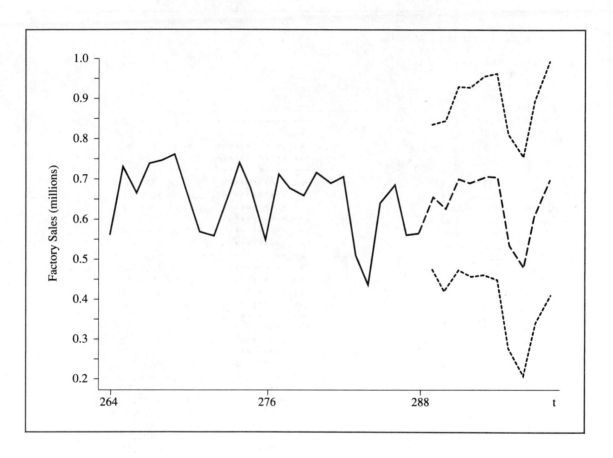

shows the last two years of observations together with these point and
interval forecasts.

Example 7.6.   In our next example we analyze a series of 204 monthly
observations on retail sales of apparel. Part of the SPSS program output
is shown in Exhibit 7.7. The variability of this series increases with its
level, so that it is appropriate to take logarithms of the data before
proceeding. The sample autocorrelations of the undifferenced series are
very large and behave quite smoothly at high lags so that some differencing
is clearly needed. For the first differenced series, the sample autocorrelations at multiples of 12 are very large, indicating the desirability of
seasonal differencing. The sample autocorrelations of the seasonally
differenced series behave fairly smoothly at high lags, so that regular

Exhibit 7.7   Part of SPSS program output for analysis of retail sales of apparel.

```
      Autocorrelations:   APPAREL

      Transformations:  natural log

            Auto- Stand.
      Lag   Corr.  Err.  -1  -.75  -.5  -.25   0   .25  .5   .75   1   Box-Ljung  Prob.
                         +----+----+----+----+----+----+----+----+
        1   .817   .070                       . :**.**************    138.320    .000
        2   .735   .069                       . :**.************      250.692    0.0
        3   .748   .069                       . :**.*************     367.803    0.0
        4   .762   .069                       . :**.*************     489.803    0.0
        5   .733   .069                       . :**.************      603.121    0.0
        6   .723   .069                       . :**.************      713.957    0.0
        7   .707   .068                       . :**.***********       820.722    0.0
        8   .708   .068                       . :**.************      928.080    0.0
        9   .667   .068                       . :**·.**********      1023.990    0.0
       10   .624   .068                       . :**.*********       1108.387    0.0
       11   .683   .068                       . :**.***********      1209.977    0.0
       12   .830   .068                       . :**.***************** 1360.899    0.0
       13   .661   .067                       . :**.**********      1456.889    0.0
       14   .581   .067                       . :**.*********       1531.477    0.0
       15   .591   .067                       . :**.*********       1609.126    0.0
       16   .604   .067                       . :**.*********       1690.564    0.0
       17   .576   .067                       . :**.*********       1765.010    0.0
       18   .565   .067                       . :**.********        1837.237    0.0
       19   .549   .066                       . :**.********        1905.782    0.0
       20   .552   .066                       . :**.********        1975.322    0.0
       21   .510   .066                       . :**.*******         2035.135    0.0
       22   .470   .066                       . :**.******          2086.234    0.0
       23   .527   .066                       . :**.********         2150.622    0.0
       24   .663   .065                       . :**.**********      2253.168    0.0
       25   .502   .065                       . :**.*******         2312.220    0.0
       26   .429   .065                       . :**.******          2355.727    0.0
       27   .439   .065                       . :**.******          2401.540    0.0
       28   .450   .065                       . :**.******          2449.857    0.0
       29   .424   .065                       . :**.*****           2493.111    0.0
       30   .414   .064                       . :**.*****           2534.424    0.0
       31   .398   .064                       . :**.*****           2572.841    .000
       32   .401   .064                       . :**.*****           2612.113    .000
       33   .360   .064                       . :**.****            2643.980    .000
       34   .326   .064                       . :**.****            2670.210    .000
       35   .377   .063                       . :**.*****           2705.485    .000
       36   .504   .063                       . :**.*******         2769.046    .000

      Plot Symbols:      Autocorrelations *     Two Standard Error Limits .

      Total cases:  204    Computable first lags:  203
```

EXHIBIT 7.7   (*Continued*)

```
     Autocorrelations:   APPAREL

     Transformations:   natural log, difference (1)

         Auto- Stand.
     Lag  Corr.  Err. -1  -.75  -.5 -.25   0   .25  .5   .75  1   Box-Ljung  Prob.
                      +----+----+----+----+----+----+----+----+
       1  -.292  .070              ***.**:  .                    17.583    .000
       2  -.284  .069              ***.**:  .                    34.299    .000
       3   .002  .069                 . * .                      34.299    .000
       4   .132  .069                 . :***                     37.966    .000
       5  -.047  .069                 . *:  .                     38.434    .000
       6   .009  .069                 . * .                      38.450    .000
       7  -.055  .069                 . *:  .                     39.099    .000
       8   .140  .068                 . :***                     43.278    .000
       9   .006  .068                 . * .                      43.286    .000
      10  -.296  .068              ***.**:  .                    62.150    .000
      11  -.261  .068               **.**:  .                    76.951    .000
      12   .905  .068                 . :**.*****************   255.473    0.0
      13  -.266  .068               **.**:  .                   270.930    0.0
      14  -.265  .067               **.**:  .                   286.409    0.0
      15   .008  .067                 . * .                     286.424    0.0
      16   .116  .067                 . :**.                    289.424    0.0
      17  -.040  .067                 . *:  .                    289.777    0.0
      18   .010  .067                 . * .                     289.799    0.0
      19  -.065  .066                 . *:  .                    290.754    0.0
      20   .144  .066                 . :***                    295.462    0.0
      21   .001  .066                 . * .                     295.462    0.0
      22  -.279  .066              ***.**:  .                    313.392    0.0
      23  -.233  .066               **.**:  .                    325.909    0.0
      24   .839  .066                 . :**.**************      489.399    0.0
      25  -.256  .065               **.**:  .                    504.733    0.0
      26  -.234  .065               **.**:  .                    517.588    0.0
      27  -.003  .065                 . * .                     517.590    0.0
      28   .115  .065                 . :**.                    520.754    0.0
      29  -.035  .065                 . *:  .                    521.044    0.0
      30  -.002  .064                 . * .                     521.044    0.0
      31  -.057  .064                 . *:  .                    521.821    .000
      32   .144  .064                 . :***                    526.845    .000
      33  -.010  .064                 . * .                     526.870    .000
      34  -.252  .064               **.**:  .                    542.568    .000
      35  -.223  .064                *.**:  .                    554.888    .000
      36   .794  .063                 . :**.*************       711.905    .000

     Plot Symbols:     Autocorrelations *     Two Standard Error Limits .

     Total cases:  204     Computable first lags after differencing:  202
```

EXHIBIT 7.7   (*Continued*)

```
     Autocorrelations:   APPAREL

     Transformations:  natural log, seasonal difference (1 at 12)

          Auto- Stand.
     Lag  Corr.  Err. -1  -.75  -.5 -.25   0   .25   .5   .75   1  Box-Ljung  Prob.
                       +----+----+----+----+----+----+----+----+
       1   .497  .072                      . :**.*******          48.246    .000
       2   .546  .071                      . :**.********         106.774    .000
       3   .553  .071                      . :**.********         166.938    0.0
       4   .413  .071                      . :**.*****           200.794    0.0
       5   .362  .071                      . :**.****            226.864    0.0
       6   .287  .071                      . :**.***             243.411    0.0
       7   .238  .070                      . :**.**              254.796    0.0
       8   .146  .070                      . :***               259.085    0.0
       9   .027  .070                      . :* .               259.236    0.0
      10   .015  .070                      . * .                259.282    0.0
      11  -.043  .070                      . *: .               259.663    0.0
      12  -.283  .070                  ***.**: .                276.210    0.0
      13  -.127  .069                    ***: .                279.569    0.0
      14  -.204  .069                  *.**: .                288.292    0.0
      15  -.220  .069                  *.**: .                298.517    0.0
      16  -.241  .069                  **.**: .                310.767    0.0
      17  -.241  .069                  **.**: .                323.093    0.0
      18  -.234  .068                  **.**: .                334.773    0.0
      19  -.288  .068                 ***.**: .                352.628    0.0
      20  -.242  .068                  **.**: .                365.352    0.0
      21  -.185  .068                  *.**: .                372.842    0.0
      22  -.266  .068                  **.**: .                388.324    0.0
      23  -.105  .067                    .**: .                390.764    0.0
      24  -.200  .067                  *.**: .                399.619    0.0
      25  -.140  .067                   ***: .                403.983    0.0
      26  -.052  .067                   . *: .                404.584    0.0
      27  -.119  .067                   .**: .                407.765    0.0
      28  -.017  .066                   . * .                407.832    0.0
      29   .041  .066                   . :* .                408.210    0.0
      30   .007  .066                   . * .                408.222    0.0
      31   .063  .066                   . :* .                409.151    .000
      32   .082  .066                   . :**.                410.722    .000
      33   .084  .065                   . :**.                412.361    .000
      34   .116  .065                   . :**.                415.549    .000
      35   .028  .065                   . :* .                415.730    .000
      36   .153  .065                   . :***               421.286    .000

     Plot Symbols:    Autocorrelations *    Two Standard Error Limits .

     Total cases:  204    Computable first lags after differencing:  191
```

EXHIBIT 7.7   (*Continued*)

```
     Autocorrelations:   APPAREL

     Transformations:  natural log, difference (1), seasonal difference (1 at 12)

         Auto- Stand.
     Lag  Corr.  Err. -1  -.75  -.5  -.25   0   .25   .5   .75   1   Box-Ljung  Prob.
                      +----+----+----+----+----+----+----+----+
       1  -.549  .072            ********.**:  .                  58.581     .000
       2   .039  .072                    . :* .                   58.882     .000
       3   .155  .071                    . :***                   63.573     .000
       4  -.093  .071                    .**: .                   65.270     .000
       5   .023  .071                    . * .                    65.371     .000
       6  -.024  .071                    . * .                    65.483     .000
       7   .040  .071                    . :* .                   65.803     .000
       8   .028  .070                    . :* .                   65.956     .000
       9  -.110  .070                    .**: .                   68.389     .000
      10   .050  .070                    . :* .                   68.908     .000
      11   .180  .070                    . :**.*                  75.546     .000
      12  -.395  .070            *****.**:  .                    107.717     .000
      13   .234  .069                    . :**.**                119.039     .000
      14  -.056  .069                    . *: .                  119.701     .000
      15  -.006  .069                    . * .                   119.707     .000
      16  -.016  .069                    . * .                   119.759     .000
      17  -.007  .069                    . * .                   119.770     .000
      18   .061  .069                    . :* .                  120.554     .000
      19  -.097  .068                    .**: .                  122.589     .000
      20  -.010  .068                    . * .                   122.609     .000
      21   .136  .068                    . :***                  126.633     .000
      22  -.240  .068            **.**:  .                       139.227     .000
      23   .253  .068                    . :**.**                153.289     0.0
      24  -.152  .067                   ***: .                   158.368     0.0
      25  -.029  .067                    . *: .                  158.552     0.0
      26   .152  .067                    . :***                  163.727     0.0
      27  -.162  .067                   ***: .                   169.633     0.0
      28   .038  .066                    . :* .                  169.962     0.0
      29   .094  .066                    . :**.                  171.975     0.0
      30  -.092  .066                    .**: .                  173.922     0.0
      31   .037  .066                    . :* .                  174.239     .000
      32   .016  .066                    . * .                   174.297     .000
      33  -.031  .065                    . *: .                  174.520     .000
      34   .121  .065                    . :**.                  177.946     .000
      35  -.213  .065            *.**:  .                        188.667     .000
      36   .226  .065                    . :**.**                200.770     .000

     Plot Symbols:     Autocorrelations *     Two Standard Error Limits .

     Total cases:  204     Computable first lags after differencing:  190
```

EXHIBIT 7.7 (*Continued*)

```
      Partial Autocorrelations:   APPAREL

      Transformations:  natural log, difference (1), seasonal difference (1 at 12)

          Pr-Aut- Stand.
      Lag  Corr.   Err. -1  -.75  -.5 -.25   0  .25  .5   .75   1
                         +----+----+----+----+----+----+----+----+
        1  -.549   .072         ********.**:   .
        2  -.376   .072         *****.**:   .
        3  -.037   .072              . *:   .
        4   .036   .072              . :* .
        5   .053   .072              . :* .
        6  -.030   .072              . *: .
        7   .006   .072              . *  .
        8   .092   .072              . :**.
        9  -.043   .072              . *: .
       10  -.097   .072              .**: .
       11   .221   .072              . :**.*
       12  -.215   .072          *.**:   .
       13  -.192   .072          *.**:   .
       14  -.197   .072          *.**:   .
       15  -.000   .072              . *  .
       16  -.011   .072              . *  .
       17  -.029   .072              . *: .
       18   .012   .072              . *  .
       19  -.029   .072              . *: .
       20  -.100   .072              .**: .
       21   .029   .072              . :* .
       22  -.240   .072          **.**:   .
       23   .218   .072              . :**.*
       24  -.117   .072              .**: .
       25  -.188   .072          *.**:   .
       26  -.062   .072              . *: .
       27  -.030   .072              . *: .
       28  -.154   .072          ***:   .
       29   .033   .072              . :* .
       30   .049   .072              . :* .
       31   .002   .072              . *  .
       32  -.102   .072              .**: .
       33   .032   .072              . :* .
       34  -.026   .072              . *: .
       35   .041   .072              . :* .
       36   .017   .072              . *  .

      Plot Symbols:      Autocorrelations *     Two Standard Error Limits .

      Total cases:  204     Computable first lags after differencing:  190
```

Exhibit 7.7   (*Continued*)

```
FINAL PARAMETERS:

Number of residuals   191
Standard error        .03935563
Log likelihood        342.81096
AIC                   -677.62193
SBC                   -664.61283


                 Analysis of Variance:

              DF   Adj. Sum of Squares    Residual Variance
Residuals     187            .30846893             .00154887


              Variables in the Model:

                B            SEB       T-RATIO   APPROX. PROB.
AR1     -.72444670      .06551068   -11.058451   0.0
AR2     -.38026987      .06593208    -5.767600    .00000003
SMA1     .73576918      .07856644     9.364930   0.0
SMA2     .05859190      .07916992      .740078    .46018115


Covariance Matrix:

                AR1          AR2         SMA1         SMA2
AR1      .00429165    .00225448    .00026669    -.00019300
AR2      .00225448    .00434704    -.00017246   -.00032976
SMA1     .00026669    -.00017246    .00617269   -.00333228
SMA2     -.00019300   -.00032976   -.00333228    .00626788


Correlation Matrix:

                AR1          AR2         SMA1         SMA2
AR1     1.0000000     .5219595     .0518151    -.0372129
AR2      .5219595    1.0000000    -.0332934    -.0631736
SMA1     .0518151    -.0332934    1.0000000    -.5357276
SMA2     -.0372129   -.0631736    -.5357276    1.0000000
```

Exhibit 7.7   (*Continued*)

```
    Autocorrelations:    ERR#1       Error for APPAREL from ARIMA

        Auto- Stand.
    Lag Corr.  Err.  -1 -.75  -.5 -.25  0  .25  .5  .75  1   Box-Ljung  Prob.
                         +----+----+----+----+----+----+----+----+
      1  -.024  .072                        .  *  .                 .115    .735
      2  -.016  .072                        .  *  .                 .166    .920
      3  -.019  .071                        .  *  .                 .237    .971
      4   .006  .071                        .  *  .                 .243    .993
      5  -.026  .071                        . *:  .                 .372    .996
      6  -.035  .071                        . *:  .                 .611    .996
      7   .001  .071                        .  *  .                 .611    .999
      8  -.059  .070                        . *:  .                1.321    .995
      9  -.008  .070                        .  *  .                1.334    .998
     10  -.036  .070                        . *:  .                1.598    .999
     11   .072  .070                        .  :* .                2.663    .994
     12  -.022  .070                        .  *  .                2.761    .997
     13   .023  .069                        .  *  .                2.874    .998
     14  -.041  .069                        . *:  .                3.225    .999
     15  -.019  .069                        .  *  .                3.302    .999
     16  -.037  .069                        . *:  .                3.584    .999
     17  -.005  .069                        .  *  .                3.589   1.000
     18  -.044  .069                        . *:  .                4.001   1.000
     19  -.135  .068                        ***:  .                7.903    .988
     20  -.089  .068                        .**:  .                9.614    .975
     21   .065  .068                        .  :* .               10.543    .971
     22  -.118  .068                        .**:  .               13.559    .916
     23   .124  .068                        .  :**.               16.917    .813
     24  -.058  .067                        . *:  .               17.670    .819
     25   .001  .067                        .  *  .               17.671    .856
     26   .029  .067                        .  :* .               17.853    .881
     27  -.081  .067                        .**:  .               19.314    .858
     28   .044  .066                        .  :* .               19.747    .874
     29   .051  .066                        .  :* .               20.330    .882
     30  -.020  .066                        .  *  .               20.419    .905
     31  -.030  .066                        . *:  .               20.623    .922
     32   .024  .066                        .  *  .               20.762    .937
     33  -.001  .065                        .  *  .               20.762    .952
     34   .041  .065                        .  :* .               21.156    .958
     35  -.057  .065                        . *:  .               21.912    .959
     36   .097  .065                        .  :**.               24.152    .934

    Plot Symbols:       Autocorrelations *      Two Standard Error Limits .
```

differencing also was needed. There is no suggestion in the sample autocorrelations of the series $(1 - B)(1 - B^{12})X_t$ that any further differencing is necessary.

Looking at the sample autocorrelations and sample partial autocorrelations of $(1 - B)(1 - B^{12})X_t$ the choice of appropriate model is perhaps not as clear cut as in the previous two examples, so that this series allows us the opportunity to illustrate the possibility of experimenting with a number of different alternative models. The first two sample partial autocorrelations are very large, whereas the next few are very small. Also,

Exhibit 7.7   (*Continued*)

Case#	APPAREL	FIT#1	LCL#1	UCL#1
205	.	5.62860	5.20799	6.08318
206	.	5.25600	4.84917	5.69696
207	.	6.76453	6.20139	7.37879
208	.	6.95686	6.30561	7.67537
209	.	7.11252	6.41402	7.88708
210	.	6.74168	6.04064	7.52409
211	.	6.49359	5.78000	7.29527
212	.	7.55562	6.68969	8.53364
213	.	7.07971	6.23360	8.04067
214	.	7.48875	6.55875	8.55063
215	.	8.27401	7.21070	9.49413
216	.	12.48755	10.82960	14.39933
217	.	6.17799	5.29829	7.20374
218	.	5.76300	4.91397	6.75871
219	.	7.36698	6.24167	8.69518
220	.	7.63903	6.42638	9.08052
221	.	7.76231	6.49200	9.28118
222	.	7.38586	6.14020	8.88423
223	.	7.10994	5.87595	8.60307
224	.	8.25695	6.78618	10.04650
225	.	7.75406	6.33797	9.48654
226	.	8.20255	6.66882	10.08902
227	.	9.06174	7.32934	11.20362
228	.	13.67234	11.00250	16.99002

there are large or moderately large sample autocorrelations and sample partial autocorrelations at and around lags 12 and 24. These considerations suggest that an appropriate model might require two regular terms and two seasonal terms. We decided to fit all nine models of this type. The values of the SBC criterion are shown in Table 7.5. (Note that, since the models contain the same number of parameters, comparisons could be made by other means if the user does not have access to a program that computes the SBC criterion. For example, if MINITAB were used, the model leading to the smallest residual mean square could be chosen.)

From Table 7.5 it can be seen that the smallest SBC value is for the ARIMA$(2, 1, 0)(0, 1, 2)_{12}$ model

$$(1 - \phi_1 B - \phi_2 B^2)(1 - B)(1 - B^{12})X_t = (1 - \Theta_1 B^{12} - \Theta_2 B^{24})a_t$$

Table 7.5   Values of SBC criterion for seasonal ARIMA models fitted to logarithms of retail sales of apparel.

Model	SBC	Model	SBC	Model	SBC
$(2, 1, 0)(2, 1, 0)_{12}$	-655.37	$(2, 1, 0)(1, 1, 1)_{12}$	-664.55	$(2, 1, 0)(0, 1, 2)_{12}$	-664.61
$(1, 1, 1)(2, 1, 0)_{12}$	-650.15	$(1, 1, 1)(1, 1, 1)_{12}$	-658.59	$(1, 1, 1)(0, 1, 2)_{12}$	-658.66
$(0, 1, 2)(2, 1, 0)_{12}$	-651.84	$(0, 1, 2)(1, 1, 1)_{12}$	-660.92	$(0, 1, 2)(0, 1, 2)_{12}$	-661.00

From the output in Exhibit 7.7 it can be seen that the fitted model is

$$(1 + 0.724B + 0.380B^2)(1 - B)(1 - B^{12})X_t$$
$$(0.066)\quad(0.066)$$
$$= (1 - 0.736B^{12} - 0.059B^{24})a_t$$
$$(0.079)\quad\quad(0.079)$$

$$(7.11.8)$$

Three of the estimated parameters are large compared with their standard errors, but the second seasonal moving average parameter is very small. At this stage the analyst might want to drop this term, and fit an ARIMA$(2, 1, 0)(0, 1, 1)_{12}$ model. This is a sensible course of action, though the estimated parameter is so small in this case that much the same forecasts will result. The reader is invited to verify this contention.

The residual autocorrelations from the fitted model 7.11.8 are all quite small, and the Box-Ljung statistics fail to provide any grounds for questioning the adequacy of that model. We tried several alternative models with additional parameters, but none of their estimates turned out to be statistically significant. Indeed, there is already a degree of over-fit in equation 7.11.8, since the second seasonal moving average term appears to be redundant. The final portion of Exhibit 7.7 shows forecasts of retail sales of apparel for the next 24 months, based on the fitted model 7.11.8.

Example 7.7. For our final example we analyze a series of 42 quarterly observations on sales of Illinois Power. This small sample size is toward the lower end of what is generally recommended as adequate for ARIMA analysis, particularly for seasonal data. Still, it is interesting to explore what can be achieved with so few observations.

Part of the SPSS program output is shown in Exhibit 7.8. The sample autocorrelations of the undifferenced series are persistently large, and appear to exhibit strong seasonal behavior. It certainly appears that differencing of some kind is desirable. For the first differenced series, the sample autocorrelations at multiples of 4 are very large, suggesting the necessity for seasonal differencing. For the seasonally differenced series, the sample autocorrelations at high lags are not overly large compared with their standard errors, and a case could be made that seasonal differencing alone is adequate. Nevertheless, the pattern of these sample autocorrelations is somewhat smooth, suggesting that both regular and seasonal differencing might be desirable. The sample autocorrelations of $(1 - B)(1 - B^4)X_t$ provide no suggestion that yet more differencing is necessary.

Looking at the sample autocorrelations and sample partial autocorrelations of $(1 - B)(1 - B^4)X_t$ does not suggest just a single model as uniquely plausible. This is not surprising with such a short series—after differencing we are left with just 37 observations. The sample autocorrelation and partial autocorrelation at lag 4 are quite large, while those at lags 8, 12, and 16 are small. This suggests that a single seasonal parameter—either autoregressive or moving average—should be sufficient. Since the first sample autocorrelation is large, at least one regular parameter will also be required. The second partial autocorrelation is also large, suggesting that a single autoregressive parameter alone would be insufficient. In addition, the large sample autocorrelation at lag 6 might indicate the desirability of a second regular parameter in conjunction with the seasonal parameter. We decided to fit all six models involving two regular parameters and one seasonal parameters. The values of the SBC criterion for these models are shown in Table 7.6. (Again, since the models contain the same number of parameters, they could also be compared through residual mean squares.)

The smallest SBC value is for the ARIMA$(2, 1, 0)(1, 1, 0)_4$ model

$$(1 - \phi_1 B - \phi_2 B^2)(1 - \Phi_1 B^4)(1 - B)(1 - B^4)X_t = a_t$$

The remainder of the output shown in Exhibit 7.8 relates only to this model. From that output, we see that the estimated model can be written

$$(1 + 0.390B + 0.329B^2)(1 + 0.335B^4)(1 - B)(1 - B^4)X_t = a_t$$
$$(0.160) \quad (0.163) \qquad (0.164)$$

All of the parameter estimates are a little more than twice the corresponding standard errors, so that none of these parameters appear to be redundant. The residual autocorrelations are generally quite small compared with their standard errors, and the Box-Ljung statistics are very small. The fitted model therefore appears to be adequate. The final part

TABLE 7.6   Values of SBC criterion for seasonal ARIMA models fitted to Illinois Power sales.

Model	SBC	Model	SBC
$(2,1,0)(1,1,0)_4$	363.25	$(2,1,0)(0,1,1)_4$	363.62
$(1,1,1)(1,1,0)_4$	363.59	$(1,1,1)(0,1,1)_4$	363.88
$(0,1,2)(1,1,0)_4$	363.34	$(0,1,2)(0,1,1)_4$	363.61

Exhibit 7.8   Part of SPSS program output for analysis of Illinois Power sales.

```
    Autocorrelations:    ILLPOWER
         Auto- Stand.
    Lag  Corr.  Err.  -1  -.75  -.5  -.25   0   .25   .5   .75  1   Box-Ljung  Prob.
                      +----+----+----+----+----+----+----+----+
     1   -.039  .149                     .    *:    .                  .069     .793
     2    .363  .147                     .    :*****.*                 6.153     .046
     3   -.195  .145                     . ****:    .                  7.948     .047
     4    .613  .143                     .    :*****.******           26.225     .000
     5   -.235  .141                     .*****:    .                 28.980     .000
     6    .232  .140                     .    :*****.                 31.754     .000
     7   -.312  .138                  ******:    .                    36.891     .000
     8    .367  .136                     .    :****.**                44.206     .000
     9   -.396  .134                  ***.****:    .                  52.993     .000
    10    .153  .132                     .    :***  .                 54.342     .000
    11   -.274  .130                   *****:    .                    58.808     .000
    12    .257  .127                     .    :*****                  62.861     .000
    13   -.311  .125                   *.****:    .                   69.041     .000
    14    .200  .123                     .    :****.                  71.677     .000
    15   -.184  .121                     .****:    .                  73.999     .000
    16    .221  .119                     .    :****.                  77.467     .000

    Plot Symbols:      Autocorrelations *      Two Standard Error Limits .

    Total cases:  42     Computable first lags:  41
```

Exhibit 7.8   (*Continued*)

```
     Autocorrelations:   ILLPOWER
     Transformations:  difference (1)
          Auto- Stand.
     Lag  Corr.  Err.  -1  -.75  -.5  -.25  0   .25  .5  .75  1     Box-Ljung  Prob.
                       +----+----+----+----+----+----+----+----+
       1  -.711  .151        ********.*****:         .              22.298    .000
       2   .471  .149               .    :*****.***                 32.323    .000
       3  -.661  .147         *******.*****:         .              52.577    .000
       4   .818  .145               .    :*****.**********           84.474    .000
       5  -.653  .143         *******.*****:         .             105.348    .000
       6   .489  .141               .    :*****.****                117.411    .000
       7  -.589  .139          ******.*****:         .             135.419    .000
       8   .713  .137               .    :****.*********            162.567    .000
       9  -.647  .135         *******.****:          .             185.651    .000
      10   .485  .133               .    :****.*****               199.008    .000
      11  -.476  .130           *****.****:          .             212.312    .000
      12   .553  .128               .    :****.******              230.879    .000
      13  -.544  .126          ******.****:          .             249.481    .000
      14   .438  .124               .    :****.****                262.010    .000
      15  -.386  .121             ***.****:          .             272.101    .000
      16   .425  .119               .    :****.****                284.863    .000
     Plot Symbols:      Autocorrelations *     Two Standard Error Limits .
     Total cases:  42    Computable first lags after differencing:  40
```

Exhibit 7.8   (*Continued*)

```
Autocorrelations:   ILLPOWER
Transformations:  seasonal difference (1 at 4)

        Auto- Stand.
Lag    Corr.  Err.  -1  -.75  -.5  -.25   0    .25   .5   .75   1   Box-Ljung  Prob.
                     +----+----+----+----+----+----+----+----+
  1    .378   .156              .         :*****.**              5.858     .016
  2    .206   .154              .         :**** .                7.654     .022
  3    .203   .152              .         :**** .                9.443     .024
  4   -.034   .150              .       *:      .                9.494     .050
  5    .112   .147              .         :**   .               10.068     .073
  6   -.044   .145              .       *:      .               10.161     .118
  7   -.106   .143              .      **:      .               10.708     .152
  8   -.070   .140              .       *:      .               10.954     .204
  9   -.205   .138              .    ****:      .               13.165     .155
 10   -.158   .136              .    ***:       .               14.515     .151
 11   -.111   .133              .     **:       .               15.211     .173
 12   -.167   .131              .    ***:       .               16.841     .156
 13   -.154   .128              .    ***:       .               18.285     .147
 14   -.164   .126              .    ***:       .               19.996     .130
 15   -.105   .123              .     **:       .               20.725     .146
 16   -.015   .120              .        *      .               20.740     .189

Plot Symbols:     Autocorrelations *      Two Standard Error Limits .

Total cases:  42     Computable first lags after differencing:  37
```

Exhibit 7.8   (*Continued*)

```
     Autocorrelations:   ILLPOWER
     Transformations:  difference (1), seasonal difference (1 at 4)
          Auto- Stand.
     Lag  Corr.  Err.  -1  -.75  -.5  -.25   0   .25   .5   .75   1      Box-Ljung  Prob.
                       +----+----+----+----+----+----+----+----+
       1  -.354  .158              *.*****:       .               5.033     .025
       2  -.088  .156                  . **:      .               5.352     .069
       3   .182  .153                  .    :**** .               6.755     .080
       4  -.319  .151              ******:        .              11.200     .024
       5   .214  .149                  .    :**** .              13.259     .021
       6  -.178  .147                  . ****:     .             14.740     .022
       7   .039  .144                  .    :*     .             14.812     .038
       8   .100  .142                  .    :**    .             15.311     .053
       9  -.090  .139                  .  **:      .             15.731     .073
      10   .068  .137                  .    :*     .             15.976     .100
      11   .032  .134                  .    :*     .             16.034     .140
      12  -.020  .132                  .    *      .             16.057     .189
      13   .033  .129                  .    :*     .             16.121     .243
      14  -.082  .126                  .  **:      .             16.538     .282
      15  -.029  .123                  .   *:      .             16.594     .344
      16  -.001  .121                  .    *      .             16.594     .412

     Plot Symbols:      Autocorrelations *    Two Standard Error Limits .

     Total cases:  42     Computable first lags after differencing:  36

     Partial Autocorrelations:   ILLPOWER
     Transformations:  difference (1), seasonal difference (1 at 4)
          Pr-Aut- Stand.
     Lag  Corr.  Err.  -1  -.75  -.5  -.25   0   .25   .5   .75   1
                       +----+----+----+----+----+----+----+----+
       1  -.354  .164              *******:       .
       2  -.244  .164                 . *****:      .
       3   .069  .164                 .    :*       .
       4  -.289  .164                 .******:       .
       5   .037  .164                 .    :*       .
       6  -.246  .164                 . *****:      .
       7  -.007  .164                 .    *        .
       8  -.079  .164                 .  **:        .
       9   .040  .164                 .    :*       .
      10  -.082  .164                 .  **:        .
      11   .116  .164                 .    :**      .
      12  -.005  .164                 .    *        .
      13   .106  .164                 .    :**      .
      14  -.083  .164                 .  **:        .
      15  -.011  .164                 .    *        .
      16  -.123  .164                 .  **:        .
```

Exhibit 7.8   (*Continued*)

```
    Plot Symbols:        Autocorrelations *     Two Standard Error Limits .
    Total cases:  42     Computable first lags after differencing:  36
    FINAL PARAMETERS:
    Number of residuals   37
    Standard error        29.206779
    Log likelihood        -176.20863
    AIC                   358.41726
    SBC                   363.25002
                  Analysis of Variance:
                    DF  Adj. Sum of Squares Residual Variance
    Residuals       34         29609.008            853.03593
                  Variables in the Model:
                      B          SEB        T-RATIO   APPROX. PROB.
    AR1     -.38950799    .16011600    -2.4326612       .02040181
    AR2     -.32893162    .16291711    -2.0190122       .05142735
    SAR1    -.33463792    .16408398    -2.0394308       .04923983
    Covariance Matrix:
                   AR1          AR2          SAR1
    AR1      .02563713    .00722870    -.00253154
    AR2      .00722870    .02654198     .00257184
    SAR1    -.00253154    .00257184     .02692355
    Correlation Matrix:
                   AR1          AR2          SAR1
    AR1     1.0000000     .2771142     -.0963573
    AR2      .2771142    1.0000000      .0962081
    SAR1    -.0963573     .0962081     1.0000000
```

EXHIBIT 7.8   (*Continued*)

```
    Autocorrelations:    ERR#1    Error for ILLPOWER from ARIMA
          Auto- Stand.
    Lag  Corr.  Err.  -1  -.75  -.5  -.25   0   .25  .5  .75   1    Box-Ljung  Prob.
                      +----+----+----+----+----+----+----+----+
      1  -.027  .158                   .    *:    .                    .030    .863
      2  -.039  .156                   .    *:    .                    .092    .955
      3  -.056  .153                   .    *:    .                    .223    .974
      4  -.027  .151                   .    *:    .                    .255    .993
      5   .095  .149                   .    :**   .                    .663    .985
      6  -.210  .147                   . ****:    .                   2.708    .845
      7   .077  .144                   .    :**   .                   2.989    .886
      8  -.020  .142                   .    *     .                   3.008    .934
      9   .012  .139                   .    *     .                   3.016    .964
     10  -.004  .137                   .    *     .                   3.017    .981
     11   .056  .134                   .    :*    .                   3.194    .988
     12   .049  .132                   .    :*    .                   3.330    .993
     13   .018  .129                   .    *     .                   3.349    .996
     14  -.084  .126                   .   **:    .                   3.790    .997
     15  -.099  .123                   .   **:    .                   4.436    .996
     16   .054  .121                   .    :*    .                   4.637    .997
    Plot Symbols:       Autocorrelations *    Two Standard Error Limits .

    Case# ILLPOWER    FIT#1    LCL#1    UCL#1
       43     .       439.63   380.26   499.00
       44     .       366.40   276.84   435.95
       45     .       368.41   294.25   442.58
       46     .       333.58   250.51   416.66
       47     .       461.07   348.59   573.55
       48     .       386.01   259.90   512.12
       49     .       390.43   254.13   526.73
       50     .       351.46   202.55   500.37
```

of Exhibit 7.8 shows forecasts from this model for the next eight quarters, together with the limits of the associated 95% intervals.

The reader may be harboring the suspicion that we have chosen particularly straightforward examples to illustrate seasonal ARIMA model building, leaving him or her to flounder in the intricacies of the many more difficult cases thrown up by the real world outside the comfortable environment of textbooks. After all, the general seasonal ARIMA class of models is quite complex, whereas in only one of our examples were as many as four parameters needed, and even here one of these seemed to be redundant. In fact, we reiterate our earlier assertion that typically in practice very simple models will prove adequate. Our examples were not chosen because they are unusually easy, but rather as an accurate representation of the types of series that, in our experience, are generally observed in practice.

7.12 SUMMARY OF THE BOX-JENKINS APPROACH

Since the publication of Box and Jenkins (1970), the approach to time series forecasting outlined in this chapter has attracted a good deal of attention, and has proved useful in a wide range of applications. The essence of this approach, and in a sense its most attractive feature, is the provision of a broad class of possible generating models, and consequently a wide variety of possible forecast functions, the choice of a particular one being based on the observed characteristics of the given data. The model-fitting procedure proceeds through an iterative three-stage process of model selection, parameter estimation, and model checking. Both the theoretical and practical details of this methodology are quite complicated. For the practitioner, the best advice is to acquire experience through trying out the method on several real data sets, always keeping in mind the *principle of parsimony*. The object of good model building is not to develop a highly complex structure, but to develop the simplest construct that appears to be compatible with the major features exhibited by the available data. Such parsimonious models will rarely yield disappointing forecast performance.

The Box-Jenkins approach allows the analyst to *think* about the data, and consequently about how a given time series might best be predicted. As we have said, it is precisely this that makes the methodology so appealing. However, this feature has also led to reservations about and criticisms of the ARIMA model-building approach to forecasting. Unfortunately, thought takes time and effort, and is not invariably rewarding. Certainly some experience is needed before the manager can attack forecasting problems with any great confidence using the methods of this chapter. The manager's life might be more pleasant if all business forecasting problems could be satisfactorily solved without the effort of thought, perhaps through the routine processing of data by some pre-written computer algorithm. Such fully automatic forecasting procedures are superficially attractive, but it stretches credibility to believe that they will invariably produce near-optimal, or even adequate, predictions for the wide range of time series met in the business world. In fact, a number of computer packages have been developed for the fully automatic fitting to time series data of ARIMA models, without the need for manual intervention or user judgment. Some of these are discussed by Hill and Fildes (1984), Libert (1984), Bewley (1988), and Texter and Ord (1989). We feel these may be useful when it is required to analyze a large number of series in a short amount of time, but prefer the methods of this chapter when the analyst has available the time for careful thought. Of course, as we suggested in Chapter 6, there will be occasions when it is simply not possible to devote time and effort to every individual time series that has to be predicted. In those circumstances, the use of an exponential smoothing algorithm is an attractive option. In a number of empirical studies these algorithms have been found, *in the aggregate*, to perform moderately well in comparison to the Box-Jenkins approach. Of course, these aggregate results will provide little consolation to the analyst with a single series that is particularly ill-suited to the exponential smoothing algorithm being used. Only through a procedure that allows the study of the individual characteristics of the data at hand can the analyst be justifiably optimistic about the predictor being employed. On occasion, if only by chance, a particular exponential smoothing algorithm will yield better forecasts than a carefully fitted ARIMA model. However, if the analyst has sensibly followed the Box-Jenkins methodology, only very rarely will really poor forecasts result.

A further attraction of the model-building approach of this chapter lies in the possibilities for its extension to situations where data are available on several related time series, and forecasts of one might be based on past values of all of them, presumably opening up the prospect of more accurate predictions. This possibility calls to mind the regression models of Chapters 3 and 4. Indeed ARIMA modeling and regression modeling are not different in kind, but rather similar in spirit. The possibility is therefore open for the alliance of the two, as we will briefly discuss in Chapter 9.

EXERCISES

7.1 The accompanying table gives 57 annual observations on building expenditures as a percentage of gross national product in the

United States. Fit autoregressive models of all orders up to five. Select one of these fitted models for forecasting, and predict the next six values of this series.

t	X_t	t	X_t	t	X_t	t	X_t
1	12.7	16	8.9	30	11.3	44	9.7
2	12.0	17	4.3	31	11.1	45	10.3
3	10.5	18	2.5	32	11.1	46	10.6
4	9.7	19	2.7	33	11.4	47	10.6
5	8.5	20	6.8	34	10.8	48	9.8
6	6.1	21	8.6	35	10.8	49	8.8
7	5.2	22	10.1	36	10.7	50	8.9
8	5.7	23	10.4	37	10.9	51	9.2
9	5.8	24	11.7	38	10.6	52	9.7
10	7.9	25	10.7	39	10.7	53	9.7
11	7.7	26	10.6	40	10.1	54	8.8
12	8.2	27	10.7	41	9.8	55	8.1
13	9.1	28	11.3	42	10.0	56	7.6
14	8.7	29	11.7	43	10.0	57	7.9
15	9.6						

7.2 The accompanying table shows 120 monthly observations on soybean meal price, in dollars per ton, at Decatur, Illinois. Fit autoregressive models of all orders up to five. Choose one of those fitted models for forecasting, and predict price for the next six months.

t	X_t	t	X_t	t	X_t	t	X_t	t	X_t
1	171.8	25	129.5	49	163.3	73	183.8	97	192.5
2	152.0	26	131.3	50	152.3	74	175.6	98	191.3
3	147.8	27	129.4	51	174.2	75	162.3	99	184.8
4	115.7	28	127.7	52	171.0	76	155.1	100	190.7
5	109.0	29	155.8	53	180.0	77	164.8	101	192.0
6	98.3	30	185.4	54	171.2	78	161.1	102	183.9
7	137.3	31	190.5	55	171.6	79	189.7	103	180.7
8	149.3	32	177.5	56	164.0	80	207.1	104	168.6
9	148.1	33	180.7	57	163.8	81	243.3	105	161.8
10	170.9	34	172.5	58	175.8	82	240.2	106	157.2
11	147.5	35	179.1	59	177.8	83	261.1	107	175.0
12	151.5	36	196.0	60	191.1	84	220.2	108	178.0
13	128.9	37	207.8	61	184.4	85	215.3	109	180.2
14	116.4	38	211.4	62	190.3	86	208.6	110	175.7
15	117.9	39	227.7	63	195.0	87	206.3	111	178.7
16	122.4	40	274.3	64	190.1	88	223.1	112	187.2
17	118.8	41	250.9	65	189.4	89	221.1	113	183.9
18	120.1	42	215.5	66	210.9	90	199.0	114	176.1
19	122.3	43	168.5	67	204.8	91	202.6	115	191.3
20	137.0	44	140.0	68	189.2	92	198.5	116	234.7
21	137.4	45	144.8	69	194.6	93	192.3	117	232.7
22	128.6	46	134.9	70	183.1	94	180.6	118	227.5
23	119.4	47	162.9	71	182.1	95	178.8	119	225.1
24	124.3	48	161.6	72	185.0	96	187.0	120	218.0

7.3   The accompanying table shows 168 monthly observations on the price in cents per bushel of No. 2 yellow corn at Chicago, Illinois. Fit autoregressive models of all orders up to five. Select one of these models for forecasting, and predict price for the next six months.

t	X_t	t	X_t	t	X_t	t	X_t	t	X_t
1	126	35	131	69	289	103	233	137	342
2	126	36	166	70	279	104	222	138	343
3	125	37	159	71	254	105	215	139	351
4	129	38	163	72	258	106	220	140	319
5	132	39	158	73	267	107	226	141	277
6	136	40	166	74	271	108	224	142	268
7	139	41	206	75	272	109	227	143	257
8	137	42	253	76	266	110	234	144	242
9	155	43	218	77	280	111	238	145	264
10	144	44	240	78	295	112	252	146	261
11	142	45	249	79	299	113	262	147	263
12	153	46	251	80	283	114	268	148	269
13	159	47	250	81	283	115	305	149	277
14	160	48	275	82	251	116	284	150	273
15	156	49	293	83	233	117	274	151	256
16	153	50	305	84	248	118	280	152	244
17	151	51	301	85	253	119	259	153	211
18	158	52	266	86	251	120	271	154	209
19	150	53	271	87	253	121	252	155	236
20	129	54	289	88	255	122	266	156	241
21	117	55	319	89	237	123	261	157	248
22	112	56	377	90	222	124	261	158	281
23	109	57	350	91	205	125	267	159	291
24	126	58	378	92	184	126	265	160	320
25	123	59	358	93	184	127	311	161	323
26	121	60	359	94	181	128	341	162	329
27	123	61	333	95	212	129	347	163	328
28	125	62	311	96	220	130	346	164	356
29	128	63	293	97	220	131	333	165	355
30	128	64	285	98	221	132	344	166	349
31	130	65	284	99	235	133	359	167	361
32	129	66	285	100	257	134	346	168	332
33	139	67	292	101	253	135	343		
34	131	68	313	102	251	136	344		

7.4   The time series X_t is generated by the first-order autoregressive model

$$X_t = C + \phi_1 X_{t-1} + a_t$$

Show that, standing at time n, the forecast of X_{n+h} is given by

$$\hat{X}_n(h) = (1 + \phi_1 + \cdots + \phi_1^{h-1})C + \phi_1^h X_n$$

Discuss the behavior of this predictor when $|\phi_1| < 1$, as h becomes large.

7.5 The accompanying exhibit shows the first 10 sample autocorrelations and sample partial autocorrelations for a nonseasonal stationary time series of 120 observations. Discuss the problem of selecting an appropriate model to fit to this series.

Autocorrelations:

```
      Auto- Stand.
 Lag  Corr.  Err. -1  -.75  -.5 -.25   0   .25   .5   .75   1
                   +----+----+----+----+----+----+----+----+
   1  .754  .090                      . :***.***********
   2  .613  .090                      . :***.********
   3  .482  .089                      . :***.******
   4  .405  .089                      . :***.****
   5  .346  .089                      . :***.***
   6  .383  .088                      . :***.****
   7  .316  .088                      . :***.**
   8  .262  .087                      . :**.**
   9  .179  .087                      . :**.*
  10  .155  .087                      . :***
```

Partial Autocorrelations:

```
      Pr-Aut- Stand.
 Lag  Corr.   Err. -1  -.75  -.5 -.25   0   .25   .5   .75   1
                    +----+----+----+----+----+----+----+----+
   1   .754  .091                      . :***.***********
   2   .102  .091                      . :** .
   3  -.024  .091                      . * .
   4   .055  .091                      . :* .
   5   .029  .091                      . :* .
   6   .209  .091                      . :**** 
   7  -.127  .091                      .***: .
   8  -.040  .091                      . *: .
   9  -.072  .091                      . *: .
  10   .062  .091                      . :* .
```

7.6 The accompanying exhibit shows the first 10 sample autocorrelations and sample partial autocorrelations for a nonseasonal stationary time series of 120 observations. Discuss the problem of selecting an appropriate model to fit to this series.

Autocorrelations:

```
      Auto- Stand.
 Lag  Corr.  Err. -1  -.75  -.5 -.25   0   .25   .5   .75   1
                   +----+----+----+----+----+----+----+----+
   1  -.239  .090               *.***:    .
   2  -.264  .090               *.***:    .
   3   .063  .089                  . :*    .
   4  -.156  .089                .***:    .
   5   .019  .089                  . *    .
   6   .065  .088                  . :*    .
   7   .008  .088                  . *    .
   8   .125  .087                  . :***
   9  -.091  .087                .**: .
  10   .003  .087                  . *    .
```

Partial Autocorrelations:

Lag	Pr-Aut- Corr.	Stand. Err.	-1	-.75	-.5	-.25	0	.25	.5	.75	1
			+----+----+----+----+----+----+----+----+								
1	-.239	.091				*.***:		.			
2	-.341	.091				***.***:		.			
3	-.123	.091				. **:		.			
4	-.321	.091				**.***:		.			
5	-.207	.091				****:		.			
6	-.209	.091				****:		.			
7	-.161	.091				.***:		.			
8	.003	.091				. *		.			
9	-.091	.091				. **:		.			
10	.033	.091				. :*		.			

7.7 The accompanying exhibit shows the first 10 sample autocorrelations and sample partial autocorrelations for a nonseasonal stationary time series of 120 observations. Discuss the problem of selecting an appropriate model to fit to this series.

Autocorrelations:

Lag	Auto- Corr.	Stand. Err.	-1	-.75	-.5	-.25	0	.25	.5	.75	1
			+----+----+----+----+----+----+----+----+								
1	.748	.090				.	:***.***********				
2	.750	.090				.	:***.***********				
3	.712	.089				.	:***.**********				
4	.600	.089				.	:***.********				
5	.575	.089				.	:***.*******				
6	.522	.088				.	:***.******				
7	.478	.088				.	:***.******				
8	.456	.087				.	:**.******				
9	.456	.087				.	:**.******				
10	.373	.087				.	:**.****				

Partial Autocorrelations:

Lag	Pr-Aut- Corr.	Stand. Err.	-1	-.75	-.5	-.25	0	.25	.5	.75	1
			+----+----+----+----+----+----+----+----+								
1	.748	.091				.	:***.***********				
2	.433	.091				.	:***.*****				
3	.196	.091				.	:****				
4	-.149	.091				.***:		.			
5	-.019	.091				. *		.			
6	.022	.091				. *		.			
7	.041	.091				. :*		.			
8	.035	.091				. :*		.			
9	.116	.091				. :**		.			
10	-.142	.091				.***:		.			

7.8 Fit an appropriate nonseasonal ARIMA model to the data of Exercise 7.1 on building expenditures, and use the fitted model to obtain forecasts for the next six years.

7.9 Fit an appropriate nonseasonal ARIMA model to the series of Exercise 7.2 on soybean meal price, and use the fitted model to obtain forecasts for the next six months.

7.10 Fit an appropriate nonseasonal ARIMA model to the data of Exercise 7.3 on corn price, and use the fitted model to derive forecasts for the next six months.

7.11 The accompanying table shows 160 quarterly observations on U.S. real gross national product. Fit an appropriate nonseasonal ARIMA model to the logarithms of these data, and obtain forecasts for the next four quarters.

t	X_t	t	X_t	t	X_t	t	X_t
1	1148.2	41	1671.6	81	2408.6	121	3233.4
2	1181.0	42	1666.8	82	2406.5	122	3157.0
3	1225.3	43	1668.4	83	2435.8	123	3159.1
4	1260.2	44	1654.1	84	2413.8	124	3199.2
5	1286.6	45	1671.3	85	2478.6	125	3261.1
6	1320.4	46	1692.1	86	2478.4	126	3250.2
7	1349.8	47	1716.3	87	2491.1	127	3264.6
8	1356.0	48	1754.9	88	2491.0	128	3219.0
9	1369.2	49	1777.9	89	2545.6	129	3170.4
10	1365.9	50	1796.4	90	2595.1	130	3179.9
11	1378.2	51	1813.1	91	2622.1	131	3154.5
12	1406.8	52	1810.1	92	2671.3	132	3159.3
13	1431.4	53	1834.6	93	2734.0	133	3186.6
14	1444.9	54	1860.0	94	2741.0	134	3258.3
15	1438.2	55	1892.5	95	2738.3	135	3306.4
16	1426.6	56	1906.1	96	2762.8	136	3365.1
17	1406.8	57	1948.7	97	2747.4	137	3451.7
18	1401.2	58	1965.4	98	2755.2	138	3498.0
19	1418.0	59	1985.2	99	2719.3	139	3520.6
20	1438.8	60	1993.7	100	2695.4	140	3535.2
21	1469.6	61	2036.9	101	2642.7	141	3577.5
22	1485.7	62	2066.4	102	2669.6	142	3599.2
23	1505.5	63	2099.3	103	2714.9	143	3635.8
24	1518.7	64	2147.6	104	2752.7	144	3662.4
25	1515.7	65	2190.1	105	2804.4	145	2721.1
26	1522.6	66	2195.8	106	2816.9	146	3704.6
27	1523.7	67	2218.3	107	2828.6	147	3712.4
28	1540.6	68	2229.2	108	2856.8	148	3733.6
29	1553.3	69	2241.8	109	2896.0	149	3781.2
30	1552.4	70	2255.2	110	2942.7	150	3820.3
31	1561.5	71	2287.7	111	3001.8	151	3858.9
32	1537.3	72	2300.6	112	2994.1	152	3920.7
33	1506.1	73	2327.3	113	3020.5	153	3970.2

t	X_t	t	X_t	t	X_t	t	X_t
34	1514.2	74	2366.9	114	3115.9	154	4005.8
35	1550.0	75	2385.3	115	3142.6	155	4032.1
36	1586.7	76	2383.0	116	3181.6	156	4059.3
37	1606.4	77	2416.5	117	3181.7	157	4095.7
38	1637.0	78	2419.8	118	3178.7	158	4112.2
39	1629.5	79	2433.2	119	3207.4	159	4129.7
40	1643.4	80	2423.5	120	3201.3	160	4133.2

7.12 The accompanying table shows an index of the prices received by farmers for all crops over a period of 62 years. Fit an appropriate nonseasonal ARIMA model to the logarithms of these data, and predict prices for the next six years.

t	X_t	t	X_t	t	X_t	t	X_t	t	X_t
1	121	14	98	27	263	40	222	53	394
2	136	15	103	28	255	41	227	54	504
3	156	16	108	29	224	42	232	55	452
4	159	17	118	30	233	43	240	56	443
5	164	18	80	31	265	44	239	57	433
6	139	19	82	32	267	45	230	58	456
7	134	20	90	33	240	46	238	59	501
8	142	21	108	34	242	47	225	60	539
9	135	22	145	35	231	48	225	61	580
10	115	23	187	36	235	49	217	62	524
11	75	24	199	37	225	50	225		
12	57	25	202	38	223	51	242		
13	71	26	228	39	222	52	257		

7.13 The accompanying table shows the United Kingdom–United States exchange rate, in terms of dollars per pound, over a period of 144 months. Fit an appropriate nonseasonal ARIMA model to this series, and predict the exchange rate for the next six months.

t	X_t	t	X_t	t	X_t	t	X_t	t	X_t
1	2.359	30	2.282	59	1.853	88	2.221	117	1.714
2	2.446	31	2.187	60	1.924	89	2.321	118	1.696
3	2.474	32	2.116	61	1.924	90	2.331	119	1.635
4	2.485	33	2.112	62	1.942	91	2.369	120	1.616
5	2.533	34	2.052	63	1.912	92	2.379	121	1.576
6	2.574	35	2.050	64	1.851	93	2.401	122	1.532
7	2.528	36	2.023	65	1.824	94	2.411	123	1.490
8	2.473	37	2.028	66	1.837	95	2.403	124	1.541
9	2.417	38	2.023	67	1.890	96	2.348	125	1.574
10	2.433	39	1.960	68	1.945	97	2.411	126	1.554
11	2.387	40	1.848	69	1.962	98	2.296	127	1.530
12	2.319	41	1.794	70	2.004	99	2.236	128	1.503

t	X_t	t	X_t	t	X_t	t	X_t	t	X_t
13	2.233	42	1.759	71	1.968	100	2.187	129	1.494
14	2.275	43	1.790	72	1.994	101	2.088	130	1.495
15	2.356	44	1.784	73	2.004	102	1.985	131	1.478
16	2.383	45	1.722	74	2.012	103	1.876	132	1.431
17	2.416	46	1.631	75	2.044	104	1.828	133	1.407
18	2.395	47	1.641	76	2.067	105	1.821	134	1.441
19	2.391	48	1.679	77	2.067	106	1.846	135	1.453
20	2.344	49	1.715	78	2.118	107	1.894	136	1.425
21	2.336	50	1.713	79	2.266	108	1.911	137	1.390
22	2.335	51	1.719	80	2.243	109	1.885	138	1.374
23	2.324	52	1.719	81	2.181	110	1.847	139	1.324
24	2.333	53	1.720	82	2.139	111	1.807	140	1.315
25	2.362	54	1.725	83	2.146	112	1.774	141	1.257
26	2.394	55	1.741	84	2.197	113	1.811	142	1.226
27	2.438	56	1.744	85	2.264	114	1.758	143	1.239
28	2.374	57	1.766	86	2.297	115	1.732	144	1.183
29	2.320	58	1.820	87	2.213	116	1.728		

7.14   The time series X_t is generated by the ARIMA(0, 1, 1) model

$$X_t - X_{t-1} = a_t - \theta_1 a_{t-1}$$

Show that, standing at time n, the optimal forecasts of $\hat{X}_n(h)$ are the same for all $h = 1, 2, \ldots$

7.15   The time series X_t is generated by the ARIMA(0, 2, 2) model

$$(1 - B)^2 X_t = (1 - \theta_1 B - \theta_2 B^2) a_t$$

Let $\hat{X}_n(h)$ denote the optimal forecast of X_{n+h} made at time n. Show that

$$\hat{X}_n(h) = 2\hat{X}_n(h - 1) - \hat{X}_n(h - 2)   h = 3, 4, \ldots$$

Hence show that the forecast function is a linear trend

$$\hat{X}_n(h) = \alpha + \beta h   h = 1, 2, 3, \ldots$$

where

$$\alpha = 2\hat{X}_n(1) - \hat{X}_n(2)   \beta = \hat{X}_n(2) - \hat{X}_n(1)$$

7.16   The accompanying exhibit shows the first 40 sample autocorrelations and sample partial autocorrelations for a monthly stationary time series of 240 observations. Discuss the problem of selecting an appropriate model to fit to this series.

Autocorrelations:

```
      Auto- Stand.
Lag   Corr.  Err.    -1  -.75  -.5 -.25   0   .25  .5   .75   1
                      +----+----+----+----+----+----+----+----+
  1   .510   .064                         .  :**.*******
  2   .186   .064                         .  :**.*
  3   .044   .064                         .  :*.
  4  -.104   .064                       .**:  .
  5  -.172   .064                      ***:  .
  6  -.161   .063                      ***:  .
  7  -.123   .063                       .**:  .
  8  -.067   .063                        . *:  .
  9   .091   .063                         .  :**.
 10   .201   .063                         .  :**.*
 11   .325   .063                         .  :**.****
 12   .532   .063                         .  :**.********
 13   .194   .063                         .  :**.*
 14  -.080   .062                       **:  .
 15  -.189   .062                     **.*:  .
 16  -.180   .062                     **.*:  .
 17  -.203   .062                     **.*:  .
 18  -.146   .062                      *.*:  .
 19  -.062   .062                       .*:  .
 20  -.003   .062                       . *  .
 21   .096   .061                        .  :**
 22   .169   .061                        .  :*.*
 23   .179   .061                        .  :*.**
 24   .196   .061                        .  :*.**
 25  -.009   .061                        .  *  .
 26  -.183   .061                     **.*:  .
 27  -.255   .061                    ***.*:  .
 28  -.211   .060                     **.*:  .
 29  -.235   .060                    ***.*:  .
 30  -.131   .060                      *.*:  .
 31  -.017   .060                       . *  .
 32   .017   .060                       . *  .
 33   .046   .060                        .  :*.
 34   .068   .060                        .  :*.
 35   .033   .059                        .  :*.
 36  -.015   .059                       . *  .
 37  -.144   .059                      *.*:  .
 38  -.174   .059                      *.*:  .
 39  -.166   .059                      *.*:  .
 40  -.092   .059                       **:  .
```

Partial Autocorrelations:

```
      Pr-Aut- Stand.
Lag   Corr.   Err.  -1  -.75  -.5  -.25   0   .25   .5   .75   1
                    +----+----+----+----+----+----+----+----+
  1    .510    .065                         . :**.*******
  2   -.099    .065                         .**:   .
  3   -.013    .065                         . *    .
  4   -.144    .065                         ***:   .
  5   -.068    .065                         . *:   .
  6   -.036    .065                         . *    .
  7   -.020    .065                         . *    .
  8   -.001    .065                         . *    .
  9    .149    .065                         . :***
 10    .095    .065                         . :**.
 11    .211    .065                         . :**.*
 12    .383    .065                         . :**.*****
 13   -.355    .065                    ****.**:   .
 14   -.098    .065                         .**:   .
 15   -.103    .065                         .**:   .
 16    .114    .065                         . :**.
 17   -.066    .065                         . *:   .
 18    .023    .065                         . *    .
 19   -.021    .065                         . *    .
 20    .022    .065                         . *    .
 21   -.056    .065                         . *:   .
 22    .020    .065                         . *    .
 23   -.049    .065                         . *:   .
 24   -.064    .065                         . *:   .
 25    .016    .065                         . *    .
 26   -.005    .065                         . *    .
 27   -.030    .065                         . *:   .
 28   -.098    .065                         .**:   .
 29   -.115    .065                         .**:   .
 30    .053    .065                         . :*   .
 31    .017    .065                         . *    .
 32   -.064    .065                         . *:   .
 33   -.055    .065                         . *:   .
 34   -.052    .065                         . *:   .
 35   -.026    .065                         . *:   .
 36   -.037    .065                         . *:   .
 37   -.065    .065                         . *:   .
 38    .094    .065                         . :**.
 39    .030    .065                         . :*  .
 40    .041    .065                         . :*  .
```

7.17 The accompanying exhibit shows the first 40 sample autocorrelations and sample partial autocorrelations for a monthly stationary time series of 240 observations. Discuss the problem of selecting an appropriate model to fit to this series.

Autocorrelations:

Lag	Auto-Corr.	Stand. Err.	Plot
			−1 −.75 −.5 −.25 0 .25 .5 .75 1
			+----+----+----+----+----+----+----+----+
1	−.443	.064	******.**: .
2	.086	.064	. :**.
3	−.007	.064	. * .
4	−.161	.064	***: .
5	.074	.064	. :* .
6	−.023	.063	. * .
7	−.030	.063	. *: .
8	.126	.063	. :***
9	.022	.063	. * .
10	−.068	.063	. *: .
11	.221	.063	. :**.*
12	−.467	.063	******.**: .
13	.198	.063	. :**.*
14	−.041	.062	.*: .
15	−.066	.062	.*: .
16	.172	.062	. :*.*
17	−.099	.062	**: .
18	.052	.062	. :*.
19	−.018	.062	. * .
20	−.024	.062	. * .
21	−.051	.061	.*: .
22	.060	.061	. :*.
23	−.107	.061	**: .
24	.091	.061	. :**
25	.027	.061	. :*.
26	−.072	.061	.*: .
27	.150	.061	. :*.*
28	−.119	.060	**: .
29	.043	.060	. :*.
30	.003	.060	. * .
31	−.048	.060	.*: .
32	.019	.060	. * .
33	.021	.060	. * .
34	−.019	.060	. * .
35	.128	.059	. :*.*
36	−.097	.059	**: .
37	−.017	.059	. * .
38	.067	.059	. :*.
39	−.065	.059	.*: .
40	.037	.059	. :*.

```
Partial Autocorrelations:

    Pr-Aut-  Stand.
Lag  Corr.   Err.  -1  -.75  -.5 -.25   0   .25  .5   .75   1
                   +----+----+----+----+----+----+----+----+
  1  -.443   .065            ******.**:   .
  2  -.137   .065               ***:   .
  3  -.032   .065                . *:   .
  4  -.210   .065              *.**:   .
  5  -.121   .065                .**:   .
  6  -.063   .065                . *:   .
  7  -.096   .065                .**:   .
  8   .050.  .065                . :* .
  9   .139   .065                . :***
 10   .012   .065                . * .
 11   .270   .065                . :**.**
 12  -.294   .065             ***.**:   .
 13  -.162   .065               ***:   .
 14  -.062   .065                . *:   .
 15  -.125   .065                .**:   .
 16  -.043   .065                . *:   .
 17  -.070   .065                . *:   .
 18  -.035   .065                . *:   .
 19  -.075   .065                .**:   .
 20   .039   .065                . :* .
 21  -.002   .065                . * .
 22   .020   .065                . * .
 23   .045   .065                . :* .
 24  -.175   .065               ***:   .
 25  -.020   .065                . * .
 26  -.089   .065                .**:   .
 27   .019   .065                . * .
 28   .040   .065                . :* .
 29  -.008   .065                . * .
 30   .044   .065                . :* .
 31  -.031   .065                . *:   .
 32   .004   .065                . * .
 33  -.024   .065                . * .
 34   .006   .065                . * .
 35   .137   .065                . :***
 36  -.092   .065              .**:   .
 37  -.020   .065                . * .
 38  -.028   .065                . *:   .
 39   .113   .065                . :**.
 40   .070   .065                . :* .
```

7.18 The accompanying table shows an index of industrial production
      in the United States over 168 months. Fit an appropriate seasonal
      ARIMA model to these data, and predict the index for the next 12
      months.

t	X_t	t	X_t	t	X_t	t	X_t	t	X_t
1	106.5	35	125.2	69	125.9	103	141.9	137	152.6
2	109.1	36	121.8	70	125.4	104	146.9	138	156.5
3	109.4	37	122.7	71	123.8	105	152.0	139	151.0
4	108.8	38	128.1	72	119.8	106	152.6	140	155.4
5	108.6	39	128.8	73	122.1	107	149.7	141	155.8
6	110.8	40	128.6	74	127.1	108	146.0	142	152.4
7	104.5	41	129.6	75	128.6	109	146.9	143	146.4
8	108.0	42	133.0	76	128.7	110	152.7	144	139.1
9	110.4	43	126.4	77	129.9	111	154.5	145	136.6
10	108.0	44	130.3	78	133.5	112	151.3	146	142.7
11	105.1	45	134.8	79	126.0	113	152.8	147	142.0
12	104.1	46	135.3	80	131.7	114	156.9	148	139.4
13	105.5	47	132.9	81	134.6	115	149.0	149	138.5
14	108.3	48	126.7	82	134.0	116	152.7	150	141.8
15	108.6	49	126.3	83	132.2	117	157.1	151	136.2
16	108.8	50	129.8	84	128.1	118	156.2	152	140.5
17	109.5	51	130.8	85	128.8	119	152.4	153	141.2
18	112.5	52	129.9	86	133.6	120	147.7	154	138.5
19	105.4	53	131.7	87	135.7	121	148.0	155	134.8
20	108.8	54	135.3	88	136.2	122	152.7	156	131.2
21	113.5	55	127.3	89	137.2	123	153.2	157	133.5
22	113.9	56	131.4	90	141.5	124	148.1	158	138.1
23	111.6	57	135.5	91	134.1	125	143.5	159	140.5
24	108.5	58	133.1	92	138.2	126	145.0	160	141.9
25	115.5	59	125.5	93	142.4	127	137.2	161	143.9
26	115.6	60	114.9	94	142.7	128	142.9	162	149.7
27	116.8	61	111.8	95	139.5	129	148.6	163	147.0
28	118.7	62	113.0	96	134.9	130	150.2	164	153.3
29	118.4	63	111.8	97	134.8	131	149.5	165	158.4
30	121.8	64	113.0	98	139.6	132	146.3	166	158.4
31	114.2	65	113.8	99	141.4	133	146.4	167	154.7
32	120.5	66	119.2	100	144.2	134	151.7	168	151.4
33	125.5	67	114.5	101	144.2	135	152.7		
34	126.8	68	121.4	102	148.8	136	151.5		

7.19 The accompanying table shows 132 monthly observations on total consumer credit outstanding, in billions of dollars, in the United States. Fit an appropriate seasonal ARIMA model to the logarithms of these data, and predict credit outstanding for the next 12 months.

t	X_t	t	X_t	t	X_t	t	X_t	t	X_t
1	116.9	28	154.5	55	181.2	82	263.2	109	310.6
2	116.7	29	156.6	56	183.9	83	267.1	110	309.1
3	117.4	30	158.7	57	186.3	84	273.6	111	310.7
4	119.1	31	160.4	58	187.6	85	273.8	112	313.4
5	120.9	32	162.8	59	189.3	86	274.8	113	315.4
6	123.3	33	163.6	60	193.5	87	277.3	114	318.6
7	124.5	34	163.5	61	194.3	88	281.2	115	320.8
8	126.7	35	163.5	62	194.5	89	285.7	116	324.7
9	128.0	36	164.6	63	197.1	90	289.9	117	328.3
10	128.9	37	162.6	64	200.6	91	293.2	118	328.8
11	130.5	38	161.5	65	204.1	92	298.0	119	328.9
12	133.2	39	160.1	66	208.5	93	302.0	120	333.0
13	135.0	40	160.2	67	211.6	94	304.4	121	328.8

t	X_t	t	X_t	t	X_t	t	X_t	t	X_t
14	135.4	41	160.8	68	216.1	95	307.4	122	327.4
15	136.7	42	162.0	69	219.3	96	312.0	123	327.1
16	138.6	43	164.1	70	221.6	97	311.0	124	328.3
17	141.1	44	166.0	71	224.8	98	310.1	125	329.3
18	143.9	45	167.3	72	230.5	99	309.1	126	331.9
19	146.0	46	168.2	73	229.8	100	307.8	127	332.5
20	148.6	47	169.1	74	230.2	101	305.7	128	333.8
21	149.9	48	172.4	75	233.2	102	304.4	129	335.9
22	151.4	49	170.9	76	236.9	103	303.9	130	334.9
23	153.0	50	170.6	77	242.3	104	305.7	131	337.0
24	155.1	51	171.2	78	248.6	105	306.9	132	343.4
25	154.1	52	173.5	79	252.5	106	307.2		
26	153.6	53	175.5	80	257.6	107	308.1		
27	153.2	54	178.7	81	261.1	108	313.4		

7.20   The accompanying table shows 156 monthly observations on end-of-month retailers' inventories in durable goods stores, in billions of dollars. Fit an appropriate seasonal ARIMA model to this series, and forecast inventories for the next 12 months.

t	X_t	t	X_t	t	X_t	t	X_t	t	X_t
1	17.83	33	22.04	65	31.79	97	43.61	129	51.87
2	18.15	34	22.69	66	31.68	98	44.65	130	53.90
3	18.62	35	23.74	67	31.11	99	45.99	131	55.44
4	18.94	36	23.82	68	29.86	100	47.21	132	53.82
5	18.87	37	24.23	69	30.69	101	47.16	133	54.54
6	19.05	38	25.16	70	31.53	102	46.88	134	55.06
7	18.94	39	25.99	71	32.07	103	46.40	135	55.70
8	17.64	40	26.84	72	31.64	104	44.76	136	56.49
9	17.68	41	27.38	73	31.86	105	45.51	137	57.62
10	17.34	42	27.72	74	32.65	106	47.69	138	58.49
11	17.25	43	27.48	75	33.85	107	49.35	139	58.69
12	17.48	44	25.55	76	34.43	108	49.55	140	57.18
13	18.16	45	26.01	77	34.46	109	50.88	141	57.17
14	19.24	46	26.84	78	34.68	110	51.58	142	59.21
15	20.37	47	27.85	79	34.35	111	53.04	143	60.45
16	20.93	48	27.64	80	32.82	112	54.11	144	58.44
17	21.39	49	27.96	81	33.90	113	55.35	145	57.87
18	21.48	50	28.65	82	34.79	114	55.70	146	57.37
19	21.19	51	29.30	83	36.03	115	56.03	147	58.34
20	20.18	52	29.56	84	35.90	116	53.16	148	58.35
21	20.98	53	29.79	85	36.35	117	51.83	149	57.93
22	21.24	54	29.82	86	37.04	118	53.73	150	58.98
23	21.48	55	28.89	87	38.38	119	55.07	151	59.01
24	21.27	56	27.32	88	38.67	120	53.20	152	58.62
25	21.59	57	28.31	89	38.86	121	52.50	153	59.86
26	22.17	58	30.15	90	39.02	122	53.35	154	60.94
27	22.95	59	31.75	91	38.83	123	54.57	155	60.81
28	23.43	60	31.59	92	37.23	124	55.15	156	58.90
29	23.73	61	31.48	93	37.95	125	54.55		
30	23.53	62	30.82	94	39.15	126	54.05		
31	22.68	63	31.25	95	40.43	127	53.10		
32	21.13	64	31.59	96	40.37	128	51.61		

7.21 The accompanying table shows 168 monthly observations on an index of newspaper advertising. Fit an appropriate seasonal ARIMA model, and obtain forecasts for the next 12 months.

t	X_t	t	X_t	t	X_t	t	X_t	t	X_t
1	91.8	35	113.6	69	83.6	103	68.2	137	116.6
2	88.8	36	102.1	70	98.9	104	76.0	138	111.1
3	67.7	37	73.2	71	100.3	105	76.6	139	99.8
4	111.4	38	71.7	72	90.3	106	86.6	140	92.7
5	113.3	39	89.9	73	82.2	107	91.4	141	93.8
6	105.1	40	92.2	74	80.0	108	78.3	142	108.0
7	92.3	41	91.6	75	91.2	109	78.4	143	123.3
8	100.7	42	82.8	76	97.8	110	86.0	144	109.1
9	100.5	43	73.4	77	96.6	111	91.8	145	97.5
10	110.1	44	79.2	78	89.7	112	95.3	146	99.6
11	113.3	45	81.8	79	84.5	113	102.8	147	114.8
12	104.6	46	88.8	80	84.1	114	93.3	148	121.4
13	85.1	47	98.0	81	87.8	115	79.6	149	119.6
14	86.6	48	83.3	82	91.1	116	88.7	150	111.1
15	103.1	49	77.4	83	95.2	117	92.9	151	102.9
16	101.0	50	74.7	84	87.3	118	106.7	152	95.8
17	111.2	51	85.7	85	76.0	119	103.3	153	100.1
18	100.7	52	89.4	86	73.6	120	96.2	154	102.0
19	89.7	53	92.7	87	88.3	121	91.9	155	124.2
20	99.5	54	84.5	88	82.1	122	83.3	156	110.0
21	104.5	55	73.9	89	87.0	123	104.2	157	96.6
22	112.1	56	74.9	90	86.5	124	102.9	158	101.0
23	111.7	57	77.4	91	71.3	125	115.5	159	116.4
24	111.5	58	90.2	92	74.3	126	104.3	160	103.6
25	90.0	59	89.6	93	79.0	127	93.8	161	108.3
26	87.8	60	82.4	94	82.2	128	96.6	162	105.4
27	105.9	61	85.1	95	80.5	129	102.2	163	88.8
28	103.5	62	83.0	96	76.3	130	119.3	164	101.6
29	112.4	63	94.9	97	73.0	131	118.2	165	96.9
30	103.7	64	100.4	98	72.2	132	105.8	166	109.1
31	93.1	65	97.7	99	83.9	133	97.9	167	117.3
32	99.8	66	93.2	100	79.8	134	91.3	168	98.8
33	99.2	67	83.8	101	83.5	135	109.9		
34	109.7	68	81.6	102	84.4	136	121.7		

7.22 The accompanying table shows 42 quarterly observations on sales of Vulcan Materials in millions of dollars. Fit an appropriate seasonal ARIMA model to this series, and forecast sales for the next four quarters.

t	X_t	t	X_t	t	X_t
1	167.97	15	266.86	29	202.70
2	205.20	16	254.47	30	284.45
3	213.14	17	199.52	31	298.58
4	196.98	18	261.13	32	267.44

t	X_t	t	X_t	t	X_t
5	164.29	19	272.19	33	217.51
6	187.73	20	238.96	34	293.72
7	198.31	21	157.54	35	307.24
8	169.08	22	218.72	36	257.74
9	154.58	23	227.87	37	232.02
10	199.89	24	197.68	38	295.68
11	233.83	25	168.86	39	306.60
12	232.22	26	237.95	40	271.01
13	202.40	27	270.11	41	197.04
14	259.15	28	246.35	42	266.40

7.23   The accompanying table shows 120 monthly observations on the total number of persons, in thousands, employed in the wholesale distribution of beer and ale (SIC 5181). Fit a suitable seasonal ARIMA model to this series, and forecast employment in this industry for the next 12 months.

t	X_t	t	X_t	t	X_t	t	X_t	t	X_t	t	X_t
1	86.8	25	91.1	49	91.2	73	92.2	97	91.7		
2	86.9	26	91.6	50	91.1	74	92.5	98	92.0		
3	87.2	27	91.6	51	91.5	75	92.7	99	92.5		
4	87.9	28	91.9	52	92.2	76	93.6	100	93.6		
5	89.6	29	93.4	53	93.4	77	95.1	101	95.2		
6	91.3	30	95.9	54	95.7	78	97.6	102	97.6		
7	93.0	31	97.6	55	96.3	79	98.2	103	98.2		
8	92.1	32	97.0	56	96.2	80	97.7	104	98.0		
9	90.4	33	94.7	57	93.6	81	95.7	105	96.3		
10	89.6	34	93.5	58	92.8	82	94.3	106	95.9		
11	89.4	35	93.4	59	92.8	83	93.7	107	95.9		
12	89.6	36	92.9	60	92.3	84	93.9	108	96.1		
13	87.2	37	91.0	61	92.0	85	92.8	109	93.9		
14	86.7	38	90.4	62	91.7	86	91.9	110	93.8		
15	88.7	39	90.9	63	92.2	87	93.1	111	94.8		
16	88.8	40	91.6	64	93.1	88	93.2	112	95.4		
17	90.6	41	93.2	65	94.8	89	94.2	113	97.0		
18	92.5	42	95.6	66	96.6	90	97.2	114	99.9		
19	93.3	43	96.6	67	97.4	91	98.0	115	101.2		
20	93.8	44	96.3	68	97.1	92	97.6	116	100.7		
21	92.3	45	93.7	69	95.3	93	95.2	117	98.9		
22	92.3	46	92.2	70	93.6	94	94.1	118	98.3		
23	92.1	47	92.7	71	93.5	95	93.6	119	98.0		
24	92.6	48	92.6	72	93.7	96	93.1	120	98.1		

7.24   The accompanying table shows 240 monthly observations on the index of industrially generated electricity used in the commercial printing industry. Fit a suitable seasonal ARIMA model to the logarithms of this data, and predict electricity usage of this industry for the next 12 months.

t	X_t	t	X_t	t	X_t	t	X_t	t	X_t
1	40.6	49	43.2	97	56.2	145	67.8	193	95.7
2	41.7	50	43.7	98	58.4	146	69.5	194	99.1
3	42.4	51	44.6	99	58.3	147	70.2	195	96.4
4	43.0	52	45.0	100	57.3	148	69.0	196	100.2
5	45.0	53	46.7	101	59.0	149	72.6	197	100.8
6	48.6	54	50.0	102	63.8	150	79.5	198	108.2
7	49.7	55	55.9	103	69.2	151	86.8	199	117.8
8	53.3	56	54.0	104	73.4	152	90.2	200	126.4
9	54.3	57	57.6	105	73.9	153	88.6	201	122.0
10	51.1	58	52.2	106	67.0	154	83.3	202	114.5
11	47.7	59	49.2	107	62.6	155	78.8	203	108.5
12	44.4	60	47.0	108	59.9	156	74.7	204	103.0
13	40.8	61	45.8	109	57.4	157	71.2	205	101.0
14	41.3	62	47.6	110	60.4	158	73.9	206	102.5
15	43.3	63	47.1	111	58.7	159	74.2	207	103.8
16	45.1	64	49.1	112	59.5	160	76.4	208	106.8
17	46.3	65	49.6	113	61.1	161	79.3	209	106.4
18	50.2	66	54.6	114	68.1	162	84.2	210	117.8
19	53.2	67	56.2	115	74.0	163	86.1	211	118.7
20	55.6	68	60.5	116	75.9	164	94.8	212	128.2
21	55.4	69	58.2	117	74.6	165	93.5	213	128.7
22	52.6	70	54.9	118	69.0	166	86.0	214	115.9
23	47.5	71	50.6	119	64.4	167	82.3	215	112.8
24	44.4	72	48.3	120	63.1	168	80.1	216	104.6
25	40.7	73	48.2	121	60.9	169	77.8	217	107.2
26	41.5	74	48.2	122	62.9	170	77.7	218	109.1
27	41.9	75	48.4	123	62.8	171	78.8	219	110.4
28	43.6	76	49.9	124	62.7	172	81.7	220	108.1
29	45.2	77	51.2	125	64.9	173	82.1	221	113.5
30	48.6	78	57.0	126	69.3	174	91.9	222	119.8
31	50.5	79	61.6	127	75.0	175	99.3	223	128.4
32	52.0	80	63.5	128	78.0	176	103.0	224	132.1
33	53.7	81	66.3	129	79.3	177	102.4	225	131.7
34	47.6	82	59.1	130	71.5	178	97.8	226	126.3
35	46.4	83	55.1	131	67.9	179	91.6	227	117.2
36	43.1	84	52.3	132	62.3	180	90.1	228	113.4
37	41.4	85	53.0	133	63.1	181	85.0	229	109.6
38	42.7	86	54.9	134	65.5	182	86.7	230	108.0
39	42.1	87	54.1	135	65.1	183	87.7	231	109.6
40	42.4	88	57.1	136	65.7	184	89.9	232	110.6
41	43.9	89	58.8	137	66.8	185	93.3	233	115.8
42	48.7	90	64.6	138	74.0	186	104.7	234	126.5
43	53.0	91	66.1	139	80.7	187	112.0	235	134.0
44	54.3	92	71.0	140	87.6	188	116.7	236	139.0
45	52.9	93	70.3	141	87.2	189	115.0	237	138.5
46	49.2	94	66.4	142	80.3	190	109.9	238	126.2
47	47.3	95	60.5	143	75.0	191	101.0	239	121.3
48	44.8	96	57.6	144	71.5	192	98.2	240	113.8

7.25 The accompanying table shows 264 monthly observations on the number of new business incorporations in the United States. Fit an appropriate seasonal ARIMA model to this series, and forecast new incorporations for the next 12 months.

t	X_t	t	X_t	t	X_t	t	X_t	t	X_t
1	24187	54	26012	107	37728	160	49294	213	55956
2	21623	55	29168	108	39722	161	50763	214	55226
3	22685	56	24992	109	44818	162	54357	215	49118
4	23496	57	23895	110	37759	163	47726	216	57048
5	21734	58	25615	111	46674	164	53515	217	53527
6	23202	59	22109	112	43486	165	49890	218	56588
7	22614	60	23888	113	47065	166	49331	219	68601
8	20045	61	26473	114	44766	167	47924	220	57458
9	21330	62	22755	115	44914	168	51969	221	59729
10	21431	63	26677	116	44812	169	52885	222	59235
11	19177	64	28440	117	40330	170	51501	223	53443
12	22685	65	28117	118	47922	171	57003	224	60447
13	23372	66	27493	119	40567	172	54257	225	54126
14	19698	67	30105	120	41167	173	54338	226	54494
15	25752	68	36030	121	47016	174	55878	227	49207
16	24389	69	26944	122	41569	175	52040	228	58240
17	23899	70	29885	123	45007	176	53326	229	58031
18	26266	71	24078	124	44479	177	47118	230	55905
19	24898	72	29348	125	43436	178	55216	231	68521
20	23698	73	30350	126	41420	179	49585	232	56133
21	22748	74	27184	127	46151	180	51844	233	62141
22	24007	75	35216	128	41865	181	55769	234	61041
23	22799	76	32714	129	44923	182	49789	235	51157
24	26051	77	29210	130	49023	183	57493	236	56332
25	25715	78	33938	131	39691	184	58827	237	51014
26	24340	79	31469	132	48940	185	59491	238	53175
27	30003	80	30585	133	46960	186	54841	239	50156
28	26414	81	30944	134	42935	187	55706	240	53927
29	28030	82	30749	135	51278	188	54587	241	62098
30	28331	83	29845	136	52032	189	52639	242	54072
31	26103	84	33562	137	48115	190	60455	243	63755
32	26118	85	33863	138	51729	191	51015	244	56210
33	24761	86	30420	139	52176	192	57958	245	58120
34	26736	87	39712	140	45762	193	60114	246	55720
35	23991	88	35130	141	48305	194	55153	247	49588
36	26059	89	36577	142	49002	195	61222	248	53699
37	30114	90	39909	143	43533	196	63652	249	45758
38	26841	91	35963	144	48650	197	59407	250	52781
39	31967	92	39169	145	42680	198	59227	251	45720
40	29304	93	36110	146	42511	199	58698	252	50394
41	30476	94	36723	147	52574	200	52527	253	54227
42	29003	95	34586	148	48845	201	55476	254	48419
43	27609	96	38008	149	46008	202	59764	255	55917
44	26542	97	36986	150	48876	203	48098	256	55735
45	23158	98	35249	151	45282	204	68845	257	56618
46	26931	99	43130	152	45572	205	54401	258	51654
47	24268	100	38690	153	45461	206	55406	259	52949
48	23145	101	41960	154	45029	207	65536	260	51838
49	28617	102	43060	155	44354	208	62679	261	47840
50	25338	103	39242	156	59750	209	55548	262	54000
51	28270	104	42406	157	48099	210	61412	263	46419
52	30948	105	38845	158	43756	211	58362	264	52951
53	30297	106	41001	159	53796	212	53787		

7.26 The accompanying table shows 264 monthly observations on exports from New Zealand in millions of New Zealand dollars. Fit an appropriate seasonal ARIMA model to the logarithms of these data, and predict New Zealand's exports for the next 12 months.

t	X_t	t	X_t	t	X_t	t	X_t	t	X_t	t	X_t
1	58	54	93	107	172	160	463	213	735		
2	90	55	115	108	180	161	524	214	895		
3	69	56	123	109	157	162	455	215	920		
4	63	57	75	110	199	163	481	216	728		
5	68	58	89	111	225	164	382	217	958		
6	62	59	76	112	221	165	445	218	1101		
7	55	60	106	113	228	166	415	219	1152		
8	55	61	123	114	379	167	493	220	1046		
9	36	62	146	115	176	168	520	221	1188		
10	44	63	114	116	260	169	381	222	955		
11	68	64	143	117	229	170	508	223	970		
12	58	65	130	118	219	171	660	224	877		
13	65	66	136	119	249	172	548	225	816		
14	86	67	112	120	275	173	576	226	801		
15	87	68	107	121	284	174	627	227	809		
16	84	69	127	122	286	175	541	228	931		
17	75	70	102	123	266	176	483	229	765		
18	89	71	111	124	319	177	490	230	903		
19	60	72	149	125	308	178	511	231	833		
20	79	73	137	126	347	179	577	232	916		
21	53	74	190	127	277	180	570	233	1029		
22	72	75	221	128	249	181	516	234	922		
23	70	76	158	129	229	182	625	235	1068		
24	82	77	183	130	232	183	646	236	897		
25	91	78	192	131	210	184	568	237	1031		
26	114	79	124	132	290	185	750	238	988		
27	91	80	155	133	252	186	664	239	901		
28	104	81	141	134	300	187	685	240	973		
29	83	82	146	135	309	188	510	241	889		
30	89	83	113	136	334	189	584	242	999		
31	87	84	155	137	244	190	600	243	986		
32	78	85	144	138	384	191	675	244	1077		
33	85	86	164	139	264	192	728	245	1143		
34	75	87	175	140	279	193	503	246	1156		
35	93	88	182	141	261	194	653	247	1057		
36	91	89	141	142	319	195	843	248	977		
37	89	90	149	143	354	196	602	249	900		
38	105	91	125	144	304	197	770	250	878		
39	114	92	152	145	319	198	783	251	907		
40	80	93	115	146	373	199	671	252	1180		
41	85	94	127	147	410	200	708	253	785		
42	105	95	118	148	361	201	610	254	1146		
43	91	96	143	149	418	202	602	255	1241		
44	83	97	115	150	408	203	676	256	1011		
45	72	98	130	151	318	204	690	257	1226		
46	77	99	114	152	369	205	564	258	1145		
47	76	100	164	153	353	206	811	259	1007		
48	115	101	155	154	397	207	900	260	1094		
49	75	102	154	155	439	208	671	261	1207		
50	132	103	141	156	443	209	908	262	940		
51	84	104	141	157	386	210	814	263	1257		
52	120	105	150	158	479	211	770	264	1432		
53	111	106	179	159	528	212	868				

SELECTED BIBLIOGRAPHY

Abraham, B., & J. Ledolter (1983). *Statistical Methods for Forecasting*. New York: Wiley.

Ansley, C. F., & P. Newbold (1980). Finite sample properties of estimators for autoregressive—moving average models, *Journal of Econometrics*, *13*, 159–183.

Bewley, R. (1988). AUTOBOX: A review. *Journal of Applied Econometrics*, *3*, 240–244.

Box, G. E. P., & G. M. Jenkins (1970). *Time Series Analysis, Forecasting and Control*. San Francisco: Holden Day.

Box, G. E. P., & D. A. Pierce (1970). Distribution of residual autocorrelations in autoregressive integrated moving average time series models. *Journal of the American Statistical Association*, *65*, 1509–1526.

Davies, N., & P. Newbold (1980). Forecasting with misspecified models, *Applied Statistics*, *29*, 87–92.

Dickey, D. A., W. R. Bell, & R. B. Miller (1986). Unit roots in time series models: tests and implications. *The American Statistician*, *40*, 12–26.

Granger, C. W. J., & M. Morris (1976). Time series modeling and interpretation. *Journal of the Royal Statistical Society A*, *139*, 246–257.

Granger, C. W. J., & P. Newbold (1986). *Forecasting Economic Time Series* (2nd ed.). Orlando, Fl.: Academic Press.

Hill, G., & R. Fildes (1984). The accuracy of extrapolation methods: an automatic Box-Jenkins package sift. *Journal of Forecasting*, *3*, 319–323.

Jenkins, G. M. (1979). *Practical Experiences with Modelling and Forecasting Time Series*. Lancaster: GJP Publications.

Jenkins, G. M. (1982). Some practical aspects of forecasting in organizations. *Journal of Forecasting*, *1*, 3–21.

Jenkins, G. M., & G. McLeod (1982). *Case Studies in Time Series Analysis*. Lancaster: GJP Publications.

Ledolter, J., & B. Abraham (1981). Parsimony and its importance in time series forecasting. *Technometrics*, *23*, 411–414.

Libert, G. (1984). The M-competition with a fully automatic Box-Jenkins procedure. *Journal of Forecasting*, *3*, 325–328.

Ljung, G. M., & G. E. P. Box (1978). On a measure of lack of fit in time series models. *Biometrika*, *65*, 297–303.

Nelson, C. R. (1973). *Applied Time Series Analysis for Managerial Forecasting*. San Francisco: Holden Day.

Newbold, P. (1983). ARIMA model building and the time series analysis approach to forecasting. *Journal of Forecasting*, *2*, 23–35.

Pankratz, A. (1983). *Forecasting with Univariate Box-Jenkins Models: Concepts and Cases*. New York: Wiley.

Texter, P. A., & J. K. Ord (1989). Forecasting using automatic identification procedures: A comparative analysis. *International Journal of Forecasting*, *5*, 209–215.

Vandaele, W. (1983). *Applied Time Series and Box-Jenkins Models*. Orlando, Fl.: Academic Press.

Appendix 7.1
The Autocorrelation Patterns Implied by ARMA Models

In this appendix we establish the pattern of the autocorrelations of the stationary ARMA(p, q) model

$$\dot{X}_t - \phi_1 \dot{X}_{t-1} - \cdots - \phi_p \dot{X}_{t-p} = a_t - \theta_1 a_{t-1} - \cdots - \theta_q a_{t-q}$$

$$(A.7.1)$$

where

$$\dot{X}_t = X_t - \mu$$

Now, in Section 7.5 we showed that the stationary first-order autoregressive model can be written

$$\dot{X}_t = a_t + \phi_1 a_{t-1} + \phi_1^2 a_{t-2} + \phi_1^3 a_{t-3} + \cdots$$

In the same way, the stationary series $\dot{X}_t$ of equation A.7.1 can be expressed as a linear function of a_{t-j}; $j = 0, 1, 2, \ldots$; that is, we can write

$$\dot{X}_t = a_t + \psi_1 a_{t-1} + \psi_2 a_{t-2} + \psi_3 a_{t-3} + \cdots \qquad (A.7.2)$$

where the ψ_i are functions of the autoregressive and moving average parameters ϕ_i and θ_j. It follows immediately from equation A.7.2 that $\dot{X}_t$ has mean zero, so that X_t has mean μ.

Multiplying through equation A.7.2 by a_{t+j} and taking expectations gives

$$E(a_{t+j} \dot{X}_t) = E(a_{t+j} a_t) + \psi_1 E(a_{t+j} a_{t-1}) + \psi_2 E(a_{t+j} a_{t-2})$$

$$+ \psi_3 E(a_{t+j} a_{t-3}) + \cdots$$

Then, for $j > 0$, since a_t is white noise, each expectation on the right-hand side of this equation is zero, so that

$$E(a_{t+j} \dot{X}_t) = 0 \qquad j = 1, 2, 3, \ldots \qquad (A.7.3)$$

Next, multiplying through equation A.7.1 by $\dot{X}_{t-k}$ and taking expectations gives

$$E(\dot{X}_t\dot{X}_{t-k}) - \phi_1 E(\dot{X}_{t-1}\dot{X}_{t-k}) - \cdots - \phi_p E(\dot{X}_{t-p}\dot{X}_{t-k})$$

$$= E(a_t\dot{X}_{t-k}) - \theta_1 E(a_{t-1}\dot{X}_{t-k}) - \cdots - \theta_q E(a_{t-q}\dot{X}_{t-k})$$

The expectations on the left-hand side of this equation are the autocovariances of X_t, whereas, if $k > q$, every expectation on the right-hand side is zero, by virtue of equation A.7.3. We therefore have

$$\gamma_k = \phi_1\gamma_{k-1} + \cdots + \phi_p\gamma_{k-p} \qquad k = q + 1, q + 2, \ldots$$

Finally, dividing through by the variance of X_t, it follows that the autocorrelations obey

$$\rho_k = \phi_1\rho_{k-1} + \cdots + \phi_p\rho_{k-p} \qquad k = q + 1, q + 2, \ldots \quad (A.7.4)$$

In the special case where $q = 0$, so that X_t obeys a pure AR(p) model, A.7.4 specializes to the Yule-Walker equations

$$\rho_k = \phi_1\rho_{k-1} + \cdots + \phi_p\rho_{k-p} \qquad k = 1, 2, 3, \ldots$$

Appendix 7.2
Data Series

Daily volume on NYSE (in millions of shares).

Day	Volume	Day	Volume	Day	Volume	Day	Volume	Day	Volume
1	71.34	51	79.52	101	78.19	151	128.00	201	99.74
2	112.98	52	118.00	102	69.06	152	121.20	202	149.54
3	159.99	53	64.06	103	105.66	153	131.20	203	186.90
4	137.59	54	86.46	104	81.89	154	171.00	204	81.02
5	107.10	55	87.17	105	96.04	155	77.96	205	92.26
6	109.57	56	87.34	106	96.74	156	81.47	206	91.62
7	98.66	57	79.76	107	84.84	157	91.88	207	92.76
8	99.41	58	69.07	108	83.44	158	93.61	208	83.90
9	101.79	59	73.67	109	82.12	159	71.50	209	63.20
10	93.79	60	104.87	110	67.84	160	75.45	210	95.20
11	92.75	61	81.47	111	69.05	161	128.10	211	91.89
12	109.01	62	71.59	112	84.66	162	116.10	212	107.36
13	98.34	63	85.68	113	67.51	163	83.13	213	96.81
14	93.36	64	87.98	114	79.12	164	69.64	214	84.73
15	82.01	65	92.86	115	85.46	165	57.66	215	101.25
16	103.05	66	101.75	116	94.90	166	70.56	216	110.80
17	113.47	67	86.62	117	89.00	167	90.66	217	88.58
18	111.10	68	71.57	118	99.09	168	70.84	218	83.62
19	103.72	69	78.99	119	123.38	169	57.46	219	55.61
20	103.12	70	80.28	120	98.40	170	62.11	220	69.79
21	113.51	71	96.33	121	72.85	171	69.25	221	73.94
22	107.10	72	99.62	122	82.60	172	91.92	222	81.53
23	111.33	73	73.87	123	78.84	173	84.11	223	83.14
24	109.10	74	98.15	124	77.66	174	74.41	224	69.73
25	109.09	75	85.04	125	90.77	175	101.36	225	83.24
26	107.64	76	75.68	126	69.23	176	77.98	226	81.62
27	128.19	77	73.08	127	69.96	177	110.58	227	73.91
28	92.22	78	87.06	128	66.10	178	137.42	228	76.52
29	78.46	79	83.52	129	65.85	179	88.79	229	95.47
30	91.80	80	98.00	130	74.83	180	107.76	230	86.30
31	94.87	81	88.53	131	74.01	181	119.97	231	75.86
32	81.75	82	72.74	132	89.54	182	92.03	232	75.58
33	76.60	83	110.55	133	86.05	183	120.64	233	95.30
34	71.89	84	107.08	134	75.48	184	76.38	234	81.25
35	90.08	85	91.91	135	73.42	185	86.25	235	88.70
36	100.22	86	98.58	136	82.89	186	100.20	236	96.58
37	102.62	87	72.76	137	76.64	187	88.88	237	81.00
38	99.14	88	81.61	138	85.23	188	78.95	238	81.14
39	91.01	89	100.59	139	79.09	189	73.63	239	80.24
40	92.81	90	101.81	140	77.99	190	89.36	240	78.71

Daily volume on NYSE (in millions of shares). (*Continued*)

Day	Volume	Day	Volume	Day	Volume	Day	Volume	Day	Volume
41	82.01	91	82.78	141	74.37	191	92.40	241	80.84
42	108.27	92	64.90	142	90.52	192	76.70	242	95.06
43	69.87	93	88.25	143	90.41	193	82.95	243	89.49
44	83.59	94	89.21	144	101.40	194	46.36	244	169.08
45	90.08	95	90.31	145	72.33	195	76.84	245	139.63
46	80.63	96	81.27	146	86.91	196	94.27	246	93.72
47	73.17	97	73.38	147	127.50	197	87.02	247	101.25
48	84.47	98	88.03	148	172.80	198	92.19	248	55.55
49	102.65	99	82.69	149	236.60	199	87.59	249	46.70
50	77.25	100	99.04	150	203.10	200	82.93	250	70.10
								251	77.07
								252	80.26

Percentage of advancing stocks of all stocks traded on NYSE.

Day	Advances	Day	Advances	Day	Advances
1	27.22	51	58.35	101	39.07
2	37.85	52	56.22	102	55.06
3	29.20	53	51.97	103	35.85
4	42.77	54	45.48	104	39.38
5	34.81	55	40.43	105	44.23
6	14.14	56	37.74	106	50.94
7	31.81	57	53.76	107	54.19
8	48.51	58	45.22	108	44.43
9	41.22	59	41.82	109	47.80
10	61.06	60	28.39	110	44.01
11	38.43	61	56.70	111	47.57
12	31.27	62	43.17	112	32.46
13	33.96	63	41.18	113	37.05
14	34.63	64	41.26	114	41.94
15	38.45	65	28.80	115	38.52
16	36.96	66	40.71	116	34.84
17	53.40	67	63.47	117	23.63
18	49.01	68	27.05	118	41.31
19	37.83	69	26.67	119	27.11
20	45.02	70	32.25	120	13.94
21	52.17	71	31.55	121	28.25
22	45.06	72	8.22	122	64.21
23	42.98	73	20.06	123	53.38
24	33.13	74	39.69	124	44.48
25	13.35	75	32.32	125	42.57
26	14.83	76	49.22	126	35.21
27	51.66	77	35.52	127	41.78
28	41.31	78	39.26	128	31.85
29	43.96	79	57.54	129	64.71
30	21.40	80	47.40	130	37.14
31	21.41	81	46.34	131	34.85
32	46.39	82	20.93	132	25.33
33	26.43	83	39.41	133	32.91

Percentage of advancing stocks of all stocks traded on NYSE. (*Continued*)

Day	Advances	Day	Advances	Day	Advances
34	35.17	84	16.91	134	25.29
35	35.65	85	50.68	135	43.16
36	48.95	86	52.74	136	21.47
37	43.16	87	40.68	137	26.73
38	32.88	88	37.94	138	36.94
39	49.24	89	42.34	139	45.56
40	19.04	90	36.29	140	23.67
41	26.72	91	48.25	141	30.66
42	39.57	92	40.30	142	56.92
43	35.26	93	37.83	143	29.65
44	34.57	94	38.84	144	21.98
45	33.33	95	34.51	145	48.01
46	46.23	96	58.24	146	41.81
47	35.21	97	42.78	147	20.31
48	44.97	98	34.70	148	23.12
49	40.79	99	22.68	149	38.19
50	62.48	100	39.36		

Private housing units started per 1000 of population.

Year	Starts	Year	Starts	Year	Starts
1	6.807	20	7.245	39	7.581
2	6.249	21	8.763	40	5.926
3	4.179	22	9.253	41	6.502
4	2.679	23	9.786	42	7.514
5	2.047	24	12.817	43	7.230
6	1.073	25	9.626	44	7.016
7	0.740	26	9.543	45	9.913
8	0.996	27	8.976	46	11.288
9	1.735	28	9.515	47	9.720
10	2.488	29	9.922	48	6.314
11	2.605	30	7.987	49	5.383
12	3.123	31	7.116	50	7.084
13	3.931	32	7.902	51	9.065
14	4.565	33	8.532	52	9.120
15	5.292	34	6.929	53	7.766
16	2.639	35	7.148	54	5.687
17	1.397	36	7.845	55	4.727
18	1.026	37	8.510	56	4.587
19	2.330	38	7.968		

Number of active oil wells in United States.

Year	Oil Wells	Year	Oil Wells	Year	Oil Wells
1	333070	18	474990	35	553920
2	340990	19	488520	36	542227
3	349450	20	498940	37	530990
4	363030	21	511200	38	517318
5	369640	22	524010	39	508443
6	380390	23	551170	40	497378
7	389010	24	569273	41	497631
8	399960	25	574905	42	500333
9	404840	26	583141	43	499110
10	407170	27	591158	44	508000
11	412220	28	594917	45	484311
12	415750	29	596385	46	526835
13	421460	30	588675	47	537523
14	426280	31	588225	48	557009
15	437880	32	589203	49	580142
16	448680	33	583302	50	603290
17	465870	34	565289		

Plant & equipment expenditures (billions of dollars).

Year	Quarter 1	2	3	4
1	8.06	9.72	9.07	9.90
2	7.72	9.07	8.93	10.18
3	8.27	9.80	9.71	10.61
4	8.39	10.14	10.40	11.84
5	10.00	11.85	11.70	13.42
6	11.20	13.63	13.65	15.93
7	13.33	16.05	15.92	18.22
8	14.46	16.69	16.20	18.12
9	15.10	16.85	16.79	19.03
10	16.04	18.81	19.25	21.46
11	17.47	20.33	20.26	21.66
12	17.68	20.60	20.14	22.79
13	19.38	22.01	21.86	25.20
14	21.50	24.73	25.04	28.48
15	24.10	28.16	28.23	31.92
16	25.82	28.43	27.79	30.74
17	25.87	29.70	30.41	34.52
18	29.20	33.73	34.82	38.06
19	32.35	37.89	38.67	44.91

Factory sales of passenger cars in the United States (millions).

Year	Jan	Feb	Mar	Apr	May	Jun	Jul	Aug	Sep	Oct	Nov	Dec
1	0.6702	0.6079	0.6541	0.6892	0.7118	0.6875	0.6609	0.1678	0.4818	0.8040	0.7485	0.7540
2	0.7262	0.6811	0.7180	0.7864	0.7350	0.7406	0.5703	0.2373	0.5733	0.4115	0.6792	0.8843
3	0.7980	0.7747	0.9574	0.8610	0.8327	0.8940	0.7540	0.3330	0.4529	0.8556	0.9085	0.8838
4	0.7980	0.7663	0.9198	0.8110	0.7878	0.8186	0.4884	0.1438	0.6218	0.8353	0.8326	0.7751
5	0.6512	0.5256	0.6841	0.6598	0.7503	0.7653	0.4255	0.2316	0.6010	0.6454	0.6830	0.8139
6	0.7870	0.7032	0.8007	0.7827	0.9169	0.8137	0.6246	0.1931	0.6564	0.9352	0.8766	0.7321
7	0.8754	0.7074	0.7633	0.7143	0.7202	0.7771	0.4652	0.3464	0.7516	0.8568	0.6821	0.6240
8	0.5714	0.5552	0.5262	0.6613	0.7244	0.8053	0.4816	0.2724	0.4936	0.3925	0.3641	0.5988
9	0.7107	0.7578	0.8652	0.7504	0.7673	0.8098	0.4905	0.4848	0.7578	0.7935	0.7735	0.6234
10	0.6980	0.7483	0.8065	0.7791	0.8429	0.8042	0.4119	0.3985	0.8593	0.8957	0.8734	0.7060
11	0.9005	0.8551	0.9412	0.8440	0.9409	0.9213	0.7140	0.4403	0.7169	0.9555	0.8878	0.5400
12	0.5999	0.5519	0.6160	0.6811	0.7369	0.6696	0.5421	0.4441	0.6622	0.8320	0.5480	0.4475
13	0.3914	0.4105	0.4926	0.5862	0.6126	0.6321	0.5045	0.4846	0.6675	0.7456	0.6059	0.5795
14	0.6474	0.6820	0.8345	0.7890	0.7756	0.8501	0.5588	0.5184	0.6521	0.6908	0.7661	0.7327
15	0.6837	0.6757	0.9531	0.8155	0.8683	0.9514	0.6795	0.5054	0.7389	0.8744	0.7672	0.6859
16	0.6570	0.6748	0.9091	0.8694	0.9187	0.8855	0.5889	0.5277	0.7379	0.8941	0.8424	0.6596
17	0.7371	0.7092	0.8829	0.7613	0.9216	0.8199	0.5870	0.4490	0.6297	0.7865	0.6407	0.4940
18	0.5134	0.6186	0.6487	0.5724	0.5185	0.5440	0.4322	0.2987	0.5290	0.6747	0.5600	0.4897
19	0.4385	0.4750	0.6202	0.6446	0.6702	0.7122	0.5127	0.3447	0.5239	0.5195	0.4253	0.3703
20	0.2731	0.3204	0.4691	0.4876	0.5096	0.5611	0.4390	0.3556	0.4294	0.4305	0.4073	0.3663
21	0.4568	0.4741	0.5748	0.5287	0.5867	0.6436	0.4609	0.4923	0.6268	0.6776	0.6360	0.5806
22	0.6467	0.6820	0.7719	0.6649	0.6989	0.6765	0.5166	0.5190	0.5376	0.6860	0.6683	0.5528
23	0.7327	0.6593	0.7358	0.7438	0.7600	0.6770	0.5650	0.5536	0.6381	0.7386	0.6583	0.5400
24	0.7126	0.6751	0.6552	0.7135	0.6850	0.7061	0.5048	0.4257	0.6372	0.6842	0.5560	0.5608

Retail sales of apparel (billions of dollars).

Year	Jan	Feb	Mar	Apr	May	Jun	Jul	Aug	Sep	Oct	Nov	Dec
1	1.412	1.245	1.603	1.548	1.659	1.650	1.532	1.670	1.690	1.846	1.870	3.017
2	1.481	1.295	1.574	1.858	1.774	1.771	1.668	1.747	1.789	1.867	2.041	3.245
3	1.555	1.421	1.884	1.817	1.936	1.903	1.735	1.935	2.031	2.122	2.268	3.520
4	1.839	1.675	2.100	2.302	2.198	2.274	2.004	2.225	2.273	2.344	2.558	3.916
5	1.959	1.754	2.138	2.467	2.373	2.296	2.186	2.473	2.323	2.444	2.556	3.927
6	2.063	1.874	2.422	2.278	2.612	2.420	2.308	2.672	2.565	2.696	2.825	4.580
7	2.311	2.073	2.406	2.793	2.588	2.608	2.598	2.723	2.742	2.927	3.039	4.909
8	2.308	2.191	2.632	2.927	2.693	2.673	2.619	2.919	2.867	3.085	3.383	5.268
9	2.402	2.271	3.113	2.998	3.109	3.104	2.972	3.450	3.488	3.518	3.948	6.116
10	2.844	2.554	3.336	3.453	3.382	3.344	3.175	3.824	3.541	3.736	4.125	6.108
11	3.085	2.824	3.399	3.599	3.650	3.415	3.388	4.067	3.731	4.081	4.346	6.603
12	3.447	3.064	3.625	4.163	3.916	3.813	3.778	4.350	4.136	4.456	4.499	7.023
13	3.507	3.351	3.937	4.266	4.150	3.846	4.020	4.374	4.151	4.395	4.762	7.232
14	3.428	3.145	4.118	4.266	4.264	4.178	4.043	4.555	4.312	4.617	5.169	7.910
15	4.342	4.167	5.055	5.548	5.534	5.485	4.897	5.678	5.474	5.587	6.474	9.551
16	4.590	4.395	5.722	5.962	6.090	5.664	5.419	6.596	5.900	6.309	7.268	10.384
17	5.048	4.731	6.594	6.169	6.794	6.115	5.947	7.106	6.449	6.826	7.570	11.426

Illinois Power quarterly sales (millions of dollars).

Year	Quarter			
	1	2	3	4
1	271.252	198.694	239.725	254.621
2	340.855	245.517	245.119	275.284
3	350.659	283.418	352.636	291.546
4	401.388	282.358	305.519	291.272
5	370.372	242.155	281.258	273.579
6	355.900	245.259	303.818	278.888
7	325.701	253.727	347.735	292.360
8	333.657	270.879	391.961	288.223
9	327.354	280.319	391.813	313.144
10	315.851	305.155	425.458	349.226
11	358.862	310.678		

8 Econometric Forecasting Models, Leading Indicators, and Expectations

8.1 THE ECONOMETRIC APPROACH TO FORECASTING

In Chapters 6 and 7 we discussed some methods for the forecasting of future values of a time series based exclusively on information from its own past. In one sense, the ARIMA model-building approach of Chapter 7 is quite sophisticated. A careful search is made for an appropriate time series model, and hence for an appropriate algorithm for projecting forward recent local patterns in the series, through a sophisticated statistical analysis of the observed data. However, viewed in another way, this approach can be regarded as quite naive. No account is taken of the broader context in which a time series is generated. The data analyzed could equally well be rainfall in Tibet, birth rate in Outer Mongolia, or the demand for coconuts in Lapland. The general method of analysis—though not the form of forecast function eventually used—would be the same in any case. The only distinction would be in the labels that we attach to our time series.

We hasten to assert that we do not view the single series forecasting methods of Chapters 6 and 7 as worthless. Past observations on a time series will almost invariably yield important information about its likely future movements. Indeed, on many occasions, little or no additional worthwhile information may be available to the analyst. In addition, the single series forecasting methods are relatively quickly implemented, and will often yield forecasts of sufficiently high quality for the purposes at hand. It is in such circumstances that these approaches have in practice proved valuable for attacking a wide variety of forecasting problems. Nevertheless, the single series approaches to forecasting are, in a sense, somewhat distasteful. In implementing such an approach, we choose, in effect, to completely ignore whatever relevant subject matter knowledge, expertise, or theories may be available, except that any forecasts derived might subsequently be judgmentally modified on such grounds. In practice, it is not a good strategy to ignore *any* relevant information when preparing forecasts.

The construction of the models of Chapter 7 was based exclusively on the evidence provided by the observed data—that is, on purely statistical grounds. It might also pay to incorporate what is known from subject matter theory into the model-building process. Such theory is likely to postulate *behavioral* relationships among time series of interest. This inevitably moves us to a position in which forecasts of future values of a time series can be based, not only on its own past, but also on the past of other related series. In this and the next three sections of this chapter, we introduce an approach where subject matter theory is not only introduced into the forecasting process, but brought firmly to the forefront. The objective will still be, as in Chapter 7, to build models of the process that might have generated our data, but now these models will be rooted as firmly as possible in subject matter theory.

The approach to statistical model building, outlined in Chapter 7, was based on a three-stage cycle of model selection, parameter estimation, and model checking. The relevance of such an approach is certainly not restricted to the construction of ARIMA models. Indeed, in broad outline it constitutes a prescription for sound statistical model building in general. In ARIMA model building, each stage of the cycle is based exclusively on data analysis. In the approach discussed here, subject matter theory is injected into this process. It is at the first stage—model selection—where this is most crucial. The intention is that such theory be allowed to suggest a particular model, or perhaps a set of possible models, for further analysis. The role of the data is then in the estimation of the model parameters, in the comparison of competing alternative models, and in the checking of model adequacy. Theory, too, may have a part to play in these activities. For example, a fitted model may appear quite satisfactory on purely statistical grounds, but involve parameter estimates whose signs or magnitudes are nonsensical from a subject matter perspective. This would presumably stimulate a search for an alternative model. It is also possible to incorporate *a priori* knowledge or belief about the signs or magnitudes of parameters explicitly into an estimation algorithm, though in practice this seems to be done quite infrequently.

The broad outline to building behavioral models that we have discussed thus far is relevant for a wide range of subjects. When it is applied to the analysis of economic data, it is referred to as the **econometric approach.** Economic theory is allowed to suggest a model, or models, for analysis; the parameters of these models are estimated on the basis of available data, and the adequacy of the fitted models should be carefully checked. We have already discussed analyses of just this sort. The regression models of Chapters 3 and 4 aim at describing the relationship between a dependent variable on the one hand, and a set of independent variables on the other. If our aim is to explain the behavior of a dependent variable of interest, and perhaps also to predict its future behavior, we presumably appeal to theory to at least suggest a set of possibly relevant independent variables. It is also possible that theory may indicate, for example, an appropriate functional form for the relationship, or, as we saw in Chapter 4, some time lag structure. Thus, the analysis of economic data through the regression models of Chapters 3 and 4 can be regarded as belonging to the econometric approach, and predictions developed from such models are often termed **econometric forecasts.** One aspect of this approach is that the fitted models are tools of direct relevance to the problem of *conditional forecasting.* They can be employed to obtain forecasts of future values of a dependent variable, assuming particular future values for the independent variables. If *unconditional forecasts* of a dependent variable are required, it is necessary first to go outside of the estimated model structure to obtain forecasts of the independent variables. In this sense we might say that, although the fitted models themselves may be useful aids to unconditional forecasting, alone they are not sufficient for this task.

The regression models of Chapters 3 and 4 are the most basic tools available for econometric forecasting. However, the general econometric approach postulates a broader class of models. This is so because economic theory frequently suggests that the values taken by quantities of interest are determined through the *simultaneous interaction* of different economic forces. In consequence, it may be necessary, rather than concentrating on a single equation, to depict behavior of interest through a set of simultaneous equations. These considerations lead to the construction of **simultaneous equations econometric models.** Such models involve individual equations, similar in form to regression equations. However, whereas a single regression equation determines the expected value of a dependent variable in terms of several independent variables, a simultaneous equations econometric model postulates the *joint determination* of a set of dependent variables in terms of the independent variables. In the next three sections we will provide a brief introduction to some of the issues involved in building such models, and to their use in forecasting. This material, then, is a natural continuation and extension of our discussion in Chapters 3 and 4 on regression analysis.

8.2   SIMULTANEOUS EQUATIONS ECONOMETRIC MODELS

A system of simultaneous econometric equations determines jointly the values of a set of dependent variables, termed in this context **endogenous variables,** as functions of the values of independent variables, referred to as **exogenous variables.** The distinction between the two sets of variables is that the values of the exogenous variables are assumed to influence the endogenous variables, but the values of the endogenous variables are assumed not to influence the exogenous variables. This is precisely the distinction between dependent and independent variables in the single equation regression models of Chapters 3 and 4. Since the system of equations is intended to determine the values of the endogenous variables, a complete system will involve the same number of equations as endogenous variables.

Simultaneity in an econometric system leads to certain problems, for which special statistical treatment is required. Suppose for now that, following from some economic theory, a system of equations has been postulated. These equations will involve unknown parameters, and an attempt must be made to estimate these parameters, based on available data. We can concentrate on a single equation that is part of such a system. This equation might represent, for example, demand for some product, or aggregate consumption in a national economy. Such an equation will resemble, in form, the regression equations of Chapters 3 and 4, so that it is tempting to estimate its parameters through the usual least squares methods. Certainly it will be possible to compute least squares estimates. However, there are two potential difficulties:

1. It is quite possible that no consistent estimators of the parameters of the equation of interest exist. This is known as the **identification problem.**
2. Even when consistent estimators do exist, if an equation contains more than one endogenous variable ordinary least squares parameter estimators will generally be inconsistent, so that alternative estimators may be preferable.

To illustrate these issues, let us consider the usual simple paradigm for a simultaneous econometric system, where the price and quantity traded of a product in a perfectly competitive market are determined in equilibrium at the point where demand and supply functions intersect. Suppose that our interest is in estimating demand and supply relationships, and that we are comfortable in assuming simple functional forms such as linearity. Now, let

Y_{1t} = Quantity of product traded at time t

Y_{2t} = Price of product at time t

Then, since for markets in equilibrium quantities demanded and supplied will be the quantity actually traded, the demand and supply equations can be written, assuming linearity, as

Demand: $$Y_{1t} = \alpha_1 + \beta_{12}Y_{2t} + \epsilon_{1t} \qquad (8.2.1a)$$

Supply: $$Y_{1t} = \alpha_2 + \beta_{22}Y_{2t} + \epsilon_{2t} \qquad (8.2.1b)$$

Here, the α's and β's are fixed parameters, and the ϵ's are random variables with zero means, incorporated as usual because in practice no simple relationship between observed values of variables will hold precisely. Economic theory suggests that, the higher the price, the lower will be quantity demanded, so that the parameter β_{12} in equation 8.2.1a should be negative. Similarly, the higher the price, the greater the quantity of the product that producers would be willing to supply, so that β_{22} in equation 8.2.1b should be positive.

In this simple example, the nature of the identification problem is quite transparent from visual inspection of equations 8.2.1. The two equations are of precisely the same form. Therefore, if this system represents a complete specification of market behavior, it will be impossible, however much data are available, to separately estimate the demand and supply functions. Suppose, for example, we simply estimated the regression of quantity on price. Would we have achieved an estimate of the demand function or of the supply function? In general, what would result is an estimate of a "mongrel relationship" between quantity and price that is some compound of these two functions. Since neither of equations 8.2.1 can be consistently estimated, both are said to be **unidentified.** The position can be seen in Figure 8.1. Here we have drawn a demand schedule DD, and a supply schedule SS. Market equilibrium is at the point at which these lines intersect, and likely observation values will be scattered around that point. Over time we would observe data around such an equilibrium, and the observations would trace out neither demand nor supply behavior. The difficulty is that we cannot observe individual demand and supply relations. We only observe equilibrium price and quantity, where these functions intersect.

FIGURE 8.1   Observations around a demand-supply equilibrium.

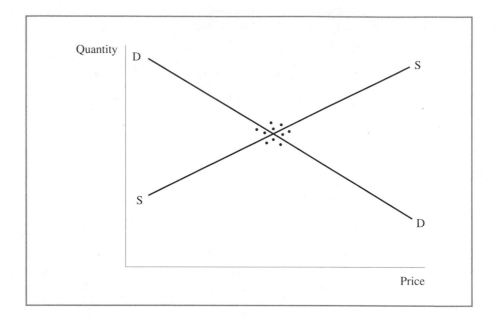

Fortunately, the position is far from hopeless, as economic theory suggests that the specification 8.2.1 is incomplete. For example, demand for many products will depend on consumers' income as well as price. Denoting this additional variable, which will be exogenous, as

$$X_{1t} = \text{Consumers' income}$$

leads to the more elaborate specification, with additional parameter γ_{11},

Demand: $Y_{1t} = \alpha_1 + \beta_{12}Y_{2t} + \gamma_{11}X_{1t} + \epsilon_{1t}$ (8.2.2a)

Supply: $Y_{1t} = \alpha_2 + \beta_{22}Y_{2t} + \epsilon_{2t}$ (8.2.2b)

Since these two equations are not identical, there is some hope for their identification. In fact, one of them is identified and one is not. Initial intuition on this point is frequently faulty, for it is the *supply* equation that is identified. This is most easily seen graphically; consider Figure 8.2. Here we have drawn a supply function SS, and a demand function D_0D_0, corresponding to some initial level of consumers' income. Equilibrium is again at their intersection, and in practice data points around that equilibrium should be observed. Suppose now that the product of interest is one for which, as consumers' income rises, demand at every price level

FIGURE 8.2   Observations around some demand-supply equilibria.

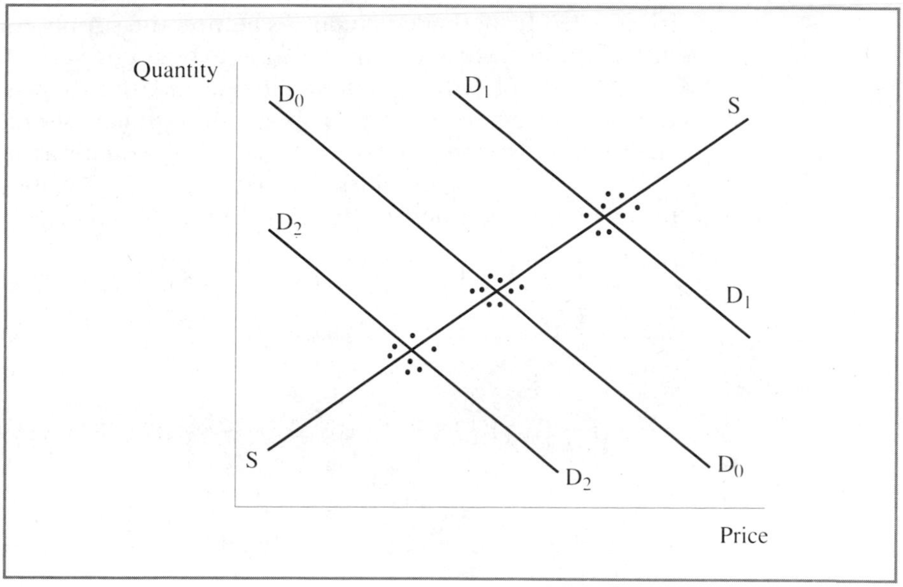

increases. Then, an increase in income above the initial level would lead to a new demand function, such as $D_1 D_1$, a corresponding new competitive equilibrium, and the possibility of observing data points around that equilibrium. Similarly, if consumers' income falls below the initial level, a demand function such as $D_2 D_2$ results, together with the possible observation points plotted in Figure 8.2 around the new equilibrium. Looking at all the observation points plotted in Figure 8.2, we see that they are grouped along the supply line SS. This explains why it is possible to estimate the parameters of the corresponding supply function equation 8.2.2b. Identification of the supply function is achieved by the introduction in the system of a relevant exogenous variable X_{1t}, *which is excluded from that equation.*

The demand equation could also be similarly identified. Suppose that, in addition to price, the quantity of the product that producers would be willing to supply depends on the exogenous variable

$$X_{2t} = \text{Cost of factors of production}$$

This leads to the pair of equations

Demand: $Y_{1t} = \alpha_1 + \beta_{12} Y_{2t} + \gamma_{11} X_{1t} + \epsilon_{1t}$ $(8.2.3a)$

Supply: $Y_{1t} = \alpha_2 + \beta_{22} Y_{2t} + \gamma_{22} X_{2t} + \epsilon_{2t}$ $(8.2.3b)$

In this model, both equations are identified: it is possible to obtain consistent estimators of the parameters of each. The demand equation is identified because the exogenous variable X_{2t} appears in the system, but is excluded from that equation. As before, the supply equation is identified through the exclusion from it of the exogenous variable X_{1t}.

The simple two-equations model, and the discussion of its identification, can be extended. The general linear simultaneous equations econometric system consists of a set of M equations in which the values of M endogenous variables, $Y_1, Y_2, \ldots, Y_M$, are jointly determined in terms of K exogenous variables, $X_1, X_2, \ldots, X_K$. The general format is

$$\alpha_1 + \beta_{11}Y_{1t} + \cdots + \beta_{1M}Y_{Mt} + \gamma_{11}X_{1t} + \cdots + \gamma_{1K}X_{Kt} + \epsilon_{1t} = 0$$

$$\alpha_2 + \beta_{21}Y_{1t} + \cdots + \beta_{2M}Y_{Mt} + \gamma_{21}X_{1t} + \cdots + \gamma_{2K}X_{Kt} + \epsilon_{2t} = 0$$

$$\vdots \qquad\qquad \vdots \qquad\qquad \vdots$$

$$\alpha_M + \beta_{M1}Y_{1t} + \cdots + \beta_{MM}Y_{Mt} + \gamma_{M1}X_{1t} + \cdots + \gamma_{MK}X_{Kt} + \epsilon_{Mt} = 0$$

$$(8.2.4)$$

where the α's, β's, and γ's are fixed parameters, and the ϵ's are error terms.

To begin, one of the parameters associated with any endogenous variable in an equation can, with no loss of generality, be set to -1. For example, the first equation in 8.2.4 might be written as

$$Y_{1t} = \alpha_1 + \beta_{12}Y_{2t} + \cdots + \beta_{1M}Y_{Mt}$$
$$+ \gamma_{11}X_{1t} + \cdots + \gamma_{1K}X_{Kt} + \epsilon_{1t} \qquad (8.2.5)$$

It can then be shown that it is necessary, if identification is to be based on the exclusion of variables, that the total number of variables, exogenous plus endogenous, excluded from an equation be at least equal to one less than the number of equations in the system. Thus, in the simple two-equations models discussed earlier, identification of an equation requires that at least one variable be excluded from it. (Of course, the excluded variable must truly belong in the system, in the sense that it appears with a non-zero parameter in the other equation.)

The general system 8.2.4 is not then, as it stands, identified. Identification of an equation in that system can be achieved through the knowledge that at least $(M - 1)$ of its parameters are zero. What is the source of such knowledge? It can only be provided by economic theory. For example, from such theory we might postulate the simple system 8.2.3. Theory tells us that the demand for a product does not depend on the cost of its factors of production, and that the quantity that producers would be willing to supply does not depend on consumers' income. In this way, theory has provided the restrictions necessary to identify these equations. In general, economic theory will postulate a system of behavioral equations like 8.2.4, but with some variables excluded from individual equations. Such representations are called the **structural form** of the model; the structure is that imposed by economic theory.

We have seen that identification can be achieved by the exclusion of at least $(M - 1)$ variables from an equation. It often happens that more than this minimal number of variables is excluded. For example, suppose we introduce into our simple demand-supply model the further exogenous variable

$$X_{3t} = \text{Price of a competing product}$$

A plausible model might now be

Demand: $Y_{1t} = \alpha_1 + \beta_{12}Y_{2t} + \gamma_{11}X_{1t} + \gamma_{13}X_{3t} + \epsilon_{1t}$ $(8.2.6a)$

Supply: $Y_{1t} = \alpha_2 + \beta_{22}Y_{2t} + \gamma_{22}X_{2t} + \epsilon_{2t}$ $(8.2.6b)$

The demand equation remains *just identified;* there is just one variable excluded from it. However, two variables—one more than is strictly necessary for identification—are excluded from the supply equation. In consequence it is said to be **over-identified.** Over-identifying restrictions of this sort, provided by economic theory, are certainly not without value. In essence, they can be used to develop superior estimates of the model parameters.

The Structural Form and the Reduced Form

The **structural form** of an econometric model is the form that would be postulated by an economist on the basis of theory. It is also the form in which the economist would be directly interested, as its parameters convey direct economic meaning, measuring such things as the response to price change of demand for a product. It is therefore important to estimate the parameters of the structural form, as set out for example in equations 8.2.3 and 8.2.4.

There is, however, an alternative form of simultaneous equations econometric models that is of practical interest. For the general econometric system of M equations, as in 8.2.4, the **reduced form** of the model is obtained by solving these equations to yield a new system of equations in which each endogenous variable is expressed as a function of all the exogenous variables, and an error term. Thus, corresponding to 8.2.4, the reduced form equations are

$$Y_{1t} = \Pi_1 + \Pi_{11}X_{1t} + \cdots + \Pi_{1K}X_{Kt} + V_{1t}$$

$$Y_{2t} = \Pi_2 + \Pi_{21}X_{1t} + \cdots + \Pi_{2K}X_{Kt} + V_{2t} \qquad (8.2.7)$$

$$\vdots \qquad\qquad \vdots \qquad\qquad \vdots$$

$$Y_{Mt} = \Pi_M + \Pi_{M1}X_{1t} + \cdots + \Pi_{MK}X_{Kt} + V_{Mt}$$

Here the Π's are fixed parameters, which will be functions of the α's, β's, and γ's, and the V's are error terms, depending on the ϵ's of equation 8.2.4. For example, after a little algebra, it is easy to see that the reduced form of the two-equations system 8.2.3 is

$$Y_{1t} = \Pi_1 + \Pi_{11}X_{1t} + \Pi_{12}X_{2t} + V_{1t} \qquad (8.2.8a)$$

$$Y_{2t} = \Pi_2 + \Pi_{21}X_{1t} + \Pi_{22}X_{2t} + V_{2t} \qquad (8.2.8b)$$

where

$$\Pi_1 = \frac{\alpha_1\beta_{22} - \alpha_2\beta_{12}}{\beta_{22} - \beta_{12}} \qquad \Pi_{11} = \frac{\gamma_{11}\beta_{22}}{\beta_{22} - \beta_{12}} \qquad \Pi_{12} = \frac{-\beta_{12}\gamma_{22}}{\beta_{22} - \beta_{12}}$$

$$\Pi_2 = \frac{\alpha_1 - \alpha_2}{\beta_{22} - \beta_{12}} \qquad \Pi_{21} = \frac{\gamma_{11}}{\beta_{22} - \beta_{12}} \qquad \Pi_{22} = \frac{-\gamma_{22}}{\beta_{22} - \beta_{12}}$$

$$V_{1t} = \frac{\beta_{22}\epsilon_{1t} - \beta_{12}\epsilon_{2t}}{\beta_{22} - \beta_{12}} \qquad V_{2t} = \frac{\epsilon_{1t} - \epsilon_{2t}}{\beta_{22} - \beta_{12}}$$

If we think of the endogenous variables as dependent variables, and of the exogenous variables as independent variables, the reduced form equations have precisely the same format as the multiple regression models of Chapter 4. This is the source of their interest. For our purposes, there are two important uses of the reduced form:

1. Estimation of the parameters of the reduced form can provide a useful intermediate step in procedures for the estimation of the structural form parameters.
2. The reduced form is the natural vehicle for the computation of conditional forecasts of future values of the endogenous variables, given assumptions about future values of the exogenous variables.

Estimation of the Structural Form Parameters: Two-Stage Least Squares

The question of how to estimate the parameters of the structural form of a simultaneous equations model can only be sensibly addressed in the context of assumptions that can be made, for example, about the behavior of the error terms. The usual starting point is with a natural extension of the standard assumptions that we considered in Chapter 4 for the multiple regression model. Specifically, with reference to equation 8.2.4, we will assume:

1. The quantities X_{jt} are either fixed numbers or they are realizations of random variables that are uncorrelated with all the error terms ϵ_{it} $(i = 1, \ldots, M)$.
2. The error terms ϵ_{it} $(i = 1, \ldots, M)$ all have mean zero.
3. For given i, the error terms ϵ_{it} have a common variance, say σ_i^2 $(i = 1, \ldots, M)$. Also, for given i and j, the error terms ϵ_{it} and ϵ_{jt} have a common covariance, say σ_{ij}, for all observation periods t.
4. No error term in time t is correlated with any error term in any other time period.

These assumptions are the most generous that can realistically be made, in the sense that they yield the most straightforward possible case for parameter estimation.

Suppose now that the above assumptions do hold, and that the aim is to estimate the parameters of a single equation that is part of a structural system. It will be assumed that the equation of interest is identified, since otherwise no progress can be made. Identification assures us that consistent parameter estimators do exist. However, it is known that, in general, if the equation of interest contains more than one endogenous variable, the usual ordinary least squares parameter estimators will be inconsistent. For example, suppose that, given data on the relevant variables, we want to estimate the demand equation 8.2.3a. Even if that equation is correctly specified, and our assumptions are correct, the estimation by the ordinary least squares methods of Chapter 4 of the regression of quantity traded on price and income will *not* yield consistent estimators of the parameters of that equation. Essentially the problem arises because, even though the exogenous variable X_{1t} is, by assumption, uncorrelated with the error term ϵ_{1t}, the endogenous variable Y_{2t} will be correlated with ϵ_{1t}. (This follows since Y_{2t} depends on ϵ_{1t} through the reduced form equation 8.2.8b.)

Because ordinary least squares estimators are inconsistent in the simultaneous equations model framework, econometricians have developed a number of alternative estimation procedures that do yield consistent parameter estimators, as well as having other desirable properties. Here we will just briefly outline one such procedure. As its name implies, the method of **two-stage least squares** proceeds in two stages, applying ordinary least squares at each stage. We will assume that the equation of interest has been written in the general form of equation 8.2.5, with an endogenous variable on the left-hand side, and both endogenous and exogenous variables, with associated parameters, on the right-hand side.

Economic theory will have suggested certain restrictions on the equation, so that not all variables that are in the system will actually be present in this equation. The method of two-stage least squares proceeds as follows:

Stage 1:   Estimate the reduced form of equations 8.2.7, one equation at a time, by ordinary least squares. This is appropriate, as no endogenous variables appear on the right-hand sides of these equations. Denote by $\hat{\Pi}$ the least squares estimates of the parameters Π. Then the fitted, or in-sample predicted, values for the endogenous variables from these regressions are

$$\hat{Y}_{it} = \hat{\Pi}_i + \hat{\Pi}_{i1}X_{1t} + \cdots + \hat{\Pi}_{iK}X_{Kt} \qquad i = 1, 2, \ldots, M$$

Stage 2:   In structural form equations such as 8.2.5 replace actual endogenous variables Y_{it} on the right-hand side, but not on the left-hand side, by the corresponding reduced form fitted values $\hat{Y}_{it}$, obtained at stage 1. Estimate the resulting equation by ordinary least squares.

To illustrate, suppose we want to estimate the parameters of the demand equation 8.2.3a, in which the endogenous variable Y_{2t} (price) appears on the right-hand side. The first stage, then, involves the estimation by ordinary least squares of the reduced form equation 8.2.8b, yielding parameter estimates $\hat{\Pi}_2$, $\hat{\Pi}_{21}$, and $\hat{\Pi}_{22}$, and fitted values

$$\hat{Y}_{2t} = \hat{\Pi}_2 + \hat{\Pi}_{21}X_{1t} + \hat{\Pi}_{22}X_{2t}$$

At the second stage, the regression of Y_{1t} on $\hat{Y}_{2t}$ and X_{1t} is estimated by ordinary least squares. This procedure yields consistent estimators of the parameters α_1, β_{12}, and γ_{11} of equation 8.2.3a. This process yields consistent parameter estimators, because, although Y_{2t} is correlated with ϵ_{1t}, its proxy $\hat{Y}_{2t}$ is not. Computer programs for the estimation of simultaneous equations models by two-stage least squares and other procedures are quite widely available.

It should be noted that stage 1 provides *initial* estimates of the reduced form parameters. In general, superior estimates of these parameters can subsequently be obtained, if required for the generation of forecasts, for example, by solving the estimated structural equations for the endogenous variables in terms of the exogenous variables, as we will illustrate in Section 8.3. This allows information about the structural form, provided by economic theory, to be incorporated into the estimation of the reduced form parameters.

The estimation procedure we have discussed is appropriate when the assumptions hold. It requires modification if one or more of them breaks down, as would occur, for example, if the error terms were autocorrelated. We will not pursue these details here.

When time series data are analyzed, it is very common for the econometric models to include lagged values of the endogenous variables. In the present context, these are often referred to as **predetermined variables,** as their values have been determined before the current time period. For purposes of identification and estimation, as discussed in this section, predetermined variables can be treated as if they were additional exogenous variables.

Simultaneous equations econometric models form the basis for an important approach to forecasting. Accordingly, we felt it necessary to provide a brief overview of some statistical problems involved in the analysis of such models. However, our treatment of these problems has been far from complete. To do more would be too much of a digression from our primary focus, which is forecasting. The reader interested in a more detailed account of the subject matter of this section can find it in one or more of the several econometrics textbooks referenced in the bibliography at the end of this chapter.

8.3 FORECASTING FROM A SIMULTANEOUS EQUATIONS MODEL: AN ILLUSTRATION

We will illustrate the application of simultaneous equations econometric models to forecasting through a very simple fictitious macroeconomic model. Modern models of national economies are extremely complex, and the reader should be cautioned that the example presented here is merely a pedagogical tool. It is a gross oversimplification of actual models, intended only to illustrate the mechanics of forecast generation. In Section 8.4 we will indicate the various ways in which such a simple model might be elaborated in practice. Suppose that our interest is in a particular national economy, whose behavior is depicted through relationships among five endogenous variables and two exogenous variables. The variables in our model are

$$Y_{1t} = \text{Consumption expenditure}$$

$$Y_{2t} = \text{Investment outlays}$$

$$Y_{3t} = \text{Tax receipts}$$

$$Y_{4t} = \text{Value of imports}$$

$$Y_{5t} = \text{Gross national product}$$

$$X_{1t} = \text{Government expenditures}$$

$$X_{2t} = \text{Value of exports}$$

All variables are measured in terms of the nation's currency, adjusted for inflation—that is, in real terms.

Assume that a model has been specified, and its parameters estimated, yielding the following results for the structural form

$$Y_{1t} = 10 + 0.70(Y_{5t} - Y_{3t}) + \epsilon_{1t} \qquad (8.3.1a)$$

$$Y_{2t} = 2 + 0.10Y_{5t} + \epsilon_{2t} \qquad (8.3.1b)$$

$$Y_{3t} = 8 + 0.30Y_{5t} + \epsilon_{3t} \qquad (8.3.1c)$$

$$Y_{4t} = 2 + 0.09Y_{5t} + \epsilon_{4t} \qquad (8.3.1d)$$

$$Y_{5t} = Y_{1t} + Y_{2t} + X_{1t} + X_{2t} - Y_{4t} \qquad (8.3.1e)$$

where the ϵ's are error terms. The system is complete in the sense that it contains the same number of equations as endogenous variables. Equation 8.3.1a relates consumption expenditures to disposable income; that is, the difference between gross national product and taxes. The next three equations relate, in turn, investment, taxes, and imports to gross national product. Finally, equation 8.3.1e is an *identity,* in which gross national product is defined as the sum of consumption, investment, and government spending, plus exports less imports. It therefore contains no error term, and has no parameters to be estimated.

Equations 8.3.1, which constitute the structural form of the model, are of the type that might be specified by a simple-minded economist. They are not, however, in the most convenient form for forecasting. Simultaneous equations models of this sort are tools for the conditional forecasting of future values of the endogenous variables, given assumed future values for the exogenous variables. Therefore, it is natural to express each endogenous variable in terms of the exogenous variables in the reduced form. Solving the equations 8.3.1 leads to the estimated reduced form

$$Y_{1t} = 8.712 + 0.98X_{1t} + 0.98X_{2t} + V_{1t} \qquad (8.3.2a)$$

$$Y_{2t} = 2.88 + 0.2X_{1t} + 0.2X_{2t} + V_{2t} \qquad (8.3.2b)$$

$$Y_{3t} = 10.64 + 0.6X_{1t} + 0.6X_{2t} + V_{3t} \qquad (8.3.2c)$$

$$Y_{4t} = 2.792 + 0.18X_{1t} + 0.18X_{2t} + V_{4t} \qquad (8.3.2d)$$

$$Y_{5t} = 8.8 + 2X_{1t} + 2X_{2t} + V_{5t} \qquad (8.3.2e)$$

where the error terms V_{it} are linear functions of the ϵ_{jt}'s of equation 8.3.1. Suppose now that we are standing at time period n, and want to predict future values of the endogenous variables in some time period, say time

$(n + 1)$. These predictions will have to be based on assumptions about future values of the exogenous variables. Forecasts are then obtained directly from estimated reduced form equations such as equation 8.3.2, setting t equal to $(n + 1)$, and replacing unknown future error terms $V_{i,n+1}$ by their means of zero. For example, suppose that government expenditures and the value of exports in the next time period are expected to be

$$X_{1,n+1} = 500 \qquad X_{2,n+1} = 100$$

Then, directly from equations 8.3.2, forecasts of consumption, investment, tax receipts, imports, and gross national product for that time period are

$$\hat{Y}_{1,n+1} = 8.712 + (0.98)(500) + (0.98)(100) = 597$$

$$\hat{Y}_{2,n+1} = 2.88 + (0.2)(500) + (0.2)(100) = 123$$

$$\hat{Y}_{3,n+1} = 10.64 + (0.6)(500) + (0.6)(100) = 371$$

$$\hat{Y}_{4,n+1} = 2.792 + (0.18)(500) + (0.18)(100) = 111$$

$$\hat{Y}_{5,n+1} = 8.8 + (2)(500) + (2)(100) = 1,209$$

These forecasts can be viewed in two ways. They can be thought of as *conditional* forecasts of the five endogenous variables, assuming that the future levels of government expenditures and value of exports will be 500 units and 100 units, respectively. Alternatively, if we regard 500 units and 100 units as forecasts of the exogenous variables, obtained from some external source, then the forecasts of the endogenous variables are *unconditional*. Simultaneous equations econometric models are not self-sufficient tools for unconditional forecasting, as they provide no useful information about likely future values of the exogenous variables. Conditional forecasting is the natural application of such models. This has been said to be a strength, but is also a weakness. For policy analysis, it can be argued that conditional, or "what if," forecasts are precisely what is required. Government agencies responsible for economic policy will have available various options, and it would be useful to attempt to estimate the impact of alternative strategies on economic activity. For example, at least in theory, government has some control over such policy instruments as its own spending levels. Rational decision making requires an assessment of the likely future consequences of alternative courses of action. When the exogenous variables in an econometric model are the values of policy variables over which the decision maker has some control, the merit of conditional forecasts in policy analysis is obvious. Of course, however successful might be the single series ARIMA models of Chapter 7 in generating good quality, unconditional forecasts, they are of no direct value in the kind of conditional forecasting required for the evaluation of policy options. (That is not to say, however, that those models cannot be extended to incorporate information on other variables. On the contrary, we will see in Chapter 9 how that is possible.) Although econometric models are ideally suited to conditional forecasting, generally some of the exogenous variables in such models are not instruments under the control of a policy maker. For example, as is quite typical of far more elaborate macroeconometric models, our simple example includes exports as an exogenous variable. This is not surprising since demand for the exports of a country will depend on external factors, such as world trade conditions. Thus, even if the kind of conditional forecasts for policy purposes that we have discussed are required, it is likely to be necessary to obtain from somewhere forecasts of some of the exogenous variables in the model. One possibility is to use single series methods, such as ARIMA model building, for this purpose. More often, these variables are predicted through informal judgmental means. The subject matter knowledge and expertise of the analyst is exploited, but not through the construction of formal models.

We must repeat that our analysis is this section is not intended as an accurate representation of the activities of modern macroeconometric model builders and forecasters. Our aim has been the more modest one of introducing a model that is sufficiently simple to allow the mechanics of the forecasting process to be transparent. Of course, modern macroeconomists, having access to substantial computing power for the analysis and reduced form solution of models, are not bound by such a constraint. In addition, modern theory suggests quite sophisticated specifications for individual segments of a macroeconomic model. Our rather casual discussion of the specification of equations 8.3.1 is certainly not intended to do justice to recent theoretical developments. We do not, in any case, have the space to do so.

8.4 MACROECONOMETRIC FORECASTS

Our apologies to our macroeconomist friends for the relative crudity of the model on which we based the discussion of Section 8.3 have, we hope, been sufficiently profuse. We turn now to the more difficult task of providing a flavor of the content of modern macroeconomic forecasting and the econometric models on which the forecasts are based. What is the value of all of this in the business world? Individual corporations do not function in isolation. Certainly, in looking to the future, the corporate analyst needs to carefully consider local microeconomic factors. However, few corporations can isolate themselves entirely from trends in the broader national economy, or indeed at the present time in the international economy. In business planning, it will often be important to take a view on the likely future course of such macroeconomic variables as national income, interest rates, and price inflation. Several consulting groups specialize in the development of macroeconomic forecasts, generally based on a sophisticated macroeconomic model. Forecasts are typically available in disaggregated form, at the level of individual industries. Many corporations subscribe to one or another of these services. Of course, it is quite feasible for a corporation to develop macroeconomic forecasts in-house. However, this is a very expensive enterprise, requiring substantial amounts of time, computing effort, and highly skilled and expensive people. It is certainly less expensive to simply purchase the forecasts, and, unless there is good reason to believe that an in-house team could develop a product that is either noticeably superior or more relevant, this would seem to be the wiser course. Nevertheless, it is important for the business analyst to have some understanding, at least in general terms, of the process generating the forecasts, and also of their limitations. Our goal in this section is to provide such an understanding.

It may be useful to take the simple model 8.3.1 as a starting point, and ask how, in practice, such a structure might be elaborated. It is instructive to compare the model 8.3.1 with a small macroeconometric model discussed by Klein (1988). The Klein model is an elaboration of ours in a number of important dimensions.

1. The Klein model contains an additional endogenous variable, short-term interest rate.
2. Since there is a sixth endogenous variable in the system, there must necessarily be a sixth equation. This equation incorporates a new exogenous variable—money supply—and relates the ratio of gross national product to money to the interest rate.
3. The specification of equations is more careful than ours; for example, in the Klein model both consumption and investment depend on the interest rate, as well as on gross national product.
4. The specification of the Klein model, by contrast with equations 8.3.1, is not static. Rather, the individual equations involve a number of lagged values of the endogenous variables.
5. The functional relationships in the Klein model are not all linear. This certainly makes it more difficult to find the reduced form equations, in which the endogenous variables will be nonlinear functions of the exogenous and pre-determined variables. In fact, in these circumstances, the estimated structural form is solved numerically through a specially programmed computational algorithm to yield values of the endogenous variables for any given values of the exogenous variables.

The Klein model is certainly more sophisticated than ours; it is bigger, and its structure involves lags, nonlinearities, and more careful behavioral specification. Modern macroeconometric models have all these qualities, and yet the Klein model of six equations is also no more than a tool for exposition. In practice, models of national economies in current use are very much larger. Indeed, as Klein notes, models used in the description of modern developed economies may contain more than 1000 equations! What is the source of such monstrous size? In part, extra equations are required to explain the behavior of additional macroeconomic variables of interest, such as employment, wages, and prices. (Desai and Weber (1988) describe a sophisticated model incorporating equations for the behavior of these variables, together with a very sophisticated statistical analysis of that model.) Most of the growth in model size, compared with the small structures discussed here, comes about through **disaggregation** of gross quantities such as consumption and investment into segments. A model will contain not one consumption equation, but several, and will treat consumer spending on different types of goods and services separately.

In summary, the modern macroeconometric model is a very large system of simultaneous nonlinear equations, postulated through an appeal to economic theory, and with at least some care taken over the specification of appropriate lags. As the reader can imagine, collecting all of the necessary data, estimating the model parameters, and solving the model to obtain forecasts are far from trivial tasks. The computational requirements are heavy; the requirement for skilled personnel is even heavier. Indeed, these models are not simply specified once and for all and then left to generate forecasts. The requirement still exists to supply to the models judgmental forecasts of exogenous variables. In addition, the models are frequently revised or updated, as their proprietors' understanding of the economy evolves, or as it is believed that the structure of the economy has altered. The reader should now be able to see why we suggested that a corporation will generally prefer to purchase forecasts from a consulting group, rather than undertake these activities itself.

The typical progression from fitted macroeconometric model to the publication of forecasts is not as straightforward as we have pretended up to this point. In spite of the size and apparent sophistication of these models, and of the enormous amounts of time and effort spent on their construction, they are rarely trusted to produce forecasts without the benefit of the injection of expert human judgment into the process. Of course, as we have already indicated, the models cannot be used to predict future values of the exogenous variables, and economists generally prefer to do this judgmentally rather than through some formal statistical model, such as the ARIMA models of Chapter 7. One consequence of this is that, however excellent the econometric models might be in representing actual economic behavior, the quality of any unconditional forecasts of endogenous variables will depend on the quality of forecasts of the exogenous variables used. This issue has not received much attention, though it is obviously important. However, some results of Ashley (1983, 1985, 1988) do highlight the potential problem involved. It is entirely possible that an econometric model could be adequately specified; yet, if forecasts of exogenous variables are sufficiently poor, one might do better in the prediction of endogenous variables to work with a less completely specified model that ignored these exogenous variables altogether.

To some extent, the use of judgment in the prediction of future values of the exogenous variables is inevitable. However, in practice, most macroeconomic forecasts involve the injection of judgment at two other points in the forecasting process, where such injection is purely optional. First, however much care has been put into adequate model specification, an economist may decide at any point in time that particular equations in the system are not representing, or are not likely to represent in the near future, economic activity sufficiently well. For example, it might have been observed that, over the last few time periods, a certain equation has been yielding persistently positive or persistently negative errors, suggesting a tendency to underestimate or overestimate the actual values of some endogenous variable. Alternatively, the economist may be aware of extraneous factors, not specifically incorporated into the formal model, that are likely to influence the future behavior of particular variables. Under either circumstance, it is common practice to make some allowance by modifying individual equations in the system. These modifications are sometimes called constant term adjustments, as they typically involve changing the estimated values of the constant, or intercept, terms in individual model equations. Once individual equations have been adjusted, the system is then solved for the endogenous variables in terms of assumed or predicted future values of the exogenous variables. This yields forecasts. However, these forecasts may be modified judgmentally by economists if they are inconsistent with strongly held prior beliefs. It can be seen, then, that finally published macroeconomic forecasts rely on a good deal of expert judgment as well as on formal quantitative models. The role of judgment in macroeconomic forecasting, based on an econometric model, is discussed more fully and illustrated by Young (1982), while McNees (1990) provides evidence on gains in forecast accuracy from judgmental modifications.

We do not wish to leave the reader with the impression that we view the judgmental content of macroeconomic forecasts as in any sense undesirable. The sensible forecaster will try to incorporate into the prediction process all relevant information and expertise that is at hand, and not all of this will be easily quantifiable or lend itself to inclusion in a formal model. An interesting question does arise, however. To what extent are forecasts produced by groups of macroeconomists truly based on their econometric models, and to what extent do they merely measure the subjective judgments of these economists? The question is really impossible to answer, as the two elements are inextricably entangled in practical forecasting exercises. For example, it is reasonable to expect that the discipline of building a formal model will itself sharpen and modify the economist's intuition about the way the economy behaves. Still, an outsider who is overly impressed by the scale and sophistication of modern macroeconomic forecasting models might reflect on the fact that very often the model builders themselves are not sufficiently impressed to allow the models to generate forecasts without unnecessary human intervention.

Modern macroeconomic forecasting models represent theoretical and empirical analysis on a very grand scale. Moreover, the judgmental modifications involved should properly be viewed as perfectly reasonable in principle, since not all human expertise can be captured in any formal model. The resulting forecasts, then, might be seen as resulting from a blend of very high-powered theory, empirical analysis, and expert judgment. It is tempting, in looking from the outside at such enterprises, to gaze with awe and admiration. Yet, these endeavors have not in fact met with unmixed applause, even from economists. The sheer scale of the modern models has itself been a source of scepticism.

For example, Zellner (1988) doubts the value of very complicated models in economics, or indeed in any other branch of science, in either understanding the past or predicting the future. Indeed, Zellner goes further, suggesting that concentration on such models may have "significantly impeded the progress" of the subject. The comments of some statisticians, notably Jenkins (1979), on this subject have been a good deal more scathing. At the heart of this controversy is the issue of *parsimony*, which we have raised several times previously in this book, notably in Chapter 7. The real world—particularly that part of it involving the behavior of real people—is an exceedingly complicated place, and to some extent it is this observation that motivates the building of complicated models. However, one interpretation of the principle of parsimony, which is thoroughly imbedded in the scientific method, asserts that no formal model can ever completely describe the complex real world. Far from embracing the thought that bigger is better, the scientist should aim for simplicity, searching for those major enduring truths, or near-truths, that can be unearthed from study of theory and data. Indeed, casual observation does seem to suggest that the most important scientific truths are relatively simple. That any formal model of a national economy, however large, will inevitably leave us a very considerable distance from an accurate description of real human behavior is easily argued. Economic activity results from decisions made by individual agents—consumers or managers. Theory about such activity is inevitably based on the assumption that these agents behave rationally, and much modern theory requires in effect that individuals succeed continually in solving quite complex mathematical constrained optimization problems. As theory, there is no harm in all of this. As a description of the way real people actually behave, it is patently absurd. However, it may have a good deal of practical value. It is quite possible that such idealized theory can provide a serviceable *approximation* to the actual behavior of economic agents, *in the aggregate*. Nevertheless, it is quite clear that any formal model, however large, can be no more than a potentially useful idealization of a far more complex reality. In these circumstances, it is doubtful that greater utility necessarily results from larger models.

The discussion of the previous paragraph will no doubt have seemed rather esoteric to the pragmatically inclined manager. Few managers will have the time, and even fewer the inclination, to become thoroughly acquainted with the intricate workings of one of the large modern macroeconomic models. Moreover, given the element of judgment involved in the procedures, a thorough formal understanding of the complete forecast-generating mechanism is unattainable. A more down-to-earth attitude would ask, regardless of their source, how accurate are the forecasts. Over the years a good many empirical studies have evaluated the quality of macroeconometric models and forecasts. The available evidence is not, however, completely clear. In part this is because some studies have assessed the quality of actual forecasts, some have attempted to evaluate particular models, as forecasting tools without the aid of human judgment, while others have done both. Of course, the question of how the forecasts should be evaluated needs to be confronted. We will discuss the principles behind forecast evaluation in some detail in Chapter 13.

It is clear that the quality of a set of forecasts is most sensibly assessed through comparison of accuracy with a set of competing forecasts. Many published studies have compared forecasts derived from econometric models with predictions obtained from the single series ARIMA models of Chapter 7, and more recently with multivariate generalizations of those ARIMA models. The results of some early studies, many of which are summarized in Granger and Newbold (1986), were far from encouraging for the macroeconometric model builders. Now, it is clear that, if an econometric model predicts poorly in comparison with a simple ARIMA alternative, the dynamic specification of the econometric model must be at fault. Perhaps because of the disappointing results of the early evaluation studies, econometricians have, over the years, incorporated increasingly sophisticated dynamic specifications into their models. It is almost certainly not coincidental that subsequent studies such as McNees (1982, 1986), and Dhrymes and Peristiani (1988) have shown econometric forecasts to be more successful in competition against simple time series models, although Ashley (1988) is pessimistic on the question of how far into the future the forecasts are of much value. Given the difference in the scales of effort involved, it is difficult to be overly impressed by findings that large econometric models usually forecast better than simple ARIMA models. One should really expect more. Ideally, ARIMA forecasts should contain no useful information about the future that is not already incorporated in the econometric forecasts.[1] The results of a number of studies, including Longbottom and Holly (1985), suggest that this is often not the case. It seems that scope for further improvement in the quality of macroeconometric forecasts still remains.

What is the bottom line to all of this? If we were asked for forecasts of macroeconomic variables such as gross national product, interest rates or price inflation over, say, the next two or three years, we would consult one or more of the several model-building groups that have established a successful track record over the years. We would not, however, be overly impressed by the apparent sophistication of the models on which the forecasts were based, and certainly not by the fact that the forecasts are advertised as computer-generated. Indeed, we would be well aware of the heavy judgmental element in the forecasting process, and grateful for it, since virtually every study that has looked at the question has found a good deal of gain in forecast quality resulting from the judgmental modifications. In spite of the considerable and impressive efforts that have been put into their generation, we would be aware of the fact that these forecasts will not invariably be reliable. Very serious errors have been made in the past, and no doubt will be made on occasion in the future. Modern macroeconomic forecasting is part art, and part science. It is not, and never will be, an exact science. We might also be inclined to hedge our bets, obtaining forecasts from two or three groups, and combining them to form composite forecasts, using methods to be discussed in Chapter 12.

8.5   Leading Indicators

We are all familiar with the empirical observation that the progression through time of a nation's economic activity is not characterized by continual steady growth. Rather, measures of that activity, such as gross national product, grow quite rapidly over some periods of time, while over others they are flat, and may actually be falling. National economies, then, tend to move through alternating periods of growth and recession. Many economists refer to this type of behavior as **business cycles,** though economic cycles certainly do not exhibit the degree of regularity in either

---

1.   This is the notion of *conditional efficiency* of one set of forecasts with respect to another, to be discussed in Chapter 13.

intensity or duration typically found in cyclical data, such as daily temperature cycles, in the physical sciences. It is sometimes argued that, as a practical matter, it is far more important to be able to anticipate *turning points* in economic activity than to have especially accurate forecasts in those time periods where growth rates are more stable. We would not want to put undue emphasis on this point of view; forecasts at all times are important. However, for planning purposes, advance warning that the economy is about to enter a new phase of expansion or contraction is clearly valuable to the manager.

Proponents of the econometric model-building approach, discussed in the previous sections of this chapter, would argue that sensibly constructed models should be perfectly capable of producing good forecasts around turning points, and indeed that they have often done so. Nevertheless, beginning in the 1930s at the National Bureau of Economic Research, principally through the work of Wesley Mitchell and Arthur Burns, an alternative approach to the prediction of turning points in economic activity has evolved. The goal of this research has been to identify time series whose movements, particularly around peaks and troughs, anticipate those of broad economic activity. Such series are called **leading indicators.** (Also in this research, series that are broadly synchronized with gross national product are identified as **coincident indicators,** whereas those that turn later are identified as **lagging indicators.**) Given a set of individual time series that are thought to be leading indicators, a single composite series, or **index of leading indicators,** can be constructed. The goal, then, is to develop an index that, at least around turning points, can successfully anticipate changing trends in the economy. In the United States, figures for leading indicators have been published monthly by the Department of Commerce in *Survey of Current Business* since 1961. This approach has proved sufficiently attractive that similar indices are now produced by government agencies in many industrialized countries. Research on the leading indicators approach continues, through the work of Geoffrey Moore and his colleagues, at the Center of International Business Cycle Research at Columbia University (previously at Rutgers University).

For many years, the Department of Commerce index of leading indicators has been developed from a set of constituent time series, whose number and membership has changed from time to time. A recently used set included the following series:

1. average work week of production workers, manufacturing
2. average weekly unemployment insurance claims
3. value of manufacturers' new orders for consumer goods and materials
4. index of consumer expectations
5. index of stock prices

6.   contracts and orders for plant and equipment
7.   index of building permits
8.   vendor performance
9.   change in manufacturers' unfilled orders for durable goods
10.   percent change in sensitive materials prices
11.   real money supply (M_2)

The precise details of how the individual series are amalgamated in the formation of a composite index need not detain us; they are, in fact, rather *ad hoc*, though intuitively plausible.[2] The choice of components for the index, and the weights they receive, is far from arbitrary. These determinations are based on the following factors:

1.   The leading indicators approach is sometimes disparagingly referred to as measurement without theory. By contrast with the formal econometric model building approach, there is some justice in this complaint. Certainly no carefully specified theoretical model is developed. However, at least on a fragmented basis, it is required that there be some support in *economic theory* for the claim that a variable should lead general economic activity before it is included in the index. Such justifications are not difficult to find for many of the 11 variables listed above. For example, it is reasonable to expect an increase in new orders to lead to a subsequent increase in production. Again, if a sustained period of decline in unfilled orders is observed, producers can be expected to restrain output in the coming months.

2.   It is also required that the series used have desirable *statistical properties*, such as consistency of definition over time and freedom from serious measurement errors.

3.   *Conformity with the business cycle,* with turning points in the broad economy being anticipated, is crucially important.

4.   It is also useful if the leading indicator series *perform well outside of the neighborhood of turning points*, having the same broad upswings and downswings as the usual measures of economic activity.

5.   A danger in the leading indicators approach is the possibility for generating false signals. Occasional random blips in an indicator series could be wrongly interpreted as signalling a true turning point. Accordingly, *smoothness* in the time series that make up the index of leading indicators is desirable. In the terminology of Chapter 5, series with substantial irregular components are not very useful for this purpose.

6.   The index of leading indicators is a tool for forecasting the future. Therefore, the sooner the index for a particular month is available

2.   The interested reader is referred to *The Handbook of Cyclical Indicators*, U.S. Government Printing Office, Washington, D.C., 1984.

for publication, the better. It is therefore important that observations on the component series be *promptly available*. Since its individual components series are subject to subsequent revision, so is the index itself. It is important that the promptly available data not, on the average, differ too much from the more accurate estimates which may not be available until several months later.

The index of leading indicators, published monthly, is widely cited in the press, and carefully studied by many in the business and financial communities. As a forecasting tool, it is typically applied graphically and informally, and paid most attention when there is some suggestion of a possible turning point. To see how this sort of descriptive analysis might proceed, consider Figure 8.3.

FIGURE 8.3   U.S. indices of leading economic indicators and industrial production, January 1970–April 1992.

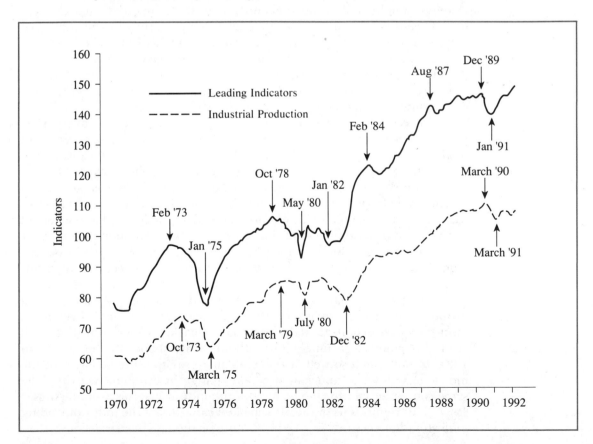

In the figure we have graphed monthly observations from January 1970 through April 1992 of United States industrial production and an index of leading economic indicators. Also, on the graph we have noted a number of interesting dates around turning points in the business cycle. One difficulty in this kind of informal approach is that the precise dating of turning points is to some extent arbitrary. In part this is because economic time series have non-negligible random components, so that their progression through time will not be completely smooth; there are likely to be minor ups and downs through time which, in retrospect, signal nothing of lasting importance. Moreover, the economy is most unlikely to move from boom to bust, or bust to boom, in a single month. Peaks and troughs tend to be somewhat flat, extending over several months. A consequence of these issues is that a turning point in either the indicators or the economy itself is difficult to recognize until a few months after the event.

What emerges from Figure 8.3 appears to be a picture of two time series whose broad movements are similar, with substantial direction changes in industrial production anticipated somewhat by similar changes in the leading indicators. The first interesting feature in the industrial production series is a marked downturn from a peak in October 1973. In fact, the leading indicators had peaked in February of that year, after which a slight decline, which eventually became steeper, set in. A rather sharp recovery in industrial production began after March 1975, while the leading indicators turned two months earlier.

The economy then grew quite steadily for a period of about four years, until a slow-down, and subsequent decline, whose starting point might be dated around March 1979. This appears to have been anticipated by similar behavior of the leading indicators after the peak in October 1978. The very sharp trough in production in July 1980 was anticipated by similar behavior in the indicators two months earlier. This recovery was not really maintained, and it seems reasonable to date sustained recovery from December 1982. The corresponding trough in the indicator series, beginning in January 1982, is much flatter. Nevertheless, it is clear from Figure 8.3 that the indicators did anticipate this recovery by a few months.

We have next marked on our graph of the leading indicator series a pronounced peak in February 1984. No such clear peak is evident in industrial production, though there was a marked slow-down in growth after this point for a time. Thus, although the shapes of the graphs in 1984 do not match so well, it remains fair to say that the behavior of the indicator series had anticipated a real change in economic activity. The same cannot be said for the turning of the indicator series around August 1987. This reminds us of the oft-repeated canard that the index of leading indicators has successfully predicted nine of the last five recessions!

The decline in the leading indicators from a peak in December 1989 does appear to have anticipated by about three months a similar decline in the economy. However, the growth of the indicators since January 1991 provides rather too rosy a forecast of industrial production compared with the actual outcome.

A more wide-ranging analysis of the ability of an index of leading indicators to warn of impending growth cycle peaks and troughs was reported by Klein and Moore (1983). These authors analyzed long series of data from the United States and several other countries, reporting encouraging findings. Their United States data covered 28 years, from 1948 to 1975. In that period they identified nine peaks and nine troughs. For an index of leading indicators, the corresponding turning point occurred in the same month as that of the growth cycle on two occasions, while the leading indicators actually did lead at the other 16 turning points. Over all 18 business cycle turning points, the average lead of the indicator series was six months; it was three months or less on nine occasions. It is certainly useful to have such early warning signals. However, these results are not quite as impressive as they might appear at first sight. It would take two or three months of observations beyond a peak or trough in the leading indicator series to establish with much certainly that what has really occurred is a turning point rather than mere random fluctuations. Therefore, very often the index of leading indicators would be signalling an event that is already in progress, rather than providing a great deal of advance warning.

Although indices of leading indicators were designed as descriptive statistics, aimed particularly at aiding the prediction of turning points in economic activity, a number of authors, including Neftci (1979), Auerbach (1982), and Koch and Rasche (1988), have attempted to incorporate them in formal forecasting models. These authors have asked if a model in which such series as industrial production are related to the leading indicators can yield better forecasts than would result from predicting industrial production exclusively from its own past, based for example on the ARIMA models of Chapter 7. They report some gains in forecast accuracy when the index of leading economic indicators is used in this way.

There seems to be ample evidence that the index of leading economic indicators has some value as a forecasting tool, particularly around turning points in the economy. It is possibly best used informally, perhaps as a supplement to other forecasting methods. In this way it provides a readily available, and often, but not always, an easily interpreted signal of an impending change in trend. Unfortunately, the timing of turning points in the economy is not very reliably estimated in this way. Often the index of leading indicators will turn within three months of a turning point in the business cycle; however, the lead can be a good deal longer, and, indeed, false signals can be generated. The index of leading indicators may be most useful when its movements confirm forecasts obtained from other sources, such as econometric models.

For many years in the developed economies price inflation was at very modest rates, and therefore caused little concern. However, in the 1970s and early 1980s many developed countries experienced serious bouts of inflation, with some disruptive effects on economic activity. These experiences were sufficiently traumatic that concern about price inflation is often well to the forefront in the minds of policy makers, consumers, managers, and particularly participants in financial markets. This concern has stimulated interest in the possibility of discovering leading indicators of inflation, the more so since economists' forecasts of inflation are generally somewhat less reliable than those of gross national product. A particular index of leading indicators of inflation is discussed by Klein (1986), who reports its prediction performance to be generally quite satisfactory.

The leading indicators approach to forecasting is qualitatively different from that based on building formal econometric models. In Chapters 6 and 7 we discussed procedures for forecasting future values of a time series based only on its past behavior. No account in that methodology is paid to the fact that the variable in which we are interested may be related to other variables, and that such relationships might possibly be exploited for forecasting purposes. Both the leading indicators and the econometric model-building approaches take as their point of departure the search for relationships between variables, basing these searches on an understanding of the way in which the economy behaves. However, there the similarity ends. The econometric approach attempts the construction of formal models, firmly grounded in often quite sophisticated economic theory. The leading indicators approach is far more informal and *ad hoc*. At the outset, attention is paid to the importance of *timing* in forecasting, so that the relationships of most interest are those in which changes in one variable are anticipated by changes in another. Certainly, economic theory provides some clues in the selection of indicators. However, no attempt is made to build a formal model reflecting the analysts' theoretical understanding of the way the economy behaves. To many economists, this casual attitude to theory has been a source of considerable irritation. However, to the manager this need be no great cause for concern if useful and reliable predictions can be extracted from the leading indicators. We believe that indices of leading indicators impound different information than is contained in other types of forecasts. Moreover, while formal models are based on an assumption of stable relationships over time, this is less of a concern in the leading indicators approach, where admittedly the lag between changes in the index and changes in the series being anticipated may vary in length, and the relationships involved may vary in strength.

The available studies suggest that, when looking to the future, information impounded in indices of leading indicators should not be entirely ignored; in practice, it has not been.

8.6   SURVEYS OF EXPECTATIONS

In the field of marketing, the collection, analysis and interpretation of survey data, as an aid to the understanding and prediction of behavior, is very much in the mainstream of the subject. In macroeconomics, it is not. Nevertheless, a considerable amount of survey data, intended as an aid to the prediction of economic variables, is collected. Many of these surveys are carried out privately—on behalf of particular industry groups, for example—and their findings are not publicly available. However, there are some regular large-scale surveys whose results are widely reported. Broadly, those surveys that have as at least indirect goals the generation of information useful in the prediction of economic activity can be classified into three types:

1. Information may be obtained from *consumers,* or households, in an attempt to assess public sentiment about the state of the economy, expectations about future economic trends, and possible future purchase plans.
2. Relevant *corporate managers* are questioned about future plans for their organizations, particularly investment plans.
3. *Professional economists* are surveyed about their expectations of the future, and forecasts of specific macroeconomic variables are elicited.

The types of information that might reasonably be expected from these three groups, and the rationales behind the use of such information for forecasting, are quite different. Indeed, perhaps the only unifying theme is that a sample of individuals from a particular target population is questioned in each case.

Information, including expectations and data aimed at assessing consumer sentiment about the economy, has for many years been collected on a monthly basis from surveys of households both by the Survey Research Center at the University of Michigan and the Conference Board. This information is readily available, and quite widely reported. Whether it is sensible to view the expectations of such nonexperts as useful forecasts is problematic. Nevertheless, a broad measure of consumer sentiment, such as the index developed from the survey results by the Survey Research Center, may well contain useful information about the likelihood of purchase of big ticket items, such as automobiles. When consumers view the present and the future with optimism they are far more likely to commit to major purchases, and to take on additional debt to do so. Pessimism is likely to lead to retrenchment, and perhaps the running down of existing debt levels. It is in this area that businesses are likely to find most useful measures of consumer sentiment, though it must be acknowledged that such sentiment, even in the aggregate, can be quite fickle. The Survey Research Center index of consumer expectations is now incorporated in the Department of Commerce index of leading indicators.

In asking those managers who will be involved in the actual decision-making process about investment intentions, we are presumably on somewhat firmer ground. Survey information of this sort is collected regularly by both the Department of Commerce and McGraw-Hill. One attraction to having such information is that corporate investment can prove quite difficult to forecast accurately by other means. Presumably senior managers know what the investment intentions of their corporations are, and these plans should be pretty firm in the short run. Over the longer run, however, such plans can be quite radically altered in the light of changing economic conditions, and the surveyed managers may not be best-placed to anticipate changes in the economic climate. Therefore, although it is reasonable to hope that these surveys could provide reasonable inputs to forecasting business investment in the short term—say, 12 to 18 months ahead—it is more optimistic to expect them to be as valuable in looking much further ahead.

Since 1968, the National Bureau of Economic Research, in collaboration with the American Statistical Association, has carried out quarterly surveys of a group of professional economists who are engaged in forecasting. Summary of the forecasts, particularly consensus forecasts calculated as the medians of the individual predictions, is published, and is widely available. Some discussion of this survey, its methodology, and an analysis of its findings is provided by Zarnowitz (1984, 1985). The forecasting results are generally encouraging. The participants in this kind of survey are professional economists, who may or may not base their individual forecasts on formal econometric models, as well as their own professional judgments. Hence, the consensus forecast may not be radically different in kind from the macroeconomic forecasts discussed earlier in this chapter. Apart from its easy accessibility, this approach offers two possible advantages. First, there may be gains in accuracy from combining the predictions of several economists in the production of an overall composite forecast. We will discuss the combination of forecasts in Chapter 12. Here, it provides a means of incorporating the experience and insights of a number of authorities into the forecast-generating mechanism. In essence, the advantage of a combined forecast over a forecast from a single source is the same as that of investing in a portfolio of common stock rather than in the stock of a single corporation. Risk—in our case, the chance of a very large forecasting error—is reduced. Second, the extent of the diversity of opinions of economists about future values of quantities such as inflation provides a measure of the *uncertainty* in the profession about coming trends. It is often useful, as well as having a point forecast, to have at least an informal assessment of the associated degree of uncertainty.

Survey data have sometimes been incorporated into formal models, with the aim, which is typically successful, of producing improvements in forecast accuracy. An example of this approach to the prediction of inflation is provided by Lahiri and Zaporowski (1987). This may be the way in which survey data can most profitably be used in forecasting. To the purist macroeconometrician, leading indicators and surveys of expectations may seem redundant. Under this view, the determinants of economic activity will all be represented in a carefully specified model, following the prescriptions of modern theory. Thus, any useful information about the future that is contained in either the leading indicators or the surveys should already be impounded in the model. In principle, we might agree. In practice, we might also agree if the forecasting track record of macroeconomic models were better. The behavior of modern industrial economies is so intricate that it cannot be adequately captured in a model. Forecasting such behavior is likely to continue to be extremely difficult, and it is wise to look for guidance to a variety of different sources, even when some of these sources may not be firmly grounded in abstract economic theory.

EXERCISES

8.1   Distinguish between the members of the following pairs:
   (a)   "structural form" and "reduced form"
   (b)   "endogenous variables" and "exogenous variables"
   (c)   "conditional forecasts" and "unconditional forecasts"

8.2   (a)   Carefully explain what is meant by "the identification problem" in the context of simultaneous equations econometric models.
   (b)   Explain why the method of ordinary least squares is often not employed in the estimation of a regression equation that is part of a simultaneous equations econometric system.

8.3   Consider the pair of equations 8.2.2, which constitute a demand/ supply system.
   (a)   Write down the reduced form equations, expressing their parameters as functions of the parameters of the structural equations.

(b) Explain how the supply equation 8.2.2b can be estimated by the method of two-stage least squares.

(c) Explore the consequences of attempting to apply the method of two-stage least squares to the estimation of the parameters of the demand equation 8.2.2a.

8.4 Consider the pair of equations 8.2.6, which constitute a demand/supply system. Set out the reduced form equations, expressing the parameters and error terms in those equations as functions of the parameters and error terms of the structural form equations.

8.5 The following two-equations model was estimated as an aid to the prediction of local advertising expenditures, using annual observations[3]:

$$Y_{1t} = -41.9 + 0.48Y_{1,t-1} + 0.019Y_{2t} + \epsilon_{1t}$$

$$Y_{2t} = 1922 + 0.38X_t + \epsilon_{2t}$$

where

Y_{1t} = Real local advertising expenditures per household

Y_{2t} = Real value of retail sales per household

X_t = Real disposable income per household

Real local advertising expenditures per household in the current year are

$$Y_{1n} = 155.7$$

If real disposable income per household in the next three years is expected to be

$$X_{n+1} = 12,798 \qquad X_{n+2} = 12,962 \qquad X_{n+3} = 13,216$$

obtain point forecasts of real local advertising expenditures per household in these three years.

8.6 Consider the following simple two-equations model for price and wage inflation.

$$Y_{1t} = 3.1 + 0.80Y_{2t} - 0.62X_{1t} + \epsilon_{1t}$$

$$Y_{2t} = 2.2 + 0.65Y_{1t} - 0.33X_{2t} + \epsilon_{2t}$$

3. The model was fitted by N. K. Dhalla, "Short-term forecasts of advertising expenditures." *Journal of Advertising Research 19*, no. 1 (1979):7–14.

where

$$Y_{1t} = \text{Annual percentage change in prices}$$

$$Y_{2t} = \text{Annual percentage change in wages}$$

$$X_{1t} = \text{Annual percentage change in productivity}$$

$$X_{2t} = \text{Percentage of the labor force unemployed}$$

Suppose that next year annual percentage change in productivity and percentage of the labor force unemployed are expected to be

$$X_{1,n+1} = 2.5 \qquad X_{2,n+1} = 6.4$$

Find point forecasts for percentage changes in prices and wages.

8.7   Carefully explain the philosophical distinctions between the econometric model-building and leading indicators approaches to macroeconomic forecasting.

8.8   Continue, using more recent data, the analysis of Figure 8.3. Obtain data after April 1992 on the United States indices of leading economic indicators and industrial production. Plot these data on a graph, and write a summary of your findings. How does the index of leading indicators behave in advance of turning points in the economy?

8.9   What would you expect to learn from a survey of consumer sentiments? Explain which economic variables this information might be useful in predicting, and which it would not.

SELECTED BIBLIOGRAPHY

Ashley, R. (1983). On the usefulness of macroeconomic forecasts as inputs to forecasting models. *Journal of Forecasting, 2,* 211–223.

Ashley, R. (1985). On the optimal use of suboptimal forecasts of explanatory variables. *Journal of Business and Economic Statistics, 3,* 129–131.

Ashley, R. (1988). On the relative worth of recent macroeconomic forecasts. *International Journal of Forecasting, 4,* 363–376.

Auerbach, A. J. (1982). The index of leading indicators: "Measurement without theory" thirty five years later. *Review of Economics and Statistics, 64,* 589–595.

Desai, M. & G. Weber (1988). A Keynesian macroeconometric model of the U.K.: 1955–1984. *Journal of Applied Econometrics, 3,* 1–33.

Dhrymes, P. J. & S. C. Peristiani (1988). A comparison of the forecasting performance of WEFA and ARIMA time series methods. *International Journal of Forecasting, 4,* 81–101.

Granger, C. W. J. & P. Newbold (1986). *Forecasting Economic Time Series* (2nd ed.). Orlando, Fl.: Academic Press.

Jenkins, G. M. (1979). *Practical Experience with Modelling and Forecasting Time Series.* Lancaster, England: Gwilym Jenkins and Partners.

Judge, G. G., R. C. Hill, W. E. Griffiths, H. Lutkepohl, & T. C. Lee (1988). *Introduction to the Theory and Practice of Econometrics* (2nd ed.). New York: Wiley.

Kelejian, H. H. & W. E. Oates (1989). *Introduction to Econometrics* (3rd ed.). New York: Harper and Row.

Klein, L. R. (1988). The statistical approach to economics. *Journal of Econometrics, 37,* 7–26.

Klein, L. R. (ed.) (1991). *Comparative Performance of U.S. Econometric Models.* Oxford: Oxford University Press.

Klein, P. A. (1986). Leading indicators of inflation in market economies. *International Journal of Forecasting, 2,* 403–412.

Klein, P. A. & G. H. Moore (1983). The leading indicator approach to economic forecasting—retrospect and prospect. *Journal of Forecasting, 2,* 119–135.

Koch, P. D. & R. H. Rasche (1988). An examination of the Commerce Department leading indicator approach. *Journal of Business and Economic Statistics, 6,* 167–187.

Lahiri, K. & M. Zaporowski (1987). More flexible use of survey data on expectations in macroeconomic models. *Journal of Business and Economic Statistics, 5,* 69–76.

Longbottom, J. A. & S. Holly (1985). The role of time series analysis in the evaluation of econometric models. *Journal of Forecasting, 4,* 75–87.

Maddala, G. S. (1992). *Introduction to Econometrics* (2nd ed.). New York: MacMillan.

McNees, S. K. (1982). The role of macroeconometric models in forecasting and policy analysis in the United States. *Journal of Forecasting, 1,* 37–48.

McNees, S. K. (1985). Forecasting accuracy of alternative techniques: A comparison of U.S. macroeconomic forecasts. *Journal of Business and Economic Statistics, 4,* 5–23.

McNees, S. K. (1988). On the future of macroeconomic forecasting. *International Journal of Forecasting, 4,* 359–362.

McNees, S. K. (1990). The role of judgment in macroeconomic forecasting accuracy. *International Journal of Forecasting, 6,* 287–299.

Neftci, S. N. (1979). Lead-lag relations, exogeneity and prediction of economic time series. *Econometrica, 47,* 101–113.

Wallis, K. F. (1989). Macroeconomic forecasting: a survey. *Economic Journal, 99,* 28–61.

Wallis, K. F. & J. D. Whitley (1991). Sources of error in forecasts and expectations: U.K. economic models, 1984–8. *Journal of Forecasting, 10,* 231–253.

Young, R. M. (1982). Forecasting with an econometric model. *Journal of Forecasting, 1,* 189–204.

Zarnowitz, V. (1984). The accuracy of individual and group forecasts from business outlook surveys. *Journal of Forecasting, 3,* 11–26.

Zarnowitz, V. (1985). Rational expectations and macroeconomic forecasts. *Journal of Business and Economic Statistics, 3,* 293–311.

Zellner, A. (1988). Bayesian analysis in econometrics. *Journal of Econometrics, 37,* 27–50.

9 Regression Models, Exponential Smoothing Algorithms, and ARIMA Models: Relationships and Extensions

9.1 INTRODUCTION

The bulk of this book is devoted to the introduction of three quantitative approaches to forecasting: regression models, exponential smoothing algorithms, and ARIMA time series models. Regression models were discussed in Chapters 3 and 4, and their simultaneous equations extensions in Chapter 8. In Chapters 6 and 7 we introduced exponential smoothing algorithms and ARIMA models as devices to facilitate the prediction of future values of a time series from its own past history.

We have presented these as three distinct approaches to forecasting, and the major distinctions among them should be pretty clear. In building regression models, emphasis is placed on relationships among variables, so that forecasts of one variable will be based, in part, on the values of others, whereas our discussions in Chapters 6 and 7 were restricted to the prediction of future values of a particular variable exclusively on the basis of its own past values. Both regression and ARIMA analysis are based on the fitting to observed data of formal models. To some extent the structures of these models are determined by either the characteristics of the available data or subject matter theory, or both. The fitted models are then projected forward to derive forecasts. By contrast, the exponential smoothing approach to forecasting is more *ad hoc* in character. Models are not explicitly built. Rather, a collection of intuitively plausible prediction algorithms that have proved useful in practical applications has been assembled. The chief advantage of exponential smoothing is that future values of a very large number of time series can be routinely predicted with a minimum of manual intervention and expense.

In the business world, a great many practical forecasting exercises are based on one or another of these three approaches. Our purpose in this chapter is to explore their similarities and possibilities for their amalgamation. We will try, then, to unify some of the material from earlier chapters to provide the reader with a more coherent picture of the quantitative forecasting methodology. In truth, the subject matter of forecasting is so fragmented that it is particularly important to explore possibilities for unification, where they exist, rather than leave the reader with the impression that what is on offer is merely a bewildering array of wholly distinct methodologies from which a choice must somehow be made.

In the next three sections of this chapter we explore the relationship between certain exponential smoothing algorithms and ARIMA models. In particular it will be shown that, while model building plays no overt part in exponential smoothing, many of the algorithms in fact yield forecasts that are identical to those that follow from specific ARIMA models. In effect, then, it is possible that practical application of the two approaches could lead to the same forecasts. Such equivalencies have been studied for many years, dating back to Muth (1960). Later sections of the chapter are intended to move us away from the notion that ARIMA and regression models are disjoint entities from which the analyst must choose. We will see, rather, that it is quite straightforward to construct a global model of which the regression models of Chapter 4 and the ARIMA models of Chapter 7 are special cases. For our purposes the precise details of these global models, and of the methods through which they are fitted to data, are less important than the recognition of the possibility of unifying the regression and ARIMA approaches to forecasting. Accordingly, we will not devote a great deal of space to these details.

This chapter does not explain how to forecast; it is intended to draw together material on regression, exponential smoothing, and ARIMA models in order to clarify some of their features and the relationships among them.

9.2 CONSTANT PREDICTION FUNCTIONS

We begin our study of the relationship between exponential smoothing and ARIMA models by returning to the simple exponential smoothing algorithm of Section 6.2. Given a time series, X_t, the current level of the series at time t, L_t, is found through the algorithm

$$L_t = \alpha X_t + (1 - \alpha)L_{t-1} \qquad (9.2.1)$$

where the smoothing constant α is a number between zero and one. Standing at time t, all future values X_{t+h} of the series are then predicted by the current level, so that the forecasts are

$$\hat{X}_t(h) = L_t \qquad h = 1, 2, 3, \ldots$$

These forecasts, made at fixed time t, are all the same, so that we describe this as a **constant prediction function.** (Figure 6.1 provides an illustration.)

Now, as in Chapter 6, let e_t denote the error that is made when X_t is predicted at time $(t - 1)$, so that

$$e_t = X_t - L_{t-1} \qquad (9.2.2)$$

After a little algebra it is now possible to transpose the simple exponential smoothing algorithm to a familiar ARIMA form. First, replacing t by $(t - 1)$ in equation 9.2.1 gives

$$L_{t-1} = \alpha X_{t-1} - (1 + \alpha)L_{t-2}$$

Then, using equation 9.2.2 to substitute for L_{t-1} and L_{t-2} in this expression yields

$$X_t - e_t = \alpha X_{t-1} + (1 - \alpha)(X_{t-1} - e_{t-1})$$

so that

$$X_t - X_{t-1} = e_t - (1 - \alpha)e_{t-1} \qquad (9.2.3)$$

Equation 9.2.3 relates the original time series X_t to the one-step prediction errors e_t from the simple exponential smoothing algorithm.

Finally, setting

$$e_t = a_t \qquad 1 - \alpha = \theta$$

in equation 9.2.3 we have

$$X_t - X_{t-1} = a_t - \theta a_{t-1} \qquad (9.2.4)$$

This is the ARIMA(0, 1, 1) model of Chapter 7, where the first difference of a time series obeys a first-order moving average model. To establish the equivalence of this model and simple exponential smoothing in forecasting, it is only necessary then to show that, when forecasts are derived from equation 9.2.4, the error terms a_t are indeed the one-step forecast errors. This follows from our general analysis in Section 7.10. Specifically, suppose that we are standing at time $(t - 1)$ and want to predict X_t, which is assumed to be generated by the model 9.2.4. Then

$$X_t = X_{t-1} + a_t - \theta a_{t-1}$$

and the forecast is

$$\hat{X}_{t-1}(1) = X_{t-1} - \theta a_{t-1}$$

with error

$$X_t - \hat{X}_{t-1}(1) = a_t$$

A review of Section 7.10 should make it clear that this result is quite general. The error term a_t in any ARIMA model is the one-step forecast error, made when X_t is predicted at time $(t - 1)$.

We have now succeeded in establishing that forecasting through simple exponential smoothing is equivalent to prediction through a specific ARIMA model—the ARIMA(0, 1, 1) model 9.2.4, with moving average parameter θ equal to one minus the smoothing constant α. Notice that the usual restriction in exponential smoothing, that the smoothing constant takes a value between zero and one, implies that the moving average parameter θ of the equivalent ARIMA(0, 1, 1) model must also be between zero and one. This is more restrictive than is required in the usual time series ARIMA model analysis, where θ is permitted to take any value between -1 and 1.

In Chapter 6, we saw that, in practical exponential smoothing exercises, an appropriate value of the smoothing constant is often chosen objectively through the minimization of the sum of squares of in-sample one-step forecast errors. This is analogous to the estimation from sample data of the moving average parameter θ of the ARIMA(0, 1, 1) model 9.2.4.

There is a limited sense, then, in which forecasting through exponential smoothing and through an ARIMA model are equivalent. Suppose that data on a particular time series are available. If, by some means or another, it is decided to proceed through simple exponential smoothing with objective choice of smoothing constant, and if the ARIMA model-building methodology suggests that an ARIMA(0, 1, 1) model is appropriate, then the two approaches will yield more or less identical forecasts. (In practice, small differences will arise in the forecasts through differences in the computational algorithms in which the smoothing constant and the moving average parameter are estimated.) This equivalence holds only if the estimate of the moving average parameter in the ARIMA model is positive.

The equivalence established here between simple exponential smoothing and a particular ARIMA model can be viewed in two different ways, depending on one's perspective. From the viewpoint of an adherent of the ARIMA model-building approach to forecasting, simple exponential smoothing offers no new possibilities. It simply generates forecasts that could be obtained from a specific ARIMA model. Moreover, if that model is indeed appropriate for the prediction of future values of a particular time series, this fact should be revealed through careful application of the ARIMA model-building methodology. Besides parameter estimation, that methodology incorporates model selection and checking stages which should allow the intelligent choice, based on evidence in the data, of an appropriate model from a broad general class of models, of which the ARIMA(0, 1, 1) model is but one specific member. Thus, if a given time series is best predicted through simple exponential smoothing, this conclusion is likely to emerge from application of the ARIMA model-building methodology, and the ARIMA(0, 1, 1) model (or something close to it) will be fitted. Equally important, that methodology should reveal those cases for which the ARIMA(0, 1, 1) model is clearly not appropriate, and consequently where simple exponential smoothing is likely to yield quite poor forecasts. Such well-developed procedures for model selection and checking are not available within the exponential smoothing framework.

An adherent of exponential smoothing can also take some comfort from the equivalence of forecasting through simple exponential smoothing and the ARIMA(0, 1, 1) model. Experience suggests that this particular ARIMA model is quite often fitted in practice to actual business and economic time series, arguing that the intuition behind simple exponential smoothing accords well with observation, and that frequently this algorithm will be appropriate for forecasting. Moreover, resources will often be unavailable for the careful analysis of every member of a large set of time series, and it is certainly reassuring to learn that, had such resources been available, they would quite often lead to the same forecasts that would follow the application of some "all purpose" algorithm such as simple exponential smoothing to all series. In addition, it is often required to predict future values of time series for which only a relatively short past history is available. Here, given little evidence on which to base judgments, the ARIMA model-building methodology will not be very reliable, and it may be preferable to work with an algorithm, such as simple exponential smoothing, which is known to be appropriate for many similar series.

As we will see, prediction from a number of other exponential smoothing algorithms can be shown to be equivalent to forecasting from specific ARIMA models. The above comments apply also to those cases.

In Section 6.5 we discussed an approach which is still quite popular, known as general exponential smoothing. Here a deterministic function of time is fitted to data, not by least squares, but by discounted least squares. The simplest possible case of this arises when the deterministic function of time is just a constant. Then, in the notation of 6.5.10 and 6.5.11, standing at time t future values of a series are predicted by

$$\hat{X}_t(h) = a(t) \qquad h = 1, 2, \ldots$$

where the value $a(t)$ is chosen to minimize

$$S = \sum_{j=0}^{t-1} \delta^j [X_{t-j} - a(t)]^2 \qquad 0 < \delta < 1 \qquad (9.2.5)$$

Now, it can be shown that, approximately for moderately large t,

$$a(t) = (1 - \delta)X_t + \delta a(t - 1) \qquad (9.2.6)$$

(The reader was asked to establish this result in Exercise 6.12.) Comparison of equation 9.2.6 with equation 9.2.1 reveals the equivalence of this algorithm to simple exponential smoothing, with smoothing constant α equal to one minus the discount parameter δ. Of course, the implication is that this algorithm also is equivalent to forecasting from the ARIMA(0, 1, 1) model.

9.3 LINEAR TREND PREDICTION FUNCTIONS

Consider now Holt's linear trend algorithm of Section 6.3. Here, a time series X_t is viewed as having local level and slope components, L_t and T_t, estimated through the recurrence equations

$$L_t = \alpha X_t + (1 - \alpha)(L_{t-1} + T_{t-1}) \qquad (9.3.1a)$$

$$T_t = \beta(L_t - L_{t-1}) + (1 - \beta)T_{t-1} \qquad (9.3.1b)$$

In equations 9.3.1 the parameters α and β are smoothing constants whose values are generally set between zero and one, perhaps through an objective procedure, choosing those numbers for which the sum of squared in-sample one-step forecast errors is a minimum. At time t, future values of the time series are then predicted from

$$\hat{X}_t(h) = L_t + hT_t \qquad h = 1, 2, 3, \ldots$$

These forecasts, made from a fixed time period, all lie on a straight line, so that we describe this as a **linear trend prediction function.** (An illustration of forecasts obtained from an application of Holt's linear trend algorithm is provided in Figure 6.4.)

Let e_t denote the error made in predicting X_t at time $(t - 1)$, so that

$$e_t = X_t - \hat{X}_{t-1}(1) = X_t - L_{t-1} - T_{t-1} \qquad (9.3.2)$$

Now, after a little tedious algebra, it is possible to derive from equations 9.3.1 and 9.3.2 the form of an ARIMA model that generates the same forecasts as Holt's linear trend algorithm.

First, substituting from equation 9.3.2 into equation 9.3.1a gives

$$L_t = \alpha X_t + (1 - \alpha)(L_{t-1} + T_{t-1})$$
$$= \alpha(L_{t-1} + T_{t-1} + e_t) + (1 - \alpha)(L_{t-1} + T_{t-1})$$

so that

$$L_t = L_{t-1} + T_{t-1} + \alpha e_t \qquad (9.3.3)$$

Then, substituting from equation 9.3.3 into equation 9.3.1b gives

$$T_t = \beta(L_t - L_{t-1}) + (1 - \beta)T_{t-1}$$
$$= \beta(T_{t-1} + \alpha e_t) + (1 - \beta)T_{t-1}$$

so that

$$T_t - T_{t-1} = \alpha\beta e_t \qquad (9.3.4)$$

from which it follows that

$$T_t - 2T_{t-1} + T_{t-2} = (T_t - T_{t-1}) - (T_{t-1} - T_{t-2}) \qquad (9.3.5)$$
$$= \alpha\beta(e_t - e_{t-1})$$

Next, using equations 9.3.3 and 9.3.4 we find

$$L_t - 2L_{t-1} + L_{t-2} = (L_t - L_{t-1}) - (L_{t-1} - L_{t-2})$$
$$= T_{t-1} - T_{t-2} + \alpha(e_t - e_{t-1})$$

so that

$$L_t - 2L_{t-1} + L_{t-2} = \alpha\beta e_{t-1} + \alpha(e_t - e_{t-1}) \qquad (9.3.6)$$

Finally, using equation 9.3.2, we can write

$$X_t - 2X_{t-1} + X_{t-2} = (L_{t-1} - 2L_{t-2} + L_{t-3})$$
$$+ (T_{t-1} - 2T_{t-2} + T_{t-3}) + (e_t - 2e_{t-1} + e_{t-2})$$

so that, from equations 9.3.5 and 9.3.6, we find

$$X_t - 2X_{t-1} + X_{t-2} = \alpha\beta e_{t-2} + \alpha(e_{t-1} - e_{t-2})$$
$$+ \alpha\beta(e_{t-1} - e_{t-2}) + (e_t - 2e_{t-1} + e_{t-2})$$

Therefore

$$X_t - 2X_{t-1} + X_{t-2} = e_t - (2 - \alpha - \alpha\beta)e_{t-1} + (1 - \alpha)e_{t-2} \qquad (9.3.7)$$

Now, in equation 9.3.7, set

$$a_t = e_t \qquad \theta_1 = 2 - \alpha - \alpha\beta \qquad \theta_2 = -(1 - \alpha) \qquad (9.3.8)$$

so that

$$X_t - 2X_{t-1} + X_{t-2} = a_t - \theta_1 a_{t-1} - \theta_2 a_{t-2}$$

or, introducing the back-shift operator B,

$$(1 - B)^2 X_t = (1 - \theta_1 B - \theta_2 B^2)a_t \qquad (9.3.9)$$

Recalling our discussion of Chapter 7, equation 9.3.9 is the generating equation of an ARIMA(0, 2, 2) model, where the second difference of a time series follows a second-order moving average process. We have established then that an ARIMA(0, 2, 2) model can generate the same forecasts as Holt's linear trend algorithm. Once again, there is an equivalence between prediction from a commonly used exponential smoothing algorithm and from a specific member of the general ARIMA class.

To illustrate, in Example 7.3 of Section 7.9 we fitted the ARIMA(0, 2, 2) model to annual data on the number of active oil wells in the United States. The fitted model achieved was

$$(1 - B)^2 X_t = a_t - 0.856 a_{t-1} + 0.372 a_{t-2}$$

so that, in the notation of equation 9.3.9, the moving average parameter estimates are

$$\theta_1 = 0.856 \qquad \theta_2 = -0.372$$

Then, from equations 9.3.8, we find

$$1 - \alpha = 0.372$$

so that

$$\alpha = 0.628$$

and

$$2 - \alpha - \alpha\beta = 0.856$$

Hence

$$2 - 0.628 - 0.628\beta = 0.856$$

giving

$$\beta = 0.822$$

It follows that prediction of this time series from our fitted ARIMA(0, 2, 2) model is equivalent to forecasting from Holt's linear trend algorithm with smoothing constants 0.628 and 0.822. In practice, if the values of the smoothing constants are chosen objectively, the Holt algorithm should yield for such series forecasts that are very similar to those obtained from a fitted ARIMA(0, 2, 2) model, though there will be modest differences due to the use of different estimation procedures. It is useful to reinforce a point made in the previous section. In our ARIMA analysis of the oil wells data in Chapter 7, the fitted model finally achieved was arrived at through a careful systematic analysis of the properties of the available data, so that it is possible to have a degree of faith in its merits as a forecasting tool for this particular series. It is possible that an analyst may have chosen to predict this series through Holt's linear trend predictor. However, such a choice would be based on little more than inspired guesswork.

In Section 6.5, we discussed Brown's double smoothing algorithm, which is equivalent to the case of general exponential smoothing where a linear trend function is estimated by discounted least squares. We showed that double smoothing is simply a special case of Holt's linear trend algorithm. It necessarily follows that particular ARIMA(0, 2, 2) models yield the same forecasts as double smoothing.

Some Other Nonseasonal Exponential Smoothing Algorithms

The most popular exponential smoothing algorithms are those that project linear trend forecast functions. They have been widely and successfully applied to predict future values of a broad range of business and economic time series. However, as we saw in Section 6.5, other exponential smoothing algorithms, with different forecast functions, are sometimes used. Some, but not all, of these also have equivalent ARIMA model representations.

The damped trend algorithm, set out in equation 6.5.1 is given by

$$L_t = \alpha X_t + (1 - \alpha)(L_{t-1} + \phi T_{t-1}) \qquad 0 < \alpha < 1 \qquad 0 < \phi \le 1$$

$$T_t = \beta(L_t - L_{t-1}) + (1 - \beta)\phi T_{t-1} \qquad 0 < \beta < 1$$

with forecasts obtained from

$$\hat{X}_t(h) = L_t + \sum_{i=1}^{h} \phi^i T_t \qquad h = 1, 2, \ldots$$

This is a generalization of Holt's linear trend algorithm, reducing to the latter in the special case in which the parameter ϕ is equal to one. After a little algebra, whose details are similar to that which led to equation 9.3.7, it can be shown that forecasts from the nonseasonal damped trend algorithm are equivalent to those from the ARIMA(1, 1, 2) model

$$(1 - \phi B)(1 - B)X_t = (1 - \theta_1 B - \theta_2 B^2)a_t \qquad (9.3.10)$$

where

$$\theta_1 = 1 + \phi - \alpha - \phi\alpha\beta \qquad \theta_2 = -\phi(1 - \alpha)$$

The derivation of this result is left as an exercise to the reader. Comparison of equation 9.3.10 to equation 9.3.9 makes the position clear. If Holt's linear trend algorithm is appropriate, the time series requires differencing twice to achieve stationarity. On the other hand, the damped trend algorithm implies just a single differencing, leading to a model with a single autoregressive parameter ϕ, as well as two moving average parameters. If a time series is indeed generated by the model 9.3.10, with a value of ϕ much less than one, this should emerge pretty clearly from an examination of the sample autocorrelations and partial autocorrelations of the first differenced series.

In the method of general exponential smoothing, discussed in Section 6.5, a deterministic function of time is fitted to the data through discounted least squares, using a discount parameter δ with a value between zero and one. Often, for nonseasonal series polynomials in time are used as fitting functions. We have already seen that, for a constant fitting function this is equivalent to forecasting through simple exponential smoothing, while a linear trend fitting function leads to a special case of Holt's linear trend algorithm. More generally, if the fitting function is a polynomial of degree k, McKenzie (1976) has shown that general exponential smoothing is equivalent to prediction from the subset of ARIMA$(0, k + 1, k + 1)$ models

$$(1 - B)^{k + 1}X_t = (1 - \delta B)^{k + 1}a_t$$

In fact, considerable practical experience in the analysis of actual business and economic time series suggests that almost never is it necessary to difference a series more than twice to achieve stationarity. Thus, although in principle general exponential smoothing permits a wide array of possible predictors, most of these are unlikely to be of much practical value. McKenzie also establishes an equivalence between certain other general exponential smoothing predictors and particular members of the ARIMA class of models.

As we have seen in this and the previous section, most exponential smoothing predictors in common use for nonseasonal time series have quite simple ARIMA model equivalents. (The exponential trend algorithm of Section 6.5 is an exception.) For this reason, we judge the value of exponential smoothing in the nonseasonal case to be quite limited. Provided the analyst has available a sufficiently long series—say, at least 40 observations—it should be possible through careful analysis within the ARIMA model-building framework to fit appropriate models for forecasting. These models may or may not be equivalent to particular exponential smoothing algorithms. In sections 2 and 9 of Chapter 7 we fitted what seemed to be appropriate ARIMA models to four nonseasonal time series. These were:

Daily stock volume: ARIMA$(1, 0, 0)$

Daily observations on percent advances of number of issues traded: ARIMA$(0, 0, 1)$

Annual observations on number of private housing units started: ARIMA$(0, 1, 3)$

Annual observations on number of active oil wells: ARIMA$(0, 2, 2)$

As we have already seen, the model fitted to the oil wells data is equivalent to forecasting from Holt's linear trend algorithm. However, the other three models are not equivalent to any commonly employed exponential smoothing algorithms. The ARIMA class of models offers a far richer array of alternative predictors than does exponential smoothing, and, given sufficient data, the ARIMA model-building methodology offers a procedure that should give the analyst a good chance of choosing an appropriate model in individual applications. Moreover, given available modern computing hardware and software resources, an experienced analyst should be able to fit ARIMA models quite quickly. In recent years, these computing advances have done much to mitigate the advantage through exponential smoothing of the capability for handling a large number of series in a short amount of time. The role of exponential smoothing in the analysis of nonseasonal series should accordingly be quite limited, perhaps to just the analysis of short series.

9.4   LINEAR TREND PLUS SEASONAL DUMMIES PREDICTION FUNCTIONS

The discussion of the previous two sections develops our view that, for the prediction of nonseasonal time series, the standard exponential smoothing algorithms have relatively little to offer in comparison with a careful ARIMA model-building analysis. This view is by no means universally shared. However, modern computing technology now allows a full ARIMA analysis to proceed quite rapidly. Moreover, that analysis contemplates the possibility of a very wide array of alternative prediction functions, together with a soundly based methodology for selecting a predictor whose merits are supported by the evidence of the available data. Virtually all exponential smoothing algorithms in common use are equivalent to quite simple members of the general ARIMA class of models, and are therefore readily available for selection in the ARIMA analysis, if they are supported by the data.

In this section we discuss the case of seasonal time series, where the position is rather different. In the previous section we saw that a linear trend prediction function is often appropriate for nonseasonal time series. If the series is seasonal, it is obviously desirable that seasonal patterns be reflected in the prediction function. One possibility is a linear trend on which are superimposed "seasonal dummies," summing to zero over every span of one year. A number of forecasting procedures in common use yield such prediction functions. An extensive discussion and comparison of some of them is provided by Newbold (1988).

One predictor of this type is the additive seasonality variant of the Holt-Winters algorithm. In Section 6.4 we applied this algorithm to some

Figure 9.1   Quarterly sales and forecasts from Holt-Winters additive seasonal algorithm.

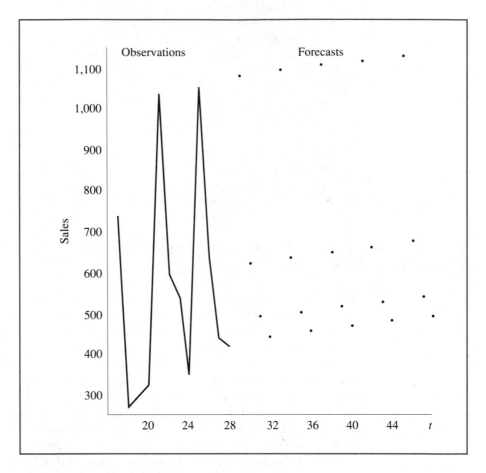

quarterly sales data. Figure 9.1, which is an extension of Figure 6.5, shows the resulting forecasts several years ahead. Forecasts into the distant future, derived in this way, cannot be expected to be too reliable; algorithms of this sort were designed for, and are most useful in, short-term forecasting. However, Figure 9.1 does clarify the nature of the forecast function. The predictions follow an upward linear trend, with a repeating seasonal pattern superimposed.

Let X_t be a seasonal time series, observed at s periods each year. Then the additive variant of the Holt-Winters algorithm estimates local level, L, slope, T, and seasonal factor, F, through the recurrence equations

$$L_t = \alpha(X_t - F_{t-s}) + (1 - \alpha)(L_{t-1} + T_{t-1})$$

$$T_t = \beta(L_t - L_{t-1}) + (1 - \beta)T_{t-1}$$

$$F_t = \gamma(X_t - L_t) + (1 - \gamma)F_{t-s}$$

where the fixed parameters α, β, and γ are smoothing constants. Standing at time t, forecasts of future values of the time series are then obtained through

$$\hat{X}_t(h) = L_t + hT_t + F_{t+h-s} \qquad h = 1, 2, \ldots, s$$

$$= L_t + hT_t + F_{t+h-2s} \qquad h = s + 1, s + 2, \ldots, 2s$$

and so on. It is possible to show that prediction through this algorithm is equivalent to forecasting from a particular ARIMA model. (The details of the derivation, which we omit, are similar to those of the previous section.) The equivalent ARIMA model is

$$
\begin{aligned}
(1 &- B)(1 - B^s)X_t \\
&= a_t - \theta_1 a_{t-1} - \theta_2 a_{t-2} - \cdots - \theta_s a_{t-s} - \theta_{s+1} a_{t-s-1}
\end{aligned}
\qquad (9.4.1)
$$

where B is the back-shift operator, a_t the white noise error series, and

$$\theta_1 = 1 - \alpha - \alpha\beta \qquad \theta_j = -\alpha\beta \qquad (j = 2, \ldots, s - 1)$$

$$\theta_s = 1 - \alpha\beta - \gamma(1 - \alpha) \qquad \theta_{s+1} = -1 + \alpha + \gamma(1 - \alpha)$$

$$(9.4.2)$$

Notice that this model implies the application of both the regular difference operator, $(1 - B)$, and the seasonal difference operator, $(1 - B^s)$, to achieve stationarity. According to equation 9.4.1, the differenced series $(1 - B)(1 - B^s)X_t$ then obeys a moving average process of order $(s + 1)$.

On the surface, then, we have established formal equivalence between the additive variant of the Holt-Winters exponential smoothing algorithm and a specific ARIMA model. However, from a practical point of view, this result has very little substantive content. In practice, the Holt-Winters algorithm and an ARIMA model-building analysis will yield different forecasts. In fact, it can be shown that any model of the general form equation 9.4.1 yields a prediction function that is a linear trend plus seasonal dummies. However, this model involves $(s + 1)$ parameters θ_j—

that is, 13 parameters for monthly data. The principle of parsimony suggests that it would typically be unwise to fit such elaborate models to data with any reasonable hope of developing successful forecasts. It is more sensible to seek variants of the general model involving just a few unknown parameters. As we have seen, the Holt-Winters algorithm provides one such variant where, according to equation 9.4.2, the moving average parameters of equation 9.4.1 are all functions of the three smoothing constants α, β, and γ. Moreover, this variant is not one that would emerge through the usual ARIMA model-building exercise of Section 7.11, where attention is usually concentrated on the class of multiplicative seasonal ARIMA models.

As we noted in Section 7.11, a particular model of this class that often in practice emerges from the ARIMA analysis as being appropriate is the "airline model"

$$
\begin{aligned}
(1 - B)(1 - B^s)X_t &= (1 - \theta_1 B)(1 - \Theta_1 B^s)a_t \\
&= a_t - \theta_1 a_{t-1} - \Theta_1 a_{t-s} + \theta_1 \Theta_1 a_{t-s-1}
\end{aligned}
\qquad (9.4.3)
$$

where θ_1 and Θ_1 are fixed parameters. As can be seen, this is quite distinct from the model implied by the additive variant of the Holt-Winters algorithm, and the two will not generate the same forecasts. In fact, as Newbold (1988) shows, all ARIMA models of the general form of equation 9.4.1, of which the Holt-Winters algorithm and the airline model are two distinct special cases, can also be expressed as exponential smoothing algorithms, in both recurrence and error-correction forms. There is, then, a close *formal* connection between exponential smoothing and ARIMA models in the seasonal case. It is the practical need to work with a parsimonious model that leads to differences when the two approaches are applied to data.

We do not find the rationale behind the development of either particular exponential smoothing algorithms, such as Holt-Winters, or multiplicative seasonal ARIMA models sufficiently compelling to assert that one or the other is uniquely attractive as a tool for practical forecasting. Of course, an attraction of the ARIMA model-building methodology remains the facility to entertain a broad range of models, and hence a range of forecast functions, of which linear trend plus seasonal dummies is but one possibility, together with the ability to select among them on the basis of data evidence. Nevertheless, Holt-Winters and other exponential smoothing algorithms do provide alternative plausible predictors that have enjoyed some practical success, and that will not emerge from an ARIMA model-building exercise. The case for abandoning exponential smoothing altogether in favor of ARIMA model building for forecasting a time series from its own past is far less strong for seasonal series than for nonseasonal series. On the contrary, intuitive plausibility, practical success, and computational convenience render Holt-Winters and some of the other seasonal exponential smoothing algorithms discussed in Chapter 6 quite attractive.

There is an exponential smoothing algorithm that is equivalent to the ARIMA airline model 9.4.3. McKenzie (1984) has shown that the variant of general exponential smoothing in which a linear trend plus seasonal dummies is fitted to data by discounted least squares, with discount parameter δ, is equivalent to prediction from the model

$$(1 - B)(1 - B^s)X_t = (1 - \delta B)(1 - \delta^s B^s)a_t$$

This is simply a special case of equation 9.4.3, with both moving average parameters depending on the single discount parameter δ. It is difficult to see it as an attractive special case, particularly since the analysis of actual time series rarely suggests this particular relationship between the two moving average parameters. Indeed, this result argues the general inadequacy of working with just a single parameter in general exponential smoothing, especially in the analysis of seasonal time series.

In practice, the multiplicative seasonal variant 6.4.7 of the Holt-Winters algorithm is often employed. The relationship between this algorithm and ARIMA models is explored in some detail by Abraham and Ledolter (1986). In fact, the multiplicative seasonal Holt-Winters algorithm has no equivalent ARIMA representation, a conclusion that strengthens our assertion that, in the seasonal case, exponential smoothing offers interesting and intuitively appealing possibilities that are not available in practice through an ARIMA model-building exercise.

9.5 REGRESSION MODELS WITH ARIMA ERROR STRUCTURES

Although exponential smoothing is not based on the construction of formal models, certain models are, in a sense, implicit in the development of forecasts from particular exponential smoothing algorithms. It is the model construction aspect that provides the linkage between the regression methods of Chapters 3 and 4 and the ARIMA models of Chapter 7. As we have presented them, these appear to constitute two quite distinct approaches to forecasting. Regression models are employed to formulate behavioral relationships among variables, as might be postulated by subject matter theory, while ARIMA model building provides quite a sophisticated basis for the prediction of future values of a time series exclusively from its own past history. Now, in some circumstances aspects of each of these approaches might be quite appealing. If worthwhile subject matter theory is available, it is desirable to incorporate it into a forecasting exercise, and the regression model framework will often provide a useful basis for accomplishing this. On the other hand, the forecaster must necessarily be conscious of the evolution of historical patterns, which will often be of more value than the understanding of contemporaneous relationships among variables. After all, the forecasting problem is essentially dynamic rather than static in character. The ARIMA model framework can be very useful for capturing such evolutionary patterns.

In fact, it is not at all necessary to choose to attack a forecasting problem through either regression models or ARIMA models. Since both are relatively simple parametric statistical models, it is quite straightforward in principle to write down a broader model incorporating each as special cases. Moreover, it is often not too difficult to analyze actual data in the context of this more general model, and hence to develop forecasts embodying both the regression and ARIMA components. Consider the model

$$Y_t = \alpha + \beta_1 X_{1t} + \beta_2 X_{2t} + \cdots + \beta_K X_{Kt} + \epsilon_t \qquad (9.5.1a)$$

$$\phi(B)(1 - B)^d \epsilon_t = \theta(B) a_t \qquad (9.5.1b)$$

Equation 9.5.1a is simply the usual multiple regression model linking a dependent variable Y and K independent variables $X_1, X_2, \ldots, X_K$, with an error term ϵ_t. However, extending the models of Chapter 4, equation 9.5.1b permits these error terms to follow a general ARIMA(p, d, q) model. The notation here is that of Chapter 7, so that B is the back-shift operator, and the error term a_t is white noise. In other words, these errors are taken to have zero means, equal variances, and to be uncorrelated with one another.

We have already met three special cases of the general model 9.5.1:

(i)   If the error term ϵ_t of equation 9.5.1a is white noise, so that equation 9.5.1b reduces to

$$\epsilon_t = a_t$$

then we simply have the basic multiple regression model under the standard assumptions of Section 4.1.

(ii)   In Section 4.5 we discussed the problem of autocorrelated errors in regression equations, concentrating in particular there on the special case where the errors obey a first order autoregressive model—that is, an ARIMA(1, 0, 0) process

$$\epsilon_t - \phi\epsilon_{t-1} = a_t$$

This possibility is, of course, less general than is allowed by equation 9.5.1b. The first-order autoregressive model has, in practice, often proved useful in representing the time series behavior of the error terms in a regression equation. However, this simple model is by no means invariably adequate, and it can certainly be useful to entertain the possibility of employing other members of the general ARIMA class for this purpose.

(iii)   In the special case of equation 9.5.1a where

$$\beta_1 = \beta_2 = \cdots = \beta_K = 0$$

the independent variables no longer appear in 9.5.1a. The implication now is that the dependent variable simply follows an ARIMA model, and that the independent variables are of no value in its prediction, at least within the framework of the model 9.5.1.

Our purpose in this section is not to explore technical issues concerning the model 9.5.1, or the details of its fitting to data. Rather, we want to note here, and in the following section, that regression and ARIMA models need not be viewed as competing bases for the forecasting of business and economic time series. Rather, both can be seen as basic building blocks that may be valuable in the construction of more general and more versatile forecasting models. The ability to incorporate the ARIMA structure in a more general framework, such as the model 9.5.1, constitutes a significant advantage over exponential smoothing algorithms. It is difficult to extend the exponential smoothing methods of Chapter 6 in any satisfactory way to allow the incorporation into the forecast of information on related time series.

In fact, it is not difficult in principle to fit models of the general form of equation 9.5.1 to data. In outline, a workable methodology proceeds as follows:

(i)   As a first step, the regression equation 9.5.1 is fitted by ordinary least squares, pretending for now that the error terms ϵ_t are white noise.

(ii) The residuals $\hat{\epsilon}_t$ from the first step fitted regression are estimates of the error terms ϵ_t. Consequently, the sample autocorrelations and partial autocorrelations of these residuals provide estimates of the autocorrelations and partial autocorrelations of the errors. These residual sample autocorrelations and partial autocorrelations are then employed, precisely as in Section 7.9, to suggest an appropriate ARIMA(p, d, q) structure for the regression errors from the general class 9.5.1b.

(iii) Once a specific model has been selected from the general class, the regression parameters $\alpha, \beta_1, \ldots, \beta_K$ of 9.5.1a and the autoregressive and moving average parameters of equation 9.5.1b can be jointly estimated through efficient statistical methods. A number of statistical program packages, including SPSS, have this option available.

(iv) Given that a model has been fitted, the appropriateness of the assumed ARIMA structure can be checked, as discussed in Section 7.5. The residual autocorrelations can be examined, and more elaborate structures tried.

9.6 TRANSFER FUNCTION–NOISE MODELS

The model discussed in the previous section is quite general, yet it has a potentially serious limitation, particularly when one thinks in terms of forecasting. The relationship portrayed in equation 9.5.1a between the dependent variable and the independent variables is entirely static in character. The implication of the model is that a change in an independent variable in the current time period will have an impact on the dependent variable in that period, but not in future time periods. Contemplation of the behavior of real business and economic processes suggests that such an assumption will often be unwarranted. Moreover, if our interest is in forecasting, the timing, or **dynamics,** of relevant relationships is likely to be more important than their general static character. Accordingly, it is important to consider the possibility of formulating models that can capture various possibly dynamic structures in relationships. We raised this same issue in Section 4.4, when introducing regression models with lagged dependent variables. The models to be introduced here can be viewed as generalizations of those models.

For ease of exposition, we consider a dependent variable, Y, influenced by a single independent variable, X. It is assumed that the value taken by the dependent variable in the current time period depends linearly on the values of the independent variable in the current and all previous time periods. Such a relationship can be represented by the model.

$$Y_t = \alpha + V_0 X_t + V_1 X_{t-1} + V_2 X_{t-2} + V_3 X_{t-3} + \cdots + \epsilon_t \quad (9.6.1)$$

In this expression, $\alpha, V_0, V_1, \ldots$ are fixed parameters, and ϵ_t is an error term with mean zero. The implication of this model is that an increase of one unit of the independent variable in the current time period leads to an expected increase in the dependent variable of V_0 units in the current period, a further expected increase of V_1 units in the next period, an additional expected increase of V_2 units two time periods ahead, and so on. Hence, the model allows the possibility that the impact on the dependent variable of a change in the value of the independent variable is distributed over the current and all future time periods. This accords with both theory and experience of the behavior of business and economic systems.

Unfortunately, as it stands, the model equation 9.6.1 is of little practical value, as it contains an infinite number of parameters V_j, which obviously cannot be independently estimated from a finite amount of data. Moreover, in practice, truncation of the infinite sum in equation 9.6.1 at some appropriately high lag will often yield a model with too many parameters, thus violating the principle of parsimony. Such models may appear to fit quite well to observed data, but will often yield disappointingly poor forecasts when projected forward. What is required instead is a class of models capable of approximating the general behavior represented in equation 9.6.1 with a relatively small number of unknown parameters. To see how this might be achieved, we again use the back-shift operator notation, so that

$$B^j X_t \equiv X_{t-j} \qquad j = 0, 1, 2, \ldots$$

In that notation, equation 9.6.1 can be written

$$Y_t = \alpha + (V_0 + V_1 B + V_2 B^2 + V_3 B^3 + \cdots)X_t + \epsilon_t \quad (9.6.2)$$

Now, for many practical purposes, it will be possible to approximate the infinite order polynomial in B in this expression by a ratio of finite order polynomials, writing approximately

$$V_0 + V_1 B + V_2 B^2 + V_3 B^3 + \cdots = \frac{\omega_0 + \omega_1 B + \cdots + \omega_r B^r}{1 - \delta_1 B - \cdots - \delta_s B^s}$$

where the ω's and δ's are fixed parameters. Substitution in equation 9.6.2 then yields

$$Y_t = \alpha + \frac{\omega_0 + \omega_1 B + \cdots + \omega_r B^r}{1 - \delta_1 B - \cdots - \delta_s B^s} X_t + \epsilon_t \quad (9.6.3)$$

Often, in practical applications, it is found that a model of the form equation 9.6.3 fits data very well with just a small number of parameters—that is, with low values of r and s. A very simple example of this model is provided by

$$Y_t = \alpha + \frac{\omega_0}{1 - \delta_1 B} X_t + \epsilon_t$$

or, equivalently,

$$Y_t = \alpha + \omega_0 X_t + \omega_0 \delta_1 X_{t-1} + \omega_0 \delta_1^2 X_{t-2} + \omega_0 \delta_1^3 X_{t-3} + \cdots + \epsilon_t$$

This is precisely the structure of the regression model with a single lagged dependent variable, introduced in Section 4.4. Its implication is that a one-unit increase in the dependent variable in the current time period leads to an expected increase of ω_0 units in the dependent variable in that time period, a further expected increase of $\omega_0 \delta_1$ units in the next time period, an additional expected increase of $\omega_0 \delta_1^2$ units two time periods ahead, and so on. Since δ_1 is typically a positive number less than one, the impact of a change in the independent variable on the dependent variable dampens out in distant future time periods.

The model 9.6.3 is completed by permitting, exactly as in equation 9.5.1b, the error terms ϵ_t to follow an ARIMA(p, d, q) process, so that we have

$$Y_t = \alpha + \frac{\omega_0 + \omega_1 B + \cdots + \omega_r B^r}{1 - \delta_1 B - \cdots - \delta_s B^s} X_t + \epsilon_t \qquad (9.6.4a)$$

$$\phi(B)(1 - B)^d \epsilon_t = \theta(B) a_t \qquad (9.6.4b)$$

where again a_t is a white noise error term. This is sometimes called a **transfer function–noise model.** The transfer function part of the model, represented by equation 9.6.4a, depicts how the impact of a change in the independent variable is transferred to current and future values of the dependent variable. Equation 9.6.4b describes the behavior over time of the noise, or error term, ϵ_t.

The transfer function–noise class of models allows the analyst to be able to represent very general linear relationships between a dependent variable and an independent variable. In principle, it is easily extended to the case of several independent variables. This class of models, then, represents a natural generalization of both the regression models of Chapter 4 and the ARIMA models of Chapter 7. Viewed in this way, these models are not competitors, but rather building blocks through which, in any practical application, the analyst may be able to construct an appropriate forecasting model.

Box and Jenkins (1970) proposed a methodology through which, in practice, an appropriate transfer function–noise model from the general class of equation 9.6.4 might be fitted to data, and exploited for forecasting purposes. As was the case for the fitting of ARIMA models, discussed in Chapter 7, that methodology involves an iterative cycle of model selection, parameter estimation, and model checking. At the model selection stage, appropriate values are chosen for the integers r and s of equation 9.6.4a as well as the orders p, d, and q in the error structure of the ARIMA form, equation 9.6.4b. The parameters of equations 9.6.4a and 9.6.4b are jointly estimated, and the adequacy of the fitted model is then checked. The details of this methodology are quite intricate, and we will not pursue them here. The interested reader may refer to Granger and Newbold (1986), or Abraham and Ledolter (1983). A discussion of the application of these methods to the analysis of seasonal time series is provided by Abraham (1985).

An alternative representation of these models is sometimes favored by economists. For convenience, we again restrict attention to the case of a dependent variable, Y, and a single independent variable, X. Consider the model

$$Y_t = \alpha + \phi_1 Y_{t-1} + \cdots + \phi_p Y_{t-p} + \beta_0 X_t + \beta_1 X_{t-1} \qquad (9.6.5)$$
$$+ \cdots + \beta_r X_{t-r} + a_t - \theta_1 a_{t-1} - \cdots - \theta_q a_{t-q}$$

where α, β_i, ϕ_i, θ_i are fixed parameters and a_t is white noise. Equation (9.6.5) is sometimes referred to as an **ARMAX model.** Notice that, in the special case where the β's are all zero, it reduces to an ARMA(p, q) model for the dependent variable Y_t. The model allows, in general, for lagged dependent, and lagged independent variables. In the special case where the θ's are all zero the other model parameters are easily estimated by ordinary least squares. In the more general case of non-zero θ's, a nonlinear regression algorithm is required for parameter estimation.

9.7 INTERVENTION ANALYSIS

In Section 9.6 we introduced the transfer function–noise model (equation 9.6.4) as a quite sophisticated means of depicting the dependence of one time series on another. Essentially this same model has another use. In Chapter 7 we saw how ARIMA models could be used to represent the behavior over time of a single time series, and how fitted ARIMA models could then be employed to develop forecasts. Implicit in this whole approach is an underlying assumption of *stability* over time in the environment through which the time series evolves—today is to yesterday as yesterday was to the day before. Often this assumption of stability will provide a serviceable approximation to reality, but occasionally it will not. It may happen that, at some identifiable point in the past, the relevant environment of a time series of interest has undergone a discrete qualitative change. For example, a competitor may have introduced an attractive and heavily advertised alternative to a product whose sales are being monitored. Such an intervention is very likely to have an impact on the behavior of the time series of interest, and, if this is the case, the simple ARIMA models will be incapable of capturing this impact, and hence will be unlikely to yield satisfactory forecasts.

When a significant intervention has interrupted the stable behavior of a time series of interest, it is important to attempt to explicitly model its impact. Box and Tiao (1975) introduced a procedure, known as **intervention analysis,** for this purpose. Essentially, these authors proposed the use of the transfer function–noise class of models 9.6.4, but with X_t a dummy variable series, defined to take the value zero up to the point in time that the intervention occurs, and the value one thereafter. This approach allows a rich array of alternative possibilities for the impact of the intervention on the future course of the time series of interest. Two recent applications of this approach have been provided by Abraham (1987) and Leone (1987). Abraham analyzes the impact of mandatory seat belt and speed limit legislation on road traffic fatalities, while Leone examines the effects of such interventions as changes in advertising on product sales.

Intervention analysis is most often used in an attempt to estimate the impact of an intervention. Nevertheless, if a time series has been interrupted in this way, a far more reliable forecasting model is likely to result when explicit account of the intervention is taken into the structure of the forecasting model.

9.8 SIMULTANEOUS EQUATIONS REGRESSION MODELS AND TIME SERIES ANALYSIS

In Sections 9.5 and 9.6, we saw how time series models and concepts could be incorporated into the single equation regression framework of Chapter 4. However, in Chapter 8 we noted another possible extension of the single equation regression model. Often, the observed values of business and economic variables arise through the simultaneous interaction of economic forces. This led us to consider simultaneous equations econometric models.

The ARIMA time series models of Chapter 7 can also be extended to represent the simultaneous evolution of a set of several series. Here, for simplicity, we will briefly discuss only the pure autoregressive variants of these multiple time series models. Such models are sometimes called **vector autoregressions.** A vector autoregression relating a set of M time series consists of a set of M simultaneous linear equations. In each equation, the current value of one time series is expressed as a linear function of the past values of all series in the set, plus a white noise error term. For example, given a set of three time series, (X_{1t}, X_{2t}, X_{3t}), the vector autoregression of order p is

$$X_{1t} = \alpha_1 + \phi_{111}X_{1,t-1} + \cdots + \phi_{p11}X_{1,t-p} + \phi_{112}X_{2,t-1} + \cdots$$
$$+ \phi_{p12}X_{2,t-p} + \phi_{113}X_{3,t-1} + \cdots + \phi_{p13}X_{3,t-p} + a_{1t}$$

$$X_{2t} = \alpha_2 + \phi_{121}X_{1,t-1} + \cdots + \phi_{p21}X_{1,t-p} + \phi_{122}X_{2,t-1} + \cdots$$
$$+ \phi_{p22}X_{2,t-p} + \phi_{123}X_{3,t-1} + \cdots + \phi_{p23}X_{3,t-p} + a_{2t}$$

$$X_{3t} = \alpha_3 + \phi_{131}X_{1,t-1} + \cdots + \phi_{p31}X_{1,t-p} + \phi_{132}X_{2,t-1} + \cdots$$
$$+ \phi_{p32}X_{2,t-p} + \phi_{133}X_{3,t-1} + \cdots + \phi_{p33}X_{3,t-p} + a_{3t}$$

where the α's and ϕ's are fixed parameters and the a's are white noise errors. These equations can be fitted to observed data, one at a time, by ordinary least squares.

Granger and Newbold (1986) discuss the fitting to data, and derivation of forecasts from, a range of multiple time series models. One difficulty, that should be clear from our example of a vector autoregression, is that unless the number of time series in the set under study is very small, multiple time series models may contain a very large number of parameters. The principle of parsimony then suggests that disappointing results will emerge when such models are projected forward for forecasting. What is desirable, then, is some means of arriving at simple, less heavily parameterized variants of general multiple time series models. One possibility is that subject matter theory might suggest restrictions on these general model formulations. An attraction of the simultaneous equations econometric model framework of Chapter 8 lies precisely here. Well-conceived theory can be useful in narrowing the field of search when seeking an appropriate model to link a set of time series. Perhaps this way the analyst can arrive, after some experimentation in trying different lag structures, at a model that is faithful to theory, that fits the available data well, and that is not too heavily parameterized. In the absence of such theory, it is really too optimistic to expect to be able to satisfactorily model the relationships among, say, 10 to 20 time series, given the type and quantity of data likely to be available in practice. The ARIMA model-building methodology of Chapter 7, though it can be extended for the case of a small number of related time series, simply cannot be usefully extended to handle even a moderately large number of related series. Like it or not, in this case the analyst will inevitably be driven to a dependence on subject matter theory to achieve a manageable model, or set of alternative models.

Exercises

9.1   The time series X_t is generated by the ARIMA(0, 1, 1) model

$$X_t - X_{t-1} = a_t - 0.6a_{t-1}$$

where a_t is white noise. Is there an exponential smoothing algorithm that generates the same forecasts as this model? If so, write down the recurrence form of that algorithm.

9.2   The time series X_t is generated by the ARIMA(0, 2, 2) model

$$(1 - B)^2 X_t = a_t - 1.1a_{t-1} + 0.5a_{t-2}$$

where B is the back-shift operator, and a_t is white noise. Is there an exponential smoothing algorithm that generates the same forecasts as this model? If so, write down the recurrence form of that algorithm.

9.3   Consider the damped trend algorithm

$$L_t = \alpha X_t + (1 - \alpha)(L_{t-1} + \phi T_{t-1})$$
$$T_t = \beta(L_t - L_{t-1}) + (1 - \beta)\phi T_{t-1}$$

with forecasts derived from

$$\hat{X}_t(h) = L_t + \sum_{i=1}^{h} \phi^i T_t \qquad h = 1, 2, \ldots$$

Prove that the same forecasts follow from the ARIMA(1, 1, 2) model

$$(1 - \phi B)(1 - B)X_t = (1 - \theta_1 B - \theta_2 B^2)a_t$$

where B is the back-shift operator, a_t is white noise, and

$$\theta_1 = 1 + \phi - \alpha - \phi\alpha\beta \qquad \theta_2 = -\phi(1 - \alpha)$$

9.4   The time series X_t is generated by the ARIMA(1, 1, 2) model

$$(1 - 0.60B)(1 - B)X_t = (1 - 0.86B + 0.30B^2)a_t$$

where B is the back-shift operator, and a_t is white noise. Is there an exponential smoothing algorithm that generates the same forecasts as this model? If so, write down the recurrence form of that algorithm.

9.5 Consider the additive seasonal variant of the Holt-Winters algorithm, with smoothing constants α, β, and γ. Prove that the same forecasts can be obtained from the ARIMA model defined by equations 9.4.1 and 9.4.2.

9.6 Carefully explain why we say that in practice, when applied to monthly data, the additive seasonal variant of the Holt-Winters algorithm and the Box-Jenkins ARIMA model-building methodology will not yield the same forecasts.

9.7 Let Y_t be a dependent variable and X_t an independent variable whose relationship can be represented by the model

$$Y_t = \alpha + \beta X_t + \epsilon_t$$

$$\epsilon_t = a_t - \theta_1 a_{t-1} - \theta_2 a_{t-2}$$

where a_t is white noise. Given a sample of 100 pairs of observations on (X_t, Y_t), explain how, in practice, you would arrive at this model from an analysis of the available data.

9.8 The relationship between a dependent variable Y_t and an independent variable X_t is given by the transfer function–noise model

$$Y_t = \alpha + \frac{\omega_0 + \omega_1 B}{1 - \delta_1 B} X_t + \epsilon_t$$

$$\phi(B)(1 - B)^d \epsilon_t = \theta(B) a_t$$

Write

$$V(B) = V_0 + V_1 B + V_2 B^2 + \cdots = \frac{\omega_0 + \omega_1 B}{1 - \delta_1 B}$$

so that

$$(1 - \delta_1 B)(V_0 + V_1 B + V_2 B^2 + \cdots) = \omega_0 + \omega_1 B$$

Hence find $V_0, V_1, V_2, \ldots$ as functions of ω_0, ω_1, δ_1, and discuss the expected behavior of current and future values of the dependent variable resulting from a one-unit increase in the independent variable.

SELECTED BIBLIOGRAPHY

Abraham, B. (1985). Seasonal time series and transfer function modeling. *Journal of Business and Economic Statistics, 3,* 356–361.

Abraham, B. (1987). Application of intervention analysis to a road fatality series in Ontario. *Journal of Forecasting, 6,* 211–219.

Abraham, B., & J. Ledolter (1983). *Statistical Methods for Forecasting.* New York: Wiley.

Abraham, B., & J. Ledolter (1986). Forecast functions implied by autoregressive integrated moving average models and other related forecast procedures. *International Statistical Review, 54,* 51–66.

Box, G. E. P., & G. M. Jenkins (1970). *Time Series Analysis, Forecasting and Control.* San Francisco: Holden Day.

Box, G. E. P., & G. C. Tiao (1975). Intervention analysis with applications to economics and environmental problems. *Journal of American Statistical Association, 70,* 70–79.

Granger, C. W. J., & P. Newbold (1986). *Forecasting Economic Time Series* (2nd ed.). Orlando, Fl.: Academic Press.

Harrison, P. J. (1967). Exponential smoothing and short-term sales forecasting. *Management Science, 13,* 821–842.

Ledolter, J., & G. E. P. Box (1978). Conditions for the optimality of exponential smoothing forecast procedures. *Metrika, 25,* 77–93.

Leone, R. P. (1987). Forecasting the effect of an environmental change on market performance: an intervention time series approach. *International Journal of Forecasting, 3,* 463–478.

McKenzie, E. (1976). An analysis of general exponential smoothing. *Operations Research, 24,* 131–140.

McKenzie, E. (1984). General exponential smoothing and the equivalent ARIMA process. *Journal of Forecasting, 3,* 333–344.

Mills, T. C. (1990). *Time Series Techniques for Economists.* Cambridge: Cambridge University Press.

Muth, J. F. (1960). Optimal properties of exponentially weighted forecasts. *Journal of the American Statistical Association, 55,* 299–306.

Nerlove, M., & S. Wage (1964). On the optimality of adaptive forecasting. *Management Science, 10,* 207–224.

Newbold, P. (1988). Predictors projecting linear trend plus seasonal dummies. *The Statistician, 37,* 111–127.

Roberts, S. A. (1982). A general class of Holt-Winters type forecasting models. *Management Science, 28,* 808–820.

Theil, H., & S. Wage (1964). Some observations on adaptive forecasting. *Management Science, 10,* 198–206.

Some Other Quantitative Forecasting Methods

10.1 INTRODUCTION

Authors of a book on forecasting have the difficult task of deciding which approaches to discuss at all, and on which to put most emphasis. Our own emphasis here is decidedly on formal quantitative methods, though in Chapter 11 we will briefly outline judgmental approaches to forecasting. Within the quantitative approach, we have concentrated on three general methodologies: regression models, exponential smoothing algorithms, and ARIMA models. These three approaches were chosen because they are soundly and plausibly based, they are very widely used, and all have enjoyed some measure of practical success in real world applications to business and economic forecasting problems. The regression, exponential smoothing, and ARIMA model-building approaches to forecasting are quite distinct in character, philosophy, and technical details, so that it is easy for the reader to get the impression that the subject of forecasting is somewhat fragmented, consisting of disjointed methodologies, rather than constituting a coherent whole. In Chapter 9 we tried to dispel this impression by outlining relationships among these three forecasting approaches, and considering possibilities for their integration.

Unfortunately, at this point we must confirm the reader's original impression. At the present time the subject of quantitative forecasting is indeed seriously fragmented. The degree of coherence we have been able to suggest is possible only because of our concentration on just three methodologies. In fact, very many more quantitative forecasting methodologies have, at one time or another, been proposed and implemented, and computer programs for several of them are quite widely available. Even were we so inclined, it would be impossible to provide any reasonable discussion of every available method. Indeed, the subject has now reached the sad state where forecasting computer program packages are available for which it is difficult to find any adequate written account of the underlying methodology, and even more difficult to find any convincing justification or rationale for that methodology. For this reason alone, encyclopedic coverage would be impossible.

In this chapter, we will introduce *some* other quantitative forecasting methods. As we have indicated, we will not attempt a discussion of every method currently in use. Instead, we try to provide the reader with a feeling for the broad spectrum of possibilities, in order to make our discussion manageable. Some of the methods we will introduce are obvious extensions or modifications of procedures discussed in previous chapters of this book, others are in some senses related to these procedures, whereas others are clearly distinct. Our selection here is based in part on our own judgment as to which procedures are likely to offer good chances of success in practical implementations, in part on a goal to provide a broad and balanced coverage of types of methodology and problems, and in part on pedagogy. The last of these is necessary to eliminate those methods for which any adequate discussion would be far more technically involved than appears to be warranted by their apparent merits. We will concentrate throughout on the problem of predicting future values of a time series exclusively on the basis of its own past. Some of the methods to be discussed can in principle be extended to the case where information on related time series is also available, though generally in practice such extensions are problematic and have not been very thoroughly explored.

A few heroic attempts, notably Harvey (1984), have been made at a synthesis of at least a moderate number of the quantitative forecasting methods in current use. However, these are invariably quite technical and do not achieve a full coverage of the vast array of possible methods. Indeed, if after all of this the reader is left with the impression that the subject of forecasting is currently made up of a veritable morass of alternative methods, with disappointingly little cohesion, that view would not be far from our own. We offer three explanations for this state of affairs. First, there really is no such thing as a generic forecasting problem.

In practice, forecasting problems have their own distinctive features, so that it should not be surprising to find that there exists no generic solution algorithm for "the forecasting problem." Rather, attempts must often be made to modify particular solution algorithms, or perhaps develop entirely new algorithms, to deal with particular problem features. Second, as we have seen in our discussion of exponential smoothing, from the early days approaches to forecasting have often been based on *ad hoc* procedures, grounded in little more than intuitive plausibility. It appears that the capacity of the human imagination to devise new algorithms with at least a degree of superficial plausibility is virtually limitless. Third, as we have been at pains to emphasize, any successful forecasting model—whether explicitly built, or implicit in some prediction algorithm—is likely to be parsimonious, in the sense that it involves just a small number of unknown parameters. Such models do not, of course, represent truth. They are intended to be simple, convenient, and useful approximations to the complex real world process that generates the data. Once the view is taken that the object of model building is not the discovery of truth, but of a rather crude approximation to that truth, any number of possible avenues for approximation are opened. Some of these will appear to be more plausible than others, but it is not reasonable to expect any one to be uniquely compelling. For example, though we would be prepared to mount a very sturdy defense of the appeal of ARIMA models for nonseasonal time series, as noted in Chapter 9 the case for multiplicative seasonal ARIMA models in the seasonal time series case, to the exclusion of other possibilities, is far less strong. Given the possibility of a number of different types of approximating models, and given the very different types of data that might in practice be observed for business and economic time series, it would be optimistic to hope that practical experience would point very clearly down one particular avenue. Certainly that hope has not yet been realized.

We do believe that a thorough understanding of regression analysis, exponential smoothing algorithms, and ARIMA model-building methods are essential for the modern forecaster, and that one or another of these approaches, sensibly applied, and perhaps modified or extended, should be adequate for a great many forecasting problems. The procedures to be discussed in this chapter are all less widely used than these. Nevertheless, some understanding of the possibilities they offer can be useful. We include these further methods, then, not merely for completeness, but because they can on occasion offer the potential for success in some practical applications. Some forecasting problems met in practice can be quite troublesome, in the sense that it is difficult to find any approach that generates predictions of adequate quality. In those cases, the sensible forecaster, rather than staying with some favorite approach, will try a range of alternative possible approaches, if only out of desperation!

10.2 STRUCTURAL MODELS

In Chapter 5 we introduced the concept of a time series being made up of trend, seasonal, and irregular *components*. This components view of time series has considerable intuitive appeal, and indeed in the early days of time series analysis much effort was devoted to procedures for isolating the individual components in an observed series. These procedures were informal, based as we saw in Chapter 5, on the method of moving weighted averages, employing systems of weights that were somewhat arbitrarily chosen. This general approach still constitutes the basis of the seasonal adjustment methods in most common practical use. The problem of seasonal adjustment is, of course, that of extracting the seasonal component from the historical record of an observed time series. However, for many years, seasonal adjustment aside, the components approach to time series analysis fell into relative disuse. Attention was focused instead on model building, particularly on the ARIMA class of time series models. An approach to time series analysis and forecasting through the construction of formal models has four attractions:

1. Any assumptions that are being made about the behavior of the time series are quite explicit in the model structure.
2. Data, and any other considerations, can be used to provide the analyst with a means of assessing which particular model might be appropriate in any application.
3. The complete specification of a formal model provides the basis for the development of efficient methods for the estimation of fixed parameters.
4. The analyst has the ability to check whether any assumed model provides an adequate description of the behavior of observed data.

For these reasons, the ARIMA model-building methodology has enjoyed widespread popularity. However, a criticism of the ARIMA model approach has been that *intuitive interpretation* of these models is often not easy.

In fact, some, though not all, ARIMA models can be viewed in terms of the familiar decomposition of a time series into trend, seasonal, and irregular components. However, such interpretations are indirect consequences of particular ARIMA models. An alternative possibility, proposed by Harvey and Todd (1983), is to set out to build a formal model of a time series that directly and explicitly incorporates this decomposition. In this view it is assumed that a time series possesses some structure— specifically that it is the sum of independent trend, seasonal, and irregular components. The resulting models are then called **structural models.** The approach to structural model building, as outlined by Harvey and Todd, is to be applied to business and economic time series and has two important further characteristics:

(i) Separate plausible models are postulated for the individual trend, seasonal, and irregular components (and possibly also for a separate cyclical component).

(ii) In specifying these models, it is acknowledged that *global* specifications of trend and seasonality will typically be inadequate. Rather, *local* trend and seasonal patterns that evolve through time are posited.

Harvey and Todd concentrated on a single structural model, known as the **basic structural model,** and much subsequent work has been devoted to this model, or simple variants of it. Let X_t denote the observed value of a series at time t, and write the structure

$$X_t = T_t + S_t + a_t \qquad (10.2.1)$$

where

T_t = trend component at time t

S_t = seasonal component at time t

a_t = irregular component at time t

In the basic structural model, the irregular component is assumed to be white noise. Also, in that model, trend is taken to be *locally linear*. To see how the concept of local linearity might be formally modeled, consider for the moment the possibility of a global linear trend, which could be written

$$T_t = \alpha + \beta t$$

where α and β are fixed parameters. In consequence, the change in the trend term from one time period to the next would simply be equal to the slope parameter β; that is,

$$T_t = T_{t-1} + \beta$$

Now, if trend is not fixed, but instead evolves over time, we might add an error term a_{1t} to the right-hand side of this expression. In addition, we drop the assumption that the slope is fixed, giving

$$T_t = T_{t-1} + \beta_{t-1} + a_{1t} \qquad (10.2.2)$$

It is further assumed that the change in the slope term from one time period to the next is given by a random variable a_{2t}, so that

$$\beta_t = \beta_{t-1} + a_{2t} \qquad (10.2.3)$$

Suppose now that the time series of interest is seasonal, involving s periods per year, so that s is 4 for quarterly data and 12 for monthly data. Now, a very simple representation of a *fixed* pattern of seasonality would depict the seasonal components S_t by dummy variables, summing to zero over every s consecutive time periods. As a model of local seasonality, Harvey and Todd propose that the sum of s consecutive values of the seasonal component sum to a random variable a_{3t}, so that

$$\sum_{j=0}^{s-1} S_{t-j} = a_{3t} \qquad (10.2.4)$$

The set of equations 10.2.1 through 10.2.4 constitute the basic structural model of Harvey and Todd, with the assumption that a_t, a_{1t}, a_{2t}, a_{3t} are independent white noise error terms with different variances. (These four error variances are the unknown fixed parameters of the model.)

The basic structural model fits into a general framework, known as the *state space representation*, which has been extensively studied for many years by engineers. This need not concern us, except to note that for such a representation an algorithm known as the *Kalman filter* is available to allow the computationally efficient estimation of parameters and derivation of forecasts.

Some properties of the basic structural model, and in particular its relationship to other forecasting approaches, have been studied by Maravall (1985), and Newbold (1988). Note first that equations 10.2.1 through 10.2.4 constitute a single model, rather than a class of models. It is no more general than the Holt-Winters additive seasonal algorithm or a specific ARIMA model, such as the airline model. In fact, in common with that Holt-Winters algorithm and the airline model, the basic structural model generates a forecast function that is a linear trend plus seasonal dummies. We discussed such forecast functions in Section 9.4, noting there that different efficient parameterizations of the general class of possibilities would lead to distinct forecasts. In fact, the basic structural model produces different forecasts than the Holt-Winters algorithm or the airline model (or, indeed, any seasonal ARIMA model that is at all likely to be fitted in practice). The basic structural model, then, offers for seasonal time series a genuine alternative to those methods discussed in previous chapters. That is not the case for nonseasonal time series.

Eliminating the term S_t from equation 10.2.1, and consequently equation 10.2.4, leaves us with a model that generates the same forecasts as Holt's linear trend algorithm, and consequently, as noted in Section 9.3, a subset of the ARIMA(0, 2, 2) models.

Whether the forecasts generated by the basic structural model for seasonal time series have any compelling intuitive appeal depends on our view of the specification 10.2.4 as a plausible representation of evolving seasonality. It is difficult to see this as a uniquely plausible formulation. Indeed, Harvey (1984) has proposed an alternative.

The possibilities of the structural model approach are discussed in considerable detail by Harvey (1989). Harvey discusses many variants of the model, and illustrates a general approach to model building.

The great advantage of structural models is their facility for incorporating time series model-building methods into the traditional components decomposition framework. In principle, the resulting models have strong intuitive appeal, and are straightforward to interpret. (Unfortunately, as shown by Ghysels (1987), if an economic time series is viewed as the output of some behavioral mechanism, its decomposition into independent components has less theoretical appeal.) Some evidence on the forecast performance of simple structural models is encouraging, and the possibility exists that analysis based on structural models could provide a real alternative to the Box-Jenkins ARIMA analysis of Chapter 7.

10.3 BAYESIAN FORECASTING

In statistical analysis, Bayes' theorem provides a mechanism for the updating of probability assessments as new information becomes available. Now, in forecasting, we almost inevitably revise our view about the future as new data, or other types of information, are acquired. In this sense, then, virtually any forecasting method could be described as "Bayesian." In this section, however, our concern is with a specific forecasting methodology that has been called, by its developers, Bayesian forecasting. This methodology was introduced by Harrison and Stevens (1971, 1976). Some further discussion of subsequent developments, practical implementation, and empirical performance is provided by Fildes (1983, 1984).

At least in its basic variant, the objective of **Bayesian forecasting** is the prediction of future values of a time series from its own past. Virtually all of our discussion to date on this problem—particularly the exponential smoothing algorithms of Chapter 6, and the ARIMA model-building methodology of Chapter 7—implicitly assumes a degree of stability in the evolution through time of a series. Proponents of Bayesian forecasting argue that, particularly for time series of product sales, such an assumption will often be too idealistic. In Chapter 9, we briefly discussed how a known or suspected structural change, occurring at some known point in time, could be incorporated through intervention analysis into the ARIMA model-building framework. As we saw, intervention analysis has proved useful in practical forecasting exercises in circumstances where the environment in which a time series evolves experiences discrete qualitative changes at one or a small number of time points. There are, however, two practical difficulties with this methodology. First, the model-building exercise that is involved can be quite time consuming, whereas, realistically or not, many practitioners would prefer an approach that is closer to being fully automatic. More seriously, it might be argued that, for some products, sales behavior is susceptible to a number of structural changes, whose causes and timing will not be readily identifiable; for example, rolling changes in marketing strategy. Under this view, what is required is a procedure that, as new data become available, continually allows for the *possibility* of structural change of various sorts, preferably on-line in an automated fashion. It is this ambitious goal at which Bayesian forecasting takes aim, with the added advantage of allowing users to incorporate subjective views about the process under study and its likely future course into the analysis.

The Bayesian forecasting approach of Harrison and Stevens has its roots in exponential smoothing, though through particular models that are equivalent to specific exponential smoothing algorithms. Here these models are formulated in a form similar to that of Section 10.2 rather than in ARIMA form. Although treatment of seasonal time series is possible, we will restrict our discussion to a specific nonseasonal formulation. The time series X_t under study is assumed to be generated by the model

$$X_t = T_t + a_t \qquad (10.3.1a)$$

$$T_t = T_{t-1} + \beta_t + a_{1t} \qquad (10.3.1b)$$

$$\beta_t = \beta_{t-1} + a_{2t} \qquad (10.3.1c)$$

where a_t, a_{1t}, a_{2t} are independent white noise processes with respective variances σ^2, σ_1^2, σ_2^2. Notice that equation 10.3.1 is precisely the same as the basic structural model 10.2.1 through 10.2.3, with the seasonal term omitted, except that β_t rather than β_{t-1} appears on the right-hand side of equation 10.3.1b. In fact, this modification has no operational significance, and can be thought of simply as a relabeling of the same quantity. (Harvey (1984) discusses the general relationship between the Harrison/Stevens models and the basic structural model in the seasonal case.)

The important distinction between the structural modeling approach and Bayesian forecasting is that, in the former the variances of the white noise errors in equation 10.3.1 are regarded as fixed parameters to be estimated, whereas in the latter structural changes in the process are represented by changes in these variances. We will see shortly how this is achieved. The point of departure of Bayesian forecasting from other forecasting methods is that, at any point in time, the process generating the data is regarded as being in one of four possible states. These are

(i)   *No change.* Here the structure of the time series is in a steady state: no abrupt structural change has occurred. If the series remains in this state over the whole observation period, the methods of Chapters 6 and 7 should be adequate for its analysis.

(ii) *Step change.* In this state the time series experiences an abrupt change in level, that is maintained over subsequent observation periods.

(iii) *Slope change.* Here an abrupt shift in the slope, or growth rate, of the time series is exhibited. Again this change in structure is maintained for some time.

(iv) *Transient.* In this state an odd extremely high or extremely low observation occurs. The cause of this phenomenon is quite temporary, so that subsequently the series reverts to its normal behavior pattern. By their nature, such transients are unpredictable and convey no useful information about subsequent behavior patterns.

These four states are illustrated in Figure 10.1.

In Bayesian forecasting, the four possible contemplated states are represented by values assigned to σ^2, σ_1^2, σ_2^2, the variances of the white noise error terms a_t, a_{1t}, a_{2t} in the model 10.3.1. The magnitudes of these variances are indicated in Table 10.1. Equations 10.3.1b and 10.3.1c determine respectively the evolution of the level and slope of the time series. Consequently, a step change, or abrupt change in level, will be reflected in a large absolute number for the realized value of a_{1t}; that is, a large variance for this random variable. Similarly, an abrupt slope change corresponds to a large value for the variance of the random variable a_{2t}. Generally, the error term a_t of equation 10.3.1a will be of normal magnitude, representing the outcomes of the usual random occurrences continually influencing the behavior of the time series. However, on occasion a large transient disturbance in the evolutionary pattern of the

TABLE 10.1   Error variances for four states in Bayesian forecasting.

State	σ^2	σ_1^2	σ_2^2
No change	Normal	0	0
Step change	Normal	Large	0
Slope change	Normal	0	Large
Transient	Large	0	0

FIGURE 10.1   Four states in Bayesian forecasting.

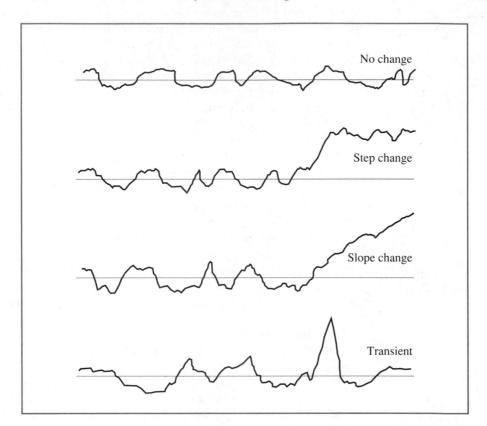

No change

Step change

Slope change

Transient

series will occur. This corresponds to a large variance for the random variable a_t.

The analysis of a time series through the Bayesian forecasting algorithm does not assume knowledge of the particular state prevailing at any point in time, but attempts to assess probabilities for each of the four states based on the observed data. These probabilities are used to weight the forecasts that would result if the analyst knew the true state. The technical details of this methodology are quite intricate, and will not be explored here. The forecasting algorithm can be automated, but the user is required to specify relative magnitudes for the large error variances of Table 10.1, and also prior probabilities, reflecting subjective belief about the chances of occurrence of the four states in the absence of any data. As Fildes (1983) indicates, the performance of this forecasting method can be quite sensitive to the choices that are made for these quantities.

Fildes' empirical evaluation of the standard automated version of Bayesian forecasting is not encouraging. In spite of the additional complexity of the method, he reports no substantial accuracy gains over simpler approaches, such as exponential smoothing. It is possible, however, that the approach would be more useful in those cases where the analyst has important prior information about the series under study.

The important issue when considering the adoption of Bayesian forecasting is the analyst's judgment on the relative stability of the time series of interest. If the series exhibits structural shifts of the type anticipated by this methodology, it would be reasonable to expect it to perform relatively well. On the other hand, if a time series is fairly stable, one could not be too optimistic about a procedure that attempts to make some allowance for situations that do not arise. Moreover, in the stable state Bayesian forecasting does not permit the same flexibility as ARIMA analysis in allowing for a wide range of possible generating models. Fildes (1983) does report some robustness in forecast performance, implying perhaps that Bayesian forecasting may not sacrifice too much in forecasting accuracy in those stable situations for which it was not designed, while offering the prospect of substantial gains in the analysis of more volatile time series. Given the available evidence, it is difficult to recommend Bayesian forecasting as the standard approach through which an analyst should attack all, or even most, problems of predicting a time series from its own past. On the other hand, it might prove quite valuable for analyzing those volatile time series for which the standard methods have failed to yield forecasts of adequate quality.

10.4 STEPWISE AUTOREGRESSION

Stepwise autoregression, introduced by Newbold and Granger (1974) and further discussed by Granger and Newbold (1986), was designed for the prediction of a time series from its own past in a fashion that could be automated, so that a large number of series could be analyzed relatively quickly and cheaply. In this sense, stepwise autoregression provides an alternative to the exponential smoothing algorithms of Chapter 6.

In building regression models to explain the behavior of a dependent variable, it sometimes happens, when no well-conceived subject matter theory is available for guidance, that the analyst has available a very large number of potential independent variables for inclusion in the regression. Given only a limited amount of data, it would be very poor strategy to simply fit the full regression involving all of these independent variables. The principle of parsimony suggests that little of value would be learned from such an exercise, and that the resulting fitted model would be likely to prove a mediocre forecasting tool. A number of alternative strategies, including stepwise regression, have been developed to attack this problem, with the objective of allowing the data to suggest a relatively simple, lightly parameterized model. This approach can also be applied to the fitting of the autoregressive time series models, discussed in Section 7.2.

Let X_t be a time series. Then, the autoregressive model of order K can be written

$$X_t = C + \phi_1 X_{t-1} + \phi_2 X_{t-2} + \cdots + \phi_K X_{t-K} + a_t \quad (10.4.1)$$

where $C, \phi_1, \ldots, \phi_K$ are fixed parameters, and a_t is an error term, assumed to be white noise. In Section 7.2 we saw that the $(K + 1)$ unknown parameters of this model could be efficiently estimated by ordinary least squares. This can provide a successful forecasting model, provided that the number K of autoregressive parameters is small compared with the number of available sample observations. However, in many practical applications, only relatively short time series of observations are available, while the analyst might suspect that the present is influenced by the somewhat distant past, suggesting the desirability of a moderately large value for K in equation 10.4.1. If the full model 10.4.1 is to be fitted, then, there is the possibility of having to estimate a large number of unknown parameters on the basis of a small number of observations. A **stepwise regression algorithm** might prove useful in such circumstances.

In stepwise autoregression, the aim is to take the completely specified model 10.4.1 as just a starting point. This model involves the K autoregressive parameters $\phi_1, \phi_2, \ldots, \phi_K$ on all lagged values of the time series, up to the maximum permitted lag K. However, it will often be the case that a good fit of the data can be achieved through a model involving only a few of these lagged values of the time series and their associated parameters. Stepwise autoregression is the application of a stepwise regression algorithm in a systematic search for such a simplified model structure. There are a number of variants of stepwise regression. Our preference is for a variant involving the **backward elimination** of terms in the full model. As applied in the present context, this proceeds by fitting the complete model 10.4.1 at the first stage. Almost inevitably, not all of the estimated parameters in the fitted model will be statistically significant. In that case, the least significant is dropped from the model. The algorithm then proceeds, step by step, eliminating at each step that lagged value whose contribution to the model fit is smallest, provided that contribution is not statistically significant. However, it may be that lagged values that have been dropped at previous steps can profitably be reintroduced into the model to achieve a superior fit. This possibility is checked at each step before further deletions are made. In outline, then, stepwise autoregression proceeds as follows:

(i)   Fit the complete model 10.4.1. If all parameter estimates are statistically significant, the algorithm terminates. Otherwise, drop the lag term X_{t-i} associated with the least significant parameter estimate from the model.

(ii) At each subsequent step we begin with an achieved fitted model.

   (a) Does any lag X_{t-i} excluded from this model yield a significant improvement in fit when added to it? If so, add that lag that produces the greatest improvement in the model fit. Proceed in this way until further additions fail to yield a significant gain in the fit of the autoregression.

   (b) At this point, check whether there is any lag X_{t-i} whose deletion would lead to an insignificant reduction in the goodness of fit of the autoregression. If so, drop that X_{t-i} whose deletion has the smallest impact on this goodness of fit.

(iii) At this stage, a new model has been developed. Return to (ii) and continue in this way until a model has been achieved for which the addition of all omitted lags fails to significantly improve the fit, and the exclusion of any included lag leads to a significant worsening of the fit.

It generally happens that the fitted model derived from this stepwise autoregression algorithm contains just a small number of parameters. The arithmetic calculations involved in stepwise autoregression are quite intricate, but they are easily automated, and computer programs for stepwise regression have long been widely available. Once a fitted autoregressive model has finally been obtained in this way, forecasts of future values of a time series are easily derived, as described in Section 7.2.

In practice, if the time series X_t is not stationary, it may be preferable to difference the data before applying stepwise autoregression. For many nonseasonal business and economic time series the algorithm would then be applied to $(1 - B)X_t$, and for seasonal time series to $(1 - B)(1 - B^s)X_t$, rather than to the original data. The user must also select the maximum permitted lag K of the autoregression in equation 10.4.1. Newbold and Granger (1974) recommended $K = 13$ for most purposes, though preferring $K = 25$ for monthly seasonal time series.

An apparent attraction of stepwise autoregression, in common with many other forecasting algorithms, is that it provides the user with an answer after only routine effort. This can lull the unwary into a false sense of security. We have been at pains to stress elsewhere that all that emerges from an apparently sophisticated computer forecasting algorithm is not necessarily golden. The possession of such an algorithm does not relieve the analyst of the obligation to think about the underlying methodology. In fact, in spite of their apparent plausibility, it is difficult to find any sense in which stepwise regression methods produce optimal results. Suppose that the model finally achieved involves m parameters. It cannot be guaranteed that this is the best fitting of all possible models with this number of parameters. (An alternative procedure, fitting all possible regressions, can circumvent this problem, though at greater computational cost.) Stepwise autoregression then is essentially an *ad hoc* forecasting method. Like all such methods, it must be judged on its intuitive plausibility and its success in practical implementations. In an extensive empirical evaluation, Newbold and Granger (1974) reported that forecasts from stepwise autoregression were, roughly, about as accurate as those from Holt's linear trend algorithm and the Holt-Winters algorithm. In Chapter 12, we will introduce the possibility of combining stepwise autoregression forecasts with those from the exponential smoothing algorithms in the production of a superior composite forecast.

10.5 POWER TRANSFORMATIONS

In this section we discuss an approach which is not, by itself, a forecasting method, but which might possibly be incorporated in existing methods. The possibility is one to which we have briefly and tentatively alluded in previous chapters, when analyzing the logarithms of original data. Most, though not all, of the forecasting methods we have discussed to this point generate **linear predictors**—that is, forecasts that are linear functions of the available data. Certainly, this allows a rich array of possibilities, and will often lead to forecasts of adequate quality. However, it might be suspected that, on occasions, a nonlinear predictor would be preferable. For example, we have considered methods, such as Holt's linear trend algorithm, that allow for locally linear trend. However, for many time series, such as product sales, it may be more reasonable to think in terms of growth rate, or exponential trend, suggesting an analysis of the logarithms of the original data.

The possibility of fitting models to, or applying forecasting algorithms to, either the original data or their logarithms leads to two questions:

(i) Might we consider other *transformations* than the logarithm of the original data?
(ii) How can we determine which, if any, transformation of the data is appropriate?

In both time series and regression analysis, attention has focused most often on the class of **power transformations,** introduced by Box and Cox.[1]

---

1. These authors discussed theoretical and practical aspects of this approach, in a non-forecasting context, in Box, G. E. P. and D. R. Cox (1964). An analysis of transformations. *Journal of the Royal Statistical Society B, 26,* 211–243.

Consider the case of a single time series X_t, for which n observations are available. The concept involved here is that the same transformation should be applied to each observation, so that rather than necessarily working with the original X_t, the analyst contemplates first raising each observation to some power λ. (We are assuming here a series of positive observations.) In fact, the Box-Cox approach involves the analysis of the transformed series $X_t(\lambda)$, defined as

$$X_t(\lambda) = (X_t^\lambda - 1)/\lambda \quad \text{if } \lambda \neq 0$$
$$X_t(\lambda) = \log X_t \quad \text{if } \lambda = 0$$

$(10.5.1)$

The rationale for this definition is that it allows the natural incorporation of the logarithmic transformation, for it can be shown that, as λ approaches zero, the function $(X_t^\lambda - 1)/\lambda$ approaches $\log X_t$. Notice that, for values of λ between zero and one, we can regard equation 10.5.1 as providing transformations of the data that are intermediate between the logarithmic transformation and no transformation.

We do not claim that the application of power transformations is invariably necessary. On the contrary, experience suggests that such an elaboration will often be of limited value. However, these transformations are sometimes employed in practical forecasting exercises, and can be useful when there is uncertainty about the shape of local trend in a time series. Consider, for example, the possibility of predicting the time series X_t from its own past, either through exponential smoothing or ARIMA model building. These approaches could of course be applied equally well to transformed variants of the original time series. This would lead directly to forecasts of future values of the transformed series. Forecasts of future values of the original series could then be obtained by applying the inverse transformation.[2]

If power transformations are contemplated, the user is left with the task of determining what is the most appropriate transformation to use. One possibility is to try a grid of possible values of the transformation parameter λ of equation 10.5.1. Often it will be adequate to consider only values in a range from zero to one, so that use of $\lambda = 0, 0.2, 0.4, 0.6, 0.8,$ 1 should suffice. Each choice of λ yields a transformed series, $X_t(\lambda)$, which is subsequently analyzed. Now, let $\hat{\sigma}_\lambda^2$ denote an estimate of the one-step ahead forecast error variance when the series $X_t(\lambda)$ is predicted. For example, $\hat{\sigma}_\lambda^2$ would be the average of the squared in-sample one-step

2. Technically, as Granger, C. W. J. and P. Newbold (1976), Forecasting transformed series, *Journal of the Royal Statistical Society B, 38,* 189–203, suggest, a case can be made for a modest modification of this simple approach to deriving forecasts of the untransformed series.

forecast errors for exponential smoothing, and the estimated variance of the white noise error term when an ARIMA model is fitted. The value eventually chosen for the power transformation is then that number λ for which

$$g(\lambda) = \frac{n \log \hat{\sigma}_\lambda^2}{2} + (1 - \lambda) \sum_{t=1}^{n} \log X_t$$

is smallest.

This approach to power transformations has been most often applied in the forecasting literature in the context of fitting ARIMA models. Some practical methodological issues in such applications are discussed by Hopwood, McKeown, and Newbold (1984). The evidence on the potential forecasting gains to be obtained in this way is rather mixed and not very encouraging. Following the analysis of a set of macroeconomic time series, Nelson and Granger (1979) report no gains, on the average, in forecast quality following from the additional elaboration of introducing the power transformation into the ARIMA model. On the other hand, Hopwood, McKeown, and Newbold (1981) find some modest improvement in the quality of forecasts of corporate earnings per share when the possibility of a power transformation of the data is allowed.

10.6 PERIODIC AUTOREGRESSIVE MODELS

We have noted on a number of occasions that the ARIMA model-building methodology, as it is usually implemented, is somewhat less widely embraced in the case of seasonal time series than in the nonseasonal case. In particular, a number of authors, including Osborn (1990), have questioned the validity of the seasonal difference operator that occurs so frequently in practice in fitted ARIMA models.

It might therefore be worth paying attention to the possibility of fitting models to either the undifferenced or first differenced series, but with no seasonal differencing. If this is done, seasonality can be partially modelled by incorporating a different mean, or mean change, for each period of the year. It is also possible to go further, allowing the other model parameters to depend on the period of the year. When these other parameters are exclusively autoregressive, these considerations lead to the periodic autoregressive model, advocated by Osborn (1988) and Osborn and Smith (1989). In the case of a quarterly time series X_t (which could be the first difference of an observed series), the periodic autoregressive model is

$$\phi^{(j)}(B)(X_{j+4i} - \mu_j) = a_{j+4i}; \qquad j = 1, \ldots, 4; \qquad i = 0, 1, 2, \ldots$$

where B is the usual back-shift operator, and a_t an error term assumed to be white noise. The index i in this expression refers to years, while the index j denotes the particular quarter within a year. The four means (or mean changes) μ_1, μ_2, μ_3 and μ_4, allow different means for each quarter, and much of the seasonality of the time series will be captured in differences among these means. The distinctive feature of this model, however, is that the autoregressive parameters are also permitted to differ from one quarter to the next, so that four sets of autoregressive parameters are estimated in this model. Osborn and Smith (1989) reported some encouraging evidence on the quality of forecasts obtained from this model.

In principle, the use of periodically varying parameters need not be restricted to pure autoregressions. Tiao and Grupe (1980) introduced periodic ARMA models. These impose a somewhat heavier computational burden, and appear to have been applied only infrequently in practice.

10.7   CALENDAR EFFECTS

As with Section 10.5, the subject of this section is not a separate forecasting methodology, but the possibility of the elaboration of a methodology discussed earlier. Here our interest is in the prediction of a monthly seasonal time series from its own past. Now, the essence of seasonal variation rests on the observation that, while month-to-month variations can be expected in a time series precisely because of the location of months within the annual cycle, many of the characteristics of one April, for example, will be the same as those of any other April. We thus assume, in approaches such as the Holt-Winters algorithms of Section 6.4 and the seasonal ARIMA models of Section 7.11, a certain amount of stability. Certainly these approaches allow for an evolving seasonal pattern over time, but the implicit assumption is that, as far as assessing the impact of the time of year on an observation, one April is pretty much like any other. For a great many seasonal time series, this assumption is perfectly adequate, and both the Holt-Winters algorithms and seasonal ARIMA models have enjoyed much success in a wide variety of forecasting applications. Unfortunately, it is important to recognize for some applications that all Aprils are *not* created equal. This is an important consequence of the peculiarities in the construction of our calendar, and the difficulties that sometimes follow from it are often referred to as the problem of **calendar effects.** The two most important aspects of this problem are

1. *Trading day variations.* For some time series, notably product retail sales, one would not expect uniformity across days of the week. Rather, we might suspect that total sales in a month would depend

on the number of Mondays, Tuesdays, and so on in that month. For many consumer products, Saturday is an important trading day, and, all other things the same, higher sales might be expected in months with five Saturdays than in months with four. Unfortunately, the number of Mondays, Tuesdays, etc. that fall in a particular month changes from one year to the next. (The month of February does not even have the same total number of days every year.) This phenomenon is often referred to as the problem of trading day variations.

2. *Holiday effects.* Christmas falls at the same time every year. Consequently, its location in the calendar is simply an unchanging attribute of the month of December (and perhaps, in some instances, to a certain extent of the months of January and November). Because it is unchanging, the location of Christmas in December is simply subsumed in the December seasonal effect, and therefore causes no difficulty in the application of the methods of Chapters 6 and 7. Unfortunately, not all holidays have a fixed location in our calendar. For example, Easter can occur at any time from March 22 to April 25. If the time series in which we are interested is one whose values are likely to be influenced by the Easter holiday, then the assumption of stability in the annual cycle clearly fails. If the magnitude of the "Easter effect" is sufficiently serious, some attempt will have to be made to account for it.

As we have described them, calendar effects are something of a nuisance in the analysis of seasonal time series. If they are ignored, and do in fact have a substantial impact on the time series of interest, they can clearly impede any attempt, by whatever means, at understanding the underlying seasonal patterns in a time series. For example, suppose that sales of a retail product appear to be unusually high in June of this year. This might be interpreted as suggesting a rise in the underlying trend, but could in fact be no more than a consequence of the fact that this June has five Saturdays, while last June had four. Ignoring important calendar effects, then, could lead to unnecessarily poor forecasts, resulting from a faulty interpretation of the causes of recent developments in the behavior of a time series. There is, however, a positive side to all of this for the forecaster. If, in a particular application, the importance of calendar effects is recognized, and if the analyst is able in some way to make a reasonable assessment of their impacts on the behavior of a time series, it should be possible to exploit this understanding to produce superior forecasts. In essence, the analyst will have learned more about the **systematic component** in the behavior of the series. Successful forecasting, of course, depends on the ability to isolate systematic behavior. Suppose, for example, that it is possible to estimate, with some reliability, the impact of the location of Easter and of the number of Mondays, Tuesdays, and so on in the month on the behavior of a monthly time series. Such estimates should be very useful for forecasting, as we know, as far ahead as we care to know, the precise construction of the calendar. This is in contrast with the usual regression methods of Chapter 4, where, even if a relationship can be determined, future values of independent variables, required to predict the dependent variable, will typically not be known with certainty.

Attention to calendar effects has been paid for some years in the literature of both seasonal adjustment and forecasting. Most of the forecasting literature, including for example Liu (1980, 1986), Hillmer (1982), and Bell and Hillmer (1983), has concentrated on allowing for these effects in the context of an ARIMA model. In principle, such allowance should also be straightforward within the framework of other models, such as the structural models of Section 10.2. We view this as an important strength of the model-building approach to time series analysis and forecasting. If the analyst follows the discipline of formal model construction, then the assumptions made about the process under study should be quite explicit. It should then be relatively straightforward to contemplate, where it appears to be desirable, the relaxation of any assumptions, and the consequent elaboration of a model. We find it difficult to see how allowance for calendar effects can readily and reliably be made within the framework of such *ad hoc* approaches to forecasting as exponential smoothing, though the consequences of ignoring such effects will be the same whether, for example, the ARIMA model-building approach or the Holt-Winters algorithm is applied to a monthly seasonal time series.

To illustrate what might be done, we will discuss here the incorporation of trading day variations in a seasonal ARIMA model, following Hillmer (1982). The approach is essentially that of Section 9.5, employing regression models with an ARIMA error structure. The influence of the number of Mondays, Tuesdays, etc. in a month is postulated in the regression part of the model. Let Y_t denote observations on a monthly time series of interest. Then Hillmer considers the model

$$Y_t = \beta_1 X_{1t} + \beta_2 X_{2t} + \cdots + \beta_6 X_{6t} + \beta_7 X_{7t} + \epsilon_t \quad (10.7.1a)$$

$$\phi(B)\Phi(B^{12})(1 - B)^d(1 - B^{12})^D \epsilon_t = \theta(B)\Theta(B^{12})a_t \quad (10.7.1b)$$

In equation 10.7.1a ϵ_t is an error term, and the quantities X_{it} ($i = 1, \ldots, 7$) provide information about the number of trading days of different sorts in the month t. Specifically,

$$X_{1t} = \text{Number of Mondays in the month}$$
$$- \text{Number of Sundays in the month}$$

$$X_{2t} = \text{Number of Tuesdays in the month}$$
$$- \text{ Number of Sundays in the month}$$

$$\vdots$$

$$X_{6t} = \text{Number of Saturdays in the month}$$
$$- \text{ Number of Sundays in the month}$$

$$X_{7t} = \text{Total number of days in the month}$$

This specification may seem unduly cumbersome. After all, precisely the same thing could be accomplished by defining a different set of seven independent variables—number of Mondays in the month, number of Tuesdays in the month, . . . , number of Sundays in the month. However, these independent variables would be strongly correlated with one another, leading to imprecise estimates of their associated parameters.

The error specification 10.7.1b is precisely the multiplicative seasonal ARIMA model discussed in Section 7.11. Here a_t is white noise, B the back-shift operator, and the regular and seasonal autoregressive and moving average parameters are carried in

$$\phi(B) = 1 - \phi_1 B - \cdots - \phi_p B^p$$

$$\Phi(B^{12}) = 1 - \Phi_1 B^{12} - \cdots - \Phi_P B^{12P}$$

$$\theta(B) = 1 - \theta_1 B - \cdots - \theta_q B^q$$

$$\Theta(B^{12}) = 1 - \Theta_1 B^{12} - \cdots - \Theta_Q B^{12Q}$$

In essence, the methodology for fitting to data the model 10.7.1 is that outlined in Section 9.5. However, Hillmer suggests proceeding by first using the sample autocorrelations of the observed series Y_t, and its differences, to assess the amount of differencing needed—that is, to choose values for d and D in equation 10.7.1b. The remainder of the analysis then begins by regressing through ordinary least squares $(1 - B)^d (1 - B^{12})^D Y_t$ on $(1 - B)^d (1 - B^{12})^D X_{it}$ $(i = 1, \ldots, 7)$. The autocorrelations and partial autocorrelations of the residuals from this fit are then employed to suggest the numbers of regular and seasonal autoregressive and moving average parameters required in Equation 10.7.1b.

Allowance for holiday effects, such as the location in the calendar of Easter, can also be made through the addition of further appropriately defined independent variables to the right-hand side of Equation 10.7.1a. Perhaps surprisingly, this turns out to be more tricky than the modeling of trading day variations. Experience suggests that it is important to allow not only for which month contains Easter, but also for where in that month Easter falls. Some details of a workable approach to this problem are discussed by Bell and Hillmer (1983).

Very often, but not invariably, the allowance for calendar effects will prove in practice to be an unnecessary elaboration of the usual methods for analyzing and forecasting monthly seasonal time series. It is for the analyst, familiar with the genesis of the time series of interest, to determine in any particular application whether such effects are likely to be important. Analyses in the articles cited in this section suggest that on occasion the incorporation of calendar effects into a model can lead to worthwhile gains in forecast accuracy.

10.8   ARARMA Models

An intriguing generalization of the ARIMA models of Chapter 7 is discussed by Parzen (1982), and Newton and Parzen (1984). Essentially, these authors generalize the differencing element in ARIMA model analysis. If a time series is stationary, it can be fitted by an appropriate ARMA model, which is then projected forward to derive forecasts. However, many business and economic time series met in practice are not stationary. In such circumstances, it may be possible to apply a simple transformation to the observed data to derive a series that is stationary. In ARIMA model building, the differencing transformation is used for this purpose. Here, we consider the possibility of applying instead more general autoregressive transformations. An ARMA model can then be fitted to the transformed series. Since differencing—the "I" part of "ARIMA"—is replaced here by an autoregressive transformation, the resulting models are called **ARARMA models.**

In practice, a number of alternative types of autoregressive transformation of a time series of interest might be tried, depending on the characteristics of the series. The analyst has some freedom of choice here, and can exercise some judgment. However, an automated variant of ARARMA model building can be developed by concentrating on a particular subset of autoregressive transformations that has proved useful. Let X_t $(t = 1, \ldots, n)$ be a set of n observations on a nonstationary series. We consider transformations to the new series $\tilde{X}_t$ defined by

$$\tilde{X}_t = X_t - \phi_\tau X_{t-\tau} \qquad t = \tau + 1, \ldots, n \qquad (10.8.1)$$

where τ is a positive integer and ϕ_τ a parameter. In practice, both of these quantities need to be determined. For a given value τ, the parameter ϕ_τ is estimated by least squares, as the number $\hat{\phi}_\tau$ for which

$$S = \sum_{t=\tau+1}^{n} (X_t - \phi_\tau X_{t-\tau})^2$$

is a minimum; that is

$$\hat{\phi}_\tau = \frac{\displaystyle\sum_{t=\tau+1}^{n} X_t X_{t-\tau}}{\displaystyle\sum_{t=\tau+1}^{n} X_{t-\tau}^2} \qquad (10.8.2)$$

It remains to choose the integer τ. This can be done by comparing the sums of squared errors from regressions for different values of τ, modifying for changes in the effective number of observations in the regressions. Specifically, a maximum permitted value M is chosen, and all values $\tau = 1, 2, \ldots, M$ are considered. The estimates 10.8.2 are calculated, and hence the error functions

$$\text{Err.}(\tau) = \frac{\displaystyle\sum_{t=\tau+1}^{n} (X_t - \hat{\phi}_\tau X_{t-\tau})^2}{\displaystyle\sum_{t=\tau+1}^{n} X_t^2}$$

The value of τ for which this function is smallest, $\hat{\tau}$, is then chosen.

Having reached this stage, the transformation 10.8.1 is applied to the data, with τ set to $\hat{\tau}$, and the parameter ϕ replaced by the corresponding least squares estimate. An ARMA model can then be fitted to the transformed series, $\tilde{X}_t$, using the methods of Chapter 7. The usual procedures, discussed in Chapter 7, can then be applied to forecasting future values of the stationary series $\tilde{X}_t$. Substitution of these forecasts into equation 10.8.1 then leads directly to forecasts of the original series X_t.

To the best of our knowledge, the ARARMA model-building approach is little used in practical business forecasting, and we have no experience of its application. However, this brief discussion is included here because of the superior performance of this approach in a large empirical study of the application of several forecasting methods reported by Makridakis et al. (1982).

EXERCISES

10.1   Consider the nonseasonal variant of the basic structural model

$$X_t = T_t + a_t$$

$$T_t = T_{t-1} + \beta_{t-1} + a_{1t}$$

$$\beta_t = \beta_{t-1} + a_{2t}$$

where a_t, a_{1t}, a_{2t} are independent white noise processes.
(a)   Show that it follows from this specification that we can write

$$(1 - B)^2 X_t = a_t - 2a_{t-1} + a_{t-2} + a_{1t} - a_{1,t-1} + a_{2,t-1}$$

where B is the back-shift operator.
(b)   Let

$$Z_t = a_t - 2a_{t-1} + a_{t-2} + a_{1t} - a_{1,t-1} + a_{2,t-1}$$

Show that all autocorrelations beyond the second of Z_t are zero. Hence deduce that the nonseasonal variant of the basic structural model is equivalent to a subset of the ARIMA(0, 2, 2) models.

10.2   Consider the basic structural model defined by equations 10.2.1 through 10.2.4, where a_t, a_{1t}, a_{2t}, a_{3t} are white noise processes.
(a)   Show that equation 10.3.4 implies

$$(1 - B^s)S_t = a_{3t} - a_{3,t-1}$$

(b)   Hence show that the basic structural model specification implies

$$(1 - B)(1 - B^s)X_t = a_t - a_{t-1} - a_{t-s} + a_{t-s-1}$$
$$+ a_{1t} - a_{1,t-s} + a_{2,t-1} + a_{2,t-2}$$
$$+ \cdots + a_{2,t-s} + a_{3t} - 2a_{3,t-1} + a_{3,t-2}$$

Deduce that $(1 - B)(1 - B^s)X_t$ obeys a moving average model of order $s + 1$. Discuss the likelihood of this particular specification being identified by the ARIMA model-building methodology of Section 7.11.

10.3   Discuss the differences between Bayesian forecasting and the incorporation of intervention analysis into the ARIMA model-building framework.

10.4   Consider the data of Exercise 7.12 on prices received by farmers for all crops. Fit appropriate ARIMA models to the transformed series, $X_t(\lambda)$ defined by equation 10.5.1, for $\lambda = 0, 0.2, 0.4, 0.6, 0.8, 1$. Choose the most appropriate λ, and forecast the next six values of the series.

10.5   Consider the data of Exercise 7.13 on the United Kingdom-United States exchange rate. Fit appropriate ARIMA models to the transformed series, $X_t(\lambda)$, defined by equation 10.5.1, for $\lambda = 0, 0.2,$

0.4, 0.6, 0.8, 1. Choose the most appropriate λ, and forecast the next five values of the series.

10.6 Carefully discuss the problem of calendar effects in the analysis and forecasting of monthly seasonal time series. List as many possible effects of this sort as you can, and suggest possible time series for which you would expect them to be important.

SELECTED BIBLIOGRAPHY

Bell, W. R., & S. C. Hillmer (1983). Modeling time series with calendar variation. *Journal of the American Statistical Association, 78*, 526–534.

Fildes, R. (1983). An evaluation of Bayesian forecasting. *Journal of Forecasting, 2*, 137–150.

Fildes, R. (1984). Bayesian forecasting. In S. Makridakis et al. (Eds.), *The Forecasting Accuracy of Major Time Series Methods*. New York: Wiley.

Ghysels, E. (1987). Seasonal extraction in the presence of feedback. *Journal of Business and Economic Statistics, 5*, 191–194.

Granger, C. W. J., & P. Newbold (1986). *Forecasting Economic Time Series* (2nd ed.). Orlando, Fl.: Academic Press.

Harrison, P. J., & C. F. Stevens (1971). A Bayesian approach to short term forecasting. *Operational Research Quarterly, 22*, 341–362.

Harrison, P. J., & C. F. Stevens (1976). Bayesian forecasting. *Journal of the Royal Statistical Society B, 38*, 205–247.

Harvey, A. C. (1984). A unified view of statistical forecasting procedures. *Journal of Forecasting, 3*, 245–275.

Harvey, A. C. (1989). *Forecasting, Structural Time Series Models and the Kalman Filter*. Cambridge: University Press.

Harvey, A. C., & P. H. J. Todd (1983). Forecasting economic time series with structural and Box-Jenkins models: a case study. *Journal of Business and Economic Statistics, 1*, 299–307.

Hillmer, S. C. (1982). Forecasting time series with trading day variation. *Journal of Forecasting, 1*, 385–395.

Hopwood, W. S., J. C. McKeown, & P. Newbold (1981). Power transformations in time series models of quarterly earnings per share. *Accounting Review, 56*, 927–933.

Hopwood, W. S., J. C. McKeown, & P. Newbold (1984). Time series forecasting models involving power transformations. *Journal of Forecasting, 3*, 57–61.

Liu, L. M. (1980). Analysis of time series with calendar effects. *Management Science, 26,* 106–112.

Liu, L. M. (1986). Identification of time series models in the presence of calendar variation. *International Journal of Forecasting, 2,* 357–372.

Makridakis, S., A. Anderson, R. Carbone, R. Fildes, M. Hibon, R. Lewandowski, J. Newton, E. Parzen & R. Winkler (1982). The accuracy of extrapolation (time series) methods: results of a forecasting competition. *Journal of Forecasting, 1,* 111–153.

Maravall, A. (1985). On structural time series models and the characterization of components. *Journal of Business and Economic Statistics, 3,* 350–355.

Nelson, H. L., & C. W. J. Granger (1979). Experience with using the Box-Cox transformation when forecasting economic time series. *Journal of Econometrics, 10,* 57–69.

Newbold, P. (1988). Predictors projecting linear trend plus seasonal dummies. *The Statistician, 37,* 111–127.

Newbold, P., & C. W. J. Granger (1974). Experience with forecasting univariate time series and the combination of forecasts. *Journal of the Royal Statistical Society A, 137,* 131–146.

Newton, H. J., & E. Parzen (1984). Forecasting and time series model types of 111 economic time series. In S. Makridakis et al. (Eds.), *The Forecasting Accuracy of Major Time Series Methods.* New York: Wiley.

Osborn, D. R. (1988). Seasonality and habit persistence in a life cycle model of consumption. *Journal of Applied Econometrics, 3,* 255–266.

Osborn, D. R. (1990). A survey of seasonality in U.K. macroeconomic variables. *International Journal of Forecasting, 6,* 327–336.

Osborn, D. R., & J. P. Smith (1989). The performance of periodic autoregressive models in forecasting seasonal U.K. consumption. *Journal of Business and Economic Statistics, 7,* 117–127.

Parzen, E. (1982). ARARMA models for time series analysis and forecasting. *Journal of Forecasting, 1,* 67–82.

Tiao, G. C., & M. R. Grupe (1980). Hidden periodic autoregressive moving average models in time series data. *Biometrika, 67,* 365–373.

Judgmental Methods and Technological Forecasting

11.1 INTRODUCTION: THE VALUE OF JUDGMENT

If you want forecasts of product sales for next month, it may be useful to consult a statistician. If you want to predict what products will be selling in what quantities in your industry in 20 years time, consult experts in the relevant areas of research and development, corporate strategy, marketing, and so on. The authors of this book are statisticians, and our main focus is on those forecasting techniques where the experience of the recent past might reasonably be expected to provide useful guidance as to what will happen in the not-too-distant future. We might, for example, be fairly confident in taking a shot at predicting the monthly demand for electricity in central Illinois over the next year. However, we would be far less confident of the value of our expertise if asked to forecast what will be the pattern of energy consumption in 20 years time. The eventual outcome will depend on questions best answered by experts in a range of fields, including economics, politics, geology, and engineering. Will a cartel of oil-producing countries succeed in imposing huge price increases? What is the potential for further substantial discoveries of oil, and at what price would the development of new fields be economic? What reserves of natural gas remain to be tapped? If there are to be substantial price increases, what are the prospects for further energy conservation by the public and by industry? Will the energy picture be disturbed by political upheavals in the Middle East? What is the potential for alternative sources of energy at competitive costs? What part will be played by government in providing incentives to production or disincentives to consumption? A well-thought-out attack on this problem clearly requires an approach that is very different from the approaches to forecasting on which we have concentrated in this book. It is not our intention here to discuss this or any similar forecasting problem in great detail. However, it is useful to see how it might require an approach that is radically different from those of previous chapters of this book.

We have concentrated on the use of formal quantitative models or algorithms in forecasting. Such objective approaches can be expected to be valuable when the most important determinants of the behavior of interest are quantifiable, and when the system being studied is sufficiently stable that it is reasonable to extrapolate the future from the past. However, they will be far less useful if, as is possible in the energy sector over the next 20 years, political or technical developments render a current formal model obsolete. A number of points emerge from these considerations:

1. Formal quantitative models will often be very useful for short-run forecasting, but they may be of less relevance for prediction in the very long-term, where historical patterns might be expected to break down, as a result, for example, of technological and social changes. The question of how far ahead it is reasonable to project from a formal model is a difficult one. The answer depends more on the context than the calendar, for some processes have been and can be expected to be far more stable than others. For example, the prediction of the total population of the United States in ten years time in this way might be quite reasonable. However, we would be far more reluctant to attempt to forecast the market for computers this far ahead.

2. In many instances, the most important determinants of the long-term outlook are likely to be difficult or impossible to quantify. Thus, what may be required is not a different type of formal model, but rather the abandonment of the formal model-building approach. The best approach to long-term forecasting may be less structured, more informal, and rest primarily on subjective judgment.

3. In our example of the long-term energy outlook, we have indicated the possible value of expertise in a number of fields, including politics, economics, geology, and technology. An appeal to expert judgment— possibly to the judgment of experts in a number of areas—is often

the most useful aid to an understanding of the factors relevant to the long-term future.

4. For the longer term, technological developments may need to be anticipated to achieve reasonable forecasts. Other qualitative changes, such as those in the political area, could also be relevant.

We have emphasized that, in long-term forecasting, purely or primarily judgmental approaches may be more appropriate than a formal quantitative approach to prediction. Of course, in practice there is no reason why any forecasting problem cannot be attacked exclusively through subjective judgment rather than the more objective methods we have discussed in earlier chapters. When valuable expertise is available, it should certainly be used, and even when a formal quantitative approach is employed, the ingredient of human judgment can be and often is profitably incorporated. For example, suppose that forecasts are generated by one of the simple single series projection methods of Chapters 6 or 7. These procedures provide an extrapolation of recent trends that will typically be quite adequate for short-run prediction *in a stable environment*. However, in sales forecasting for example, management may be aware of certain factors suggesting either higher or lower sales than would be expected from consideration only of past trends. In that case the quantitative forecasts could be subjectively modified in an attempt to allow for the impact of these factors. Often such modifications are made quite informally. However, Cholette (1982) provides a formal mechanism for amalgamating ARIMA forecasts with so-called benchmarks, which may be predictions from expert judgment, in the production of an overall forecast. On occasion the analyst may have available a record of the performance over time of both time series and purely judgmental forecasts. The latter, for example, might be predictions made by the sales force. An examination of this record could suggest appropriate weights to be used in forming a *composite forecast*. This possibility will be discussed in Chapter 12.

In Chapters 3 and 4 we discussed the use of regression models in forecasting, and more complex econometric models were considered in Chapter 8. If such behavioral models are to be built, the injection of judgment into the process is inevitable. After all, in constructing a regression model, we do not merely look for significant correlations between a dependent variable and every conceivable independent variable. Such an exhaustive search would almost certainly lead to apparent success simply by chance. Rather, statistical behavioral models are constructed through the interplay of subject matter hypotheses, proposed through expert knowledge, and empirical evidence. Einhorn and Hogarth (1982) forcefully make the point that expert judgment should invariably play a part in the assessment of statistical evidence. As a trivial example, the so-called "Super Bowl Stock Market Predictor Theory" asserts that a victory in the Super Bowl for a member of the old American Football League is bearish for the market, while a win for a member of the original National Football League is bullish. This rule correctly predicted the direction of the stock market in 23 of the years after the first 26 Super Bowls. The statistical evidence is very strong on the surface, but an ounce of judgment would dissuade one from betting on it!

In Chapter 8, we saw that judgment plays an even larger part in macroeconomic forecasting than it does in sensible econometric model specification. A national economy is a hugely complex entity whose intricacies are not easily captured in a formal statistical model, however sophisticated the structure of that model. The available evidence suggests that model builders correctly believe that the production of good forecasts requires judgmental intervention and modification beyond the usual judgmental projection of exogenous variables.

It can be seen then that judgmental forecasting need not be something that is distinct from the use of formal quantitative algorithms or models. On the contrary, soundly based expert judgment should be of value whether or not a formal model is constructed. In much of the rest of this chapter we will concentrate on purely judgmental approaches to forecasting. These range in sophistication from simple visual trend extrapolation to technological forecasting approaches such as *Delphi*. They also vary greatly in cost, depending on the amount of expertise that is to be purchased. As we have already indicated, the necessary expertise extends well beyond the statistical, and consequently the details of practical forecasting exercises of this type are beyond the scope of this book. We will provide here just a brief review of some of the issues that are involved. The bibliography at the end of the chapter provides ample scope for further reading.

11.2   JUDGMENTAL EXTRAPOLATION

It is important to distinguish between two different types of judgmental forecasting. We have introduced the notion that subject matter expertise can be, and very often should be, an important element in a forecasting exercise. However, the literature on judgmental forecasting discusses also the possibility of projecting future values merely from the visual inspection of the graph of a time series, independent of any subject matter knowledge. This very crude form of judgmental forecasting is sometimes called **judgmental extrapolation,** or **bold freehand extrapolation.** It might also properly be characterized as *non-expert judgment*, since no understanding of the physical process generating a time series is required. The only expertise needed is the ability, just from the visual inspection of the graph of a series, to guess future movements with some accuracy. We view this approach as quite different in kind from the application of subject matter expertise, knowledge, and insight to a forecasting problem.

Judgmental extrapolation certainly has one attraction: It requires minimal expenditures of time, effort and money. (Of course, fully automatic quantitative approaches, such as exponential smoothing, may be even less expensive when forecasts of a large collection of time series are required.) The obvious question to be asked concerns the abilities of individuals to achieve any degree of success with such a simple approach. Unfortunately, the published literature on this issue is far from definitive. Lawrence (1983), and Lawrence, et al. (1985) report impressive results from judgmental extrapolation compared with the more formal time series projection methods of Chapters 6 and 7. However, far less favorable findings are reported by Hogarth and Makridakis (1981), and Carbone and Gorr (1985). Willemain (1989, 1991) provides some evidence that, when presented with graphs of forecasts, individuals can make adjustments that improve the forecasts, *when these forecasts are seriously suboptimal.* Our own position is firmly in the camp of the skeptics. We would not otherwise have written Chapters 6 and 7, which occupy a substantial portion of this book. We simply do not believe that human judgment, unburdened with subject matter knowledge, can provide an adequate substitute either for the careful model-building approach of Chapter 7 or the sensible choice of an exponential smoothing algorithm whose value is supported by a wealth of practical experience. Certainly some time series met in practice exhibit so much regularity that almost any reasonable approach, including judgmental extrapolation, will achieve very similar forecasts. However, many more series do not, and for these more difficult cases our faith in judgmental extrapolation is about on a par with that in astrology.

To the reader who wishes to try his or her hand at bold freehand extrapolation, we have very little guidance to offer, since we have no particular faith in our own abilities in this regard. Our only advice is based on a study of the methods of Chapters 6 and 7. It seems quite clear that, although the behavior of an observed time series might exhibit considerable variability and volatility, optimally the forecast function should be considerably smoother. It is clearly foolish in a forecast function to attempt to mimic the unpredictable, random behavior present in any time series. To illustrate, Figure 11.1 shows data generated from the random walk model, where period-to-period changes are zero-mean white noise. It follows that the best forecast of all future changes is zero, so that the optimal prediction, based on the past, for the future is simply the most recent observation. The observations of Figure 11.1 certainly exhibit a good deal of action: They are far from constant. Nevertheless, the optimal forecast of all future values is simply, as shown in the figure, constant equal to the last observation. We assert this not because we claim any particular skill in

FIGURE 11.1 Observations generated by a random walk, and optimal forecasts.

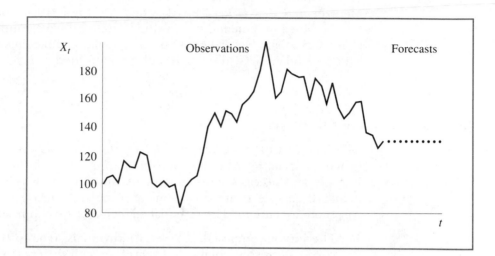

judgmental extrapolation, but because we generated a series with this characteristic.

For the reader who suspects that he or she possesses particular occult powers allowing divination of the future from a casual contemplation of the past, we can only suggest putting these powers to the test. Take a collection of time series, and leave aside a few observations at the end of each for assessing the quality of your forecasts. Then generate forecasts using either the Box-Jenkins approach or an appropriate exponential smoothing algorithm. Compare these forecasts with those that you obtain from judgmental extrapolation. (In Chapter 13 we will discuss some procedures for the evaluation of forecasts.) If you succeed in consistently beating the formal quantitative approaches, there are two possibilities: Either you are not properly applying the ARIMA approach (re-read Chapter 7), or you have unusual perceptual abilities (ignore everything you read in Chapters 6 and 7, and consider a career as a fortune-teller).

11.3 EXPERT JUDGMENT

We move now to the more serious possibility of basing forecasts exclusively on judgment derived from subject matter expertise. In spite of the development over the years of various formal quantitative approaches to forecasting, and of the growth in computing resources that has made these approaches increasingly accessible to practitioners, it is quite clear from surveys of management that purely judgmental methods continue to be extremely popular. Findings along these lines are reported by Mentzer and Cox (1984), Sparkes and McHugh (1984), and Dalrymple (1987). Much judgmental forecasting is quite informal, and defies formal characterization. Nevertheless, three popular management approaches, which we now briefly discuss, have been identified.

Jury of Executive Opinion

The title "jury of executive opinion" is often given as a formal description of what is generally the most informal approach to business forecasting. Put simply, forecasts of quantities of interest, such as future product demand, emerge from discussions at a meeting of a group, or jury, of corporate executives. The essential elements of this approach are

1. The jury is composed of several individuals, from different areas of corporate responsibility, and therefore with different types of expertise and knowledge. The group therefore has available inputs from executives in marketing, finance, production, research and development, and so on.
2. The final verdict emerges in some way following face-to-face discussion among the jury members, with each interpreting and weighing the views of the others in a quite informal way. The eventual forecast then might be regarded as resulting from a synthesis of the expert judgments of the individuals in the group.

The precise mechanism through which the final forecast is achieved varies somewhat from one corporation to another, and perhaps also from one application to another. One possibility is that, following the discussions, individual jury members write down their own forecasts, which are then averaged. Alternatively, a consensus forecast may be arrived at through more extensive discussions. This latter approach is typically informal, and essentially nonquantitative, though jury members may be presented with relevant quantitative, and also qualitative, information prior to the meetings. Sniezek (1989) discusses alternative ways of organizing groups for the generation of judgmental forecasts.

The most obvious characteristic of the jury of executive opinion approach, and one that is often cited as an advantage, is its simplicity. This does not, however, necessarily imply that the approach is inexpensive, as quite substantial blocks of the time of high-salaried executives may be taken up by the meetings. A more compelling advantage is that this is an obvious and direct, and perhaps the only feasible, way to incorporate the considerable experience of a range of high-level corporate executives in the forecast-generating process. The value of product knowledge in sales forecasting is stressed by Edmundson, Lawrence, and O'Connor (1988).

In addition to cost, perhaps the major disadvantage is the tautological one of the absence, or low level, of objectivity in forecasts based on subjective judgment. Moreover, it is not at all clear that group dynamics will lead to the wisest consensus forecast. For example, too much weight may be given to the views of those executives who are most articulate, or have the strongest and most forceful personalities. Additionally, deference to the views of those with the most senior positions in the organization may be unwarranted. There may also be a tendency for the group to be swayed by the views of its most optimistic members. Given the unstructured way in which the forecast eventually emerges, it is difficult to attach responsibility for poor forecast performance to individual executives. Moreover, the group will typically be slow to realize whose views are most reliable, and whose should be most heavily discounted, since the time that elapses between making the forecast and observing the outcome will have dulled the memories of the jury participants. Furthermore, a group of senior executives is likely to feel comfortable in taking a medium- or long-term view, but is unlikely to have the expertise to assess month-to-month variations in sales due to seasonal factors. Thus, even in the circumstances in which the jury of executive opinion approach appears to be appropriate, supplementation by more formal methods may be required when interest is in the short run. A further reservation about this and other subjective approaches arises from the tendency of people to overreact to recent unexpected and dramatic events. This phenomenon is discussed by De Bondt and Thaler (1985) in connection with stock market prices.

Sales Force Composite Forecasts

Many products are sold by sales representatives attached to particular geographic locations. Sales force members are in regular and frequent contact with customers and potential customers, and might be expected to have useful insights into purchasing intentions, at least over horizons of about a year. There is much to be said for the desirability of incorporating these insights into sales forecasts. The most direct way to do this is to simply ask individual sales force members to predict sales of each product for which they are responsible in their own territories. These forecasts can then be aggregated to form sales force composite predictions over the whole country, or indeed on an international basis. Of course, the possibility for a regional breakdown of the forecasts implicit in this approach can also be valuable.

A possible difficulty with this approach is that individual sales force members may be quite unrealistic in their projections. It may be desirable for senior sales managers to review these individual predictions, and to modify them if deemed necessary. Alternatively, the responsibility for forecasting might simply be put in the hands of the more senior sales executives.

The advantages of the sales force composite approach are the ability to disaggregate forecasts by region, and the use of the information gleaned by those members of the corporation closest to customers. However, although it is clear that sales force members should be in possession of valuable information, at least of a qualitative sort, their ability to translate this information into the production of accurate forecasts is less clear. One potential problem is a tendency toward optimism. More seriously, the expertise that the salespeople have will be at the *microeconomic* level; it is likely to relate to the relative strengths of the markets for the products they sell. However, future demand levels for virtually all products will be strongly influenced by *macroeconomic* developments—an area in which sales staff will have considerably less expertise.

The type of expertise available to a corporation's sales force will be very different from that required to build an ARIMA time series model, or a regression model that is to be used for forecasting. Intuition suggests that the intelligent incorporation of this expertise into the forecast-generating mechanism should prove useful. This conjecture may well be worth checking in those cases where sales staff have routinely produced forecasts. As suggested in Section 11.1, the combination of sales force forecasts with a more formal quantitative approach is an attractive possibility.

Surveys of Expectations and Anticipations

It is possible to go one step beyond consulting the sales force by surveying customers, or potential customers, in attempting to predict product demand. The type of survey employed will depend to a great extent on the type of market for the product. If there is a relatively small number of business companies who are potential customers, quite strenuous efforts can be made to elicit from managers in these companies estimates of future product demand, and the likely distribution of that demand among competing suppliers. Of course, the value of such contacts with major purchasers extends far beyond demand forecasting. They provide valuable feedback on perceived product quality and on product characteristics considered most desirable by these important customers.

For consumer products, where the potential market consists of a substantial segment of the whole population, a sample survey of actual and potential buying patterns may be carried out by a market research group. Again, the value of such market research does not lie only in the forecasting area. Information can be obtained about perceptions of the product and its competitors, as well as data on penetration in different market segments, brand loyalty, and so on. All of this should prove valuable in marketing. Of course, substantial market research efforts on particular products will not be routinely mounted due to high costs; therefore, this approach to forecasting will not be available for demand for mature products. However, market research surveys are particularly valuable in attempting to assess the likely demand for new products.

The Quality of Judgmental Forecasts

Attempts to assess the practical merits of various forecasting methodologies are fraught with difficulties. All forecasting problems have unique characteristics, so that it is hard to generalize from whatever empirical evidence happens to be available. The problem becomes even more difficult when we consider forecasting through expert judgment. Quite simply, there is no replicable forecasting methodology called "expert judgment." In any particular exercise, all depends on the specific features of the forecasting problem, the worth of the expertise focused on the problem, and what alternative forecasting approaches are available. The discovery of a particular group of experts who have enjoyed success in one area tells us nothing about whether there exists a group of experts who will forecast successfully in a different area. In the same way, if a particular group has a poor record in predicting some quantity it may be that some other group can predict that same quantity quite effectively.

The value of purely judgmental forecasts is likely to be problem area specific. There are particular areas where it is easy to believe on *a priori* grounds that informal expert judgment is likely to be the best bet in predicting the future. It could be that quantitative information is sparse or unavailable, or that the most important determinants of the future appear to be discrete qualitative developments. It is not difficult to imagine circumstances in which what seems to be the most relevant available information simply cannot be incorporated into any formal model, so that any model built would be a crude, unsophisticated approximation of the world, and therefore of little value. Certainly it is easy to believe that the forecasting of political events falls into this category. Ascher (1982) firmly makes the point that formal quantitative models are likely to be of limited value in this area. Austin and Yoffie (1984) stress the importance of political forecasting in management decision making, and discuss the integration of political forecasting into the overall prediction and decision-making process. Certainly this is an area in which management would welcome access to expertise, in both domestic and international politics. The extent to which such expertise is actually available, however, is not clear. For example, an important question for corporations with substantial international operations concerns the political riskiness of different countries, and political risk analysis is now a well-established profession in corporate management. However, Mumpower, Livingston, and Lee (1987) present evidence suggesting that the evaluations of these analysts differed little from those of a group of undergraduate students.

As we have already suggested, in business applications forecasts are very frequently based exclusively on expert judgment, even when a formal quantitative approach is perfectly feasible. There is no systematic record of the relative performances of judgmental and quantitative approaches to forecasting where these are competitors or potential competitors: The published evidence is spotty. Asked to predict what would be found, we would expect that on occasions judgmental forecasting would do quite well, while on others its performance might be relatively poor. The evidence seems to support this conjecture. For example, Armstrong (1983) summarizes evidence on the prediction of annual corporate earnings indicating a generally superior performance for judgmental forecasts, whether prepared by management or financial analysts, compared with time series extrapolation methods. On the other hand, Brandt and Bessler (1983) find for agricultural prices ARIMA forecasts that outperform those based on expert judgment. In a survey of developments in forecasting, Makridakis (1986) concludes that, on the whole, judgmental forecasts tend to be no more accurate than those based on quantitative models, noting in addition that the judgmental approach may be more costly. Brown (1988) suggests that the judgmental forecaster has the advantage when he or she can exert influence over the event being predicted, can self-select items to be predicted, and possesses inside information.

Depending on one's perspective, one might be surprised to learn that forecasts by experts are often inferior to those generated from very simple time series extrapolation methods. After all, these simple quantitative approaches cannot incorporate the wealth of knowledge, experience, and insight of the human expert. Two problems in particular are potentially important. First, when forecasts are prepared internally by management, there is a tendency toward bias. Second, individuals appear to exhibit far more certainty than is warranted about their predictions. Tyebjee (1987) distinguishes and studies three sources of upward bias in forecasts of new product sales. These are

1. *The postdecision audit bias.* In the product planning stage, a number of alternatives may be considered. Only those products expected to achieve most market success will actually be developed, so that although some new products inevitably will meet with little market success, only those that are expected to sell well will have been marketed.

2. *The advocacy bias.* Executives involved in the planning of the development of a new product will naturally become attached to its virtues, and in selling the product to their colleagues are likely to overstate

its market potential, emphasizing positive indications while neglecting or down-playing those factors mitigating against a strong market performance.

3. *The optimism bias.* There is some tendency for human judgment to be clouded by optimism. This is particularly likely when executives who have taken part in the planning and development of a product contemplate its market prospects.

It is well known that humans tend to be more confident than is justified in their knowledge of factual information. In the same way, as Fischoff and MacGregor (1982) demonstrate, they seem to be more confident than is warranted in their predictions of future events. These authors presented subjects with questions about whether particular events would or would not occur, and asked for probabilistic assessments of the more likely outcomes. In the aggregate, the actual frequencies of occurrence were noticeably lower than those implied by these subjective probabilities. This finding is important and disturbing in evaluating judgmental forecasts, since very often in practice decisions will be based not simply on the predictions themselves, but also on the strength of belief in these predictions. In forecasting it is important not only to assess the most likely outcome, but also to achieve a realistic understanding of the degree of uncertainty surrounding future developments.

11.4 TECHNOLOGICAL FORECASTING: DELPHI

In Section 11.1 we introduced the idea that, for forecasting in the long term, even in situations where it was possible to fit formal quantitative models to historical data, the relevance of such models was likely to be severely reduced by environmental changes which could best be anticipated, if at all, judgmentally. Recognition of this fact, combined with the need to plan rationally for the longer run has led to the development of a number of approaches designed to predict changes in the environment. Since many of these changes involve technological developments, this activity is often known as **technological forecasting.** The methodology of technological forecasting has been applied to the anticipation of developments not generally thought of as technological. Also, in principle there is no reason why many of these procedures need be restricted to viewing the longer term, though in practice this has typically been the case.

The best known approach to technological forecasting is the **Delphi method,** developed at the Rand Corporation. Delphi is discussed in detail and illustrated in many articles and books, including Helmer (1966, 1968), Martino (1970, 1983), Linstone and Turoff (1975), Gordon (1968), Welty

(1972), and Parenté, et al. (1984). The major features of a Delphi exercise are the following:

1. A *panel of experts* is assembled; it is important that there be several experts, though their particular areas of expertise may differ, such diversity being essential in many practical applications. By contrast with the jury of expert opinion approach of Section 11.3, the panel members do not meet, so that conclusions are not influenced by the interaction of individual personalities.

2. Panel members are provided with questions of the what, if, or when variety. At the least specific level, management may want to know what products are likely to be developed in a particular industry. More specifically, either initially or at some later stage, panel members may be presented with particular conjectures, or *scenarios*, and asked both if and when certain developments will occur. Answers to "if" questions may be phrased in terms of subjective probabilities.

3. Since panel members will have access to different information, and will interpret the information that they have in different ways, it can be expected that their first-round responses will present a wide diversity of views. Such a range of opinions may fail to provide the decision maker with clear guidelines. The panel may, however, move closer to consensus through a process of **iterative consultation.**

4. This iterative consultation process is stimulated by providing panel members with feedback from the previous round of consultations. Panel members' views are summarized and summary statements are provided to all members. In this way something closer to a consensual group view may emerge in successive rounds of consultations. Panel members whose positions differ substantially from the group median may be asked to provide written justifications to assess the strength of opinion. If deviant views are not strongly held, some shift towards the group norm can be expected, whereas if they are strongly held their justifications may provide valuable input to the process.

5. Although iterative consultation and feedback will often move the panel closer to consensus, and to some extent are designed to do so, consensus is not essential. A single group forecast is not the only useful goal. It is also valuable to know on what aspects of the future there is serious disagreement among experts, since management may then be able to plan for multiple eventualities.

As we have noted, unlike the jury of expert opinion, Delphi panel members do not meet. A difficulty of this is that individual panel members do not have immediate access to the knowledge of others. The process of iteration and feedback is designed to disseminate that knowledge in a framework free from personal interactions.

It is difficult to evaluate the worth of a Delphi exercise for two reasons. First, the great majority of its applications—and certainly those for which it was designed—have involved looking many years ahead using panels whose members have a good deal of technical expertise. Thus a considerable amount of time needs to have elapsed before it is possible to form any view of the merits of what was achieved in consulting the Delphi panel. Further, although scholars may be able to replicate some of the ingredients of a Delphi exercise in forming a panel to predict shorter run phenomena, the costs of assembling a sizeable group with genuine technical expertise are very high. The extent to which one can generalize, as some have attempted, from results derived from panels of students is far from clear. A second difficulty is that, given the types of problems often presented to Delphi panels in practice, it is hard to see what alternative approaches are available for comparison. Certainly, some doubts have been expressed. For example, although Brockhoff (1984) notes that the iteration process achieves a pull of extreme forecasts to the group median, he is more doubtful that a pull toward the true future outcome is achieved. Parenté, et al. (1984) attempt to assess the impact of various features of a Delphi exercise on forecast accuracy. The clearest finding concerns the worth of basing predictions on some kind of group average rather than using the projections of individuals. The value of the iterative process is less clear-cut: It appears to improve forecasts of when events will occur, but not of if they will occur. However, the panels used in this study were composed of student volunteers, and, as we have indicated, it may be rash to imply similar conclusions for panels of the kinds of experts typically employed in real world Delphi exercises.

11.5 OTHER APPROACHES TO TECHNOLOGICAL FORECASTING

It is extremely difficult to try to visualize the longer term future, and even more difficult to formalize the processes involved in trying to understand that future. Almost inevitably, the insights of subject matter experts—often from a diversity of subjects—are crucial, and the task is to attempt the synthesis of these judgments to form a coherent view. A number of alternative general approaches, most of which are summarized in Martino (1983), have been applied. Here we are able only to touch on a few of the issues involved. (The journal *Technological Forecasting and Social Change* reports many developments in this area.)

Cross-Impact Analysis

The cross-impact approach is often used in conjunction with Delphi, and is most relevant to assessing the chance that a particular event will occur, perhaps in some specific time frame. Cross-impact analysis, discussed by Linstone and Turoff (1975), and Helmer (1977), was designed in recognition of the fact that one's view of the chance of occurrence of one event may depend strongly on an assessment of whether some other event will occur. Moreover, these events may be in very different fields, with expertise in one implying little or no special knowledge of the other. For example, we might be interested in the possibility of substantial increases in the price of oil at some point in the next decade—a possibility on which economists and geologists might be expected to have useful views. However, the oil price could be strongly influenced by disruptions of supplies following political or military upheavals in the Middle East—the province of experts in international politics. The point is simply that it may not be sufficient to look at individual potential occurrences in isolation. Instead, it is useful to ask questions of the sort: "If A happens, then what is the chance that B will happen." Formally, the concept involved here is the specification of **conditional probabilities.**

Cross-impact analysis constitutes an attempt to assess the interdependence of uncertain future events. It is important for the decision maker to achieve some understanding of what developments are likely to substantially influence the area of interest. Better forecasts might then be achieved through a serious study of these potential influential developments. Moreover, if at some stage in the future such an influential development does indeed occur, the decision maker will be better placed to understand its potential impact. A difficulty in this approach is that it can be extremely hard to anticipate future causal links, and that the nature and direction of these relationships will often be far from clear, and indeed could be quite complex. For example, we have suggested that the market for oil could be influenced by political developments in the Middle East. However, it is entirely possible that future Middle East political changes could themselves be induced by movements in the oil markets.

La Prospective

La Prospective, discussed by Godet (1982), was developed in France, and is less well known in Anglo-Saxon countries: Certainly it has a rather Gallic flavor. It rejects formal quantitative models of the past, leading to single forecasts of the future of specific variables. Rather, the emphasis is on a multiplicity of possible futures, brought about through the activities of individuals, through qualitative developments. The future is seen as resulting from the interactions of many events, studied through cross-impact analysis, related through structures that are dynamic, and evolving over time. An important ingredient is the study of the power, strategies and resources of the individual actors whose actions will determine the future. The organization commissioning these forecasts may well be one of the influential actors involved, so that forecasting is not simply viewed as a passive activity; rather, the future is an entity in which the organization is an active participant, so that the exercise involves not simply estimating the future but quite naturally evaluating the merits of specific actions that might be taken by the organization. The end product of the analysis involves the writing of scenarios of the future, on which organizational strategies might be based. More formal methods might be applied to assess probabilities of occurrences of particular scenarios.

Scenario Writing

The writing of scenarios, in which views of possible futures are verbally exposited, is not in itself a method of forecasting, but plays an important part in many approaches to technological forecasting. Such scenarios are the result of imagination and expertise, and are intended to concentrate the minds of decision makers on potential outcomes. Scenarios are particularly useful for this purpose when, as is often the case, the future is sufficiently obscure that there is some merit in anticipating an array of potential developments. The process of scenario construction itself has received relatively little consideration from corporate forecasters, though as Jungermann (1985) points out, important psychological considerations are involved. It is difficult to assess the value of scenarios. Their worth as aids to quantitative sales forecasting has been questioned by Schnaars and Topol (1987). In particular, these authors found that the presentation of multiple scenarios did not improve the quality of judgmental sales forecasts, which turned out to be inferior to quantitative extrapolations. Moreover, despite predictions to the contrary of advocates of the merits of scenarios, their use did not lessen the surprise of forecasters at unexpected outcomes. Thus, although it is claimed that multiple scenarios better prepare management to face a turbulent environment, the available evidence fails to support such a claim. It appears that, if scenarios are to play a valuable part in preparing an organization to face the future, management needs to be educated in their sensible use and interpretation. Some discussion of technical methods for the analysis of scenarios is provided by Brauers and Weber (1988). Further discussion and illustration of implementations is provided by Huss (1988) and Schoemaker (1991).

11.6 SUMMARY

Our primary interest is in the use of formal quantitative methods in business forecasting, and our chief purpose in writing this book is to introduce the reader to these methods. Nevertheless, it must be admitted that on many occasions less formal judgmental approaches are employed. In many of these instances, the formal quantitative approach is a viable alternative, and may well be preferable, though the use of some element of judgment in conjunction with formal models is frequently advantageous. In spite of our advocacy of the objective approaches discussed in previous chapters, we acknowledge their limitations, recognizing that the simple extrapolation of the past into the future cannot provide answers to all forecasting problems faced by the managerial decision maker. On the contrary, it will often be necessary to look so far ahead that it is likely that any formal model will be rendered obsolete by qualitative environmental changes. Such changes will be difficult to anticipate by any means, but it appears that some kind of appeal to the judgments of subject matter experts offers the best prospects. In this chapter we have been able to provide only a brief overview of judgmental approaches to forecasting: To do more would take us far from our main theme. Forecasting problems for which the judgmental approach is most suitable are inevitably idiosyncratic, so that generalizations are of limited value. Moreover, these often involve the application of expert knowledge in such fields as politics and technology, to which we can lay no particular claims. Readers interested in more details, and specific applications of judgmental and technological forecasting exercises are invited to study some of the articles and books cited in the extensive bibliography at the end of this chapter.

EXERCISES

11.1 How good are your friends at judgmental extrapolation? Find a time series, and, holding out a few values at the end, graph the remaining observations. Invite a sample of your friends to project the series forward. Note the extent of the diversity of their projections. Now, use a formal approach—either build an ARIMA model, or employ an exponential smoothing algorithm. Compare the judgmental and quantitative forecasts with the actual outcomes.

11.2 (a) From among your friends, assemble a Delphi panel. Choose a possible future event, and try to obtain an assessment of if and when it will occur. Discuss any movement toward consensus that is observed during the Delphi iterations.

(b) Look at the same forecasting problem as in part (a), but now through constituting from among your friends a jury of executive opinion, with yourself as chairperson. Compare and contrast the processes through which the final prediction was achieved in these two cases.

SELECTED BIBLIOGRAPHY

Ang, S., & M. O'Connor (1991). The effect of group interaction processes on performance in time series extrapolation. *International Journal of Forecasting, 7*, 141–149.

Armstrong, J. S. (1983). Relative accuracy of judgmental and extrapolative methods in forecasting annual earnings. *Journal of Forecasting, 2*, 437–447.

Armstrong, J. S. (1985). *Long-range Forecasting: From Crystal Ball to Computer* (2nd ed.). New York: Wiley.

Ascher, W. (1982). Political forecasting: The Missing Link. *Journal of Forecasting, 1*, 227–239.

Austin, J. E., & D. B. Yoffie (1984). Political forecasting as a management tool. *Journal of Forecasting, 3*, 395–408.

Ayres, R. U. (1969). *Technological Forecasting and Long Range Planning.* New York: McGraw-Hill.

Brandt, J. A., & D. A. Bessler (1983). Price forecasting and evaluation: An application in agriculture. *Journal of Forecasting, 2*, 237–248.

Brauers, J., & M. Weber (1988). A new method of scenario analysis for strategic planning. *Journal of Forecasting, 7*, 31–47.

Brockhoff, K. (1984). Forecasting quality and information. *Journal of Forecasting, 3*, 417–428.

Brown, L. D. (1988). Comparing judgmental to extrapolative forecasts: It's time to ask why and when. *International Journal of Forecasting, 4*, 171–173.

Carbone, R., & W. Gorr (1985). Accuracy of judgmental forecasting of time series. *Decision Sciences, 16*, 153–160.

Cetron, M. J., & C. A. Ralph (1971). *Industrial Application of Technological Forecasting.* New York: Wiley.

Cholette, P. A. (1982). Prior information and ARIMA forecasting. *Journal of Forecasting, 1*, 375–383.

Clarke, A. C. (1973). *Profiles of the Future* (2nd ed.). New York: Harper and Row.

Dalrymple, D. J. (1987). Sales forecasting practices: Results from a United States survey. *International Journal of Forecasting, 3*, 379–391.

De Bondt, W. F. M., & R. Thaler (1985). Does the stock market overreact? *Journal of Finance, 40*, 793–805.

Edmundson, B., M. Lawrence, & M. O'Connor (1988). The use of non-time series information in sales forecasting: A case study. *Journal of Forecasting, 7*, 201–211.

Einhorn, H. J., & R. M. Hogarth (1982). Prediction, diagnosis, and causal thinking in forecasting. *Journal of Forecasting, 1,* 23–36.

Fischoff, B. (1988). Judgmental aspects of forecasting: Needs and possible trends. *International Journal of Forecasting, 4,* 331–339.

Fischoff, B., & D. MacGregor (1982). Subjective confidence in forecasts. *Journal of Forecasting, 1,* 155–172.

Flores, B. E., D. L. Olson, & C. Wolfe (1992). Judgmental adjustment of forecasts: a comparison of methods. *International Journal of Forecasting, 7,* 421–433.

Gerstenfeld, A. (1971). Technological forecasting. *Journal of Business, 44,* 10–18.

Godet, M. (1982). From forecasting to "La Prospective": A new way of looking at futures. *Journal of Forecasting, 1,* 293–301.

Gordon, T. J. (1968). The Delphi method: An illustration. In J. Bright (Ed.), *Technological Forecasting for Industry and Government.* Englewood Cliffs, N.J.: Prentice-Hall.

Helmer, O. (1966). *Social Technology.* New York: Basic Books.

Helmer, O. (1968). Analysis of the future: The Delphi method. In J. Bright, (Ed.), *Technological Forecasting for Industry and Government.* Englewood Cliffs, N.J.: Prentice-Hall.

Helmer, O. (1977). Problems in futures research—Delphi and causal cross-input analysis. *Futures, 9.*

Hogarth, R. M., & S. Makridakis (1981). Forecasting and planning: An evaluation. *Management Science, 27,* 115–138.

Huss, W. R. (1988). A move toward scenario analysis. *International Journal of Forecasting, 4,* 377–388.

Jungermann, H. (1985). Inferential processes in the construction of scenarios. *Journal of Forecasting, 4,* 321–327.

Lawrence, M. J. (1983). An exploration of some practical issues in the use of quantitative forecasting models. *Journal of Forecasting, 2,* 169–179.

Lawrence, M. J., R. H. Edmundson, & M. J. O'Connor (1985). An examination of the accuracy of judgmental extrapolation of time series. *International Journal of Forecasting, 1,* 25–35.

Linneman, R. E., & H. E. Klein (1979). The use of multiple scenarios by U.S. industrial companies. *Long Range Planning, 12,* 83–90.

Linstone, H., & M. Turoff (1975). *The Delphi Method: Techniques and Applications.* Reading, Mass.: Addison-Wesley.

Makridakis, S. (1986). The art and science of forecasting: An assessment and future directions. *International Journal of Forecasting, 2,* 15–39.

Martino, J. (1970). The precision of Delphi estimates. *Technological Forecasting and Social Change, 1,* 292–299.

Martino, J. (1983). *Technological Forecasting for Decision Making* (2nd ed.). Amsterdam: North Holland.

Mentzer, J. T., & J. E. Cox (1984). Familiarity, application, and performance of sales forecasting techniques. *Journal of Forecasting, 3,* 27–36.

Mumpower, J. L., S. Livingston, & T. J. Lee (1987). Expert judgments of political riskiness. *Journal of Forecasting, 6,* 51–65.

Parenté, F. J., J. K. Anderson, P. Myers, & T. O'Brien (1984). An examination of factors contributing to Delphi accuracy. *Journal of Forecasting, 3,* 173–182.

Salancik, J. R., W. Wenger, & E. Helfer (1971). The construction of Delphi statements. *Technological Forecasting and Social Change, 3,* 65–73.

Schnaars, S. P., & M. T. Topol (1987). The use of multiple scenarios in sales forecasting: An empirical test. *International Journal of Forecasting, 3,* 405–419.

Schoemaker, P. J. H. (1991). When and how to use scenario planning: A heuristic approach with illustration. *Journal of Forecasting, 10,* 549–564.

Sniezek, J. A. (1989). An examination of group process in judgmental forecasting. *International Journal of Forecasting, 5,* 171–178.

Sparkes, J. R., & A. K. McHugh (1984). Awareness and use of forecasting techniques in British industry. *Journal of Forecasting, 3,* 37–42.

Tyebjee, T. T. (1987). Behavioral biases in new product forecasting. *International Journal of Forecasting, 3,* 393–404.

Welty, G. (1972). Problems of selecting experts for Delphi exercises. *Academy of Management Journal, 15,* 121–124.

Willemain, T. R. (1989). Graphical adjustment of statistical forecasts. *International Journal of Forecasting, 5,* 179–185.

Willemain, T. R. (1991). The effect of graphical adjustment on forecast accuracy. *International Journal of Forecasting, 7,* 151–154.

Zentner, R. D. (1982). Scenarios: Past, present and future. *Long Range Planning, 15,* 12–20.

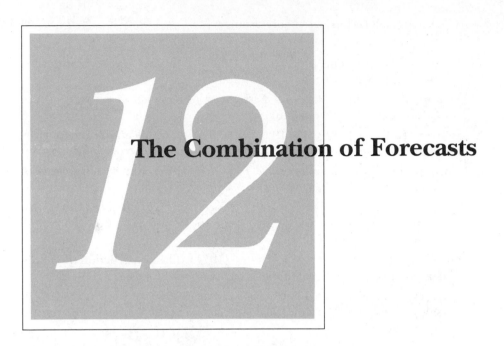

The Combination of Forecasts

12.1 WHY COMBINE FORECASTS?

In previous chapters, we have discussed three broad approaches to quantitative forecasting: behavioral models, exponential smoothing algorithms, and ARIMA time series models. Some other quantitative approaches were briefly discussed in Chapter 10. Additionally, in Chapter 11 we saw that judgmental methods can be valuable. This array of possibilities leads naturally to the question of what approach should be employed for any particular forecasting problem. In Chapter 9 we showed how various quantitative forecasting approaches are related, and indicated circumstances in which particular quantitative procedures might be most appropriate. In addition, in Chapter 11, we noted the possible value of modifying quantitative forecasts on judgmental grounds. Nevertheless, there simply does not exist a uniquely satisfactory answer to the question of what is likely to be the best approach for a specific problem. Certainly, it is possible to point to a number of factors that are relevant in making this choice. These would include the resources available to an investigator, the value to the organization of high-quality forecasts, the past behavior of the variable to be predicted, the investigator's insights into the causes of that behavior, and the relevant information available to the investigator. Thus, even if a purely quantitative approach is to be employed, some judgment is necessary in the selection of that approach. In this chapter we explore the assertion that it is not necessary, and frequently not desirable, to select at the outset a single forecast or a single approach to forecasting from competing alternatives. Instead, it may be better to form a **composite, or combined, forecast** from two or more alternative forecasts.

In subsequent sections of this chapter we will describe some formal procedures that have been successfully used in combining individual forecasts. Here we will discuss the factors that might persuade the analyst to consider this possibility. Briefly, some or all of the following eight considerations will often be relevant in specific forecasting exercises.

1. Often, two or more alternative forecasts will already be available to the investigator.
2. Almost invariably, an investigator will have available two or more distinct methodologies for the generation of plausible forecasts.
3. A formal combination scheme provides an attractive methodology for the amalgamation of judgmental and quantitative forecasts.
4. When alternative forecasts are available, the investigator will rarely have enough information to assert with any great conviction that one is best.
5. Even when a particular forecast appears to be better than its competitors, it does not necessarily follow that those competitors have no further value.
6. In quantitative forecasting, one could think of building a model that includes all competing models as special cases. This, however, will often be impractically or undesirably complex.
7. Combination is a simple, sensible solution to the problem of what to do with two or more competing forecasts. Such solutions frequently work well in practice.
8. In fact, a very large volume of accumulated empirical evidence suggests that the combination of forecasts often works very well in practice.

In the remainder of this section we will explore these points in a little more detail. Corporate analysts often need to take a view about future movements of national economic variables, such as gross domestic product, prices, and interest rates. As we indicated in Chapter 8, such forecasts are provided by several public and private agencies. Therefore, either a choice has to be made, or some means of combining these predictions must be found. The fact that so many alternatives are available suggests that no single forecasting group has achieved a dominant position in this important area.

If forecasts are to be prepared in-house, there are, as we have seen in previous chapters, a great many methodological approaches that can be taken. Of course, for specific problems, some of these may clearly be inappropriate. However, often there is some uncertainty as to which will be the best approach to follow in attacking a particular forecasting problem. In these circumstances the analyst may feel more comfortable experimenting with two or more methods rather than relying on a single one. In particular, if expert judgments are available, it might be useful to combine these with the results of a more formal quantitative approach.

When two or more forecasts are available, one possibility is simply to select one of them. This choice could be based on the analyst's judgment that a specific approach to the forecasting problem is more likely than others to yield satisfactory results. However, very often it will not be possible to arrive at such a conclusion with any great confidence. Some guidance may be provided by the past records of the competing approaches, so that the procedure that performed best in the recent past can be chosen. This is certainly an attractive possibility if a single forecast must be chosen, but typically the available records will be quite short, so that it will be difficult to ascertain the extent to which an apparently superior performance is due to chance and the extent to which it derives from an inherently better forecast-generating mechanism. Again, then, the analyst is likely to be reluctant to abandon all but a single forecast.

In fact, even if one has a great deal of confidence that, for a given problem, a particular forecasting approach is very likely to outperform its competitors, it does not necessarily follow that this approach should be used to the exclusion of the others. If forecaster A or forecasting method A does consistently better than forecaster B or forecasting method B, does it necessarily follow that, given A, B is worthless? It does not. In spite of its inferior performance, B may nevertheless contain useful information not present in A. Two competing forecasts will generally be based on different assumptions about the process generating the quantity to be predicted; they may employ different information, or use the available information in different ways. Therefore, even if A is clearly superior, it may be possible to incorporate the information in the inferior forecast to produce a combined forecast that performs better than either individual forecast. It is this point that makes most attractive the possibility of combining individual forecasts, and accounts for much of the success of the methods we will be discussing in this chapter. Also, as we will see in Chapter 13, the idea that a superior forecast might be improved through combination with another prediction is the basis for an important approach to the evaluation of forecasts.

Many quantitative forecasting methods are based explicitly on the fitting of a model to historical data. This model is then viewed as having generated the observed data, and is projected forward to derive forecasts of future values. As we saw in Chapter 9, even for quantitative methods such as exponential smoothing where no explicit model is postulated, it may nevertheless be possible to write down a formal generating model for which the prediction algorithm yields optimal forecasts. Two forecasting models can, at least in principle, allow the development of a broader model that includes the two alternative models as special cases, rather than merely combining the individual forecasts. The available data could then be used to check the adequacy of the competing individual models. This is an attractive possibility, and one that is often employed in practice. However, on many occasions its attractions will be more academic than practical. Often the conglomerate model will be unwieldy, having a complex structure involving many unknown parameters. As we have emphasized several times in previous chapters, such models violate the principle of parsimony, so that although they are likely to provide an apparently good fit of historical data, they will often yield disappointingly poor forecasts. Indeed, when the individual forecasting models are themselves complex—as might be the case with the econometric models discussed in Chapter 8—the construction of conglomerate models would be practically impossible. Therefore, the far more straightforward alternative of combining forecasts rather than models is often the only viable possibility. This problem can arise even in the apparently simple case of forecasting a series from its own past. For example, combining a seasonal ARIMA model with the model implied by the multiplicative variant of the Holt-Winters algorithm would be a daunting task.

Faced with the question of what to do with two or more alternative forecasts, the idea of combining, and methods usually employed to derive combined forecasts, are simple, straightforward, and intuitively appealing solutions. Such solutions to apparently complex problems often work well in practice, and, as we will see, a large volume of accumulated empirical evidence strongly suggests that this is the case with forecast combination.

12.2 THREE PROCEDURES FOR THE COMBINATION OF FORECASTS

We assume now that an investigator has available two or more different forecasts of the same quantity. Some or all of these may have been provided by outside agencies, or all could have been generated by the investigator using different, apparently plausible forecasting models. In either case the objective is to combine these forecasts to produce a single composite prediction.

The quantity to be predicted will be denoted X_t, a value which will of course be unknown at the time the forecasts are made. For notational simplicity we will use $f_{1t}, f_{2t}, \ldots, f_{kt}$ to denote k alternative forecasts of this quantity. Thus the f_{it} are forecasts available now of the value at some specified future time of the variable of interest. In many circumstances, it is attractive to form a composite forecast that is a **weighted average** of the individual forecasts. This is achieved by assigning weights $w_1, w_2, \ldots, w_k$, between zero and one, to the individual forecasts, with these weights summing to one. The combined forecast is then calculated as

$$f_{ct} = w_1 f_{1t} + w_2 f_{2t} + \cdots + w_k f_{kt} \qquad 0 \le w_i \le 1 \qquad \sum_{i=1}^{k} w_i = 1$$

$$(12.2.1)$$

Thus, in the special case where there are just two alternative forecasts, the combined forecast is

$$f_{ct} = w_1 f_{1t} + w_2 f_{2t} \qquad 0 \le w_i \le 1 \qquad w_1 + w_2 = 1$$

which can be written

$$f_{ct} = w_1 f_{1t} + (1 - w_1) f_{2t} \qquad 0 \le w_1 \le 1 \qquad (12.2.2)$$

Notice that it follows that the composite forecast defined in equation 12.2.2 must lie between the two individual forecasts, being equal to one or the other only in the extreme cases where the weight w_1 is equal to zero or one. In this sense we can think of the composite forecast as a compromise between the two individual predictions. Similarly, the composite forecast defined in equation 12.2.1 will lie between the smallest and the largest of the individual predictions.

We now show that the weighted average linear combination defined in equation 12.2.1 has the additional attractive feature of ensuring that the composite forecast will be *unbiased* when the individual forecasts are themselves unbiased. Any forecast will be in error, and the study of past forecast errors forms the core of the procedures for the evaluation of forecasts to be discussed in the next chapter. Let e_{it} denote the error resulting when the forecast f_{it} is used to predict X_t, so that we can write

$$e_{it} = X_t - f_{it} \qquad (i = 1, 2, \ldots, k)$$

Now, before the actual outcome X_t is observed, these errors can be regarded as random variables, and a forecast will be said to be unbiased if the associated error has mean zero. In that case, there would be no reason to expect, on the average, the forecast to be too high or too low. Unbiasedness, then, is a desirable property in any forecast, and one which will generally result from a reasonable forecasting methodology. Suppose now that the k individual forecasts are all unbiased, so that the associated errors all have expectation zero; that is,

$$E(e_{it}) = 0 \qquad (i = 1, 2, \ldots, k)$$

If the composite forecast is formed as the weighted average 12.2.1, the error of that forecast will be

$$
\begin{aligned}
e_{ct} = X_t - f_{ct} &= X_t - (w_1 f_{1t} + w_2 f_{2t} + \cdots + w_k f_{kt}) \\
&= w_1(X_t - f_{1t}) + w_2(X_t - f_{2t}) + \cdots + w_k(X_t - f_{kt}) \\
&= w_1 e_{1t} + w_2 e_{2t} + \cdots + w_k e_{kt}
\end{aligned}
$$

Then, if each of the individual forecasts is unbiased, each e_{it} has expectation zero, from which it follows that

$$E(e_{ct}) = 0$$

so that the combined forecast is also unbiased.

We see that not only is the formation of a composite predictor as a weighted average of the individual forecasts an intuitively appealing approach, it also ensures unbiasedness when the individual forecasts exhibit no bias, as will often be the case in practice. It remains to determine the weights to be allocated to the constituent forecasts in forming the composite. Three very straightforward approaches will be discussed in the remainder of this section.

1. A Simple Average: The Equal Weights Case

Suppose that we have a set of k forecasts, $f_{1t}, f_{2t}, \ldots, f_{kt}$, of an unknown future value X_t. The most straightforward way to combine these individual forecasts is to assign them equal weights in forming a composite forecast. The combined forecast is then just the simple average of the individual forecasts

$$f_{ct} = \frac{(f_{1t} + f_{2t} + \cdots + f_{kt})}{k}$$

To see the potential gains from the combination of forecasts, let f_{1t} and f_{2t} be a pair of unbiased forecasts of X_t, with errors e_{1t} and e_{2t}. Denote by σ_1^2 and σ_2^2 the variance of these forecast errors and by ρ the correlation between them. Then, the average of the two forecasts is

$$f_{ct} = \frac{(f_{1t} + f_{2t})}{2}$$

and the error of the combined forecast is

$$e_{ct} = X_t - f_{ct} = \frac{(e_{1t} + e_{2t})}{2}$$

As we have already noted, the combined forecast is unbiased; its error variance is

$$E(e_{ct}^2) = \frac{1}{4} E[(e_{1t} + e_{2t})^2]$$

$$= \frac{(\sigma_1^2 + \sigma_2^2 + 2\rho\sigma_1\sigma_2)}{4}$$

Suppose that the two individual forecasts are of equal quality, in the sense that their error variances are the same. Denoting by $\sigma^2 = \sigma_1^2 = \sigma_2^2$ the common error variance, it then follows that the variance of the error of the composite forecast is

$$\sigma_c^2 = E(e_{ct}^2) = \frac{(\sigma^2 + \sigma^2 + 2\rho\sigma^2)}{4}$$

$$= \frac{\sigma^2(1 + \rho)}{2}$$

Notice that the variance of the error of the composite forecast is strictly less than the error variance, σ^2, of the individual forecasts unless the correlation, ρ, between the individual forecasts is equal to one. (This occurs where the individual forecasts are identical, so there would be no point in combining them.) We see that, if there is not a very high positive correlation between the individual forecast errors, the combined forecast can have much smaller error variance than the constituent forecasts. Therefore, if forecasts of roughly equal quality are averaged it is likely that gains in precision will result, where here we equate a gain in precision with a decrease in forecast error variance.

We can think of these gains in expected forecast accuracy as resulting from the **diversification of risk** that follows when two or more forecasts are aggregated. In any specific instance, any forecasting method, however good, can by chance be in substantial error. If this forecast is aggregated with others, the impact of a very large error in an individual forecast will be damped in the composite predictor. This diversification of risk is precisely the phenomenon that renders attractive the formation of a portfolio of risky investment securities. Therefore we can think of combination as the development of a **portfolio of forecasts.**

The chief advantage of using a simple average to form the composite predictor, in addition to its simplicity, is that no further information is required. The chief disadvantage is that, even if information on the quality of previous forecasts produced by the individual methods or individual forecasters is available, that information is not used in choosing the weights assigned in the composite forecast. This seems particularly unsatisfactory if we know that, in the past, one forecasting method has performed very much worse than another. We would then be reluctant to give these two methods the same weight in forming a combined forecast. In the remainder of this section we will discuss two approaches to combination where the weights assigned to individual forecasts are determined by past performance. For now we note that the advantages claimed for the equal weights case are most likely to materialize if the individual forecasts are of roughly equal quality. If the analyst has good reason to suspect that one forecast is likely to be substantially inferior to the others, it may be best to exclude this forecast altogether, and apply equal weights combination only to those forecasts in which the analyst has a reasonable degree of faith.

2. Weights Inversely Proportional to the Sum of Squared Errors

If two or more forecasts are to be combined, and a record of the past performance of the individual forecasts is available, it may be desirable to use that record in determining what weights to assign to the individual forecasts in the composite. In developing an appropriate weighting scheme, two factors should be kept in mind.

1. We will generally prefer to give relatively high weights to those forecast methods that have performed best in the recent past, and relatively low weights to those methods whose performance has been poorest.
2. It may be desirable to allow the weighting scheme to *adapt* over time to account for the possibility that the relative performances of the individual forecasting methods may change through time.

These factors can be accounted for by basing the weights on the few most recent sets of forecasts for which corresponding outcomes are available. For example, if we are at time $(t - 1)$ and attempting to predict X_t, the n most recent outcomes will be $X_{t-1}, X_{t-2}, \ldots, X_{t-n}$. Similarly, if we are standing at time $(t - 2)$ trying to predict X_t with a two-steps ahead forecast, we will have observed the quality of two-steps ahead forecasts of $X_{t-2}, X_{t-3}, \ldots, X_{t-n-1}$. For purposes of exposition, we will assume that one-step ahead forecasts are to be combined and that the weights to be used will be based on the quality of the n most recent one-step ahead forecasts. The generalization to the case where forecasts further ahead are to be combined is straightforward, requiring only an obvious notational adjustment. The position then is that we want to choose the weights to be used in equation 12.2.1, given that we have available the forecasts $(f_{1,t-1}, f_{2,t-1}, \ldots, f_{k,t-1}), \ldots, (f_{1,t-n}, f_{2,t-n}, \ldots, f_{k,t-n})$ that were made through the k forecasting methods of the known quantities $X_{t-1}, X_{t-2}, \ldots, X_{t-n}$.

Now, it is natural to judge the quality of these individual forecasts through the sizes of the errors made

$$e_{i,t-j} = X_{t-j} - f_{i,t-j} \qquad (i = 1, \ldots, k \qquad j = 1, \ldots, n)$$

The larger the magnitude of the errors made, the poorer the performance of a particular forecasting method. Accordingly, one approach, to be discussed in more detail in Chapter 13, to the assessment of forecast quality is through the *sum of squared forecast errors*. These sums of squared errors for the k individual forecast methods over the last n time periods are

$$\sum_{j=1}^{n} (X_{t-j} - f_{i,t-j})^2 = \sum_{j=1}^{n} e_{i,t-j}^2 \qquad (i = 1, \ldots, k)$$

The smaller is this sum of squared forecast errors, the better by this criterion has been the recent performance of a forecasting method. Hence, the smaller is the sum of squared forecasts errors the higher, all other things being equal, would be the weight that we would want to associate with a particular forecast method in forming a composite predictor.

One possibility with this property is to make the weight attached to forecasts from the ith method inversely proportional to the sum of squared errors achieved by this method over the n most recent time periods. Then, the weights of equation 12.2.1 would be such that

$$w_i \propto \left(\sum_{j=1}^{n} e_{i,t-j}^2 \right)^{-1} \qquad (i = 1, \ldots, k)$$

If these weights are to sum to one, it follows that they must be given by

$$w_i = \frac{\left(\sum\limits_{j=1}^{n} e_{i,t-j}^2\right)^{-1}}{\left(\sum\limits_{j=1}^{n} e_{1,t-j}^2\right)^{-1} + \cdots + \left(\sum\limits_{j=1}^{n} e_{k,t-j}^2\right)^{-1}} \qquad (i = 1, \ldots, k)$$

$$(12.2.3)$$

In the special case where just two forecasts are to be combined, the formula 12.2.3 simplifies to

$$w_1 = \frac{\left(\sum\limits_{j=1}^{n} e_{1,t-j}^2\right)^{-1}}{\left(\sum\limits_{j=1}^{n} e_{1,t-j}^2\right)^{-1} + \left(\sum\limits_{j=1}^{n} e_{2,t-j}^2\right)^{-1}}$$

$$(12.2.4)$$

$$= \frac{\sum\limits_{j=1}^{n} e_{2,t-j}^2}{\sum\limits_{j=1}^{n} e_{1,t-j}^2 + \sum\limits_{j=1}^{n} e_{2,t-j}^2}$$

To use either equation 12.2.3 or 12.2.4 to choose combining weights, it only remains to select the number n of past forecast errors to be employed. This choice may depend on how much past information is available. If the analyst has access to moderately long records of past performance, the choice must balance the desirability for using a moderately large value of n to achieve reasonable estimates of past performance and a value that is sufficiently small to allow the weights to adapt over time in response to relative changes in the qualities of the individual methods. Experience suggests that values of n in the range from six to twelve will usually be satisfactory. The issue here is essentially that of *stationarity*. If dramatic changes in performance of one forecaster or another might be expected— perhaps because of modifications in the methodology used—a long record of past performance may not be a good indicator of what to expect in the future. The question of how to allow for non-stationarity in determining appropriate weights in a combining scheme is a topic of recent research concern. Some useful discussion is provided by Miller, Clemen and Winkler (1992).

To illustrate, Table 12.1 shows six consecutive months of product

TABLE 12.1   Data for the combination of sales forecasts.

t	X_t	f_{1t}	f_{2t}	e_{1t}	e_{2t}	e_{1t}^2	e_{2t}^2
1	725	692	711	33	14	1,089	196
2	714	719	733	−5	−19	25	361
3	752	741	769	11	−17	121	289
4	768	758	784	10	−16	100	256
5	773	781	793	−8	−20	64	400
6	761	774	788	−13	−27	169	729
7		766	784				
					Sums	1,568	2,231

sales figures, together with two sets of forecasts of these sales that had been made in the previous month. Also shown are one-step ahead forecasts for month seven. These are to be combined, using equations 12.2.2 and 12.2.4 to obtain a composite forecast for month seven. The table provides the calculations for the sums of squared errors for the individual forecasts for the first six months. These are

$$\sum_{t=1}^{6} e_{1t}^2 = 1,568 \qquad \sum_{t=1}^{6} e_{2t}^2 = 2,231$$

Thus, directly from equation 12.2.4 we find that the weight to be attached to the first forecast is

$$w_1 = \frac{2,231}{1,568 + 2,231} = 0.59$$

The combined forecast for month seven is then, from equation 12.2.2,

$$f_c = (0.59)(766) + (0.41)(784) = 773$$

This is a weighted average of the two individual forecasts: It is somewhat closer to the first than the second, reflecting the better performance, on the average, of the first forecast method in the previous six months.

3. Regression-Based Weights

The use of weights that are inversely proportional to the sum of squared forecast errors, though plausible, and in practice often very successful, is somewhat *ad hoc*. It also suffers from the disadvantage of often giving more weight than is desirable to really poor forecasting methods, though it is obviously better than the simple average in this respect.

An alternative approach is to view the problem in the context of a regression model. Suppose, for now, that there are just two forecasts to combine, with weights w_1 and w_2 summing to one, so that

$$w_2 = 1 - w_1$$

We can think of the actual observation as being the weighted average of the two forecasts, plus a term that is the error e_{ct} made in using the combined forecast to predict X_t. We can then write

$$X_t = w_1 f_{1t} + (1 - w_1)f_{2t} + e_{ct}$$

or, equivalently,

$$(X_t - f_{2t}) = w_1(f_{1t} - f_{2t}) + e_{ct}$$

This can be viewed as being in the form of a regression model, with dependent variable $(X_t - f_{2t})$, independent variable $(f_{1t} - f_{2t})$, slope parameter w_1, no intercept parameter, and error term e_{ct}.

Now, if as before we are in possession of the last n observations and their associated forecasts, this information can be used to compute least squares estimates of the regression parameter w_1. We can write

$$(X_{t-j} - f_{2,t-j}) = w_1(f_{1,t-j} - f_{2,t-j}) + e_{c,t-j} \qquad (j = 1, 2, \ldots, n)$$

The least squares estimate of the parameter w_1 is

$$\hat{w}_1 = \frac{\displaystyle\sum_{j=1}^{n} (f_{1,t-j} - f_{2,t-j})(X_{t-j} - f_{2,t-j})}{\displaystyle\sum_{j=1}^{n} (f_{1,t-j} - f_{2,t-j})^2}$$

Now, the individual forecast errors are

$$e_{it} = X_t - f_{it} \qquad (i = 1, 2)$$

and it follows since

$$f_{1t} - f_{2t} = e_{2t} - e_{1t}$$

that

$$\hat{w}_1 = \frac{\sum\limits_{j=1}^{n} e_{2,t-j}^2 - \sum\limits_{j=1}^{n} e_{1,t-j}e_{2,t-j}}{\sum\limits_{j=1}^{n} e_{1,t-j}^2 + \sum\limits_{j=1}^{n} e_{2,t-j}^2 - 2\sum\limits_{j=1}^{n} e_{1,t-j}e_{2,t-j}} \qquad (12.2.5)$$

Comparing formulas 12.2.4 and 12.2.5 we see that they differ in that the former does not contain the term that is the sum of the products of the individual forecast errors.

To illustrate, consider again the data of Table 12.1, for which

$$\sum_{t=1}^{6} e_{1t}e_{2t} = 721$$

Formula 12.2.5 then gives for the weight to be attached to the first forecast

$$\hat{w}_1 = \frac{2,231 - 721}{1,568 + 2,231 - (2)(721)} = 0.64$$

The combined forecast for month seven, obtained through the use of regression-based weights, is then

$$f_c = (0.64)(766) + (0.36)(784) = 772$$

For this particular example, the two approaches yield virtually identical results, though this will not always be the case. Notice also in this example that the regression-based approach assigns more weight to the forecast method with the better record than does use of a weight inversely proportional to the sum of squared forecast errors. This is quite typical, though not inevitable: The phenomenon occurs when, as is usually the case,

$$\sum_{j=1}^{n} e_{1,t-j}e_{2,t-j} > 0$$

so that the sample correlation between the individual forecast errors is positive.

One difficulty with the regression-based approach is that formula 12.2.5 does not necessarily yield values between zero and one for the weights. However, it is surely implausible to assign a *negative* weight to any forecast in which one has some faith. Therefore, it is common practice to substitute zero for any negative value resulting when formula 12.2.5 is computed, and correspondingly to constrain the maximum possible value to one.

The procedure just discussed can be extended to the case where there are k forecasts to be combined, using weights $w_1, w_2, \ldots, w_k$. Since these weights are required to sum to one, we can write

$$w_k = 1 - w_1 - w_2 - \cdots - w_{k-1}$$

The regression model is then

$$X_t = w_1 f_{1t} + w_2 f_{2t} + \cdots + w_{k-1} f_{k-1,t}$$
$$+ (1 - w_1 - w_2 - \cdots - w_{k-1}) f_{kt} + e_{ct}$$

The weights can then be estimated by applying least squares to

$$(X_{t-j} - f_{k,t-j}) = w_1 (f_{1,t-j} - f_{k,t-j}) + w_2 (f_{2,t-j} - f_{k,t-j})$$
$$+ \cdots + w_{k-1} (f_{k-1,t-j} - f_{k,t-j}) + e_{c,t-j} \qquad j = 1, \ldots, n$$

If any of these weight estimates turns out to be negative, the corresponding forecast should be dropped from further consideration and the regression equation re-estimated by least squares. This procedure is continued until all remaining weight estimates are positive.

The procedures for the combination of forecasts that we have described to this point are appropriate when the individual forecasts are unbiased. However, Granger and Ramanathan (1984) have argued that this will not always be true. In such circumstances, the regression-based approach is easily appropriately modified, by fitting the model

$$X_t = \alpha + \beta_1 f_{1t} + \beta_2 f_{2t} + \cdots + \beta_k f_{kt} + e_{ct}$$

but now without restricting either α to be zero or the β_j to sum to one. This model is fitted by least squares to the available historical record, and then projected forward to derive the required composite forecast.

In many ways, the regression-based approach is more theoretically satisfactory than the alternatives we have discussed. It does, however, have two drawbacks:

1. The error terms in the regression equations may be autocorrelated—indeed, for forecasts beyond one step ahead they will be. Thus the least squares estimates of the weights can be inefficient.
2. Very often only a small number of data points will be available for

estimating the regression parameters, and even when many are available the analyst may prefer to use just a few so that the forecast weights can adapt quite quickly over time. Given a small sample, least squares can be quite inaccurate.

For these reasons the use of regression-based weights is in practice often not preferable to the two simpler approaches to the combination of forecasts discussed earlier in this section.

Because of its record of practical success, the topic of forecast combination has attracted a good deal of research attention, and the procedures discussed here are by no means the only possibilities that have been proposed. Bates and Granger (1969), and Newbold and Granger (1974) discussed not only the use of weights inversely proportional to the sum of squared errors and the regression-based approach, but also some closely related procedures. However, empirical investigation failed to suggest any marked advantage for these variants over the methods discussed in this section.

There has been an explosion of interest in the topic of forecast combination in the last few years, and it is not possible even to summarize here either the many technical issues that have been raised or the scope of practical implementations. Two excellent commentaries are provided by Clemen (1989) and Granger (1989). Certainly alternative, more elaborate, schemes for forecast combination have been proposed. Nevertheless, empirical evidence suggests that the straightforward approaches discussed in this section will generally prove satisfactory. The issue of which particular scheme to employ in choosing combining weights is to a certain extent problem-specific. If a sufficiently long record of historical experience is available, the best advice is to experiment with several possibilities, settling eventually on the one that proves most successful for the problem at hand. If this is infeasible, our preference is for weights inversely proportional to the sum of squares of the last six to twelve forecast errors—the number depending on the analyst's assessment of the likely degree of stationarity in relative performances of the individual forecasts.

12.3   Empirical Evidence on the Combination of Forecasts

Perhaps the most remarkable fact about the combination of forecasts is that the wealth of empirical evidence that has accumulated over the years has pointed so clearly to a number of conclusions:

1. Almost whatever forecasts are combined, and whatever individual forecasting methods are included in the composite, the combined

forecast performs extremely well. Very often the combined forecast turns out to be superior to all the individual forecasts: Almost invariably it is at worst very close to what, in the event, emerges as the most successful of the individual forecasts.

2. In spite of its simplicity, the simple average combined forecast frequently performs very well.

3. In the aggregate, it appears that using weights inversely proportional to the sum of squared forecast errors is preferable to the use of regression-based weights.

4. In those cases where a small number of forecasts are to be combined, and some are considerably better than others, the simple average and, to a lesser extent, weights inversely proportional to the sum of squared errors, are less successful. In such circumstances regression-based weights can be used, or inferior forecasts dropped before applying either of the other approaches.

It is possible, at least to a limited extent, that there is some bias in the accumulated mass of published literature indicating the excellent performance of composite forecasts; after all, it is presumably easier to publish such positive findings than the negative conclusion that no benefit resulted from combination. However, this reservation cannot hold for a number of very large-scale studies in which individual forecasting methods, together with composite methods, have been evaluated over large collections of time series. Much of the empirical evidence on the performance of combined forecasts is summarized by Mahmoud (1984) and Clemen (1989).

A number of studies have evaluated the effectiveness of combining forecasts from extrapolation methods, such as exponential smoothing and single series ARIMA model building. That the simple average can do very well in such circumstances is confirmed by the large-scale studies reported by Makridakis et al. (1982), Makridakis and Winkler (1983), and Schnaars (1986).

Much of the more recent interest in the combination of forecasts was stimulated by the work of Bates and Granger (1969). These authors considered the use of weights inversely proportional to the sum of squared forecast errors and the use of regression-based weights, as well as some closely related procedures. Newbold and Granger (1974) evaluated, for a collection of 80 monthly time series, one-step ahead forecasts obtained from the Holt-Winters exponential smoothing algorithm, stepwise autoregression, and fitted ARIMA models. Forecasts were combined in pairs, and as a set of three. In the aggregate, the ARIMA forecasts were superior, in terms of one-step ahead errors, to the other two sets. Table 12.2 summarizes some of the results of pairwise combinations of ARIMA and each of the other two forecasts, using methods (2) and (3) of Section 12.2 for determining the weights: forecasts are compared, for each of the 80

TABLE 12.2   Percentage of series for which ARIMA forecasts are outperformed
by (A) ARIMA combined with Holt-Winters, (B) ARIMA combined
with stepwise autoregression.

Method (2)			Method (3)	
A	B	n	A	B
50.00	53.75	3	46.25	42.50
55.00	52.50	6	41.25	38.75
57.50	53.75	9	47.50	38.75
56.25	55.00	12	45.00	37.50

time series, in terms of average squared error. It can be seen from Table
12.2 that when weights are inversely proportional to the sum of squared
past forecast errors, ARIMA combined with either of the other two
methods outperforms ARIMA alone for a modest majority of these time
series. The use of regression-based weights was somewhat less successful.

Table 12.3 provides some results on the combination of Holt-Winters
and stepwise autoregressive forecasts. Here the results are more striking.
Whatever combination method is used, the composite forecast is superior
to either individual forecast on a clear majority of occasions. Again the
advantage is more pronounced when weights inversely proportion to the
sum of squared past forecast errors are used. Finally, Table 12.4 summarizes some of the results from the combination of all three forecasts.
Compared with the results in Table 12.2, it emerges that further gains
are achieved when a third forecast is incorporated into the composite.

The findings of this study on the combination of forecasts generated
by various single series extrapolation methods suggest that gains in
accuracy can, in the aggregate, be achieved through the use of a composite
forecast instead of what appears to be the best individual method alone.
Also it was found, on the average, that the use of weights based on the

TABLE 12.3   Percentage of series for which combined Holt-Winters and stepwise
autoregression forecasts outperformed (A) Holt-Winters and
(B) Stepwise autoregression.

Method (2)			Method (3)	
A	B	n	A	B
67.50	78.75	3	60.00	65.25
67.50	78.75	6	57.50	65.25
68.75	77.50	9	57.50	71.25
68.75	76.25	12	60.00	71.25

TABLE 12.4   Percentage of series for which ARIMA forecasts are outperformed by ARIMA combined with both Holt-Winters and stepwise autoregression.

Method (2)	n	Method (3)
65.00	3	52.50
60.00	6	47.50
63.75	9	52.50
62.50	12	51.25

inverse of the sum of squared past forecast errors was superior to the use of regression-based weights. Similar conclusions emerged from a larger study, reported by Winkler and Makridakis (1983). These authors combined forecasts generated by ten single series methods over 1,001 time series. Forecast horizons beyond one-step ahead were also considered in this study.

The apparently superior performances of weights based on the inverse of the sum of squared forecast errors, and indeed equal weights, compared with the regression-based approach, in these large-scale studies are of course aggregate findings, and should not be taken to imply that regression-based weights will necessarily be inferior in any particular application. This issue is discussed by Bunn (1985). The regression-based approach is likely to be preferable when one or more of the individual forecasts is clearly inferior to the others. An alternative would be to discard the clearly inferior forecasts before using one of the other two weighting schemes.

The evidence discussed so far in this section relates to the combination of forecasts from different single series projection methods. However, other types of forecasts have also been successfully included in composites. For example, Granger and Newbold (1986) and Fullerton (1989) provide examples of the combination of ARIMA and econometric forecasts, Clemen and Winkler (1986) provide some evidence on the combination of several econometric forecasts, and Lawrence, Edmundson, and O'Connor (1986) demonstrate the value of incorporating judgmental forecasts into a composite. Many other citations of successful implementations are cited in an excellent annotated bibliography provided by Clemen (1989).

In spite of the volume of accumulated evidence on its practical success, the combination of forecasts has not been universally enthusiastically embraced, particularly by academic economists. In an interesting philosophical discussion of the subject, Winkler (1989) suggests that this may reflect confusion on the distinction between "model" and "truth." No model, however elaborate, or however sophisticated the mathematical theory behind its construction, is anything more than a possibly convenient *approximation* to reality. There are, of course, occasions when it is useful to pretend that a model is truth. For example, procedures for the estimation of model parameters are often based on this fiction. However, there are occasions on which belief in fiction is dangerous. In fact, we can never build a model that is true. Moreover, given limited amounts of data, it is not difficult to reach a point at which increasing model complexity leads to deteriorating forecast performance. It is perfectly reasonable to believe that a number of relatively simple models can yield good forecast performance, and that combining these forecasts can generate further gains in forecast quality that would not follow from a model that is a cumbersome composite of the individual models.

EXERCISES

12.1   Why is the combination of forecasts often an attractive option in practice? Develop a realistic example of a case where an analyst might opt for the combination of individual forecasts.

12.2   When individual forecasts are combined, a weighted average is frequently used. Explain why this is so.

12.3   Let f_{1t} and f_{2t} be two unbiased forecasts of X_t, with errors e_{1t} and e_{2t}. Denote by σ_1^2 and σ_2^2 the two error variances, and by ρ the correlation between these errors. Let the weighted average composite forecast be

$$f_{ct} = w_1 f_{1t} + (1 - w_1)f_{2t}$$

with error

$$e_{ct} = X_t - f_{ct} = w_1 e_{1t} + (1 - w_1)e_{2t}$$

(a)   Show that the variance of the error of the composite forecast is

$$\sigma_c^2 = w_1^2 \sigma_1^2 + (1 - w_1)^2 \sigma_2^2 + 2\rho w_1(1 - w_1)\sigma_1 \sigma_2$$

(b)   Show that this expression for the variance of the error of the composite forecast can be written as

$$\sigma_c^2 = (\sigma_1^2 + \sigma_2^2 - 2\rho\sigma_1\sigma_2)w_1^2 - 2(\sigma_2^2 - \rho\sigma_1\sigma_2)w_1 + \sigma_2^2$$

$$= (\sigma_1^2 + \sigma_2^2 - 2\rho\sigma_1\sigma_2)\left[w_1 - \frac{\sigma_2^2 - \rho\sigma_1\sigma_2}{\sigma_1^2 + \sigma_2^2 - 2\rho\sigma_1\sigma_2}\right]^2$$

$$+ \frac{\sigma_1^2\sigma_2^2(1 - \rho^2)}{\sigma_1^2 + \sigma_2^2 - 2\rho\sigma_1\sigma_2}$$

(c)   Using the result in (b), show that the value of the weight w_1 for which the variance of the error of the composite forecast is smallest is

$$w_1 = \frac{\sigma_2^2 - \rho\sigma_1\sigma_2}{\sigma_1^2 + \sigma_2^2 - 2\rho\sigma_1\sigma_2}$$

(d)   The value of w_1 in (c) is often called the optimal weight. In practice it cannot be found, since σ_1^2, σ_2^2 and ρ will not be known.

(i)   Show that the regression-based weight 12.2.5 follows from substituting for σ_1^2, σ_2^2, and ρ their natural sample estimates based on the last n sets of forecast errors.

(ii)   Show that the weight 12.2.4 follows from substituting zero for ρ and the natural estimates based on the last n sets of forecast errors for σ_1^2 and σ_2^2.

(e)   Using the result of (b), show that if the optimal weight w_1 of (c) is used, the variance of the error of the composite forecast is

$$\sigma_c^2 = \frac{\sigma_1^2\sigma_2^2(1 - \rho^2)}{\sigma_1^2 + \sigma_2^2 - 2\rho\sigma_1\sigma_2}$$

(f)   Using the result of (e), show that if the optimal weight w_1 is used,

$$\sigma_c^2 < \sigma_1^2$$

except in the special cases

$$\sigma_1^2 = 0$$

$$\rho = \sigma_1/\sigma_2$$

(g)   Show that the optimal weight w_1 of (c) is between zero and one provided ρ is not bigger than σ_1/σ_2 or σ_2/σ_1.

12.4   The accompanying table shows product sales for six consecutive months and two sets of one-month ahead forecasts of these sales. Also shown are forecasts for the seventh month. Assume that both sets of forecasts are unbiased.

t	X_t	f_{1t}	f_{2t}
1	672	649	663
2	653	661	658
3	731	695	711
4	596	643	628
5	618	631	615
6	592	580	602
7		640	613

(a) Find the composite forecast for month seven based on equal weights.

(b) Find the composite forecast for month seven based on weights inversely proportional to the sums of squares of the last six sets of forecast errors.

(c) Find the composite forecast for month seven based on a regression approach using the last six sets of forecast errors.

12.5 The accompanying table shows orders received for a product over six consecutive months and two sets of one-month ahead forecasts of these orders. Also shown are forecasts for the next month. Assume that both sets of forecasts are unbiased.

t	X_t	f_{1t}	f_{2t}
1	882	903	921
2	1,014	947	930
3	963	986	980
4	1,098	1,011	1,001
5	1,173	1,132	1,111
6	980	998	990
7		1,012	1,028

(a) Find the composite forecast for month seven based on equal weights.

(b) Find the composite forecast for month seven using weights inversely proportional to the sums of squares of the last six sets of forecast errors.

(c) Using the regression-based approach with the last six sets of forecast errors, find a composite forecast for month seven.

12.6 Discuss the relative advantages of equal weights, weights inversely proportional to the sum of squared forecast errors, and regression-based weights in the combination of forecasts.

12.7 The accompanying table shows earnings per share (in dollars) of a corporation over eight consecutive quarters and forecasts made one quarter previously by two financial analysts. Also shown are the analysts' forecasts for the next quarter. Assume that both analysts produce unbiased forecasts.

t	X_t	f_{1t}	f_{2t}
1	8.25	9.25	9.00
2	12.50	10.25	11.25
3	13.25	12.00	13.00
4	10.50	12.00	11.50
5	13.75	12.50	12.50
6	17.50	15.25	16.50
7	14.75	15.25	15.75
8	12.25	13.00	13.50
9		14.25	12.75

(a) Find the composite forecast for quarter nine based on equal weights.

(b) Find the composite forecast for quarter nine based on weights inversely proportional to the sums of squares of the last four sets of forecast errors.

(c) Find the composite forecast for quarter nine based on weights inversely proportional to the sums of squares of the last eight sets of forecast errors.

(d) Find the composite forecast for quarter nine using the regression method based on the last four sets of forecast errors.

(e) Find the composite forecast for quarter nine using the regression method based on the last eight sets of forecast errors.

(f) How would you compute a composite forecast for quarter nine if you suspected bias in the individual forecasts?

12.8   The accompanying table shows product sales for six consecutive months and three sets of one-month ahead forecasts of these sales. Also shown are forecasts for the seventh month. Assume that all three sets of forecasts are unbiased.

t	X_t	f_{1t}	f_{2t}	f_{3t}
1	2,863	2,793	2,841	2,727
2	2,631	2,730	2,601	2,702
3	2,280	2,451	2,316	2,149
4	2,395	2,428	2,287	2,319
5	2,260	2,302	2,387	2,192
6	2,387	2,309	2,469	2,273
7		2,591	2,380	2,469

(a) Find the composite forecast for month seven based on equal weights.

(b) Find the composite forecast for month seven based on weights inversely proportional to the sums of squares of the last six sets of forecast errors.

(c)   Find the composite forecast for month seven using the regression approach with the last six sets of forecast errors.

12.9   The accompanying table shows demand for a product over 12 consecutive months, together with three sets of one-month ahead forecasts. Also shown are forecasts for the next month. Assume that all three sets of forecasts are unbiased.

t	X_t	f_{1t}	f_{2t}	f_{3t}
1	971	901	989	998
2	1,129	1,056	1,042	1,087
3	1,135	1,191	1,183	1,079
4	1,362	1,280	1,395	1,423
5	1,287	1,359	1,327	1,186
6	1,079	1,010	1,031	1,143
7	1,120	1,035	1,080	991
8	986	923	995	1,067
9	923	959	902	1,015
10	834	729	875	806
11	898	795	843	930
12	875	806	821	810
13		982	871	998

(a)   Find the composite forecast for month 13 based on equal weights.

(b)   Find the composite forecast for month 13 based on weights inversely proportional to the sums of squares of the last six sets of forecast errors.

(c)   Find the composite forecast for month 13 based on weights inversely proportional to the sums of squares of the last 12 sets of forecast errors.

(d)   Find the composite forecast for month 13 based on the regression approach using the last six sets of forecast errors.

(e)   Find the composite forecast for month 13 based on the regression approach using the last 12 sets of forecast errors.

(f)   How would you proceed if you suspected that the individual forecasts were biased?

12.10   The accompanying table shows the U.S. unemployment rate over 33 consecutive quarters, together with five sets of one-quarter ahead forecasts, made respectively by the U.C.L.A. Business Forecasting Project, Merrill Lynch Economics Inc., The Conference Board, Data Resources Inc., and Wharton E.F.A. Inc. Also shown are forecasts for the next quarter. Assume that all five sets of forecasts are unbiased. (Data compiled from various issues of the *Statistical Bulletin*. New York: The Conference Board.)

t	X_t	f_{1t}	f_{2t}	f_{3t}	f_{4t}	f_{5t}
1	6.1	6.6	6.4	6.3	6.1	6.3
2	7.5	7.2	7.2	7.3	6.6	6.5
3	7.6	7.9	8.3	8.2	7.9	8.1
4	7.5	8.2	7.9	7.4	7.8	7.7
5	7.3	7.7	7.5	7.8	7.7	7.6
6	7.4	7.5	7.8	7.5	7.4	7.4
7	7.2	7.6	7.8	7.7	7.6	7.6
8	8.3	8.0	7.7	7.8	8.0	8.1
9	8.8	9.3	8.0	8.9	9.2	9.3
10	9.5	9.2	9.5	9.5	9.2	9.2
11	9.9	9.7	9.7	9.7	9.6	9.6
12	10.7	10.4	10.2	10.5	10.3	10.2
13	10.4	11.0	10.9	10.6	11.0	10.8
14	10.1	10.2	10.3	10.2	10.2	10.2
15	9.4	9.6	9.4	9.8	9.6	9.7
16	8.5	9.0	9.1	8.7	8.9	9.1
17	7.9	8.1	8.2	7.8	8.1	8.0
18	7.5	7.6	7.7	7.7	7.6	7.7
19	7.5	6.9	7.3	6.9	6.9	6.9
20	7.1	7.3	7.1	7.5	7.3	7.3
21	7.3	7.1	7.3	7.2	7.2	7.1
22	7.3	7.3	7.2	7.4	7.4	7.4
23	7.1	7.3	7.4	7.3	7.3	7.2
24	7.0	7.1	7.2	7.1	7.2	7.2
25	7.1	7.1	6.9	6.7	6.9	7.0
26	7.2	6.4	6.9	7.1	7.0	7.0
27	6.9	7.0	7.2	7.3	7.0	7.2
28	6.8	6.9	6.9	7.1	6.9	7.1
29	6.7	6.8	6.8	7.2	6.8	6.8
30	6.2	6.6	6.7	6.3	6.6	6.7
31	6.0	6.0	6.0	6.0	6.1	6.0
32	5.9	6.2	6.0	6.0	6.0	6.0
33	5.7	6.3	6.2	5.9	5.9	6.0
34		5.9	5.5	5.4	5.7	5.6

(a) Find all composite forecasts based on equal weights for quarter 1 through quarter 34.

(b) Find the sums of squared forecast errors for all individual forecasts and the equal weights composite forecasts over the period quarter 1 through quarter 33. Comment on your findings.

(c) Find all composite forecasts based on weights inversely proportional to the sums of squares of the last eight sets of forecast errors for quarter 9 through quarter 34.

(d) Find the sums of squared forecast errors for all individual forecasts and the composite forecasts of part (c) over the period quarter 9 through quarter 33. Comment on your findings.

(e) Find the composite forecast for quarter 34 based on the regression approach, using all information from the previous 33 quarters.

12.11   The accompanying table shows annualized U.S. percentage growth in gross national product over 33 consecutive quarters, together with five sets of one-quarter ahead forecasts, made respectively by the U.C.L.A. Business Forecasting Project, Merrill Lynch Economics Inc., The Conference Board, Data Resources Inc., and Wharton E.F.A. Inc. Also shown are forecasts for the next quarter. Assume that all five sets of forecasts are unbiased. (Data compiled from various issues of the *Statistical Bulletin*. New York: The Conference Board.)

t	X_t	f_{1t}	f_{2t}	f_{3t}	f_{4t}	f_{5t}
1	1.1	−5.0	−2.3	1.0	−0.9	−1.7
2	−9.1	−2.4	−5.1	−8.5	−4.9	−2.5
3	1.0	−4.7	−5.0	−6.0	−3.6	−5.1
4	5.0	−0.3	0.4	3.0	1.3	2.2
5	6.5	0.7	−1.1	−1.6	−0.9	0.6
6	−1.9	−0.1	−2.5	1.5	0.4	0.4
7	−0.6	−0.9	−1.3	−3.0	−0.8	0.1
8	−5.2	−5.3	0.8	−4.0	−3.4	−1.8
9	−3.9	−5.0	−2.5	−2.2	−2.8	−3.4
10	1.7	−1.7	2.0	−0.7	−1.4	2.2
11	0.8	1.5	3.5	0.3	2.1	3.1
12	−2.5	0.7	2.8	1.0	2.1	2.2
13	3.1	3.1	4.1	4.8	2.8	4.1
14	8.7	4.5	3.8	6.9	3.7	5.4
15	7.9	7.0	7.3	7.1	6.8	8.0
16	4.5	5.1	4.9	8.5	5.4	6.2
17	8.3	6.1	5.1	6.2	5.6	5.4
18	7.5	5.2	2.5	2.8	3.8	3.7
19	2.7	5.8	5.2	5.2	5.3	6.1
20	3.9	2.5	4.5	3.0	2.3	3.3
21	1.3	5.0	4.5	2.9	3.2	4.6
22	1.7	5.1	3.5	3.7	3.2	3.1
23	3.3	5.0	3.5	3.1	3.5	3.9
24	2.4	3.2	2.1	3.3	2.0	2.2
25	3.2	2.5	4.8	4.3	2.7	2.8
26	1.1	5.0	3.8	2.8	2.6	2.9
27	2.9	3.3	1.6	2.0	2.6	2.5
28	1.7	3.7	1.9	2.3	2.6	1.2
29	4.3	3.9	1.6	1.2	2.5	3.0
30	2.3	3.1	0.7	2.8	2.2	0.9
31	3.8	5.5	2.3	3.8	3.2	1.6
32	4.2	−1.4	3.2	2.0	2.3	1.4
33	2.3	−7.2	−0.8	1.5	0.4	−0.2
34		−3.6	3.1	2.8	1.5	1.6

(a)   Find all composite forecasts based on equal weights for quarter 1 through quarter 34.

(b)   Find the sums of squared forecast errors for all individual forecasts and the equal weights composite forecasts over the period quarter 1 through quarter 33. Comment on your findings.

(c) Find all composite forecasts based on weights inversely proportional to the sums of squares of the last eight sets of
forecast errors for quarter 9 through quarter 34.

(d) Find the sums of squared forecast errors for all individual
forecasts and the composite forecasts of part (c) over the
period quarter 9 through quarter 33. Comment on your
findings.

(e) Find the composite forecast for quarter 34 based on the
regression approach, using all information from the previous
33 quarters.

12.12 Review recent publications in the forecasting journals such as the
Journal of Forecasting or the *International Journal of Forecasting*. Find
an article in which forecasts have been combined. Write a review
of this article, describing the methodology employed and the
empirical findings.

Selected Bibliography

Bates, J. M., & C. W. J. Granger (1969). The combination of forecasts.
Operational Research Quarterly, 20, 451–468.

Bunn, D. W. (1975). A Bayesian approach to the linear combination of
forecasts. *Operational Research Quarterly, 26*, 325–329.

Bunn, D. W. (1981). Two methodologies for the linear combination of
forecasts. *Journal of the Operational Research Society, 32*, 213–222.

Bunn, D. W. (1985). Statistical efficiency in the linear combination of
forecasts. *International Journal of Forecasting, 1*, 151–163.

Clemen, R. T. (1989). Combining forecasts: a review and annotated
bibliography. *International Journal of Forecasting, 5*, 559–583.

Clemen, R. T., & J. B. Guerard (1989). Econometric GNP forecasts:
incremental information relative to naive extrapolation. *International
Journal of Forecasting, 5*, 417–426.

Clemen, R. T., & R. L. Winkler (1986). Combining economic forecasts.
Journal of Business and Economic Statistics, 4, 39–46.

Diebold, F. X. (1988). Serial correlation and the combination of forecasts.
Journal of Business and Economic Statistics, 6, 105–111.

Diebold, F. X., & P. Pauly (1987). Structural change and the combination
of forecasts. *Journal of Forecasting, 6*, 21–40.

Figlewski, S. (1983). Optimal price forecasting using survey data. *Review
of Economics and Statistics, 65*, 13–21.

Figlewski, S., & T. Urich (1983). Optimal aggregation of money supply forecasts: Accuracy, profitability and market efficiency. *Journal of Finance, 28,* 695–710.

Fullerton, T. M. (1989). A composite approach to forecasting state government revenues: case study of the Idaho sales tax. *International Journal of Forecasting, 5,* 373–380.

Granger, C. W. J. (1989). Combining forecasts—twenty years later. *Journal of Forecasting, 8,* 167–173.

Granger, C. W. J., & P. Newbold (1986). *Forecasting Economic Time Series* (2nd ed.). Orlando, Fl.: Academic Press.

Granger, C. W. J., & R. Ramanathan (1984). Improved methods of combining forecasts. *Journal of Forecasting, 3,* 197–204.

Gupta, S., & P. C. Wilton (1987). Combination of forecasts: An extension. *Management Science, 33,* 356–372.

Gupta, S., & P. C. Wilton (1988). Combination of economic forecasts: An odds-matrix approach. *Journal of Business and Economic Statistics, 6,* 373–379.

Lawrence, M. J., R. H. Edmundson, & M. J. O'Connor (1986). The accuracy of combining judgmental and statistical forecasts. *Management Science, 32,* 1521–1532.

Lobo, G. J. (1991). Alternative methods of combining security analysts' and statistical forecasts of annual corporate earnings. *International Journal of Forecasting, 7,* 57–63.

Mahmoud, E. (1984). Accuracy in forecasting: A survey. *Journal of Forecasting, 3,* 139–159.

Makridakis, S., et al. (1982). The accuracy of extrapolation (time series) methods. *Journal of Forecasting, 1,* 111–153.

Makridakis, S., & R. L. Winkler (1983). Averages of forecasts: Some empirical results. *Management Science, 29,* 987–996.

Miller, C. M., R. T. Clemen, & R. L. Winkler (1992). The effect of nonstationarity on combined forecasts. *International Journal of Forecasting, 7,* 515–529.

Newbold, P., & C. W. J. Granger (1974). Experience with forecasting univariate time series and the combination of forecasts. *Journal of the Royal Statistical Society A, 137,* 131–165.

Newbold, P., J. K. Zumwalt, & S. Kannan (1987). Combining forecasts to improve earnings per share prediction: An examination of electric utilities. *International Journal of Forecasting, 3,* 229–238.

Phillips, R. F. (1987). Composite forecasting: An integrated approach and optimality reconsidered. *Journal of Business and Economic Statistics, 5,* 389–395.

Reeves, G. R., & K. D. Lawrence (1982). Combining multiple forecasts given multiple objectives. *International Journal of Forecasting, 1,* 271–279.

Schnaars, S. P. (1986). A comparison of extrapolation models on yearly sales forecasts. *International Journal of Forecasting, 2,* 71–85.

Trabelsi, A., & S. C. Hillmer (1989). A benchmarking approach to forecast combination. *Journal of Business and Economic Statistics, 7,* 353–362.

Winkler, R. L. (1989). Combining forecasts: a philosophical basis and some current issues. *International Journal of Forecasting, 5,* 605–609.

Winkler, R. L., & S. Makridakis (1983). The combination of forecasts. *Journal of the Royal Statistical Society A, 146,* 150–157.

The Evaluation of Forecasts

13.1 THE IMPORTANCE OF EVALUATION: COST OF ERRORS

We have devoted considerable space in this book to the discussion of the production of a specific product—forecasts. However, as any production manager knows, it is essential also to pay particular attention to product *quality*, and not merely to the mechanics of the production process. In this chapter we will attempt to redress the balance somewhat by considering procedures for the *evaluation* of forecast quality. Perhaps for most readers it is unnecessary for us to stress the importance of forecast evaluation. After all, considerable amounts of money, time, and effort are expended in the production of forecasts intended as inputs to business decision making at all levels, where the potential gains or losses accruing from superior or inferior decisions can be substantial. It seems self-evident then that management will want to check that forecasts of adequate quality are being made available. However, we have noticed a tendency for some users to become obsessed with the sophistication and complexity of particular forecasting methodologies, perhaps taking too much for granted the assumption that turning such heavy artillery loose on a problem will be successful. This issue appears to have become increasingly germane with the development of numerous computer packages for forecast generation. There is a tendency for users, without making the effort to understand the limitations of the underlying methodologies, to put unwarranted faith in computer-generated predictions. However, the acid test must surely be based on the accuracy of the forecasts rather than the aesthetic appeal of the forecast-generating mechanism.

Taking for granted now the desirability of evaluating forecasts, we turn to a discussion of how this might be done, of the difficulties that are raised, and of some approaches to evaluation that have been proposed and implemented. The following two assertions should be fairly uncontroversial:

1.   The central criteria should rest on *forecast performance*.
2.   Evaluation should concentrate as much as possible on *real forecasts*.

The first is an argument for the importance of the bottom line. Certainly it is important that forecasts be generated through some intellectually plausible mechanism, and certainly it is legitimate to remain skeptical when apparently good forecasts have been generated by an implausible mechanism. Nevertheless, however appealing the methodology employed, it is essential to check that satisfactory forecasts are being produced. These checks should not be based, for example, on how closely some model fits sample data, but rather on the record of this model when projected forward to produce real forecasts. In practice, as is clear from survey results reported by Carbone and Armstrong (1982), other criteria than accuracy are important to practitioners evaluating forecasts and forecasting methods. Obviously, these involve the cost and time required as well as the ease of use and implementation. Somewhat less obviously, ease of interpretation is also thought to be important. Clearly some balance needs to be struck between the cost of forecast generation and the benefits from more accurate forecasts. Just where this balance point is located depends in any application on the potential gains to the organization that might flow from more accurate forecasts. We are less convinced by the argument that forecasting methods need to be kept so simple that they are easily understood by senior management. After all, senior managers should be well placed to understand the gains from more accurate forecasts, and, where such gains can be demonstrated, to rely on the expertise of subordinates on methodological details. One can derive benefit from driving an automobile without fully understanding exactly how it works, though some general understanding is certainly useful.

The major motivation for the evaluation of forecasts is not to distribute credit or blame to forecasters, but to assess whether the system currently being implemented is doing an adequate job, and whether through some modification, which could be major or minor, a better job might be done. The best way to approach the issue is through the realization that, in the event, any forecasts will turn out to be in error to some extent. Presumably, when errors are made the organization will incur some costs. It is therefore desirable to review the record and analyze forecast errors that have been made in the past, with a view to assessing the prospects for avoiding the most costly errors in the future. Such a review could be either subjective or objective. A subjective review would presumably concentrate on the largest errors, attempting to understand why these were made, and to seek information, available at the time the forecasts were prepared, that could have been employed to produce more accurate forecasts. Viewed in this way the subjective approach can be very helpful to the forecaster intent on learning how to do the job more effectively. Unfortunately, human nature being what it is, there is a great temptation to explain away all forecast errors as resulting from developments that could not possibly have been foreseen at the time the forecasts were made. Of course, in reality this attitude will sometimes be justified. However, it is not likely to lead to significant future improvements in forecast quality. For this reason, it is important that more objective approaches to forecast evaluation also be adopted.

Most of the objective approaches which will be discussed in the next two sections of this chapter are based in one way or another on the analysis of forecast errors. Let e denote the error in a forecast, and suppose that a cost C can be associated with that error. Then cost will be a function of error, and we can write

$$C = C(e)$$

On some occasions it may be possible to determine fairly precise dollar costs that would be incurred as a result of future forecast errors, but more often this is not the case as the decision making environment will be too complex for such accounting. In particular, at the time the forecast is made, any error costs would occur some time in the future, and so they also would have to be predicted. In the absence of any problem-specific cost of error function, analysts typically resort to assuming some simple, plausible function involving relative costs. There are many possibilities that might be used here, and the following three characteristics of cost of error functions will often be reasonable:

1. If the forecast is perfect, so that the error is zero, there will be no error cost; that is,

$$C(0) = 0$$

2. The larger is any positive forecast error, the greater should be the associated cost; thus, if e_1 and e_2 are two possible positive errors

$$C(e_1) > C(e_2) \text{ if } e_1 > e_2 > 0$$

Similarly, for negative errors,

$$C(e_1) > C(e_2) \text{ if } e_1 < e_2 < 0$$

3. The cost of error function will often be *symmetric*, so that the cost of a positive error will be same as that of a negative error in the same amount; that is,

$$C(e) = C(-e)$$

It is difficult to argue with the appeal of the first two of these characteristics. However, there will be occasions when the third is not appropriate. For example, consider the production of some perishable commodity for which demand must be predicted. The cost of overproduction might be different than the cost of underproduction in the same amount. The former leads to waste of unsalable goods, whereas the latter will result in foregone profits, and perhaps also good will losses. There is no particular reason to expect the two marginal costs to be the same. In general, it is desirable that forecasts be unbiased, but, as Granger (1969), and Zellner (1986) have shown, in the presence of asymmetric cost of error functions, biased forecasts will be preferable. Asymmetric cost of error functions, then, require not only special treatment in forecast evaluation, but also some modification of the usual forecasting methodologies. We will not discuss this issue further here.

Figure 13.1 shows the two symmetric cost of error functions that are employed in practice far more than any others. These are:

1. The **quadratic cost of error function,** in which the cost of an error of any amount is taken to be proportional to the squared error; that is,

$$C(e) \propto e^2$$

2. The **absolute error cost function,** where error cost is assumed proportional to absolute error, so that

$$C(e) \propto |e|$$

Although both of these functions are quite popular, the quadratic cost of error function is used more often in practice. There are two reasons for this. First, the quadratic function attaches a relatively higher penalty than

FIGURE 13.1   Two cost of error functions. (a) Quadratic cost of error function.
(b) Absolute error cost function.

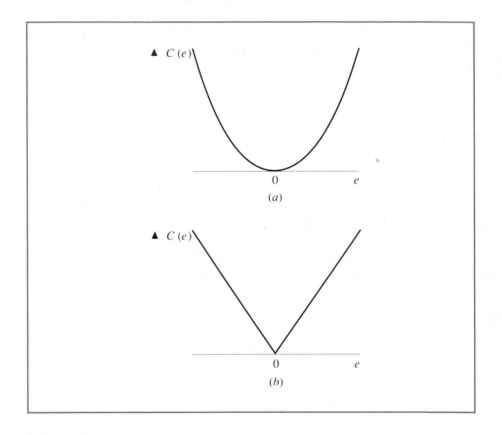

does the absolute function to forecast errors of very large magnitude. In many applications, where modest errors can be easily tolerated but very large errors may have severe consequences, this is precisely what is required. Secondly, the obvious relationship between the quadratic cost of error function and the method of least squares allows, as we will see in the next two sections, considerable further analysis of forecast errors.

In subsequent sections of this chapter, we will concentrate on situations where the two simple cost of error functions of Figure 13.1, particularly the quadratic cost function, are appropriate. However, it must be noted that there are circumstances where this particular approach is not the most suitable. As we have already suggested, there are specific applications for which it is possible to accurately specify error costs, in which case this should be done. For example, Boothe and Glassman (1987) evaluate various procedures for exchange rate forecasting in terms of profitability in forward market speculation. Obviously, if the motivation for forecasting is exclusively for this type of speculation, profitability is the relevant criterion for evaluating the forecasts. On some occasions, while finding it difficult to specify precise costs, users may feel strongly that neither of the functions of Figure 13.1 is appropriate in particular circumstances. Indeed, sometimes an approach exclusively through cost of error functions does not adequately capture users' views of what is most important in forecast quality. Perhaps the most common occurrence of this view is manifest in the attention that is sometimes paid to the anticipation of *turning points* in business and economic time series. For example, if a particular procedure is relatively successful in predicting turning points, some additional inaccuracy in average performance of forecasts over the whole business cycle may be tolerable. In fact, it is quite difficult to formalize an approach to forecast evaluation that pays special attention to turning points, partly because, as we noted in Chapter 8, it is nontrivial to determine whether or not a turning point has occurred, even after the event. Kling (1987) provides some discussion on the evaluation of turning point forecasts.

Finally, as argued by Einhorn and Hogarth (1982), there are occasions on which the outcome is not independent of the forecast. Predictions are made as an aid to decision making, and in some circumstances decision makers may be in a position to react by making moves that will influence the eventual outcome either in the direction of or away from what was predicted. For example, the forecast of a severe economic recession next year could stimulate government policy makers to take steps aimed at preventing this eventuality. In circumstances where the forecaster and decision maker are more than mere passive observers of the quantity being predicted, the evaluation of forecasts through the comparison of predictions and outcomes is less attractive, and in extreme cases may be pointless. Perhaps the best that can then be done is to fall back on a very careful and thorough examination of the methodology employed in generating forecasts.

13.2 MEAN SQUARED ERROR AND ALTERNATIVE MEASURES

The objective approaches to forecast evaluation to be discussed in the remainder of this chapter necessarily require an accumulation of evidence of actual forecast performance, and are therefore directly applicable only in circumstances where a forecast procedure has been in operation for quite some time, and where records have been kept. In practice this requirement is quite restrictive, and will certainly be frustrating to the analyst eager to try out a new methodology, or who is applying existing methods for the first time. In these circumstances it may be possible to simulate a forecasting record. For example, if prediction is to be based on the fitting of some model to data, the available data could be broken into two parts. The first part would be used for model building, and the model thus achieved could be projected forward to derive "forecasts" of the known values in the more recent part of the observation period.

When evaluating forecasts it is important to separate predictions for different horizons, so the one-step ahead forecasts, two-steps ahead forecasts, and so on are evaluated separately. This is important since, to make sense of the performance records, it is necessary to deal with homogeneous sets of information. Additionally, some methods may be relatively successful in very short-run forecasting, while others may be better in predicting further ahead. Such information would naturally be valuable to the analyst.

Objective measures of forecast performance are based on aggregate quality over some period of time, the appropriate statistical aggregates depending on assumed cost of error functions. We will illustrate through an example for which some calculations are set out in Table 13.1. The

TABLE 13.1   One-step ahead forecasts, and some error-based performance measures.

t	X_t	f_{1t}	e_{1t}	e_{1t}^2	$|e_{1t}|$	$100|e_{1t}|/X_t$
0	220					
1	225	226	−1	1	1	0.4444
2	229	228	1	1	1	0.4367
3	225	237	−12	144	12	5.3333
4	230	235	−5	25	5	2.1739
5	237	229	8	64	8	3.3755
6	241	231	10	100	10	4.1494
7	250	247	3	9	3	1.2000
8	239	245	−6	36	6	2.5105
9	245	236	9	81	9	3.6735
10	245	243	2	4	2	0.8163
11	251	246	5	25	5	1.9920
12	263	245	18	324	18	6.8441
13	242	253	−11	121	11	4.5455
14	245	251	−6	36	6	2.4490
15	247	248	−1	1	1	0.4049
16	247	247	0	0	0	0.0000
17	229	239	−10	100	10	4.3668
18	222	228	−6	36	6	2.7027
19	214	210	4	16	4	1.8692
20	227	218	9	81	9	3.9648
				1205	127	53.25

table shows 21 consecutive monthly sales figures, X_t, for a product for which demand is not seasonal. Also shown are one-step forecasts, f_{1t}, of the last twenty of these values. Thus, f_{1t} is the forecast of X_t made one month previously. Evaluation is then based on the set of one-step forecast errors

$$e_{1t} = X_t - f_{1t} \qquad t = 1, 2, \ldots, 20$$

Three measures of average forecast quality, based on forecast errors, are often computed in practice:

1. If the quadratic cost of error function is appropriate, then it is natural to calculate the average of the squared forecast errors, or the **mean squared error.** If n forecast errors e_t are available, this is

$$\text{M.S.E.} = \sum_{t=1}^{n} e_t^2 / n$$

2. Similarly, based on an absolute cost of error function, we would calculate the **mean absolute error**

$$\text{M.A.E.} = \sum_{t=1}^{n} |e_t| / n$$

3. Often it is convenient for purposes of interpretation to express absolute error in terms of a percentage of the quantity being predicted, leading to the **mean absolute percentage error**

$$\text{M.A.P.E.} = \sum_{t=1}^{n} 100 |e_t| / nX_t$$

For the example of Table 13.1, these three statistics are

$$\text{M.S.E.} = 1{,}205/20 = 60.25$$

$$\text{M.A.E.} = 127/20 = 6.35$$

$$\text{M.A.P.E.} = 53.25/20 = 2.66$$

Thus we see, for example, that the forecasting procedure that is in operation is yielding predictions whose errors have magnitudes that are on average 2.66% of the quantity being predicted. For ease of interpretation in terms of the original units of measurement, *root mean squared error* is often calculated. In our example, this is $\sqrt{60.25} = 7.76$.

The mean squared error, mean absolute error, and mean absolute percentage error are all useful statistics for describing the record of an operational forecasting system. They do not, however, provide much direct information about whether something better might be achieved. If the analyst has available a competing set of forecasts, then the two sets can be compared through any or all of these three criteria. Obviously, the set for which the criterion statistic is smaller will be judged to be better. Frequently, however, no alternative forecasts will be available. In these circumstances it is common to compare performance with a set of **naïve forecasts.** The idea here is that a good deal of time, effort, and expense will have been devoted to the production of forecasts, and it would be interesting to learn what, if anything, has been gained compared with what could have been achieved through some very simple, or naïve, decision rule. Forecasts based on such a rule are easily developed, and can be compared with the forecasts of interest through mean squared error, mean absolute error, or mean absolute percentage error. The choice of appropriate naïve forecasts for comparison depends to some extent on the characteristics of the forecasting problem. The following four possibilities have often proved useful:

1. For many nonseasonal business and economic time series, it is useful to view the most recent observation as a serviceable crude forecast of all future values. Thus, for one-step ahead prediction, the naïve forecast would be

$$f_{2t} = X_{t-1}$$

Table 13.2 sets out some calculations for this naïve forecast of the series of Table 13.1. The mean squared error, mean absolute error, and mean absolute percentage error are

$$\text{M.S.E.} = 1{,}625/20 = 81.25$$

$$\text{M.A.E.} = 145/20 = 7.25$$

$$\text{M.A.P.E.} = 61.33/20 = 3.07$$

We see that, by each criterion, the original forecasts outperformed the naïve alternatives. This should certainly be at least mildly reassuring to the analysts who produced these forecasts. Comparison of the criterion functions for the two sets of predictions provides a measure of relative quality. For example, the ratio of the mean squared errors is

$$\frac{\text{M.S.E.(1)}}{\text{M.S.E.(2)}} = 60.25/81.25 = 0.7415$$

TABLE 13.2   Error-based performance measures for a naïve predictor.

t	X_t	f_{2t}	e_{2t}	e_{2t}^2	$|e_{2t}|$	$100|e_{2t}|/X_t$
1	225	220	5	25	5	2.2222
2	229	225	4	16	4	1.7467
3	225	229	−4	16	4	1.7778
4	230	225	5	25	5	2.1739
5	237	230	7	49	7	2.9536
6	241	237	4	16	4	1.6598
7	250	241	9	81	9	3.6000
8	239	250	−11	121	11	4.6025
9	245	239	6	36	6	2.4490
10	245	245	0	0	0	0.0000
11	251	245	6	36	6	2.3904
12	263	251	12	144	12	4.5627
13	242	263	−21	441	21	8.6777
14	245	242	3	9	3	1.2245
15	247	245	2	4	2	0.8097
16	247	247	0	0	0	0.0000
17	229	247	−18	324	18	7.8603
18	222	229	−7	49	7	3.1532
19	214	222	−8	64	8	3.7383
20	227	214	13	169	13	5.7269
				1625	145	61.33

so that the original forecasts have mean squared error that is 74.15% of that of the naïve forecasts. It is usual to take square roots, giving a ratio of root mean squared errors of 0.861, to return to the original units of measurement. This is, in effect, a version of a statistic, originally proposed by Theil (1966), which is frequently calculated in evaluation exercises. The Theil statistic is

$$U = \left[\frac{\sum_{t=1}^{n} (X_t - f_{1t})^2}{\sum_{t=1}^{n} (X_t - X_{t-1})^2} \right]^{1/2}$$

and provides a measure of the extent to which a set of forecasts is superior to the naïve "no change" forecasts.

2. Some business and economic time series exhibit quite long periods of steady growth, so that a prediction of no change would be foolish. For such series, a preferable naïve alternative is to predict all future changes by the most recent observed change. Then, for one-step ahead prediction, the naïve forecast would be

$$f_{2t} = X_{t-1} + (X_{t-1} - X_{t-2}) = 2X_{t-1} - X_{t-2}$$

3. Neither of the above two naïve predictors takes into account the possibility of seasonality, and both would perform very poorly for strongly seasonal time series. Clearly, in evaluating forecasts of a seasonal series it would be useful to have available some more reasonable naïve alternative. It is often useful to predict all future period-to-period changes by the period-to-period changes in the most recently observed year. Thus, for a seasonal time series of period s, naïve one-step ahead forecasts would be

$$f_{2t} = X_{t-1} + (X_{t-s} - X_{t-s-1})$$

4. On some occasions, particularly in macroeconomic forecasting, very complex and expensive forecasting exercises are attempted. Large behavioral models are built with considerable care, and the generation of forecasts also involves considerable expert judgment. By comparison, the three alternatives just considered seem ridiculously simple, and it is often felt that more serious competitors are required. These are generally based on the prediction of a time series from its own past, using the methods of Chapters 6 and 7. Thus, expensively produced forecasts are often compared with predictions from appropriately fitted ARIMA models. These can be thought of as quite sophisticated naïve alternatives. Occasionally, to save time in the production of the alternative forecasts, either an exponential smoothing algorithm or a pure autoregressive model is used in place of a full ARIMA model-building exercise.

As the survey results of Carbone and Armstrong (1982) indicate, in practice mean squared error is used more often than mean absolute error or mean absolute percentage error in forecast evaluation. In the remainder of this and the following section we will concentrate on further approaches to forecast evaluation that are related to mean squared error and relevant when a quadratic cost of error function is assumed.

Decomposition of Mean Squared Error

Let f_t ($t = 1, 2, \ldots, n$) be a set of forecasts of the actual values X_t. Then, the mean squared error is

$$\text{M.S.E.} = \sum_{t=1}^{n} (X_t - f_t)^2/n \qquad (13.2.1)$$

Theil (1958) proposed an interesting decomposition, which has frequently been calculated in practice, of prediction mean squared error into three components, which have useful interpretations. This, and a further less useful decomposition, have been discussed by Granger and Newbold (1973, 1986), and Ahlburg (1984). After some algebra, the statistic 13.2.1 can be written

$$\text{M.S.E.} = (\bar{f} - \bar{X})^2 + (S_f - rS_x)^2 + (1 - r^2)S_x^2 \quad (13.2.2)$$

Here $\bar{f}$ and $\bar{X}$ are the means of the forecasts and observations, so that

$$\bar{f} = \sum_{t=1}^{n} f_t/n \qquad \bar{X} = \sum_{t=1}^{n} X_t/n$$

S_f and S_x are the standard deviations of these two sets of values, defined as

$$S_f = \left[\sum_{t=1}^{n} \frac{(f_t - \bar{f})^2}{n} \right]^{1/2} \qquad S_x = \left[\sum_{t=1}^{n} \frac{(X_t - \bar{X})^2}{n} \right]^{1/2}$$

where division is by n rather than $(n - 1)$. Finally, r is the correlation between the observed and predicted values, so that

$$r = \sum_{t=1}^{n} \frac{(f_t - \bar{f})(X_t - \bar{X})}{nS_f S_x}$$

To see the rationale for this decomposition, note first that, at least for symmetric cost of error functions, it is desirable that the forecasts be unbiased, so that the errors have mean zero. Of course, for any sample we would not expect the average of the forecast errors to be precisely zero, but the difference between the averages of the sample means of the actual and predicted series should be quite small. Hence, the first term on the right-hand side of equation 13.2.2 should be relatively small.

Having compared the means of the observed and predicted series, it is natural also to compare their sample standard deviations. Now, it might at first sight seem desirable also that these two standard deviations should be approximately the same. In fact, however, this is not generally true. To the extent that perfect forecasts are unachievable, the standard deviation of the predictor series should ideally be *less* than that of the actual series. Intuitively this is so because it would be suboptimal to incorporate in the forecasts a random element matching any unpredictable irregularities in the observed series. It can be shown that, ideally, the standard deviation of the predictor series should be equal to the product of the standard deviation of the actual series and the correlation between the two series. Hence, the second term on the right-hand side of equation

13.2.2 should also be quite small. The decomposition 13.2.2 is sometimes written

$$UM + UR + UD = 1$$

where

$$\left. \begin{array}{l} UM = (\overline{f} - \overline{X})^2/\text{M.S.E.} \\ UR = (S_f - rS_x)^2/\text{M.S.E.} \\ UD = (1 - r^2)S_x^2/\text{M.S.E.} \end{array} \right] \qquad (13.2.3)$$

The three proportions UM, UR, and UD are sometimes called the **bias proportion,** the **regression proportion,** and the **disturbance proportion.** (The terminology follows from the fact that UM compares the *means,* while the other two statistics relate to the regression of actual on predicted values: UR assesses the extent to which the slope of this *regression* is different from one, whereas UD provides a measure of the relative size of the *disturbances,* or error terms in this regression.) We will discuss this breakdown further in the following section, when we consider the value of regressing the observations on the predictions. In computing Theil's decomposition the analyst is looking ideally for very small values of UM and UR, and consequently a value close to one for UD. A high value of UM would indicate bias in the forecasts, whereas a high value for UR would suggest either too much or too little variability in the forecasts.

For the data of Table 13.1, we have already found

$$\text{M.S.E.} = 60.25$$

In addition, a little arithmetic yields

$$\overline{f} = 237.10 \qquad \overline{X} = 237.65 \qquad S_f = 11.1799$$
$$S_x = 11.8080 \qquad r = 0.7744$$

Substituting these values into equation 13.2.3 then yields

$$UM = 0.005 \qquad UR = 0.069 \qquad UD = 0.926$$

Certainly the proportions UM and UR appear to be quite small, though the reader is entitled to ask just what values would be regarded as satisfactorily small. We will provide one answer to this question in the next section through the fitting of the regression of actual on predicted values. It has to be added that a satisfactory decomposition of this sort does not constitute sufficient evidence to claim that the forecasts are of high quality, or that superior predictions cannot be found. It merely indicates the presence of certain desirable properties in the mean and standard deviation of the forecasts.

13.3   EFFICIENCY AND CONDITIONAL EFFICIENCY

The concept of efficiency plays an important part in the theory of statistical estimation. Essentially the same concept has attracted the attention of analysts interested in the evaluation of forecasts. As in any evaluation exercise, conclusions need to be drawn in terms of some implicit cost of error function. Partly because of theoretical tractability, forecast efficiency is almost invariably discussed in terms of a quadratic cost of error function. Then, for any particular problem, one predictor is said to be more efficient than another, at a particular lead time, if it yields smaller expected squared forecast error. Thus, the comparison of the observed performance of two predictors in terms of mean squared error can be viewed as a determination of which was the more efficient over the observations period. So far this breaks no new ground. However, in statistical estimation theory, it is possible to determine in certain circumstances that a particular estimator is the most efficient in a broad class of possible estimators. For example, we saw in Chapters 3 and 4, as a result of the Gauss-Markov theorem, that in regression models for which the standard assumptions can be made, least squares estimators have minimum variance in a wide class of unbiased estimators of the model parameters. It is interesting to ask if it is possible to test for efficiency of this sort in a set of forecasts. Two approaches along these lines have been proposed and implemented in the literature.

Let X_t $(t = 1, \ldots, n)$ be a set of observations on a time series, for which forecasts f_t are available. Mincer and Zarnowitz (1969) discuss the regression of X_t on f_t; that is,

$$X_t = \alpha + \beta f_t + \epsilon_t \qquad (13.3.1)$$

where ϵ_t is an error term. Clearly, for well-behaved forecasts, we would expect to find $\alpha = 0$ and $\beta = 1$, so that

$$X_t = f_t + \epsilon_t$$

where the ϵ_t have mean zero. Then a plot of the observations X_t against the forecasts f_t would consist of a set of points distributed around the line of perfect forecasts

$$X_t = f_t$$

FIGURE 13.2   Plot of observations and forecasts of Table 13.1.

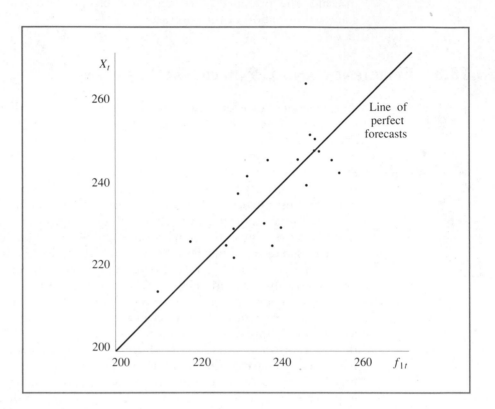

Figure 13.2 shows such a plot for the data of Table 13.1. Viewed in this way these forecasts seem quite satisfactory. Mincer and Zarnowitz propose to test for forecast efficiency by estimating the regression equation 13.3.1 and testing the hypothesis that both $\alpha = 0$ and $\beta = 1$. In effect, this is a test of the hypothesis that the forecasts f_t are the most efficient in the class of possible predictors $(\alpha + \beta f_t)$, where α and β are any fixed numbers. We will refer to this concept as **Mincer-Zarnowitz efficiency.** Unfortunately, the class of predictors considered here is very narrow. Many alternative forecasts with which we would wish comparison do not belong to this class. Certainly it would be unreasonable for the forecaster to be complacent because her or his predictions appeared to be Mincer-Zarnowitz efficient. They could still be substantially poorer than other easily obtained alternative predictions.

Although we do not view the Mincer-Zarnowitz concept as a fully satisfactory characterization of forecast efficiency, we do believe that there is some value in fitting the regression 13.3.1, as useful information about forecast quality can be obtained. We will assume for now that the error terms ϵ_t have mean zero, fixed variance, and are not autocorrelated, so that least squares estimation is appropriate. Our aim is to test the null hypothesis

$$H_0: \alpha = 0, \beta = 1$$

Let S_1 denote the sum of squared forecast errors, so that

$$S_1 = \sum_{t=1}^{n} (X_t - f_t)^2$$

and let S_2 denote the sum of squared residuals from the fitted regression, so that if a and b are the least squares estimates of α and β

$$S_2 = \sum_{t=1}^{n} (X_t - a - bf_t)^2$$

The test of our null hypothesis is based on the statistic

$$F = \frac{(S_1 - S_2)/2}{S_2/(n - 2)} \qquad (13.3.2)$$

The null hypothesis of Mincer-Zarnowitz efficiency is rejected if the statistic 13.3.2 exceeds the tabulated significance points of the F-distribution with $(2, n - 2)$ degrees of freedom.

To illustrate this procedure, we will test for Mincer-Zarnowitz efficiency in the forecasts of Table 13.1, for which we have already found

$$S_1 = 1,205$$

The fitted least squares regression is

$$X_t = \underset{(37.38)}{43.71} + \underset{(0.157)}{0.818f_{1t}} \qquad R^2 = 0.600 \qquad d = 1.650 \qquad (13.3.3)$$

where, as usual, figures in parentheses below coefficient estimates are estimated standard errors, R^2 is the coefficient of determination, and d is the Durbin-Watson statistic. Also, we found the sum of squared residuals

$$S_2 = 1,116.1$$

The test statistic 13.3.2 is then

$$F = \frac{(1{,}205 - 1{,}116.1)/2}{1{,}116.1/18} = 0.72$$

Since the tabulated 5% point for the F-distribution with (2, 18) degrees of freedom is 3.55 we are not close to being able to reject the null hypothesis of Mincer-Zarnowitz efficiency at the 5% significance level, confirming the visual impression in Figure 13.2 that there is no cause for concern on this score.

Mincer-Zarnowitz efficiency is intimately connected with Theil's decomposition of forecast mean squared error, equation 13.2.2. Specifically, it can be shown, through a little tedious algebra, that the proportions UM and UR, defined in equation 13.2.3 are both zero if and only if the regression 13.3.1 yields least squares estimates $a = 0$, $b = 1$. In Section 13.2 we raised the question as to what values would be regarded as too high for these proportions. A sensible answer to this would be if they are sufficiently high that the test statistic 13.3.2 is large enough to allow rejection of the null hypothesis of Mincer-Zarnowitz efficiency at some low significance level, such as 5%.

There are two possible further benefits from fitting the regression 13.3.1 of observations on forecasts. First, the coefficient of determination, R^2, provides a measure of the strength of association between the actual values and the forecasts. Thus, in line with our discussion in Chapter 4, we might claim that 60.0% of the variability in the observations of Table 13.1 is, by virtue of the fitted regression 13.3.3, explained by the linear relation between the observed values and the forecasts in this sample. Of course, we could measure the strength of this association through the sample correlation, $r = 0.7744$, found in Section 13.2: The coefficient of determination is simply the square of the sample correlation. There is, however, some difficulty in the interpretation of these measures of forecast quality. A relatively high value of R^2 may indicate nothing more than that the series of interest is quite easy to predict, whereas a low value of R^2 does not necessarily imply that in practice anything better can be achieved. The point is critical when we are attempting to predict the levels of typical business or economic time series. Such nonseasonal series generally follow quite smooth paths through time, so that a high correlation between predicted and actual levels is easily achieved. However, it is far more difficult to obtain a large correlation between predicted and actual changes in such series. Thus, the value of the coefficient of determination in equation 13.3.3, and similar regressions, will generally be very different if we take changes in the variable of interest as the quantity to be predicted rather than levels of that series. For this reason, the interpretation of the coefficient of determination in such regressions is far less clear than might at first sight seem to be the case. In exactly the same fashion, Figure 13.2 appears to demonstrate a reassuringly close relationship between forecasts and observations. However, as the reader is invited to verify, a plot of actual changes against predicted changes presents a far less convincing picture. In our view, this suggests that assessments of the quality of forecasts based only on a crude comparison of actual and predicted values are of limited worth. Rather, the question of the quality of a set of forecasts is best approached through comparison with some alternative predictions. For example, these alternatives could be one or other of the naïve forecasts introduced in Section 13.2. These are sometimes termed **benchmarks** for comparison.

The regression 13.3.3 was estimated from one-step ahead forecasts. Now, optimally the errors from such forecasts should not be autocorrelated. This is so since otherwise forecast errors would be correlated with information that was known at the time the predictions were made. In that case, the forecast errors would be predictable to some extent, so that better predictions could have been obtained. The regression 13.3.3 provides a means of testing for autocorrelation in the forecast errors, as well as Mincer-Zarnowitz efficiency. The Durbin-Watson statistic can be used to test for autocorrelated errors. The computed statistic, 1.650, exceeds the upper bound tabulated value, $d_u = 1.41$, for a 5% level test, so that there is little evidence of autocorrelation in these forecast errors.

Consecutive forecast errors at horizons beyond one-step ahead will typically be autocorrelated. Indeed, it can be shown that, for optimal h-steps ahead forecasts, these errors should follow a moving average model of order $(h - 1)$. It follows that, strictly speaking, the estimation of the regression equation 13.3.1 by ordinary least squares, and consequent hypothesis tests, are valid only for one-step ahead forecasts f_t. In principle, for a series of h-steps ahead forecasts, a test for Mincer-Zarnowitz efficiency could be based on the estimation of equation 13.3.1 with the error terms taken to follow a moving average model of order $(h - 1)$. In practice, however, this is rarely done as only quite short series of forecasts are typically available. The procedures discussed here are most often applied only to one-step ahead forecasts.

As we have already suggested, the direct comparison of forecasts and observations, although useful, is not an adequate basis for evaluation. Rather, if asked how good are some forecasts, a natural answer must be: "Compared with what?" It is important to compare one's forecasts with some alternatives. On some occasions the analyst will have available a second set of forecasts for comparison. On others, as we saw in Section 13.2, comparison with a set of naïve forecasts might be interesting. In Section 13.2 we compared sets of forecasts through their mean squared errors. We are thus able to say by how much, over the sample period, one set of forecasts has outperformed another. However, although it might be reassuring to an analyst to find that a set of forecasts, whose derivation required a good deal of time and effort, turned out to be superior to some simple naïve alternatives, this can hardly provide grounds for complacency. As we discussed in Chapter 12, the fact that one set of forecasts is better than another does not necessarily imply that the poorer forecasts are worthless; they may contain useful information about the quantity being predicted. It might be possible to find a *combined forecast* that outperforms both individual forecasts. This idea led Granger and Newbold (1973, 1986) to introduce the concept of **conditional efficiency.** One set of forecasts is said to be conditionally efficient with respect to another if combining the second set with the first produces no gain in mean squared error compared with using the first set alone. For one-step ahead forecasts, the regression-based approach to combining, discussed in Section 12.2, provides a test of conditional efficiency that can be easily carried out.

Let f_{1t} and f_{2t} be two forecasts of the quantity X_t. It is often reasonable to assume that these forecasts are unbiased, and to consider composite forecasts that are weighted averages of the individual forecasts. Then, if w is the weight attached to the second forecast, we can write

$$X_t = (1 - w)f_{1t} + wf_{2t} + \epsilon_t$$

or

$$(X_t - f_{1t}) = w(f_{2t} - f_{1t}) + \epsilon_t \qquad (13.3.4)$$

where ϵ_t is the error of the combined forecast. Then, if forecasts are to be combined in this way, conditional efficiency of f_{1t} with respect to f_{2t} is equivalent to $w = 0$ in equation 13.3.4. Thus, a test for conditional efficiency can be based on estimating equation 13.3.4 by least squares, and comparing the least squares estimate of w with its estimated standard error through the usual t-ratio. The null hypothesis of conditional efficiency then is

$$H_0: w = 0$$

This is naturally tested against the alternative that a positive weight is attached to f_{2t} in the composite predictor; that is,

$$H_1: w > 0$$

We evaluated the forecasts of Table 13.1 in comparison with the naïve forecasts of Table 13.2 in this way. The fitted regression 13.3.4 was

$$(X_t - f_{1t}) = \underset{(0.282)}{0.228(f_{2t} - f_{1t})}$$

The t-ratio is only 0.809, and thus provides no substantial evidence against the hypothesis that the forecasts of Table 13.1 are conditionally efficient with respect to the naïve no change forecasts. This provides us with a stronger endorsement of the forecasts f_{1t}. In Section 13.2 we saw that these have smaller mean squared error than the naïve forecasts. We can now assert that there are no real grounds for suspecting that the naïve forecasts contain any useful information not present in f_{1t}.

Comparison of the regression equations 13.3.1 and 13.3.4 suggests that it is possible to test simultaneously for Mincer-Zarnowitz efficiency and conditional efficiency. Consider the regression of the observations X_t on the pair of forecasts (f_{1t}, f_{2t})

$$X_t = \alpha + \beta_1 f_{1t} + \beta_2 f_{2t} + \epsilon_t \qquad (13.3.5)$$

Then, it follows from our definitions that the forecasts f_{1t} are both Mincer-Zarnowitz efficient and conditionally efficient with respect to the forecasts f_{2t} if and only if $\alpha = 0$, $\beta_1 = 1$, and $\beta_2 = 0$. It is required then to test the null hypothesis

$$H_0: \alpha = 0, \quad \beta_1 = 1, \quad \beta_2 = 0$$

This is achieved through fitting by least squares the regression equation 13.3.5. As before, let S_1 denote the sum of squared errors of the forecasts f_{1t}. Also, denote by S_3 the sum of squared residuals from the fitted regression 13.3.5, so that

$$S_3 = \sum_{t=1}^{n} (X_t - a - b_1 f_{1t} - b_2 f_{2t})^2$$

where a, b_1, and b_2 are the least squares estimates of the parameters α, β_1, and β_2. The test of our null hypothesis is then based on the statistic

$$F = \frac{(S_1 - S_3)/3}{S_3/(n - 3)} \qquad (13.3.6)$$

The null hypothesis that the forecasts f_{1t} are both Mincer-Zarnowitz efficient and conditionally efficient with respect to the forecasts f_{2t} is rejected if the statistic 13.3.6 is bigger than tabulated significance levels of the F-distribution with $(3, n - 3)$ degrees of freedom.

Applying this test to the data of Tables 13.1 and 13.2, we use, as before,

$$S_1 = 1,205$$

The fitted least squares regression 13.3.5 is

$$X_t = \underset{(38.18)}{41.04} + \underset{(0.316)}{0.635 f_{1t}} + \underset{(0.290)}{0.194 f_{2t}}$$

The sum of squared residuals from this fitted regression is

$$S_3 = 1,087.5$$

Hence, the test statistic 13.3.6 is

$$F = \frac{(1,205 - 1,087.5)/3}{1,087.5/17} = 0.61$$

Since the tabulated 5% point of the F-distribution with $(3, 17)$ degrees of freedom is 3.20, the evidence against the null hypothesis that the forecasts f_{1t} are both Mincer-Zarnowitz efficient and conditionally efficient with respect to the forecasts f_{2t} is very weak. No serious indicators of inefficiencies of these sorts in the forecasts f_{1t} are apparent. Certainly, this is good news for the producers of these forecasts. If a set of forecasts turns out not to be conditionally efficient with respect to some competitor, this suggests that some modification of the forecast generating mechanism is desirable. One possibility is to simply combine the two sets of forecasts in the future. Alternatively, a thorough review of the model or mechanism used to derive the original forecasts might be carried out. This could suggest either some alternative procedure, or some elaboration of that currently in operation. Unfortunately, conditional efficiency of one set of forecasts with respect to another tells us little about how well our forecasts would compare with other possible competitors. In this sense, the concepts of forecast efficiency discussed here are quite restrictive. All we achieve from our test based on the regression 13.3.5 is an assessment of whether the forecasts f_{1t} are most efficient in the class $(\alpha + \beta_1 f_{1t} + \beta_2 f_{2t})$, where α, β_1, and β_2 are any fixed numbers. In practice, then, it is important to evaluate forecasts through comparison with the most serious alternatives that the analyst can find.

In line with our earlier discussion, tests of conditional efficiency based on the ordinary least squares fits of the regressions 13.3.4 and 13.3.5 are only strictly valid for one-step ahead forecasts, where the error terms are not autocorrelated. For series of consecutive h-steps ahead forecasts it would be necessary to modify this approach by allowing the error terms of the regression equations to follow moving average models of order $(h - 1)$. Typically, this requires longer series of forecasts than will be available to the analyst.

As we have already suggested, frequently forecasts derived from sophisticated and expensive exercises, such as the construction of large econometric models, are evaluated through comparison with benchmark predictions obtained from relatively straightforward time series extrapolation methods. Examples of this type of study include Nelson (1972), Cooper and Nelson (1975), Longbottom and Holly (1985), Nelson and Peck (1985), Brodie and De Kluyver (1987), and Clemen and Guerard (1989). Often the comparison is not simply in terms of observed mean squared error, for one could not really be very satisfied with the results of an expensive exercise unless it yields forecasts that are conditionally efficient with respect to the benchmark extrapolations. Thus, the fitting of regressions such as 13.3.4 and 13.3.5 has been found to be particularly valuable in assessing the success of major forecasting exercises.

13.4 A PLETHORA OF EVALUATION CRITERIA

We began this chapter by urging the importance of the evaluation of forecasts, having little doubt that the great majority of readers would readily agree with us on this score. Indeed, perhaps the most natural reaction to our claim that forecast evaluation is well worthwhile would be: "Yes, of course. How is it done?" Our answer to this question may be frustrating, for there is no single right, or indeed wholly satisfactory, way to go in the evaluation of forecasts. In practical evaluation exercises, many different criteria have been applied, and most of these are capable of yielding useful information on forecast quality. Some further possibilities are outlined by Stekler (1991).

In previous sections of this chapter we have introduced some of the most widely used and generally useful of these criteria. In practice, it will typically be best to base forecast evaluation on a range of different types of information, rather than on the calculation of a single statistic aimed at providing a definitive measure of prediction quality. No such statistic is available, and it is for this reason that a multitude of evaluation criteria have been proposed and implemented.

To a certain extent, the criteria that will be most relevant will differ from one problem to another. In part this may occur because different cost of error functions are appropriate for different problems. Also, the goals of forecasting will differ from one exercise to another. Certainly "accuracy," broadly defined, will always be critical, but this must be balanced against the costs of forecasting, and assessed in the context of what is realistically attainable. Some forecasting exercises require the routine prediction of very large numbers of time series. Considerable individual attention to each series will not be feasible, and probably not justifiable in a cost-benefit sense. On the other hand, there are forecasting problems for which additional accuracy is well worth having, and on which considerable efforts are spent. It is reasonable to demand far more stringent criteria of forecast adequacy in the latter case than in the former. Stekler (1987) discusses yet a different problem, where large numbers of alternative forecasts of the same quantity are available.

In the case of routine forecasting exercises, where relatively little special attention can be paid to each individual series, it may be sufficient to calculate forecast mean squared errors, or similar measures based on appropriate cost of error functions, to check whether the forecasts are sufficiently accurate for the task at hand. It might also be worthwhile to check whether simple, easily implemented modifications can improve forecast accuracy. For example, one-step errors could be checked for autocorrelation. Also, Mincer-Zarnowitz efficiency can be checked, or, equivalently, Theil's decomposition of forecast mean squared error computed. Comparison with some simple naïve alternative might also be useful, since in this context it may turn out that such a naïve predictor is preferable to what is currently being used.

When it is thought sufficiently important to spend much effort on the production of accurate forecasts of a times series, it should also be worthwhile to enquire more closely as to whether more can be done by modifying the current system, or perhaps abandoning it altogether in favor of another that promises more success. This suggests more stringent standards for forecast evaluation. Effort should be spent in developing credible alternative forecasts for comparison, and the analyst should not be satisfied merely to beat these competitors. Rather, the tougher requirement of conditional efficiency should be checked. Any shortcomings detected may suggest possible improvements for the future. For example, suppose that forecasts are developed through a sophisticated system of econometric equations, over whose construction some pain was taken. These predictions could be compared with alternatives based on some time series approach—perhaps involving the prediction of a series from just its own past. The ARIMA model-building methods of Chapter 7 have been found to provide quite healthy competition in this context. If the econometric model forecasts are not conditionally efficient with respect to the ARIMA forecasts, it is possible that either the dynamic specification or the assumed error structure of the model is at fault. This can be carefully checked, and any necessary modifications made.

This chapter has had two themes. First, it is important to evaluate forecasts. Predictions should not be filed away and forgotten after they are made. It is important to keep records, and to compare forecasts with eventual outcomes. Second, a number of procedures for forecast evaluation are available, the most appropriate depending on the problem context.

EXERCISES

13.1 We have analyzed the forecasts of Table 13.1. Consider now, based on these data, the actual and predicted changes in this time series.

(a) (i)   Plot a graph of predicted change against actual change.
     (ii) Find the sample correlation between predicted change and actual change.
     (iii) Fit by least squares the regression of actual change on predicted change.

(b) Compare the results in part (a) with those found in this chapter relating actual and predicted levels.

13.2 The table shows 21 observations and one-step forecasts for the last 20 of these.

t	X_t	f_{1t}	t	X_t	f_{1t}
0	1,275		11	821	711
1	1,204	1,132	12	910	843
2	1,053	1,150	13	874	892
3	972	1,021	14	964	883
4	850	811	15	893	915
5	619	759	16	1,014	972
6	523	501	17	1,047	1,136
7	575	493	18	1,192	1,257
8	584	525	19	1,073	1,240
9	793	618	20	1,060	1,013
10	772	799			

(a) Find and interpret the mean squared error, root mean squared error, mean absolute error, and mean absolute percentage error for these forecasts.

(b) Compare these forecasts with naive "no change" forecasts through Theil's U statistic.

(c) Find and interpret Theil's decomposition of mean squared forecast error.

(d) Estimate the linear regression of X_t on f_{1t} and discuss your findings. Include an interpretation of the coefficient of determination and the Durbin-Watson statistic, and test for Mincer-Zarnowitz efficiency.

(e)   Let f_{2t} denote the series of naive "no change" forecasts. Test whether the forecasts f_{1t} are conditionally efficient with respect to the forecasts f_{2t} by considering weighted averages of these two sets of forecasts.

(f)   Test jointly for Mincer-Zarnowitz efficiency and conditional efficiency of the forecasts f_{1t} with respect to the forecasts f_{2t}.

13.3   Discuss the relevance of the combination of forecasts to forecast evaluation. Illustrate your answer by analyzing the data of Table 12.1.

13.4   The table shows 26 observations and one-step forecasts for the last 25 of these.

t	X_t	f_{1t}	t	X_t	f_{1t}
0	725		13	853	897
1	876	782	14	692	823
2	925	943	15	714	651
3	978	991	16	784	720
4	1,281	1,039	17	851	870
5	962	1,093	18	796	809
6	954	901	19	758	723
7	897	853	20	592	694
8	951	911	21	650	672
9	992	999	22	751	683
10	798	903	23	723	690
11	711	759	24	701	718
12	790	743	25	991	753

(a)   Find and interpret the mean squared error, root mean squared error, mean absolute error, and mean absolute percentage error for these forecasts.

(b)   Compare these forecasts with naive "no change" forecasts through Theil's U statistic.

(c)   Find and interpret Theil's decomposition of mean squared forecast error.

(d)   Plot a graph of actual values against forecasts, and interpret the resulting picture.

(e)   Estimate the regression of X_t on f_{1t} and discuss your findings.

(f)   Let f_{2t} denote the series of naive "no change" forecasts. Test whether the forecasts f_{1t} are conditionally efficient with respect to the forecasts f_{2t} by considering weighted averages of these two sets of forecasts.

(g)   Test jointly for Mincer-Zarnowitz efficiency and conditional efficiency of the forecasts f_{1t} with respect to the forecasts f_{2t}.

13.5   Optimally, the errors for h-steps ahead forecasts should follow a moving average model of order $(h - 1)$. Explain why this is so, and discuss the consequences for forecast evaluation.

13.6   In the regression

$$X_t = \alpha + \beta f_t + \epsilon_t$$

the least squares estimates of α and β are

$$b = \frac{\sum (f_t - \bar{f})(X_t - \bar{X})}{\sum (f_t - \bar{f})^2}$$

and

$$a = \bar{X} - b\bar{f}$$

(a)   Show that $b = 1$ if and only if

$$S_f = rS_x$$

where S_f and S_x are the forecast and actual standard deviations, and r is the correlation between the predicted and actual values.

(b)   Show that, if $b = 1$, $a = 0$ if and only if

$$\bar{X} = \bar{f}$$

(c)   Hence show that the bias proportion and regression proportion, UM and UR, in Theil's decomposition are both zero if and only if $a = 0$ and $b = 1$.

13.7   Consider the regression of X_t on f_t (equation 13.3.1), and the notation (equations 13.2.1 through 13.2.3) of Theil's decomposition.

(a)   Show that the sum of squared residuals from the fitted regression 13.3.1 can be written

$$S_2 = \sum_{t=1}^{n} (X_t - a - bf_t)^2 = nS_x^2(1 - r^2)$$

(b)   Hence show that the statistic 13.3.2 for testing Mincer-Zarnowitz efficiency can be written

$$F = \frac{(S_1 - S_2)/2}{S_2/(n-2)} = \frac{(n-2)}{2} \left[\frac{UM + UR}{1 - UM - UR} \right]$$

13.8   Refer to the data of Exercise 2 of Chapter 7, showing 120 observations on soybean meal price. Hold out the last 20 observations for forecasting purposes. Fit an ARIMA model to the first 100 observations, and use the fitted model to generate series of forecasts one-step ahead, two-steps ahead, and so on. Evaluate these forecasts.

13.9 Refer to the data of Exercise 21 of Chapter 7, showing 168 observations on newspaper advertising. Hold out the last 24 observations for forecasting purposes. Fit a seasonal ARIMA model to the first 144 observations, and use the fitted model to generate series of forecasts one-step ahead, two-steps ahead, and so on. Evaluate these forecasts, including a comparison with Holt-Winters forecasts of this series.

13.10 Refer to the data of Exercise 12.10, showing forecasts of the U.S. unemployment rate. Compare the mean squared errors of the two sets of forecasts f_{2t} and f_{3t}. Is either of these conditionally efficient with respect to the other?

13.11 Refer to the data of Exercise 12.11, showing forecasts of growth rates in U.S. gross national product. Compare the mean squared errors of the two sets of forecasts f_{4t} and f_{5t}. Is either of these conditionally efficient with respect to the other?

13.12 Suppose that you had available two sets of forecasts—one derived from a regression model and one from an ARIMA model. After further analysis, you find that neither of these forecasts is conditionally efficient with respect to the other. How would you react?

SELECTED BIBLIOGRAPHY

Ahlburg, D. A. (1984). Forecast evaluation and improvement using Theil's decomposition. *Journal of Forecasting, 3,* 345–351.

Boothe, P., & D. Glassman (1987). Comparing exchange rate forecasting models: Accuracy versus profitability. *International Journal of Forecasting, 3,* 65–79.

Brodie R. J., & C. A. De Kluyver (1987). A comparison of the short term forecasting accuracy of econometric and naïve extrapolation models of market share. *International Journal of Forecasting, 3,* 423–437.

Carbone, R., & J. S. Armstrong (1982). Evaluation of extrapolative forecasting methods. *Journal of Forecasting, 1,* 215–217.

Clemen, R. T., & J. B. Guerard (1989). Econometric GNP forecasts: incremental information relative to naive extrapolation. *International Journal of Forecasting, 5,* 417–426.

Cooper, J. P., & C. R. Nelson (1975). The ex-ante prediction performance of the St. Louis and FRB-MIT-Penn. econometric models and some results on composite predictors. *Journal of Money, Credit & Banking, 7,* 1–32.

Einhorn, H. J., & R. M. Hogarth (1982). Prediction, diagnosis, and causal thinking in forecasting. *Journal of Forecasting, 1,* 23–36.

Granger, C. W. J. (1969). Prediction with a generalized cost of error function. *Operational Research Quarterly, 20,* 199–207.

Granger, C. W. J. & P. Newbold (1973). Some comments on the evaluation of economic forecasts. *Applied Economics, 5,* 35–47.

Granger, C. W. J., & P. Newbold (1986). *Forecasting Economic Time Series* (2nd ed.). Orlando, Fl.: Academic Press.

Kling, J. L. (1987). Predicting the turning points of business and economic time series. *Journal of Business, 60,* 201–238.

Longbottom, J. A., & S. Holly (1985). The role of time series analysis in the evaluation of econometric models. *Journal of Forecasting, 4,* 75–87.

Mincer, J., & V. Zarnowitz (1969). The evaluation of economic forecasts. In J. Mincer (ed.). *Economic Forecasts and Expectations.* New York: National Bureau of Economic Research.

Nelson, C. R. (1972). The prediction performance of the FRB-MIT-Penn. model of the U.S. economy. *American Economic Review, 62,* 902–917.

Nelson, C. R., & S. C. Peck (1985). The NERC fan: A retrospective analysis of the NERC summary forecasts. *Journal of Business and Economic Statistics, 3,* 179–187.

Stekler, H. O. (1987). Who forecasts better? *Journal of Business and Economic Statistics, 5,* 155–158.

Stekler, H. O. (1991). Macroeconomic forecast evaluation techniques. *International Journal of Forecasting, 7,* 375–384.

Theil, H. (1958). *Economic Forecasts and Policy.* Amsterdam: North Holland.

Theil, H. (1966). *Applied Economic Forecasting.* Amsterdam: North Holland.

Zellner, A. (1986). Biased predictors, rationality and the evaluation of forecasts. *Economics Letters, 21,* 45–48.

14 An Overview of Business Forecasting Methods

14.1 THE IMPORTANCE OF METHODOLOGY

We began the first chapter of this book with a section on The Importance of Forecasting. It is not our intention to preach that message again here; the unconverted reader presumably would not have come this far. Taking the importance of forecasting as established, the bulk of this book is devoted to an account of various approaches to prediction that can be used or adapted to attack real business and economic problems. We also stressed in the first chapter, and at a number of points subsequently, that there is no such thing as the forecasting problem, and consequently no such thing as the right way to forecast. All forecasting problems have unique characteristics, so that the forecaster is obliged to think carefully about how best to approach their solution. That, however, is far from saying that there can be no worthwhile body of knowledge and understanding with which the forecaster should be familiar. It is certainly not necessary to reinvent the wheel on each occasion a new forecasting problem is met.

The position of the forecaster is a little like that of the coach of a football team. Each opponent will provide a distinct challenge. Each will have its own strengths and weaknesses, and each will attempt particular and somewhat novel strategies in the course of a game. Nevertheless, the coach will have prepared for the season by developing a playbook, and specific challenges in a game will be met by what it is hoped will be appropriate selections from the playbook. The bulk of the material introduced in this volume can be regarded as forming the foundation for a forecaster's playbook. The practical forecaster should be able to select, and perhaps refine, one of the approaches discussed here to usefully attack a very wide range of forecasting problems.

Our position is not that a single approach to all forecasting problems is desirable, or even sensible, but that a *methodical* attack on a particular problem should be rewarding. There is a methodology, or set of methodologies, useful for forecasting. The methods we have outlined in this book have proved useful in a great many real world forecasting applications. It is therefore incumbent on the forecaster to understand these methods, so as to be in a position to reliably conjecture which might be most appropriate for a particular practical problem, and what, if any, modifications or elaborations of the chosen method may be desirable. Having recognized the uniqueness of individual forecasting problems, it is equally important to recognize the importance of methodology.

We said a little in Chapter 11 about purely judgmental approaches to forecasting, but concentrated most attention in this book on more formal forecasting methodologies, particularly regression, exponential smoothing, and ARIMA models. We did so in part because we felt more qualified to introduce the reader to these formal methods than to instill the capacity for sound judgment. Additionally, however, we believe strongly in the value of a methodological approach to forecasting. Such an approach allows, and indeed should force, the forecaster to think in a disciplined way about the problem at hand. Thus, the goal should not be to force a particular formal solution algorithm onto a specific problem. Rather, the forecaster should define the important features of a problem, determine what general methodological approaches are available for attacking problems with such features, determine which assumptions behind these approaches are appropriate and, if they are not, determine whether or not suitable modifications can be made. We do not pretend that it will always be easy to answer all these questions, but do assert the value of a framework in which they can be asked. In employing a particular forecasting algorithm, the forecaster is taking a view about the way the world, or at least that part of immediate interest, behaves. The importance of a forecasting methodology lies precisely in the formalization of a view of the world. If this view seems hopelessly unrealistic, the forecaster is still left with a framework into which realism might be introduced.

Most of our discussion has concentrated on what particular forecasting methods can do. A proper understanding of these methods should render the forecaster equally aware of what they cannot do. To take just one example, the Holt-Winters exponential smoothing algorithms have proved extremely useful for routine short-term forecasting of seasonal time series. However, they are no more than attempts to employ recent past patterns of evolution to make sensible conjectures about likely future patterns. If the investigator knows of other important determinants of future behavior, or strongly suspects that for some reason important changes in behavior patterns will emerge, the basic Holt-Winters algorithms will not be a sensible choice for forecasting. It is in this sense that we have urged the importance of thinking simultaneously about both methodology and the features of the specific forecasting problem at hand.

14.2 THE IMPORTANCE OF UNDERSTANDING METHODOLOGY AND DATA

We begin with a true story: All names have been omitted to protect the guilty. Not too long ago, one of us was called by a former student, who had ventured into the real world. He asked for information about a certain forecasting method, whose details had not been well-documented in the literature. It emerged from the discussion that this request was prompted by his boss, who had purchased a computer package based on this method and had attempted to implement that package to conduct an important forecasting function in the organization. The obvious suggestion, of course, was to ask his boss for the necessary information. However, it turned out that this individual had only the haziest notion of how forecasts were generated by the computer package, and even less idea of why. We have no way of assessing how common is this story. We hope that such cases are rare, but fear that they are far from unique.

It might be argued that in order to drive an automobile one does not need to understand the intricate technical details of how and why it works. Nevertheless, a general understanding is certainly useful, and complete ignorance is positively dangerous. Successful business forecasting is considerably more difficult than successfully driving an automobile: The road ahead is far less clearly marked. It would certainly be convenient, except possibly for authors of books such as this, if there existed a single all-purpose algorithm, suitable for application, without the necessity of thought, to every forecasting problem. However, as we have been at pain to stress, this is not, and cannot be, the case. In the real world, forecasting problems of quite diverse characteristics are met, calling for quite different solution approaches. A procedure that works well for one problem may perform quite poorly for another. Therefore it is essential that the forecaster exercise sound judgment when deciding how to attack a particular problem. Such judgment, of course, necessarily requires an understanding of the various methodological approaches to forecasting. It is essential to understand both what can be and what cannot be accomplished within a particular methodological framework. Virtually all of the forecasting methods discussed in this text have been programmed, and the computer packages are quite widely available. However, possession of such a package is certainly not an adequate substitute for an understanding of the underlying methodology. Certainly such packages are convenient tools for carrying out tedious arithmetic calculations, but they are no more than that.

We have perhaps stressed the obvious. If one is to analyze data, familiarity with the methodological tools of analysis is an essential prerequisite. The desirability of familiarity with the data themselves is perhaps equally obvious. Yet, we have frequently seen data fed through standard algorithms with little or no regard for any possible peculiarities in the numbers. In forecasting, as in other areas of applied statistics, the importance of a careful look at the data before any intricate technical analysis is attempted cannot be stressed too heavily. As a minimum, a graph of a time series should be examined prior to further analysis. Does such a graph suggest any unusual data points, and if so can an explanation for these aberrant values be found? Such unusual points can exert quite a strong influence on data analysis through the standard methods, which might consequently yield implausible conclusions. Again, following analysis, it is good practice to study residuals from a fitted model, or in-sample one-step ahead forecast errors. Unusually large values can suggest the presence of extreme data points. It may be desirable to clip such observations, rendering them more nearly normal before applying the standard analytical tools. One possible procedure for doing so was suggested in Section 5.6.

Many practitioners, discussing the art of forecasting, have drawn attention to the havoc that can be caused by difficult data points, or apparent abrupt changes in structure. This issue is raised by Jenkins (1982), Brown (1982), and Klein (1984), writing from otherwise quite different perspectives. Indeed, Brown strikes a nerve in claiming that many time series met in the real world are quite different from those found in textbooks! It is certainly true that authors, such as ourselves, have the luxury of choosing from a great many possible examples. Almost inevitably, the examples that get into the books are "textbook examples," in the sense of being relatively free from complications. It is not that we prefer to attack easy problems, but cogent exposition does dictate that straightforward application of the methodology being illustrated should be more or less appropriate for the data at hand. Of course, the real world does throw up the kind of data sets that would never find their way into textbooks, though not, in our experience, as frequently as Brown claims. Just what can and should be done in such circumstances depends on the problem context. Ideally, the causes of unusual data points should be sought, and, where possible, these causes should be explicitly modeled. Often this is infeasible, in which case a certain amount of judicious clipping will generally be preferable to the routine analysis of the raw data through some algorithm that was not designed to handle such data. This approach is quite informal, but no less valuable for that.

14.3   THE IMPORTANCE OF JUDGMENT

In this book we have concentrated heavily on forecasting methods. As we stressed in the previous section, a good understanding of these methods is essential for the forecaster. Sensibly applied, they should provide an excellent foundation for approaching a broad range of different forecasting problems. In Chapter 11 we devoted just a small amount of space to a discussion of purely judgmental forecasting procedures. In part, this rather cursory treatment resulted from the fact that we felt we had relatively little to say about the sound exercise of human judgment. Obviously sound judgment is preferable to unsound, and, to a certain extent, it is a capacity accumulated through experience. However, our concentration on more formal approaches to forecasting was also dictated partly by our belief in the virtues of formalization. The discipline of thinking about a problem within a formal framework should persuade the forecaster to carefully consider what is being implicitly assumed about the world, and the extent to which these assumptions are appropriate for the problem at hand. We are deeply suspicious of the subject matter "expert" who claims to be able to predict purely through informal contemplation, based in some mysterious fashion on his or her own "expertise" and experience. Certainly, we have seen very successful forecasts achieved in this manner, but we have also seen very poor ones! Given the nature of the world, it is inevitable that, at some time or another, forecasts will go wrong. When forecasts are based exclusively on subjective judgment, it is difficult, if not impossible, to trace the source of serious errors. This is far less difficult when forecasts are based on a formal model, whose assumptions are clearly spelled out. The sensible forecaster will attempt to understand the causes of past errors to learn more about the system, exploiting the knowledge gained in the production of better forecasts in the future.

In addition to our discussion of Chapter 11, we have alluded at various places in this book to the importance of judgment. We feel, however, that the message in these passing references may have been drowned in the mass of technical detail about various forecasting methodologies. It is important therefore to set the record straight here. The successful practical forecaster is not a mere technocrat. It is important that the application of sophisticated methodological tools be associated with sensible judgment. One aspect of the necessity for sound judgment was discussed in the previous section. However sophisticated the tools at the forecaster's command, it is necessary to think carefully about the features of the problem under investigation before selecting and adapting a methodology for its solution. There is no solution algorithm—no formula into which one can substitute—for making this selection. In short, judgment based on an understanding of the methodological tools available, the problem context, and the available data, is essential. We are aware of attempts to develop "expert systems" for forecasting, aimed at relieving the analyst of the burden of thought, but we are not convinced of their potential worth.

Suppose that a formal methodological approach has been appropriately chosen for attacking a forecasting problem. Many of the procedures discussed in previous chapters of this book will then produce an answer without further judgmental intervention. However, expert practitioners almost unanimously agree that, on occasions, *judgmental modification* of formally derived forecasts is likely to be valuable. (See, for example, Jenkins (1982), Brown (1982), Chatfield (1988), and our discussion in Chapter 8 on econometric forecasting.) To understand this, it is useful to think of forecasts as being based on some **information set,** containing all relevant information available at the time predictions are made. Some of this information will undoubtedly be quantitative, and presumably quite readily assimilated by a formal forecasting algorithm or model. However, various sorts of qualitative information may be less amenable to such formal analysis. That is certainly not grounds for ignoring this type of information. One possible approach is to proceed with the formal derivation of forecasts, but to consider modifying these forecasts judgmentally if expert opinion suggests the desirability of such a course. Such modifications will typically be made informally, often in a meeting between the forecasters who know what information is already incorporated into the formal forecasts, and subject matter experts whose insights may lead to the consideration of other relevant factors.

This marriage—generally a loosely structured marriage of convenience—between formal analysis and informal expert judgment represents the best practice in modern business forecasting. In a sense, its appeal is obvious. That judgment and technology should be happily married in this way accords with our intuition. However, Jenkins (1982) offers some words of caution. We can all agree, *in principle*, that sound judgment should be valuable in forecasting. That, however, is a far cry from claiming that, *in practice*, the "expert" judgment that is actually available really will be sound. If forecasts are to be modified in this way, it is sensible to *monitor* forecast performance to check whether in fact more good than harm is being accomplished through the modifications. The intuitive appeal of judgmental modification should not blind us to its possible dangers. The informal assessments of "experts" may well reflect prejudices and misconceptions as well as informed insights. Just as it is important to check the adequacy of a formal model, it is equally important to assess the practical value of informal modifications to forecasting. As we will stress again in section 14.7 of this chapter, the evaluation of forecasts is extremely important, whatever their source.

14.4   THE BEST FORECASTING METHOD?

The title of this section was provoked by a paper of Chatfield (1988), asking "What is the 'best' method of forecasting?" It is natural that this question be asked, but, in common with Chatfield, we find it impossible to produce a definitive answer. Quite simply, as we have repeatedly stressed, the diversity of characteristics of practically occurring business forecasting problems is such that no single forecasting method will invariably be appropriate, much less best. Indeed, we would go further. Faced with a specific forecasting problem, whose parameters are well defined, an honest analyst is often unable to assert with any great certainty that a particular methodological approach will be best. It should be possible to propose one or two potentially fruitful lines of attack, but a certain amount of experimentation in trying out these alternatives will often prove useful.

Of course, as authors of a textbook on business forecasting, we have inevitably provided our own partial answer to the question raised here in selecting the topics on which to place more emphasis. We have chosen to emphasize formal quantitative approaches to forecasting, and within that framework have concentrated most heavily on regression methods, exponential smoothing algorithms, and ARIMA models. We do not claim that this choice either reflects brilliant original insight or is likely to provoke great controversy. To the contrary, these three approaches are very much in the mainstream of modern business forecasting, the well-equipped forecaster would be expected to have a good understanding of all of them, and one or another, perhaps suitably modified and adapted, should be appropriate for a very wide range of practical problems. We regard these three approaches as building blocks on which the analysis of many forecasting problems can be sensibly based.

To appreciate the range of problems for which these quantitative methods might prove useful, it is worthwhile to summarize their features in outline. Exponential smoothing algorithms were designed for situations where short-term forecasts of a very large number of time series were routinely and regularly required, as in product sales forecasting for inventory control. It is for this purpose that they are most suited. Forecasts of future values of a time series are computed exclusively on the basis of current and past values of the series, through computationally efficient algorithms requiring a minimum of costly expert intervention. By contrast with the model builder, the exponential smoother takes no explicit view of the way the world evolves; rather, the various exponential smoothing algorithms have been developed as intuitively plausible prediction tools for projecting behavior of such characteristics as trend and seasonality in a time series. The exponential smoother typically does not think of the resulting forecasts of individual time series as best in the usual sense, but sees these algorithms as capable of generating good, if not optimal, forecasts for the great majority of members of a large class of time series. Nevertheless, it is interesting to note, as we did in Chapter 9, that specific exponential smoothing algorithms do yield optimal forecasts when time series are generated by particular models. Just these models, or something quite close to them, often emerge as appropriate when a model-building exercise is applied to business and economic time series. It is this fact that accounts for the practical success of exponential smoothing, and hence for the continued popularity of this simple approach to forecasting.

The ARIMA model-building approach to forecasting, developed by Box and Jenkins, also predicts a time series from its past history, though as noted in Chapter 9 it can be extended to incorporate other information also. This possibility for extension constitutes an advantage over exponential smoothing. As we saw in Chapter 7, the ARIMA model builder contemplates a wide range of possible models that might have generated a particular time series, and then uses the available data in a systematic way to determine an apparently appropriate model. By contrast with the routine application of an exponential smoothing algorithm, ARIMA model building requires the careful study of the characteristics of the observed data, leading to a prediction algorithm tailored specifically to those characteristics. Consequently, ARIMA model building is more labor intensive, and therefore more costly, than exponential smoothing. The payoff should be that the analyst has reasonable grounds for confidence that the prediction algorithm employed ought to be suitable for the specific problem at hand, by contrast with the more vague assurance that exponential smoothing generally yields adequate forecasts. Satisfactory results, *in the aggregate*, from the application of exponential smoothing would not at all deter us from a marked preference for ARIMA analysis in any *individual* application that was at all important, as for example if we had to bet our own money on the outcome. After all, the time series at hand might be one of those for which exponential smoothing turned out to be far from optimal.

Regression analysis also concentrates on formal model building, but here the primary focus of interest is in relationships among variables rather than the description of historical patterns in a single variable. To the extent that such relationships can make an important contribution to the quality of forecasts, regression methods of one sort or another become valuable, though as we stressed in Chapter 9 regression and ARIMA models need not be viewed as competitors: It is possible to construct models incorporating the features of both. The forecaster is likely to move away from single series time series methods, such as those of Chapters 6 and 7, when subject matter theory suggests strong relationships of interest and relevant data for the modeling of these relationships are available. It must be emphasized, however, that the possession of an elaborate theory, such as those that give rise to the sophisticated econometric models of Chapter 8, does not excuse the analyst from concern about the time series properties of the data. The intimate connection between forecasting and time cannot be broken by theory. Among other consequences of this assertion is the importance of the careful specification of the time series structure of the error terms in a regression equation. One other consideration—the horizon at which forecasts are required—might influence the choice between a behavioral model and a simpler single series approach to forecasting. In business and economic problems, broadly speaking, the importance of uncovering relationships becomes more pronounced the further ahead one wants to forecast. Consider the following example: In the United States, for reasons that to us are neither clear nor convincing, money supply figures are published weekly. From time to time these weekly announcements have caused considerable interest on Wall Street. (At other times, the "sages of the Street" have been especially preoccupied with monthly balance of trade figures.) Now, economic theory certainly has something to say about the determinants of the growth in money, but such theory necessarily involves longer run relationships, and has little or nothing to say about the determinants of change from one week to the next. Thus, even were other relevant economic data available on a weekly basis, we would prefer single series methods for predicting money supply a week or two ahead. However, regression models should be potentially much more valuable if forecasts were required a year or two ahead.

A number of authors have attacked the question posed in this section by organizing forecasting competitions among various methods. Often these have involved applying a number of methods to just a very few forecasting problems, so that any generalization beyond these problems is unreasonable. Those that have analyzed a large number of problems, including Newbold and Granger (1974), Reid (1975), Makridakis and Hibon (1979), and Makridakis, et al. (1982), have concentrated on procedures for forecasting a time series from its own past. These exercises are certainly not without value, but their findings have not been as clear cut as one might have hoped, and indeed these results are subject to a range of interpretations. We agree with the conclusion of Chatfield (1988) that these competitions raise about as many questions as they answer. Certainly, we know of no experienced forecasters whose prior preferences (prejudices?) have been altered as a result. One difficulty is that, for those methods that demand some judgment or skill in application, the competitions may be assessing the abilities of particular practitioners as much as the worth of the methods.

14.5 THE IMPORTANCE OF THE FORECASTER

It is sometimes suggested, tongue in cheek, that forecasting is the second oldest profession. More seriously, we would urge that forecasting is, and should be, a profession. Taking as common ground the importance of forecasts in business decision making, it must be added that the task is too difficult to be safely entrusted to either an amateur or a machine.

Forecasting is an activity requiring knowledge, experience, and sound judgment for its successful practice. The good forecaster is in a position to make a substantial impact on the corporate bottom line. Certainly, anyone can, for a time, accumulate by chance a successful forecasting record—but only for a time. Of course, the well-equipped forecaster cannot expect to enjoy an unbroken string of successes indefinitely. Nevertheless, as in any other profession, genuine expertise is hard won, and pays off in the long run.

The professional forecaster requires all of the following:

1. A good knowledge and understanding of the various technical forecasting methods. By this we mean a great deal more than knowledge of where to locate the relevant computer packages! It is important to understand why particular methods are likely to work well in certain circumstances, and why they are not in others.
2. The ability to communicate with subject matter experts who understand possible sources of data anomalies and can postulate theoretical explanations for developments in the process of interest.
3. A good feel for real data, so as to assess possible changes in structure or unusual observations.
4. The judgment to select, and where necessary appropriately modify, a suitable methodology for attacking a given problem.
5. The ability to weigh the judgments of experts in assessing how, if at all, a prediction derived from some formal quantitative methodology should be subjectively modified.

These qualities are by no means easily acquired. Certainly they cannot all be obtained by simply reading a book! The accumulation of practical experience is at least as important as technical knowledge. No machine today, or in the foreseeable future can match the human expert in these qualities. We believe the world would be poorer if such a machine existed: Undoubtedly, we would be! The professional forecaster is a specialist, who should be consulted on a wide range of problems. Even if one subscribes to the view of a forecasting expert, such as Chatfield (1986), that the simplest methods are generally best, judgment is required for their appropriate application, as well as for identifying those cases in which more is required. Forecasting is both too important and too difficult to be left to managers in other areas as a part-time occupation. Certainly sales managers will have some insight into likely future product demand, for example, but these people will have neither the time nor the inclination to equip themselves with the forecaster's skills. It is for this reason that we are skeptical of such approaches to forecasting as the sales force composite method of Section 11.3.

Indeed, we are skeptical of all purely judgmental approaches to forecasting, and would reject them in all cases where a more formal analysis was feasible. Just as the forecaster with good technical knowledge and no capacity for judgment is incomplete, so is the forecaster who relies excessively on judgment and is deficient in technical knowledge. The complete forecaster is an important member of any organization, with specialist expertise that could be useful in many fields of corporate activity. Like many other specialists—in quality control, for example—the forecaster is in a position to make an appreciable contribution to the success of the organization. It is obviously important that the job be done well. It is less obvious that the job invariably is, or will be, done well. All forecasters are not equally proficient, and talent in this area, as in other specialities, should be eagerly sought, carefully nurtured, and generously rewarded!

14.6   TO MODEL, OR NOT TO MODEL: AN INTERESTING QUESTION?

In this book we have discussed approaches to forecasting through model building, principally regression analysis and ARIMA modeling, and also through *ad hoc* algorithms, particularly exponential smoothing, where no formal model is explicitly built. Although we have made comments at various places on the relative merits of different approaches, it may be useful here to explicitly set out our views on the general merits of these two approaches.

Academic statisticians and university statistics courses, at any level, will differ considerably from one another in emphasis on the importance of various aspects of the subject. This lack of uniformity is entirely healthy, reflecting lively professional debate on directions in the subject. Nevertheless, there is much common ground. Virtually any academic statistician and any university statistics course will stress the role of such basic concepts as the following: uncertainty (as measured by probability statements), random variables, inference (for example: point estimation, confidence intervals, and hypothesis testing), and model building. Now, quantitative forecasting calls for the analysis and interpretation of data, and so is very much in the province of the professional statistician. Yet, in practical business forecasting, prediction is often accomplished through *ad hoc* techniques, such as exponential smoothing, where little or no attention is paid to these concepts viewed by the academic statistician as quite fundamental. (Much the same could be said of practical seasonal adjustment.) Is this observation just another illustration of the folk "wisdom" that the academy is out of touch with the "real world"? Our response to this question can perhaps be anticipated from both our own affiliations and our punctuation of the previous sentence!

There are certainly occasions on which it will be impractical to invoke the heavy artillery of a formal statistical model-building exercise. Sometimes very little relevant data are available. The occasionally witnessed spectacle of subjecting a small data set of dubious quality to complex formal analysis is both unedifying and unrewarding. It is unreasonable to expect to learn much from a sophisticated analysis, whatever its theoretical appeal, of such data. In these circumstances, simpler techniques, preferably supplemented by good judgment, are all that may be warranted. On other occasions, it may be felt that few resources can be afforded for attacking a particular forecasting problem. A case of this sort arises, as we have noted before, in routine sales forecasting, when forecasts for a very large number of time series are required, and little attention can be paid to every individual series. In these circumstances, various *ad hoc* approaches to forecasting can be useful, though it should be added that the forecaster who is unable to devote much effort to a problem ought to be correspondingly sanguine about the likely outcome.

In posing the question of this section, we have in mind those situations where formal model building and the more *ad hoc* methods are both feasible approaches to a forecasting problem. In our judgment, the question of which avenue to follow then is not an interesting one. It is like asking whether or not we should think. The requirement to think is certainly a tiresome inconvenience, but, at least for readers who have read this far through this book, it should generally prove rewarding. This is the essence of our preference for formal model building. The model builder has available a convenient framework for thinking about the characteristics of the problem at hand, and for determining appropriate forecasts on the basis of these characteristics. A range of alternative possible models of the data-generating process can be contemplated, and a particular model chosen on the basis of both empirical evidence and subject matter theory. Reliable statistical techniques are available for the estimation of any unknown parameters in the chosen model, and the adequacy of the achieved model that has been fitted to the available data can be assessed through a range of checks. These checks may suggest the desirability of modifications to, or elaborations of, the initially chosen model. In this way, model building can be viewed as an exercise in learning about the system of interest. The forecaster has available a number of basic model types, such as regression and ARIMA models, that have often proved to be successful forecasting tools. However, perhaps the greatest advantage of model building is the facility for incorporating distinctive problem features through the elaboration of such basic models. We saw some examples of such possibilities in Chapter 10, where we discussed particular elaborations of ARIMA models, allowing for example for calendar effects in seasonal time series.

Any model-building exercise is founded on assumptions about the way the world behaves. These assumptions are explicitly made, so that questions of their validity can readily be raised. It should be clear which factors have been explicitly taken into account in developing the forecasts, and, equally important, it should also be clear which factors have not been taken into account. The careful and thoughtful model builder will often be rewarded with successful forecasts. But the world is not invariably kind, and on occasion poor forecasts will result whatever approach is used. In these cases, the model builder should be far better placed than the *ad hoc* analyst to trace the sources of serious forecasting errors. This too can aid in learning about the system, and may lead to improvements in model specification, and hence in the quality of forecasts in the future.

14.7 COMBINATION AND EVALUATION: NEGLECTED OPTIONS?

Two assertions about business forecasting, made previously, need to be repeated here. First, many problems met in practice are difficult, in the sense that it is hard to achieve forecasts of adequate quality. Second, in particular applications the analyst often will not be in a position to assert with much justified confidence that the methodological approach employed is the best that can be done. The professional forecaster, then, will sometimes face a situation where it is suspected that the forecasts are inadequate and that better results could have been achieved. Poor forecasts, then, should not be met with a shrug of the shoulders and a lecture on the inherent difficulty of the problem. The sensible forecaster will try to learn from past errors, and thus improve future performance.

Two consequences follow from all of this. First, since it is impossible to have complete assurance that any particular method will do well, much less be optimal, in a given application, the possibility is open for the fruitful combination of forecasts derived from different methods or sources. Second, it is important to evaluate the quality of forecasts through comparison with eventual outcomes. We have learned in the last few years about the importance of quality control in a number of aspects of corporate endeavor: Forecasting should be no exception. Our conviction of the importance of the combination and evaluation of forecasts has led us to devote a separate chapter in this book to each of these topics. Both topics have been the subject of some academic interest over the years. However, in our experience, they have been too often neglected by practitioners. In this sense, we would claim that the academy is ahead of the real world, and has something of real value to offer it.

What are the sources of this apparent neglect? Too often, when faced with a forecasting problem, the analyst is tempted to hastily embrace a single methodological approach. This methodology may be a particular favorite of the analyst—one that is quite well understood, with which he or she has enjoyed some measure of success in the past, and for which relevant computing software is readily available. Little or no thought is given to the possibility that alternative approaches, capable of exploiting different information or of employing the same information in a different way, may have something of value to contribute. In short, the focus of the analyst may be too narrow to contemplate the real benefits that can accrue from the combination of forecasts. In the real world, the life of the practitioner is dominated by tasks that must be completed. It is all too easy in this world to view the development of forecasts, or of an algorithm for deriving forecasts, as the completion of a task, that is then forgotten when moving on to other tasks. This is a pity, as the analyst who does not subsequently return to evaluate forecast performance is deprived of a potentially valuable educational experience.

The combination of forecasts is that rare and beautiful entity—a simple, easily understood idea that actually works well in practice. The notion of combining information from different sources has considerable intuitive appeal, the formation of a composite forecast as a weighted average is perfectly straightforward, and the basing of weights on the quality of past forecasts is obviously plausible. The empirical results with which we are familiar from combination exercises of this sort are, to say the least, gratifying. In part these results are explained by the tendency of averaging forecasts together to reduce the chances of very large errors. As we have already noted, this is essentially the same phenomenon as the reduction in the probability of large losses from investment in a portfolio of securities rather than in a single security. The temptation to embrace just a single prediction algorithm, particularly when considerable effort has been spent on its development, is quite understandable. However, the more mature view, as taken by Marriott and Tremayne (1988), recognizes the difficulty of incorporating all relevant problem features in a single model without achieving undesirable complexity. It will often be preferable, rather than working toward some horribly complex model, to try one or two simpler approaches to forecasting, and then combine their results.

If anything, the evaluation of forecasts has been even more neglected by practitioners than the combination of forecasts. Yet, the virtues of evaluation are surely even more transparent than those of combination. It is simply not reasonable for the forecaster to take the attitude that all that can be done has been done, and any serious forecasting errors are merely the consequences of cruel fate. It is unpleasant to dwell on one's errors, but we know of no better way to avoid the repetition of similar errors. The wise forecaster will view evaluation as equally important as the development of the forecasts. We stress that we have in mind here the evaluation of real post-sample forecasts. Certainly, in developing a prediction algorithm, it is useful, for a number of reasons, to look at the behavior of in-sample forecast errors. However, often the development of a forecasting algorithm or model involves a good deal of experimentation, where various alternative specifications are tried. It is often not too difficult, given sufficient ingenuity, to achieve a model that provides a good fit of sample data. The true worth of such a model can, however, only be reliably evaluated through an assessment of its post-sample forecasts.

14.8   Forecasting the Future of Forecasting

We have written a book on forecasting without making any forecasts of consequence. In part, this reflects natural caution. Forecasts of the United States economy that turned out to be hopelessly inaccurate at the time of publication would not do a great deal for our sales! However, here we will depart, in a very modest way, from this strategy.

In writing a book such as this, it is only possible to present a snapshot view of the art and science of business forecasting at one point in time. The subject is, however, a very exciting one. Important developments have been seen in the recent past, and the safest possible prediction is that further such developments will be seen in the future. The following are our own forecasts of the future of forecasting.

1. Developments in computing hardware and software, many of which have recently occurred, will greatly increase the accessibility to practitioners of a whole range of forecasting methods. As we have said

elsewhere, this is, in our view, something of a mixed blessing. In an ideal world, these developments would be entirely beneficial. In the real world, the temptation to employ computer programs as a substitute for thought rather than as a supplement to it is a cause for some concern.

2. The increase in computing power, allied with interest in management information systems, should yield substantial improvements in the scope and quality of data bases available to the forecaster.

3. Following from our first point, it should be a good deal easier in the future for the analyst to experiment with a number of alternative methodologies. This could, in turn, lead to increased interest in the combination of forecasts.

4. Additional computing power should also make it easier to modify the standard methods to deal with specific peculiarities of individual forecasting problems, rather than the routine application of these methods to all problems.

5. The subject of forecasting is one in which *ad hoc* methods are well entrenched, and widely viewed as respectable. The temptation to develop more such methods, particularly given the potential rewards from marketing the associated software, will prove irresistible. Some of these will even prove useful: More will be used. The undisciplined development of prediction algorithms with weak theoretical foundations is inevitable. Sensible forecasters will be properly cautious before embracing these developments.

6. More attention will be paid to the development of methods that attempt to account, in some systematic way, for changes in the structure of the process under study.

7. Inevitably, spectacularly inaccurate forecasts will occasionally be made, even by expert practitioners. Equally inevitably, some of these will receive far more press coverage than the many more relatively accurate forecasts that are made.

8. In some areas, notably those connected with financial markets, there will be a great many forecasters. Some of these, if only by chance, will enjoy for a time an impressive track record. These people will come to be regarded as having almost mystical powers, and their future utterances will be treated far more seriously than any objective assessment of their methods would warrant. Following these "gurus" could prove expensive.

9. Forecasting will come to be viewed by business as a critically important activity. Professional forecasters will enjoy enhanced status in their organizations. They will become truly knowledgeable experts, and will be seen and rewarded as such. This is more optimistic conjecture than honest forecasting, but is a good note on which to end.

SELECTED BIBLIOGRAPHY

Brown, R. G. (1982). The balance of effort in forecasting. *Journal of Forecasting, 1,* 49–53.

Chatfield, C. (1986). Simple is best? *International Journal of Forecasting, 2,* 401–402.

Chatfield, C. (1988). What is the 'best' method of forecasting? *Journal of Applied Statistics, 15,* 19–38.

DeRoeck, R. (1991). Is there a gap between forecasting theory and practice? A personal view. *International Journal of Forecasting, 7,* 1–2.

Fildes, R. (1992). Influencing forecasting practice. *International Journal of Forecasting, 8,* 1–2.

Jenkins, G. M. (1982). Some practical aspects of forecasting in organizations. *Journal of Forecasting, 1,* 3–21.

Klein, L. R. (1984). The importance of the forecast. *Journal of Forecasting, 3,* 1–9.

Makridakis, S. (1991). Forecasting in the 21st century. *International Journal of Forecasting, 7,* 123–126.

Makridakis, S., A. Andersen, R. Carbone, R. Fildes, M. Hibon, R. Lewandowski, J. Newton, E. Parzen, & R. Winkler (1982). The accuracy of extrapolation (time series) methods: Results of a forecasting competition. *Journal of Forecasting, 1,* 111–153.

Makridakis, S., & M. Hibon (1979). Accuracy of forecasting: An empirical investigation. *Journal of Royal Statistical Society A, 142,* 97–145.

Marriott, J. M., & A. R. Tremayne (1988). Alternative statistical approaches to time series modelling for forecasting purposes. *The Statistician, 37,* 187–197.

Newbold, P., & C. W. J. Granger (1974). Experience with forecasting univariate time series and the combination of forecasts. *Journal of Royal Statistical Society A, 137,* 131–165.

Reid, D. J. (1975). A review of short-term projection techniques. In H. A. Gordon (Ed.), *Practical Aspects of Forecasting.* London: Operational Research Society.

Schultz, R. L. (1992). Fundamental aspects of forecasting in organizations. *International Journal of Forecasting, 7,* 409–411.

Appendix
Statistical Tables

TABLE A.1   Standard Normal Distribution
Let Z be a standard normal random variable. For selected
probabilities α, the table gives numbers Z_α, such that
$\alpha = P(Z > Z_\alpha)$.

α	.50	.40	.30	.20	.10	.05	.025	.010	.005
Z_α	0.000	0.253	0.524	0.842	1.282	1.645	1.960	2.326	2.576

TABLE A.2   Student's t Distribution
Let t_v be a Student's t random variable with v degrees of freedom.
For selected probabilities α, the table gives numbers $t_{v,\alpha}$, such that
$\alpha = P(t_v > t_{v,\alpha})$.

v	α				
	.100	.050	.025	.010	.005
1	3.078	6.314	12.706	31.821	63.657
2	1.886	2.920	4.303	6.965	9.925
3	1.638	2.353	3.182	4.541	5.841
4	1.533	2.132	2.776	3.747	4.604
5	1.476	2.015	2.571	3.365	4.032
6	1.440	1.943	2.447	3.143	3.707
7	1.415	1.895	2.365	2.998	3.499
8	1.397	1.860	2.306	2.896	3.355
9	1.383	1.833	2.262	2.821	3.250
10	1.372	1.812	2.228	2.764	3.169
11	1.363	1.796	2.201	2.718	3.106
12	1.356	1.782	2.179	2.681	3.055
13	1.350	1.771	2.160	2.650	3.012
14	1.345	1.761	2.145	2.624	2.977
15	1.341	1.753	2.131	2.602	2.947
16	1.337	1.746	2.120	2.583	2.921
17	1.333	1.740	2.110	2.567	2.898
18	1.330	1.734	2.101	2.552	2.878
19	1.328	1.729	2.093	2.539	2.861
20	1.325	1.725	2.086	2.528	2.845
21	1.323	1.721	2.080	2.518	2.831
22	1.321	1.717	2.074	2.508	2.819
23	1.319	1.714	2.069	2.500	2.807
24	1.318	1.711	2.064	2.492	2.797
25	1.316	1.708	2.060	2.485	2.787
26	1.315	1.706	2.056	2.479	2.779
27	1.314	1.703	2.052	2.473	2.771
28	1.313	1.701	2.048	2.467	2.763
29	1.311	1.699	2.045	2.462	2.756
30	1.310	1.697	2.042	2.457	2.750
40	1.303	1.684	2.021	2.423	2.704
60	1.296	1.671	2.000	2.390	2.660
∞	1.282	1.645	1.960	2.326	2.576

TABLE A.3 Chi-square Distribution

Let χ_v^2 be a chi-square random variable with v degrees of freedom. For selected probabilities α, the table gives numbers $\chi_{v,\alpha}^2$, such that $\alpha = P(\chi_v^2 > \chi_{v,\alpha}^2)$.

v	α									
	.995	.990	.975	.950	.900	.100	.050	.025	.010	.005
1	0.0^4393	0.0^3157	0.0^3982	0.0^2393	0.0158	2.71	3.84	5.02	6.63	7.88
2	0.0100	0.0201	0.0506	0.103	0.211	4.61	5.99	7.38	9.21	10.60
3	0.072	0.115	0.216	0.352	0.584	6.25	7.81	9.35	11.34	12.84
4	0.207	0.297	0.484	0.711	1.064	7.78	9.49	11.14	13.28	14.86
5	0.412	0.554	0.831	1.145	1.61	9.24	11.07	12.83	15.09	16.75
6	0.676	0.872	1.24	1.64	2.20	10.64	12.59	14.45	16.81	18.55
7	0.989	1.24	1.69	2.17	2.83	12.02	14.07	16.01	18.48	20.28
8	1.34	1.65	2.18	2.73	3.49	13.36	15.51	17.53	20.09	21.96
9	1.73	2.09	2.70	3.33	4.17	14.68	16.92	19.02	21.67	23.59
10	2.16	2.56	3.25	3.94	4.87	15.99	18.31	20.48	23.21	25.19
11	2.60	3.05	3.82	4.57	5.58	17.28	19.68	21.92	24.73	26.76
12	3.07	3.57	4.40	5.23	6.30	18.55	21.03	23.34	26.22	28.30
13	3.57	4.11	5.01	5.89	7.04	19.81	22.36	24.74	27.69	29.82
14	4.07	4.66	5.63	6.57	7.79	21.06	23.68	26.12	29.14	31.32
15	4.60	5.23	6.26	7.26	8.55	22.31	25.00	27.49	30.58	32.80
16	5.14	5.81	6.91	7.96	9.31	23.54	26.30	28.85	32.00	34.27
17	5.70	6.41	7.56	8.67	10.09	24.77	27.59	30.19	33.41	35.72
18	6.26	7.01	8.23	9.39	10.86	25.99	28.87	31.53	34.81	37.16
19	6.84	7.63	8.91	10.12	11.65	27.20	30.14	32.85	36.19	38.58
20	7.43	8.26	9.59	10.85	12.44	28.41	31.41	34.17	37.57	40.00
21	8.03	8.90	10.28	11.59	13.24	29.62	32.67	35.48	38.93	41.40
22	8.64	9.54	10.98	12.34	14.04	30.81	33.92	36.78	40.29	42.80
23	9.26	10.20	11.69	13.09	14.85	32.01	35.17	38.08	41.64	44.18
24	9.89	10.86	12.40	13.85	15.66	33.20	36.42	39.36	42.98	45.56
25	10.52	11.52	13.12	14.61	16.47	34.38	37.65	40.65	44.31	46.93
26	11.16	12.20	13.84	15.38	17.29	35.56	38.89	41.92	45.64	48.29
27	11.81	12.88	14.57	16.15	18.11	36.74	40.11	43.19	46.96	49.64
28	12.46	13.56	15.31	16.93	18.94	37.92	41.34	44.46	48.28	50.99
29	13.12	14.26	16.05	17.71	19.77	39.09	42.56	45.72	49.59	52.34
30	13.79	14.95	16.79	18.49	20.60	40.26	43.77	46.98	50.89	53.67
40	20.71	22.16	24.43	26.51	29.05	51.81	55.76	59.34	63.69	66.77
50	27.99	29.71	32.36	34.76	37.69	63.17	67.50	71.42	76.15	79.49
60	35.53	37.48	40.48	43.19	46.46	74.40	79.08	83.30	88.38	91.95
70	43.28	45.44	48.76	51.74	55.33	85.53	90.53	95.02	100.4	104.2
80	51.17	53.54	57.15	60.39	64.28	96.58	101.9	106.6	112.3	116.3
90	59.20	61.75	65.65	69.13	73.29	107.6	113.1	118.1	124.1	128.3
100	67.33	70.06	74.22	77.93	82.36	118.5	124.3	129.6	135.8	140.2

Reproduced with permission from C. M. Thompson, "Tables of percentage points of the chi-square distribution," *Biometrika, 32* (1941).

TABLE A.4 *F* Distribution

Let F_{ν_1,ν_2} be a random variable having an F distribution, with numerator degrees of freedom ν_1 and denominator degrees of freedom ν_2. For probabilities $\alpha = 0.05, 0.01$, the table gives numbers $F_{\nu_1,\nu_2,\alpha}$, such that

$$\alpha = P(F_{\nu_1,\nu_2} > F_{\nu_1,\nu_2,\alpha})$$

$\alpha = .05$

Numerator ν_1

Denominator ν_2	1	2	3	4	5	6	7	8	9	10	12	15	20	24	30	40	60	120	∞
1	161.4	199.5	215.7	224.6	230.2	234.0	236.8	238.9	240.5	241.9	243.9	245.9	248.0	249.1	250.1	251.1	252.2	253.3	254.3
2	18.51	19.00	19.16	19.25	19.30	19.33	19.35	19.37	19.38	19.40	19.41	19.43	19.45	19.45	19.46	19.47	19.48	19.49	19.50
3	10.13	9.55	9.28	9.12	9.01	8.94	8.89	8.85	8.81	8.79	8.74	8.70	8.66	8.64	8.62	8.59	8.57	8.55	8.53
4	7.71	6.94	6.59	6.39	6.26	6.16	6.09	6.04	6.00	5.96	5.91	5.86	5.80	5.77	5.75	5.72	5.69	5.66	5.63
5	6.61	5.79	5.41	5.19	5.05	4.95	4.88	4.82	4.77	4.74	4.68	4.62	4.56	4.53	4.50	4.46	4.43	4.40	4.36
6	5.99	5.14	4.76	4.53	4.39	4.28	4.21	4.15	4.10	4.06	4.00	3.94	3.87	3.84	3.81	3.77	3.74	3.70	3.67
7	5.59	4.74	4.35	4.12	3.97	3.87	3.79	3.73	3.68	3.64	3.57	3.51	3.44	3.41	3.38	3.34	3.30	3.27	3.23
8	5.32	4.46	4.07	3.84	3.69	3.58	3.50	3.44	3.39	3.35	3.28	3.22	3.15	3.12	3.08	3.04	3.01	2.97	2.93
9	5.12	4.26	3.86	3.63	3.48	3.37	3.29	3.23	3.18	3.14	3.07	3.01	2.94	2.90	2.86	2.83	2.79	2.75	2.71
10	4.96	4.10	3.71	3.48	3.33	3.22	3.14	3.07	3.02	2.98	2.91	2.85	2.77	2.74	2.70	2.66	2.62	2.58	2.54
11	4.84	3.98	3.59	3.36	3.20	3.09	3.01	2.95	2.90	2.85	2.79	2.72	2.65	2.61	2.57	2.53	2.49	2.45	2.40
12	4.75	3.89	3.49	3.26	3.11	3.00	2.91	2.85	2.80	2.75	2.69	2.62	2.54	2.51	2.47	2.43	2.38	2.34	2.30
13	4.67	3.81	3.41	3.18	3.03	2.92	2.83	2.77	2.71	2.67	2.60	2.53	2.46	2.42	2.38	2.34	2.30	2.25	2.21
14	4.60	3.74	3.34	3.11	2.96	2.85	2.76	2.70	2.65	2.60	2.53	2.46	2.39	2.35	2.31	2.27	2.22	2.18	2.13
15	4.54	3.68	3.29	3.06	2.90	2.79	2.71	2.64	2.59	2.54	2.48	2.40	2.33	2.29	2.25	2.20	2.16	2.11	2.07
16	4.49	3.63	3.24	3.01	2.85	2.74	2.66	2.59	2.54	2.49	2.42	2.35	2.28	2.24	2.19	2.15	2.11	2.06	2.01
17	4.45	3.59	3.20	2.96	2.81	2.70	2.61	2.55	2.49	2.45	2.38	2.31	2.23	2.19	2.15	2.10	2.06	2.01	1.96
18	4.41	3.55	3.16	2.93	2.77	2.66	2.58	2.51	2.46	2.41	2.34	2.27	2.19	2.15	2.11	2.06	2.02	1.97	1.92
19	4.38	3.52	3.13	2.90	2.74	2.63	2.54	2.48	2.42	2.38	2.31	2.23	2.16	2.11	2.07	2.03	1.98	1.93	1.88
20	4.35	3.49	3.10	2.87	2.71	2.60	2.51	2.45	2.39	2.35	2.28	2.20	2.12	2.08	2.04	1.99	1.95	1.90	1.84
21	4.32	3.47	3.07	2.84	2.68	2.57	2.49	2.42	2.37	2.32	2.25	2.18	2.10	2.05	2.01	1.96	1.92	1.87	1.81
22	4.30	3.44	3.05	2.82	2.66	2.55	2.46	2.40	2.34	2.30	2.23	2.15	2.07	2.03	1.98	1.94	1.89	1.84	1.78
23	4.28	3.42	3.03	2.80	2.64	2.53	2.44	2.37	2.32	2.27	2.20	2.13	2.05	2.01	1.96	1.91	1.86	1.81	1.76
24	4.26	3.40	3.01	2.78	2.62	2.51	2.42	2.36	2.30	2.25	2.18	2.11	2.03	1.98	1.94	1.89	1.84	1.79	1.73
25	4.24	3.39	2.99	2.76	2.60	2.49	2.40	2.34	2.28	2.24	2.16	2.09	2.01	1.96	1.92	1.87	1.82	1.77	1.71
26	4.23	3.37	2.98	2.74	2.59	2.47	2.39	2.32	2.27	2.22	2.15	2.07	1.99	1.95	1.90	1.85	1.80	1.75	1.69
27	4.21	3.35	2.96	2.73	2.57	2.46	2.37	2.31	2.25	2.20	2.13	2.06	1.97	1.93	1.88	1.84	1.79	1.73	1.67
28	4.20	3.34	2.95	2.71	2.56	2.45	2.36	2.29	2.24	2.19	2.12	2.04	1.96	1.91	1.87	1.82	1.77	1.71	1.65
29	4.18	3.33	2.93	2.70	2.55	2.43	2.35	2.28	2.22	2.18	2.10	2.03	1.94	1.90	1.85	1.81	1.75	1.70	1.64
30	4.17	3.32	2.92	2.69	2.53	2.42	2.33	2.27	2.21	2.16	2.09	2.01	1.93	1.89	1.84	1.79	1.74	1.68	1.62
40	4.08	3.23	2.84	2.61	2.45	2.34	2.25	2.18	2.12	2.08	2.00	1.92	1.84	1.79	1.74	1.69	1.64	1.58	1.51
60	4.00	3.15	2.76	2.53	2.37	2.25	2.17	2.10	2.04	1.99	1.92	1.84	1.75	1.70	1.65	1.59	1.53	1.47	1.39
120	3.92	3.07	2.68	2.45	2.29	2.17	2.09	2.02	1.96	1.91	1.83	1.75	1.66	1.61	1.55	1.50	1.43	1.35	1.25
∞	3.84	3.00	2.60	2.37	2.21	2.10	2.01	1.94	1.88	1.83	1.75	1.67	1.57	1.52	1.46	1.39	1.32	1.22	1.00

$$\alpha = .01$$

Numerator v_1

Denominator v_2	1	2	3	4	5	6	7	8	9	10	12	15	20	24	30	40	60	120	∞
1	4052	4999.5	5403	5625	5764	5859	5928	5982	6022	6056	6106	6157	6209	6235	6261	6287	6313	6339	6366
2	98.50	99.00	99.17	99.25	99.30	99.33	99.36	99.37	99.39	99.40	99.42	99.43	99.45	99.46	99.47	99.47	99.48	99.48	99.50
3	34.12	30.82	29.46	28.71	28.24	27.91	27.67	27.49	27.35	27.23	27.05	26.87	26.69	26.60	26.50	26.41	26.32	26.22	26.13
4	21.20	18.00	16.69	15.98	15.52	15.21	14.98	14.80	14.66	14.55	14.37	14.20	14.02	13.93	13.84	13.75	13.65	13.56	13.46
5	16.26	13.27	12.06	11.39	10.97	10.67	10.46	10.29	10.16	10.05	9.89	9.72	9.55	9.47	9.38	9.29	9.20	9.11	9.02
6	13.75	10.92	9.78	9.15	8.75	8.47	8.26	8.10	7.98	7.87	7.72	7.56	7.40	7.31	7.23	7.14	7.06	6.97	6.88
7	12.25	9.55	8.45	7.85	7.46	7.19	6.99	6.84	6.72	6.62	6.47	6.31	6.16	6.07	5.99	5.91	5.82	5.74	5.65
8	11.26	8.65	7.59	7.01	6.63	6.37	6.18	6.03	5.91	5.81	5.67	5.52	5.36	5.28	5.20	5.12	5.03	4.95	4.86
9	10.56	8.02	6.99	6.42	6.06	5.80	5.61	5.47	5.35	5.26	5.11	4.96	4.81	4.73	4.65	4.57	4.48	4.40	4.31
10	10.04	7.56	6.55	5.99	5.64	5.39	5.20	5.06	4.94	4.85	4.71	4.56	4.41	4.33	4.25	4.17	4.08	4.00	3.91
11	9.65	7.21	6.22	5.67	5.32	5.07	4.89	4.74	4.63	4.54	4.40	4.25	4.10	4.02	3.94	3.86	3.78	3.69	3.60
12	9.33	6.93	5.95	5.41	5.06	4.82	4.64	4.50	4.39	4.30	4.16	4.01	3.86	3.78	3.70	3.62	3.54	3.45	3.36
13	9.07	6.70	5.74	5.21	4.86	4.62	4.44	4.30	4.19	4.10	3.96	3.82	3.66	3.59	3.51	3.43	3.34	3.25	3.17
14	8.86	6.51	5.56	5.04	4.69	4.46	4.28	4.14	4.03	3.94	3.80	3.66	3.51	3.43	3.35	3.27	3.18	3.09	3.00
15	8.68	6.36	5.42	4.89	4.56	4.32	4.14	4.00	3.89	3.80	3.67	3.52	3.37	3.29	3.21	3.13	3.05	2.96	2.87
16	8.53	6.23	5.29	4.77	4.44	4.20	4.03	3.89	3.78	3.69	3.55	3.41	3.26	3.18	3.10	3.02	2.93	2.84	2.75
17	8.40	6.11	5.18	4.67	4.34	4.10	3.93	3.79	3.68	3.59	3.46	3.31	3.16	3.08	3.00	2.92	2.83	2.75	2.65
18	8.29	6.01	5.09	4.58	4.25	4.01	3.84	3.71	3.60	3.51	3.37	3.23	3.08	3.00	2.92	2.84	2.75	2.66	2.57
19	8.18	5.93	5.01	4.50	4.17	3.94	3.77	3.63	3.52	3.43	3.30	3.15	3.00	2.92	2.84	2.76	2.67	2.58	2.49
20	8.10	5.85	4.94	4.43	4.10	3.87	3.70	3.56	3.46	3.37	3.23	3.09	2.94	2.86	2.78	2.69	2.61	2.52	2.42
21	8.02	5.78	4.87	4.37	4.04	3.81	3.64	3.51	3.40	3.31	3.17	3.03	2.88	2.80	2.72	2.64	2.55	2.46	2.36
22	7.95	5.72	4.82	4.31	3.99	3.76	3.59	3.45	3.35	3.26	3.12	2.98	2.83	2.75	2.67	2.58	2.50	2.40	2.31
23	7.88	5.66	4.76	4.26	3.94	3.71	3.54	3.41	3.30	3.21	3.07	2.93	2.78	2.70	2.62	2.54	2.45	2.35	2.26
24	7.82	5.61	4.72	4.22	3.90	3.67	3.50	3.36	3.26	3.17	3.03	2.89	2.74	2.66	2.58	2.49	2.40	2.31	2.21
25	7.77	5.57	4.68	4.18	3.85	3.63	3.46	3.32	3.22	3.13	2.99	2.85	2.70	2.62	2.54	2.45	2.36	2.27	2.17
26	7.72	5.53	4.64	4.14	3.82	3.59	3.42	3.29	3.18	3.09	2.96	2.81	2.66	2.58	2.50	2.42	2.33	2.23	2.13
27	7.68	5.49	4.60	4.11	3.78	3.56	3.39	3.26	3.15	3.06	2.93	2.78	2.63	2.55	2.47	2.38	2.29	2.20	2.10
28	7.64	5.45	4.57	4.07	3.75	3.53	3.36	3.23	3.12	3.03	2.90	2.75	2.60	2.52	2.44	2.35	2.26	2.17	2.06
29	7.60	5.42	4.54	4.04	3.73	3.50	3.33	3.20	3.09	3.00	2.87	2.73	2.57	2.49	2.41	2.33	2.23	2.14	2.03
30	7.56	5.39	4.51	4.02	3.70	3.47	3.30	3.17	3.07	2.98	2.84	2.70	2.55	2.47	2.39	2.30	2.21	2.11	2.01
40	7.31	5.18	4.31	3.83	3.51	3.29	3.12	2.99	2.89	2.80	2.66	2.52	2.37	2.29	2.20	2.11	2.02	1.92	1.80
60	7.08	4.98	4.13	3.65	3.34	3.12	2.95	2.82	2.72	2.63	2.50	2.35	2.20	2.12	2.03	1.94	1.84	1.73	1.60
120	6.85	4.79	3.95	3.48	3.17	2.96	2.79	2.66	2.56	2.47	2.34	2.19	2.03	1.95	1.86	1.76	1.66	1.53	1.38
∞	6.63	4.61	3.78	3.32	3.02	2.80	2.64	2.51	2.41	2.32	2.18	2.04	1.88	1.79	1.70	1.59	1.47	1.32	1.00

TABLE A.5 Durbin-Watson Statistic

Let the statistic d have the null distribution of the Durbin-Watson test statistic, and let d_α be the number for which $P(d < d_\alpha) = \alpha$. For $\alpha = 0.05, 0.01$, the table gives numbers d_L and d_U such that $d_L \le d_\alpha \le d_U$, for regressions with n observations and K independent variables.

$\alpha = .05$

	K									
	1		2		3		4		5	
n	d_L	d_U	d_L	d_U	d_L	d_U	d_L	d_U	d_L	d_U
15	1.08	1.36	0.95	1.54	0.82	1.75	0.69	1.97	0.56	2.21
16	1.10	1.37	0.98	1.54	0.86	1.73	0.74	1.93	0.62	2.15
17	1.13	1.38	1.02	1.54	0.90	1.71	0.78	1.90	0.67	2.10
18	1.16	1.39	1.05	1.53	0.93	1.69	0.82	1.87	0.71	2.06
19	1.18	1.40	1.08	1.53	0.97	1.68	0.86	1.85	0.75	2.02
20	1.20	1.41	1.10	1.54	1.00	1.68	0.90	1.83	0.79	1.99
21	1.22	1.42	1.13	1.54	1.03	1.67	0.93	1.81	0.83	1.96
22	1.24	1.43	1.15	1.54	1.05	1.66	0.96	1.80	0.86	1.94
23	1.26	1.44	1.17	1.54	1.08	1.66	0.99	1.79	0.90	1.92
24	1.27	1.45	1.19	1.55	1.10	1.66	1.01	1.78	0.93	1.90
25	1.29	1.45	1.21	1.55	1.12	1.66	1.04	1.77	0.95	1.89
26	1.30	1.46	1.22	1.55	1.14	1.65	1.06	1.76	0.98	1.88
27	1.32	1.47	1.24	1.56	1.16	1.65	1.08	1.76	1.01	1.86
28	1.33	1.48	1.26	1.56	1.18	1.65	1.10	1.75	1.03	1.85
29	1.34	1.48	1.27	1.56	1.20	1.65	1.12	1.74	1.05	1.84
30	1.35	1.49	1.28	1.57	1.21	1.65	1.14	1.74	1.07	1.83
31	1.36	1.50	1.30	1.57	1.23	1.65	1.16	1.74	1.09	1.83
32	1.37	1.50	1.31	1.57	1.24	1.65	1.18	1.73	1.11	1.82
33	1.38	1.51	1.32	1.58	1.26	1.65	1.19	1.73	1.13	1.81
34	1.39	1.51	1.33	1.58	1.27	1.65	1.21	1.73	1.15	1.81
35	1.40	1.52	1.34	1.58	1.28	1.65	1.22	1.73	1.16	1.80
36	1.41	1.52	1.35	1.59	1.29	1.65	1.24	1.73	1.18	1.80
37	1.42	1.53	1.36	1.59	1.31	1.66	1.25	1.72	1.19	1.80
38	1.43	1.54	1.37	1.59	1.32	1.66	1.26	1.72	1.21	1.79
39	1.43	1.54	1.38	1.60	1.33	1.66	1.27	1.72	1.22	1.79
40	1.44	1.54	1.39	1.60	1.34	1.66	1.29	1.72	1.23	1.79
45	1.48	1.57	1.43	1.62	1.38	1.67	1.34	1.72	1.29	1.78
50	1.50	1.59	1.46	1.63	1.42	1.67	1.38	1.72	1.34	1.77
55	1.53	1.60	1.49	1.64	1.45	1.68	1.41	1.72	1.38	1.77
60	1.55	1.62	1.51	1.65	1.48	1.69	1.44	1.73	1.41	1.77
65	1.57	1.63	1.54	1.66	1.50	1.70	1.47	1.73	1.44	1.77
70	1.58	1.64	1.55	1.67	1.52	1.70	1.49	1.74	1.46	1.77
75	1.60	1.65	1.57	1.68	1.54	1.71	1.51	1.74	1.49	1.77
80	1.61	1.66	1.59	1.69	1.56	1.72	1.53	1.74	1.51	1.77
85	1.62	1.67	1.60	1.70	1.57	1.72	1.55	1.75	1.52	1.77
90	1.63	1.68	1.61	1.70	1.59	1.73	1.57	1.75	1.54	1.78
95	1.64	1.69	1.62	1.71	1.60	1.73	1.58	1.75	1.56	1.78
100	1.65	1.69	1.63	1.72	1.61	1.74	1.59	1.76	1.57	1.78

TABLE A.5. (*Continued*)

$$\alpha = .01$$

	K									
	1		2		3		4		5	
n	d_L	d_U	d_L	d_U	d_L	d_U	d_L	d_U	d_L	d_U
15	0.81	1.07	0.70	1.25	0.59	1.46	0.49	1.70	0.39	1.96
16	0.84	1.09	0.74	1.25	0.63	1.44	0.53	1.66	0.44	1.90
17	0.87	1.10	0.77	1.25	0.67	1.43	0.57	1.63	0.48	1.85
18	0.90	1.12	0.80	1.26	0.71	1.42	0.61	1.60	0.52	1.80
19	0.93	1.13	0.83	1.26	0.74	1.41	0.65	1.58	0.56	1.77
20	0.95	1.15	0.86	1.27	0.77	1.41	0.68	1.57	0.60	1.74
21	0.97	1.16	0.89	1.27	0.80	1.41	0.72	1.55	0.63	1.71
22	1.00	1.17	0.91	1.28	0.83	1.40	0.75	1.54	0.66	1.69
23	1.02	1.19	0.94	1.29	0.86	1.40	0.77	1.53	0.70	1.67
24	1.04	1.20	0.96	1.30	0.88	1.41	0.80	1.53	0.72	1.66
25	1.05	1.21	0.98	1.30	0.90	1.41	0.83	1.52	0.75	1.65
26	1.07	1.22	1.00	1.31	0.93	1.41	0.85	1.52	0.78	1.64
27	1.09	1.23	1.02	1.32	0.95	1.41	0.88	1.51	0.81	1.63
28	1.10	1.24	1.04	1.32	0.97	1.41	0.90	1.51	0.83	1.62
29	1.12	1.25	1.05	1.33	0.99	1.42	0.92	1.51	0.85	1.61
30	1.13	1.26	1.07	1.34	1.01	1.42	0.94	1.51	0.88	1.61
31	1.15	1.27	1.08	1.34	1.02	1.42	0.96	1.51	0.90	1.60
32	1.16	1.28	1.10	1.35	1.04	1.43	0.98	1.51	0.92	1.60
33	1.17	1.29	1.11	1.36	1.05	1.43	1.00	1.51	0.94	1.59
34	1.18	1.30	1.13	1.36	1.07	1.43	1.01	1.51	0.95	1.59
35	1.19	1.31	1.14	1.37	1.08	1.44	1.03	1.51	0.97	1.59
36	1.21	1.32	1.15	1.38	1.10	1.44	1.04	1.51	0.99	1.59
37	1.22	1.32	1.16	1.38	1.11	1.45	1.06	1.51	1.00	1.59
38	1.23	1.33	1.18	1.39	1.12	1.45	1.07	1.52	1.02	1.58
39	1.24	1.34	1.19	1.39	1.14	1.45	1.09	1.52	1.03	1.58
40	1.25	1.34	1.20	1.40	1.15	1.46	1.10	1.52	1.05	1.58
45	1.29	1.38	1.24	1.42	1.20	1.48	1.16	1.53	1.11	1.58
50	1.32	1.40	1.28	1.45	1.24	1.49	1.20	1.54	1.16	1.59
55	1.36	1.43	1.32	1.47	1.28	1.51	1.25	1.55	1.21	1.59
60	1.38	1.45	1.35	1.48	1.32	1.52	1.28	1.56	1.25	1.60
65	1.41	1.47	1.38	1.50	1.35	1.53	1.31	1.57	1.28	1.61
70	1.43	1.49	1.40	1.52	1.37	1.55	1.34	1.58	1.31	1.61
75	1.45	1.50	1.42	1.53	1.39	1.56	1.37	1.59	1.34	1.62
80	1.47	1.52	1.44	1.54	1.42	1.57	1.39	1.60	1.36	1.62
85	1.48	1.53	1.46	1.55	1.43	1.58	1.41	1.60	1.39	1.63
90	1.50	1.54	1.47	1.56	1.45	1.59	1.43	1.61	1.41	1.64
95	1.51	1.55	1.49	1.57	1.47	1.60	1.45	1.62	1.42	1.64
100	1.52	1.56	1.50	1.58	1.48	1.60	1.46	1.63	1.44	1.65

Reproduced with permission from J. Durbin and G. S. Watson, "Testing for serial correlation in least squares regression, II," *Biometrika, 38* (1951).

Name Index

Subject Index